Mass Media Revolution

Now in its Third Edition, *Mass Media Revolution* remains a dynamic guide to the world of mass media, enhancing its readers' development as critical media consumers. The text employs a storytelling narrative style and integrated, chapter-specific rich media and dynamic web components, providing a seamless learning experience. It features a wealth of expanded content—with particular attention to diversity in the media industry, reality TV, ethics and social media, and the evolution of online journalism. Chapter content, both print and online, is aligned to the ACEJMC national academic standards. Along with student video resources, this text includes an accompanying instructor resource manual and PowerPoint slides.

Mass Media Revolution

Third Edition

J. Charles Sterin and
Tameka Winston

Routledge
Taylor & Francis Group

NEW YORK AND LONDON

Third edition published 2018
by Routledge
711 Third Avenue, New York, NY 10017

and by Routledge
2 Park Square, Milton Park, Abingdon, Oxon, OX14 4RN

Routledge is an imprint of the Taylor & Francis Group, an informa business

First edition published by Pearson Education Inc. 2012
Second edition published by Routledge 2016

Library of Congress Cataloging-in-Publication Data
A catalog record for this book has been requested

Video segments produced by J. Charles Sterin

ISBN: 9781138232648 (hbk)
ISBN: 9781138232655 (pbk)
ISBN: 9781315311814 (ebk)

Typeset in Syntax
by Apex CoVantage, LLC

Visit the companion website: www.routledge.com/sterin

Dr. Sterin dedicates this book to his wife Pauline,
without whose unwavering love and support
this work would not have been possible.

Dr. Winston dedicates this book to her husband and best friend Calvin,
thanks for always supporting my endeavors.
You're the true definition of a devoted husband.
Love you always.

Brief Contents

Contents

Key ACEJMC Learning Objectives

CHAPTER 1
- Understand concepts and apply theories in the use and presentation of images and information.
- Conduct research and evaluate information by methods appropriate to the communications professions in which they work.
- Think critically, creatively and independently.

CHAPTER 2
- Demonstrate an understanding of the history and role of professionals and institutions in shaping communications.

CHAPTER 3
- Apply tools and technologies appropriate for the communications professions in which they work.
- Think critically, creatively, and independently.

CHAPTER 4
- Write correctly and clearly in forms and styles appropriate for the communications professions, audiences and purposes they serve.

CHAPTER 5
- Write correctly and clearly in forms and styles appropriate for the communications professions, audiences and purposes they serve.

CHAPTER 6
- Write correctly and clearly in forms and styles appropriate for the communications professions, audiences and purposes they serve.

CHAPTER 7
- Apply tools and technologies appropriate for the communications professions in which they work.
- Think critically, creatively, and independently.

CHAPTER 8
- Write correctly and clearly in forms and styles appropriate for the communications professions, audiences and purposes they serve.
- Conduct research and evaluate information by methods appropriate to the communications professions in which they work.

- Think critically, creatively and independently.
- Understand concepts and apply theories in the use and presentation of images and information.

CHAPTER 9
- Critically evaluate their own work and that of others for accuracy and fairness, clarity, appropriate style and grammatical correctness.
- Demonstrate an understanding of professional ethical principles and work ethically in pursuit of truth, accuracy, fairness and diversity.

CHAPTER 10
- Think critically, creatively and independently.
- Critically evaluate their own work and that of others for accuracy and fairness, clarity, appropriate style and grammatical correctness.
- Demonstrate an understanding of professional ethical principles and work ethically in pursuit of truth, accuracy, fairness and diversity.

CHAPTER 11
- Demonstrate an understanding of professional ethical principles and work ethically in pursuit of truth, accuracy, fairness and diversity.
- Understand and apply the principles and laws of freedom of speech and press for the country in which the institution that invites ACEJMC is located, as well as receive instruction in and understand the range of systems of freedom of expression around the world, including the right to dissent, to monitor and criticize power, and to assemble and petition for redress of grievances.

CHAPTER 12
- Understand concepts and apply theories in the use and presentation of images and information.
- Think critically, creatively and independently.

CHAPTER 13
- Understand and apply the principles and laws of freedom of speech and press for the country in which the institution that invites ACEJMC is located, as well as receive instruction in and understand the range of systems of freedom of expression around the world, including the right to dissent, to monitor and criticize power, and to assemble and petition for redress of grievances.
- Think critically, creatively and independently.
- Critically evaluate their own work and that of others for accuracy and fairness, clarity, appropriate style and grammatical correctness.
- Demonstrate an understanding of professional ethical principles and work ethically in pursuit of truth, accuracy, fairness and diversity.

CHAPTER 14
- Understand and apply the principles and laws of freedom of speech and press for the country in which the institution that invites ACEJMC is located, as well as receive instruction in and understand the range of systems of freedom of expression around the world, including the right to dissent, to monitor and criticize power, and to assemble and petition for redress of grievances.
- Demonstrate an understanding of gender, race, ethnicity, sexual orientation and, as appropriate, other forms of diversity in domestic society in relation to mass communications.
- Demonstrate an understanding of the diversity of peoples and cultures and of the significance and impact of mass communications in a global society.

CHAPTER 15

- Demonstrate an understanding of gender, race, ethnicity, sexual orientation and, as appropriate, other forms of diversity in domestic society in relation to mass communications.
- Demonstrate an understanding of the diversity of peoples and cultures and of the significance and impact of mass communications in a global society.
- Think critically, creatively and independently.
- Critically evaluate their own work and that of others for accuracy and fairness, clarity, appropriate style and grammatical correctness.

CHAPTER 16

- Contribute to knowledge appropriate to the communications professions in which they work.
- Demonstrate an understanding of gender, race, ethnicity, sexual orientation and, as appropriate, other forms of diversity in domestic society in relation to mass communications.

Preface

This book, along with its closely integrated media-rich website, has been written and designed to appeal to today's digital native students. Technologically savvy, they enter college already skilled in the essentials for social and academic survival: Facebook and Tumblr accounts, Twitter feeds, smartphones, blogs—the list goes on. They spend more time online than in the library, text more than they talk and, most importantly, are accustomed to consuming media as they please and from an ever-widening variety of platforms, most often at the same time.

Mass media has always moved toward convergence driven by technological change, only now the change is happening so fast it's harder to demonstrate and teach. *Mass Media Revolution* by its very nature is an example of **media convergence**. Its blend of **storytelling narrative** with video and **digital assets** makes it a mass communication text for the digital age. Its digital resources and **learner-centered approach** revolutionize how mass communication can be studied, experienced and taught today. Superior coverage of emerging and evolving technology, diversity, and history; a custom-built digital program; and unparalleled assessment tools encourage modern media literacy and an active learning experience. Through its engaging storytelling approach that places media history and facts in context and a wealth of digital resources, *Mass Media Revolution* draws students into today's mass media world while enhancing their development as critical consumers of mass media. An extraordinarily diverse range of media content, developed specifically by the author of *Mass Media Revolution* to enrich the narrative of the text and exemplify the real-world applications of the concepts and theories presented, helps instructors take full advantage of the educational capabilities of the Web while saving time in class preparation.

Mass Media Revolution's approach reflects the way students consume mass media today—in narrative bites—highlighting the relevance of topics and experiences to their own lives as both mass media consumers and media technology users. Tracing the connections between historical events and current events and trends, *Mass Media Revolution* gives students the tools they need to understand how mass media function today and how the various media emerged from a rich history of technological innovation, economic ambition and cultural shifts. Students will learn to think critically about how mass media technologies influence our lives and to envision and analyze how the media of today might affect the media of tomorrow. Additionally, the alignment of print and digital content to national academic accreditation standards for the course (ACEJMC) supports contemporary instruction and the goal of furthering student media literacy.

Features of the Third Edition

Unparalleled Digital Integration: The third edition allows for a seamless digital learning experience that can be tailored to meet the needs and preferences of instructors and students. Digital assets are integrated with the instructional content and users may access the multimedia from their desktop, laptop, tablet or mobile devices at massmediarev.com.

Author-Created Video Assets: Video clips enhance the third edition. They range from a discussion on innovation and the impact of mass media technologies with Richard Saul Wurman (Chapter 3) to the cutting-edge creation of the *XCOM* video game by Firaxis (Chapter 7) to the operation of a successful hyperjournalism site, TownDock.net (Chapter 13).

Fully Assignable Digital Assets: *Mass Media Revolution, 3e*'s extensive digital assets can now be integrated into daily class activities with greater ease and flexibility. Critical assessment questions accompany every video referenced within the book. In addition, the *3e*'s website includes multiple-choice questions for each of these videos as well as assignable essay questions.

Emphasis on Media Convergence: Discussion of media convergence has been expanded throughout the book. A new section in Chapter 1, "Mass Media Convergence in the Digital Age," discusses historical convergence and the way rapidly expanding technology has accelerated the process. Streamlined content in Chapter 3 focuses the discussion on technological convergence in mass media including the "cloud." Later chapters discuss social media and the ways it is changing consumer access to and ownership of mediated content, including coverage of political activist Aung San Suu Kyi in Chapter 14 and the impact of social media coverage on governmental policies.

Enhanced Coverage of Social Media and its impact on mainstream media, democratic institutions, and economic and social aspects of society.

Enhanced Coverage of Diversity Issues in media, including expanded sections on the contributions of African-Americans to the history and evolution of the music industry.

Theory Coverage: The coverage of theory has been increased throughout this new edition. Chapter 1 now includes new coverage on the ancient roots of communication as well as a new section on "Theoretical Building Blocks of Mass Media" covering research such as textual analysis, content coding, social learning theory, agenda setting, cultivation effect and the uses and gratifications theory. Chapter 8 includes new coverage of Edward L. Bernays and his work in establishing the psychological models and methodologies in public relations, as well as of social psychologist Solomon Eliot Asch and his studies on the effects of propaganda on groups.

Videos and Media: Integrated throughout are more than 50 videos, created and/or selected by author J. Charles Sterin, that directly complement the narrative of each chapter. A variety of compelling approaches and perspectives, ranging from TV-news-magazine-style interviews to mini-documentaries, present rich content to students in familiar formats. Students can explore the contemporary mass media landscape through exclusive interviews with some of the top names in media today—interviews conducted specifically for *Mass Media Revolution*. Mini-documentaries allow students to experience what it is like to work in the mass media industry by revealing a day in the life of contemporary media professionals, including producers at a hit record label, a video game developer, and various public relations professionals. Students will hear directly from media professionals who work at such organizations as National Public Radio and MTV/Gigantic Productions. Assignable Video Quizzes help students reinforce their learning by highlighting specific mass media concepts with visual coverage of current events, scholarly interviews and professional commentary. The results of these Video Quizzes report directly to the instructor's gradebook.

Working in Mass Media Today: Written by a skilled filmmaker and television producer, *Mass Media Revolution* provides students with a broad understanding of the practical aspects of working in the mass media today. Chapter 16 covers numerous careers in media, providing "a day in the life" videos highlighting individuals practicing their craft. Chapter 14, **Media Impact on the Global Stage**, explores the impact and importance of mass media on international relations, as well as the contacts between and confrontations among nations and cultures around the world, including new coverage of the use of social media to cover military action in Gaza and the role of social media in bringing about social and democratic change in Egypt. Chapter 15, **Stories of Diversity in American Media**, provides an overview of the cultural dynamics of the media industry and the challenges of representing diversity through narrative examples and multiple videos.

Chapter Openers and Learning Objectives: The stories presented in these chapter-opening vignettes define the primary theme and set the stage for that chapter's narrative. Learning objectives, informed by Bloom's taxonomy, clearly outline what students need to learn, consider and evaluate from each chapter by highlighting key concepts and reinforcing the significance of related video clips.

Critical Thinking Questions: At the end of each chapter, and running as a selectable layer associated with every video segment, students are tested on their understanding of the key ideas and concepts presented in both the text and videos. These questions also allow students to apply what they learned in the chapter to their own everyday experiences with mass media.

Chapter Summaries: Organized by key topics, Chapter Summaries at the end of each chapter assist with study and review of key concepts. The summaries reinforce what the students have read and viewed online while increasing student exposure to the chapter's content. This deconstruction allows students to get to the core of the material quickly and efficiently, and provides a context for what they have learned within the larger scope of the mass media field.

ACEJMC Accreditation Standards Grid: This list, found on page xix, aligns each chapter's content with the learning objectives established by the Accrediting Council on Education in Journalism and Mass Communication to help professors see how the material meets accreditation standards for the course.

Visual Narrative: More than 400 color photographs provide students with a vibrant visual narrative. Photos have been carefully researched and selected to effectively illustrate key topics in the text and develop visual literacy, while representing up-to-date events and important people and information.

About the Authors

J. Charles Sterin is an award-winning documentary filmmaker, investigative television journalist and screenwriter. Over the course of his 40-year career, Sterin has produced over 60 hours of television documentaries, including episodes of A&E Network's prime-time series *Investigative Reports* and *Ancient Mysteries*, and documentary specials aired on PBS. Sterin co-produced a national media project with 10 of the world's leading humanist thinkers (including anthropologist Margaret Mead, psychologist Carl Rogers and anthropologist Ashley Montagu) and was selected by the Poynter Institute to produce its seminal PBS documentary series *NewsLeaders* on the leading figures of American news media. He has also authored 26 screenplays, two of which he has re-authored as novels; the most recent, *Hell Scrolls*, was published in the summer of 2013.

Sterin is fascinated with the future of media technologies, especially the evolution of the Internet, mass media convergence and artificial intelligence-based expert systems. He has developed innovative approaches to producing short-form documentary videos in integrated content delivery platforms for "blended" online training and higher education. In 2001, Sterin joined the faculty of the University of Maryland–University College (UMUC)—a world leader in web-enhanced and online college programs— where he has applied his interests in the evolution of mass media and media-based blended learning applications to the creation of a number of UMUC's mass communication courses. Through these popular courses, Sterin has introduced thousands of students across the country and around the world to the study of mass media.

Tameka Winston is the Department Chair and an award-winning Professor in the Department of Communications at Tennessee State University (TSU). She is also an author and Sirius XM radio host. Winston has been working at the collegiate level for 15 years, and is a popular and respected professor and student mentor at TSU. Winston's passion for education has made her a popular conference speaker and she has a growing national reputation. She was recently awarded the prestigious "2017 Woman of Achievement Award" by the Nashville Business Journal, joining the ranks of previous recipients including Megan Barry, the first female mayor of Nashville, TN. She was also among the finalists for the 2016 Nashville's Emerging Leaders Award sponsored by the Nashville Area Chamber of Commerce and YP Nashville.

Acknowledgments

This work was possible in part because my first edition lead editor, Jeanne Zalesky, maintained an unshakable belief in the approach and success of this project. She was able to see that the future of academic publishing calls for disruptive innovation, and she fought for this book with courage and vision at every stage of the process. My second edition development editor, Barbara Heinssen, supplied brilliant, painstaking editing and contributed significantly to the evolving vision of *Mass Media Revolution*. I want to thank our third edition researcher Joe Ritchie for his valuable contributions to the process. And we would like to also thank our third edition editor Laura Briskman for her flexibility and support during the transition process to our new publisher.

Section I

Paving the Way to Today's Mass Media

1

Introduction to the Mass Media Revolution

John Moore/Staff

CHAPTER OUTLINE

The Style and Approach of *Mass Media Revolution*

Sneak Peek at *MMR*, 3e Movie trailer of things to come as you experience *Mass Media Revolution*, 3e.

Studying the Mass Media
Theoretical Building Blocks of Mass Media
Mass Communication Models, Theories and Research Chart

Marshall McLuhan, Explorations Marshall McLuhan's legacy and impact as a mass media futurist.

Audience Trends
Why Research Audiences?

How Ratings Work Discussion of measurement techniques used to place values on television and radio programming.

Culture and Mass Media: Sharing What We Know
From My Village to the Global Village
Mass Media Convergence in the Digital Age
Conclusion: Understanding *New* Mass Media from a Critical Perspective

LEARNING OBJECTIVES

1. Evaluate how well the author's storytelling approach, the book's media features and the book's presentation of historical concepts clarify the role of mass media in our 21st-century world.
2. Explain the concept of media convergence and how technology has changed the nature of mediated communication.
3. Classify the foundational concepts, theories and trends that converge within the dynamic field of mass media.
4. Explain the importance of audience interest to the success of media industries.
5. Illustrate the ways in which audience demographics impact media content.
6. Outline the ways in which electronic media has contributed to the ongoing trend toward cultural convergence and a globalizing worldview.
7. Assess the impact of information overload on an individual's ability to process and filter media messages.

THIS BOOK

and its media-rich Website will show you why understanding the significance of the Digital Age and developing your own media literacy is vital to understanding the world you live in today. Many of you, having been born into and then grown up in a world of technology and the Internet, may already understand a great deal about the mass media. We refer to you as digital natives. Those who are transitioning into the Digital Age, we refer to as digital immigrants.

As digital natives, you are already fully immersed participants in many aspects of mass media, often simultaneously. You are active in social media, regularly communicating with hundreds of "friends" on Twitter or Facebook; you likely use your smartphones as combined texting and media portal devices; you rely on the Internet for much, if not most, of your television and movie viewing. Much of your news probably comes from Internet sites and blogs. As digital natives, you expertly weave your way in and out of converged media—music, games, movies and television, magazines and books—into a vast nonlinear, user-selectable and programmable, media-rich digital fourth dimension.

Being fluent in today's mass media technologies and being an active participant on the Internet, however, should not represent the entirety of your mass media experience. With the multitude of media channels and content constantly bombarding us today, it is vital that we all become skilled and informed mass media consumers. In fact, it is our responsibility. The mass media of the 21st century are dynamic, complex and all-encompassing. We need to understand mass media's evolution to identify and analyze the forces that are influencing and guiding where the mass communication industries are heading in the future—in your lifetime.

Those of you who are reading this book and exploring its many media components may already be looking forward to careers in mass media—as journalists, artists, Web developers, filmmakers, television program creators or video game developers. Your opportunities and entry points are vastly broader than and different from those experienced by preceding generations. While these

> The mass media of the 21st century are dynamic, complex and all-encompassing. We need to understand mass media's evolution to identify and analyze the forces that are influencing and guiding where the mass communication industries are heading in the future—in your lifetime.

opportunities continue to increase exponentially, so do the expectations of the degree of critical knowledge, skills and abilities you must bring with you to succeed in these fields. *Mass Media Revolution* has been designed to guide you on your way, to help you become a more knowledgeable, more effective and more critical mass media consumer and participant.

1.1
goodluz/Fotolia

THE STYLE AND APPROACH OF *MASS MEDIA REVOLUTION*

Technological transformation affects how we all operate as mass media consumers, and it is now in the process of forcing immense changes in how media producers—from news reporters to entertainment organizations—create and distribute their media content.

This onslaught of news reporting and commentary, along with the increasingly available information and entertainment options, makes it imperative that all of us develop the skills to identify and understand media bias, select the content we want, and skillfully navigate between what is of value and what is just the thunderous noise. We also must manage these sometimes-intimidating tasks without suffering from what author and media critic Richard Saul Wurman was the first to call *information anxiety*:

> [**Information anxiety**] is produced by the ever-widening gap between what we understand and what we think we should understand. It is the black hole between data and knowledge, and what happens when information doesn't tell us what we want or need to know.[1]

In this book, we explore contemporary issues and challenges of mass media in a revolutionary way. As the author, I have made some assumptions about you, the reader and media user. First, this book assumes that you already know quite a lot about mass media from the valid perspective of your own extensive experience. Second, to critically enhance what you may already know, this highly visual book, with its integrated media resources, provides you with the stories behind the media and presents topics in a way that aims to challenge and provoke you to reconsider your own views and ideas. Some of the chronicles and stories you might have already heard; others you will likely find new and surprising. The primary goal is to encourage you to think more critically about your own views of mass media in society and cultures, to increase your real-world knowledge about how the mass media work, to encourage you to develop your own individual interpretations and conclusions and to enhance your understanding and appreciation of mass media's profound effects on all of our lives.

You bring your own developed skills and learning styles to this course. The book and its integrated media components were designed to flexibly adapt to *your* learning style—whether you follow a linear approach (A-B-C-D) or a more dynamic, nonlinear approach (A-B-G-Q-A), similar to your interactive experience on the Web. The practice of using both the printed and online content will help you learn about the mass media in an experiential, interactive way—much like how you currently access information.

1.2

Architect, graphic designer, author and pioneer in the study of how to make information widely understandable, Richard Saul Wurman coined the popular terms "information architecture" and "information anxiety."

Randy Duchaine/Alamy Stock Photo

Media as Storytellers

From my perspective as a practitioner and educator of mass media, to understand how the industries have evolved and how they operate today, it helps to view all mass media as a form of storytelling. In many ways, most media content captures our attention with some sort of (and often controversial) story, whether it's an exposé on the extramarital affairs of a famous sports figure or a feature about a young president's fight to achieve universal health care. These stories hold our interest; they influence our personal views and beliefs. Throughout this book and the accompanying media, I emphasize an anecdotal approach. Rather than

Rather than present you with static lists of facts and theories, *Mass Media Revolution* strives to present ideas through illuminating and memorable stories, photographs and videos, connecting theories to their place in time and the theorists' own experiences so that you may immediately engage in the world of mass media.

present you with static lists of facts and theories, *Mass Media Revolution* strives to present ideas through illuminating and memorable stories, photographs and videos, connecting theories to their place in time and the theorists' own experiences so that you may immediately engage in the world of mass media.

As in cultures and civilizations that have preceded our own, regardless of technological sophistication, the power of the story lies in its ability to create shared images and shared ideas through skillful use of language and other aspects of communication; to express ideas and beliefs, values and aesthetics—to "paint with words" and images. As you will see in Chapter 2, well-constructed and well-told stories can unite vast segments of a population by creating a communal experience, and thus a collective meaning. Stories are what we use to better understand and respond to the ever-changing world around us. Story-delivered messages have the added power of enabling us to identify with the characters and situations, creating an increased level of ownership, or affinity, with the message being communicated. The power of mass communicated stories can never be overestimated.

Inspiring Debate Through Bias and Controversy

As you will learn throughout the book and media, and particularly in Chapter 10, all media are somewhat biased. Some media content is more biased by design and intent, whereas other sources express bias because of the nature of the medium itself. Textbooks are no exception. As an author, I have tried to be honest, open and forthcoming about my own bias with the aim of encouraging readers to openly explore their own ideas and opinions about the topics under discussion. The important thing to remember as you read and interact with this content is that there are no perfect theories that explain everything in mass communication. The goal of *Mass Media Revolution* is to encourage you to develop your own thoughts about how mass communication systems work and where they are headed and to further your exploration and critical assessment of different viewpoints.

As you make your way through the stories of mass media, keep in mind that many of the topics are controversial. The mass media play such a pivotal role in the progress of cultures, societies and nations that to study it is to confront contentious debates about race, religion, politics, the power of governments and the rights, or lack of rights, of individuals and groups. However checkered mass media's role has been in society, the significance of that role cannot be denied. History reveals that the mass media are responsible for sustaining racial and ethnic stereotypes as well as breaking them down and removing barriers to social and cultural diversity. Mass media, at its best, can facilitate the free flow of information ideas; at its worst, it can perpetuate lies and falsehoods through subtle manipulation of facts or outright propaganda.

Experience and Scholarship

As a mass media practitioner and academic, I encourage experiential learning using multimedia. The experiential approach of this book and accompanying media seeks to further enhance your study of mass media topics, philosophies, issues and trends. In every chapter of this book, you will notice video content that was produced to promote integrative mass media learning. A video player icon signals the availability of these videos, showing you when the chapter's narrative is being extended online. Here's a "sneak peek"

A Sneak Peek at *MMR*, 3e
View this movie trailer of things to come as you experience *Mass Media Revolution*, 3e.

trailer; these clips come from the many short "mini-documentary" videos that make up a significant portion of *Mass Media Revolution, 3e.* ▶

Applying Historical Context to Mass Media

To understand fully the dynamics of present-day mass media, we need to build a historical context that tracks the common themes that recur in the industries' evolutions. In other words, to appreciate where we are today, we need to understand what it took to get us here. For this reason, this book spends time walking you through the history of mass media (particularly in Chapter 2), to demonstrate how long chains of technology-driven revolutions (each made possible by the cumulative advances that came before) make the mass media story all the more fascinating. Consider, for instance, how the innovative progression of cell phones has changed the world—from early personal digital assistant (PDA) technologies to Apple's iPhone. The proliferation and advancement of cell phone technologies especially the rapid global spread of "smartphones" such as the iPhone and Android, have made communication and media so widely accessible and mobile that they are changing cultures around the world. In this way, every revolutionary change in mass media has served as the new media of its time.

> To understand fully the dynamics of present-day mass media, we need to build a historical context that tracks the common themes that recur in the industries' evolutions. In other words, to appreciate where we are today, we need to understand what it took to get us here.

As you will learn, mass media contribute in a major way to changing the existing social, political, religious and cultural orders. According to author and media historian Irving Fang, for an information and mass media revolution to succeed, the technological and content innovations must provide a new means for communicating within societies that are already poised to undergo revolutionary change.[2] For example, the German goldsmith and printer Johannes Gutenberg (1398–1468) unleashed the new media of his era by inventing the wooden printing press, and then using it to print and distribute the Christian Bible to a broader, more socially diverse audience than ever before. His invention contributed to a cultural, religious and social revolution throughout 15th-century Europe. Historians widely agree that Europe of the 15th century was already poised for such revolution; Gutenberg's mass media innovation greatly facilitated that process.

Throughout history, mass media-facilitated change has almost always had tumultuous beginnings. Entrenched cultural forces tend to fight to preserve the status quo, which they have a key stake in maintaining. Forces of change generally win the culture wars, but victory often comes only after long periods of struggle. Humankind adjusts and evolves, but the pace of transformation is speeding up exponentially. We are all witness to and participants in the revolutionary transformations brought about, in part, by the new media of our day. Mass media have not only served as major catalysts and facilitators for cultural and social change, but have also represented the primary means by which societies and cultures tell their stories to the next generations. Storytelling is inseparable from mass media, and it has allowed the media to exert tremendous influence over society.

STUDYING THE MASS MEDIA

In this book, we study mass media from various perspectives and theoretical viewpoints. This chapter introduces you to the most common of those theories, including media literacy, media dynamics and media effects. In the early part of the 20th century, the study of media and communication took place primarily in the speech/rhetoric departments of colleges and universities. These departments focused on developing theories of mass media in the context of studying rhetoric (writing or speaking as a means of communication or persuasion) and human communication and explored how rhetoric influences public speaking, interpretation of literature, drama, debate and verbal interaction within small groups. As early as the 1940s, researchers in university psychology, sociology and cultural anthropology departments started to focus more on a collaborative and scientific exploration of the emerging electronic media: What was their potential impact on human communication? On information delivery? On the access to and transfer of knowledge?

1.3

Marble Head of Aristotle
(384–322 b.c.)

Hulton Archive/Stringer

1.4

Portrait of Confucius
(551–472 b.c.)

Leemage

The study of communication actually began about 2,400 years ago, when ancient philosophers such as Aristotle in Greece and Confucius in China recognized the relationship between good governance and good communication between rulers and the people they governed. Confucius believed that spoken and written words served as forces for social change and could significantly influence how both individuals and even entire societies behaved. Aristotle also recognized the power of spoken and written words, especially when they were expressed persuasively and in the right setting by a well-respected person. He believed that in the right combination, words could shape what people thought and how they acted. What is remarkable about Aristotle (384–322 b.c.) and Confucius (551–472 b.c.) is that at roughly the same time in history—during an ancient era when most people rarely traveled more than a few miles from their homes and very few people were even literate—they both recognized how words can influence, delight, inspire and guide people.[3]

This inevitable coming together of mass media, communication and information technology research quickly became a dominant force in academia. It also paralleled the equally rapid convergence of mass media environments and media content, and fueled the extraordinary increase in the number of jobs that require basic understanding of mass media systems and processes. This mediated communication affords us the ability to exchange ideas and information quickly, effectively and across geographical and cultural barriers. As a result, the media have become the central component to the prosperity of individuals, organizations, nations and societies.

Media Convergence

Since the early 20th century, most communication has occurred through the use of technology that extends our connections far beyond face-to-face discussion. The obvious role of evolving communication and mass media technologies in shaping our lives and driving dynamic social, cultural and political change helped push scientists in disciplines such as cultural anthropology, sociology and psychology to formally study "mass communication" and to develop theories on how these processes actually work. Although both the concepts and research tools have undergone significant refinements over time, the ideas first described by philosophers such as Aristotle and Confucius are still at the core of the study of mass media. Contemporary mass communication scholars and researchers examine how technology is used to communicate and influences individuals and groups when they are physically apart from each other.

Since the mid-19th century, a steady and increasingly rapid series of technological developments starting with the invention of the telegraph and telephone gave more and more people the ability to communicate, regardless of their geographical location. As you will learn throughout this book, technological innovation is ever-evolving and continues to grow exponentially. The timeline "The Evolution of Media Technologies" (found in Chapter 2) demonstrates the rapid pace at which technological change is driving media convergence. Convergence is not a new phenomenon; what is new is the pace of technological change that drives convergence. The past 30 years has brought us more choices and more individual capabilities and options for both personal expression and social change than were seen in the previous 300 years.

Changes in the way we communicate have likewise changed the way researchers theorize and study communication. On the one hand, we now have previously unimagined resources to express ourselves to ever-increasing circles of geographically and culturally dispersed people—think Facebook and Twitter. On the other hand, we are bombarded daily by a cacophony of media messages that require us to become skilled at determining what we pay attention to versus what we ignore. Moreover, the concept of "private" communication appears to be rapidly disappearing as we put more and more aspects of our lives and our personal information online.

These rapidly evolving technologically driven changes beg the question: Which mass communication theories are most useful and most important for us to know about? This is not an easy question to answer because there is no single theory that encompasses all aspects of human use of and participation in mass communication and mass media. In fact, most often the best and most useful results come from the application of a range of theories, resulting in an integrated snapshot of how various aspects of mass media appear to be working.

Mass Media Defined

Before we explore the common perspectives for studying and analyzing the mass media, we must first agree upon a good operational definition for mass media and the role each media industry plays in human communication. Mass media comprise the communication platforms that enable the exchange of information and meanings (content) between individuals and groups. These messages are shared via a common system of language or symbols on or along a platform or conduit (medium) that is equally accessible by all parties in the exchange. A mass media platform refers to the entire gamut of technology-based communication media—from the telephone to sophisticated Internet technology.

Many examples and stories discussed in *Mass Media Revolution* illustrate and help explain how the mass media operate and influence what we know, what we believe and how our society and culture progress. An individual skilled in "reading" mass media texts can decipher the media message, appreciate and analyze the content from social and cultural perspectives, and determine the validity and effectiveness of that message in context. Academics and researchers call this mass media content "media literacy." Media literacy is the term commonly used to describe the identification, study and analysis of all processes involved in creating and consuming media content across all media types and platforms. In other words, media literacy is the ability to understand how mass media work and how they influence all aspects of our lives.

media literacy is the ability to understand how mass media work and how they influence all aspects of our lives.

Media literate people are not only better able to understand and convey ideas, but also better equipped to understand how media technologies and media biases affect the vast array of information, news and media content available. Moreover, they are better able to seek out alternative sources of information, viewpoints and entertainment. In this sense, media literate people are more responsible citizens of their society, their nation and the increasingly linked and interdependent global community. While the origin of this term is credited to scholars and researchers working in the realm of mass communication, it is commonly used by all persons who consume or produce media.

Media dynamics refers to all of the various processes and influences that go into shaping mass media content—from creative issues; to economics and business models; to political influences; to technological advances and limitations; to social, cultural and even religious pressures and trends. Media effects, or *media influence*, refers to ideas and theories about how mass media influence people—as individuals, as families, as communities, as nations. Media effects theory looks at how media content, from news to entertainment, influences the way we see our neighbors, the world and ourselves. Media effects can be studied at the individual issue or specific-story level, it can focus on the forms and genres of mass media, or it can focus more broadly on various platforms for the delivery of media content— broadcast television versus Internet, for example. This book focuses primarily on the multiple ways the mass media influence society and culture, along with the platforms and processes through which media industries exert their influence, so one could say that this book is *all* about media dynamics and media effects.

THEORETICAL BUILDING BLOCKS OF MASS MEDIA

The two-page chart, "Mass Communication Models, Theories and Research," outlines how some major theories help us to understand the workings of mass communication. The following are examples of how we can apply these theories to what we actually experience in the mass media.

Textual analyses are used by researchers who have an interest in carefully examining mass media products, such as TV shows. In this context, the word "text" or "textual" does not necessarily refer to a book or written material but perhaps to a single television program, a group of programs, songs, movies or video games. Communication researchers often look at "texts" to determine how people or groups are portrayed, often applying what is called social learning theory. Social learning theory states that we gain important information about other people through observation and then apply these learned models to how we see ourselves.

For example, many Muslim Americans were concerned about how they were being portrayed in the media following the September 11, 2001, attacks on the World Trade Center and the Pentagon. Researchers using textual analyses examined popular TV shows including *Lost* and *24* to question the role of entertainment media in promoting a more complex discussion about contemporary and historical depictions of Muslims. Instead of finding well-rounded portrayals, the research showed that many recent TV and film dramas still project negative stereotypes about Muslims and the Islamic religion—depictions that have become increasingly negative after 9/11.[4]

A more rigorous kind of textual analysis is called content coding. Content coding occurs when a team of trained "coders" analyzes a specific TV program, film, advertising campaign, video game or blog to measure and report on certain attributes of the content. For example, if researchers want to see if television news is reporting on minorities in a fair and unbiased manner, they will record the major networks' news programs and keep track of each time minorities are included as part of a news story. Content coding would look at the number and kinds of minorities involved in each story and the factual quality of the reporting and then record any bias in the reporting by logging particular words, phrases or images used.

While rooted in social learning theory, content coding draws from other mass communication theories such as agenda setting and cultivation effect. In agenda setting, researchers seek to find out if the amount of news coverage that a story receives affects both how much and in what way audiences view that story. For example, although the cable news networks might spend 25 percent of their airtime covering the primaries leading up to national elections, the majority of audiences might not rate campaign news stories as being very important to them until very close to Election Day. On the other hand, if the national news media focus attention on a particularly horrific child molestation case, people may rate that subject as highly important to them; this may be in part because so many people are parents and thus have a personal affinity with the victims in the story. As a theory, agenda setting was first suggested in 1968 by communication scholars Maxwell McCombs and Donald L. Shaw as a method—incorporating both content coding and public opinion research—for studying how people rate the importance of specific news stories, and how certain news stories influence the public agenda while other stories have little lasting impact.[5]

> In agenda setting, researchers seek to find out if the amount of news coverage that a story receives affects both how much and in what way audiences view that story.

Another important mass communication theory is known as the cultivation effect; this suggests that people over time are "cultivated" to have certain beliefs about the world based upon their exposure to mass media, especially television. Developed in the late 1960s by George Gerbner, the cultivation effect occurs when viewers of mass media begin to assume that what they see on TV is representative of the "real world." Gerbner and his colleagues found that the public in some cities assumed their community was much more violent than it actually was according to police statistics. This media-driven misperception of reality occurred in part because the TV audiences received a constant fare of violent scenes both on fictional programs and the local and national news.[6] Gerbner, who grew up in Hungary before World War II and left when the Communists overtook the country in 1956, believed that there can be political gains for a government in keeping the population fearful of each other, complacent about greater police power and willing to accept increasing regulations that take away personal freedoms or personal privacy in the service

Mass Communication

How Do Mass Media Communicate Their Messages?

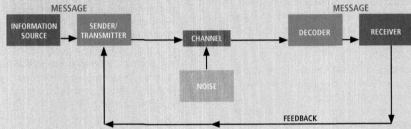

THE SHANNON-WEAVER MODEL

Also referred to as the linear model of communication, this model comprises eight primary components:

- Source—the source/creator (writers, producers, media organizations) of the message; before delivering a message, the sender must consider how best to organize and deliver the message to ensure that it reaches the receiver (also known as encoding).
- Message—the content (all forms of "text": print, visual, audio and digital).
- Sender/Transmitter—the sender/transmitter encodes the message into signals (words, images, gestures) that represent the intended meaning of the message.
- Channel—the medium (books, newspapers, magazines, radio, television, film, Internet) that carries the message.
- Decoder—the content manager (editors, producers, Web page hosts and monitors) that filters the message.
- Receiver—the audience (readers, viewers, listeners).
- Noise—anything and everything that interferes with the transmission of the message (traffic heard through an open window, a person's head obstructing your view of the movie screen, internal dialogue, stress).
- Feedback—the receiver's response (letter to the editor, blog post, e-mail, text) to the message.

Factors That Affect Mass Communication:
- Communication environment—the setting in which communication occurs (online, face-to-face, alone with a book, in a theater with other viewers); the setting profoundly affects the meaning of the message received.

The Goal of Mass Communication:
- Shared meaning—a continuum of understanding about the message between sender and receiver.

Concerns About the Linear Model:
- Communication is not linear—Although researchers have not abandoned the Shannon-Weaver model as an approach to studying the way mass media communicate, some suggest that it is an unrealistic model because communication is a

dynamic and interactive process and individuals do not function as passive senders and receivers. This is especially true in the Digital Age, as information does not have to be consumed linearly (from beginning to end) and individuals are able to respond and participate in the creation and communication of messages.

THE TRANSACTIONAL MODEL

It shows how the sender and he receiver are constantly encoding and decoding messages, providing feedback to each other, and being affected by noise—all at the same time.

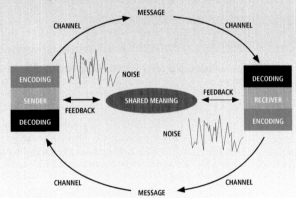

CRITICAL/CULTURAL APPROACHES TO COMMUNICATION STUDIES

This scholarly approach combines qualitative and quantitative analysis to examine what individuals bring to a message that might affect their interpretation of its meaning. Critical cultural theory assumes that those controlling mass media forward messages that maintain their cultural, social or political agenda. Critical studies consider how mass media portrayals of ideology, ethnicity, social class, sexuality and gender contribute to the way media consumers view their own and others' cultural positions and status. For example, a critical cultural scholar might observe a news broadcast and ask questions about which cultural status quo is being maintained by the story, which stories are not being covered in the news and why, and how the choices of news coverage reflect a social or cultural norm.

THEORIES

How Do We Study The Effects Of Mass Media?

EARLY APPROACHES

- **Hypodermic Needle Theory or Magic Bullet Theory**
  Based on the work of Yale psychologist Harold Lasswell, who studied World War II propaganda, this model suggests that mass media can at times inject false information and manipulative ideas into the public consciousness, thereby manipulating the public agenda. This theory assumes that the public, as mass media consumers, are passive and uncritical of media-delivered information and will automatically accept whatever the media put forth as facts and truth. (See Chapter 10.)

- **Minimal Effects Model**
  Based on studies conducted in the 1940s by the Columbia University sociologist Paul Lazarsfeld, this model argues that the media have only a minimal effect on media consumers. At most, it suggests, the media merely reinforce current behaviors and attitudes. This theory also suggests that media consumers are passive. (See Chapter 7.)

- **Uses and Gratifications Model**
  Originally based on studies conducted in the 1940s, this model argues that the media have only a minimal effect on media consumers. At most, it suggests, the media merely reinforce current behaviors an attitudes. This theory also suggests that media consumers are passive. (See Chapter 7.)

CONTEMPORARY APPROACHES

- **Social Learning Theory**
  Based on theories from social psychology first developed by University of Connecticut psychologist Julian Rotter in the 1950s, this theory considers how people learn new behaviors through a process of observing and modeling.

- **Agenda-Setting Theory**
  Based on the work of communication scholar Maxwell McCombs from his groundbreaking study of voter behavior in the 1968 U.S. presidential election, this theory suggests that the media's focus and framing of stories, issues and events will determine what audiences will talk about—thereby setting the public agenda. (See Chapters 9, 10, 11, 13, and 14.)

- **Cumulative Effects Theory**
  Based on the writings of German political scientist Elisabeth Noelle-Neumann, this theory suggests that the powerful effects of mass media build up to a certain point, rather than occurring immediately. (See Chapters 8 and 10.)

- **Cultivation Effect**
  This model assumes that if media consumers watch television in great enough quantities, they will perceive television's depictions of reality to be consistent, accurate and true. In other words, the media nurture or shape the media consumer's idea of reality.

- **Spiral of Silence**
  Developed in the 1970s and 1980s by Elisabeth Noelle-Neumann, this theory suggests that individuals will not (for fear of social isolation) express their views if they believe their views represent the minority. As a consequence, the media overinflate acceptance of what is considered the "majority" view.

RESEARCH

How Do We Analyze Media Messages?

EARLY APPROACHES

- **Propaganda Analysis**
  First developed by scientists working at the Institute for Propaganda Analysis in the late 1930s, this analysis helps us to more clearly identify when specific media content is intentionally structured to spread ideas and to manipulate audiences into accepting those ideas.

- **Public Opinion Research**
  First developed in the mid-19th century and refined throughout the 20th century, this method uses survey and sampling techniques, along with sophisticated statistical analysis, to gain insights into citizens' behavior, opinions and attitudes, especially during political elections.

- **Social Psychology Studies**
  First appearing in the 1920s and refined in subsequent decades, these methodologies measure the effects of different forms of media content, such as movies, television programs, TV advertising and video games, on individual behavior—in particular, on antisocial behaviors.

- **Content Analysis**
  Studies developed to focus specific media messages use Harold Lasswell's four-question guide: "Who says what to whom, why, to what extent and with what effect?"

CONTEMPORARY APPROACHES

- **Textual Analysis**
  First developed by Indiana University sociologist Alfred R. Linde-smith in the 1930s and 1940s and later expanded by Yale psychologist Harold Lasswell, this approach conducts systematic analysis of cultural content via examination of seemingly minor things. For example, in a textbook, the item considered could be the number of times a certain key phrase is used: What does that frequency say about the larger message of the book?

- **Audience Measurement**
  Originally using media diaries and now electronic and computer-based monitoring, this research method tracks the media-consuming behaviors—radio listening, television program watching, and more recently Website visits—of small numbers of statistically representative (and usually paid) volunteers. Observations are then used to help determine larger audience preferences and behaviors.

of keeping violence at bay. As with agenda setting, Gerbner and his colleagues relied upon public opinion research to track rising public fear of violence and to find the correlation between those most fearful people and the heaviest TV viewers.

During the early and mid-20th century, researchers looked more closely at the relationship between mediated communication and power. The idea was simple: those people and organizations that can get their messages out to the most people will have more power than those who cannot be heard. One of the earliest and most influential scholars to explore the relationship between media message proliferation and power was Antonio Gramsci, who wrote many of his most important works while a prisoner of war in World War I. Gramsci wrote about the way those who have less power agree to remain in their subservient social position because of the messages they hear through school, laws or religion. Many contemporary mass media scholars assert that the media play an important role in creating hegemonic power for governments and large corporations—both having the ability to send out persistent messages to vast segments of the general public that justify social and economic inequities and make those who are poorer or weaker "complicit" in maintaining the current power structures. Those scholars who view communication studies as mainly about issues of power in a society often identify themselves as Marxist or critical theorists; their work tends to be highly interpretive, seeking the underlying or "counterhegemonic" messages in the media.

> Many contemporary mass media scholars assert that the media play an important role in creating hegemonic power for governments and large corporations

Most media theorists agree, and most of us as media consumers easily recognize, that the core of mass media is always various forms of "selling." Selling ideas, products, candidates, lifestyles, religious beliefs—even fantasies. The scholars who study media in the realm of "selling" are most interested in what will change people's beliefs, attitudes and behaviors.[7] To find out which tools are most effective, researchers use concepts from social psychology to measure the kinds of effects various types of media content and messages generate. Researchers carefully analyze people's responses, using sophisticated statistical methods and models. Some of the more important findings from this area of applied mass communication research are the inoculation theory, social judgment theory and the elaboration likelihood model. All three theories have demonstrated that people can be encouraged or discouraged from using reason to make decisions regarding many aspects of their day-to-day lives. These three theories also attempt to explain when, where and in what situations people will be persuaded by certain kinds of communications.

Another popular mass communication theory focuses on how people use technology for their own need fulfillment, sense of connection and happiness. The uses and gratifications theory is rooted in research conducted on the attachment TV viewers felt in the 1950s to the hosts of

1.5

In the Digital Age, media literacy is of critical importance. Think about the media you consume on a regular basis. Are you aware of the media dynamics influencing your news and entertainment? How do you consume media most frequently?

BananaStock/ Thinkstock

game shows. Based on this earlier research, media scholars have demonstrated that people do not merely "consume" mass media, but "actively use" media to enhance their lives.[8] With the advent of the Internet, researchers began to reexamine this theory to see how children and adults use the Internet, electronic games, mobile media devices, social networking and instant messaging to maintain relationships and build self-identity.

Passive and Active Media

Mass media platforms can be either active or passive. Active media platforms allow for the exchange of information between users who share in creating the media content and messages. The Internet is the most obvious example of such a platform, as it is where we regularly find ourselves acting as both users and co-creators of content. Passive media platforms allow for little or no direct input into the content from the user, such as when we watch a movie or television program. While this content is no doubt useful, entertaining and educational, we have control only over what, when, where and how we choose to watch a film or program. This same concept applies to most books, magazines and music that we buy—that is, we are most often passive consumers of the media content.

The Digital Age, with its rapid convergence of media and media delivery platforms, offers the average media consumer more opportunities to become an active participant in media content. Internet Websites, blogs, broadcast news and entertainment programs, e-books, music file-sharing sites and many other platforms are quickly offering ever-more options and opportunities for users to participate in the selection and even the creation of the media content they want.

Media Framing

Mass media framing is often a topic of great controversy and inspires debates in which the media, particularly the news media, are accused of presenting stories and issues to fit the "reality" that it wants the public—the receivers—to accept. Even in the most stringent attempts at "balanced journalism," the news media have an influence on their audience's perception of the story. (We explore this topic in detail as part of our discussion of media bias in Chapter 10.)

Framing, or bias, can be as basic as what a particular news organization elects to cover as its "top stories" or who it suggests is responsible for a problem or its solution. The audience of a television news broadcast might be able to detect that a story or a reporter is biased, but the question of great interest to mass media researchers is whether the detection of framing results in the audience becoming critical media consumers. Might the media effect be so powerful that the majority of the audience accepts even framed and biased reporting as a balanced and fair representation of reality?

Research has shown that media framing does have an effect on the way audiences interpret stories and issues. This effect on the audience is of critical importance because the success of the media, especially the U.S. commercial model (which we discuss in greater detail in Chapter 9), is almost totally dependent on audience reaction and acceptance—on whether and when audiences select and then stay tuned into a particular media outlet. This is true to such an extent that it is common to hear media producers, platform operators or researchers say that in mass media the audience "rules."

Today's multiple mass media channels are constantly placing demands on our attention as well as diminishing the quality of the media content and messages—a trend that challenges our ability to categorize the content we are able to receive and use effectively. This relationship is why most media creators and media organizations—be they broadcasting networks, Webcasters, publishers, authors, artists, musicians or even the editor of your school newspaper—work to maximize the amount of information that they can deliver by increasing the quality and attractiveness of the mass media platform that they use to communicate with media consumers.

This scientific model of mass media communication—the widely accepted model used for understanding how things work in the natural world—uses hypothesis, observation and evaluation to help us to filter the morass of information and retain only the most meaningful items. The model can be applied to all forms

1.6

Here we see a crowd watching Russian president Putin; in what ways is the photojournalist who took this image attempting to "frame a media message"?

Sergei Ilnitsky/AFP/Newscom

of communication, from the direct and interpersonal, to the highly complex and technological. Proponents and defenders of the scientific view use theoretical modeling to make it easier to identify, understand and reduce the barriers to effective mass media communication within highly complex systems and environments. To build a working understanding of how mass media communicate knowledge, ideas and stories, we must combine scientific models with a basic understanding of how we as human beings come to understand and communicate with the world around us.

To build a working understanding of how mass media communicate knowledge, ideas and stories, we must combine scientific models with a basic understanding of how we as human beings come to understand and communicate with the world around us.

The Humanistic Approach to Communication

Philosopher-psychologists such as Abraham Maslow and Carl Rogers described in their writings the humanistic approach to the study and understanding of human communication. Maslow based his work on the study of the lives of individuals he termed "self-actualized." Rogers based his theories on both his work as a psychotherapist and his later work in international conflict resolution. According to Maslow, all human communication revolves around a basic hierarchy of human needs, which begins with basic physiological needs and moves through safety, love and esteem to self-actualization. Maslow found this hierarchy of needs to be common in all cultures and theorized that it is the basis of all human communication. As individuals move through the process of satisfying this hierarchy of needs, he suggested, higher and more complex communication becomes possible.

Today, Maslow's hierarchy of human needs is more broadly interpreted and applied to allow for the fact that most of us work on various need levels simultaneously. Maslow's highly optimistic and positive view of human potential and social interaction emphasizes freedom of choice to understand why and how human beings communicate. In combination with the more scientific Shannon–Weaver model (which covers the information source, the message, the receiver, the sender, the channel—see the following graphic illustrating this model and any noise that may interrupt the communication process), Maslow's work brings us closer to understanding how at the core of mass media, we are all participants in complex multilevel exchanges of information.

1.7

Maslow's Hierarchy of Human
Needs

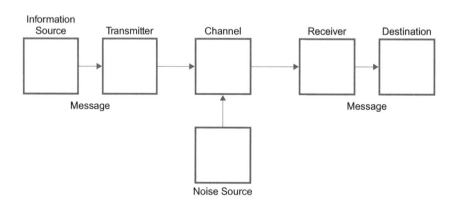

**The Need for
Self-actualization**
Experience purpose and
meaning and realize
all inner potential.

Esteem Need
The need to be a unique individual with
self-respect and to enjoy general
esteem from others.

Love and Belonging Needs
The need for belonging; to receive and give love,
appreciation, friendship.

Security Need
The basic need for social security in a family and a society
that protects against hunger and violence.

The Physiological Needs
The need for food, water, shelter and clothing.

1.8

Shannon-Weaver Model

Information
Source | Transmitter | Channel | Receiver | Destination

Message

Message

Noise Source

Carl Rogers, another influential American psychologist in the mid-20th century, also contributed to our growing knowledge of how mass media operate as vehicles of human communication. While Rogers is considered one of the founding fathers of modern psychotherapy, his later work on the roots of social conflict is considered a major contribution that helped aid our understanding of the impact of mass media on culture and society. According to Rogers, problems can arise when people attempt to communicate and force their worldviews and beliefs onto others. He tested this theory by investigating mass media effects on intergroup conflict in South Africa and Northern Ireland; these studies earned him a Nobel Peace Prize nomination.

Rogers's research into the complexities of human communication ultimately led him to the conclusion that it is impossible to understand entirely the meaning of what people are communicating; therefore, we should accept all communicated meaning at face value only. In view of our limited ability to decipher messages, Rogers's advocates are becoming skillful and capable mass media consumers—listeners, viewers, readers and so forth. He persuasively argues that critical listening (and viewing) interrupts the passage of unfiltered content to the media consumer and helps prevent premature judgments and evaluations that would otherwise alter the content. Rogers's efforts to apply these theories to conflict mediation in the 1970s among highly volatile groups in Northern Ireland and the Middle East had extraordinarily positive results, albeit within small groups. Yet, despite the success of his studies, many experts outside the humanistic movement question the validity of his research and results. Whether Rogers's theories have valuable implications for the study of mass communication is an interesting question to ponder.

Linking the Medium and the Message

To many in the field, the founding father of mass media theory was the Canadian philosopher, educator and media critic Marshall McLuhan—one of the truly outstanding theorists and writers on the subject of the impact of mass media on society. McLuhan's analysis of modern mass media and the link between "medium and message" has had a profound impact on our awareness and understanding of the role of mass media. It was especially critical in its shaping of society through the 20th century and into the dawning of the 21st century. McLuhan's book *Understanding Media: The Extensions of Man* focused on the practical and operational reality that all personal and social communication are inseparable from the medium within which the message is communicated.

As the media of human communication have evolved with the introduction of new technologies, from the printing press through the telephone, radio, television and now the Internet, the very nature of the way humans associate with one another has also changed. In McLuhan's view, the technological mechanisms that enable human communication are inseparable from the dynamics of how mass communication really works, and thus also inseparable from the content of the messages being exchanged. The implications of this theoretical viewpoint are manifest. It is impossible, for example, to disconnect the effects of a television news story from the medium through which it is being delivered to us. The impact of a given news story about a terrorist bombing becomes inseparable from the real-time video footage that enables us to experience the story almost in real time as it is unfolding. McLuhan's futurist predictions about where communication and mass media technologies were headed, which he first introduced in the early 1960s, are presented in the video, "Marshall McLuhan, *Explorations*." This television broadcast on his work and ideas first aired on May 5, 1960. ▶

▶ **Marshall McLuhan, Explorations**
Marshall McLuhan—his legacy and impact as a mass media futurist.

AUDIENCE TRENDS

The expansion of mass media technologies has brought with it a parallel increase in audience demand for more information and more knowledge; an understanding of this audience trend links inextricably to our study of mass media. This demand helps drive the innovation and growth of an ever-wider interdependent union between technology, content and audience. The dynamic interchange between advertisers (whose financial support underlies much of mass media production and distribution) and content delivery organizations (television broadcast and cable companies, publishers, Internet content providers and Internet services companies) strives to attract and keep audiences; after all, without audience retention, media industries would not survive financially. In other words, in most areas of mass media, the audience rules.

As we explore in Chapter 9, entire media industries continue to evolve and reinvent their operating, marketing and business models in response to their careful projections about what audiences want now and in the future. Consider, for instance, the consumer demand for (and thus success of) reality television programs—from the lighthearted *America's Funniest Home Videos* (1989), which invited viewers to submit hilarious moments from their home video collections; to the more *Lord of the Flies*-sequel wilderness show *Survivor* (2000); to the exciting around-the-world adventures of *The Amazing Race* (2001). Clearly, this trend in television and cable programming has not only become popular over the last 20 years, but, with the spate of shows within the last 10 years, has driven home the point that there appears to be no shortage of "reality" topics to cover. Media organizations invest huge sums of money trying to correctly predict what audiences want in an effort to adjust their content and delivery styles quickly so that they may both reap the financial rewards of meeting these demands and direct the next new wave of trends.

When it came to foreseeing how audiences would eventually want to receive their news, for example, innovative media researcher Frank N. Magid (1932–2010) made some successful predictions. In the 1970s, Magid conducted audience research that resulted in the reinvention of how television news programs were produced. It used to be that both national and local news broadcasts featured a single news anchor—usually a middle-aged white man who read news stories from a stack of papers on his desk in front of a static background. Magid changed this scenario by convincing television news organizations to build their broadcasts around co-anchors, many more of whom were women of various ethnicities. To humanize these broadcasts, co-anchors would engage in dialogue and commentary about the news stories on which they were reporting.

Magid also encouraged news programs to include more soft human-interest stories, add interesting graphics and greatly increase the overall pace of the reporting. News anchors were told to stop reading from papers on their desks and to engage more directly with their viewers using teleprompters to emphasize a more natural, conversational telling of a news story. Those networks and local stations that followed Magid's audience research-based recommendations quickly shot to the top in the ratings, resulting in higher advertising revenues for their news broadcasts, which had traditionally been considered more of a public service than a market-sensitive revenue generator. Magid went so far as to invent terms for this new audience-responsive news program format for local stations, calling it either Action News or Eyewitness News—terms still found in the titles of many local television news programs today.[9]

1.9

Frank N. Magid changed the face of television news by convincing organizations to build their broadcasts around co-anchors, who would engage with their viewers through dialogue and commentary about the news.

ColorBlin Images/Belnd

WHY RESEARCH AUDIENCES?

Audiences rule the production, packaging and marketing of the content and format of mass media, so they are also constantly being researched and surveyed. Researchers working for media content producers and advertisers use sophisticated techniques of identifying audience demographics—such factors as age, sex, race, educational levels, geographic location and psychographics, as well as attitudes, social and cultural values, interests and lifestyles—to identify exactly who their audience is and what they want. More specifically, demographic analysis allows content providers to target and attract new viewers, listeners, readers and Website users. As audience research has grown increasingly more sophisticated and thus more accurate, media content producers and especially advertisers have successfully managed to narrowly tailor their content and define their audiences—a process known as *narrowcasting* (and discussed in greater detail in Chapter 8 on advertising and public relations and Chapter 10 on media bias and political media). Today, media research firms such as A. C. Nielsen and Arbitron dominate the audience research industry to such a degree that their work has a huge impact on which new media content, especially television and radio content, is produced. To understand how these companies' audience feedback systems work, view the video segment titled "How Ratings Work." ▶

▶ **How Ratings Work**
Discussion of measurement techniques used to place values on television and radio programming.

Advertisers need the ability to target those audience segments in which they are interested, often within the specified geographic areas they service. For this purpose, the geographic distribution of media audiences in the United States is broken into 250 geographic regions called Designated Market Areas (DMAs). Many urban regions are considered crossover DMAs, especially for television and radio markets. For example, the Washington, D.C.–Baltimore, Maryland, area is one of these crossover DMAs because radio stations, television stations and newspapers service both metropolitan areas simultaneously. The rapid growth of television services and the Internet has changed how media producers and advertisers approach audiences, and it presents both new challenges and new opportunities to the process of identifying and reaching desired audience segments. The growth of media formats and media channels in the late 20th and early 21st century also makes it easier for content producers and advertisers to reach their targeted audiences, especially in the case of special audiences such as children, minorities and the elderly.

In the early days of television, advertisers for series such as *The Lone Ranger* and *Superman* knew that a portion of the audience was children; therefore, commercials typically sold children's toys and games. However, advertisers had a hard time determining exactly what percentage were children and which age group made up the regular audience. By comparison, today advertisers selling toys or games for children ages 6 to 12 today can buy commercial spots on programs geared toward this specific age group, running on the Nickelodeon Channel or the Disney Channel, and know with a great deal of statistical certainty the demographics of the audience they are reaching. In the same way, an advertiser promoting a retirement community can buy commercial spots on a travel program geared toward audiences ages 50 and older running on the Travel Channel and know that it is reaching the precise segment of the audience that is their market. Of course, there is a counterforce to these efforts to more narrowly identify audiences—namely, the ever-increasing globalization of mass media, especially through the Internet.

CULTURE AND MASS MEDIA: SHARING WHAT WE KNOW

All mass media operate within a social/cultural context. To aid us in our understanding of mass media within cultural contexts, and for the purposes of this book, we will define culture as the integrated and dynamic social system of behaviors, characteristics, customs, language, artifacts and symbols that distinguish one social group from another. Culture also comprises the distinct processes, methods, styles and media that group members use to communicate with one another.[10] A social group generally consists of two or more people who interact with one another. Social groups are not a recently developed concept—even the earliest humans formed and lived within social groups. Human communication evolved along a social interaction continuum, starting with the smallest family unit and proceeding upward to large ethnic units. Communication systems and processes develop simultaneously within and between each type of social group and one or more larger units along the social interaction continuum.

We rely on culture to distinguish one social group from another. Culture gives individuals within a group their social anchor and identity and establishes the rules that enable individuals to engage with one another effectively. To some extent, culture consists of the methods and media through which the members in the group are able to communicate. As we move up the social continuum, the mounting size and complexity of a society requires increasingly dynamic means of communicating with ever-larger groups in ways that allow smaller groups to retain a knowledge of who they are and where they belong. This is where the tool of mass media comes in: The multiple aspects and forms of mass media that we explore throughout this book, taken together, are the primary means by which culture is communicated—within a society, between societies and from one generation to the next.

> The multiple aspects and forms of mass media that we explore throughout this book, taken together, are the primary means by which culture is communicated—within a society, between societies and from one generation to the next.

The Challenge of Cross-Cultural Communication

American anthropologist Clyde Kluckhohn (1905–1960) identified more than 160 definitions of "culture." Some of these definitions envisage culture as communicable knowledge; others view culture as a totality of the collective history of a society. All definitions of culture have at their core the ability to communicate, or a component of communicating, the knowledge, history, styles and symbols of a society, along with the means and methods of the communication itself. Culture incorporates all learned and shared elements of a society that can be transmitted between its participants and passed down through generations. It encompasses mutual ways of thinking and behaving that emanate from social groups and that are reinforced, controlled or regulated by commonly accepted authorities within that group (e.g., parents, leaders, officials, governments, courts). Culture, and how it is communicated, is the principal bridge—and sometimes barrier—to interaction and exchange between societies. The more different cultural groups are from one another, the more critical and challenging communication between them becomes.[11]

> Culture, and how it is communicated, is the principal bridge—and sometimes barrier—to interaction and exchange between societies.

As we explore in other chapters, although the United States does not produce the most film and television content worldwide, its media content certainly is the most sought after and valued internationally; as such, the United States dominates the world's film and television industry. American culture has become so pervasive that it is viewed as a threat by countries that adhere to a stricter, more traditional code of social rules and cultural etiquette. Some countries, such as France, make a concerted effort to limit the amount of U.S.-produced film and television content allowed within their borders in the effort to decrease that perceived threat. Cultural conservatives in France, for example, believe that this kind of cultural patrimony is the only way to protect the French language, customs and society. Fortunately, in the face of advancing mass communication technology, efforts to impose such barriers appear to be failing. Even though many countries in the world—the United States, China and Russia, just to name a few—are so diverse that individuals tend to identify themselves with multiple, yet sometimes conflicting, social groups, the rapid growth and globalization of mass media are forcing an unprecedented melding of cultures.

The Media's Influence on Religion and Beliefs

Cultures, like individuals, change through the communication of information. Worldviews tend to expand; culture evolves; individuals experience personal growth. Such feats would be significantly hampered if access to information were blocked. Information blocking is not uncommon in authoritarian regimes; this is the case today and has been throughout history, in countries ranging from Iran to North Korea to Burma. Their strongest adversary, however, is the mass media. As a system of industries whose primary role is to share information, the mass media represent one of the major vehicles influencing the way people view politics, society, culture and religion; in some instances, the mass media may even *incite* change. (A more in-depth

discussion of the profound effects of mass media in a global context appears in Chapter 14.) For now, to illustrate how mass media can encourage or damage cross-cultural communication, let's consider the current conflict between the United States and the Middle East.

One cannot fully appreciate the dynamics of mass media's impact on culture and society without considering how dominant religions and belief systems influence the perception and consumption of mass media content. For example, even though the majority of the U.S. population is Christian (75 percent of the total population), that majority supports the idea of secularism as protected by the U.S. Constitution. Therefore, American mainstream media do not often advance an overtly religious agenda.[12] Secularism (the separation of religion from political or civic affairs) is not supported by all governments, cultures and religious leaders, however. Many nations in the Middle East, for example, are largely dominated by Islamic culture, which does not support the separation of governing principles and religious beliefs and practices. As a result of these stories, followers of Islam are often wrongly accused of violent extremism and terrorism and Americans of selfishness, materialism and immorality. Of course, in media-blocked countries, these false impressions are exacerbated by limited or no access to media outlets that report objectively and factually on the state of cross-cultural affairs.

In the United States, strong proponents on one end of the political, religious or social spectrum may simply opt to ignore the media that inform media consumers about the opposing perspective. This (lack of) response can be just as much of a hindrance to effective cross-cultural communication as national controls imposed on information and media access. Unfortunately, even expression of a common culture through responsible mass media does not always assure common ground will be found. History is replete with examples of violent conflicts between groups that actually shared religious beliefs and worldviews. For example, consider the historic conflict between the Catholics and Protestants in

1.10

Psy/Ops officers work to bridge extreme cultural differences in an effort to "win minds and hearts" in war-torn Afghanistan.

DOD/Handout

1.11

Despite critical claims that U.S. media is a negative influence, many countries throughout the world imitate American media styles and programs.

Orlando Sierra/Staff

Northern Ireland. When Carl Rogers conducted conflict resolution work in Northern Ireland, he found that once young adults from both sides of the conflict were brought together and asked to debate what the media identified as the roots of their conflict, they were able to share an objective view that incorporated aspects of both sides of the story. This process made it less likely that they would return to being violent combatants.[13]

Another process that we examine when studying the mass media effects on cultures and religions is cultural aesthetics. Simply put, cultural aesthetics relates to what is considered "in good taste" within a specific cultural context. Cultural aesthetics determines a culture's mode of dress and unique art and crafts; it also guides the way a group communicates important information about its social structure, values and worldview. Amish groups in the United States, for instance, live a primarily agricultural lifestyle and choose to restrict their use of and access to modern technologies such as electricity, telephones, television and radio. The most traditional Amish groups continue to travel by horse-drawn wagons and opt not to own or operate cars. Many people may wonder how such a culture can survive in the current Digital Age—yet the Amish population in Lancaster County, Pennsylvania, has actually tripled since 1960, which indicates that the culture has survived and thrived into the 21st century.[14]

The Amish are a private people who live according to the literal interpretation of the Christian Bible. While they welcome visitors, they also believe that photographing or videotaping someone who might be recognizable is "forbidden by the Biblical prohibition against making any 'graven image.'"[15] For many people in the United States, Europe and Japan, the Academy Award-winning film *Witness* (1985), about a young Amish boy who witnesses a murder, was their first introduction to the Amish people.[16] To this day, these Mennonite groups continue to live by the Scripture and believe that as long

1.12

The Amish in America are just one of many cultural groups that have withstood the world's dramatic transition into the Digital Age.

George Sheldon/Shutterstock.com

as they stay separate from mainstream American culture, their community will only strengthen and endure. The more they tend to shy away from the media, the greater the public interest in their culture and way of life.

As mass media have evolved technologically, cultures have found it increasingly easier to use these forums to communicate their values and worldviews. This continually enhanced cultural exchange has been an important element in our continual movement toward what Marshall McLuhan first called the global village.

Global Access, Global Threats

Regardless of cultural or political identity, information is the primary currency and the main product of our contemporary age. The worldwide reach of digitally delivered broadcast television and radio, the Internet and the digital infrastructure of mass-distributed publishing all combine to form the information transportation system of the Digital Age. Unlike the media infrastructure of the past, however, much of this digital network is either inconsistently regulated or not regulated at all. Although efforts to update and enforce "rules of the road" for information and mass media delivery systems continue to be made, the exponential rate of innovation and growth of the electronic media that constitute the world's digital highways is such that it is proving very difficult to regulate and enforce. (This will be more fully explored in Chapter 11.)

> Regardless of cultural or political identity, information is the primary currency and the main product of our contemporary age.

Today's progressive technologies and the globalization of mass media are driving an environment—some would say *forcing* an environment—of cultural convergence, characterized by the breaking down of the demarcations between cultural contexts. Media theorists such as Marshall McLuhan, and such leading disciples as Paul Levinson, view this technology-driven cultural convergence as an inevitable and highly desirable stage in human evolution. Writers such as Ray Kurzweil, a leading researcher and inventor in the field of artificial intelligence, suggest that we are just beginning to experience the profound impact of technology, which is the real driving force behind cultural convergence today.[17] Meanwhile, other writers, such as Richard Saul Wurman, are trying to emphasize the importance of developing skills to help people handle the demands associated with information and communication overload, which has become such an indelible consequence of cultural convergence. To paraphrase McLuhan's famous words, mass media are helping move the world inescapably toward a highly interconnected global village.

FROM MY VILLAGE TO THE GLOBAL VILLAGE

In his book *Understanding Media: The Extensions of Man*, McLuhan wrote, "The effects of technology do not occur at the levels of opinions or concepts, but alter the sense ratios (balance of our senses) and patterns of perception steadily and without resistance."[18]

McLuhan's theory suggests that the most significant influence of mass media derives from how they affect our basic processes of perception and thinking. Technology-driven mass communication—more specifically, worldwide television, radio and the Internet—have a profound effect on the way we perceive and think. McLuhan believed that the evolving growth and proliferation of mass media, especially television and the Internet, has already diminished and will continue to weaken individual identification with specific cultures and nations, and represents the single most important driving force toward global cultural convergence, which he was the first to term "the global village."

Some communication theorists have misinterpreted McLuhan's theories as implying that the "content" of mass communication does not matter. On the contrary, what McLuhan suggested is that when considering the content of mass media and the medium (channel) over which it is being transmitted, from the perspective of media effects, the two are inseparable. Researchers have now largely accepted McLuhan's theories, some five decades after they were first published. The preponderance of research supports the link that McLuhan posited as existing between the social and cultural impact and implications of electronic media and the ongoing trend toward cultural convergence and a globalizing worldview. Only time will tell if this continuing process will result in the global village that McLuhan envisioned.

Proximity and Media Space

According to McLuhan and the theorists who have followed in his footsteps, the success, evolution and, some suggest, survival of the human species depend largely on mass communication's ability to instantaneously transform societies. Such transformation naturally results in an altering of how we view and participate in our world. At the same time, the powers and opportunities that media technologies afford their participants place increasing demands upon them as citizens of a global village. Information and communication are being transmitted at the speed of light, so all events and information in the world are theoretically occurring simultaneously. Given enough technological capability, all information and communication will be made available to every individual in the world at the same time. Obviously, this theory of simultaneous occurrence and access poses significant logistical, economic and even class issues that may never be fully resolvable. Kurzweil and his followers, however, are postulating that this mass consciousness might very well become practical sometime late in the 21st century.[19]

> Given enough technological capability, all information and communication will be made available to every individual in the world at the same time.

It is interesting to note that when theorizing on the impact of electronic communication on man and society, McLuhan consistently refers back to his concept of proximity, which involves minimizing distance via digital media. These repeated mentions of proximity imply that all mass media are transmitted electrically in some way. Publishing now is digitized, with print newspapers such as the *USA Today* and the *International Herald Tribune* converging onto online platforms. In McCluhan's own words:

> There is no time or space separating events. Information and images bump against each other every day in massive quantities, and the resonance of this interfacing is like the babble of a village tavern or gossip session. The absence of space brings to mind the idea of a village. . .[20]

The simultaneous media space in which we live today is a multidimensional electronic environment whose center is everywhere at once and whose boundaries are nonexistent. It cannot be subdivided in the same manner as our old concepts of space and environment; rather, media space "is both compressed and indivisible, and at the same time expanding."[21] What does this trend mean for personal privacy? Will this proximity and the technological innovations that are driving it lead to more cross-cultural understanding and tolerance—or less, as we scramble to redefine and reestablish individual and social boundaries? These are just some of the complex questions that are challenging mass media theorists and researchers today.

Media Hegemony

Media hegemony theorists take another view of mass media in the late 20th and early 21st centuries. Media hegemony refers to dominance of the media by a particular group; theorists believe that mass media cause individuals to accept dominant images of society, culture and public policy as routine and valid because their dominance permits them to be perceived as such. Media hegemony theorists suggest that news and other mass media—delivered content inherently support a "media class" of society that is controlled by national and global capitalist and multinational corporate interests. This belief is part of the escalating protests against economic globalization that have materialized at meetings of world-scale bodies such as the World Trade Organization.

> Even as we acknowledge that the worldwide proliferation of the Internet is perhaps the greatest technological advancement in human history, we must recognize how it has brought with it many new challenges and threats to the stability of world economies and security.

Although its proponents describe this media hegemony view as a pervasive international phenomenon, research does not support their theories. In fact, it appears that without the spotlight shined on them by the Internet, today's anti-globalization groups would not be able to have the voice or impact that they are having on the stage of international policy. Even as we acknowledge that the worldwide proliferation of the Internet is perhaps the greatest technological advancement in human history, we must recognize how it has brought with it many new challenges and threats to the stability of world economies and security. Nevertheless, our ready access to various modes of communication and technology-based media content has proved to be the great equalizer of our era. In many ways, everyone on the Internet is alike, regardless of nationality, race, socioeconomic class or geographic location. What separates us on the Internet is simply access speed (bandwidth), processing speeds and communication and technical skills.

For instance, consider the countless numbers of people—both inside and outside the borders of the United States—who are able to receive a broadcast television or radio signal; they can interpret the images and "read" the language. They are all consumers of broadcast content. Thus everyone who has access to the Internet is entering a massive global mass media playing field on nearly equal footing. Just surf the Web for the growing number of independent video sites—the huge size, widespread reach and varied content on YouTube is just one example—or surf a shortwave radio dial for some of the many independent radio stations, or tune into one of the many public-access community TV channels. You will quickly discover that technology is moving toward equalizing broadcast media as well.

MASS MEDIA CONVERGENCE IN THE DIGITAL AGE

While *Mass Media Revolution* consistently emphasizes convergence as the primary trend in mass media in these times, it also recognizes the issue of appropriate technologies as a key factor in understanding mass media. In other words, just because technological innovation enables individuals, communities and societies to communicate through mass media via ever-more complex systems, it does not automatically mean that these systems are the *best* platforms for certain forms of communicating. No matter how "wired" our world becomes, people still desire and seek out human contact for sharing beliefs and ideas. The social nature of our species means that it is highly unlikely that we will evolve away from this basic human need. What will change, however, are the many options we have for where and how we make our connections with others. We are all participants in the dynamic world of mass information and communication exchange; our lives and our futures are, for the most part, tied to it.

Perhaps the most illustrative example of convergence in mass communication is the 2010 introduction of Apple's iPad—a Web-enabled, mobile, multimedia tablet computer. While this new technology represents the physical culmination of convergence, it also exemplifies the next stage in the evolution of mass media—convergence of content and businesses. Media convergence is bringing both unimagined opportunities and options for consumers, while at the same time presenting challenges to media content producers and providers. This movement is forcing the reinvention of business models and in some cases threatening the very existence of traditional forms of media, including newspapers, broadcast television networks, major music labels, authors and publishers of books, and reporters and editors of news outlets.

The very speed of communication and information transfer made possible by the onward march of new technologies offers at once a great power and a great challenge. Technology has made the majority of our communication immediate, leaving us with less time to make judgments on the relevance, reliability and truthfulness of the messages we encounter. Confronting the blur of available information and "voices" competing for our attention, we are challenged to pick out what is important and valuable from the noise—the cacophony of messages that demand our attention and response.

> Technology has made the majority of our communication immediate, leaving us with less time to make judgments on the relevance, reliability and truthfulness of the messages we encounter.

And the challenges facing all of us as media consumers keeps growing with the impact and proliferation of ever-changing social media platforms. According to recent research, 2.44 billion people will regularly utilize different social media platforms by 2018—an increase from 970,000 in 2010. We send over 30 million messages on Facebook and almost 350,000 tweets per minute. Social media is becoming one of the primary ways that we communicate, retrieve news and current events. In effect we are all living parallel lives online, in large part because of social media. Social media today impacts the way we conduct business, learn about the world around us and even how we behave as humans.[22]

Dealing With Information Bombardment

We are bombarded with information from the mass media, from electronic communication nodes (cell phones, e-mails, tablets), from print media (newspapers, magazines, books), from the "snail mail" stuffed in our mailboxes, and from oral communication from supervisors, co-workers, neighbors, friends and family. The sheer volume of information vying for our attention, and the timing and methods of its delivery, combine to make selecting and using all of the information and media content available to us a daily challenge. Innovations in technology are making active and informed participation in the process possible for a large majority of citizens. Yet this same technology is flooding us with political advertising and analysis, commentary from talk-show pundits and talk radio, political mailings and e-mails—all of which combine to test even the most motivated citizen's ability to extract usable, valid information from the onslaught of political spin—misinformation that attempts to hide the truth of an event or an issue.

Fortunately, most of us are gifted with an extraordinary ability to "tune out" and ignore stimuli that are not immediately relevant or that we are incapable of processing. In other words, as part of being effective mass media consumers, we learn to practice information and media content filtering so as to avoid media and information overload. Without this innate skill to quickly determine which information is immediately relevant and to dismiss the rest as distracting noise, everyday tasks such as driving a car would be impossible to accomplish safely. Recent studies on how drivers are being dangerously distracted by the addition of information and communication technology into the driving environment—smart phones, GPS navigation devices, handheld computers, stereo radio/CD players, onboard DVDs, even onboard miniature microwave ovens—have reinforced the fact that we automatically limit the incoming stimuli that we can attend to at any given moment.

In a now-classic study conducted by Daniel Simmons of the University of Illinois, a group of test subjects were asked to count the number of ball passes made while watching a video of an exciting basketball game. In the middle of the video, the researchers had a woman in a gorilla suit move into the center of the frame and wave her arms. Almost half of the test subjects stated that they never noticed the gorilla in the video, even though it plainly appeared in the center of their view. For this group, the appearance of the gorilla was unanticipated, out of context and irrelevant to the other information they were processing or the task they were trying to perform. So they just did not "see" the gorilla. This same phenomenon explains the reports of drivers who hit pedestrians or bicyclists who appear "out of nowhere," while driving the same route they drive every day, and simultaneously talking on their cell phones. The unfortunate pedestrian who might cross such a driver's path is certainly there in the crosswalk, but her appearance is unanticipated and at that split second unconsciously judged irrelevant as compared to the other stimuli that the driver is trying to process. The pedestrian loses her life because her image was relegated to the surrounding "noise." The driver cries in horror that he "never saw her," and he really didn't: The pedestrian was part of the noise that his brain had learned to tune out.[23]

The evolution in mass media technologies that has led to where we find ourselves in the early decades of the 21st century is also bringing about a human evolution: the ability to process, both effectively and simultaneously, increasingly larger amounts of information. Think back to just 10 years ago and try to remember the quantity of daily information you had to deal with, the media that delivered it and the state of the communication devices you operated at the time. Now try to imagine what you will be able to do—what you will *have to be able* to do—by the year 2020 or 2030. The theory of technological determinism suggests that as technologies develop and advance, so must the structure and values of our society and culture, and so must we as human beings—we, who from our earliest history, have demonstrated our incredible ability to learn and to adapt.

Media Access Versus Media Overload

Much of this discussion of information overload and information anxiety is drawn from the compelling and entertaining books written by Richard Saul Wurman, a graphic designer, architect, professor and recipient of National Endowment for the Arts (NEA) fellowships and Guggenheim and Chandler awards. Wurman's ideas about information anxiety and information filtering offer a range of insights that should be required reading for anyone who has anything to do with communication and communicating. Wurman writes:

> A weekday edition of the *New York Times* contains more information than the average person was likely to come across in a lifetime in seventeenth-century England. More new information has been produced in the last 30 years than in the previous 5,000. About 1,000 books are published internationally every day, and the total of all printed knowledge doubles every eight years.[24]

This burgeoning quantity of information, in combination with the escalating number of mass media channels and amount of content that we face most days, acts to blur the distinction between meaningful information and useless information, between available facts and useful knowledge. For example, we live in the most image-rich era in history, yet human beings have a limited, albeit evolving, capacity to receive, process and transmit images effectively. This constraint requires that we limit, and thereby inevitably distort, our perception of the world. We cannot perceive everything that is coming to us, and we are automatically selective about what we do notice. The greater the number of images demanding our attention at any given time, the more selective we are forced to become and, therefore, the more distorted our worldview becomes. Our image-rich mass media also contribute to creating some of the forms of media bias that we explore later in this book.

Another way to look at this phenomenon is that the more we have to pick and choose from, the more likely we are to develop some form of information anxiety. To deal with information anxiety, Wurman advocates the following approach: Realize that you will never understand everything because there is simply too much information available. Then develop a "theory" of personal media-content processing that serves as an "intellectual armature" and allows only certain facts in. Other inconsequential facts can be screened out, untouched, not to be worried about.

Today's content creators, including journalists, have a responsibility to create and deliver their material in a manner that contributes to the user's ability to effectively process the usable knowledge. Ideas are the building blocks of our understanding of facts, but too many facts delivered in an unbalanced, untimely way cloud our understanding. The effective media consumer is able to recognize information that is both relevant and useful, thereby rising above the flood of information "noise." Messages and media that attract and focus the receiver's attention through clarity of image and information automatically create affinity paths, which direct the media consumer toward a given message or content.

> To deal with information anxiety, Wurman advocates the following approach: Realize that you will never understand everything because there is simply too much information available. Then develop a "theory" of personal media-content processing that serves as an "intellectual armature" and allows only certain facts in. Other inconsequential facts can be screened out, untouched, not to be worried about.

CONCLUSION: UNDERSTANDING *NEW* MASS MEDIA FROM A CRITICAL PERSPECTIVE

This chapter presented a brief overview of some of the many theoretical approaches and the research aimed at increasing the understanding of the dynamics and impact of mass media. The debate between opposing theories continues to rage, as researchers have yet to come up with a widely supported, unified theory of the processes and effects of mass media. With the continued growth and change in mass-communication technologies, such a unified theory is certain to remain a moving target. Throughout this book, we will explore the stories, people and technological advances that combine to make mass media one of the most important driving forces behind the advancement of humankind and will consider how the mass media affect all of our lives. The goal of this book, supported by its Web-based video resources, is to help you better understand the history and workings of your mass media world. In doing so, it will contribute to your becoming a more effective and more critical mass media consumer/participant.

CHAPTER SUMMARY	KEY TERMS
The Style and Approach of *Mass Media Revolution* Introduces the unique storytelling style of *Mass Media Revolution* as well as the basic building blocks the text uses to critically explore the major theories and processes of mass media from both a historical and present-day perspective. **Visual Media** **Sneak Peek at *MMR*, 3e** Movie trailer of things to come as you experience *Mass Media Revolution*, 3e.	digital natives digital immigrants mass media rhetoric
Studying the Mass Media Explores the foundational concepts of the study of mass media and describes what is required for individuals to become media literate and effective mass media consumers.	mediated communication media convergence mass media platform media literacy media dynamics media effects
Theoretical Building Blocks of Mass Media Presents an outline of the major theories and principal theorists that contribute to our understanding of the interrelated aspects and processes of mass media. **Visual Media** **Mass Communication Models, Theories and Research Chart** **Marshall McLuhan, Explorations** In this 1960 broadcast, mass media theorist McLuhan predicts the future of mass media communication and technologies. 1. How relevant and predictive are McLuhan's visions of mass media—first published in the mid-20th century—on today's mass media? 2. How accurate was McLuhan's futurist conception of the "global village" when applied to today's cross-cultural conflicts?	textual analysis social learning theory content coding agenda setting cultivation effect public opinion research social psychology inoculation theory social judgment theory elaboration likelihood model active media platforms passive media platforms mass media framing scientific model of mass media communication hierarchy of human needs Shannon–Weaver model
Audience Trends Examines the important role audience plays in the development of media content and outlines how advertisers track audience demographics.	teleprompters Action News or Eyewitness News
Why Research Audiences? Looks at the methods and techniques used to measure mass media audiences, determine the impact of specific media content and predict trends in the type of mass media content audiences will want in the near and moderate term future. **Visual Media** **How Ratings Work** Discussion of measurement techniques used to place values on television and radio programming. 1. How does audience research of current television programs and series influence which new programs and series are developed?	audience demographics Designated Market Area

2. How effective are audience rating services, such as the Nielson ratings, in predicting audience trends today, when more and more viewers are accessing TV programs via video-on-demand and Web-based television services?	
Culture and Mass Media: Sharing What We Know Explains the important role played by mass media in both the evolution of cultures as well as how cultures communicate within each society and cross culturally.	culture social group cultural aesthetics global village cultural convergence proximity media space media hegemony
Mass Media Convergence in the Digital Age Explores how innovation and evolution in modern mass media technologies in the Digital Age are at once causing and enabling the merging of previously separate mass media platforms.	affinity paths appropriate technologies convergence of content and businesses noise spin technological determinism information overload information filtering

NOTES

1   Wurman, R. S. (2001). *Information anxiety 2*. Que Publications.
2   Fang, I. (1997). *A history of mass communications*. Focal Press.
3   Lu, X. (2004). *Rhetoric of the Chinese cultural revolution: The impact on Chinese thought, culture, and communication*. University of South Carolina Press.
4   Hirji, F. (2011). Through the looking glass: Muslim women on television—an analysis of 24, lost, and little Mosque on the Prairie. *Global Media Journal: Canadian Edition, 4*(2).
5   McCombs, M. E., & Shaw, D. L. (1993). The evolution of agenda-setting research: Twenty-five years in the marketplace of ideas. *Journal of Communication, 43*.
6   Signorelli, N., & Gerbner, G. (1995). Violence on television: The cultural indicators project. *Journal of Broadcasting and Electronic Media, 39*(2).
7   Perloff, R. M. (1993). *The dynamics of persuasion*. Lawrence Erlbaum Associates.
8   Bryant, J., & Zillmann, D. (Eds.). (2002). *Media effects: Advances in theory and research*. Lawrence Erlbaum Associates.
9   Sullivan, P., & Magid, F. N. (2010, February 8). Creator of "Action News" format and chatty co-anchor "happy talk." *Washington Post.*
10   Author's composite definition of culture used in his lectures.
11   Kluckhohn, C. (1959). Review: "Man's way: A preface to the understanding of human society," by Walter Goldschmidt. *American Anthropologist, 61*, 1098–1099.
12   Newport, F. (2015, December 24). Percentage of Christian Drifting. *Gallup.* Retrieved from www.gallup.com/poll/187955/percentage-christians-drifting
13   From the author's on-camera interviews with Dr. Carl Rogers as part of his Explorer's of Humankind media project in 1978–1980.
14   (2015). *The Amish & the plain people*. Retrieved from www.800padutch.com/amish.shtml
15   Ibid.
16   (2015). *Amish Country News*. Retrieved from www.amishnews.com/amisharticles/amishinmedia.htm
17   Kurzweil, R. (2000). *The age of spiritual machines*. Penguin.
18   McLuhan, M. (2003). *Understanding media: The extensions of man*. Gingko Press.

19 Kurzweil, R. (2000). *The age of spiritual machines*. Penguin.

20 Beneditti, P., & DeHart, N. (1997). *Forward through the rearview mirror: Reflections on and by Marshall McLuhan*. MIT Press.

21 Ibid.

22 Guzman, A., & Vis, F. (2016, April 7). *6 Ways social media is changing the world*. World Economic Forum. Retrieved from www.weforum.org/agenda/2016/04/6-ways-social-media-is-changing-the-world/

23 Simons, D. J., & Chabris, C. F. (1999). Gorillas in our midst: Sustained inattentional blindness for dynamic events. *Perception, 28*, 1959–2074.

24 Wurman, R. (2001). *Information anxiety 2*. Que Publications.

2
Mass Media
A Brief Historical Narrative

Patricia Hofmeester/Shutterstock.com

CHAPTER OUTLINE

The Roots of Mass Media Networks
The Power and Influence of Media Publishers
The Impact of Music and Images on Culture and Society

The History of Radio
Following three decades of competing innovations, patent battles and competitions between rival governments, radio at last moved beyond point-to-point communications.

The Evolution of Media Technologies Timeline

The Digital Age
Conclusion: Mass Media Converge

News Stories
Discussion of how during times of national and international crisis, television news plays an essential role in shaping public opinion.

LEARNING OBJECTIVES

1. Outline the historical roots of mass media networks from the Chinese Song Dynasty through the Western European Renaissance.
2. Characterize the historical and cultural impact of the printing press on Western society and culture post 1450.
3. Explain the impact sound and image media have on U.S. ideology, government and politics.
4. Evaluate how advances in mass media technologies that facilitate the dissemination of information influence American culture and society.
5. Describe how media convergence and the pace of technological change in the past 30 years has impacted our ability to communicate.

SU DONGPO

also known as Su Shi, was a renowned Chinese artist, poet and storyteller who lived between 1037 and 1101 a.d. during the Song Dynasty. He was also a mandarin, a public official in the Chinese empire, who served in a high position in the emperor's civil service. As he aged, Su Shi also became increasingly more outspoken—and this vociferousness, in turn, often resulted in conflict with a more powerful and corrupt political faction led by Wang Anshi, the emperor's favorite advisor. Su Shi's open conflicts with Wang Anshi, and his protests against the corruption and abuse of power that Wang represented, won Su Shi wide favor and a legendary reputation among the people, but also resulted in his being exiled from court to distant provinces three times. He eventually landed on Hainan Island in 1094.

Through a series of message runners—the early Chinese version of a postal service—Su Shi received word from his brother, another well-placed mandarin in the emperor's civil service, of an ominous development: Wang had manipulated the emperor into establishing a new, onerous tax on merchants and farmers, and had been given wide-ranging authority to collect the new taxes through force. Worse yet, as their fee for enforcing

the emperor's new tax mandate, members of Wang's political faction were given the right to retain one-third of all goods and property they confiscated from tax evaders.

What could Su Shi do to block this egregious abuse of power by Wang? He no longer had any direct voice at court, and his exile on Hainan Island made it difficult for him to travel through the provinces. Even so, Su Shi felt compelled to try to temper the response of local village leaders, who

were certain to meet Wang's forces with small militias of their own, resulting in skirmishes that might quickly escalate into a full-scale civil war.

Fortunately, Su Shi understood the power of storytelling as the traditional method of capturing the hearts and minds of the masses. He had seen the impact of captivating stories and had watched how quickly well-told tales spread through the populace—from storyteller to storyteller, from village to village, from province to

2.1

David Page/Alamy Stock Photo

province. Su Shi's stories, calling attention to the corrupt policies of Wang Anshi and his political faction at the imperial court, spread through the land like wildfire. Within weeks, his tale was everywhere, uniting people throughout China in a shared idea of how good government should work, and informing them about how dangerous to civil peace a corrupting power at the top can be. The mass sharing of Su Shi's stories served as a vehicle to create the impression that the people were uniting against the emperor because of the abuses of Wang and his followers. Fearing civil war and the loss of the "Mandate of Heaven"—the ancient Chinese belief that the emperor's power to rule is a moral right granted by Heaven— the emperor capitulated to Su Shi's demands: he rescinded the new tax, disbanded Wang's army and diminished his authority and influence at court. Su Shi's stories worked.

From his island exile, Su Shi had used the mass medium of his day to change the public agenda, taking what must have initially seemed like a foolhardy stand against decisions made by the emperor and his government. Su Shi understood a key point about power: that the perceived will of the masses could be even more powerful than their actual physical presence in persuading the government to act justly. The account of Su Shi illustrates how stories, when well structured and well told, can rouse sentiment and produce solidarity across a vast population, creating a shared experience and, therefore, a shared meaning. Stories inspire a sense of identification with the characters and situations they present. They also help to establish a level of ownership—that is, affinity—with the messages they communicate. The influence of stories delivered through mass media can never be overestimated.

THE ROOTS OF MASS MEDIA NETWORKS

As Chapter 1 suggested, the power of a story lies in its ability to use language and performance skillfully to generate meaning through images and ideas—to "paint with words." To be considered mass media content, often referred to as the media message, a story must travel to a broad audience by way of a network. Today mass media networks—systems designed to communicate messages to a large number of people at once—are generally technology based, although this has not always been the case. Su Shi, for example, relied on a loosely linked network of oral storytellers, who fanned out across the great expanse of Imperial China, disseminating his story across the land. While this approach was not a technological method, as a mass media network, it was certainly effective.

For Su Shi's accounts decrying corruption to produce such a dramatic impact, they had to spread rapidly—without the loss of their basic narrative structure and primary message. Su Shi's vast and varied audience, which included everyone from rural villagers to townspeople and city dwellers, had to hear the same message in context to ensure the impact of that message. The government in distant Peking also had to perceive that the overwhelming majority of the people believed that the emperor and his representatives were corrupt, to the degree that it could threaten their authority to govern. A captivating story told well and effectively, through an effective mass media network, can become a potent force of social, cultural and political change—as powerful as weapons and armies. The more efficient and effective the mass media network is in creating an overwhelmingly accepted view, the more powerful (and potentially dangerous, depending on one's perspective) it can become.

The Storytellers

The Iroquois Confederacy, also known as the Six Nations, comprised the Seneca, Mohawk, Oneida, Onondaga, Cayuga and Tuscarora tribes of Native Americans. These large tribes had a long history of engaging in often devastating wars with one another. Although they had different cultures and spoke different dialects, the Six Nations came together starting around 1142. By the 1780s, they formed what amounted to a united multistate nation stretching from the eastern shores of Lake Erie and Lake Ontario, north through much of eastern Canada, and south through northern New York, New Hampshire and Vermont. As a united nation, the Iroquois Confederacy fought against the French and their tribal allies, and sometimes fought skirmishes

2.2

The Iroquois Confederacy relied on storytelling to communicate laws across its multiple member tribes, establishing itself as one of the earliest, most effective mass media networks.

SuperStock

against English colonies as well. This coalition reached the apex of its power in the late 17th and early 18th centuries, when its population numbered nearly 12,000 to 15,000—quite large by the standards of the day.

The Iroquois Confederacy established a constitution called Gayanasha-gowa, or "Great Law of Peace." It entered into treaties with other tribes, as well as the North American colonies of European nations. In June 1776, the Confederacy was even invited to send representatives to meet with the Continental Congress. From their writings, we know that both Benjamin Franklin and Thomas Jefferson were inspired by the Iroquois Confederacy when making their respective contributions to the Declaration of Independence and the U.S. Constitution.[1]

How did the Iroquois Confederacy accomplish all of these astounding feats when it had no written language? What its members held in common was an evolving worldview and history, which were communicated among the member tribes and from one generation to the next via their shared mass medium: storytelling. Tribal storytellers held high status and were among the few tribal leaders who understood and spoke the multiple dialects of the member tribes. In this way, the Iroquois storytellers simultaneously served as linguistic, political and cultural bridges. Although their cultures were different, the rules and norms of the member tribes were rooted in a series of common stories. These stories established and communicated the laws that governed the Iroquois Confederacy as a united people, differentiating them from surrounding tribes that were not part of the Six Nations—in many ways, representing one of the earliest examples of an effective mass media network.

The Scribes

In many cultures, the grand tradition of oral storytelling, supplemented by pictographs (such as Egyptian hieroglyphs), eventually developed into written language form. Early written languages evolved separately in China, the Middle East and Meso-america. As these written languages matured and spread into pan-cultural systems (systems that extend beyond the physical borders of a cultural region), a new class of specialists emerged—the scribes. Through mastery of the written word, scribes established significant influence over the political, economic and cultural progress of their societies.

Because scribes possessed the knowledge of and skills for written communication, they wielded enormous power in society and were held in high regard. In many cultures, very few people, including members of the upper class or economic and political elite, knew how to read or write. During the early decades of the Roman Empire (in ancient Egypt and early Greece, for example), many scribes were actually valued slaves or indentured servants. Imagine a situation where an illiterate Roman ruler

2.3

Egyptian hieroglyphs were written by scribes, many of whom were slaves.

Megapress/Alamy Stock Photo

depended solely on his literate slave-scribes for all his written communication and for all official government records. Essentially, these scribes were not just slaves, but rather the principal vehicle for communicating the ruler's will and agenda to the people—through other scribes, town criers and storytellers. This situation, which was quite common during the early years of the Roman Empire, created what amounted to a very powerful media class that could either contribute to maintaining the general peace and prosperity or, just as easily, incite political intrigue, riot or revolution, simply by manipulating the message and controlling the medium.[2]

As the number of scribes grew in these early societies, language-based knowledge grew exponentially, giving rise to the media masters we know today as philosophers, mathematicians, astronomers and inventors. This literate and skilled media class pushed the progression of their culture, and of humankind as a whole, forward—sometimes with astounding leaps of knowledge. The small but growing literate class, which controlled both the medium and the content, was also able to formulate and circulate influential belief systems through myths, allegories and compelling stories that continue to affect cultural progress today.

> The small but growing literate class, which controlled both the medium and the content, was also able to formulate and circulate influential belief systems through myths, allegories and compelling stories that continue to affect cultural progress today

Highly skilled storytellers, armed with written language, contributed to the development of many world religions through some of the most enduring examples of mass media known to humankind: the Torah, the Bible, the Koran, the Analects of Confucius and the Bhagavad Gita. These products of the early mass media have helped to forge cultures and nations, set off wars, unify diverse peoples under shared belief systems and worldviews, and shape the history of the world. Even today, they continue to influence present-day culture wars and global religion-based conflicts.

Early texts and ancient manuscripts laid the foundations of modern science. These documents and maps were authored by great astronomers, mathematicians and philosophers who are still revered today.

The Visual Artists

Although early scribes were masters of written communication, they were also artists who lavishly illustrated their scrolls, manuscripts and early scientific treatises with decorative lettering and drawings. Gutenberg's Bible, for example, included illustrations in the margins and headings, initially done by hand just before the pages were bound. Soon printers were combining woodcut block illustrations with movable type, and illustrated publications became commonplace. In fact, illustration, art and text have evolved in a side-by-side fashion since the earliest days of publishing. Clearly, art and artists have played important roles in the creation and communication of culture—from prehistoric days when primitive tribes would communicate their stories via cave paintings to today's graphic novels, which have developed into their own unique genre of mass media. Stories combined with images proved as transformative—if not more so—as the spoken or written word alone.

In some ways, maps represent one of history's earliest examples of media convergence: the partnership between text and image. Maps opened people's eyes to the world beyond and piqued the interests and curiosities of thousands. As with the doors opened by the Internet, maps left deep and profound impressions upon people's conceptualization of the world in which they lived.

Early mapmakers were more than skilled artists: They were masters of an emerging mass media that influenced and expanded world exploration and trade, established definable, defensible national boundaries and enabled the creation of empires. Maps communicated a broader worldview and encouraged technological innovations that enabled nations to build ships, develop navigational tools and conquer new lands and new peoples. In the great age of explorers, maps, in combination with journals of exploration, spurred the parallel growth of both nationalism and imperialism and became the equivalent of the modern-day bestsellers. Consider the ease with which a king or queen could raise navies and find financial backers for expeditions and new trading routes when expansionism of this nature was popularized by maps and journals. These illustrated travelogues of a sort allowed people to visualize, and vicariously live, the romance

2.4 and 2.5

The communication of culture via visual imagery spans the ages, from prehistoric cave paintings to current-day graphic novels.

Karl Weatherly/Thinkstock and © *Warner Bros./courtesy Everett Collection*

2.6

Maps were early mass media that influenced and expanded world exploration and trade.

Joao Virissimo/Shutterstock.com

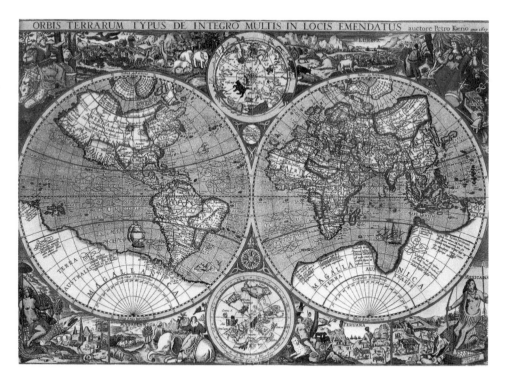

of the great adventure. Even today, as such technological innovations as Google Maps would demonstrate, maps continue to exert a powerful pull on the public psyche.

Starting in the Middle Ages, the lives of most Western peoples were dominated by the Catholic Church. As an institution, it controlled the majority of wealth throughout Europe. Moreover, its community wielded great influence over society and commerce—in effect, controlling the first media industry.

At one time, Rome's vast collection of statues and visual arts was heavily criticized by the Catholic Church; its leaders deemed the collection a demonstration of great hubris, suggesting that the Roman Republic acted as though it was more important on earth than Christ or God. The debate over whether visual arts should be denounced as idolatry or recognized as an effective way to communicate Christian beliefs and to gain followers dominated the theological and political debate within the Christian church for centuries. Ultimately, the Christian church embraced art as a means of communicating doctrine to the public and as a source of religious inspiration.

The power of the visual is not just a historical phenomenon, however. Images remain as palpable an influence today as they were in the Middle Ages. Of course, instead of serving primarily as the voice of the Church in Europe, visual images are now embraced—and exploited—by governments, corporations and the general public alike. (The power of visuals is discussed in greater detail in Chapter 8, which covers advertising and public relations, and Chapter 12, which addresses photography and the power of visual images.)

Arts, Artists and the Renaissance

The era when art and artists were at the forefront of advancing knowledge and culture in the Western world has been given a lofty name—the Renaissance. The word "renaissance" means rebirth. The Renaissance started in Italy in the 14th century and spread through Europe by the 16th century.

The leap from the deprivations and oppression of the Middle Ages to the mind-expanding arts, sciences and scholarship of the Renaissance was as revolutionary as our own leap into the Digital Age in the late 20th century. In the latter case, it seemed that many of us were just discovering the World Wide Web one day, but then, just as suddenly, were attending online classes at institutions such as the University of Phoenix. These days, instead of talking to one another face to face, we text, Tweet or use Facebook to communicate. Just 10 years ago, we carried around a cell phone to make phone calls, a camera to take photos, and an iPod to listen to music. Now a single smart phone can perform all of those functions simultaneously—a digital leap, indeed.

During the Renaissance, Leonardo da Vinci, Michelangelo, Raphael and Botticelli in Italy; van Eyck, Bruegel, van der Goes and later Dürer in Germany; and Rembrandt and Vermeer in the Netherlands were just some of the artists who were considered the media stars of their day. Not only were they renowned for having developed innovative approaches to using color, perspective, light and shadow, textures and dimensionality, but they also merged these techniques to create a "language" that communicated their message of humanism and the value of knowledge to the masses.

The Renaissance pushed forward the Protestant Reformation (a challenge to the dominance of the Roman Catholic Church), which ultimately inspired wars, counterreformation movements and the emergence of new religions and new sciences. Leaders of this era greatly expanded trade and contributed to the globalization of economics, nations and empire building. Imagine how young people of the Middle Ages—accustomed to the bleakness of farm life, the Black Death (plague) and the authoritarianism of feudal landlords—might have experienced the media revolution of the Renaissance, from which emerged a new social and economic class comprising artists, merchants and tradesmen. Out of this new social class came some of our most treasured artists and artisans, whose works continue to inspire and influence art today.[3]

> Imagine how young people of the Middle Ages . . . might have experienced the media revolution of the Renaissance, from which emerged a new social and economic class comprising artists, merchants and tradesmen

Rembrandt, for example, may have had inborn talent, but it was clearly his exposure to a wealth of new ideas and technologies that allowed him to develop into one of the greatest artists and portrait painters of the late Renaissance. His prolific body of work stands as a testament of a visionary who sought to communicate competing ideas about social class, religion, politics and emerging sciences to a mass audience. Consider, for example, his painting of Dutch surgeon and Amsterdam mayor, Nicolaes Tulp.

Dr. Tulp often gave public lectures, performing dissections and anatomy lessons on the corpses of criminals who had been hanged. The general paying public was very interested in human anatomy; as at the time, this field of study was not considered merely a subject of interest among medical students or surgeons. Thus, as a means of creating and maintaining revenue to support his work, Dr. Tulp commissioned Rembrandt to create a large painting of his anatomy lesson (The Anatomy Lesson of Dr. Nicolaes Tulp, 1632). In effect, he hired Rembrandt to create an advertisement of sorts that he hoped would attract even larger paying audiences to his public lectures. Dr. Tulp was ahead of his time: He understood early on the power of advertising and promotion. His story also points to the historical relationship between those who create media content and those who disseminate it to mass audiences—which brings us to the printers and the publishers.[4]

THE POWER AND INFLUENCE OF MEDIA PUBLISHERS

From scholars to politicians to media pundits and critics, the debate rages on as to which group exerts the most power and influence in mass media—the content producers or the content publishers. Long before broadcasting rose to dominate mass media, and long before the Internet's global reach and content interactivity, the printers ruled media.

In approximately 1045, movable type was invented in China. Given that the Chinese written language comprises more than 10,000 characters, however, it is not surprising that this innovation did not catch on quickly. In 1450, an innovative German goldsmith and engraver named Johannes Gensfleisch zur Laden zum Gutenberg invented a new system of movable type. In his printmaking approach, metal letters were placed in wooden frames, covered with oil-based ink and pressed onto paper with a large hand-cranked press. Gutenberg's innovation allowed printmakers to manufacture a number of single letters or symbols at a time using small blocks called composing sticks; these sticks were set into wooden trays and reused many times. Gutenberg's printing press revolutionized printing and gave birth to modern mass media. Its use spread rapidly throughout Europe. Indeed, by 1500, printing presses and the mass-produced books and leaflets they created had become commonplace.[5]

The Birth of Modern Mass Media

The social, cultural and political impact of the printing press and widely distributed printed media on the course of history is immeasurable. The level of literacy among all social classes, and the number and availability of educational institutions and libraries, grew exponentially. As a result of this trend, the overall literacy of the population grew, creating a culture of shared knowledge. Written information was no longer the sole domain of the few literate elite. Farmers could keep track of weather and crops, merchants could create ledgers and read contracts—oral stories and

2.7

Gutenberg's movable-type printing press revolutionized the printed media.

Dja65/Shutterstock.com

legends were no longer the only way to pass information from one generation to the next

One of Gutenberg's first publications was a Bible. His decision to produce this volume is widely believed to have marked the beginning of the dissolution of the Latin-trained, Roman Catholic clerical elite who held moral and political sway over Europe at the time. The ability to reproduce the "Word of God" through a mechanism outside the privileged elite and Church allowed more individuals to read the Bible on their own and thus develop their own ideas, interpretations and opinions about it.[6] More intellectuals began questioning the dominance of the Catholic papacy, including Martin Luther, a German monk considered the father of the Protestant Reformation. Gutenberg's printing press helped spread the word of the Protestant Reformation, making it possible for Luther to publish and widely circulate his writings, which accused the Catholic Church of exploiting its religious authority to increase its own vast wealth. Had a means of efficiently printing multiple copies of Luther's literature not existed, his reports of corruption might not have reached as many people as they did.

2.8

The arrival of the printed Bible and other text brought forth a media revolution during which ordinary people gained access for the first time to previously restricted and exclusive information.

Bruce yuanyue Bi/Alamy Stock Photo

Printing and Politics

Because Gutenberg's printing press also irreversibly connected once-separate realms of information and made them more readily available to the people, it also contributed to the expansion, and better maintenance and survival, of government. Citizens became aware of their governments' actions because those actions were reported on and criticized in widely distributed publications. Perhaps not surprising, given their penchant for self-preservation, governments quickly developed methods to control and suppress information by attempting to license the printers.

During the lead-up to the American Revolution, for example, England's King George III and Parliament understood that because colonial printers were also the principal writers and editors of radical publications, controlling them would restrict communication and the flow and availability of information and, therefore, squelch dissent. This approach had worked in England dating back to 1529, when Henry VIII first asserted his supreme power over the pope by establishing the Church of England and by issuing a list of prohibited books, thereby dictating what could and could not be published. (England officially separated from the Roman Catholic Church in 1536.) Under this system, printers could operate only under license from the Crown. (We will explore the historical roots of efforts to legislate controls on the media in Chapter 11). Suffice it to say that what worked well in England in the 16th century backfired in the American colonies in the 18th century. Indeed, England's attempt to control the press in colonial America was one of the primary abuses that led to the American Revolution.

The Newsmakers

By the early 1760s, master printers in the American colonies were operating roughly 50 printing presses and publishing more than a dozen newspapers, as well as broadsheets (large-format newspapers, typically

2.9

Large-format newspapers known as broadsheets were being printed throughout the American colonies by the early 1760s.

North Wind Picture Archives

15 by 24 inches), pamphlets and books. As these printing operations grew in size, readership and profitability, the more politically charged their publications became. The colonists, arguing amongst themselves, crept ever-closer to all-out rebellion against England. At the center of this emerging mass media maelstrom were many of the U.S. "Founding Fathers," including, the United States' first media mogul, Benjamin Franklin. (In Chapter 4, we will look at the fascinating story of Benjamin Franklin and his dual roles as Founding Father and pioneer of U.S. publishing.) The Founding Fathers recognized the essential role of the press in the maintenance and survival of American democracy. Since our nation's founding, the publishing industry has remained an integral component of U.S. society and culture.

The vital role of traditional publishing in the survival and prosperity of the nation is evident from its formation to the dawn of the Digital Age. Imagine, for example, how long the abuses of prisoners at the U.S. military base at Guantánamo Bay would have remained hidden had the news media not broken the story to the American public. Until these stories circulated, people were unaware of the harsh interrogation practices—most of which were in violation of basic human rights—being applied to the detainees. The public outcry was so intense that within days after his inauguration in January 2009, President Barack Obama issued an executive order to shut down the facility. However, Congress, as well as many state and local jurisdictions, blocked the president's efforts to move the Guantánamo Bay prisoners to alternative detention facilities within the United States, and the prison remains open.

From the very inception of the U.S. publishing industry, American media have fostered a close relationship with advertisers as a means to ensure their economic survival. Just as broadcast and print media do today, the publishers of yesteryear sold advertising to local merchants to support their print operations. Right from the start, the mass media in the United States have been integrally tied to the marketplace. Correspondingly, right from the start, newspaper and magazine publishers had to find a way to maintain the complex balance between the potentially competing interests of accurately and truthfully reporting the news while maintaining the support of their advertiser clients.

This relationship between the media and business was not all bad. By the early 1800s, it had produced a burgeoning information economy that had a significant and overall positive impact on U.S. society. It enabled readers to gain fairly unrestricted access to an ever-widening range of information and knowledge. In addition to news and public affairs, religious, scientific and literary media content flourished. This allowed 19th-century, New World America to compete with the culture of Old World Europe effectively as the nation aggressively promoted (and highly valued) the circulation of knowledge.

The economics of this early knowledge industry required educated, creative contributors, who were instrumental in the development of universities, libraries and law schools, as well as laboratories for scientific investigation and technical colleges to train skilled technicians to meet the demands of the rapidly expanding Industrial Age.

2.10

The American public and the rest of the world may not have ever known about the mistreatment of prisoners at Guantánamo Bay, had the news media not broken the story.

MCT/Contributor

The growth of media's power was not lost on early 19th-century politicians. *The National Intelligencer*, begun in 1800, became the most influential, often-quoted and politically focused newspaper in the country. This national publication had significant cultural and political influence. In fact, by the end of the Jefferson administration, it served as the political voice of the U.S. federal government. As the country became embroiled in the debate leading up to the War of 1812, however, new publishers arose to provide Americans with more objective, contrasting voices on the issues of the day, such as *The New York Evening Post* and its sister publication, *The New York Herald*. Their approach was to give their readers "correct information on all interesting subjects"—in other words, news on information not colored by the political powers in Washington, D.C.

The Rise of Yellow Journalism and Penny Presses

The movement away from control of the press by political factions gained momentum after the election of Andrew Jackson as president in 1829. This counterforce gave rise to independent advertisers as the major financiers of newspaper publishing. This trend was accompanied by the emergence of media barons—private individuals who owned or had controlling interests in publishing companies. Their control over the new publications resulted in more independent media, albeit at a cost: The media became potential vehicles for advancing the private agendas of these individuals. As a result of this changing dynamic, newspapers began to take on a new focus known as yellow journalism that would entertain, inform and overwhelm the nation and the world.

During this period of the 19th century, newspaper and magazine readership soared with advances in printing technology, the easy availability of cheap paper, improvements in low-cost transportation and circulation and increasing revenues from advertising. Mainstream publications fought for customers with the burgeoning penny press—cheap, tabloid-style newspapers that drove down the quality of reporting and editorial content and encouraged sensationalism. Not surprisingly, facts and fiction soon mingled in the rush to enthrall readers. Bizarre events and scientific hoaxes became regular fare in the publications of the day. As sales of these newspapers grew, the more prevalent these lurid accounts became, with publishers sacrificing facts for cheap entertainment in their bid to sell more papers.[7]

> With the increase in economic resources being channeled into publishing, coverage of government, legal and social issues expanded. Notably, the national press brought the political debate about slavery and states' rights to the forefront of the national agenda.

Although dangerous patterns were clearly developing in the media as publishers attempted to cash in on the culture's fascination with sensational stories, there were also positive consequences from the proliferation of newspapers. With the increase in economic resources being channeled into publishing, coverage of government, legal and social issues expanded. Notably, the national press brought the political debate about slavery and states' rights to the forefront of the national agenda.

The First Media War in the United States

In the early 1840s, following the advent of telegraph and railroad technologies, Americans began to move out into the western part of the country, in no small part due to the vision promoted by Horace Greeley, the editor of the *New York Tribune*. Greeley, along with other publishers in the East, sold settlers and adventurers on the idea that the western frontier held the promise of fulfilling America's manifest destiny—the belief that the nation was destined to expand. This image captured the imaginations of tens of thousands and was largely responsible for one of the greatest migrations in history. The reality was that the "Wild West" was actually quite different from its depiction in the stories published by Greeley, but other stories did not slow down either the migration or the media's efforts to portray the illusion of a "Golden West." In response to the persistent enticement of Greeley and his colleagues, towns began to spring up all over the western frontier, adding to the growing national network of newspapers, telegraph offices and postal services.[8]

During this era of expansionism, influential writers such as Mark Twain, Edgar Allan Poe and Ralph Waldo Emerson toured cities and frontier towns in highly popular shows that were part lecture, part stand-up comedy and social satire, and all entertainment. The growing popularity of inexpensive paperback books (first introduced in the United States in 1845) significantly increased the audiences for these shows. Due to the progressive ideas advocated by many of these writers, the Christian church viewed these tours as attempts to spread secular humanism, prompting churches to initiate an early culture war in America. Of course, that battle also played out in the press—selling yet more newspapers and magazines. (This social conflict was the precursor to the conservative Christian versus liberal secular struggle that continues to be fought in the media today.) Smoldering just below the surface of this ideological struggle was a growing political and economic conflict between the industrial North and the agrarian South over slavery.

Horace Greeley, who was always an extreme liberal on social and political issues, made his *New York Tribune* the national voice of the new liberal Republican Party and a loud and passionate media voice against slavery. In so doing, he made the *Tribune* the most widely read newspaper in the country. The views espoused by this growing popular press, led by Greeley, are credited with contributing to President Abraham Lincoln's decision to preserve the Union and to abolish slavery. Moreover, Mark Twain and other writers of the time used their popularity to rail against slavery throughout the Civil War and continued to articulate the damage that slavery had wrought on the United States for decades thereafter.

Historians consider the American Civil War to be the first modern war where rapid advancements in weaponry and communication technology enabled a more sophisticated method of military strategizing to be employed. This conflict also represents America's first "media war." Journalists and photographers told stories about the agony of war, often from the perspective of the frontline soldiers, to audiences in both the North and the South. By doing so, they made the horrors and devastation of civil war more of a reality for readers safely distant from the battlefields. Their work also takes us to the story of images and image-makers—the photographers.[9]

The Photographers

The story of photography dates back to approximately 300 b.c. In Optics, Euclid—a famed Greek philosopher and mathematician living in Alexandria, Egypt—proposed the design and effects of a pin-hole light box (camera) to study the behavior of light. By 1558, this early photographic technique, called the camera obscura, was used widely by painters to create outlines of their subjects—in particular, natural landscapes and buildings—with exacting proportions and correct visual perspective. A little more than a hundred years later, Robert Boyle and Robert Hooke, two late 17th-century English scientists, published treatises describing more sophisticated camera obscura designs. These designs utilized the telephoto lens, designed 80 years earlier by the German astronomer and inventor Johannes Kepler. By the beginning of the 18th century, commercially manufactured camera obscuras were commonly available for sale in London and other major cities of Europe.

In London in 1834, Henry Fox Talbot created the first negative-to-positive contact printing of a photograph onto paper. This chemical process involved soaking paper in silver chloride and fixing it with a sodium chloride solution. Talbot patented this process in 1841.

At about the same time in Paris, Louis Daguerre invented his daguerreotype process, involving the use of silver-coated copper plates, with images developed by combining highly toxic silver iodide and warmed mercury.

In 1851, another brave photographer-inventor in London, Frederick Scott Archer, succeeded in improving the work of his predecessors by adding another toxic and highly flammable chemical to the process—alcohol. Using glass plates rather than copper plates enabled him and later photographers to increase the resolution of their images and make almost unlimited reproductions—if they did not blow up themselves and their equipment in the process.

2.11

A camera obscura, consisting of a light-proof box with a pinhole aperture. Light enters the pinhole to form a clear, upside-down image on the back side of the camera, thus exposing the film.

Photos.com/Thinkstock

While Europe took the early lead in developing the art and technology of photography (especially the photographers in Paris), after the Civil War, American photographers took the reins, moving ahead in the development of new photographic technologies. In the late 1800s and early 1900s, electric lighting proliferated across the United States, Europe and worldwide, making it much easier to take photographs indoors.

In addition, the invention of the electric photoflash bulb to replace the hazards of exploding flash powder significantly expanded the areas where photographs could be taken. Thus, through the late 19th century and into the early 20th century, photography became the public's window into exotic places. From the jungles of Brazil to the sacred mountains of China and Japan to the natural canyons of the American West, photography allowed publishers to capture ever-greater readerships by bringing the wonders and perils of the world to an enthusiastic audience of customers.

The advent of photography around 1837 and the refinements and innovations in photographic technologies through the mid-1860s made it possible for journalists and photographers to bring home the realities of the Civil War frontlines. War correspondents and photographers were embedded (integrated) with the troops on both sides. (You will learn more about this practice in Chapter 13.)

One such photographer was Mathew Brady. As a young man, Brady was fascinated by photography. At age 16, he sought out Samuel Morse, who, in addition to having invented the coding system that made telegraphic communication possible, was a fan of the daguerreotype and was largely responsible for bringing this new technology to the United States. Brady had an abundance of natural talent and, never shy of the rich and famous, hit it off with the world-renowned inventor, soaking up everything he could about the new image-making technology. Before long, he had opened his own daguerreotype portrait studio in New York. Brady moved his studio to Washington, D.C., in 1856. There, he began photographing America's political and economic leaders as well as foreign dignitaries passing through Washington or ensconced in the growing number of foreign embassies there. At the height of his career, Brady could be considered a media goliath: He counted among his friends and patrons congressmen and senators, judges and presidents, and the leading authors, artists and actors of his day.[10]

With the outbreak of the Civil War, Brady used his substantial political contacts, including his relationship to President Lincoln, to establish a grand project to photograph the war. He organized a group of photographers, equipped them with horse-drawn wagons—mobile photographic studios of his own design—and sent them off to the frontlines to capture the carnage of war. This early attempt at documentary photography, or photojournalism, required a good deal of courage. Brady and his photographers, in their cumbersome wagons filled with the highly toxic, flammable chemical soup they were working with inside the poorly ventilated mobile studios, were constantly threatened by bullet and mortar fire from both sides of the line.

War photography had first been attempted seven years earlier during the Crimean War, but Brady's great Civil War photography project firmly established photography as the preeminent means of capturing the realities and horrors of the modern battlefield. Brady's images of war were initially sold in his own gallery. When his exhibition of war photography opened in New York in the fall of 1862, the press hailed it as a sensation. Eventually *The New York Times* and other leading publications of the day caught on to the allure of this new visual medium and began publishing war photographs. Since Brady was a staunch abolitionist, his images of the terrible human cost of the war represented the Union perspective—an early example of media bias. (We will explore the topic of media bias further in Chapter 10.)

Since Brady was a staunch abolitionist, his images of the terrible human cost of the war represented the Union perspective—an early example of media bias.

With their up-close images of death and destruction, Brady and many other Civil War photographers made a lasting impact on the way the public views war. In an 1859 essay published in the *Atlantic Monthly*, after viewing Brady's exhibit of war photos, Oliver Wendell Holmes, Sr., wrote the following words about the impact of photography:

> . . . this greatest of human triumphs over earthly conditions . . . The time is perhaps at hand when a flash of light, as sudden and brief as that of the lightning which shows a whirling wheel standing stock-still, shall preserve the very instant of the shock of contact of mighty armies that are even now gathering . . .[11]

Later, Wendell would further reflect on the power of photographic images:

> . . . Let him who wishes to know what war is like look at this series of [photographs] . . . It was nearly like visiting the battlefield to look over these views, that all the emotions excited by the actual sight of the stained and sordid scene, strewed with rags and wrecks, came back to us. . .[12]

Smaller, lighter cameras and faster film allowed World War I war correspondents to capture riveting combat images from the front. Decades later, during World War II, Robert Capra and Bert Hardy, along with other up-and-coming photojournalists, would go out to the frontlines in Europe and the Pacific and bring the war home to Americans through their poignant black-and-white and color images. Photographers were also firsthand witnesses to the devastation of the Japanese attack on Pearl Harbor, London's suffering under the incessant German bombardment of the Blitz, the campaign for North Africa, the Normandy invasion, the Battle of the Bulge and the horrors of the Holocaust. Today photojournalists such as Zoriah Miller continue to present evocative images from the wars in Afghanistan, Iraq and the Gaza Strip.

Advances in printing technologies and parallel advances in photographic equipment and processes—especially the reduction in the size of cameras—in the early 20th century enabled photography and photojournalism to become equal partners with text-based reporting. These advances also burnished photography's reputation as an art form and as a method of image-based reportage.

The Golden Age of photojournalism in the United States occurred between the 1930s and 1950s, when photo-rich news magazines and newspapers such as *Life*, *Paris Match*, *Picture Post*, *The New York Daily News* and even *Sports Illustrated* developed enormous subscriber bases in large part by publishing highly visual stories built around captivating photography. Specialty magazines such as *National Geographic* and *Popular Science* also grew in popularity for similar reasons.

In 1935, the U.S. Farm Security Administration (FSA) launched a special photography department and recruited top photojournalists to document two events: the tragedy of agricultural failures and the poverty-driven human migration resulting from the Great Depression and the environmental devastation of the Dust Bowl years. The photographers who participated in the project—including Dorothea Lange, Robert Capa, Alfred Eisenstaedt, Walker Evans, Gordon Parks, Marion Post Wolcott and W. Eugene Smith—became household names. Their remarkable and often disturbing images told the stories of human suffering without words, allowing readers to grow accustomed to viewing the world through the camera's eye. These images deeply affected American voters and generated overwhelming support for President Roosevelt's New Deal programs.[13]

2.12

Migrant Mother (Dorothea Lange), from the U.S. Farm Security Administration's Depression-era photography program.

Lange, Dorothea, photographer. Destitute pea pickers in California. Mother of seven children. Age 32. Nipomo, California. Courtesy of Library of Congress

2.13

Father and Sons Walking in Face of Dust Storm (Arthur Rothstein), from the U.S. Farm Security Administration's Depression-era photography program.

Farm Security Administration—Office of War Information Photograph Collection (/LC-USF34–004052 Rothstein, Arthur, 1915–1985. Courtesy of Library of Congress

2.14

Bud Fields and His Family at Home (Walker Evans), from the U.S. Farm Security Administration's Depression-era photography program.

Evans, Walker, photographer. Sharecropper Bud Fields and his family at home. Hale County, Alabama. Courtesy of Library of Congress

During World War II, photography served the governments on both sides of the conflict in another way. Many governments undertook extraordinary efforts to widely disseminate propaganda—negative and often false images of the enemy. Hitler's cleverly produced "documentary" photographs and films demonstrate his mastery of the art of manipulating the truth: The often-exhilarating propaganda produced by his administration hailed the wonderful destiny of the Third Reich and touted the evils of the Americans, British, Russians and Jews. In Japan, the Emperor's generals used photo propaganda to reaffirm the faith of the citizens of Japan in their imperial right to dominate Asia and the Pacific and to laud the invincibility of the Japanese army and navy.

Both U.S. President Franklin Roosevelt and British Prime Minister Winston Churchill understood the extraordinary impact of photography and films as weapons of war. In the United States, the War Department not only gave photographers and filmmakers relatively unfettered access to the troops and the frontlines, but also footed much of the costs of these expeditions, provided transportation for these photojournalists and shipped their exposed rolls of film back to London or the United States. Both the American and British war departments operated their own photography sections in support of their respective propaganda efforts.[14]

The impact of war photography extended from World War II through the Korean War and into the Vietnam War, when war photographers and film camera crews alike were able to rapidly transmit images from the frontlines to the front rooms of America. These images raised the anti-war ire of a generation and helped bring down the presidency of Lyndon Johnson, setting the stage for the social and cultural revolutions of the late 20th century.

The images of war also helped inspire anti-war folk songs. Rock songs of the late 1960s and early 1970s helped turn the Vietnam War debate into a large political movement and significantly contributed to the changing—and solidifying—public opinion against the war. This brings us to the story of the music-makers.

THE IMPACT OF MUSIC AND IMAGES ON CULTURE AND SOCIETY

Early Christian leaders understood how, like the visual arts, music could engage audiences, influence beliefs and sway the masses to the theological teachings and authority of the Church. By the 6th century, music was definitely a well-recognized component of the Catholic Mass, which helped establish the early foundations of the symbols, structure and melodic syntax of written music—all in the service of the Church.

By the Middle Ages, while remaining an important part of Christian and Jewish religious practices throughout Europe, music was also moving into the secular world as popular entertainment for the masses. Poet-singers called troubadours, often accompanied by minstrels, traveled from village to village and city to city entertaining crowds with musical storytelling, ballads and love songs. Around the 1280s, performers in the larger towns and cities throughout Europe began presenting musical plays built around traditional narratives and drawing heavily from folk songs. By the mid-14th century, the composition and performance of music, both religious and secular, was such a well-established aspect of culture (as demonstrated by the highly respected vocation of instrument design) that it helped lay the foundation for the Renaissance and the age of the great Western composers.

The Music-Makers

The Renaissance not only yielded great advances in art, science and culture, but also closely aligned music, musical performance and theater with other humanistic endeavors, including storytelling in literature. Renaissance composers created new ways for music to dramatize popular myths and stories and to entertain large audiences drawn from all classes of society. Competition between the Catholic Church and wealthy secular dynasties such as the Medici family in Italy expanded the patronage of composers and playwrights, just as it did for artists. From the city-states of Florence and Venice, to the growing city centers of France, Germany and the Netherlands, musical styles competed and combined to become a primary entertainment medium for the masses. Traveling companies of troubadours, musicians and actors continued to journey throughout Europe, while chants and choirs remained an important factor drawing audiences to church services.

From the late 15th through 18th centuries, instrumental ensembles, orchestral suites, symphonies and operas continued to evolve as mass entertainment media. Leading composers from Italy, France and Germany, including Mozart, Vivaldi, Bach, Handel, Schubert and Beethoven, emerged as international celebrities. Their works, such as Vivaldi's Four Seasons and Beethoven's Ninth Symphony, have been performed and celebrated throughout the centuries and continue to be played today.[15]

No matter what the cultural era, popular music has served as not just a form of culture and entertainment, but as one of the vehicles for delivering messages that drive social and political movements and communicate patriotic values. That role continues today.

During the American Civil War, both Union and Confederate troops wrote and distributed songs that expressed their respective high purpose and commitment to the Civil War cause. The music of both North and South expressed passionate support for the values of liberty and freedom. Battle songs, for example, were composed to rally troops and public support. Meanwhile, popular tavern songs expressed the struggle, fears and sacrifice of the common soldier. Some songs became masterpieces, expressing universal fears and longings regardless of which side of the conflict one was on. In 1861, Julia Ward Howe, a New England Puritan, created an immortal set of lyrics set to the music of the then-popular song "John Brown's Body" after visiting Union solder encampments. Her powerful lyrics are still as moving now as they were when she first wrote them. Her song, titled "The Battle Hymn of the Republic" and recognizable by generations, begins:

> Mine eyes have seen the glory of the coming of the Lord;
> He is trampling out the vintage where the grapes of wrath are stored;
> He hath loosed the fateful lightning of His terrible swift sword;
> His truth is marching on.

American music of the 18th and 19th centuries was dominated by folk songs and ballads brought by immigrants from Great Britain, slaves from Africa and others. At that time, American folk music told stories drawn from the struggles of the poor and working classes—and it continues to fill that role today. Songs about love and war, and survival and perseverance, have played an important role in the evolution of American culture, communicating mutual experiences across social classes, ethnic and racial barriers. For example, consider legendary folk singer Woody Guthrie's song, "This Land Is Your Land"; the first verses have become so iconic that the song is almost America's "unofficial" national anthem.

Few people today are aware that Guthrie wrote this classic while traveling between migrant labor camps during the Great Depression. "This Land Is Your Land" not only celebrates the vast natural beauty of America, and the strength and diversity of her people, but also protests the injustices faced by the poor and working classes in the heartland of the nation. Guthrie lived among these people, sharing their meager food and shelter and lifting their spirits with his songs. During his own lifetime, many considered Guthrie and his songs subversive and anti-American because of his willingness to criticize American culture and espouse

2.15

Woody Guthrie (1942) traveled with migrant labor camps during the Great Depression—an experience that inspired the unofficial American anthem, "This Land Is Your Land."

Aumuller, Al, photographer. [Woody Guthrie, half-length portrait, seated, facing front, playing a guitar that has a sticker attached reading: "This Machine Kills Fascists"/World Telegram photo by Al Aumuller]. Courtesy of Library of Congress

left-leaning political views. Eventually, both the song and the songwriter won their place in U.S. history. Today Guthrie's music is celebrated at folk music festivals, sung by scores of contemporary performers, and even included in the Smithsonian's National History Museum. Folk songs, especially "This Land Is Your Land," remain living examples of the power of music to move us as individuals and to contribute to social awareness and cultural change.[16]

The cultivation of social awareness and cultural change through music has opened up opportunities for people of diverse ethnic and social backgrounds to express their own voices. The African-American experience, from the days of slavery through the early decades of the 20th century, merged with the experiences of the American urban poor and working classes in the early 1900s to become jazz. Jazz is a uniquely American creation that bridged the gulf between the black and white cultures and by its very nature is rooted in free expression. American jazz played an important role in the rise of radio during its days, from the 1920s through the 1940s. The sounds, rhythms and soul of jazz reached across the broadcast airwaves and into the hearts of an America suffering from the devastating drought of the Dust Bowl and the widespread poverty of the Great Depression. The words and music of jazz helped teach the tide of early 20th-century immigrants the language and customs of their new country. (Discussed in more depth in Chapter 5.) The influence of music and its contribution to American culture is enormous—and it really soared with the advent of radio broadcasting.

The Radio Broadcasters

In 1895, while the United States was starting down the path that would lead to the Spanish-American War, a race sprang up among inventors and engineers to create the first effective system of wireless communications. A 21-year-old Italian physicist by the name of Guglielmo Marconi is popularly credited with inventing the radio, although the credit actually belongs to a Serbian-born physicist, inventor and engineer named Nikola Tesla. Tesla first demonstrated his "wireless communications" in 1893. Tesla was not as effective an entrepreneur as Marconi, however, and Marconi ended up winning the honors for inventing the first radio transmitter and receiver. More importantly, Marconi received the patents for this new communication technology, which would change the world and put mass media on the path toward the Digital Age.[17]

2.16

Natalia Aggiato/Shutterstock.com

Marconi failed to gain the financial backing he sought from the Italian government to launch his radio on a widespread basis, so in 1896 he traveled to London, where he demonstrated his invention to the chief engineer of the British Post Office. By 1899, Marconi's wireless telegraphy—signals sent electronically not through wires, but rather as electromagnetic waves—was transmitting signals across the English Channel. Not surprisingly, governments were the first to adopt the invention because this landmark technological innovation allowed effective real-time communication between ships at sea, and from ship to shore (known as point-to-point communication). As the dominant sea power of the time, Britain jumped in with both funding and political support for this upstart inventor and his new technology.

Marconi started the Wireless Signals Company to exploit his patent commercially and tried to monopolize the international wireless communication business, but his efforts quickly failed because of barriers to economic and geopolitical completion of the infrastructure necessary to support radio on a global basis. It took another three decades and a maze of competing innovations, patent battles and competitions between rival governments to move radio beyond point-to-point communications. Ultimately, the future of radio broadcasting would be led by visionaries who saw in wireless communications the potential to bring news and entertainment to

▶ **The History of Radio**
Following three decades of competing innovations, patent battles and competitions between rival governments, radio at last moved beyond point-to-point communications.

mass audiences, in the process creating unprecedented wealth for the owners of commercial stations and fledgling networks (a topic to which we will return in Chapter 9). Ongoing refinements of the initial wave of transmitters and receivers turned radio into the first broadcast mass medium and led to its Golden Age. View the following segment on the history of what was then deemed the "miracle" of radio. ▶

KDKA, the first licensed commercial broadcast station based in Pittsburgh, Pennsylvania, made its debut on November 2, 1920. Initial proliferation of commercial radio stations was slow, in part because it took some years for advertisers to catch on to radio as an effective new medium for reaching large audiences. During the early 1920s, with no advertiser support and no government backing, radio manufacturers supported commercial radio in America and Europe solely as a vehicle for selling their new mass media technology. It was not an easy sale. The first radios were difficult to set up and operate. With sets made up of crystals, coils, knobs and dials, it took some technical knowledge and a lot of patience and perseverance to tune in to broadcast stations of the period.

Just like the first adopters of today's digital technologies, many of the initial users of radios were young people who were as intrigued by the technology as they were attracted to the (limited) program offerings. This situation changed very quickly, however. As advertisers jumped into the new broadcast mass medium, more stations were established across the United States and Canada. In tandem with this increased financial base, programming improved rapidly, both qualitatively and quantitatively. In the United States, the Golden Age of commercial radio was also driven forward by the rise of the American broadcasting networks. For a more in-depth discussion of radio broadcasting, see Chapter 5.

The Filmmakers

Eadweard Muybridge successfully completed the first motion study using moving images in 1877 in an effort to settle a legendary ongoing bet between racehorse owner Leland Stanford and his rivals. Muybridge was a photographer who specialized in animal and nature subjects. Stanford, a former governor of California, had wagered with a friend on whether a horse's four feet leave the ground simultaneously during a gallop. To determine the winner of the bet, Muybridge lined up cameras side by side and, using fast shutter speeds, recorded a galloping horse. He printed the resulting photos on a glass wheel. By projecting a bright light through the glass as he turned it with a hand crank, his contraption projected moving images of the horse against a white background screen. Muybridge is credited for having invented the first moving picture with this 1879 debut of the zoopraxiscope. With this projector, he proved that a horse at full gallop actually "flies" off the ground, with all four feet in the air at the instant of mid-gallop, all in only 24 frames.[18]

2.17

In 1877, Eadweard Muybridge successfully completed the first motion picture study using moving images. He devised a series of cameras with fast shutter speeds; the cameras were triggered by strings broken by the galloping horse.

Stapleton Historical Collection/Heritage

By 1891, advances in gelatin emulsion film stock on rolls of celluloid made possible the production of short silent movie possible. In 1988, America's preeminent inventor of the time, Thomas Edison, patented the basic components of motion picture technology—perforated film that traveled from a sprocketed reel across a revolving shutter in front of a strong continuous light source. His employer, fellow inventor W. L. K. Dickson, later took this projection device concept and further developed it to create the viewing device called the kinetoscope. The first kinetoscope parlor opened in New York City in 1894, causing these new, inexpensive and immensely popular entertainment venues to spring up all over America.

By 1900, other inventors had refined the technology of projecting motion pictures, and the motion picture industry and movie house syndicates quickly became an important part of mass media in the United States. In 1895, considered the official birth year of the movies, the French Lumière brothers created 10 short films recording vaudeville theater acts, which they called actualities. When these films were shown in Paris, they captivated audiences. Edison, who always had a nose for both public attention and profits, responded by filming sporting events and even boxing matches—all distributed via movie parlor syndicates to a voracious audience clamoring for more. America was hooked on the movies.

The motion picture industry flourished in large part because its proponents understood the mass media potential of moving-picture technology. It catered to wide audiences and served as an inexpensive and easily accessible form of entertainment. The movie business was astoundingly profitable, as long as the film producers also controlled the means of distribution through networks of movie theaters that could hold large paying audiences. Such films as *The Great Train Robbery* (Edwin S. Porter, 1903) became instant sensations in the early days of the cinema. The Industrial Age had improved transportation systems and led to the expansion of the cities, which were populated primarily by an urban working class. The denizens of these densely populated cities, with money to spend and a desire for entertainment, turned out in droves to visit the newly constructed movie "palaces." New movie studios enjoyed immense profits as a result. By the 1920s and the 1930s, the Hollywood studio systems emerged as the primary driving force behind U.S. culture, with all of the social and political power and influence that came with this role of social arbiter. The movie business was, and remains, astoundingly profitable. (We will learn more about the production, distribution, exhibition and marketing forces that contributed to its success in Chapter 6.)

At the same time as dramatic films grew in popularity, documentary film production increased—due in no small part to the early work of a young wilderness guide in northern Canada. After a restless childhood in Michigan, Robert Flaherty, a hearty and adventurous young man, followed in his father's footsteps and traveled to the Hudson Bay region of northern Canada to seek his fortune as a prospector. When wealth from prospecting proved elusive, Flaherty offered his services as a guide. With funding from Canadian railroad baron Sir William McKenzie, Flaherty undertook numerous expeditions into the northern Canadian wilderness between 1910 and 1916. While experimenting with an early film camera provided by McKenzie during a wilderness trek along the shores of Hudson Bay, Flaherty found that the local Inuits were curious about the strange contraption and proved willing film subjects. With the help of his Inuit friends, who reenacted scenes of tribal life in the frozen north, Flaherty produced the first feature-length documentary film, *Nanook of the North*. It was released in 1922 to great acclaim and even greater profits.

Knowing a good thing when they saw it, Paramount Pictures executives commissioned Flaherty to travel to the South Pacific and repeat his success. Although the resulting films, *Moana* (1926) and *White Shadows on the South Seas* (MGM, 1928), did not achieve the same success as

> The motion picture industry flourished in large part because its proponents understood the mass media potential of moving-picture technology.

2.18

Edwin S. Porter's *The Great Train Robbery* (1903), a film considered to be one of the first successes of the motion picture industry.

Strobridge & Co. Lith. The Great Train Robbery.

2.19

Scene from Robert Flaherty's *Nanook of the North* (1922), the first feature-length documentary that received great acclaim and made a profit.

ZUMA Press, Inc./Alamy Stock Photo

Nanook, Flaherty's work sealed the filmmaker's reputation as a primary documentarian. The fact that much of Flaherty's work was actually less "documentary" and more "reenactments" (as these terms are commonly used today) did not prevent him from establishing himself as a pioneer of documentary filmmaking. He ultimately produced or co-produced seven more documentaries before his death in 1951. The fame accorded to these early documentary films resembles the popularity of today's reality TV shows.[19]

Visual news became available to the moviegoing public in Europe in 1910 and in the United States by 1911, in the form of newsreels. Newsreels were short film montages that featured brief, often sensationalized coverage of national and world events. The Allied Forces all employed newsreels to garner support for World War I. They played before the main feature film in movie theaters in the pre-television era, with their topics changing weekly. Newsreels remained highly popular through World War II. During the war, newsreels depicting events in the Pacific and Europe had a significant impact on American audiences back home, in particular by encouraging viewers to support the war effort through the purchase of war bonds. The vast archives of World War II newsreel footage are still used by documentary filmmakers today to produce moving historical films and television programs about this critical period in United States and world history. Newsreels remained part of the moviegoing experience in the United States until 1967, and helped lay the foundation for early television news and news magazines such as CBS's *60 Minutes*.

The Television Producers

The first patent for what was called "television" was issued to a Russian-born inventor named Paul Nipkow. Unfortunately, Nipkow's electromechanical system of photoelectric cells was unwieldy and unreliable; it produced a very blurry image made up of 48 lines of horizontal resolution. In 1925, John Logie Baird, working in England, was the first to transmit an image—albeit a very blurred geometric shape—over only a few feet. The development of an effective system to capture, transmit, receive and then display a television image proved highly challenging.

That situation changed dramatically in 1926 with the arrival on the scene of a 19-year-old farm boy from Idaho with the unlikely name of Philo T. Farnsworth. Farnsworth just happened to be an electrical engineering genius. Working from a rundown warehouse in San Francisco, he invented a system of transmitting encoded radio signals that had been captured by the first effective video camera, which Farnsworth called an "Image Dissector." A receiver equipped with a decoding circuit picked up the signals, and then literally shot the amplified signals through an electron "gun" and onto a cathode-ray tube. With the backing of two San Francisco bankers, Farnsworth hired a small staff of young engineers and worked to perfect his technology.

The Birth of Television Broadcast Systems

While Farnsworth was making great progress with his invention, David Sarnoff of RCA was aggressively building his radio network, buying up as many stations as he could while battling charges that he had created an illegal broadcasting monopoly. Sarnoff was a broadcasting visionary who realized the potential of television, but had backed the efforts of Russian-born inventor Vladimir Kosma Zworykin over Farnsworth, secretly funding his experiments to invent a successful television system. Sarnoff even sent Zworykin on what amounted to a spying mission to Farnsworth's lab in an effort to steal his rival's technology. Sarnoff tried other

2.20

Philo T. Farnsworth (1906–1971), the father of television, adjusts the first effective video camera.

questionable tactics both to block Farnsworth from negotiating licensing relationships with RCA's competitors and to buy more time for Zworykin to catch up. Farnsworth was eventually forced to sue RCA for patent theft. He won the case in 1925 by demonstrating that he had conceived his television system in 1922, and that Zworykin's patent did not present a credible electronic image scanning and transmutation technology. Despite his victory in the courts, the fight between Farnsworth and Sarnoff's RCA continued unabated while the Federal Communications Commission (FCC, which had been reconstituted from the earlier Federal Radio Commission in 1934) struggled to establish standards for television broadcasts.

By 1928, young Farnsworth had beat competing laboratories all over the world in the race to invent modern television. His outstandingly effective system transmitted 500 lines of horizontal resolution and displayed a strikingly clear black-and-white image of "live" real-time television. After years of battles with bankers and investors, and extraordinary efforts to keep secret his technology and his progress, Farnsworth finally was able to demonstrate his system to the public in 1934 at the Franklin Institute in Philadelphia, giving birth to the modern age of television. The leading radio broadcasting companies—GE, RCA and Westinghouse—lined up to compete for the purchase of Farnsworth's invention, and Farnsworth's financial future looked bright indeed.

All the players in the great battle to establish the first television broadcasting system converged on the 1939 World's Fair. At this event, Sarnoff stole the limelight by announcing the launch of NBC as the first television network. Sarnoff used the financial might and radio broadcasting dominance of RCA to trump Farnsworth and even the FCC. Television was born—and RCA was positioned to dominate the new mass medium for the foreseeable future.

The Advent of News and Entertainment Television

Unfortunately, for Sarnoff and RCA, world events intervened in the race to develop and market television technology and the first network of broadcast stations. While the worldwide financial crisis that sparked the Great Depression had not seemed to slow the progress of this technology, World War II would virtually stop television in its tracks. While it remained on a full war footing, the federal government banned the manufacture and sale of all television sets; it also put all television broadcasting licensing on hold until the end of the war. The Franklin D. Roosevelt administration and Congress saw the inevitable proliferation of television as a waste of national resources and a risk to national security. Ultimately, it would be Sarnoff's chief competitor, William Paley of CBS, who would successfully launch the television age by bringing the stars of radio entertainment, and more importantly radio news, into the new medium of television.

Soon after the war ended in 1947, both Sarnoff's NBC and Paley's CBS began broadcasting regularly scheduled television news programs: Camel News Caravan with John Cameron Swayze on NBC and Television News with Douglas Edwards on CBS. Initially these television broadcasts

2.21

Cast members William Frawley, Vivian Vance, Lucille Ball and Desi Arnaz on the set of an early television sitcom, *I Love Lucy* (1952).

Photo 12/Alamy Stock Photo

reached only the major cities on the East Coast of the United States, but within five years there were more than 100 stations broadcasting from major cities across the nation. The early TV stations broadcast only a few hours each evening in so-called prime-time. Early television programming was dominated by variety shows—essentially live radio programs "with moving pictures," hosted by former radio celebrities such as Milton Berle and Sid Caesar. Popular radio dramas as well as live stage plays evolved into the first TV dramas, packaged as prime-time evening programs such as Hallmark Hall of Fame and Kraft Television Theater.

Soon the three rapidly expanding television networks—CBS, NBC and ABC—were filling their prime-time schedules with made-for-television dramatic series. Westerns such as *Cheyenne* were especially popular in the early days of television, as they were relatively easy for the Hollywood studios to produce on their vast Southern California back lots. Daytime soap operas—so named because they were sponsored by dominant consumer products companies—were inexpensive serial dramas produced in New York that captured large audiences of post-World War II homemakers. Such situational comedies ("sitcoms") as *I Love Lucy* and *The Honeymooners* became early national prime-time hits, as did made-for-television serial dramas such as *Superman* and *The Lone Ranger*.

All three national networks also introduced quiz shows, which achieved immediate popularity in the 1950s. Ultimately, these quiz shows—for example, *The $64,000 Question*—were discovered to be "fixed"—that is, the winners were predetermined before the competition actually began, although members of the viewing public were led to believe they were witnessing an honest contest. The resulting scandal diminished the popularity and advertiser support for this program genre for almost a decade. By the mid-1950s, early-morning news-talk programs such as NBC's *The Today Show* had appeared, followed quickly by late-night talk shows such as *The Tonight Show*, which is currently the longest-running talk show in television history. While early television entertainment was establishing itself as the foundation of America's new broadcast mass media, television news was on its own trajectory—one that would soon have an extraordinary impact on U.S. ideology, government and politics. This transformation started with CBS's William Paley and his star World War II radio reporter, Edward R. Murrow.

While early television entertainment was establishing itself as the foundation of America's new broadcast mass media, television news was on its own trajectory—one that would soon have an extraordinary impact on U.S. ideology, government and politics

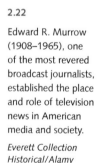

2.22

Edward R. Murrow (1908–1965), one of the most revered broadcast journalists, established the place and role of television news in American media and society.

Everett Collection Historical/Alamy Stock Photo

Because of his heroic on-air radio reports during the German bombings of London (also known as the Blitz) for CBS during World War II, Edward R. Murrow returned from Europe as one of the most recognized and revered American broadcast journalists. Murrow first ventured onto national television screens in 1948, covering the political conventions in San Francisco and New York with a direct style and forceful personality that had made him perhaps the most famous radio correspondent in history. Thanks to television, viewers across the country were able to watch Murrow as he covered the 1948 presidential conventions and debated the hot issue of the day—the Korean War—with his CBS colleague Eric Sevareid. With the help of his longtime producer (and later CBS news chief) Fred Friendly, Murrow successfully transitioned his popular radio news and commentary program *Hear It Now* to the new mass medium of television as *See It Now*. The team of Murrow and Friendly quickly built *See It Now* into a highly popular, hard-hitting, and often controversial investigative TV newsmagazine program, the predecessor to *60 Minutes*. *See It Now* essentially invented television investigative reporting and established CBS as the leading U.S. network for television news programming for many years.

Through *See It Now*, Murrow addressed controversial topics such as the plight of migrant workers in rural America in an episode titled "Harvest of Shame." Murrow's unflinching work was supported by his producers Fred Friendly and Don Hewitt (the latter would be the lead creator of *60 Minutes*) and enjoyed the behind-the-scenes backing of CBS's chairman, William Paley. Many of Murrow's investigative exposés had a significant impact on American attitudes and influenced the political response to controversial issues, but none more so than Murrow's on-air confrontation of Senator Joe McCarthy. McCarthy's egregious and anti-democratic tactics—now commonly known as McCarthyism—unfairly accused scores of Americans in government, academia and especially the entertainment industry of being communists and traitors. Murrow exposed the ugliness of McCarthy's views to the nation and helped bring this dark period of abuse of congressional power to an end. Murrow's closing argument to his national television audience on March 9, 1954, remains one of the most famous commentaries in the history of broadcast journalism:

> We proclaim ourselves—as indeed we are—the defenders of freedom abroad, what's left of it, but we cannot defend freedom abroad by deserting it at home. The actions of the junior senator from Wisconsin [McCarthy] have caused alarm and dismay amongst our allies abroad and given considerable comfort to our enemies, and whose fault is that? Not really his. He didn't create this situation of fear [of communist infiltrators and spies]; he merely exploited it, and rather successfully. Cassius was right: "The fault, dear Brutus, is not in our stars but in ourselves" . . . Good night and good luck.[20]

Murrow's broadcasts and his words have continued to echo through the decades since 1954, proving themselves as true today as when he spoke them to a national television audience searching for guidance in troubled times. This key role for mass media, especially television news, which Murrow established, has been revisited repeatedly at times of national and international crisis, as the video segment "News Stories" shows. ▶

From the national turbulence in the wake of a disastrous and costly war in Vietnam, to the national trauma caused by terrorist attacks on the United States on September 11, 2001, to the challenges and debates over an unpopular and costly war in Iraq, and beyond, Murrow's words have resonated for generations of Americans. As we will explore throughout this book, the debate over the role and impact of mass media, especially television news, rages on. The Digital Age brings with it a new age of mass media, one characterized by a convergence of newspapers, television, radio and the Internet.

THE DIGITAL AGE

Most science and technology historians attribute the invention of the modern computer to Charles Babbage's Difference Engine, which was first demonstrated in London in 1832. Babbage was a mathematician who was obsessed with organization and efficiency. Frustrated with having to use endless tables and charts to solve logarithmic problems and endless strings of multiplication and division, he spent 10 years developing his mechanical computer. A working replica of Babbage's Difference Engine,

▶ **News Stories**
Again and again during times of national and international crisis, television news, as established by Edward R. Murrow, plays an essential role.

2.23

Model of mathematician/inventor Charles Babbage's Difference Engine, considered the precursor to the modern computer.

World History Archive/Alamy Stock Photo

built on his detailed design, can be found today in the London Science Museum—and when pitted against modern computers, it proves to be astoundingly accurate. Babbage went on to design a second-generation device called the Analytical Engine, which used punch cards—early analog "memory" systems. Unfortunately, this more sophisticated early computer was never built to completion and demonstrated. Only a portion of the Analytical Engine was built before Babbage died in 1871, and the British scientific establishment blocked any further government funding due to political debate surrounding the project.[21]

The first punch cards were used as early as 1725 in France to control the operation of Jacquard textile looms, which were named after their inventor, Joseph Marie Jacquard. These memory systems controlled the complex timing of the moving parts of the loom, assuring highly accurate and consistent weaving patterns that led to the industrialization of the textile industry in Europe. While Babbage adopted this earlier technology in designing his Analytical Engine, it was Herman Hollerith who first developed a practical punch card-based tabulation system in America. Hollerith patented his innovation and eventually sold it to the U.S. government to be used for the 1890 national census. Punch cards went on to become the first mass data storage and input technology when IBM and Univac came out with the first digital computers in the early 1950s.

Toward the end of the World War II, in 1944, IBM partnered with Harvard University to build one of the first successful programmable computers, the Mark I. An electromechanical computer weighing more than five tons, the Mark I filled a large room with its components. It was constructed of thousands of relay switches, hundreds of rotating shafts and wheels, and more than 500 miles of wires. Input and output were handled via long spools of punch tape—basically continuous punch cards. The Mark I proved to be a very finicky contraption to keep running properly, although it stayed in operation for 15 years. The smallest problem could cause huge errors and big problems for its operators. One of its programmers, Grace Hopper, traced one shutdown to a moth that had gotten caught in one of the punch-tape readers—from which we get the term "computer bug." Hopper taped the deceased bug to the operations journal with the notation: "9/9 1545 (3:45 PM) Relay #70 Panel F (moth) in relay. First actual case of a bug being found."[22] In 1953, Hopper invented the first high-level computer language, which she called "Flow-Matic"; it would later evolve into the ubiquitous computer language known as COBOL.

Other vacuum tube-based mainframe computers—large data processing systems with massive storage capacities—came online during this period, the most famous being ENIAC. All of these machines where huge heat-generating, electricity-guzzling contraptions weighing hundreds of tons and filling large rooms, but with strikingly little computing power in today's terms. In fact, despite their enormous size, both the Mark I and ENIAC had less than 1 percent of the memory and processing power of even the least costly low-end computer available today. Even the average BlackBerry or iPod is thousands of times more powerful than the most powerful early mainframe computers.

By 1962, there were approximately 10,000 mainframe computers worldwide. The most powerful were housed at major research universities such as the Massachusetts Institute of Technology (MIT), corporate research organizations such as Bell Laboratories, and government agencies such as the Department of Defense.

Led by the Department of Defense Advanced Research Projects Agency (ARPA), a joint government–industry committee was established in 1963 to develop a standardized language by which these computers could communicate with one another—namely, the American Standard Code for Information Interchange (ASCII). In 1964, computer engineers at MIT, the Rand Corporation and the U.S. National Physics Laboratory joined forces to develop a protocol for packet switching, which enables computers to send and receive data through a network of communication links, initially consisting of dedicated telephone lines. In the same year, IBM introduced its System/360, the first general-purpose mainframe computer to be extensively used by large government, academic and corporate organizations.

Computers Get Linked

By 1967, a futurist by the name of Larry Roberts, who had worked for NASA, brought leading computer network developers from ARPA, MIT, Rand, Stanford Research Institute and the British National Physics Laboratory together for a conference in Ann Arbor, Michigan. While there, they began mapping out a system that would link scientists and engineers at participating research universities with the government agencies that were contracting and funding their work. This "network" of computers would allow researchers in geographically dispersed laboratories to share their work and data more efficiently.

Initial funding for this network came from the U.S. government through ARPA, so the system was named ARPANET. Within three years, the number of participating computers, or "nodes," linked into ARPANET was increasing at a rate of more than one per month. The technology for operating ever-more sophisticated networks at increasingly faster speeds (network architecture) evolved rapidly to keep pace with ARPANET's growth. Developments in the manufacture of more powerful and faster computer chips, primarily by Intel, enabled the manufacture of more powerful computers. Also, the protocols that enabled these computers to communicate with each other quickly grew more sophisticated, supporting the increasing volume of communication traffic between the participating nodes on the network.

By the end of 1973, 37 institutions were operating mainframe computers connected to ARPANET. Within just another year, daily communication traffic over ARPANET exceeded 3 million data "packets." By 1975, ARPA—now called DARPA (Defense Advanced Research Projects Agency)—in cooperation with the National Science Foundation (NSF), was supporting more than 120 universities on the network.

The Birth of the Personal Computer

In 1974, two college dropouts, Steve Jobs and Steve Wozniak, who had been attending meetings of the Homebrew Computer Club in Northern California and working part-time for arcade game manufacturer Atari, changed the direction of the Digital Age. Wozniak had already built his own computer. Using this experience as a starting point, he joined forces with Jobs to form Apple Computer Company. In 1976, the nascent firm introduced its first product to a primarily hobbyist market—the Apple I, a do-it-yourself kit that sold for $666. The following year, the fledgling company brought the Apple II to the market as the first fully assembled computer for personal use. The personal computer (PC) revolution was born.

2.24

An Apple 1 computer was first marketed to hobbyists as rows of microchips on a circuit board housed in a wooden box—a far cry from today's sleek Apple design.

Bloomberg/Contributor

In 1981, the leader in mainframe computers, IBM, introduced the IBM PC, thereby launching personal computers into the mainstream. Soon other manufacturers jumped into the burgeoning marketplace to compete with IBM and Apple. Scores of other companies sprang up to develop and sell applications software for the rapidly expanding market. Most notable was Microsoft, whose powerful new operating system called MS-DOS (the precursor to Windows) added a graphical user interface (GUI) to make personal computers more "user-friendly"; MS-DOS/Windows would eventually become the dominant operating system throughout the world.

The Internet

In 1979, the NSF agreed to fund a computer research network that would connect universities outside of the DARPA consortium. As part of this venture, a number of these universities set up ongoing newsgroup communications via networks called CSNET and BITNET. Participants in these newsgroups communicated with one another using a new file transfer protocol called "e-mail," along interconnecting networks called the Internet. The number of computers using this new Internet continued to expand exponentially, and by 1983 a system was needed to standardize node addresses, leading to the establishment of the Domain Name System (DNS).

The next year, the NSF issued its overall Internet architecture plan, called the National Computing Environment for Academic Research. Among other things, this plan established a series of regional Internet supercomputer hosting hubs, called the NSF Net Backbone. Only six years later, the NSF Network Backbone went international and opened itself up to any computer with the capability to communicate with the network—mainframe to PCs.

Also in 1989, a computer engineer named Tim Berners-Lee, working at CERN in Switzerland, introduced a hypertext-based system to facilitate hierarchal searching on the Internet. Such searches had previously required the writing of long associated strings based on Boolean algebraic formulas; in contrast, Berners-Lee's more user-friendly system supported "keyword" searching.

The dramatic growth and evolution of the Internet continued, and in 1991 Congress passed the Gore Bill, named for its author, U.S. Senator Al Gore. The Gore Bill provided funding to establish regional hosting hubs and their related infrastructure, and lifted the last barriers to full and open access for everyone to the Internet. When the Gore Bill was passed, all of the technology, protocols, network architecture plans and communications infrastructure models were finally in place to form the foundation of the World Wide Web—and the world would never be the same. The new cyberspace of the World Wide Web quickly became the dominant environment for media and communications, and the springboard to the Digital Age.

> The new cyberspace of the World Wide Web quickly became the dominant environment for media and communications, and the springboard to the Digital Age.

CONCLUSION: MASS MEDIA CONVERGE

By building and traveling along this historical road map of the key topics and issues that form the foundation of today's mass media, we are able to more easily recognize and link the historical trends in mass media with those occurring in the media we all experience today. Additionally, we gain the tools we need to start developing a more critical understanding of the dynamic changes, innovations and leaps forward that have gotten us here. By taking this broad view, we are able to identify some recurring themes in mass media: Advances in mass media technologies influence and enable advances in cultures and societies, allow for the accumulation and sharing of knowledge and innovation, and facilitate the dissemination of this knowledge to wider audiences. People, in turn, are then able to access mass media to better inform their own lives and the lives of their families and communities, and to become contributors as responsible citizens of their nations and the world.

CHAPTER SUMMARY	KEY TERMS
The Roots of Mass Media Networks Explores some of the fascinating historic roots of mass media, from the storytellers of ancient China, to indigenous tribes in North America, to the Middle Ages and Renaissance in Europe, to the precursors of American democracy.	message mass media networks pan-cultural systems scribes
The Power and Influence of Media Publishers Examines the historic impact and influence of printing and print publishing on the world and illustrates the role of publishing in the evolution of American democracy and culture.	printmaking printing press broadsheet knowledge industry yellow journalism penny press manifest destiny camera obscura daguerreotype process
The Impact of Music and Images on Culture and Society Looks at how music and photography, and eventually the broadcasting of sound and images, have influenced the evolution of society and culture. **Visual Media** **The History of Radio** Following three decades of competing innovations, patent battles and competitions between rival governments, radio at last moved beyond point-to-point communications. 1. What are two of the most important effects that the proliferation of broadcast radio had on early 20th-century America? 2. What aspect of modern radio is having a similar impact on early 21st-century American society? **The Evolution of Media Technologies Timeline** **News Stories** Discussion of how during times of national and international crisis, television news plays an essential role in shaping public opinion. 1. Name three national or international news stories appearing over the last six months that have had a significant impact on the American public similar to those shown in this video segment. 2. Why do such stories have such a broad impact on the public while many others do not?	wireless telegraphy KDKA commercial radio moving picture zoopraxiscope motion picture technology kinetoscope actualities newsreels McCarthyism
The Digital Age Introduces the key events and characters that helped to launch the Digital Age in mass media.	punch cards mainframe computers Internet Gore Bill

NOTES

1 Johansen, B. (1982). *Forgotten founders: Benjamin Franklin, the Iroquois, and the rationale for the American Revolution*. Gambit.

2 Wiener, P. (1974). *Dictionary of the history of ideas*. Charles Scribner's Sons.

3 Boorstin, D. J. (1992). *The creators: A history of heroes of the imagination*. Random House.

4 Field, D. M. (2002). *Rembrandt*. Regency House.

5 Needham, J., & Tsuen-Hsuin, T. (1985). *Science and civilisation in China*. Volume 5: Chemistry and chemical technology. Part 1: Paper and printing. Cambridge University Press.

6 DiNatale, M. (2005, August 21). The protestant reformation. *AssociatedContent.com*. Retrieved from www.associatedcontent.com/article/7179/the_protestant_reformation.html

7 Blanchard, M. A. (1998). *History of mass media in the United States*. Fitzroy Dearborn Publishers, pp. 709–710.

8 Cross, C. (1995). *Go west young man! Horace Greeley's vision for America*. University of New Mexico Press.

9 Walters, J. B. (1973). *Merchant of terror: General Sherman and total war*. Bobbs-Merrill.

10 Horan, J. (1988). *Mathew Brady: Historian with a camera*. Random House.

11 Holmes, O. W. Sr. (1859, June). The stereoscope and the stereograph. *Atlantic Monthly, 3*, 738–748.

12 Holmes, O. W. Sr. (1863, July). Doings of the sunbeam. *Atlantic Monthly, 12*, 1–16.

13 Baldwin, S. (1968). *Poverty and politics: The rise and decline of the Farm Security Administration*. University of North Carolina Press.

14 Muscio, G. (1996). *Hollywood's new deal*. Temple University Press.

15 Orrey, L., & Milnes, R. (1987). *Opera: A concise history*. Thames & Hudson.

16 Fisher, M. (2007). *Something in the air: Radio, rock, and the revolution that shaped a generation*. Random House.

17 Seifer, M. (2001). *Wizard: The life and times of Nikola Tesla: Biography of a genius*. Citadel.

18 Leslie, M. (2001, May/June). The man who stopped time. *Stanford Magazine*. Retrieved from www.stanfordalumni.org/news/magazine/2001/mayjun/features/muybridge.Html

19 Christopher, R. (2005). *Robert and Frances Flaherty: A documentary life, 1883–1922*. McGill-Queen's University Press.

20 Edwards, B. (2004). *Edward R. Murrow and the birth of broadcast journalism (Turning points in history)*. John Wiley & Sons, Inc.

21 Swade, D. (2002). *The difference engine: Charles Babbage and the quest to build the first computer*. Penguin.

22 Ifra, G. (2001). *The universal history of computing from the abacus to the quantum computer*. John Wiley & Sons, Inc.

3

Media Technologies and the Dynamics of Change

guteksk7/Shutterstock.com

CHAPTER OUTLINE

The Stages of Technological Innovation

Media Technology Format Wars A closer look at the causes and industry effects of the HD DVD and Blu-ray format wars.

Hurtling into the Future: Technology Revolutionizes Mass Media

Richard Saul Wurman on Innovation TED (technology innovation conferences) founder discusses innovation and the impact of mass media technologies.

Paul Levinson on the Future of Mass Media A modern communication and media professor's insight into the future of mass media—after McLuhan's global village.

Will Technological Convergence Be the Death of the Printed Word?

World Digital Library Project The LOC's World Digital Library project comes to fruition.

Conclusion: Adapting to Change

LEARNING OBJECTIVES

1. Explain how the various stages of technological innovation build upon one another to establish new technologies.
2. Illustrate how Moore's law helps us to predict future media technologies.
3. Evaluate how technological innovations like e-readers have impacted the business models of books, newspapers and magazines.
4. Assess the impact on society of a read–write media culture where individuals are both media consumers and media creators.

RAJASTHAN

is a state in the northwest of India. It is the largest and one of the poorest states in the country. Within Rajasthan is a city of nearly 4 million people that is home to the dusty and hardscrabble campus of the Indian Institute of Technology (IIT)—an elite technology education and research campus often referred to as the MIT of India. Here, school director and computer engineer Prem Kalra is focusing the efforts and resources of the IIT on developing inexpensive tablet computers that can meet a major challenge facing India and other nations in what was once termed the developing world—how to reach the last, the poorest and least empowered person in India, and give that person the basic tools and (teach him or her) enough skills to overcome dire poverty.

The challenge is to design and build a simplified, stripped-down tablet computer that will bring wireless Internet access to the poorest Indian family at a cost of under $50, which will be subsidized by the Indian government. The idea is neither new nor unique to India. Back in 1995, MIT Media Lab co-founder Nicholas Negroponte, speaking at the Economic Forum in Davos, Switzerland, proposed designing and building a $100 laptop computer specifically for children. The idea was beautifully simple—make a laptop computer available to all children in the developing world and to poor children in the developed world. As a step toward realizing this goal and in an effort to bridge the Digital Divide—the fissure that separates those who have financial and physical access to information technologies from those who do not—Negroponte helped found the nonprofit organization known as One Laptop Per Child (OLPC).[1] Unfortunately, the OLPC project didn't work quite as well as it had been envisioned. The advances in low-cost and lightweight mobile computing had not yet caught up with the vision. By 2007, the per unit price of $199 was above the promised $100; however, with an aggressive Give One Get One program for $399 in the United States and other Western countries, Negroponte's vision was a good first attempt.[2]

Just five years later, Professor Kalra's Aakash tablet computer—Aakash is the Hindi word for "sky"—was able to deliver on Negroponte's original idea. Kalra created an Android-based tablet that enabled people living in poor rural villages—or India's infamous urban slums—to participate in the global Web-connected world. Social networking, YouTube videos, education, news and information, and entertainment are available via wireless broadband services provided by the Indian government. The $50 Aakash tablet was the technological stepping-stone needed to help India's 220 million students climb out of the cycle of poor education and poverty. It enabled Indian students to be taught subjects by teachers, not just in India, but also in America, Canada or Australia; it opened new worlds of knowledge in science, mathematics, history and culture unimagined by their parents.

Meanwhile, OPLC continued on its innovative path, introducing the XO-3 tablet that came with a solar cell and hand-crank power option—all for less than $100—at the 2012 Consumer Electronics Show.

3.1

Mail Today/Contributor

THE STAGES OF TECHNOLOGICAL INNOVATION

The news media—from the academic and scientific to the popular and entertaining—regularly confront us with stories about the rapid growth of technology in the information age. Pundits fill broadcast airtime and print media with seemingly endless debates about whether our rapidly growing digital world is having positive or negative effects on individuals and society. What the market agrees on is that technology keeps changing at an ever-faster pace, with no slowdown in sight. As we learned in Chapter 2, this continual expansion of mass media has existed since humankind first attempted to use language and storytelling to communicate. Ideas, creativity and technological innovations ebb and flow in measurable, seemingly predictable patterns of dynamic change. These shifts are matched by transformations of the variety of mass media content as well as the capabilities, power and complexity of mass media technologies. Modernizations in mass media and their related technology—in all technological innovation—have a life cycle that progresses through identifiable stages before the process begins anew.

> Modernizations in mass media and their related technology—in all technological innovation—have a life cycle that progresses through identifiable stages before the process begins anew.

The Precursor Stage

The first stage of the innovation cycle is the precursor stage, when visionaries and futurists establish the conditions for technological change. During this stage, philosophers, artists and creative thinkers imagine new ideas, processes and machines, and bring their visions to the world through journals, drawings, collaboration and eventually professional conferences, Internet sites, blogs and wikis. Their innovations often break with cultural and scientific traditions and challenge established "truths," which their contemporaries sometimes consider outlandish. Fortunately, today's eccentric often turns into tomorrow's genius.

Leonardo da Vinci, for example, envisaged many innovations, thought about how they might be built and how they might work, and created intriguing drawings in an effort to communicate his visions

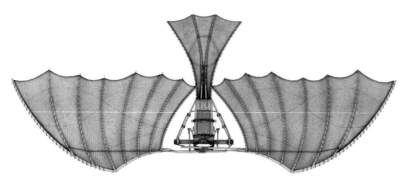

3.2

Leonardo da Vinci's glider, the precursor to today's hang glider, exemplifies the first stage of technological innovation.

Thinkstock

to the world. His notebooks contained drawings of weaponry, aircraft and physiological maps of humans and animals—all of which were considered impossible and nothing other than fantastical in the 15th and 16th centuries, though not to da Vinci. He saw vast possibilities in his ideas, which partially explains why his drawings still captivate the imagination today. Although da Vinci is considered one of humankind's greatest artists, he did not invent any of the grand machines that he envisioned due to the technological limitations of his time. That task was left to the inventors of the future.

The Invention and Development Stages

During the invention stage, innovators give birth to new technologies to solve current or anticipated problems by applying scientific thought and engineering. In other words, inventors actually build what was previously only imagined during the precursor stage. In the early years of the Digital Age, for instance, innovators discussed the possibility of developing a computer-processing technology that would become small and inexpensive enough to be accessible to everyone—that is, the personal computer. It took forward thinkers such as Steve Jobs and Steve Wozniak, the founders of Apple Computer, to figure out how to actually make this happen on a large, sensible scale. Jobs and Wozniak took ideas and technological elements that were already in existence and combined them in a new and novel way, thereby "inventing" the first practical personal computer.

The invention stage is followed by the development stage, during which the innovation is nurtured, refined and focused so that it can be successfully adopted and brought into the mainstream. In this phase, developers must identify and solve practical problems, such as those dealing with reliability and the user interface, as well as marketing and distribution challenges. Manufacturers of the required hardware and software often struggle to agree on a universal format standard during this stage, vying for the market dominance that will allow them to exert their will in the marketplace. These battles between commercial goliaths, called format wars, are heated affairs in which companies with the winning formats stand to make huge profits, while the losing companies are forced to leave the marketplace or adopt the leading technology. At the risk of loss of market share and investor equity, and sometimes for the sake of corporate survival, media content producers enter these battles and try to position their products so that they end up the winning platform—not an easy feat.

Consider, for example, the high-stakes format war between high-definition digital video discs (HD DVD) and Blu-ray optical discs. Both formats offer higher-resolution video and audio quality, as well as increased storage capacity, relative to traditional DVDs. Two significant differences separate the two formats, however: the type of laser used during the disc-production processes and the HD DVD's backward compatibility (that is, its ability to work with older technologies).

The battle between HD DVD and Blu-ray began in 2006 when the Japanese companies Toshiba and NEC released the first HD DVD players to the market, with other major manufacturers quickly following suit with their own HD DVD models. Fellow Japanese company Sony and a few other companies, however, banked on the Blu-ray technology capturing market dominance; thus they brought Blu-ray HD players to the market. Major content producers such as Hollywood film studios preferred Blu-ray technology because of its improved image quality, which was noticeably sharper and more refined, and its audio quality, which was much more akin to how a director or an audio engineer intended for sound to be experienced.

Furthermore, Blu-ray offered an array of special features not available on HD DVD, such as popup menus accessible even during movie play.[3] But, before there was a clear winner in this format war, Hollywood studios were forced to release their latest feature films, television programs and video games on *both* HD DVD and Blu-ray formats. This significantly increased studios' manufacturing costs, which in turn reduced their profits and increased their risk.[4]

By late 2007, although the HD DVD manufacturers appeared to be pulling ahead in the battle, the Blu-ray manufacturers continued to fight back by claiming an increased market share owing to new video games and cross-platform (multiplatform) video gaming devices that also supported Blu-ray HD movies. By 2008, Blu-ray had come to dominate the market, even though HD DVD still remained available. Yet, despite its increasing popularity, drawbacks to the Blu-ray existed—for example, the high cost of the players, the limited number of films available in the format, a slow load time, and a lack of backward compatibility. Thus one can fairly presume that at that time, Blu-ray's market share was partly the result of successful marketing and business strategies, rather than its superior format.[5] By mid-2012, the market share for Blue-ray had increased to 26 percent, while DVD market share hovered at a still dominant 74 percent, according to Home Media Magazine's weekly reporting of market shares. For a more in-depth look into the causes and implications of these format wars, view the video segment "Media Technology Format Wars." ▶

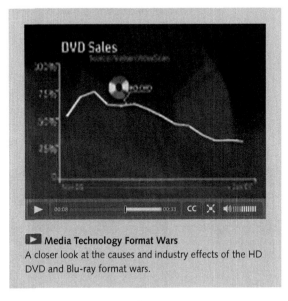

▶ **Media Technology Format Wars**
A closer look at the causes and industry effects of the HD DVD and Blu-ray format wars.

The Maturity Stage

The next phase of technological innovation is the maturity stage. In this stage, one particular mass media technology emerges as the clear winner, dominating the world market. Occasionally no other competing format exists, making it possible for one technology to mature more quickly. During the maturity stage, the vast majority of media content producers gear all of their releases toward the sole or dominant platform. As this media technology continues to evolve and is refined, it becomes fully accepted and integrated into the marketplace.

Consider, for instance, the evolution from the battery-powered, transistor/integrated circuit-based portable radio to the tape player, to the CD player, to MP3 players such as Apple's iPad—at one point, each of these devices was considered the dominant mass media device and was accepted as commonplace in everyday life. Apple's continued innovations in multiuse mobile computing devices like the iPad and the iPhone are changing what tools are considered commonplace for work, education and entertainment.

The format war between Blu-ray and HD DVD eventually led to a truce, with both formats sharing the market equally in 2012. Today's consumers are more knowledgeable, selecting the technology formats and features that best work for them. During the maturity stage, with one format's market dominance established, prices drop and the technology becomes ubiquitous. For instance, as HD television has become less of a novelty, the creative focus has turned to content: What can program producers deliver in terms of film, television and video games to captivate and sustain audience interest? The BBC/Discovery Channel documentary series *Planet Earth* (2006) was one answer to this question. With advanced, high-definition camera technology, the producers of this critically acclaimed nature series managed to capture some remarkable, never-before-seen moments of life on earth in some of its most diverse, unforgiving habitats. As a result of this series' success and popularity, an equally stunning sequel was produced: Discovery Channel's *Life* (2010). Like its predecessor, this series also met with critical acclaim.

Some media technologies stabilize once they move into the maturity stage; they remain essentially static for decades, with only small innovations being applied to their basic platforms to help improve and rejuvenate them. A good example of this phenomenon is commercial FM radio, which offers clear sound and wide-range tonal quality. Commercial FM radio was developed in the 1940s, reached a broad market by the 1960s, and remained popular, yet unchanged for the next 45 years. In 2002, commercial Radio broadcasters began switching to digital radio, in large part to better utilize smaller bandwidths—smaller slices of the crowded range of broadcast frequencies. For the average radio listener, beyond the additional cost of purchasing a new digital receiver, there is little difference between traditional FM radio and HD (digital) radio.

The Antiquity Stage

The final phase of technological innovation is the antiquity stage, when technologies become obsolete. The maturity stage of a technology is usually rather short lived, as each technological innovation sows the seeds for the many other developments that follow it. The concept of obsolescence, especially with mass media technologies, is actually the unavoidable outcome of the innovation process. Some media technologies—such as the early analog Hi-8 consumer video camcorders—reach the antiquity stage and quickly disappear. These camcorders became obsolete so quickly that many people have probably never even heard of them. Their replacements were the even smaller and more capable digital video (DV) camcorders.

Other technologies sometimes reach this stage and are later rediscovered. For example, audiophiles have long believed that digitally reproduced music lacks some of the rich depth and broad tonal range made possible by vintage audio amplifiers from the 1980s. These devices contained vacuum tubes located in the amplifier stage of the equipment. Audio engineers determined that to reproduce these same rich and varied tones, they had to develop high-end digital audio systems that included these same kinds of tiny vacuum tubes on the amplifier circuit board (and on the audio circuit cards of computers). This improvement of an old technology made it possible for digital audio systems to reproduce older, albeit higher-quality sound. As this story suggests, even in its antiquity stage, a seemingly obsolete technology can be rediscovered and reinvented—pushing the past forward into the present.[6]

3.3

The vacuum tube technology of the vintage audio amplifier was adapted to improve the depth and range of digital audio system recordings.

Konstantin Maslak/stock.adobe.com

HURTLING INTO THE FUTURE: TECHNOLOGY REVOLUTIONIZES MASS MEDIA

Multiple innovations in communication have helped to catapult mass media into a yet unknown, but far-reaching future. First was the invention of systematic written languages, followed by the invention of the movable-type printing press. Then came the introduction of electronic communications and electronic media—integrated circuits, computers, the World Wide Web and the ubiquitous cyberspace—heralding the latest quantum leap in mass communication history.

It turns out that the path of development in computer technologies follows an identifiable pattern of exponential growth, which parallels advances in modern mass media technology. Chairman Emeritus Gordon Moore of Intel Corporation and one of the inventors of the integrated circuit (IC)—a miniaturized electronic circuit that forms the basic electronic building blocks of all electronic equipment, from computers to MP3 players to the digital control boards in cars—Gordon Moore developed a measure to predict the exponential growth in computer technology known as Moore's law.

Moore was the first to recognize, as early as 1965, a clear pattern and pace of the technological growth rate, a pattern that was set in motion by the invention of the integrated circuit. Moore's law predicts that

3.4

Does this display of mass media transitioning into a converged and online universe reflect the final result of a mass media revolution?

Luis Francisco Cordero/ Shutterstock.com

Technological Growth and Moore's Law

Transistors*

- 10,000,000,000
- 1,000,000,000
- 100,000,000
- 10,000,000
- 1,000,000
- 100,000
- 10,000

Intel Dual Core Itanium® processor

Intel Core 2 Duo

Intel Itanium® 2 processor

Intel Itanium® processor
Intel Xeon™ processor

Pentium® 4 processor

Pentium® III processor

Intel® Celeron® processor

Pentium® II processor

Pentium® Pro processor

Pentium® processor

i486™ processor

i386™ processor

286

8086
8088

8080

4004
8008

Year of Introduction

1970　1975　1980　1985　1990　1995　2000　2005　2010

*Note: Vertical scale of chart not proportional to actual transistor count.

3.5

Moore's Law

As the number of transistors that can be printed on an integrated circuit doubles, the size of the integrated circuit will grow smaller at a rate of about 50 percent every 12 to 18 months.

in our age of integrated circuits and computers, technology will follow a pattern of accelerating innovation; this pattern will be based on cycles of increasing power and decreasing size of the integrated circuit. The number of transistors (microscopic digital switches) that can be printed on an integrated circuit will continue to double, while the size of the IC will continue to grow smaller at a rate of about 50 percent every 12 to 18 months. As a result, the power of computer technology doubles every year or so, while the cost of "mature" computer-based technology is halved approximately every two years.

The validity of Moore's law can easily be demonstrated: Think about the power of the first computer you or your parents purchased and the price you paid for it. Now compare that with the significantly increased power and decreased cost of the computer you use today. You have just demonstrated a proof of Moore's law.

Using predictive models such as Moore's law, historians have tracked the path of technological growth through the 20th century and into the 21st century. The speed of innovation along this path, and hence the impact of technology on culture, society and communication, has grown exponentially. While it sometimes feels as if we are moving toward technological chaos, the process continues to evolve naturally—and by extension, so do mass media. In the Digital Age, the very same innovations that pull order out of apparent chaos are simultaneously contributing to more chaos, creating a rapid spiral of change to which society must continually adapt. This begs two questions: Will this acceleration of technological change continue, or will the wave of changes slow down? And what does it mean for the Digital Age if the current pattern persists?

Dominating the Media Message

Today new ideas move through cyberspace at the speed of light, racing from one part of the world to another. This rapid dissemination of information creates the foundation of a universal culture and a universal language of invention. It also helps to drive the engines of creativity and change such that the progression of mass media makes a mockery of natural and political borders. In fact, warfare in the 21st century is far less about weapons and battlefield strategies and far more about ideological confrontations that play out in the media. In the Digital Age, the mission can no longer be about winning territory, but rather must focus on the goal of winning hearts and minds—in large part by winning the battle for mass media message dominance.

Knowledge is power and the free flow of ideas is difficult to stop once begun. The mass media remove the filters of time and space, enabling those who want to participate in the evolution of new ideas to see and judge the value of ideas for themselves. Mass media, especially Internet-based media, link knowledge and information in a network of creativity. They may well be the most powerful of all the forces hastening change in the 21st century—and perhaps the most powerful in the history of humankind.

In the Middle East, for example, the Al Jazeera television network operates much like CNN, which has been broadcasting in the region since 1985. The competition between these two networks is as much a competition between cultural histories, social norms and political ideologies as it is a competition to capture audiences—with incalculable repercussions for the people living in the region and beyond. Middle Easterners are well acquainted with this struggle. After World War II and throughout the Cold War, the Middle East was one of the prime diplomatic concerns of the Soviet Union, which used informational warfare to secure allegiances in the region while simultaneously creating anti-American sentiment.

Coping With "Future Shock"

The omnipresence of electronic media requires all of us to learn to cope with and to exploit the extraordinary capabilities now available to us. In Chapter 1, we first discussed Marshall McLuhan's 1964 prediction that advances in communication and mass media technologies would lead to a global village that would

3.6

Mass media technologies have the power to remove the filters of time and space to allow even the most remote citizen to participate in the media revolution.

© Bill Bachmann/Alamy Stock Photo

3.7

In the Middle East, the Al Jazeera network and CNN do not just compete for broadcast time, but for the social and cultural ideologies of the citizenry as well.

Thomas Koehler/Contributor

reshape human relationships. Another renowned futurist, author Alvin Toffler, called this process future shock in his 1970 best-selling book by the same name. A sociologist by training, Toffler cautioned that the rapid rate of technological change—especially in computer and media technologies—would overwhelm many people, causing widespread social upheaval as a result of what he termed information overload. We now know that Toffler was, at the very least, partially wrong. Richard Slaughter, a contemporary futurist,

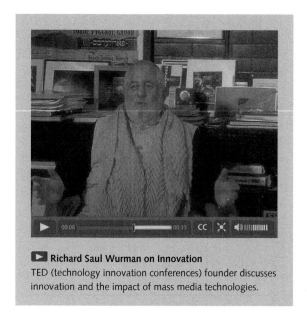

► **Richard Saul Wurman on Innovation**
TED (technology innovation conferences) founder discusses innovation and the impact of mass media technologies.

notes that one of the major flaws with Toffler's thesis was that he based his conclusions on observations gleaned solely from pop psychology, which deals primarily with external factors. For the most part, societies and cultures, as well as the majority of individuals, have proven highly adaptive to these dynamic changes.[7]

New media techniques and technologies—in publishing, broadcasting and telecommunications and on the Internet—do not so much remove and replace older media, but rather redefine and reincorporate the best components of the older technologies into the next generation. Today we tend to welcome most mass media innovations, even when they force us to struggle through short periods of chaos while we come up to speed with the latest hardware, platforms or interactive interfaces. Many of these innovations in media technology are promoted as necessary for our continued participation in the growing network of a media-unifying "digital community." In response, most of us accept an ongoing learning-curve relationship with new media. In this video segment Richard Saul Wurman, architect, designer, futurist, founder of the international TED technology innovation conferences and author of 83 books including *Information Anxiety* and *Information Anxiety 2*, shares his unique perspective on the role of innovation and the impact of mass media technologies. ►

Converging Technologies

In Chapter 1, we introduced the concept of convergence, which is a phenomenon of digital mass media. Technological convergence occurs when media delivery tools and platforms move inexorably toward assimilation into fewer media platforms—radio and television programming merging and integrating with print and delivered through cyberspace to user-programmable and interactive Web nodes, linked lists and tree data structures. Such convergence is driven by the early 21st-century urgency to migrate all media content, and eventually all knowledge and creative output, onto the World Wide Web. Is this a good thing or a bad thing? Again, the answer depends on one's perspective and the level of one's access and competence as a participant in the digital world. In his 2006 book *Convergence Culture: Where and How Media Collide*, theorist Henry Jenkins postulates that new media providers are often ambivalent about how they want users to actually have less and less control, because less control by consumers is often better for the corporate bottom line.

Knowledge, information, entertainment and even social network structures are now in constant motion. To help us keep up with the volume and speed of these messages, technology innovators bring to the market more sophisticated devices that promise to help manage our travels through the digital world.

Full participation in the evolving and globalizing Digital Age requires an individual commitment to continuous lifelong learning. It also requires the capability to access the world of vast amounts of often competing images and voices, the endless onslaught of information, the 24/7 coverage of news events from the important to the entertaining to the inane. Knowledge, information, entertainment and even social network structures are now in constant motion. To help us keep up with the volume and speed of these messages, technology innovators bring to the market more sophisticated devices that promise to help manage our travels through the digital world. Smartphones and tablet computers become our personal nodes to the converging network of communication, information, entertainment and education.

All tablets now feature color and Wi-Fi access to the Internet for browsing or e-mailing as well as high-definition quality images. They also offer unlimited storage for content generated through the

3.8

In many regions of the world today, being unwired from any form of digital device is considered unusual.

Jack Hollingsworth/Thinkstock

company producing the tablet. For example, owners of the Kindle Fire have unlimited memory for products purchased through Amazon in the Amazon "cloud." Through the cloud storage of its contents, media organizations are changing consumers' notion of "ownership." In reality, consumers are purchasing access to the mediated product through the device linked to the product. It is yet another example of converging technologies. Mobile devices are radically changing how most of us use computers to access the Internet, watch movies and TV, play games, get our news, and network and communicate with others. The rapid proliferation of reasonably low-cost mobile devices—from multifunction cell phones to tablet computers—is also forcing changes in how mass media content is produced and structured so that any given media content can work simultaneously and compatibly on any device, and even between devices. Today I'm able to start watching a movie on my home computer or flat-screen television using a service such as Netflix, pause the film should I have to leave for an appointment, and pick up where I left off viewing the film on my table computer. The term for this interconnectiveness of media content is mobility.[8]

The faster the changes in mass media, the greater the opportunities that present themselves for many of us to do more, learn more, create and innovate—and for some of us to become more overloaded and more anxious and to fall further and further behind. It is either an exciting and exquisite new world or an ever-more frightening one, depending on one's perspective. While a far cry from fulfilling Toffler's prediction of social upheaval, convergence can and has resulted in increased stress for some.

Evolving Roles of Mass Media in Society

In addition to posing individual challenges in navigating through the text and visual information presented to users, today's dynamically changing and converging mass media place a great deal of responsibility on journalists and other media professionals to serve as reliable interpreters and honest brokers of media content. The news media, for example, are now responsible for guiding their audiences into the next developmental stages of technological innovation—as evidenced by such informational resources as the technology section of *The New York Times*; the technology news and review site cnet.com; the technology news site TechNewsWorld, which offers "all tech—all the time," and the ever-popular *Wired* magazine. On the whole, the mass media are also playing a larger critical role in helping society understand how it will operate once media and media technologies enter their next stages of evolution. Consider, for instance, what the trend of participatory mass media—from talk radio to Internet blogs—did to our level of involvement in the electoral process in the United States. In the 2008 presidential election, mass media technology changed the face of political campaigning, inspired greater citizen involvement and brought political advertising, debates and speeches straight into our laps via YouTube and live streaming of campaign events.

Essentially, advances in mass media technology, the convergence of media platforms and the migration of news, education and entertainment content to cyberspace are driving media outlets to become more responsive to smaller and more tightly defined audience groups. Meanwhile, these same individuals enjoy an even more expansive menu of media content, in part because hundreds of television and radio stations can now be transmitted in the same bandwidth that, in the past, could accommodate only a dozen or so TV stations and a few dozen radio stations.

Our intellectual, social, cultural and economic lives are becoming inextricably entwined at a global level. In theory, this mass media-linked world will bring benefits to everyone eventually—for some of us sooner rather than later.

Forming a New Global Culture

The digital revolution in mass media is tearing down traditionally accepted boundaries between nations, cultures and classes—but simultaneously creating new social, economic and cultural challenges with global effects. Our intellectual, social, cultural and economic lives are becoming inextricably entwined at a global level. In theory, this mass media-linked world will bring benefits to everyone eventually—for some of us sooner rather than later. For many, this movement represents a positive advance toward realization of Marshall McLuhan's "global village." Businesses, for example, are redefining how to conduct their affairs, and more people are participating in an expanding global marketplace. One might argue that a small shop owner in New Delhi, India, is now just as much a player in the global economy as is the sales executive in a large multinational corporation headquartered in London. Yet, for those who struggle to maintain cultural patrimony—that is, the preservation of historical and social traditions deemed central to a particular group or culture—the boundary-breaking digital revolution is viewed as a threat.

The more quickly mass media and digital communications seek to bring the world together, the more forcefully traditionalists fight to preserve a slower and simpler way of life. Interestingly, many of the same changes that resisters balk at accepting are often quickly adopted as a means of promoting their own worldviews. For example, extremist groups such as al-Qaida spread their dogma decrying the introduction of technological

3.9

Even the most remote villages in Peru cannot escape the globalizing effects of mass media technology.

Danita Delimont/Alamy Stock Photo

innovation and Western thought through Websites, e-mail and sophisticated streaming video—the same technologies that they claim threaten their nation, culture, religion and beliefs.

In his book *The Future of Ideas*, Lawrence Lessig quotes 16th-century Italian diplomat and philosopher Niccolo Machiavelli's apt description of those who struggle against innovation. These words are as applicable today as they were when Machiavelli wrote them in 1513 in his best-known work, *The Prince*, a treatise on the art of political rule and control:

> Innovation makes enemies of all those who prospered under the old regime and only lukewarm support is forthcoming from those who would prosper under the new. Their support is indifferent partly from fear and partly because they are generally incredulous, never really trusting new things unless they have tested them by experience.[9]

It can be argued that groups who rail against the cultural and moral dangers of television, movies, popular music and the Internet are denying themselves and their cultures the ability to participate fully in a robustly evolving mass media world. They are exiling themselves from the vast opportunities and benefits of the Digital Age.

The Spanish philosopher and essayist George Santayana (1863–1952) said, "Those who cannot learn from history are doomed to repeat it." In the Digital Age, we use mass media to learn about not just the events but also the processes of history, to enable us to contribute to the building of our own future. The faster and more dynamically change occurs, the more important mass media become as vehicles for sharing and guiding the direction of change. With the right attitude and an open mind, we can learn from all media, from all voices and ideas, from the profound to the profane. They challenge us to take responsibility for selecting the best platforms and the most reliable and trustworthy sources and to make more informed choices about the quality and quantity of the media we consume and create. Paul Levinson, communication and media professor at Fordham University, would agree with this evaluation of the current state of mass media; his outlook on the future of mass media is showcased in the video segment titled "Paul Levinson on the Future of Mass Media."

▶ Paul Levinson on the Future of Mass Media
A modern communication and media professor's insight into the future of mass media—after McLuhan's global village.

WILL TECHNOLOGICAL CONVERGENCE BE THE DEATH OF THE PRINTED WORD?

What does the future hold for books in the Digital Age? As e-books increase in popularity, and with the refinement of digital readers such as the KoboTouch reader, the Amazon Kindle, the Barnes & Noble Nook and the Apple iPad, one cannot deny that the nature and role of books in society are changing. Indeed, some futurists maintain that books will eventually be replaced by computers, e-readers and digital libraries. Are libraries rapidly becoming cyberspace portals—gateways that we log into rather than physically visit? Are knowledge and entertainment so quickly migrating into electronic platforms and cyberspace that printed books are now entering their antiquity stage?

In 1802, Thomas Jefferson, Founding Father and third president of the United States, signed into law the legislation and approved funding to create the Library of Congress. Along with the second president of the United States, John Adams, Jefferson recognized the importance of building a great national library to serve as the central repository of knowledge and the hub of the new nation's cultural and scientific progress. Jefferson predicted that the U.S. Library of Congress would one day become the most influential national library in the world. He envisioned a center modeled after the Great Library of Alexandria created by Ptolemy II of Egypt in the 3rd century b.c. A futurist of his time, Jefferson believed that for democracy to take root and survive, vast knowledge had to be collected and made available to the nation's leaders and its citizenry to encourage and assure the free flow of ideas. During his presidency, he personally guided the acquisition of thousands of books from Europe, which was considered the 19th century's center of Western civilization. When he retired to Monticello, Virginia, in 1809, Jefferson sold his personal library of nearly 7,000 volumes—at the time the largest and most valuable collection of books in the United States—to the Library of Congress. Just as he envisioned it, Jefferson's efforts started a process that continues today, making the Library of Congress the largest, most comprehensive library in the world.[10]

While books remain of central importance, their format has evolved. The digitization of the world's vast stockpile of books and printed media (magazines, journals, drawings and photographic images) began in earnest at the British Library in the early 1990s. In 1993, the Librarian of Congress, James H. Billington, initiated a massive project to convert all of that library's vast collections to digital media, emphasizing that "the Library of Congress is becoming an even more important catalyst for the educational, competitive, and creative needs of the nation."[11] The goal of this Herculean technological challenge was to turn the Library of Congress into the largest digital repository of information and knowledge in the world, a process that continues today.

The Digitization of Libraries

What is happening at the Library of Congress is happening at every level of mass media and for every subject and discipline—science, culture, anthropology, economics, philosophy, religion, politics, art, music and entertainment. All media content is migrating onto a digital platform and into cyberspace. In this effort, the Library of Congress is not without stiff competition. For example, in 2005 Google announced its Google Library Project. Initially signing agreements with the New York Public Library and libraries of such major universities as Oxford University, Harvard University, Stanford University and the University of Michigan, Google sought to offer digitally scanned full texts of millions of books from the participating libraries online—all searchable on Google.

The Google Library Project was very controversial when it was proposed because it challenged traditional views on copyright and copyright enforcement (see Chapter 11). In 2005, the Association of American Publishers joined forces with the Authors Guild, the American Booksellers Association and five other major publishers and sued Google in federal court in an effort to stop this venture. Google argued that its Library Project would ultimately benefit publishers, authors and readers by making the world's vast collection of knowledge searchable by everyone, greatly increasing the use—and therefore the value—of published works. The company also claimed its Library Project would enhance and prolong the life of books in the 21st century. Clearly, not everyone agreed with this view.

In the years since the lawsuit was filed, the case has been settled, and Google is now working closely with these various industry associations to bring more books online. In March 2010, the company announced it would undertake a similar digitization effort in Italy, working with the National Libraries of Florence and Rome to digitize numerous out-of-copyright works, including rare books, scientific works and literature by some of Italy's most renowned poets and writers.[12]

In an effort to compete with Google, the Library of Congress launched the World Digital Library Project in partnership with UNESCO (United Nations Educational, Scientific, and Cultural Organization) in 2005—interestingly, with Google as one of the corporate sponsors. The goal of the World Digital Library project is to use cutting-edge, Web-based technologies to create the largest linked global digital library in the world. National libraries, including the Bibliotheca Alexandria (Egypt), the National Library of Brazil, the National Library and Archives of Egypt, and the National Library of Russia, joined this ambitious international effort. In its 2012 mission statement, the World Digital Library Project laid out its goals for the library.

The World Digital Library (WDL) makes available on the Internet—free of charge and in multilingual format—significant primary materials from countries and cultures around the world.

The principal objectives of the WDL are to:

- Promote international and intercultural understanding;
- Expand the volume and variety of cultural content on the Internet;
- Provide resources for educators, scholars and general audiences;
- Build capacity in partner institutions to narrow the Digital Divide within and between countries.[13]

The World Digital Library Project platform incorporates a variety of exciting user-interface tools, including a real-time language translator. This tool allows users to scan foreign-language documents using a dynamic window that automatically translates texts into user-selected languages. In addition, an intelligent voice translator will read any user-selected text as streaming audio narration, also in user-selected languages—enabling more people to access different content than was otherwise possible in the pre-Digital Age. To see the World Digital Library Project come to fruition, view the video titled "World Digital Library Project."

If you were born after 1980, the libraries with which you are familiar are nothing like the libraries used by generations before yours. Legions of computer terminals, enormous database computer servers and online resources dominate today's libraries. In fact, the main branches in most metropolitan areas provide hundreds of public-use computers. The historical role of the reference librarian has evolved from

World Digital Library Project
The LOC's World Digital Library Project comes to fruition.

serving as a guide to the physical collection on the shelves to being the expert in the complex world of information management. The smallest community library, while still housing collections of popular books, CDs and DVDs, can also serve as a primary portal into a network of hundreds of other libraries—public libraries, libraries at major universities, national libraries and even a growing number of private libraries—across the state, across the country and around the world. American historian Anthony Grafton cautions that while a digital library offers the potential for civilization to learn more about itself than ever before, it is also likely that the digitization of historical works might lead to their demise as they fall out of view and lose our attention in what seems to be an endless web of information.

Print-on-Demand Publishing

For some, the logical next step to digitizing the world's libraries is a completely new form of publishing called print-on-demand, wherein a new copy of a book or other printed resource is not printed until an order for the text has been received. The technology supporting this method of content delivery is already available and provides a viable alternative model for both publishers and consumers.

Here is how the process works: Suppose a reader is interested in a particular kind of adventure novel by a new author that she heard about while reading her favorite blog. She does a search on Google and locates a number of books by this author. She uses Google Book Search to read the first chapter of the book online and decides to buy it. To do so, the user simply clicks on the publisher's link and purchases a digital download of the entire book. Within minutes, the entire book is stored on her computer. The reader uses her high-speed color printer to print a hardcopy version and loads a few chapters onto her notebook computer, tablet or e-reader so she can read it during her train commute or on her lunch break. She might even elect to download a free audiobook version from her local library and transfer it to her iPod so she can listen to the book during her morning workouts. The option of how to access the book's content is up to the consumer, who can select the media that best suit her personal schedule and lifestyle—all made possible by book publishing's migration into the digital world and technological convergence. (We will explore some other new publishing models in Chapter 4.)

For Jason Epstein, former editorial director of Random House and founding editor of Anchor Books and *The New York Review of Books*, a print-on-demand kiosk similar to the ubiquitous bank ATMs would be the most ideal. The book buyer uses this machine's integrated computer to search for the book he wants. The machine then downloads the digital file containing all the components and content of the book. It then prints the pages, including color illustrations; gathers the printed pages together; and binds them. He also has the option of creating a customized cover by selecting a cover style and cover art downloaded from the book's master file. In just a few minutes, out comes a brand-new printed-on-demand book through a slot at the bottom—delivered like a can of soda from a vending machine, but for a much higher price, of course.

Is this machine a boon for publishing? Or is it a dangerous innovation if you happen to be the owner of a bookstore? These are just a few of the questions currently being debated by scholars, publishers, businesses, producers and consumers.

3.10

E-books have forever changed the business of book publishing.

Pixellover RM 1/Alamy Stock Photo

The E-book Market

The booming e-book market is affecting all areas of publishing. Electronic books are viewed on specialized lightweight digital readers with vertical screens that mimic the layout and look of the standard printed book page. They also have easy-to-use controls and internal wireless broadband capability to enable consumers to quickly purchase and download digitized texts.

Sony was an early entrant into the e-book market, with its line of Reader Digital Book portable e-book devices. Then in late 2007, the leading online bookseller, Amazon.com, entered the market with its own e-book called the Amazon Kindle.

The e-reader market underwent a major shift in January 2010, when Apple founder and CEO Steve Jobs introduced the company's new iPad tablet computer. The iPad represents a major leap forward in that it combines the functionality of a portable e-book device, albeit with a higher resolution and full-color display, with integrated WiFi-enabled Web browsing and media display capabilities. The iPad has made to make portable tablet computers a commonplace digital reading device for books, magazines and newspapers as well as a mobile window to all of today's vast digital content—text, images, radio and music, videos, films and television programs. In so doing, it will make yet another contribution to the pace of mass media convergence.

To stay competitive with Apple, Amazon came out with the Kindle Fire in 2011. This four-color, touch screen version of its original e-reader offers access to over 20 million movies, games, music and apps as well as reading materials. Its cloud-accelerated Web browser enables easy access to content.

This market trend is both good news and bad news for the publishing industry. The good news is that print revenue was up primarily in trade paperbacks. According to industry data, print revenue rose 3.4 percent in 2016, primarily through the growth in trade paperback sales among young adult and religious titles. The bad news is that at the same time print revenues actually decreased 4.3 percent year-to-date, a 7 percent loss compared to 2015. E-book sales also dropped by 22.7 percent from 2015.[14]

The magazine industry as a legacy medium is also experiencing rapid change as magazine publishers are forced to adapt their publications toward primarily web-based readers. Magazines have been among the first in connecting brands and audiences, and have shown a strong willingness to experiment with new E-publishing alternatives. Popular magazines such as *Parents*, *Better Homes and Gardens*, *PC Magazine* and *Wired* magazine were among the first to strongly commit to web-first publishing models. Martha Stewart and Rachael Ray are two more examples of successful producers of parallel media products with simultaneous brand extensions in broadcast television, radio, and digital media.

Does the continued evolution of digital content and the Internet really mean that books and other printed publishing will slowly disappear? Or is the rush to digitize everything and make it available in cyberspace fueling the reinvention and "rebirth" of books? The degree to which the onward march into the Digital Age has created a market for printed material is astounding. In 2004, a study by the National Education Association showed that while only 57 percent of American adults read at least one book in a given year, active computer users report reading many books in a given year. The Web abounds with not only sources of discounted books, but also thousands of Websites, forums and blogs driven by readers and books.[15]

> Does the continued evolution of digital content and the Internet really mean that books and other printed publishing will slowly disappear? Or is the rush to digitize everything and make it available in cyberspace fueling the reinvention and "rebirth" of books?

The Digitization of Newspapers and Magazines

As books and libraries undergo a transition in the Digital Age, so are newspapers and magazines. Many in fact, are fighting for their very survival. Since 2000, circulation and market penetration of newspapers have been steadily dropping. Take, for example, classified advertising. Many people might be surprised to learn that the most lucrative revenue source for newspapers in the 20th century was the sale of classified ads. Internet alternatives such as eBay and Craigslist have grown so rapidly that newspapers have scrambled to establish their own online classified ad services. However, it might be too late for all except the major national-brand newspapers, such as *The Washington Post*, *New York Times*, *Chicago Tribune*, or *Boston Globe*, to compete effectively.

Many newspapers and magazines have been forced to adopt entirely new business models as they have rushed to turn Internet versions of their publications into an integral part of their operations and of their advertising revenues. Magazines with companion Websites have continued to prosper as mass media, and the continued growth of the Internet has given birth to a number of highly successful new-technology magazines that live parallel lives in print and in cyberspace. *Wired* magazine and *Seed* magazine are two examples of publications that were established and designed to take advantage of a parallel real-world and cyberworld publishing model. Many other mainstream magazines—*Newsweek*, *Time*, *The New Yorker*, and *Sports Illustrated*, to name a few—established effective parallel business models that function both economically and editorially, attracting increased audiences and thus bringing increased advertising revenues.

Information Revolution: Innovation and Roadblocks

We have seen how mass media technologies can create profound social and political changes in a society. Such changes lead to a type of information revolution: The more information access that technology provides, the greater the instinct to diversify and disseminate information to wider audiences. Let's consider this formula in terms of Communist North Korea.

In July 1953, the United Nations Command (a U.S.-supported group of multinational military forces stationed in South Korea) and the Chinese–North Korean Command (supported by the People's Republic

3.11

Will modern printing presses such as this one enter their antiquity stage with the advent of green publishing?

Roger Bamber/Alamy Stock Photo

of China and the Soviet Union) signed the Korean Armistice Agreement, which created North Korea—the nation that its own government calls the Democratic People's Republic of Korea. It also created one of the most militaristic and repressive nations in modern history. Led first by Kim Il-sung and then, after his death in 1994, by his son Kim Young-il, the North Korean regime for decades successfully indoctrinated its people in the effort to achieve a *personality cult*—that is, an unwavering worship of the two Kims—in an attempt to strengthen their dictatorship. In addition, it successfully sustained total control over the economy, education, information and all media until the early years of the 21st century, when it became clear that managing technology-driven mass media would be a formidable task.

In the new millennium, an overwhelming tide of smuggled and inexpensive television sets, VCRs and DVD players began to flood the North Korean–Chinese border. With this flood came videotapes and DVDs of Chinese and Western television programs—all evidence of a growing black-market trade. People living near the coast or along the borders of China and South Korea were able to watch Korean and Chinese soap operas, Hollywood movies and news programs from CNN and the BBC. Of course, for a regime that practiced militaristic leadership of its people and made every effort to control the type of information that reached its citizenry, unauthorized ownership of TVs, VCRs, DVDs or any other devices that would open up media access was not just illegal, but dangerous—to *both* the government and its people.

Watching foreign films and television and listening to foreign radio broadcasts were considered antisocialist behaviors. Government agents and military forces conducted sweeps of neighborhoods and villages looking for such contraband and arrested anyone discovered with it. But the media floodgates had already opened: More and more North Koreans learned that the government of Kim Young-il had been lying about the outside world. Such exposure introduced them to the multitude of voices expressing compelling new ideas and beliefs about nations, lives and people beyond their borders. While those living in the country's interior remained isolated and largely untouched by the mass media flood, the percentage of the population that did have media access soared. In the wake of their new knowledge, North Korea's isolation and the coerced worship of its leaders quickly and progressively became difficult to maintain. While complete revolution in North Korea has yet to occur, the narrowing gap between its people and the greater media world beyond North Korean borders demonstrates how mass media can at least *catalyze* the desire for reform.

> While complete revolution in North Korea has yet to occur, the narrowing gap between its people and the greater media world beyond North Korean borders demonstrates how mass media can at least *catalyze* the desire for reform.

The Read–Write Media Culture

The massive audience migration from print to Web media sources is driving the demand for ever-more engaging and creative Web publishing as well as the convergence of print and broadcast media content into a new Internet-delivered hybrid. This trend is putting content and editorial selection power into the hands of the mass media consumers—what Lawrence Lessig, Creative Commons founder and leading authority on the impact of new mass media, calls a read–write media culture. In this culture, media content producers supply the creative, entertainment and journalistic components to consumers via technologies that enable each person to be his or her own news editor or entertainment programmer. In other words, in the Digital Age, we are simultaneously becoming media consumers and media creators; according to Lessig, we are shifting away from the traditional read-only media culture, wherein the mass media audience largely consumed, rather than produced, the media.

Indeed, we are witnessing a power shift in mass media. Content control is shifting from the large media producers and distributors, supported by the advertising industry, to the consumers of mass media. Consumers are becoming ever-more empowered to take control of the packaging and flow of media content, and advertising and production models are adapting their practices accordingly.

Who, then, is in the best position to win the mass media revolution? We all are. In the words of Marshall McLuhan:

> . . . the future work consists of learning a living (rather than earning a living) in the automation age . . . as the age of information demands the simultaneous use of all our faculties, we discover that we are most at leisure when we are most intensely involved, very much as with the artists in all ages.[16]

CONCLUSION: ADAPTING TO CHANGE

The tools of human ideas and invention—from the "mighty pen" of the days of yore to the extraordinary power of the modern-day computer and the Internet—are the means by which we bring ideas to life, share them with others, and explore and solidify our views of the world. It is common practice to blame the media and the technologies that give the media their power and influence for what we do not like and feel we cannot influence or change ourselves. The renowned Irish author George Bernard Shaw (1856–1950) wrote that "democracy is a device that ensures we shall be governed no better than we deserve."[17] In much the same way, we all get the mass media we deserve. Mass media are neither a good thing nor a bad thing; rather, it is our use of mass media that determines their value. Today, more than ever before, we are all participants in the dynamics of change—and we are all partially responsible for our future.

Are we building a future utopia or future dystopia? Science-fiction writers of the 20th century provided fictional glimpses into what the 21st century might hold. In one scenario, the rapid advance of technology brought humankind unlimited opportunities for knowledge and entertainment. In another, it heralded an apocalyptic future brought on by too much technology too fast, resulting in the ultimate technology "crash" and a return to the low-tech basics of the 19th century, with humans struggling to survive in the harsh new conditions. In a pessimistic view of the future, the mass media overwhelm us such that we become numb and lazy, cease acting as critical media consumers, and find ourselves opening the door for commercial, religious and/or political manipulation and a world where the media "haves" rebel against the media "have-nots"—setting the stage for violent social and cultural conflict.

In the end, the dynamics of change are anchored in humankind's vast ability to adapt to each quantum leap in the ceaseless advance of technology created by the idea chain. All mass media can at once serve as vehicles for the advancement of society and the means by which we learn to successfully cope with a constantly reinvented new world.

CHAPTER SUMMARY	KEY TERMS
The Stages of Technological Innovation Explores the innovation cycles for multiple technologies to demonstrate how these stages tie in to the evolution of mass media. **Visual Media** **Media Technology Format Wars** A closer look at the causes and industry effects of the HD DVD and Blu-ray format wars. 1. Why do some new media technologies such as Blu-ray become popular while others never gain widespread consumer acceptance? 2. Do new media technologies drive changes in consumer behavior or does consumer demand drive the development of new technologies?	Digital Divide format wars high-definition digital video discs (HD DVD) Blu-ray optical discs backward compatibility cross-platform maturity stage bandwidths HD (digital) radio antiquity stage
Hurtling into the Future: Technology Revolutionizes Mass Media Discusses how the development and proliferation of mass media technologies impact and even drive social and cultural progress while at the same time challenging previously well-established cultural norms. **Visual Media** **Richard Saul Wurman on Innovation** TED (technology innovation conferences) founder discusses innovation and the impact of mass media technologies. 1. Describe your own process for adopting new media technologies and coping with what Richard Saul Wurman has termed "information anxiety." 2. How does the creative process of innovation described help drive the phenomena of user-influenced, user-created mass media content? **Paul Levinson on the Future of Mass Media** A modern communication and media professor's insight into the future of mass media—after McLuhan's global village. 1. Marshal McLuhan was a futurist who made predictions about the impact of communication and mass media technologies on societies and cultures long before these technologies actually evolved to what has become commonplace today. Which of McLuhan's predictions have not come true in quite the way he envisioned them?	electronic media integrated circuit (IC) Moore's law future shock information overload technological convergence nodes cloud

Will Technological Convergence Be the Death of the Printed Word? An examination the complex relationship between technology and the printed word reveals the complex nature of today's publishing industry. **Visual Media** **World Digital Library Project** The LOC's World Digital Library project comes to fruition. 1. A visit to the most community-based or school-based libraries today—where more and more space is devoted to computer terminals and less to actual book collections—demonstrates that the way libraries function is undergoing significant change. What do you envision the "library of the future" will look like, and how will users interact with it five or 10 years from now?	print-on-demand read–write media culture

NOTES

1 Lane, F. (2007). OLPC's XO faces many challenges. *Sci-Tech Today*. Retrieved from www.sci-techtoday.com/story.xhtml?story_id=12300CLQOP4L&full_skip=1

2 Ibid.

3 Moscovciak, M. (2010, February 12). Blu-ray quick guide. *CNET Reviews*. Retrieved from http://reviews.cnet.com/2719-13817_7-286-2.html?tag=page;page

4 Shankland, S. (2005). FAQ: HD DVD vs. Blu-ray. *CNET News*. Retrieved from http://news.cnet.com/FAQ-HD-DVD-vs.-Blu-ray/2100-1041_3-5886956.html

5 Moscovciak, M. (2010, February 12). Blu-ray quick guide. *CNET Reviews*. Retrieved from http://reviews.cnet.com/2719-13817_7-286-2.html?tag=page;page

6 Many authors have described the stages of innovation, albeit somewhat differently. Those described in this chapter are the author's own construct, drawn from his many lectures and seminars on innovation and the dynamics of change in mass media.

7 Slaughter, R. (2002). Future shock re-assessed. *World Future Studies Federation Bulletin, 27*(1).

8 Armano, D. (2012, July 18). The Future Isn't About Mobile; It's About Mobility. *Harvard Business Review*. Retrieved from http://blogs.hbr.org/cs/2012/07/the_future_isnt_about_mobile_its.html

9 Machiavelli, N. (1513). *The prince*.

10 *Jefferson's library*. (2008). Retrieved from www.loc.gov/exhibits/jefferson/jefflib.html

11 Retrieved from www.loc.gov/librarianoffice

12 (2010). A digital renaissance: Partnering with the Italian Ministry of Cultural Heritage. *Official Google Blog*. Retrieved from http://googleblog.blogspot.com/2010/03/digitalrenaissancepartnering-with.html

13 Retrieved from www.wdl.org/en/about/

14 Biggs, J. (2016, September 30). Print and ebook revenue down as Amazon slashes prices. *TechCrunch* Sept. 30, 2016,. Retrieved from https://techcrunch.com/2016/09/30/print-and-ebook-revenue-down-as-amazon-slashes-prices/; Silber, T. (2016, March 1). *The untold story of how magazine media is winning: The consumer, not the print magazine, now resides at the hub of the business model. Folio*. Retrieved from www.foliomag.com/untold-story-magazine-media-winning/; Schiff, A., and Daniel, A. (2016, September 9). Offset printing versus print-on-demand. *Publishers Weekly*. Retrieved from www.publishersweekly.com/pw/by-topic/authors/pw-select/article/63094-offset-printing-versus-print-on-demand.html

15 Levy, S. (2007, November 26). Books aren't dead (they're just going digital). *Newsweek*.

16 McLuhan, M. (2003). *Understanding media: The extensions of man*. Gingko Press.

17 Shaw, G. B.

The Evolution of Media Content and Platforms

4
Print Media

Neil Fraser/Alamy Stock Photo

CHAPTER OUTLINE
Early American Newspaper Publishing

The Evolution of Printing
Insights into the history of printing and printing presses from the late 18th to the late 20th centuries and their impact on the world.

The Rise of Magazine Publishing
The Evolution of the Book Industry
Technologies Extend the Print Media
The Birth of Publishing Dynasties

Print Media Go Visual
Comic Books and the Graphic Novel
Conclusion: Will Printed Media Survive the Digital
Revolution?

Otis Chandler, *L.A. Times* The late Otis Chandler, former *L.A. Times* publisher, discusses the influence of newspapers and publishing dynasties on American culture and politics.

Al Neuharth, *USA Today* The founder of *USA Today* offers an in-depth analysis of the success and popularity of his paper.

LEARNING OBJECTIVES

1. Distinguish between the commercial press, penny press and partisan press in 19th-century America.
2. Explain how magazine publishing emerged from newspaper publishing to become the second major mass medium in America.
3. Assess the role that increased literacy rates among women in the United States impacted the 19th-century book publishing industry.
4. Explain how advances in both printing and transportation technologies helped to expand the reach of print media throughout the 19th and 20th centuries.
5. Compare and contrast the ways in which William Randolph Hearst and the Bingham family of Kentucky used their media control to influence American politics and culture.
6. Illustrate how the use of visuals impacted the 19th- and 20th-century growth of both the newspaper and magazine industries.
7. Identify the leading publishing dynasties that influenced American politics, culture and expansionism.
8. Evaluate the impact of comic books and graphic novels on popular culture.
9. Predict the impact that digital technology will have on the format of various print media in the 21st century.
10. Discuss the challenges facing print publishing in the Digital Age.

ON SEPTEMBER 15, 1982,

Al Neuharth (1924–2013), then CEO of the newspaper conglomerate Gannett Company, announced the launch of *USA Today*—the nation's first truly national daily newspaper. The paper's launch heralded a new age for newspaper publishing—one based upon an entirely new publishing model made possible by advances in digital technologies that enabled the simultaneous publication and distribution of a color and image-rich newspaper by dozens of sites located in cities throughout the United States, and soon throughout the world.

The design, layout and editorial approach of *USA Today* were revolutionary and presaged the short, synthesized, easy-to-read stories supported by a high ratio of photographs and charts that would eventually become commonplace with the advent and proliferation of the Internet and Web-based news platforms. *USA Today* was notable for its prolific use of color photographs and large colorful charts and diagrams that helped readers quickly understand otherwise complicated stories and issues. The paper's design and content

intentionally mimicked the image-rich, short-feature news reporting style of television. While some critics complained that the paper's reporting style sacrificed details that traditional newspapers delivered—turning stories into the print equivalent of TV news bites—most consumers loved the new model because it delivered important stories in a format that could be read more quickly than a traditional newspaper. Eventually many newspapers began to emulate the style of *USA Today*, also featuring shorter stories supported by color photographs and charts.[1]

USA Today's state-by-state news roundups and weather coverage predicted the growth of regional hyperlocal news sites many years before Web-based hyperlocal journalism was envisioned. The paper's inclusion of a range of opinion articles and editorials solicited from a wide range of writers—some famous, but others not—also predicted the rise of the blogosphere many years before blog sites became both routine and so influential in setting the public and political agendas in America.

Today, at a time when traditional print newspapers are struggling to retain both circulation and advertisers—with many desperately trying to migrate to the Web and many others going out of business entirely—*USA Today* is still thriving. In 2012, total readership nationally and worldwide reached 3.2 million for the printed paper and another 23.6 million for its companion Website USAToday.com. It's fascinating to note that many of *USA Today*'s groundbreaking and industry-changing accomplishments were predicted in a rare on-camera interview that *USA Today*'s founder Al Neuharth sat for with this author in 1988, just five years after its founding.

USA Today was a groundbreaking step forward in the long history of news. If the paper is at the pinnacle of American newspaper publishing in the late 20th and early 21st century, let's look at how we got here.

4.1

NetPhotos/Alamy Stock Photo

EARLY AMERICAN NEWSPAPER PUBLISHING

In 1730, 45 years before the American Revolutionary War, Benjamin Franklin was producing one of the most widely read newspapers in the colonies, *The Pennsylvania Gazette*. While at first readership comprised the colonial privileged, with time and the addition of ideological content that affected vaster segments of the population, readership expanded, inviting and embracing the concerns of artisans, shopkeepers and women. Newspapers, books and pamphlets helped bridge the gap between opposing economic and political interests, and enabled the birth of a new American nation.

Many early newspaper publishers were printers and editors who added the publishing of pamphlets—predecessors to magazines—to their printing businesses in an effort to increase their income. Other

MRS. ROSS AND THE FLAG COMMITTEE.

4.2

As the young American nation matured, its newspaper readership expanded alongside it, embracing the interests and concerns of artisans, shopkeepers and women.

North Wind Picture Archives/Alamy Stock Photo

publishers were among America's wealthy educated elite who would collaborate with printing partners by providing both financial support and editorial content, the latter often anchored in political ideologies. As the colonists' anger over England's attempts to control them grew, newspaper publishing in the 13 colonies became a tool of partisan politics (see Chapter 11).[2] Franklin, who understood the power of the press and recognized the economic viability of a *networked* mass media, influenced his fellow American publishers to formally network. As such, Franklin's media network became a principal vehicle for news and political commentary, helping to unite the colonies in the name of reform and, eventually, revolution.

> Franklin's media network became a principal vehicle for news and political commentary, helping to unite the colonies in the name of reform and, eventually, revolution.

Newspapers started in the cities and larger towns but soon spread into rural areas, mostly along major trade routes. When the First Continental Congress met in 1774 to plan a united response to England's political and economic assaults, colonial newspapers were the primary media through which the public followed the debates of their representatives. Meanwhile, letters and commentaries published in newspapers and pamphlets allowed the Continental Congress to sense the mood and direction of public opinion.

Aside from formalizing one of the first and largest news-sharing systems, Franklin established one of the first workable postal services in America and was later appointed the first postmaster general of the United States. Franklin's postal services in effect afforded him significant control over the major means of media distribution. Unfortunately, due to the slow flow of information, most newspaper content was outdated and lacked local relevance by the time it was published and read by the public.[3] The availability of current information would not change until the advent of new technologies—namely, the telegraph (discussed later in this chapter).

Newspapers Evolve to Dominate Mass Media

By the 1830s, a full century after Ben Franklin first published *The Pennsylvania Gazette*, the newspaper industry dominated mass media in the United States. It would continue to do so for approximately 160 years, while following the same basic business model. From the mid-19th century to the present day, newspaper publishing has involved three closely linked activities: the development and delivery of news, the production of news products and the financial sustenance of the news industry itself.

First and foremost, newspapers deliver news—a task that requires the work of reporters, editors and photographers. Newspapers also require production operations that print and distribute a physical product to consumers, which involves the efforts of layout artists, printers and personnel to handle distribution, transportation and logistics tasks. Since U.S. newspapers are primarily advertising supported, their survival largely depends on the talent and skills of advertising and marketing personnel. While technological advances have transformed all of these areas of operations, each of these three divisions of labor and their interdependent relationship remain just as important even as different forms of newspapers began to emerge.

Throughout newspapers' 160-year reign, three primary types of news delivery formats led the industry. First, the commercial press emerged, which mostly reported on trade and business dealings and received financial support from the

4.3

While technology may have altered the way printed news is produced and delivered, how has it also changed the relationship between editorial, production and marketing?

Andrey_Popov/Shutterstock.com

promotion of products and the sale of advertisements. The second type, the partisan press, served as the media voice of American political parties and other groups with political or ideological agendas—for example, the pre-Civil War abolitionist and anti-abolitionist movements. Its financial support came from political contributions, which turned the partisan press into the promotional arm of the day's dominant political party.

One early American journalist, Samuel Harrison Smith (1772–1845), acknowledged the press as a crucial vehicle for maintaining American democracy, a function first assumed by the Founding Fathers. Smith was a strong advocate of the free press and the citizenry—that is, the Fourth Estate, a term credited to Scottish essayist and Smith's contemporary, Thomas Carlyle (1795–1881). The Fourth Estate was responsible for checking the balance of power of the other three estates: the executive, legislative and judicial branches of government. Smith strongly believed that "Inasmuch as governments may err, every citizen has a right to expose an error in HIS OPINION committed [sic] by them."[4]

The third form of newspaper publishing was the penny press, so named because each paper cost just one penny. Penny papers catered to a growing literate audience more interested in entertainment and information than politics or ideology. This created a demand for popular advice on diverse topics, including farming and home medical treatments; the penny press also offered humor, serialized fiction and human-interest articles. Unlike the partisan press, the penny press paid for itself through the sale of individual copies, relying on advertising revenues to keep the cost of subscriptions low. The partisan papers relied heavily on subscription revenues alone.[5]

Penny press newspapers were published daily. While the price of paper and ink needed to print newspapers had decreased, making the printing of newspapers cost less, and new steam-powered presses had lowered production costs even further, penny press newspapers still did not earn enough revenue from subscriptions to cover the cost of producing a daily newspaper, let alone making the endeavor profitable. The "mainstream" partisan newspapers of the day sold a good deal of advertising to increase their revenue. Penny press papers followed suit, but were not at all particular about the advertisements they accepted and offered ad rates that were much cheaper. Their ads also reached a wider audience.

New York publisher Benjamin H. Day (1810–1889) published the first penny press newspaper in America. *The Sun*, in New York City on September 3, 1833. Like all penny press newspapers, *The Sun* was a tabloid-style (sensationalist) publication that sold for 1 cent at a time when the usual newspaper subscription cost 6 cents. It catered to working-class audiences and combined sensational reporting on crimes and political scandals, gossip about public figures and short fiction stories. Other publishers, among them Horace Greeley and Francis Story, quickly followed Day's lead. Over time, the penny press grew into a publishing phenomenon, first in the big East Coast cities and then across the country.

The Industrial Revolution Alters the Newspaper Business

The Industrial Revolution (between the 18th and 19th centuries) brought with it advancements in agriculture, manufacturing, mining and transportation that began first in Europe, then eventually North America and the rest of the world. In the United States, it represented a period of increased immigration and urbanization. Members of this new immigrant, urban population were eager to learn the language of their new homeland in order to succeed, leading to increased literacy levels. As the social, political and economic environments changed, American newspapers recognized that they, too, had to "revolutionize" to embrace this potentially lucrative new readership.

Whereas American papers previously concentrated solely on the interests of the economic and social elite, in the 19th century they became increasingly focused on the working and middle classes of urban centers. Customers tended to flock to the penny papers not just because they were affordable, but because the quality of the content had a striking local flavor—stories came from the immediate geographic area within which the new readership lived.

Penny press publishers were able to meet the increasing demand for their papers thanks to the heightened manufacturing capabilities of their new steam-powered presses, which made mass production and

4.4

Street-corner newsboys helped to increase the circulation and sales of the penny press.

Hine, Lewis Wickes, photographer. Group of Newsboys on Frankfort Street near World Building. Witness, Fred McMurry. Location: New York, New York State/Photo by Lewis W. Hine. Courtesy of Library of Congress

circulation of these papers possible. Circulation also widened with sales of the penny press by street-corner newsboys (instead of via subscription and delivery by U.S. mail). Collectively, these efforts boosted the interest in and the business of the penny press, which ultimately changed the means by which the overall newspaper industry was financed. As readership grew, so did advertising support, marking the transition from the industry's subscription-based business model to an advertising-based business model. This change in business model, of course, influenced the content and style of the papers.

Newspapers Become an Advertising-Based Business

Prior to the advent of the penny press, newspaper publishers featured advertisements that focused primarily on products or services provided by the publisher or its financiers (especially political parties that had a stake in the publication). As the penny press increased in popularity, however, papers no longer necessarily linked themselves to the publisher's advertisers. Publishers placed few restrictions on the types of products that newspapers could advertise. Anything and everything could be advertised, and publishers absolved themselves of the responsibility of monitoring advertising content. Why? Since the penny press owed its financial success in large part to advertising, the publishers' main concern was to expand readership and increase advertising revenues.

Scandal, exaggeration of news events and fabricated stories presented as real news attracted mass audiences to the penny press. As the demand for such stories rose, so did advertising sales, which further encouraged more sensational news reporting. This trend, which became known as *yellow journalism*, would be the reporting style that would help to build the Joseph Pulitzer and William Randolph Hearst publishing empires (see Chapters 2 and 9). One of the most scandal-laden, and yet most popular, newspapers of the era was the *New York Herald*, founded by the Scottish-born editor and publisher James Gordon Bennett Sr. (1795–1872). Bennett had little respect for the rights and privacy of individuals and organizations alike and was willing to capitalize on any piece of bawdy news, regardless of the ethical implications. He enjoyed shocking his readers and understood that the more scandalous the story, the more papers he could sell and the higher the advertising fees he could charge.

From the murder of prostitutes to the gambling and sexual escapades of elected officials, Bennett knew how to tantalize his readers. Records suggest that Bennett was so hated by his competitors—whom he often maliciously attacked in his editorials—that one of them, James Watson Webb, who owned the *Courier and Enquirer*, once attempted to violently attack Bennett in the middle of Wall Street. Despite Bennett's questionable journalism ethics, he became one of the most well-known innovators of his industry:

- Bennett and his reporters conducted some of the first newspaper interviews.
- Bennett was one of the first to experiment with illustrations, using images produced by woodcut printing.

- He established a cash-in-advance advertising model that was eventually adopted by a majority of newspaper and magazine publishers.
- He was one of the earliest newspaper editors to be granted an exclusive interview with a U.S. president (President Martin Van Buren in 1839).

Although the public criticized the *Herald* for its subject matter and Bennett for his antics, the newspaper's readership continued to grow. By 1866, the *New York Herald* was the most widely circulated newspaper in America.

By end of the 19th century, however, publishers began shifting away from yellow journalism. Capitalizing on their popularity and growing circulations, some newspaper publishers began to venture aggressively back into partisan politics by forming alliances with political parties, social movements and labor groups in an effort to once again influence the course of political change in America. *The New York Times* and the *Chicago Tribune* are just two examples of major mid-19th-century newspapers that became strongly aligned with national political parties.[6]

Early Communication Technologies Further Change the Industry

Samuel Morse's (1791–1872) telegraph helped to advance the newspaper publishing industry in the second half of the 19th century. Two significant changes resulted from Morse's invention.

First, the industry became stratified by wealth. Although the telegraph was a wonderful invention, it was not cheap. Telegraph operators charged by the word. Some newspapers could not afford to send and receive continuous correspondence throughout the country, which was now linked by telegraph. This inability proved a disadvantage for an industry reliant upon timeliness and relevance. In fact, other print industries claimed a definite market advantage over newspapers simply because they *were* able to afford telegraph communications.

Second, the telegraph influenced the length of newspaper stories. Given that telegraph messages were paid for by the word, reporters were forced to keep their stories as short as possible, often omitting interesting details to avoid unnecessary telegraph fees. History seems to indicate that this practice occasionally led to some essential facts being cut out as well, which forced editors to "fill in the blanks," even if that meant they had to invent details to keep the stories interesting for their readers. The shortening of information to accommodate the telegraph format led toward briefer print version and essentially introduced the more succinct news bulletin format, which avoided the longer, narrative style of traditional articles. During the Civil War, the telegraph network showed increasing signs of unreliability, making chronological reporting less effective. Since time and relevancy were of utmost importance to the industry, reporters began to use an inverted pyramid reporting structure, wherein the most important facts are presented in the lead sentences, followed by the more elaborate details that support those facts. This new style would serve as the foundation of today's 24/7 newswriting.

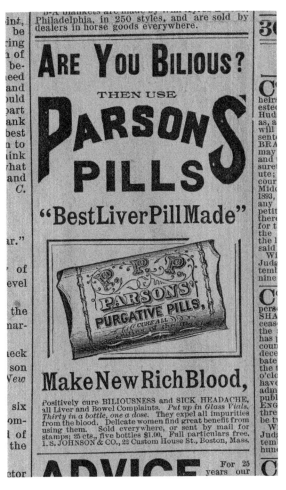

4.5

The penny press financially thrived on ads such as this one, despite the questionable content. Is regulation of advertising content a violation of free expression, or the social responsibility of a free press?

Old Paper Studios/Alamy Stock Photo

Given that telegraph messages were paid for by the word, reporters were forced to keep their stories as short as possible, often omitting interesting details to avoid unnecessary telegraph fees.

4.6

Telegraph communications not only expanded the reach of news, but its expense also limited the length of news stories to news bulletins and introduced the inverted pyramid style of reporting.

Buyenlarge/Contributor

The Establishment of News Syndicates

News syndicates, or services, are cooperatives that allow member news organizations to share stories and resources, thereby greatly increasing the capabilities of newspapers and other news reporting media. Made possible by the development of teletype technologies, telegraphic machines that printed messages typed on the transmitter's keyboard, we still find numerous news syndicates and news services operating today, the oldest and best known being the Associated Press (AP) and the United Press International (UPI). This history of news syndicates may be traced back to two groups of editors in New York: the Associated Press of the State of New York and the Associated Press of New York City. These editorial groups began cooperating to share the expense of newsgathering sometime around 1846—an early example of the consolidation and sharing of news reporting resources among affiliated newspaper and television news outlets. Nearly 50 years later, in 1897, these two groups merged to become the Associated Press we know today.[7]

All of this business and technological networking made information and news stories more available to larger segments of the United States—from the urban East to the developing central regions and even the rural Western territories. As we learned earlier, this expanded accessibility (along with other Industrial Revolution developments) contributed to record increases in literacy rates.

These rapidly growing literacy rates and the nation's ferocious appetite for reading spurred improvements in transportation, printing and the development of new kinds of print media, both as sources of information and as sources of entertainment. As a result of this steadily rising demand for information and entertainment, the newspaper industry in the 19th century helped to give birth to its sister industry—magazine publishing.[8] The evolution of both newspaper and magazine publishing was inextricably linked to the evolution of the printing press and printing technologies, as we learn from the following video segment, which presents a visual mosaic of the stages in the evolution of the printing press. ▶

THE RISE OF MAGAZINE PUBLISHING

Magazine publishing in 18th-century Europe and in America developed as an outgrowth of newspaper and pamphlet publishing. However, even then, the concept was not new. English author and journalist Daniel Defoe (1659–1731), the author of *Robinson Crusoe*, had published the first magazine, *The Review*, in 1704 as part of his political pamphleteering. Almost 40 years later, Andrew Bradford (1686–1742) published the first magazine in the colonies, *American Magazine* (1741). Bradford's publication beat Benjamin Franklin's *General Magazine, and Historical Chronicle, for all the British Plantations in North America* to the market by only three days. Although the *American Magazine* was short-lived—surviving only three months—it marked a great leap forward in American publishing.[9]

Having no children of his own to inherit his fledgling publishing dynasty, Bradford took his nephew, William Bradford III, under his wing, and mentored him in the printing business. The young William Bradford III had a strong independent streak and soon started his own publication, *The Pennsylvania Journal and Weekly Advertiser*, in December 1742. Although the younger Bradford would suffer tremendous financial losses over the course of the American Revolution due in large part to his publication of patriotic American content, his own

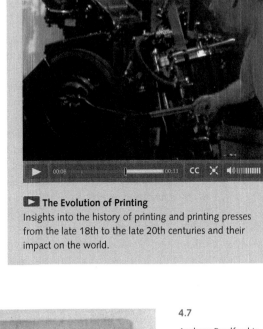

▶ **The Evolution of Printing**
Insights into the history of printing and printing presses from the late 18th to the late 20th centuries and their impact on the world.

4.7

Andrew Bradford is credited for publishing the first American colonial magazine, *American Magazine*, in 1741 and for establishing one of the nation's earliest newspaper and magazine publishing dynasties.

The American magazine, and monthly chronicle for the British colonies Praevalebit aequior. Courtesy of Library of Congress

son Thomas would resurrect the family business and turn the *Journal* into a daily paper that continued publishing until 1814.[10]

Early Business Challenges

These early attempts to build magazine publishing businesses out of newspaper publishing businesses faced a number of challenges, including issues related to distribution, publishing costs and public perception. Newspapers at the time were circulated mostly via the postal services, but the postal service found it difficult and costly to cart the heavier magazines around. The postal service, in the years before and after the American Revolutionary War, gave postmasters the authority to outright refuse to ship magazines. This changed, however, with the Postal Act of 1792. Yet, even with this act, newspapers reaped the benefits over magazines. In the early 19th century, delivery costs for a magazine amounted to between 20 percent and 40 percent of the yearly subscription—and that was not the only economic challenge facing magazine publishers.

The next problem for magazines related to their publishing costs, which were generally much higher than the publishing costs of newspapers. Only a small portion of the costs of magazine publishing could be covered by advertising, which was also in the early stages of development and which favored newspapers. Therefore, the greatest portion of magazine publishing costs had to be passed along to subscribers. Only the wealthy could afford a year's magazine subscription, as it would cost the average laborer a week's pay. Not surprisingly, this factor created a public perception that magazines were intended for the elite.

This resistance to and perception of magazines began to change around 1790 with the rise of general-interest magazines such as *New York Magazine or Literary Repository*. These new magazines were priced so that all but the poorest could afford them. Supported by an increase in audience demand and gradually decreasing postage rates; nearly 100 new magazines emerged by 1820. While American magazines owed much of their rising popularity to their intriguing content, the economics of the business made an even bigger contribution to their growth.[11]

The Economics of Magazine Publishing

Early American magazines were crudely constructed and typically contained 60 to 70 pages of content. They were printed on paper with ragged edges in small-type size, about the equivalent of that found in today's printed classified advertisements. Pictures—the mainstay of modern magazines—were a rarity. Instead, woodcuts and occasional steel or copper engravings were the most common types of illustrations in these publications. Printing images was extremely labor intensive, with a single image costing almost as much to produce as the entire textual content.

In an effort to keep costs down, early American magazine publishers took large sections of content from books and English magazines and printed them verbatim. This practice made magazines excellent vehicles for serializing books and, in essence, turned them into a running advertisement for the book publisher who produced the magazines. The practice of reprinting excerpts from published books not only greatly outnumbered original works from magazinists (authors who specifically wrote content for magazines), but also built the 18th- and 19th-century magazine publishing industry on the shoulders of copyright piracy (see Chapter 11). In contrast to contemporary attitudes toward authorship and copyright protections, magazine publishers of that era believed that they were actually doing authors and readers a publicity service by offering previously published material.

As magazines grew in popularity, national advertising soon became common and magazines quickly became primary media for promoting a wide range of companies and their products. After Congress enacted legislation that lowered the cost of mailing non-newspaper periodicals, magazine publishing became more economical and allowed a variety of magazines to enter the expanding 19th-century American consumer market. At the same time, a new professional class of writers emerged to provide creative content for scores of new magazines, which catered to a growing middle class and afforded writers new outlets for their work. As such, magazines became a more competitive source for generating income for authors.

Diversification of Magazine Audience, Style and Specialty

Prior to the Civil War, successful magazines such as *Atlantic Monthly*, *Scribner's* and *Harper's Weekly* catered to well-educated, wealthy audiences, offering highbrow literary, travel and cultural content from a conservative perspective. In the years just following the Civil War, general-interest magazines such as *Frank Leslie's Illustrated Weekly* became popular, reaching a broader readership and presenting stories and editorials that emphasized news and illustrations—much like the newspapers of the time. Gradually, the magazine industry experienced a diversification of style and specialty. Styles ranged from monthly editions to literary weeklies to specialty magazines that catered to women, religious groups and regional demographics. Some became very popular and successfully catered to specific readers, attracting many of the leading writers and poets of the time; others just as quickly folded. Among the success stories was *Godey's Lady's Book*, published by Louis A. Godey (1804–1878).

Godey's Lady's Book was one of the first U.S.-founded magazines that catered exclusively to female readers, and it became one of the premier American women's fashion magazines. While originally established to provide upper-class American women with beauty, fashion and etiquette information, as well as popular fiction aimed at female audiences, its appeal moved beyond class divisions and its readership reached more than 150,000, which was astounding for the time. Godey's magazine made a significant contribution to the early women's liberation movement with its mix of short stories, poems, articles and advice on various topics intended to educate and empower women. Some of the most notable authors whose work appeared in *Godey's Lady's Book* were Harriet Beecher Stowe, Ralph Waldo Emerson, Henry Wadsworth Longfellow, Oliver Wendell Holmes, Nathaniel Hawthorne and Edgar Allan Poe.[12]

The magazine publishing industry advanced along with printing and transportation technologies. These advancements, as noted earlier, coincided with an elevation in the nation's overall literacy levels as well as its appetite for reading. Newspapers (especially the penny press) and magazines alone could not fulfill this need. All of these factors combined to expand interest in another form of printed mass media—books.

4.8

Woodcut engravings were used to illustrate magazines and newspapers before the advent of photos. Due to the labor and expense it took to print these engravings, however, they were not a common feature.

Raimondi, Marcantonio, Approximately 1534, Artist, and Albrecht Dürer. [The Visitation]. Courtesy of Library of Congress

4.9

As magazines were able to tailor their content to appeal to a more specific audience, advertisers could better target their ads to reach a precise market of potential buyers.

Advertisements from "Godey's lady's book and magazine" for bicycles, corsets, cigarettes, elastic stockings, and other products

American women were voracious consumers of the written word in the 19th century. Their demand for literature, poetry and information helped drive the development of the book publishing industry.

THE EVOLUTION OF THE BOOK INDUSTRY

The book industry underwent drastic changes during the 1800s. Printers, who were also the publishers during the 18th century, moved away from the master–apprentice system to a wage system and formed guilds and unions to ensure fair wages for their labor. In addition to exerting more influence over pay, unions allowed printers to exercise some control over their working conditions and benefits. Owners and managers of printing press operations also became an integral part of the book production business. Moreover, for the first time, women held jobs at all levels of the process—roles that that had been restricted to men just 50 years earlier due to the arduous physical nature of the printing business. The inventions of stereotyping technology, electrotyping, Fourdrinier and Gilpin's paper-making machines, as well as technologies that sped up the binding process, radically changed the book publishing business. For example, printing technologies allowed publishers to take smaller risks by printing smaller runs (that is, fewer copies); they could then easily reprint books if sales were good.

The Social and Cultural Impact of Books

As the literacy rate rapidly increased in the United States, the social and cultural impact of books became a widely debated topic in the 19th century. While today we commonly accept and even promote the huge benefit to society that comes from books and reading, many Americans in the mid-19th century were skeptical of the benefits of reading and particularly wary of women and minority groups learning to read. Critics of general literacy claimed that the growing availability of novels and other fictional literature in magazines and newspapers contributed to laziness—and feared that women were particularly susceptible to the "dangers" of reading. While any evidence of reading being detrimental to managing a household or productivity as a whole is lacking, it is evident that American women were voracious consumers of the written word in the 19th century. Their demand for literature, poetry and information helped drive the development of the book publishing industry.

The Birth of the Novel

Often distributed serially through newspapers and magazines, the novel was long-form fiction broken down into episodes for publication over several issues, thereby attracting a large and constant readership who waited eagerly to buy the next edition. Novels portrayed stories, characters and themes that resonated with the growing middle class of the Industrial Revolution. They often told stories of class struggle, romance and intrigue, with each chapter ending in suspense. This cliffhanger encouraged readers to purchase the next issue—similar to the way many modern-day television series end their seasons with a dilemma intended to bring the audience back next season.

Improvements in paper production, bookbinding (cloth covers as an alternative to leather) and greater efficiencies in the printing process made novels—many of which sold for a dime (thus the nickname dime novel)—one of the primary forms of entertainment available to the general public starting in the mid-1850s. Dime novels were mass produced to accommodate customers of the rapidly expanding railroad system, which was revolutionizing travel and linking vast areas of the United States. These books were produced in assembly-line fashion, with publishers closely supervising their writers' quality and length, and placing demands on authors to write faster. Publishers dominated the business, with dime novelists often earning a fixed fee per book, or even per page, regardless of the success of their stories.

Dime novels appealed primarily to the working classes. While religion was no longer the centerpiece of these fictional stories, morality still had a prominent place in them. Outlaws, detectives, factory workers and prostitutes were among the many popular characters whose stories intrigued readers. Dime novels featuring adventurous traders, cavalry officers, rugged cowboys and compelling heroines can even be credited for helping inspire the great migration to the American West.

4.10

Literacy critics of the 19th century were wary of the rising number of women and minorities devouring and comprehending the written word. How would increased reading among these groups affect society and culture?

Buyenlarge/Contributor

TECHNOLOGIES EXTEND THE PRINT MEDIA

The growth of print media is closely tied to the evolution of transportation and print technologies and infrastructure. The costs of transportation and distribution represented a significant portion of the economics of publishing in the 18th and 19th centuries, and this relationship persists today. To be successful, newspapers, magazines and books needed to be affordably, reliably and effectively distributed to geographically dispersed audiences. As discussed previously, one of the major issues facing early magazine and book distributors was the postal service's refusal to ship packages weighing more than three pounds, which made it almost impossible to ship publications (other than newspapers) through national channels. Book distributors had to improvise so that publishers could get their products to distant markets, at times relying on spaces in train cargoes or even hiring passengers to carry and hand-deliver books to customers. In 1851, Congress finally permitted the postal service to accept packages that weighed more than three pounds, a move that increased the competition between books and magazines, in particular.

Further extending the reach of print media were advances in printing and bookbinding technologies. The Industrial Revolution heralded the invention of numerous machines that set in motion innovations in the production of printed mass media. For example, the Fourdrinier machine made paper from raw materials much more quickly than previous machines had done, thereby increasing paper's availability and making it less expensive to printers and publishers. More reliable and precise iron-cylinder printing presses replaced the wooden rotary-screw printing presses, which allowed the Fourdrinier to produce as many as 7,000 sheets of printed material per hour—an unthinkable volume prior to the Industrial Revolution. The spread of compulsory education in the 19th century in both Europe and the United States also meant that new generations were reading the massive amounts of text that was being manufactured.[13]

4.11

Railway postal clerks played an integral role in the distribution and dissemination of printed media across vast regions of the United States.

Hine, Lewis Wickes, photographer. Postal clerk. Location: Springfield, Missouri/Lewis W. Hine. Courtesy of Library of Congress

4.12

Sholes & Glidden Type Writer, 1874.

Everett Collection/ Newscom

Another technological leap forward for newspaper and magazine publishing was the introduction of the stereotype system. Invented by Firmin Didot (1764–1836), a French printer and engineer, the stereotype system used a soft metal printing plate, with each plate representing an entire page of a publication, including all text and graphics. This was a much more efficient method than printing directly from movable type, which had to be set by hand, letter by letter. Each plate could be used to print a full page as many times as needed and then simply melted back down to be used again.

The invention of the typewriter with the standard QWERTY keyboard developed by C. S. Sholes in the 1870s also added to the efficiency of the publishing process. After the editorial process, in which draft stories are read and corrected by editors, the typewritten stories would then be transcribed onto stereotype plates for printing. Before the invention of the typewriter, all the work done by writers and editors was handwritten. Now writers were able to use the letter keyboard to punch in words at greater speed than writing by hand.

By 1897, it was possible to print half-tone photographs on a standard newspaper printing press. This innovation ushered in the era of including black and white photos in magazines and newspapers to enhance the textual narratives of their stories. But the use of photographs to support news stories developed slowly; photos were not commonly found in newspapers until early in the 1920s. (See a further discussion of the history of photographs and news reporting in Chapter 12.)

Each of the technological innovations described here enabled the publishing industry to build new business models based on increasing publication sizes, a wider range of content and greater efficiency. The vast revenues generated by the publishing of newspapers, magazines and books, coupled with the healthy revenues generated by the growing advertising industry that subsidized newspapers and some magazines, ushered in a golden age of publishing that spanned the late 19th and the early 20th centuries. The growth of the publishing industry and early attempts at *vertical integration* (management of a chain of businesses through a single owner) created unprecedented wealth and helped solidify the prominent status of a number of U.S. publishing dynasties.

THE BIRTH OF PUBLISHING DYNASTIES

In the early 1870s, 574 newspapers were regularly published in the United States. By 1890, just 20 years later, that number had grown to more than 1,536. Newspapers in the early 20th century varied greatly in their approach to journalism, ranging from the sensationalist yellow journalism of William Randolph Hearst-owned papers to the sober-minded approach advocated by William Allen White (1868–1944), the Kansas-based "progressive" Republican newspaper editor who became an iconic voice for Middle America. At the dawning of the 20th century, newspapers had become an integral part of both the business and political communities. Even if a paper was not clearly biased in one political direction or the other, newspapers and their publishers had become the "voice of the people" and were often key players in the evolution of American democracy.[14]

The term "American publishing dynasty" usually describes the empires built by historical publishing figures such as William Randolph Hearst and Joseph Pulitzer, or 20th-century publishing and media moguls such as Rupert Murdoch and Ted Turner. While most of the major newspaper, magazine and book publishing companies today are owned by large media conglomerates, this has not always been the case (see Chapter 9). For much of the 19th and 20th centuries, powerful families controlled many of the leading publishers in the United States, especially in newspapers. The Chandler family (*Los Angeles Times*), the Ochs-Sulzberger family (*The New York Times*), the Meyer-Graham family (*The Washington Post*) and the Bingham family (*The Courier-Journal* and *The Louisville Times*) are a few prominent examples.

Such publishing dynasties often turned their substantial financial and media resources toward influencing national politics, from the election of presidents to the conduct of wars. Consider these classic examples:

- William Randolph Hearst used his yellow journalism-based empire to push the U.S. Congress and the administration of President William McKinley to promote American expansionism and to escalate conflicts between the United States and Spain into what became the Spanish-American War (1898).
- The Chandler family funded and promoted the presidential campaigns of both Richard Nixon (1969) and Ronald Reagan (1981). For an in-depth analysis of how the *Los Angeles Times* helped to influence and shape U.S. culture and politics, view the video titled "Otis Chandler, *L.A. Times*." ▶
- The Ochs-Sulzberger and Meyer-Graham families collaborated in their anti-Vietnam War reporting and editorials, first against President Lyndon Johnson (1963–1969) and then against President Richard Nixon (1969–1974).

▶ **Otis Chandler, *L.A. Times***
The late Otis Chandler, former publisher of the *L.A. Times*, discusses the influence of newspapers and publishing dynasties on American culture and politics.

Joseph Pulitzer (1847–1911) made his fortune and built his publishing empire while competing with William Randolph Hearst. Both men used yellow journalism to accomplish their empire-building visions and to push their political agendas for America. Unlike Hearst, Pulitzer went from being one of the scions of yellow journalism to being one of the models of best journalistic practices and ethics. Today, he is best known for the prize that bears his name—the Pulitzer Prize, an award given to the most highly recognized professionals in journalism and letters, drama and music.

> Unlike Hearst, Pulitzer went from being one of the scions of yellow journalism to being one of the models of best journalistic practices and ethics.

The story of the Bingham family, who maintain a newspaper publishing dynasty in Kentucky, offers an interesting 20th-century example of how a single publishing family can wield both positive and negative influences on American society and national politics. This family influenced—if not outright controlled—the

4.13

Despite the climate of southern politics during the late 1960s and early 1970s, Barry Bingham Jr. used his family's newspapers to openly support anti-segregation laws and to promote charitable programs that would aid the state's poor—whether black or white.

Bettmann/Contributor

political life of the state of Kentucky for most of the 1900s through ownership of the two major newspapers in the state (*The Courier-Journal* and *The Louisville Times*) as well as the largest radio and television stations (WHAS-Radio and WHAS-TV). Control of the business passed to current Bingham Jr. in 1971. During his years at the helm of the family's media empire, he pushed society and politics in Kentucky in liberal directions unprecedented for a southern state. His efforts included strong anti-segregation policies that opened up schools and created charitable programs for poor whites and blacks alike—earning him six Pulitzer Prizes in the process. Bingham used factual injustices and corruption to change public attitudes.

But powerful family dynasties can have their negative sides.[15] Before the death of Barry Bingham Sr. in 1988, his children fought over the spoils of the empire. Weary of family infighting, they ultimately sold the newspapers to the Gannett Corporation and the broadcasting holdings to Clear Channel Communications (1984). Their exit from the field helped to usher in a movement that saw most publishing dynasties become publicly traded corporations, merge with other media conglomerates or be broken up and entirely divested. Bingham Sr.'s daughter Sallie later wrote a tell-all book about the family's rise to power, its impact on southern politics and culture, and its eventual disintegration.[16]

The Newspaper Industry in the 20th Century

Throughout the 20th century, the publishing industry confronted a long series of technological and market challenges. In the early years of the 1900s, the press had served as a conscientious voice commenting on the effects of industrialization. Newspapers and magazines had also become a vital mass media organ of modern American business, with a strong stake in the success of the publishing industry. At the same time, publishers and editors still felt compelled to focus public attention on the woes of society and the abuses of government and big corporations, while championing the First Amendment, private ownership rights and freedom of the press.

As described earlier in this chapter, the technological innovations of the 19th century made significant contributions to the rise of newspapers, but the lack of progress in transportation and print technology led to an overall increase in costs for the industry. A revenue shift occurred, as newspapers started making more money from advertising than from sales of the papers to readers. In 1879, the estimated revenue of the newspaper industry totaled approximately $89 million, with 56 percent coming from newsstand sales and subscriptions and 44 percent from advertising. This growth continued into the new century: By 1914, the industry's revenues approached $419 million.

While the economics of multiple newspaper ownership was sound, the public grew suspicious that these major newspaper publishing companies too often promoted the interests and political agendas of their owners—that is, wealthy, politically active individuals and family dynasties. When Congress enacted the Newspaper Publicity Act of 1912, it became mandatory for newspaper companies to disclose who owned the publication and to label clearly advertisements that might be confused with news or editorial content. (See Chapter 9.)[17]

As the United States was drawn into World War I, fears grew that a free and uncensored press posed a national security risk that could weaken public support for the war effort. In 1917, President Woodrow Wilson appointed Kansas City journalist and newspaper publisher George Creel (1876–1953) to head the Committee on Public Information. This committee was empowered to exercise a significant amount of control over American's perception of World War I and standardized war coverage across the vast array of U.S. publications, both newspapers and magazines. Creel's mandate included a combination of voluntary and forced censorship and outright propaganda. He recruited more than 75,000 public speakers to deliver speeches and editorials promoting the war effort. He also commissioned artists and cartoonists to create thousands of works that the Committee on Public Information used to build public confidence in the eventual outcome of the war and to help maintain public morale.

Creel's efforts were highly successful, but his belief that such combined propaganda and censorship efforts were "expression, not repression" proved erroneous. In fact, the actions of the Committee on Public Information had a chilling effect on the freedom of the press during the war years. During his time as head of the Committee, Creel organized the news into three categories: dangerous, questionable and routine. Dangerous news might contain information about military movements or possible threats against the president and *would not be printed*. Questionable news included rumors of U.S. activity at home or abroad and reports of technological advancements that could be appropriated by America's enemies, such as the annual output of U.S. steel mills or levels of commercial shipping. Routine news encompassed everything else and *could be printed* without authorization.

During the 1920s, the newspaper industry continued to consolidate, placing the control of news reporting in the hands of a small but powerful group of publishers. By 1933, the six largest newspaper chains in the United States were the Hearst, Patterson-McCormick, Scripps-Howard, Paul Block, Ridder and Gannett companies. These six organizations controlled approximately 70 percent of the nation's daily chain circulation and 26 percent of the total circulation. One of the growing concerns about the newspaper industry in the 1920s and 1930s was that the owners were forming monopolies that not only jeopardized the function of newspapers as the Fourth Estate, but also furthered the rise of conglomerates that had a larger effect on related publishing and mass media industries. These giant publishing conglomerates also owned magazines, movie studios, radio stations and book publishing operations. Moreover, these few companies were on the path to controlling which products and services were marketed successfully to consumers and which were virtually locked out of the national marketplace.

Between the 1920s and 1930s, tabloid publications continued to grow in readership and popularity, building audiences through new applications of their old methods of sensationalism. Critics argued that the tabloids were the result of declining social morals during the era, especially during the Roaring '20s. While it is true that the tabloids attracted readership with stories about bawdy relationships, horrific murders and other bizarre happenings, they were often no worse than their mainstream newspaper counterparts of the time, which featured similar stories in an effort to attract readers and sell advertising. The advent of streetcars across the nation as a popular means of public transportation and the growing market for news that kept the interest of the common person also contributed to rise of the tabloids: with their racy headlines, multiple graphics, small size and large print, they were easy to read with one hand on the straphanger of a trolley. Meanwhile, the 1930s brought about the now common practice of including reporters' bylines, especially during the

4.14

Newspaper publisher George Creel was appointed by President Woodrow Wilson to control the public's perception of U.S. involvement in WWI through regulation of the uncensored press.

Uphold our honor—Fight for us Join Army-Navy-Marines

4.15

Walter Winchell invented the gossip column and earned national attention for his coverage of the Lindbergh baby kidnapping.

Ray Fisher/Contributor

Great Depression, as a way to mix factual reporting with commentary and analysis. Bylines helped readers to better understand the writers' increasingly complex work, in an environment where national and world politics and economics affected everyone. Journalists and editors, in turn, were learning that they needed to demonstrate that their reporting was accurate and objective.

The popularity of tabloid journalism and the rise of the gossip column in the 1920s and 1930s had a positive cultural aspect that is often overlooked today, but is well illustrated by one of the most famous gossip columnists of the period, Walter Winchell (1897–1972). Winchell's coverage of the kidnapping of famed aviator Charles Lindbergh's son and of other celebrities, from politicians to business moguls, gangsters to movie stars, brought him national notoriety not previously granted a newspaper reporter. At the height of his success in the 1920s and 1930s, Winchell's gossip column was syndicated in more than 2,000 newspapers and attracted a daily readership of more than 50 million. Winchell leveraged his newspaper audience into a weekly radio broadcast that attracted an additional 20 million listeners and continued until the late 1950s.

> Winchell's sensationalist tabloid reports on the transgressions—both factual and exaggerated—of the rich and famous, especially during the Depression years, served as a kind of social therapy for the tens of millions of Americans who were struggling mightily with daily life.

Winchell's sensationalist tabloid reports on the transgressions—both factual and exaggerated—of the rich and famous, especially during the Depression years, served as a kind of social therapy for the tens of millions of Americans who were struggling mightily with daily life. His reports were so entertaining that they helped readers to move beyond their own struggles and join in a national gossip circle. Reflecting on today's phenomenal public interest in and media saturation of celebrities such as Justin Bieber, Angelina Jolie and Jay-Z, we can easily understand the popularity of Walter Winchell's tabloid reports in a nation suffering the pains of the Great Depression and the fears of economic, social and political collapse that marked the years leading up to World War II.[18]

The 1930s also saw the U.S. government exert increased control over the media through regulation, accompanied by more deliberate efforts to influence the content of stories about government actions and policies. Today we have come to know this process as news spin. The struggle between government officials and the news media to package and control news stories, in an effort to influence reporters, editors and ultimately the American public, continued its steady evolution through the 1930s and 1940s, with a short-lived truce being declared during World War II. During that war, the vast majority of reporters and publishers saw it as their patriotic duty to fully cooperate with U.S. government censors and propaganda efforts to avoid giving "aid and comfort" to the enemy. This cooperation often meant not reporting on stories or delaying reports at the request of the War Department. This mostly voluntary cooperation was extended through the Korean War, but broke down by 1954 with the appearance of an outspoken U.S. Senator from Wisconsin named Joseph McCarthy.

In the early 1950s, Walter Winchell's support for the Red Scare fear tactics of Senator Joseph McCarthy contributed to Winchell's fall from national popularity. McCarthy used his position as the chair of a powerful Senate committee to ferret out communists and communist sympathizers that he believed had infiltrated many government agencies, especially the American media industry, from newspapers and magazines to movie studios. McCarthy was a master at manipulating the news media that covered the hearings; as a result, he initially enjoyed strong positive public opinion. The senator was an expert at forcing his way into the media, often releasing sensational charges against supposed communist sympathizers right at deadline, so that journalists were forced to decide between checking his claims, which meant missing out on breaking news, or printing his releases unvetted. Nevertheless, some newspapers, such as the *Christian Science Monitor*, *The Washington Post* and *Milwaukee Journal*, and magazines, such as *Time*, challenged McCarthy from the very start. Fortunately for the country, McCarthy's public support quickly turned negative as the news media—most prominently the television and radio reports and commentaries by Edward R. Murrow of CBS—exposed the senator's campaign to intimidate and ultimately destroy the careers of many innocent people.

During the 1960s, the United States underwent huge cultural, social and political changes. The civil rights movement, the assassination of President John F. Kennedy, and the Vietnam War were all challenges that the publishing industry encountered during that decade of change.

In fact, the late 1960s and early 1970s saw the dawning of the Digital Age in which, as Marshall McLuhan and others predicted in the 1950s, advancements in communication and mass media technologies would come to significantly define our very sense of what "the news" is and more than ever before set the public and government agendas.

One of the problems facing even the newspapers that were interested in covering the civil rights movement was the issue of differentiation. The print media could not illustrate as clearly as television or even radio the violence done to protesters. As journalists Robert Donovan and Ray Scherer note in their book *Unsilent Revolution: Television News and American Public Life*, "Police dogs looked like police dogs in newspaper and magazine photos, but on television the dogs snarled."[19]

In 1967, President Lyndon Johnson set up the Kerner Commission to try to find out why American cities were experiencing so many violent race riots. After seven months of hearings and staff investigation, the Kerner Commission released its report, the *Report of the National Advisory Commission on Civil Disorders*, in February 1968. The report became an instant best seller, and over 2 million Americans bought copies. The report's findings criticized both federal and state governments for their failed housing, education and social-service policies aimed particularly at inner-city minorities, the majority of whom at that time were poor blacks. The Kerner Commission report aimed its sharpest criticism at the mainstream media. "The press has too long basked in a white world looking out of it, if at all, with white men's eyes and white perspective that the riots resulted from black frustration at lack of economic opportunity." Rev. Martin Luther King Jr. called the report a "physician's warning of approaching death, with a prescription for life," and the report's most famous statement warned, "Our nation is moving toward two societies, one black, one white—separate and unequal."[20]

In the early 1960s, there were virtually no African-American reporters or editors working at major American newspapers—with a very few notable exceptions, such as Carl Rowan.

The cultural, economic, and political winds of change that occurred in the 1960s and 1970s played out in the mass media, with television challenging newspapers and magazines for the position of dominant media in America. These years also saw other significant changes in the newspaper industry. First, afternoon newspapers all but died out. Such papers were originally common in many moderate-size to large cities where newspapers printed two editions per day: an early edition that came out in the early mornings and a late afternoon edition. Advertisers were not interested in paying for duplicated exposure, so the afternoon paper lost profitability. Second, although newspapers increased their advertising revenues to more than $5.2 billion in 1968 and continued to beat

> The cultural, economic, and political winds of change that occurred in the 1960s and 1970s played out in the mass media.

television, whose advertising pulled in only $3.1 billion in the same year, their publishing costs rose. A number of labor strikes due to fears that technology was swallowing up traditional publishing jobs exacerbated the rise in publishing costs. Due to all these factors, overall profits were down in the newspaper industry.

The trend toward newspaper ownership consolidation continued during the 1970s, with the majority of publishing business owners and investors believing that only the largest cities could support one major newspaper from an economic standpoint. Newspaper publishers tried to find new ways to increase profitability, eventually skirting antitrust laws that prevented newspaper companies from combining their assets. In 1968, a group of publishers successfully lobbied Congress to legalize exceptions to federal antitrust laws, which allowed the formation of newspaper joint-operating agreements (JOAs) between locally competing newspaper publishers. The Supreme Court quickly ruled that JOAs were illegal. In response, Congress passed, and President Richard Nixon signed, a law that sidestepped the Court's ruling. The one overwhelming limitation of the Newspaper Preservation Act was that one of the two newspapers that were part of any JOA had to be in trouble financially—an easy legal test to overcome.

The civil rights movement and the Vietnam War had a positive impact on the professionalism of journalists and editors. Reporters, and the newspapers they worked for, once again took pride in their role as proponents of the Fourth Estate and willingly shouldered their responsibility to monitor and report on the activities of the government. That stance marked a departure from the cooperative relationship between the press and government that had characterized the previous five decades. A growing loyalty to the factual reporting of the news and to the news audience replaced journalists' loyalty to the newspaper or magazine that employed them. The new emphasis on investigative reporting and muckraking (exposing) feature articles and editorials exemplified this trend.

> A growing loyalty to the factual reporting of the news and to the news audience replaced journalists' loyalty to the newspaper or magazine that employed them.

The Newspaper Industry in the Digital Age

The Digital Age has brought with it a number of significant, if not dire, challenges to print media. The growth and proliferation of the Internet have hastened the decline of newspapers, which began with the popularization of radio and television. Through the later decades of the 20th century, while radio and television successfully won large portions of the financial base that the newspaper industry had cultivated through advertising sales, newspapers continued to provide consumers with a unique and critical perspective on the world that was not being widely duplicated by the other media. As a news content delivery device, the newspaper was still an attractive format that readers could transport with relative ease and consume on the go.

The highly successful precursor for newspapers adapting to the Digital Age actually began around the same time as the early stages of the Internet. As discussed at the start of this chapter, in 1982, Allen H. Neuharth and his team of innovative newspaper editors, technicians and marketing experts at the Gannett Company launched *USA Today*. This specially designed nationally distributed daily newspaper eventually became the largest circulated paper in publishing history, with a daily distribution of 1.9 million copies by 2009.[21] *USA Today* was able to attract this huge readership, and the attendant advertising revenues, in part by creating a national and international network of printing and distribution operations, instead of relying on highly centralized printing and distribution operations used by traditional newspapers.

To better understand the success and popularity of the paper, view the video segment titled "Al Neuharth, *USA Today*." ▶

Allen H. Neuharth
Founder/Publisher - USA Today (1982-1989)

▶ **Al Neuharth, *USA Today***

Al Neuharth, founder of *USA Today*, offers an in-depth analysis of the success and popularity of his paper.

In June 2012, Howard Kurtz, former *Washington Post* journalist, former host of CNN's *Reliable Sources* program and since 2010 the Washington bureau chief of the popular Internet news site *The Daily Beast*, was named the new head of *USA Today*. The selection of Kurtz to head up Gannett's flagship newspaper—which, although having lost many readers of its print edition, still has the largest circulation of any newspaper in America—is a clear sign of the company's commitment to position *USA Today* as a leader in the migration of news publishing into ever-new media technologies. As you can see in this video segment, this is a commitment that began with Al Neuharth and continues today with Howard Kurtz.

The advent and rapid growth of the Internet opened the floodgates of digital content and enabled the inexpensive and continuous global mass distribution of news, for the most part, without cost to the consumer. By the 1990s, the newspaper industry had been consolidating for nearly a century in its effort to adapt to the challenges of a changing marketplace. Even though a handful of large companies owned and operated the majority of American newspapers, overall the industry had not undertaken any serious innovation for decades. In addition to the lack of innovation, newspapers were unable to find ways to bolster their struggling finances. The glut of free news content on the Internet made the newspaper merely one of countless sources that consumers could turn to for their news.

In just a short time, the astounding growth and popularity of auction and classified Websites such as eBay and Craigslist effectively ripped away the substantial revenue that newspaper classifieds had been generating. Commercial advertisers also began flocking to the Internet to capitalize on the cheaper rates and wider exposure compared to what newspapers could offer. Although many newspapers slowly began to establish companion Websites, thereby enabling them to offer advertisers cross-platform options, they did so without an effective business model for translating their Internet content into advertising revenues. Unable to figure out a way to sustain the massive legacy operations that had been the foundation of the American media, many newspapers began to close their doors through the first decade of the 21st century.

In 2009, the international accounting and business consulting firm PricewaterhouseCoopers published the results of its extensive study into the future of the newspaper industry, titled *Moving into Multiple Business Models: Outlook for Newspaper Publishing in the Digital Age*. The study focused on the two key challenges facing newspaper publishers in the Digital Age: changing behavior in terms of how people access and consume news content, and the impact on and challenges for newspaper publishers, advertisers and advertising agencies and media buyers as news consumption continues to migrate away from print and onto the Internet.[22]

Also in 2009, the *Columbia Journalism Review* published a report, created by *The Washington Post* Vice President Large Leonard Downie Jr. and Columbia University's Graduate School of Journalism Professor Michael Schudson, called "The Reconstruction of American Journalism." Downie and Schudson caution against blindly making or accepting claims that newspapers are facing extinction. At the same time, they note that the real tragedy in the decline of the newspaper industry is the concomitant decrease in solid journalism—particularly local journalism—and its effect on American democracy. In addition to pointing out the impact that the Internet has had on the near monopoly once held by U.S.

4.16

With the continued trend toward increasing online newspaper subscriptions and accompanying advertising revenues, more and more traditional newspaper newsrooms are being converted to online operations.

IanDagnall Laptop Computing/Alamy Stock Photo

newspapers, their report focuses on the loss of independent investigative reporting and its centrality to any healthy democracy. Numbers posted by the Audit Bureau of Circulations substantiated the rapid decrease in newspaper readership in 2009, with *USA Today* posting a 17.2 percent loss in circulation, *The New York Times* a 7.3 percent loss, the *Los Angeles Times* an 11.1 percent loss, and (rounding out the top five) *The Washington Post* a 6.4 percent hit.[23] According to a report by PricewaterhouseCoopers, the continued decline of print newspaper readership and advertising revenues is starting to be offset by increasing online paid subscriptions, which are predicted to reach $1.2 billion annually by 2016, and the resultant parallel increase in online advertising revenues.[24]

The implications of the migration of newspapers from money-losing printed editions to less costly and thus more profitable online editions are manifest. The authors of a 2012 report, *Post Industrial Journalism—Adapting to the Present*, produced for the Tow Center for Digital Journalism at the Columbia University School of Journalism, concluded that this "tectonic shift" is nothing less than a revolution in how the business of newspaper journalism will be conducted in the 21st century:

> "In a revolution, strategies that worked for decades may simply stop working (as many already have). Strategies that seemed impossible or insane a few years ago may now be perfectly suited to the current environment. This period is not over, and the end is not even in sight; the near future will hold more such reversals, so that even up-to-the-minute strategies of a few years ago (RSS feeds and staff blogs) may fade into prosaic capabilities, while new ones (the ability to hunt for mysteries instead of secrets, the ability to bring surprising new voices to public attention) may become newly important."[25]

The early years of the 21st century have seen a migration of formerly print-only newspapers, both major dailies as well as smaller regional and local newspapers, to the Web, driven by the changing demands and demographics of audiences, the proliferation of such mobile media devices as Web-enabled cell phones and tablet computers and the financial demands of surviving in a digital media-dominated landscape. In fact, some newspapers, large and small, are being forced to move their entire publication to the Web and cease producing printed versions altogether or go out of business. A good example of this trend is the old, established New Orleans paper *The Times-Picayune*, which announced in mid-2012 that it was going entirely digital.[26]

PRINT MEDIA GO VISUAL

More than a decade into the 21st century, we take for granted that modern print media are visual in their style and presentation, offering the reader a combined textual and visual experience. As we will explore in more detail, the role and importance of images in publishing had already become established by the late 1800s. (See Chapters 8, 10 and 12.) It steadily increased throughout the 20th century, driven by a long series of technological innovations in both printing and photography.

The Use of Illustrations

The use of printed illustrations in publishing began with lithography, which was invented by German playwright and printer Alois Senefelder (1771–1834) in 1796. Lithography represented a huge leap in printing technology because only the image to be printed required ink; ink was not applied anywhere else on the plate. The lithographic plate could then be used repeatedly to produce the image with fine detail and greater longevity.

In 1896, William Randolph Hearst debuted the comic strip *Hogan's Alley* in his papers. It was not initially published in color. To drum up publicity, however, Hearst's editors added yellow to the nightshirt of a little boy featured in the strip. The gimmick became so popular that the character was given the nickname "the Yellow Kid." The Yellow Kid would later become emblematic of the sensationalist content of Hearst's yellow journalist newspapers.

The Use of Photographs

Although photographs did not find their way into magazines or newspapers directly during the Civil War, woodcarvings made from photographs did. These images began to play an important role in the relaying of events, connecting faces and places to mere names. The advent and eventual refinements to the lithography process, combined with advances in photography, entered the scene in the years prior to the American Civil War. Over time, these technologies built the foundations of the contemporary image-rich publishing that we know today.

From our modern perspective, we do not question the importance of photographs in newspapers and magazines. In contrast, some 19th-century publishers and their audiences were initially resistant to the inclusion of photographs in newspapers—and not just because of the cost factor. Perhaps these publishers simply failed to see a photograph's potential for ensuring the delivery of a more visceral, comprehensible news story. Audiences at the time were also not used to associating public figures with their likenesses: Photographs just seemed a strange phenomenon next to traditional written news. Despite this seeming resistance, Joseph Pulitzer decided to be the first to introduce widespread use of photographs in newspapers.

4.17

Richard Outcault's Yellow Kid was the inspiration for the term "yellow journalism."

Barritt, Leon, Artist. The big type war of the yellow kids/Leon Barritt. Courtesy of Library of Congress

The Photo Magazine

The early decades of the 20th century saw an expansion of the publishing industry. By the Roaring '20s, newspaper and magazine publishing experienced another boost from the parallel growth and new marketing techniques of the advertising industry. Modernization of the printing process and the greater utilization of new photographic print technologies supported this new wave of marketing. The result led to the modern symbiotic relationship between publishing and advertising (see Chapter 8). By the 1930s, these technological advances contributed to the establishment of a new subgenre of magazine publishing—the photo magazine. The person credited for bringing this subgenre to fame is Henry Luce.

Henry Luce (1898–1967) was born in the port city of Penglai, China, where his parents were Presbyterian missionaries.

4.18

Henry Luce is credited for having established the subgenre of magazines known as the photo magazine. *Life* was one of the most critically acclaimed of these photojournalistic publications.

Autumn Cruz/ZUMA Press

Educated in China, Europe and then the United States, Luce served as the managing editor of Yale University's *Yale Daily News*. This role started him on a path to becoming one of the United States' foremost magazine publishers: Luce founded *Time* magazine in 1923, *Fortune* magazine in 1930, *Life* magazine in 1927, and *Sports Illustrated* magazine in 1954, to name just a few of his offerings. Luce's publishing empire became the American media conglomerate Time Warner when it merged with Warner Communications in 1987 (the parent company of Warner Brothers Pictures); the group eventually added Turner Broadcasting (1996) and AOL (2001) to become one of the five largest media conglomerates in the world (see Chapter 9).

In 1936, Luce purchased *Life* magazine, which had originally begun publishing in 1883. Inspired by the increasing interest in documentary photography, which was successfully captivating both national and international magazine audiences, Luce intended to offer a magazine in which the images led the textual narrative. *Life* quickly became one of the most popular magazines in America, along with other photo-oriented publications such as the German magazine *BIZ* and the *Mid-Week Pictorial* (a magazine-style publication of *The New York Times* that actually predated *Life* and is considered one of the first U.S.-based photo magazines). The success of *Life* helped to establish both the format and the business model of the photo magazine. Luce remained editor-in-chief of all of the magazines he started until 1964. He used his publishing power to endorse anti-communist political agendas and conservative presidential candidates, demonstrating how once again a successful American publishing empire can, indeed, exert political influence.

> The success of *Life* helped to establish both the format and the business model of the photo magazine.

Luce was a staunch supporter of freedom of the press and the role of the Fourth Estate in democracy. Concerned that it was not functioning in society as the nation's Founding Fathers had intended, he requested that a commission be recruited to investigate the matter. In 1942, the Hutchins Commission was formed for this purpose. Five years later, the Commission concluded that the press and all of mass media should play vital roles in the development, maintenance and stability of a modern, democratic society. As such, journalists were required to uphold certain ethical standards and make decisions that would serve the greater good of the public. Later, between 1957 and 1962, *Life* magazine would be one of the first publications to address racism as an overarching issue in American society, extensively documenting both the growth of the civil rights movement as well as the integration of schools in Arkansas and Mississippi.

4.19

Henry Luce's *Life* magazine extensively documented some of the most socially significant periods in American history—the Civil Rights Movement and racial integration of the schools in the South.

Bledsoe, John T., photographer.
Courtesy of Library of Congress

The Magazine Industry Transitions to the Digital Age

President Theodore Roosevelt coined the term muckrake when he referred to certain investigative magazine journalists as being akin to a character in John Bunyan's *The Pilgrim's Progress*:

> the man who could look no way but downward, with the muck rake in his hand; who was offered a celestial crown for his muck rake, but who would neither look up nor regard the crown he was offered, but continued to rake to himself the filth of the floor.[27]

As newly empowered investigative reporters, the muckrakers were the natural heirs of the authors of the sensationalist crime stories published by the penny press. In the late 1800s, these writers' work took on a more serious tone as they attempted to connect crime and greater social woes for a national audience. Through inexpensive mass-circulation magazines, the muckrakers were able to educate America's middle class by producing serious pieces that exposed the relationships between the business world and the government, laying bare the rampant corruption and abuse of power by elected officials.

Through inexpensive mass-circulation magazines, the muckrakers were able to educate America's middle class by producing serious pieces that exposed the relationships between the business world and the government, laying bare the rampant corruption and abuse of power by elected officials.

Muckraking, which had been widespread in the early 1900s but had lost popularity between the two world wars, recovered its popularity starting in the 1960s. At the same time, the appeal of general-interest, women's magazines and photojournalism-based magazines was also surging. Magazines had become important sources of news and entertainment through their wide offerings of longer-form stories illustrated by photography and paid for by ever-higher advertising revenues.

News magazines, which originated in the 1920s and 1930s, became highly influential media outlets starting in the 1960s, driven in large part by award-winning investigative reports and exposés. News magazines began as a hybrid of the traditional newspaper and the quality magazine. Magazines such as *Time* (1923), *Newsweek* (1933) and *U.S. News & World Report* summarized the news of the daily press in weekly or monthly offerings, and combined extended news reports with stories about fashion, sports, celebrities and entertainment.

In economic terms, the move toward specialized magazines and away from the general magazine was motivated by the increasing costs of maintaining large circulations. At the same time, competition

4.20

By the 1960s, magazines enjoyed a resurgence among American consumers seeking sources of news, entertainment and photojournalism. Despite the folding of many magazines today, people still enjoy browsing through magazines.

Nick Onken

from television forced the cost of advertising down, as television could effectively reach more consumers per dollar. During the 11-year period from 1961 to 1972, more than 160 magazines were sold or merged, and approximately 760 new magazines appeared on newsstands as the industry attempted to cultivate a specialized consumer base.[28]

Content convergence onto the Internet has posed new challenges for the magazine industry. Some magazines, such as *National Geographic*, were able to successfully meet these new challenges head on, in part because they were able to adapt their content for the Web, and in part because they were able to use their Websites as integral aspects of fully integrated multimedia "packages." Such packages include Websites, printed editions, television programming and specialized short image-rich content geared to portable devices such as the Apple iPhone.

The trade publication *Advertising Age*—which is published both in hardcopy and in digital form over its subscription-based Website—reports on the magazines that have ceased publication each year because of continued economic pressures and the migration of content, advertisers and consumers to the Internet. Some have been able to reinvent themselves as Web-only content producers. Perhaps their Internet-only publishing business models will succeed in attracting and holding the numbers of site visitors that are required to bring in sufficient advertising revenues to maintain at least marginal profitability. For example, in the Fall of 2012 *Newsweek* announced that, after 80 years of publishing as a printed weekly magazine, it would cease publishing in 2013, opting for a Web-only model tied to its sister Website *The Daily Beast*. For loyal subscribers the new Web-based format offers many new interactive and media features, which may prove a popular and sustainable Web-publishing model.

COMIC BOOKS AND THE GRAPHIC NOVEL

The inclusion of photography in magazines and newspapers is not the only visual contribution to modern publishing to have occurred in the last 150 years. Cartoons and comic strips, and eventually graphic novels, have also made a significant impact. Satirical comics, for instance, date back to the mid-18th century. During the years leading up to the American Revolution, both sides of the conflict, on both sides of the Atlantic, used politically charged comics to capture public attention and to communicate their views.

Comic strips and the American comic book industry trace their origins to the late 19th century, when satirical cartoons and serialized comic strips became regular features in first newspapers and then in popular, inexpensive pulp magazines (also known as *pulp fiction*). In the 1890s, syndicated comic strips (each of which appeared in multiple newspapers) including *The Yellow Kid, Katzenjammer Kids* and *Mutt and Jeff* represented visual satires of American life, and of the social and cultural challenges of the Industrial Revolution. They became platforms for expressing, and sometimes defusing, continued racial and ethnic tensions in American society. Of the many cartoonists who built careers in the early 20th century, the story of Will Eisner stands out.

4.21

Henry "Bud" Fisher's *Mutt and Jeff* (circa 1913) was one of the first syndicated comic strips that satirized American life.

Fisher, Bud, Artist. Mutt and Jeff. "Gee! This paper says the police department is short of motorcycle cops". Courtesy of Library of Congress

Will Eisner Ushers in the Modern Comic Book

Will Eisner (1917–2005) is considered a pioneer of the modern cartoon studio and comic book publishing industry, which helped launch the graphic novel as an astoundingly popular segment of the print industry today. Eisner was born in Brooklyn, New York, in 1917. As a teenager, Eisner sold newspapers on Wall Street to help support his family. Through this job, he was exposed daily to the great comic artists of the "funny papers"—artists including E. C. Segar (*Popeye*), George Herriman (*Thimble Theatre*), Harold Gray (*Little Orphan Annie*) and Lyman Young (*Tim Tyler's Luck*).

Eisner was also drawn to satirical cartoonists featured in such highbrow publications as *The Saturday Evening Post* and *Collier's*. An insatiable reader, the young Eisner consumed a steady diet of popular period writers such as Horatio Alger, whose writings made a lasting impact on the aspiring artist. He developed a love for pulp novels and popular films. In high school, a number of teachers (notably *Batman* creator Bob Kane) encouraged him to develop his skills as an illustrator and writer.

Eisner eventually met and began cultivating what would become a longstanding working relationship with Samuel "Jerry" Iger, the editor for the magazine *Wow!*, which published comics along with its regular content. Eisner found in Iger someone with the same creative sensibilities and vision for the commercial potential of comic book publishing, a medium that at the time was considered a juvenile novelty. When *Wow!* folded after publishing only a handful of issues, the pair formed Eisner-Iger Studios. This collaboration would eventually launch a number of legendary figures in the comics industry: Bob Kane (*Batman*), Lou Fine, Jack Kurtzberg (who would later change his name to Jack Kirby and was co-creator of *Spiderman* and *The Fantastic Four*) and Mort Meskin. These artists all became giants in the comic book and graphic novel world, and their works helped to drive today's highly successful comic character-based feature films.

When entrepreneur Everett M. "Busy" Arnold decided to form his own comic book publishing company in 1938, he asked Eisner to work exclusively for him. As difficult as it was, Eisner could not pass up the opportunity and agreed to sell his share of the studio to Iger so that he could become part of Arnold's Quality Comics staff. Joined by a number of his colleagues from Eisner-Iger Studios, Eisner went to work on one of his most widely recognized publications, *The Spirit*, for which he alone assumed complete creative responsibility and to which he retained complete creative and legal rights—a privilege almost unheard of at that time.

In 1952, Eisner abandoned *The Spirit*, despite its long-running success, to pursue other more profitable and challenging projects. In 1988, the comic book industry recognized Eisner's phenomenal lifetime contributions to the genre by establishing the Eisner Award, the industry's equivalent to the film industry's Academy Award.

Jerry Siegel and Joe Shuster Introduce the Comic Book Hero

By 1929, pulp-magazine storytelling and the comic strip had become inseparable. Seminal characters such as Tarzan, Buck Rogers, Dick Tracy, Flash Gordon and the Phantom all found their way into national newspapers. In 1934, two high school students from Cleveland, Ohio, created perhaps the most important character in the history of comic books. Jerry Siegel and Joe Shuster, both second-generation Jewish immigrants, struggled with being social outcasts while sharing a love of pop culture and the American dream. Out of their adolescent struggles came a fictional hero who would capture the imagination of generations of American teenagers—Superman. The character and backstory of Superman, an individual with superhuman powers of hearing, sight, speed, strength, flight and heat-vision who pledged to use these powers in defense of truth, justice and the American way, came at the perfect time in American culture, when the nation was struggling through the Great Depression and Hitler's fascism in Germany threatened to engulf the world.

4.22

The cultural climate of America during the 1930s—emerging from the Great Depression and struggling to come to grips with a fascist leader threatening the free world—largely inspired the birth of Siegel and Shuster's *Superman*.

John Parrot/Stocktrek

Siegel and Shuster's *Superman* did not get picked up by any of the publishers to whom they pitched their story. Executives thought that Superman was too incredible a character and that readers would not relate to him. As a last-ditch effort, Siegel and Shuster sent their concept to DC Comics, which had been looking for stories for its new comic book, *Action Comics*. Executives at the company decided to take a chance on it. Even though Siegel and Shuster had dreamed of seeing *Superman* in the newspapers as a syndicated comic strip, the offer from DC Comics seemed like their last chance. For the outlandishly low fee of $130, Siegel and Shuster sold the copyright to *Superman* to DC and began creating full-length stories for *Action Comics*. Although DC ordered a cautious 200,000 copies of *Action Comics* #1, the print run quickly sold out, as did the next three print runs of the first issue. Almost overnight, *Action Comics* became the industry leader of the comic book world, selling an average of 900,000 issues every month, as opposed to the 200,000 to 400,000 issues sold by its competitors.[29]

In an attempt to follow *Superman*'s enormous success, DC Comics enlisted one of its fledgling artists, Bob Kane, to create the next big superhero character—Batman. Unlike Superman, Batman battled evil using intellect, science, technology and superior physical prowess. Kane's Batman was a dark counterpart to Siegel and Shuster's brightly garbed Superman. Kane's own artistic style was essential in developing the character's persona and world, employing unusual angle shots, distorted perspectives and a heavy use of shadow to cultivate an aesthetic quality that, by some accounts, was the comic book equivalent of the classic Orson Welles film, *Citizen Kane*.

The phenomenal success of characters such as Superman and Batman encouraged scores of publishers and entrepreneurs to cash in on the burgeoning comic book market. These companies included Dell Publishing (which acquired the rights to a number of Walt Disney characters), Fiction House (creators of *Sheena*), Quality Comics (*Plastic Man* and Will Eisner's *The Spirit*), and new-kid-on-the-block Marvel Comics, which was founded by Martin Goodman in 1939. Goodman's teenage nephew—Stanley Lieberman, who published under the name Stan Lee—ran Marvel's creative production. The comic book industry was rife with poorly drawn, poorly storied Superman and Batman knockoffs. The prevalent view at that time was that comic books were essentially lowbrow, low-priced juvenile publications. Combined with the low wages paid to comic writers and illustrators, constant deadlines, the assembly-line production process most publishers used and a lack of royalties, most comic books during this period were formulaic. Perhaps it is not surprising that one unnamed publisher would regularly instruct his staff during the industry's formative period, "Don't give me Rembrandt; give me production."[30]

4.23

Contemporary portrayals of Batman remain true to Bob Kane's original vision of him as "the Dark Knight" fighting against crime.

AF archive/Alamy Stock Photo

Comic Books Influence Society

The comic book industry, which employed a large number of liberals and Jewish Americans, vigorously supported the United States' involvement in World War II. During the war, DC Comics tried to revamp its image with American parents by forming the Editorial Advisory Board to ensure that all comic books met accepted standards for morality, which in turn made huge strides toward furthering their popularity. By 1945, the Market Research Company of America reported that 70 million Americans—nearly half of the country's entire population—avidly read comic books.

Interestingly, the economic prosperity that the country would enjoy in the aftermath of World War II led to tough times for the comic book industry. Many comic book heroes rapidly declined in popularity, with all but the strongest characters, such as Superman and Batman, facing decreasing sales of the issues devoted to them. The relevancy of comic books seemed to wane as Americans transitioned back into their peacetime lives.

In an effort to bolster struggling sales, comic book publishers began featuring char-

4.24

As a transition from the heroic tales of comic book superheroes that reflected the nation's climate throughout WWII, *Archie Comics* came along to idealize the American postwar way of life.

Lambert

acters that deviated from the accepted superhero archetype, including female superheroes in skimpy costumes who sought to attract male audiences, and everyday figures like those found in *Archie Comics*, which reflected the idealized 1950s American existence. Crime stories also became a staple of the comic industry during this period, suggesting that publishers were tapping into an undercurrent in American culture that did not find the postwar Golden Years quite so golden. Conversely, attempts to reinvigorate traditional superhero titles during the Cold War by rehashing the patriotic themes that had played so well during World War II failed. *Captain America*, for example, was brought back with stories of his fighting the United States' new enemies—Russian, Chinese and Korean Communists—but comic readers were tired of the simplistic political and social stories that had dominated the 1930s and 1940s. Although the comic book market had grown significantly since its inception, comic book readers had matured and now demanded more dynamic stories.[31]

The Transition of Comic Books

Novelty and creativity were hard to find in the comic book industry during the Cold War, partly because of the social climate, but also because publishers were afraid to take risks on new ideas. One of the few innovators during this time was EC, which originally stood for Educational Comics, but was later changed to Entertainment Comics. Following the death of comic book pioneer and EC Comics founder Max Gaines in a boating accident in 1947, the company was taken over by Gaines's son, William. At first, EC specialized in noncommercial titles, and eventually crime, romance and Western knockoffs. When these lineups did not do well, Gaines and his creative team decided to start a new trend in the comic industry—one that did not reflect its heroic beginnings.

Starting with *The Crypt of Terror* (a title later changed to *Tales from the Crypt* to placate censors), EC began producing comics that were more sophisticated than those offered by its contemporaries, employing innovative artwork and pushing the bounds of subject matter to address deeper issues of human psychology

4.25

Mad magazine, 1953. This satirical comic book was the antithesis of the tamer comics being published at the time (e.g., *Archie*); as such, it became a target of American conservatives during the Cold War.

Susan Van Etten

and other mature themes. Included in EC's new lineup were *The Vault of Horror*, *The Haunt of Fear*, *Weird Fantasy*, *Weird Science*, and a humor-based comic book called *Mad*. This alternative comics world featuring fantastic storylines, scantily clad women and portrayals of violence, crime and gore made the comic industry a major target of American conservatives during the Cold War. Eventually, it came under investigation by the Senate Subcommittee on Juvenile Delinquency, led by traditionalist crusader Estes Kefauver. As the result of the Senate's attack on the comic book industry, publishers formed the Comics Magazine Association of America (CMAA) in 1954 and appointed New York City magistrate Charles F. Murphy as the "comics czar" in an attempt at self-regulation. Within a month, Murphy had created a code for judging all comic books and engaged a full-time staff to evaluate every comic produced. Only comics that passed the CMAA's stringent criteria could display the seal of the Comics Code Authority.[32]

Sadly, EC, which had been the source of much of the innovation that went on in the comic book industry during the 1940s and 1950s, became the industry's sacrificial lamb. Max Gaines took the stand during the Senate investigation and was showcased as an enemy of decency. After the hearings and the formation of the CMAA, other comic book publishers abandoned Gaines and EC. The incredible wave of negative publicity devastated EC's sales. Distributors and newsstands began returning EC's comics unopened, with no explanation. After a number of attempts aimed at revamping his company's lineup to adjust to the new trend of sanitized comics, Gaines discontinued EC's entire line—with the exception of *Mad*, which would go on to be one of the most popular titles of all time.

The 1950s brought a recession to the comic book industry. This was in part due to the strict self-imposed code, and in part due to a lack of viable distribution companies after the American News Company, which distributed more than half of all U.S.-produced comics, withdrew from circulating magazines after its indictment on charges of engaging in monopolistic practices. While comic book content had certainly changed with the evolution of American culture, up to that point few real innovations in the form had occurred over its history. What would soon emerge, however, was a format that, while closely tied to the original comic book format, had its own style and a more lengthy and detailed storyline—the graphic novel.

The Graphic Novel

Although the roots of graphic novels trace back to the 1920s, the first truly modern graphic novel appeared in 1971 with Gil Kane and Archie Goodwin's *Blackmark*. The definition of the modern graphic novel has been debated and expanded to include entire storylines and anthologies of comic books previously published as single issues. In its purest sense, the graphic novel is an expansion of the comic book genre, which summarizes an entire story with a beginning, middle and end, and often delves into subject matters and themes of a more mature nature. Notable examples of true modern graphic novels include Richard Corben's *Bloodstar* (1976); Stan Lee and Jack Kirby's *The Silver Surfer* (1978); and Will Eisner's *A Contract with God: and Other Tenement Stories* (1978), which is considered a classic of the genre—as are Dave Sim's *Cerebus* (1977) and Frank Miller's *Batman: The Dark Knight Returns* (1986). More contemporary graphic novels that were later turned into films include Neil Gaiman's *The Sandman* (1989–1996), Frank Miller's *300* (1998), and Marjane Satrapi's *Persepolis* (2004).

Manga ("whimsical pictures"), a form of Japanese art that has evolved since the 12th century and that experienced noticeable changes after World War II, has become an enormously popular subgenre of comic books and graphic novels published in the United States. In addition to its strictly Japanese elements, modern manga reflects a blend of American and Japanese attempts to re-envision Japan as a nonmilitaristic culture following World War II, although defining manga in terms of Western political and social influence would be a great injustice.

By the early years of the 21st century, comic books and graphic novels had become the most financially stable and consistently profitable segments of the publishing industry. Publishers such as DC Comics, the largest U.S. comic book publisher and a division of Time Warner, and Marvel Comics, now a division of Disney Corporation, generate huge revenues from both publishing and films. Movie franchises drawn from popular comic book characters such as *Batman, Superman* and *Spiderman* (to name just a few) have become film industry blockbusters. The continued popularity of graphic novels has resulted in newly conceived stories and characters as well. In 2009, movie producer James Cameron brought the highly acclaimed 3-D animated feature film *Avatar* to a huge international audience. Although *Avatar* is not based on a previously published graphic novel, the creativity and success of the film reconfirmed the high profit potential for animated feature films. This recognition, in turn, has boosted the publishing value of the comic book and graphic novel, which continues to have a large audience base and serves as a wellspring of characters, stories and creative talent. The ongoing success of this genre is good news for the publishing industry at a time when most other industry genres and segments—from newspapers to magazines to book publishing—are struggling to reinvent themselves in the Internet-dominated Digital Age.

4.26

Marjane Satrapi's graphic novel *Persepolis* is an autobiographical depiction of her experiences coming of age in Iran during the 1979 revolution.

Christine Spengler Digital Press Photos/Newscom

4.27

Manga art is characterized by a superrealist aesthetic form and attempts to blend American and Japanese visions of a nonmilitaristic Japan after WWII.

Tony French/Alamy Stock Photo

The Book Industry Transitions to the Digital Age

Even with the continued growth of magazines in the mid-20th century, books—and especially novels—gained widespread popularity during this time. In part, this trend was driven by advertising, reviews and excerpts published in popular magazines. The reading of novels took on broad public appeal during the 1920s and 1930s, when paperbacks were an inexpensive entertainment escape, grabbing the attention

4.28

In the mid-20th century, science fiction increased in popularity as a result of advances in technology and digital media.

Bertrand Benoit/Shutterstock.com

of men as well as women. Adventure and science-fiction stories gained large followings during this period. Science fiction in particular benefited from the public's widespread interest in the technological progress of the mid-20th century, with many stories exploring the world of tomorrow and posing questions about how society would survive in a future technology-driven world.

From the 1950s to the 1980s, the number of book publishing houses exploded to more than 22,000 in the United States, eventually producing approximately 49,000 new titles each year. The enormous push in expanding public education after World War II brought with it the parallel rise in the demand for textbooks, resulting in a number of large media organizations such as Time Warner and CBS acquiring holdings in the book industry. Foreign investors also took interest in the American book market, with German media giant Bertelsmann purchasing U.S. publishers Doubleday, Bantam, Dell and Random House in the 1980s, for example.

The rise of the Internet and Internet-based consumerism through the closing decade of the 20th century and the opening decade of the 21st century has brought significant changes in and challenges for the book publishing and book selling industry. While small bookstores and small publishers have in many cases suffered, and while some futurists have predicted the demise of printed books in favor of digital alternatives, the book publishing industry as a whole continues to prosper, with more titles published each year than ever before. Part of the reason is that online book selling, led by the giant Amazon.com, and advances in publishing-on-demand technologies (see Chapter 3) have opened up many new opportunities not only for the larger publishing companies, but also for authors and small publishers, to market their books to a consumer market that has expanded with the growth of the Internet. Amazon has also revolutionized and brought credibility to self-publishing with its Kindle Direct Publishing program. Publishers both large and small have also jumped on the direct-to-e-book model.

> Amazon has also revolutionized and brought credibility to self-publishing with its Kindle Direct Publishing program. Publishers both large and small have also jumped on the direct-to-e-book model.

As with other media, publishers, writers and readers are engaged in a lively discussion over the future of books in the Digital Age. What might encourage readers to adopt electronic formats? Among the benefits that digital books or e-books offer are their ability to store hundreds of titles on a single device, the ability to change font sizes, near-instant access to thousands of titles through wireless connections, the ability to receive e-mail and Web pages, and the overall reduction in the cost of purchasing e-books.

Numerous companies are scrambling not only to introduce their own e-reader technology into the developing market, but also to find profitable ways to market and sell e-books. As of 2012, the three market-leading e-readers were Amazon's Kindle, Apple's iPad and Barnes and Noble's Nook. In addition, retailers have yet to discover a business model that effectively deals with the democratization of information in the Digital Age. The leading tablet companies offer their e-reader users downloads at a fraction of the cost of traditional paper books. However, efforts to digitize the entire catalog of printed knowledge, such as Google Book Search, Project Gutenberg and the Open Content Alliance, present an obstacle to the industry's efforts to distribute e-books profitably.

Similar to the issues that the music industry is facing in light of digital distribution and peer-to-peer (P2P) exchanges of content that violate traditional copyright laws, the debate is currently raging as to what content should be available free to the public via the Internet. Google Book Search, for example, offers full versions of only works that are in the public domain and merely excerpts books that are still under copyright. Even so, the book industry has attempted to limit Google's cataloguing of copyrighted material. In 2008, Google agreed in a settlement with the publishing industry to pay more than $125 million to rights holders of books that the company had scanned as well as to create a Book Rights Registry that will both document the legal status of all works and arbitrate disputes between parties claiming rights to any work in the database (see Chapter 11). Nevertheless, all of the recent attention focused on copyright issues and the migration of books into the digital world does not indicate that the global mass media market has fully accepted digital publishing. According to Publisher's Weekly, sales of e-books increased by 3.4 percent to $2.77 billion in 2011 while the sales of printed books fell by 2.5 percent.[33]

CONCLUSION: WILL PRINTED MEDIA SURVIVE THE DIGITAL REVOLUTION?

Printed mass media—newspapers, magazines and books—have played a pivotal role throughout American history. Although the vast majority of experts do not see print media disappearing completely, the future of print mass media is being determined now, in the early decades of the 21st century.

The endgame, especially for newspapers, has yet to be written and may not be as dark as it looks, especially as more and more newspapers are successfully, if often partially, migrating their content to the Web. One sign of a more positive future for newspapers is that in the last few years, through his Berkshire Hathaway investment company, billionaire and investment guru Warren Buffet has purchased 63 newspapers, mostly in small- to mid-size markets, for $142 million. Buffet clearly believes that newspapers will continue to thrive, albeit in these smaller markets, where other mass media outlets, including national Web-based news sites, do not fully nor effectively serve the needs of these communities.

Digital technologies, especially the continued growth and dominance of the Internet, are challenging publishers to develop new business models that can succeed and even flourish in the Digital Age. These innovations in publishing are, in turn, changing the combined mass media platforms that we access for news, information and entertainment and requiring new approaches and skills on the part of journalists, writers and editors to enable them to deliver content that works in both printed and digital forms. (See Chapters 3 and 13.) While old-line publishers, especially publishers of newspapers and magazines, are struggling to reinvent themselves, new opportunities are emerging for both publishing entrepreneurs and content creators to reach vast audiences—the size of which could not have been imagined just a few decades ago.

CHAPTER SUMMARY	KEY TERMS
Early American Newspaper Publishing Tells the fascinating story of newspaper publishing in early America and explains the critical role played by news publishing in the establishment and fine-tuning of American-style democracy. Visual Media **The Evolution of Printing** Insights into the history of printing and printing presses from the late 18th to the late 20th centuries and their impact on the world. 1. Compare the impact of a key component of printing technologies in the 18th to 19th centuries with the progression and growth of the Internet in the late 20th and early 21st centuries. 2. Even in the Digital Age there are many people who put time, money and effort into restoring and using old printing presses. What do you think remains the attraction of this now "antique" media technology?	commercial press partisan press Fourth Estate penny press Industrial Revolution news bulletin inverted pyramid news syndicates teletype

The Rise of Magazine Publishing Explores the rise of popular magazine publishing primarily in America and shares the next chapter in the story of American publishing, its impact and influence on American culture and the rise of the mass media consumer.	Postal Act of 1792 Subscribers magazinists *Godey's Lady's Book*
The Evolution of the Book Industry Explores the highlights in the establishment and growth of the book publishing industry and looks at the social and cultural impact of books as the overall literacy levels in America rapidly increased.	novel cliffhanger dime novel
Technologies Extend the Print Media Explains how the evolution of mass media technologies closely followed, and influenced, the stages of the Industrial Revolution through the late 18th, 19th and early 20th centuries.	Fourdrinier machine stereotype system typewriter editorial process
The Birth of Publishing Dynasties Tells the story of the influences, and the abuses, of the major American media dynasties, who together controlled virtually all American mass media between the late 18th century and mid-20th centuries, paralleling the rise and dominance of the great American industrialists, who together with the media dynasties built modern America. Visual Media **Otis Chandler, *L.A. Times*** The late Otis Chandler, former *L.A. Times* publisher, discusses the influence of newspapers and publishing dynasties on American culture and politics. 1. How does the role the *L.A. Times* played in the career of Richard Nixon compare with the influence today's newspapers have on the election process? 2. What changes within the newspaper industry make it more challenging for family ownership to pass from one generation to the next? **Al Neuharth, *USA Today*** The founder of *USA Today* offers an in-depth analysis of the success and popularity of his paper. 1. How was *USA Today* on the cutting edge of media convergence when it was founded in 1982? 2. Where in today's media do you encounter moguls who use their content to "dictate what people are to read, or think or hear"?	Pulitzer Prize Newspaper Publicity Act of 1912 Committee on Public Information dangerous news questionable news routine news tabloids bylines gossip column news spin Carl Rowan Newspaper Preservation Act
Print Media Go Visual Looks at the profound influence that illustrations and photography have had on creating modern mass media and how consumers came to expect and demand that the media they consumed delivered not merely text, but richly illustrative visual components.	lithography Hutchins Commission muckrakers news magazines
Comic Books and the Graphic Novel Tells the fascinating story of the evolution of comic books and graphic novels, which has not had a profound impact on American culture, but continues to serve as a storytelling bridge between popular printed media and dynamically visual media, such as films, television and video games.	pulp magazines syndicated comic strips Editorial Advisory Board graphic novel manga e-books Book Rights Registry

NOTES

1 In 1985, the author conducted an extensive on-camera interview with *USA Today* founder Al Neuharth as part of a 34-program PBS series called *NewsLeaders*, which the author produced and directed for the Poynter Institute.

2 Folkerts, J., & Teeter, D. (2002). *Voices of a nation: A history of mass media in the United States.* Allyn & Bacon.

3 Fang, I. (1997). *A history of mass communication*. Focal Press.

4 Folkerts, J., & Teeter, D. (2002). *Voices of a nation: A history of mass media in the United States.* Allyn & Bacon.

5 Fang, I. (1997). *A history of mass communication*. Focal Press.

6 Ibid.

7 Folkerts, J., & Teeter, D. (2002). *Voices of a nation: A history of mass media in the United States.* Allyn & Bacon.

8 Fang, I. (1997). *A history of mass communication*. Focal Press.

9 Ibid.

10 Folkerts, J., & Teeter, D. (2002). *Voices of a nation: A history of mass media in the United States.* Allyn & Bacon.

11 Ibid.

12 Ibid.

13 Ibid.

14 Ibid.

15 Bingham, S. (1989). *Passion and prejudice: A family memoir*. Alfred Knopf.

16 In 1985, the author conducted an extensive on-camera interview with Barry Bingham, Sr., as part of a 34-program PBS series called *NewsLeaders*, which the author produced and directed for the Poynter Institute.

17 Folkerts, J., & Teeter, D. (2002). *Voices of a nation: A history of mass media in the United States.* Allyn & Bacon.

18 Gabler, G. (2009, December 21). Celebrity: The greatest show on earth. *Newsweek*.

19 Donovan, R., & Scherer, R. (1992). *Unsilent revolution: Television news and American public life, 1948–1991*. Woodrow Wilson Center Press.

20 Eisenhower Foundation. (1968). Report of the National Advisory Commission on Civil Disorders. Retrieved from www.eisenhowerfoundation.org/docs/kerner.pdf

21 *Audit bureau of circulation statistics*. (2009).

22 *Moving into multiple business models: Outlook for newspaper publishing in the Digital Age*. (2006). London: PricewaterhouseCoopers. Retrieved from www.pwc.com/gx/en/entertainment-media/publications/outlooknewspaperpublishing-in-digital.jhtml

23 Ahrens, F. (2009, October 27). The accelerating decline of newspapers: Small dailies are rare bright spot in latest figures. *Washington Post*. Retrieved from www.washingtonpost.com/wp-dyn/content/article/2009/10/26/AR2009102603272.html

24 PricewaterhouseCoopers. (2012). *Global entertainment and media outlook: 2012–2016*. Newspaper digital circulation spending starts to offset print decline in EMEA. Retrieved from www.pwc.com/gx/en/global-entertainmentmedia-outlook/segment-insights/newspaper-publishing.jhtml

25 Tow Center for Digital Journalism. Retrieved from http://towcenter.org/research/post-industrialjournalism/conclusion/

26 McQuaid, J. (2012, May 24). The digital future of the Times-Picayune. *Forbes*. Retrieved from www.forbes.com/sites/johnmcquaid/2012/05/24/the-digital-future-of-thetimes-picayune/

27 Bunyan, P. (1678). *The pilgrim's progress*.

28 Wolseley, R. E. (1972). *Understanding magazines*. Iowa State University Press.

29 Wright, B. W. (2001). *Comic book nation: The transformation of youth culture in America.* Johns Hopkins University Press.

30 Ibid.

31 Ibid.

32 Ibid.

33 *Authors Guild v. Google settlement.* (2008, October 28). Retrieved from www.authorsguild.org/advocacy/articles/settlement-resources.html

5

Music and Radio

Timothy Hiatt/Stringer

CHAPTER OUTLINE

The Cultural Influence of Music and Sound Recording

Matt & Kim: Indie Rockers The indie rock group Matt & Kim go up against the major record labels.

The Birth of the Radio Broadcasting Industry

Evolution of Radio Programs An encapsulated look at the history and evolution of radio programming with Professor Bob Thompson of Syracuse University.

Popular Music: The First Cultural Shift
The Music of Revolution: The Second Cultural Shift
Musical Styles Diversify
MTV and the Birth of Music Videos
Music and Radio Transition into the Digital Age

Radio Today and Tomorrow Ron Della Chiesa and broadcast historian Bob Thompson discuss the changing world of radio.

Conclusion: Music and Radio Converge—and Endure

LEARNING OBJECTIVES

1. Illustrate how Prohibition and the Great Depression influenced the recording industry and mainstream American music in the early 20th century.
2. Explain how paid advertising impacted the way the radio and recording industries presented content to the American people.
3. Analyze the role that social issues such as civil rights played in the diversification of what came to be known as "popular" American music in the 1950s and 1960s.
4. Evaluate how counterculture movements such as Woodstock influenced the way in which the music industry came to segment audiences.
5. Characterize the ways in which MTV brought alternative music genres into the mainstream.
6. Explain how advances in recording and file-sharing technology have profoundly altered the recording industry.
7. Describe how media and content convergence has contributed to the survival of music and radio.

MATT JOHNSON

and Kim Schifino met while attending the Pratt Institute in New York, where Kim was studying illustration and Matt film. Although they can't recall exactly when they decided to start playing music together, sometime in 2004 Matt was learning how to play keyboards and Kim had picked up the drums with hopes of starting a band. Only a few months after taking up their instruments, "Matthew and Kimberly"—as they called themselves back then—debuted at a friend's loft party in the Bronx, New York. The combination of Kim's hip-hop-inspired beats and Matt's catchy synthesized melodies proved infectious, and the new group immediately started building a local following. Shortening their name to "Matt & Kim," they began to play warehouse and loft parties around New York at a frenetic pace. Although Matt & Kim recorded a demo album called To/From in 2005, they found playing live concerts both more satisfying for them as musicians and more financially lucrative for selling CDs. After two years of constant touring, they started getting invitations to play such

music festivals as Siren, Lollapalooza and South by Southwest (SXSW). In 2006, they recorded their first full album, self-titled Matt & Kim, under the indie label IHeartComix; they sold the CDs at their concerts.

During those early years, Matt & Kim learned hard lessons about how the recording industry works. Knowing nothing of the legal side of the

business, they lost nearly all the rights to their earlier works through their distribution agreement with IHeartComix. So they hired a manager whose job, in part, was to help secure the rights to their future work. Most importantly, they kept doing what they did best—entertaining live audiences with their feel-good, energetic music. Through viral marketing

00:08   00:33   CC

▶ **Matt & Kim: Indie Rockers**
Popular indie rock group Matt & Kim recount their story of going up against the major record labels.

on the Internet, and constant tour-ing, Matt & Kim gained attention on the national music scene from major record labels. They start getting calls from ad agencies that wanted to use their music for major advertising campaigns (Virgin Mobile), maga-zines (*Spin*) and television shows. The next step was signing with the independent multimedia company Fader to promote and distribute their music. Fader allowed them to main-tain creative and legal control over their work while also benefiting from the cross-media exposure that an experienced media organization can provide. For a more in-depth account of how Matt & Kim went up against the major recording labels, view their story in the video segment, "Matt & Kim: Indie Rockers." ▶

In 2009, Matt & Kim made a breakthrough onto the national music scene when the single "Daylight" from their second album, Grand, was used in the Bacardi Generations commercial, prompting a viral media frenzy on the Internet. With their music and videos available through their own Website, MySpace and YouTube, and through new promotional deals with major brands such as Pepsi's Mountain Dew Green Label Sound, fans were able to gain instant access to the band's music, increasing Matt & Kim's popu-larity exponentially and driving ticket sales for their live concerts. Using the power of the Internet and clever use of 360-degree promotions and marketing campaigns (see Chapter 8), Matt & Kim went from being just another local band to a national sensation, regularly selling out concert venues through-out the United States. Although only time will tell how successful they con-tinue to be, the future looks bright for Matt & Kim—and for scores of other talented independent artists whose careers hinge on the 21st-century evo-lution and convergence of the music and radio industries.

THE CULTURAL INFLUENCE OF MUSIC AND SOUND RECORDING

Before we explore the convergence of music and radio on the Internet, we must first consider the history that inspired the trend. In this chapter, we expand the story of the historic roots of music as part of mass media (Chapter 2) to explore music's role as a driving force of American culture and America's cultural influ-ence on the world. In modern times, the story of music and the recording industry is so interconnected with the story of radio broadcasting that we must chronicle both together.

By the late 1800s, the United States had begun to challenge Europe as the world center of music. At this same time, the United States was also emerging as the world center of technological and industrial innovation. After inventors such as Samuel Morse had developed land-based telegraph technology in the early 19th century, the next communication challenge was to find a way to transmit telegraph signals over great distances without relying on cumbersome networks of cables. The invention of sound recording, or the re-creation of sound waves, including voice, music and sound effects, marked the first real progress toward addressing this next leap forward. Although many individual inventors contributed to this effort, the man who is most widely credited with the invention of modern sound recording is Thomas Alva Edison.

The Phonograph Advances the Music Industry

In 1877, Edison completed the first working phonograph, which recorded sound as notches on a tinfoil-wrapped cylinder the size of a cardboard roll of toilet tissue. Edison was primarily interested in finding a way to record messages transmitted through telegraph and telephone lines for such business uses as dictation. In an effort to service the market he thought he was creating, Edison launched the Edison Speaking Phono-graph Company. Through this new company, Edison built exhibition models and trained technicians to tour the United States in an attempt to drum up new customers for the phonograph. The novelty of the first phonograph soon wore thin, however, forcing Edison to scramble to improve the device and to find new applications that would capture Americans' imagination—and, of course, inspire them to open their wallets.

Edison was not alone in his efforts. (See Chapter 9 for more details.) American entrepreneur Louis Glass was desperate to find a way to keep his company, which marketed Edison's machines as dictation devices, afloat. In 1889, he developed a coin-slot attachment for the phonograph and installed it in the Royal Palace Saloon in San Francisco as an entertainment device. Glass's machine, the Nickel-in-the-Slot—which would become the predecessor to the jukebox—could play only one short song, but it was an overwhelming hit with customers and sparked the coin-operated entertainment machine craze.

The popularity of the Glass coin-operated entertainment machine coincided with an innovation that first began in Boston in 1888—the nickelodeon, a small entertainment house that had seats, a screen and a piano or organ. Within a few years, coin-operated phonographs and machines that played early short silent films and animated clips had become part of the nickelodeon scene as well. All of these machines ran on either a nickel or a dime—hence the name *nickelodeon*. The nickelodeon also served as a launching pad for the early movie industry (see Chapter 4). The popularity of nickelodeons, and the recorded music and short films they offered, was further driven by the United States' emergence in the late 19th century from the cultural limitations of the Puritan and Victorian eras.

Musical Tastes Change in Changing Times

Two major events combined to help shape American music in the first few decades of the 19th century—Prohibition and the Great Depression. The Victorian era is often viewed as an era during which conservative social and religious elites made a concerted attempt to regulate morality. One of those attempts included the ratification of the 18th Amendment in 1919 prohibiting the manufacture, transportation and sale of alcohol. (Prohibition would not be repealed until 1933.) As part of the Temperance Movement, which originated as far back as the 1830s, proponents of the amendment claimed that the consumption of alcohol was the root of a rapid decline in morals that threatened American society. As soon as the sale of alcohol became illegal, vaudeville shows—satirical performances combining song and dance—all but died out, and burlesque and cabaret went underground. To make a living, many of the performers who had toured the country's theater circuit in previous years either migrated to radio or went underground as performers in speakeasies, illegal saloons and dancehalls that quickly sprang up all over the country.

Right along with alcohol, musical entertainment was a mainstay of these underground establishments. The speakeasies provided fertile ground for the birth of a new era known as the Roaring '20s and the development of a new style of music that had its roots in New Orleans jazz. During this time, the upper social classes considered much of the coin-operated machine entertainment to be lowbrow—that is, not highly intellectual or cultured. Nevertheless, it was during this period when these same coin-operated music players introduced white audiences to black musical styles and served as the gateway through which jazz and rock 'n' roll would eventually take America—and the rest of the world—by storm.

The Roaring '20s is often referred to as the Jazz Age because of how jazz came to embody the spirit of the times. Jazz grew out of ragtime, with its roots in Western European music, which blended standards from Tin Pan Alley (the music publishing district in New York City so called for its tin-pan-clash-sounding piano music) with *syncopation* (a rhythmic arrangement in which the stress falls on a beat that would normally not

> coin-operated music players introduced white audiences to black musical styles and served as the gateway through which jazz and rock 'n' roll would eventually take America—and the rest of the world—by storm.

5.1

Louis Armstrong in 1953.

Louis Armstrong, head-and-shoulders portrait, facing left, playing trumpet. Courtesy of Library of Congress

receive it) and tunes from American plantation folk music. This infectious and danceable blend of musical styles eventually led to jazz, which combined African-infused rhythms and instrumentation with a heavy dose of improvisation. The association of jazz with the underground social scene, with its illegal drinking and its overt sexuality, drove social conservatives to demonize both the form and the younger generations (as well as older progressives) who embraced it. Despite its taboo status, jazz profoundly influenced American as well as European music.

Like their vaudeville and minstrel show predecessors, jazz musicians on the radio introduced white audiences to African-American musical styles and brought new waves of profits to the record companies and broadcasting networks. Recording companies thus began producing jazz-inspired tunes, albeit toning them down to make them more palatable to "polite" society. Lyrics were altered, beats were diluted and white performers were brought in to record covers (songs and tunes performed by artists other than the original).

By the 1930s, the United States was suffering from the terrible economic downturn of the Great Depression. Due to its improvisational nature, jazz moved easily from personifying the high spirits of the Roaring '20s to symbolizing the Depression's struggle for survival. During the Depression years, people longed to make sense of their suffering. Although jazz (unlike Franklin Delano Roosevelt's "fireside chats," which we discuss in greater detail later in this chapter) did not offer a solution to the unprecedented poverty that gripped the nation, it did resonate with the difficult times being experienced by most Americans. The rhythms and lyrics of jazz helped to connect people culturally to other distractions, such as dancing and sex. According to author Piero Scaruffi, both of these connections made jazz an important coping mechanism for Americans during these hard times.[1]

New Delivery Platforms Emerge

As the cultural climate and the market demand for certain styles of music changed, technological innovators responded by providing new delivery platforms for the popular music that Americans craved. After failing to find much of a business market for his phonograph as an automated dictation device, Edison went back to the drawing board, spurred on by Glass's discovery that the public hungered after entertainment recordings. Alexander Graham Bell's graphophone and Emil Berliner's gramophone entered the marketplace as direct competitors to Edison's phonograph.

Berliner's gramophone, the predecessor to the record player, is particularly important to the story of modern music because it was the first to offer consumers interchangeable recording media in the form of a hard plastic disc, as opposed to the cylinders employed by Edison's and Bell's inventions. Unlike the cylinders, many plastic discs could be made from one original or master copy. Gramophone discs were also cheaper and sturdier than the cylinders and could be mass-produced. Moreover, they reproduced music at much higher volumes. Their introduction triggered a major shift in the music industry's focus and launched what we know today as the record industry. In an effort to design the cheapest, most reliable record player on the market in the United States, Berliner enlisted the help of Camden, N.J., machinist Eldridge R. Johnson. However, the two ended up competing against each other, with Johnson winning the competition with the Victor Talking Machine Company (1901).

Sales of home record players grew tremendously during the early 1900s, due in large part to the steady increase in the financial wealth of the average U.S. consumer. (See Chapter 9 for more details.) Nevertheless, many musicians feared that the new technology threatened their livelihoods. Live performances had been their main source of income throughout the late 19th century. Copyright laws ensuring that artists would receive royalties on recorded music were weak, so many musicians and composers believed that consumers would stop attending concerts if the recording industry succeeded. Although the technical sound quality of recorded music was initially a concern, improvements in recording technology, such as Victor's high-fidelity Red Seal records, eventually lured a number of important European opera stars such as the talented opera singer and accomplished self-promoter Enrico Caruso to make records, giving the industry a boost in credibility. Although classical music, especially opera, did not suit the tastes of the average American during the

early 20th century, such highbrow (that is, intellectual and cultured) music would keep the young recording industry from collapsing during the Great Depression, owing to its popularity among the wealthy set.

By the end of the Depression in 1939 and at the onset of World War II, although the American economy overall had recovered, record production was severely limited due to the scarcity of shellac—a hard substance produced largely in Asia and also used for military goods. In addition to a lack of raw materials, the American Federation of Musicians (AFM) had instituted a boycott on music recording to compel the recording industry to provide musicians with a larger portion of the royalties from record sales. From 1942 to 1944, AFM members did not record any new music, with one notable exception. In cooperation with U.S. government efforts to support America's troops fighting overseas, AFM allowed the recording of V-discs, which

5.2

Technological innovations such as the home record player pictured below challenged the status quo of the music industry, which had been built on live performances.

Oleg Gerasymenko/stock.adobe.com

were musical recordings produced exclusively to entertain American troops stationed around the world. World War II would also prove to be a critical period in the evolution of the radio and recording industries. The military's adoption of a number of radio and recording technologies provided funding for many technical innovations in both fields. The war also triggered what would become a decades-long battle between three of the major pioneers of modern broadcasting.

THE BIRTH OF THE RADIO BROADCASTING INDUSTRY

While the birth of the music recording industry is rooted in 19th-century American innovation (see Chapter 2), it was an Italian inventor and promoter by the name of Guglielmo Marconi who first delivered radio broadcasting—the unrestricted transmission of a signal to numerous receivers—to the world. Marconi's original intent was to develop technology that would allow telegraph messages to be sent over long distances—especially water—without the need of costly networks of cables. American entrepreneurs quickly saw the incredible potential of radio to reach mass audiences over large areas. Yet it would take development funding from the U.S. military during World War I to make radio broadcasting viable, and the results would have a sweeping impact on both U.S. culture and the record industry.

The potential profitability of commercial radio meant that major corporations, many of which had their roots in the early recording business, rushed to invest sizable capital to stake out their claims in the new radio broadcasting market (see Chapter 9). Early radio broadcasting companies such as Westinghouse and General Electric/RCA faced immediate competition for bandwidth from amateur radio hobbyists due to a lack of government regulations of broadcast radio frequencies. These minor broadcast stations offered a tremendously diverse range of content, much of which—including music—had a local flavor.

The newly created radio networks developed a two-pronged strategy in their effort to drive the many small local stations out of business. First, they attracted listeners with expensive live broadcasts, which proved far more popular with many Americans over the recorded content that smaller, limited budget stations used to fill the airtime. Second, the early radio networks lobbied the U.S. government to implement legislation that would control who could broadcast commercial radio. In response, through the Radio Act of 1927, the Federal Radio Commission (FRC)—the predecessor to today's Federal Communication Commission (FCC)—enacted radio broadcast regulations that favored the networks and nearly drove small radio stations into extinction. By the late 1930s, radio broadcasts of recorded music made their comeback to network radio as stricter copyright and licensing laws were passed to ensure that artists were able to receive royalties on their work (see Chapter 11).

The Recording Industry Links With Radio

At this juncture in history, we start seeing the linked paths of the recording industry and the radio broadcasting industry. Even while radio was becoming America's favorite in-home entertainment during the Great Depression, radio stations had to cut back on hiring live musicians. The simultaneous decrease in consumer demand for records and record players in the late 1920s forced a drop in the price of recording media, making recordings all the more attractive to radio stations as a way to fill airtime. Radio was key to the success of the recording industry, and the recording industry for the most part dictated what kind of music it was going to produce for the radio airwaves.

> Radio was key to the success of the recording industry, and the recording industry for the most part dictated what kind of music it was going to produce for the radio airwaves.

By the early 1920s, the radio broadcasting industry has emerged as a viable and prominent mass medium. Record sales almost immediately began to fall because radio offered the same thing that records did, but at no cost to the consumer. Initially, the production of radio content and the formation of radio networks were intended to drive the sales of the radios. Radio manufacturers such as RCA moved quickly to supply the rapidly expanding listener market with programming for its new radios. The first radio network, the National Broadcasting Company (NBC), was formed in 1926 when RCA acquired WEAF in New York from American Telephone & Telegraph (AT&T) and WJZ in New Jersey from Westinghouse.

While it was obvious that radio was a potential gold mine, no one really knew how to tap it as a profitable commercial enterprise. Performers who had previously created music dramas and comedies for radio networks in return for free publicity started to demand performance and licensing fees. With rising operating costs, radio stations had to find a way to remain financially viable. The solution—sell advertising. Initially, commercial sponsorship for radio broadcasts was highly unpopular with listeners. In 1923, Hugo Gernsback, an inventor and popular science-fiction author, was quoted in *The New York Times* as saying, "If the future of radio rests upon a foundation of advertising, it would be better that broadcasting did not exist at all."[2]

This single statement voiced the opinion of many consumers who were opposed to the introduction of paid advertising. However, advertiser-sponsored radio programming quickly took off, as did the profits of the radio networks, even against public opinion and in the face of inadequate attempts by the federal government to curtail radio advertising through regulation.

The Pioneers of Radio Broadcasting

It was during World War II that three of the most important figures in the history of radio broadcasting began to exert their influence on the future of the broadcasting industry: Lee De Forest (1873–1961), Edwin Howard Armstrong (1890–1954) and David Sarnoff (1891–1971).

De Forest was an American inventor and the self-proclaimed "father of radio and the grandfather of television." His big break came when he secured the patent for the Audion tube, a device that for the first time allowed the transmission and reception of the human voice. Though De Forest was sure that his Audion tube was a huge achievement, he had no idea how it worked. Figuring that out would be left to a bright young inventor from New York, 17 years his junior, and the second of the three rival radio pioneers.

Growing up, Edwin Howard Armstrong had a voracious technological curiosity. Gifted with a rare genius for engineering, Armstrong began building radio towers and working on ways to improve radio signals. During his undergraduate work at Columbia University, he took radio technology to the next stage by plotting out the theory and design for the first true regenerative radio circuit—the interconnecting electronic components that would greatly increase radio signal clarity, which he patented in 1914. De Forest attempted to patent and sell the same concept to AT&T two years later. This effort launched what would become the longest patent case in U.S. legal history, and the first of a series of legal battles between the two radio pioneers that would continue throughout their lives, taking a severe toll on both men.

On January 31, 1914, Armstrong demonstrated for the Marconi Wireless corporation how clearly and ably his regenerative circuit could pick up stations from all over the world. One chief inspector encouraged the young inventor to license his design to Marconi's company. That chief inspector became the third rival radio pioneer, David Sarnoff. David Sarnoff was not an engineer or an inventor, but rather a visionary and shrewd promoter. He rapidly moved his way up the management ladder at Marconi Wireless, promoting himself and his vision of a future dominated by radio technology. One of his early memos detailed how every American home would soon welcome radio broadcasting. When the General Electric Company bought Marconi's American business assets to form the Radio Corporation of America (RCA), Sarnoff was asked to stay on as the new company's general manager.

Armstrong, meanwhile, had enlisted in the U.S. Navy during World War I and went to work designing radio units for aviation use. During this time he developed his next major radio invention, the superheterodyne circuit, which vastly increased the sensitivity of radio receivers. Sarnoff, who had maintained a relationship with Armstrong after their initial meeting, acquired the rights to the technology. He used it as the foundation of RCA's home line of radio receivers after the war, which led to RCA's early domination of the radio electronics industry.

By 1930, despite the terrible economic conditions of the Great Depression, the radio industry endured. Radio not only captured the hearts and minds of Americans through entertainment and education, but also united many in a time of crisis, when poverty and the struggle for survival sometimes turned American against American. On March 12, 1933, three full years into the Great Depression and with U.S. banks on the verge of collapse, President Franklin Delano Roosevelt ordered all banking establishments to close. He then took to the radio airwaves to talk with the American people in what would come to be known as the "fireside chats." These chats began as more formal radio addresses in 1929, when Roosevelt was governor of New York and used these speeches to gain support for his political agenda. Once he became president, these speeches became more informal, intimate and confidence building—hence the term *fireside chat*.

Roosevelt delivered 30 "fireside chats" throughout his presidency. Some addressed the purpose and value of banking; others talked about congressional means of dealing with the Great Depression; and still others gave lessons on civics and democracy. For a decade, Roosevelt's chats helped to ease the fears of a nation. Radio also offered entertainment relief, with comedic shows such as *Abbott and Costello* and *Amos 'n' Andy*; soap operas such as *Clara, Lu, and Em*; comic strip adaptations such as *Dick Tracy* and *Little Orphan Annie*; and musical programs such as *NBC's Symphony Orchestra*. These programs, along with Roosevelt's chats and the jazz programs mentioned earlier, all helped Americans weather the Great Depression.

5.3

Listening to President Franklin Roosevelt's "fireside chats" radio addresses helped families believe in a positive future during the Great Depression.

Bettmann/Contributor

As the years went by and the country prospered, audience desire for new and different radio programming increased. In the video segment "The Evolution of Radio Programs," Syracuse University professor and broadcast history expert Bob Thompson explains the evolution of radio broadcasting as a foundation for the wide range of radio content and delivery platforms that we enjoy today. ▶

Improved Technology Spurs the Growth of Radio

One thing that both De Forest and Armstrong shared was that neither of them actually listened to commercial radio. Whereas De Forest objected to the commercialization of this medium, Armstrong couldn't stand the static produced by the amplitude modulation (AM) technology that was the broadcast format standard at the time. Armstrong dedicated himself to developing a better format, frequency modulation (FM). Armstrong's FM radio circuitry produced crystal-clear reception, which was never possible with AM, and set the new standard for quality radio broadcasting that would remain unchallenged until the advent of digital radio. Sarnoff's refusal to back Armstrong's FM radio tech-

▶ **Evolution of Radio Programs**
An encapsulated look at the history and evolution of radio programming with Professor Bob Thompson of Syracuse University.

nology turned the two former friends into lifetime business rivals, and Armstrong decided to develop and market FM on his own. Within a few years, more than half a million FM sets could be found in U.S. homes and Armstrong's broadcasting group, the Yankee Network, provided FM signals to them all.

David Sarnoff and RCA managed to get the FCC to move the FM radio spectrum from 42–50 MHz to 88–108 MHz while getting new, low-powered community television stations allocated to a new Channel 1 in the 44–50 MHz range. In fairness, the FCC was also trying to correct the plague of radio interference caused by the height of the 11-year sunspot cycle. Nevertheless, the immediate economic impact of the shift, whatever its technical merit, was devastating to early FM broadcasters. This single FCC action would render all Armstrong-era FM receivers useless within a short time as stations were moved to the new band; it also protected both RCA's AM-radio stronghold and that of the other major competing networks, CBS, ABC and Mutual. Armstrong's radio network did not survive the shift into the high frequencies and was set back by the FCC decision. This broadcast frequencies change was strongly supported by the then-telephone monopoly AT&T because the loss of FM relaying stations forced radio stations to buy wired links from AT&T.

Sarnoff would go on to launch color television and pave the way for satellite television (see Chapter 4). Despite the decades-long competition between these three pioneers of radio, or perhaps because of it, they launched and built the broadcasting industry—radio and television—that we know today. In doing so, they changed the economic and cultural face of the United States, and of much of the world, forever.[3]

POPULAR MUSIC: THE FIRST CULTURAL SHIFT

The battle to control the direction of the broadcasting industry also set the stage for one of the most revolutionary shifts in the history of music. Radio played the determining role in the buildup of a common interest in and market for jazz and rural folk music, whose themes and styles resonated with the average American. Radio-enabled popular music—music that broadly encompasses all nonclassical music styles—was on its way to becoming dominant as a cultural form, as the core focus of the recording industry and as the sound of the times.

> Radio played the determining role in the buildup of a common interest in and market for jazz and rural folk music, whose themes and styles resonated with the average American.

American folk singers and musicians reached vast audiences, as did other styles rooted in the American cultural landscape, ranging from blues to gospel to cowboy and western music. Many folk songwriters and performers used radio to express concerns about social and political issues of the day. Noteworthy among this influential group of folk music activists was Woody Guthrie, whose witty critiques of U.S. politics and personal accounts of life during the Great Depression earned him the nickname "the Dust Bowl Troubadour." The songs of Woody Guthrie and his fellow folk music activists filled the airways and sold records for the recording industry, even though many were clearly critical of the U.S. government.

Jazz continued to win radio audiences and sell records, as even those American consumers who found jazz too wild and sexually charged flocked to the sounds of the big bands—large jazz ensembles associated with the Swing Era of the late 1930s and early 1940s—and crooners, who had adopted a watered-down jazz style and extremely personal vocal techniques. The crooners' popularity was greatly enhanced by the introduction of the microphone, first patented in 1877 by Thomas Edison, to live performances. The microphone delivered amplification that, for the first time, enabled entertainers to clearly project their voices and orchestral accompaniment to large audiences. Crooning brought to national and international music stardom the likes of Nat King Cole, Bing Crosby, Dean Martin and Frank Sinatra. While a large segment of the younger generation, influenced by the free-spiritedness of the Roaring '20s, was receptive to black music, it would take the majority of white audiences at least another three decades to begin to fully accept black performers.

Rock 'n' Roll Pushes the Social Envelope

Rock 'n' roll is a slang term for "sex," which originated from blues music. Likewise, as a musical genre, the roots of rock 'n' roll may be traced back to a form of urban black music known as R&B ("rhythm and blues"). R&B had developed out of the melting pot of the black American music scene of the 1940s and 1950s, which included jazz, blues and gospel music. Rock 'n' roll arrived on the scene in the 1950s; during these early years of the genre, and into the beginning of the 1960s, it both stirred a transformation in popular music and helped push and reflect cultural change. Elvis Presley, for example, was considered controversial and inappropriate during his early career in large part because he was a white entertainer crossing racial lines. He performed music rooted in black musical traditions and culture, often laced with sexual imagery (considered taboo at the time). The United States was on the cusp of the civil rights movement, and ideas about race were starting to change. People began to recognize the unconstitutionality behind segregation. First folk singers such as Joan Baez, Harry Belafonte and Miriam Makeba, and eventually rock 'n' roll attempted to wed both black and white musical traditions—this is partly what contributed to its popularity; it was also seen as a symbolic reflection of the nation's inevitable move toward racial integration.

The country's youth were also restless—seeking an escape from the traditional and conservative lifestyle and values of their parents as well as from the political tensions that pervaded all citizens' lives at the time: Cold War threats and communist fears. Not only did they appreciate the sound of the music, but young people also gravitated toward the flamboyant appearance and audacious lifestyles of many of the leading rock 'n' roll stars of the day. Little Richard, for example, blurred gender identities and turned sexuality and racial expectations on their heads. He was considered the first "drag queen" of rock 'n' roll (later, artists such as Elton John, David Bowie, Boy George, k. d. lang and Annie Lennox would follow in his footsteps) and was criticized by some black musicians as sounding too "white."

Perhaps one of the events most remembered for pushing the social envelope and the buttons of social morality occurred when Jerry Lee Lewis—one of the pioneers of rock 'n' roll who is widely remembered today for his hit "Great Balls of Fire"—caused a scandal that nearly destroyed his career: In 1958, at the age of 23, he married his 13-year-old first cousin, Myra Gale Brown. This action threw the public in both the

United States and England into an uproar, as well as fomenting a debate over (appropriate) sexuality and the sanctity of marriage. Today, of course, Lee would have been arrested for statutory rape. At the time, his actions led to the cancelation of his European tour and his being blacklisted from the American airwaves.

Payola: Paying for Popularity

In the 1950s, even while movies and early television variety shows were helping to promote music styles and performers (see Chapter 4), radio remained the driving force behind the record industry. Such a strong market linkage between radio airtime and record sales was bound to open the door to corruption—in this case, known as payola. Payola was the practice of paying bribes to radio disc jockeys (DJs) and station owners to control which records would receive airplay over the radio. Rather than playing the music most popular with local listeners, DJs played the songs the industry paid them

5.4

Rock 'n' roll's merging of black and white sound reflected the country's inevitable move toward racial integration.

Bettmann/Contributor

to play. The practice of payola influenced which records audiences would buy, which in turn affected the economic success and even survival of recording companies. The most well-known case occurred in 1959 and involved the legendary television personality Dick Clark. As host of the *American Bandstand*, the live dance show and prime trendsetter at the time, Clark was linked to payola payments made by six of the major recording companies.

Although the radio industry did not have total control over American musical tastes, radio had become the titan of musical trendsetting. This status, of course, affected which kinds of music and which musical performers the record industry chose to produce, further increasing the power of radio. In addition to paying to get their artists played on the radio, record companies began selectively featuring artists whom they believed would be highly marketable in light of the current market trends. At the height of the payola scandal, rock 'n' roll was not just the popular music of choice, but was actually driving commercial radio's success. The powers behind radio and the recording industry became accustomed to making or breaking the careers of artists and to manipulating the evolution of American popular culture.

This payola scandal damaged America's relationship of trust with radio and tarnished the credibility of rock 'n' roll. It offended the American public, which disliked the fact that the radio and recording industries had manipulated its listening choices. Although the practice was officially outlawed in the early 1960s, new forms of payola, and resultant new legal cases, continue to crop up regularly even today. For example, in 2003 and again in 2005, the New York State attorney general filed a payola suit against the major record industry licensing agencies ASCAP and BMI for attempting to charge radio stations a small fee each time a song played over the air.

By the late 1950s, scandal after tragedy after scandal caused the corporate leadership in both the radio and record industries to focus less on the envelope-pushing rock 'n' rollers and more on squeaky-clean, relatively innocuous artists. These performers included such well-known names as Fabian, Pat Boone, Frankie Avalon, Ricky Nelson, and the groups The Shirelles and the Beach Boys. Their sound tried to build upon the legacy of the crooners, some of whom—for example, Dean Martin, Frank Sinatra and Sammy Davis Jr.—were also popular movie stars. These performers had a clean-cut look and sound, but did not write or compose most of their own music; instead, they mostly sang three-minute-long, cookie-cutter ditties about such carefree subjects as teenage love.

Since rock 'n' roll had faded off to the cultural sidelines by the end of the 1950s, American teens had few options in musical entertainment. The major record labels continued promoting the same types of artists. Many of these singers gained even more popularity by following in the footsteps of the crooners through convergent film careers. The poster-boy crossover artist for this period was Frankie Avalon, who was often teamed up with regular on-screen sweetheart and former Disney Mouseketeer Annette Funicello. Together they appeared in a series of "beach party" movies, such as *Beach Party*, *Bleach Blanket Bingo* and *How to Stuff a Wild Bikini*—which were all much more innocent than their titles might lead the reader to think. By the close of the decade, a curious competitor for manufactured mainstream music began to take America's musical landscape by storm.

Motown: The Sounds of Detroit

African-American music has impacted every area of American music, yet it is recognized as distinctly American. African-American music has not only reflected the hardships and triumphs of black Americans but it has helped dramatically shape America's national identity.

Slavery and the influx of Africans to America was in fact the introduction of a variety of ethnic groups, each with their own distinct musical traditions. Africans fashioned musical instruments such as the "banja" or "banshaw," now known as the banjo, and numerous drums and percussion instruments to create a variety of musical styles, sounds and rhythms. These styles later evolved into gospel, blues, bluegrass and country music.

On January 12, 1959, a 30-year-old aspiring writer and record producer living in Detroit, Berry Gordy Jr., used a family loan of $800 to open Tamla Records (the following year, he changed the company's name to Motown Record Corporation, which was a combination of "motor" and "town"). Gordy was a high school dropout who, following his stint in the U.S. military, became the owner/operator of a small record store and an assembly-line worker at Detroit's Lincoln-Mercury automotive plant. Gordy was also a passionate jazz fan and, as it turned out, a sharp businessperson. Jackie Wilson, who was a regular singer at a local club that Gordy frequented, became one of the first artists whom Gordy wrote for and produced. Gordy's next discovery was Smokey Robinson, who was part of a group called the Matadors (and who later changed its name to the Miracles and then to Smokey Robinson & the Miracles). Before long, Gordy was building an impressive stable of R&B acts and producing hit material at a rapid pace.

Popularized by the likes of Ray Charles, Sam Cooke and "the Godfather of Soul" James Brown, R&B had a commercial following in the United States at that time, but its reach was limited by racial barriers. Gordy's genius was to shrewdly mold Motown's talent to appeal to white audiences through the adoption of the clean-cut, mainstream aesthetic and pop sensibilities, on top of its rich authentic R&B musical core. He orchestrated the development of a unique and infectious "Motown sound" that began to take over American record sales and airwaves, prompting the ambitious Gordy to unofficially rename his studio "Hitsville, USA." Motown continued churning out chart-topper after chart-topper at a break-neck pace.

In keeping with the automotive assembly lines he had once worked on, Gordy ran Motown with mechanical precision. Along with producing hundreds of top-selling songs during the 1960s, his company was responsible for launching to musical stardom scores of legendary artists, including Diana Ross, Stevie Wonder, Marvin Gaye, the Temptations and Michael Jackson and the Jackson Five. Motown music was storming American radio and television airways; however, Motown would not be the birthplace of the next revolutionary shift in music and recording—that would come to America from across the Atlantic.

Kenneth Gamble and Leon Huff launched Philadelphia International Records in 1971 to compete with Motown. They produced over 170 gold and platinum records and a sound that is referred to as "Philly Soul." Also in 1971, in the city of Memphis, singer-songwriter Isaac Hayes was composing, arranging, producing, and recording a double album under Stax Records as the soundtrack for the movie, *Shaft*, which hit No. 1 on the Billboard Top 200 charts. Isaac Hayes the following year would become the first African-American to win an Oscar for Best Original Song for the "Theme from Shaft"—and of course the "queen of soul" Aretha Franklin.

The arrival of P-Funk in the 1970s was led by icon George Clinton and an experimental sound that included powerfully prominent bass lines and a range of styles from 1950s doo-wop, deep soul, and psychedelic rock was invented. This new form of black music was an early influence for today's rap and rock, with works that have resurfaced and have been performed by contemporary hip-hop royalty including OutKast, Snoop Dogg, Public Enemy, and Busta Rhymes. During this same period neo-soul was created by producer Kedar Massenburg as a marketing platform that launched the careers of his artists D'Angelo and Erykah Badu, and also includes artists Lauryn Hill and Maxwell Neo-soul. It combines R&B, jazz and hip-hop.[4]

The Beatles and the British Invasion

Even with the success of the Motown sound, American music fans were ready for something radically new. That music soon came from England, in what became known as the British Invasion. Influenced by American rock 'n' roll, jazz and blues artists, British musical artists developed their own brand of tougher, beat-driven music known as skiffle. Playing skiffle music was an easy and inexpensive form of entertainment in postwar England. As these groups matured and as artists developed their own unique sound, however, they discovered that their music could feed a vast U.S. market hungry for something new. British acts began to make their way overseas and onto the music charts in the early 1960s. By 1963, only three U.K. singles had cracked the U.S. top-40 pop charts: songs from the Beatles' album *All My Loving* and from the Rolling Stones' *I Want to Be Your Man*. By the next year, that number would explode to 65—with nine of the 23 No. 1 hits coming from British groups.[5]

This incredible jump in the popularity of British acts in the United States was due in no small part to a single group from Liverpool. This band, of course, was the Beatles, who created a new cultural phenomenon. Arriving on the U.K. music scene at the end of 1962, the Beatles had gained minor popularity by playing pubs and small clubs around Europe. The band was unable to land a record deal with any of the major U.K. recording companies because its sound was highly reminiscent of American rock 'n' roll. At the time, British industry executives were convinced the genre would never regain popularity. The Beatles' manager, Brian Epstein, was able to convince EMI to sign the group to a renewable

5.5

Aretha Franklin sings the National Anthem prior to the start of the Detroit Lions and the Minnesota Vikings game at Ford Field on November 24, 2016 in Detroit, Michigan.

Gregory Shamus/Staff

5.6

The Beatles make their first U.S. appearance on the *Ed Sullivan Show*, February 9, 1964—in the midst of a wave of Beatlemania.

Trinity Mirror/Mirrorpix/Alamy Stock Photo

one-year contract. While their first recording session with EMI did not produce any saleable songs, their second session in September 1962 resulted in "Love Me Do," "Please Please Me" and "From Me to You," each of which climbed the U.K. charts, with "From Me to You" rocketing all the way to No. 1. American record companies—which were also convinced that rock 'n' roll was outdated and were not interested in the more raucous style and long-haired appearance of these lads from Liverpool—showed little interest in distributing their hit singles in the United States. That would soon change.

On December 10, 1963, a five-minute news piece on the rise of Beatlemania in the United Kingdom was featured on the *CBS Evening News*, which showed throngs of teenagers going wild over the group. It prompted teens all over the United States to call in to their local radio stations requesting the Beatles' latest single, "I Want to Hold Your Hand." Virtually overnight, America buzzed with talk of the new craze, prompting the group to arrange its first American tour. Two months later, on February 7, 1964, more than 3,000 Americans waited at John F. Kennedy International Airport in New York to greet the "Fab Four." Two days later, the Beatles made their first live appearance on American television on the *Ed Sullivan Show*, one of the many popular prime-time TV variety shows at the time. That night, the number of viewers jumped to an astounding 74 million viewers—almost half the entire population of the United States.

American teenagers went crazy for the new music. Radio and record industry executives quickly realized that the Beatles—and British rock 'n' roll—were the next big wave in music and recognized that this wave was largely just a repackaging of an already existing blend of American musical styles. British bands such as the Animals, the Dave Clark 5, the Hollies, the Kinks and the Rolling Stones rode the wave of popularity started by the Beatles. The Rolling Stones were especially popular, as their even rawer sound was perceived as less wholesome than the Beatles. Their "bad boy" image would come to inspire the rise of other "British Invaders" as well other musical forms, including punk rock, glam rock, heavy metal and grunge rock—styles touched upon later in the chapter.

Studio Mixing Changes Popular Music

At the same time as fresh faces and new sounds from Britain made their way onto the American music scene, two influential names in music history tinkered with new ways to record and produce music. This initiative would have a profound effect on both the music and radio industries. After Les Paul designed and built the first solid-body electric guitar back in 1939, he began developing new methods of recording using electronic equipment. Paul used magnetized tape-recorder technology to simultaneously record multiple instruments and vocal tracks as one single, layered and cohesive whole—a practice known as multitrack recording. Paul's new method made it possible to edit live and recorded material prior to its distribution to network radio stations; this type of audio editing also meant that many instruments and voices could be combined to create radical new music mixes and previously unheard of rich levels of sound.

It would not be until legendary record producer Phil Spector adopted the tech-heavy process in the 1960s, pushing and tweaking and prodding it to produce his trademark Wall of Sound, that multitrack recording would come to dominate the music industry. The Wall of Sound had a dense, layered effect that sounded great over the radio. As part of his approach, Spector sometimes stacked a single track multiple times to produce a fuller sound.[6]

5.7

Music producer Phil Spector in his early multitrack recording studio, 1967.

Pictorial Press Ltd/Alamy Stock Photo

The emergence of the Wall of Sound also changed the relationship and power structure between artists and producers. Until this point, record producers were primarily technicians, constrained by the artist's vision and studio performance in determining the overall sound and character of an album. With multitrack recording, however, the producer became the dominant artistic voice, and artists became more like instruments to be played, switched in or switched out, depending on the sound the producer was trying to achieve. On the one hand, multitrack recording gave artists and producers a new palette for developing fantastic, rich new sounds. On the other hand, it gave music producers and record labels more control over the music that reached the public.

THE MUSIC OF REVOLUTION: THE SECOND CULTURAL SHIFT

By the mid-1960s, while radio still served as America's commercial music "hit maker," the major record labels had gained tremendous power over Americans' musical preferences, in part because of the advent of multitrack recording. Nevertheless, these big labels did not dominate musical tastes or intentions entirely. The 1960s were a turbulent time. Many high school- and college-aged people had become fed up with the conformist portrayal of life that dominated post-World War II culture. They were concerned about U.S. involvement in Vietnam, segregation and sexual discrimination. Attitudes toward the traditional roles of women and sex were changing radically. People were experimenting with

5.8

Among the social movements that inspired anti-mainstream musicians in the 1960s was Women's Liberation.

Don Carl Steffen/Contributor

drugs as a form of escapism and in an attempt to find deeper meaning to life. In this heady milieu, underground and independent artists began to emerge; they were the anti-mainstream musicians whose sound and song focused on changing political and social consciousness.

Folk Music: The Songs of Protest

The popularity of folk music, a genre characterized by untrained musicians whose compositions are passed down via oral tradition, grew immensely during the 1960s. Due to its association with the rough and tumble of society, folk music also became the voice of democracy and social change. Folk singers such as Bob Dylan; Pete Seeger; Peter, Paul and Mary; Phil Ochs; and Joan Baez influenced an entire generation of Americans—many of whom rose up in protest against the era's social injustices.

Dylan, along with a number of his contemporaries, helped to provide the sound of the counterculture movement of the 1960s—a movement that would not only leave a lasting impact on the American psyche, but also inform that generation's musical conscience. Radio and record labels would eventually notice this cultural shift and attempt to package it for mainstream commercial consumption. Musical duo Simon and Garfunkel, well known for their melodic harmonies and their songs "Sounds of Silence," "The Boxer" and "America," represented one brand of the bridging artists—artists who remained true to the changing musical landscape, but whose compositions were also much more palatable for mainstream America. As such, they garnered huge radio audiences and sold millions of albums for the record labels.

5.9

Jimi Hendrix provided a ground- and guitar-breaking performance to an audience of almost half a million fans at the Woodstock festival in 1969.

Henry Diltz/Contributor

Psychedelic Sound: When the Tide Turns

As the cultural tide began to turn, so did the musical direction of mainstream artists. The Beatles began experimenting with multi-track technology and non-Western musical styles, spicing things up with their use of psychedelic drugs, which they and many other musicians at the time believed enhanced their creative abilities and artistic expression. The resulting musical style, which came to be known as the psychedelic sound, characterized the Beatles' *Sgt. Pepper's Lonely Hearts Club Band* (1967) album.[7]

The late 1960s and 1970s saw other popular groups move toward an even more antagonistic, countercultural rock style. England's The Who, the Rolling Stones, and the Yardbirds made the shift along with the Beatles—who drew their creative influence from many music styles—as did Eric Clapton, the now three-time inductee into the Rock and Roll Hall of Fame. Newcomers Pink Floyd (from England) as well as the Doors, the Grateful Dead and Jefferson Airplane (from the United States) followed suit. Folk singer Bob Dylan altered his style to attract a different, younger crowd and inspired the formation of the folk rock (folk music characterized by a harder, more electric sound) group, the Byrds. Heavily blues-inspired rock artists Janis Joplin, Joe Cocker, Cream and Jimi Hendrix—all influential musicians of the period—also performed at the Woodstock Music & Arts Fair.

In a generation rife with social tension, where the status quo was being flipped on its head in the name of civil rights, civil liberties, the anti-war movement, peace and free love, people turned to the music of the day to hasten and give voice to their cause. This desire was partly what drew half a million people to 600 acres of farmland in Woodstock, New York, on August 15, 1969—the site of what is considered one of the largest outdoor musical festivals ever held. Documentary director Michael Wadleigh and famed director and producer Martin Scorsese, who filmed the festival, won an Academy Award for their efforts; this honor helped to bring media attention to the music and to the countercultural spirit that the concert celebrated. Beyond the celebration and the media focus on counterculture ideals, the lasting impact on the music industry was that it opened corporate America's eyes to the potential profits that lay relatively untouched in the counterculture movement and in the countercultural audience.[8]

MUSICAL STYLES DIVERSIFY

Following Woodstock, musical culture experienced an explosion of diversity during the 1970s that continues through today. The record labels and radio stations continued to cultivate the newest trends, successfully packaging rebellion, sex and youth into products that resulted in larger radio audiences, more album sales and ever-growing corporate profits. The concert legacy left behind by Woodstock was that sound mixing and recording technology further advanced; improvements in stage production audio systems allowed music groups to stage exceptional live shows in larger venues, including outdoor sports stadiums and amphitheaters. As part of this trend, arena rock bands became prominent fixtures of the 1970s music scene. High on production values and commercialization but low on creativity, radio-friendly groups such as Styx, Journey, Foreigner, Heart and REO Speedwagon looked the part of rebellious rock 'n' roll band, but created music that was far tamer than their appearances indicated, helping to make arena rock more highly acceptable to mass audiences.

Two Extremes: Hard Rock to Disco

Improvements in stage production technologies also helped give birth to hard rock—a style of music characterized by an amplified and distorted electric sound. Its emergence paved the way for the harsh instrumentals, outrageous costuming and often-violent lyrics of heavy metal, the musical roots of which can be traced to Jimi Hendrix, Led Zeppelin, Deep Purple and Cream, but it did not fully manifest itself until bands such as Black Sabbath and Judas Priest crashed onto the scene. A number of rock bands crisscrossed these young genres, attracting fans from multiple areas of the rock universe, in part because improvements in sound production and recording technologies greatly enhanced the listening experience in both recorded and live performances. Two of the most successful bands whose music crossed genres were Kiss and Blue Öyster Cult.

At the other end of the musical continuum, the improvements in multitrack studio mixing helped give birth to disco, whose dominant characteristic was its danceability. Disco music drew upon a number of different styles, including soul, funk, rock 'n' roll, Latin, jazz and classical, combined with soaring vocals, a steady four-on-the-floor beat and a driving syncopated bass line. In many regards, disco music was not new, but rather the remixing of existing musical forms so that listeners could more easily dance to them. For people from every walk of life, the dance floor was a place where the lines that previously separated people were swept away by slick fashion, sex, drugs, hot dancing, mirror balls and music that never stopped. Artists such as Donna Summers, the Bee Gees, Gloria Gaynor and Sister Sledge were leading figures of the 1970s disco scene.

Disco music revolved around dancing and nightclubs, and venues such as New York's Studio 54 became epicenters of the genre. The commercial and cultural success of disco was further advanced by Hollywood through celebrated films such as *Saturday Night Fever* (1977). One of the significant contributions made by disco is the ascent of the DJ as an entertainment celebrity. Tom Moulton, considered by many the "father of the remix," created a new art form when he began overlapping records to produce long-running, continuous tracks that could keep people dancing all night long.

The Singer-Songwriters

By the early 1980s, the recording industry and radio executives worried that rock 'n' roll was taking too much of a hit from disco's popularity. The record labels, helped by radio networks creating formula playlists, looked to support a diversity of styles in the marketplace. Pop musicians of the 1970s, including the Jackson Five, the Carpenters, Rod Stewart and Fleetwood Mac, gained a tremendous following in the 1980s as a result. In many ways, the 1980s was the era of the popular singer-songwriter. 1960s music icons Stevie Wonder, Paul Simon, John Lennon and Bob Dylan, as well as 1970s newcomers Cat Stevens, Billy Joel, Elton John, Carole King, Neil Diamond, Don McLean and Joni Mitchell successfully adjusted to the commercially changing tides, producing scores of hip, radio-friendly songs.

Punk Rock

Hard rock and its stylistic cousin, punk rock, also sought to capture niche audiences and ensure their own commercial viability. CBGB, the little rock bar located on the Bowery in New York City, is considered the home and heart of the U.S. punk rock scene. (In 2006, this famous club closed its doors.) Emerging in the 1970s, punk rock sought to challenge mainstream musical tastes as well as the dominance of the mainstream music industry. The original punk rockers include the Velvet Underground, the New York Dolls, the MC5 and the Stooges, although these groups never achieved true commercial success. Later, Patti Smith, the Ramones, Blondie, the Talking Heads and the Dead Kennedys came to be associated with the punk rock scene; these artists then paved the way for England's notorious punk rockers, who included the Sex Pistols, the Clash and the Buzzcocks.

Emerging in the 1970s, punk rock sought to challenge mainstream musical tastes as well as the dominance of the mainstream music industry.

Each group had its own cynical, caustic spin on culture, politics, sex and drugs, and many gained large fan followings through concert and album commercial success as well. More importantly, the punk

5.10

Crossover hard rock/heavy metal group KISS performs a farewell tour in Cincinnati, Ohio.

Mark Cornelison/Newscom

movement placed women in the forefront of the rock scene—introducing such well-known singers as Patti Smith, Debbie Harry, Joan Jett and Chrissie Hynde. Such women influenced the 1990s underground feminist punk movement known as Riot Grrrl—and the most popular band to emerge from this movement was Hole. Fronted by lead singer Courtney Love, this band also managed to gain mainstream success, showing that the music industry was becoming more adept at tapping into underground music phenomena. This trend would continue into the 21st century.

MTV AND THE BIRTH OF MUSIC VIDEOS

In 1981, the commercial music industry was on the verge of making a giant leap forward. This time the innovation would not be driven by the music industry's longtime relationship with the radio industry, however, but instead would come out of a new convergence with television. At 12:01 a.m. on August 1, 1981, Warner-Amex Cable in northern New Jersey began broadcasting what would prove to be the start of the next revolution in the music and recording industries. The first images transmitted were of Apollo 11 blasting off from Kennedy Space Center, followed by a montage of spacewalks on the moon, culminating in the iconic planting of the American flag on the lunar surface. However, in place of the Stars and Stripes, a multicolored, patterned animation glowed over the flag, depicting a large "M" with "TV" scrawled across its lower right side and the phrase "Music Television" below it. A narrator announced, "Ladies and gentlemen . . . rock 'n' roll," followed immediately by an aggressive distorted guitar riff. Mark Goodman, the first VJ (video jockey) then exclaimed, "This is it! Welcome to MTV Music Television—the world's first 24-hour stereo music video channel . . . the best of TV combined with the best of radio . . . Starting right now, you'll never look at music the same way again."[9]

Goodman and the young staff of the new music network had no idea of the colossal success that MTV would achieve or the enormous influence that the channel would have on the music industry. Robert W. Pittman, who had already enjoyed a successful career as a DJ and then as a radio program director, drew on his experience with original QUBE cable network, which gave birth to such other cable sensations as Nickelodeon, to build the new music television channel. Although it might not seem controversial today, Pittman's vision for MTV was a radically new one for television at the time, and network executives at Warner-Amex needed persistent reassurance that the project was financially viable. Once launched, MTV proved to be a very lucrative venture indeed and had a near immediate and unprecedented impact on the way that music was created and consumed.

Ironically, the first music video broadcasted by the station on that fateful August morning was "Video Killed the Radio Star" by the band the Buggles, which in essence forecasted the downfall of radio in deference to the video age. While radio, in fact, was not killed by the video age, the radio broadcasting industry was forced to reposition its programming in part due to the rapid rise of MTV. Before MTV, radio was the primary medium for delivering and promoting new music to audiences; indeed, radio maintained its dominant role in promoting record industry sales throughout most of the 20th century. That lofty position soon changed when audiences got a look at MTV's synthesis of music and video, enabling television to take over quickly as the most popular way of promoting artists—a role that has today migrated to the Internet, but remains built around music videos.

Prior to the advent of MTV, in a trend made possible by the proliferation of video technology, many artists were already video recording their performances or producing original scripted and elaborately staged videos for use as promotional tools for their concert tours. The roots of music videos go back to the very inception of video, but can be seen most clearly in clips recorded for the Animals' "House of the Rising Sun" and the Beatles' full-length film, *A Hard Day's Night* (1964). Even though many of MTV's early music videos were merely video collages of various pieces of concert footage covered with studio-quality recordings, the record industry quickly realized the significance of MTV's meteoric popularity and began producing more interesting original artist videos for the network. Combining young, hip VJs with cutting-edge music videos and promoting the newest countercultural trends, MTV's viewership quickly shot up. Advertisers rushed to get in on the new television music phenomenon, netting the infant channel more than $7 million in profits in its first 18 months alone. MTV was the next leap forward in the marriage between music and broadcasting—or in this case, cable television—and a push forward in media convergence that signaled the end of radio's dominance as a trendsetter in the United States and worldwide.

The birth of MTV brought about the reinvention or rise of artists who were able to tap into the new creative possibilities of music videos. A good example is Michael Jackson's 1983 music video for the title track of his new album, *Thriller*. Jackson worked with film director John Landis to produce a 14-minute mini-film/music video for *Thriller*. It became an immediate sensation on MTV, further driving the album's sales and solidifying Jackson's role as one of the most financially successful recording artists in the world and the "King of Pop." Thanks in large part to MTV's repeated showings of the *Thriller* music video, the album became the highest-selling record of all time, at 110 million copies worldwide.[10]

Alternative and Independent Music

The enormous cultural shifts in the United States between the 1960s and the 1980s provided fertile ground for creative cross-pollination between musical artists of diverse backgrounds, perspectives and tastes. The result was an explosion in the number of musical genres and subgenres. In the past, because of the control that the recording and radio industries held over the music that the public heard, many styles went unnoticed by mass audiences or found their way to public attention only by influencing more mainstream artists. The MTV phenomenon in the early 1980s opened a window of opportunity for alternative music styles.

Before MTV, radio was the primary medium for delivering and promoting new music to audiences; indeed, radio maintained its dominant role in promoting record industry sales throughout most of the 20th century. That lofty position soon changed when audiences got a look at MTV's synthesis of music and video, enabling television to take over quickly as the most popular way of promoting artists

5.11

Trinidadian-born rapper/singer Nicki Minaj has successfully used music videos on MTV and YouTube to sell millions of songs, pack concerts worldwide and become a music superstar.

Frederic J. Brown/Staff

5.12

Michael Jackson's *Thriller* music video, which first aired on MTV in 1983.

Vaughan Stephen/SIPA/Newscom

The catch-all label given to the music that did not easily fit into the popular mainstream was alternative or independent (indie) music. Independent labels signed artists and bands that had nonmainstream followings—typically low-tech, three- or four-piece groups, whose lyrics took center stage.

One such nonmainstream band was U2, whose first recordings achieved only nominal success in Europe and the United States. Over time, however, the band's rough, unpolished sound and powerful live performances, particularly from lead singer Bono, won the band a growing underground following. The group's third album, *War* (1983), was the first time the band members' unique talents combined to create a critically acclaimed sound. *War* marked U2's first successful foray into the mainstream music world, helping to solidify the band's place in both the European and American music scenes. Unlike most other mainstream groups, U2 distinguished itself not just by its musical accomplishments, but also by the path that it took to commercial success.

In the past, because of the control that the recording and radio industries held over the music that the public heard, many styles went unnoticed by mass audiences or found their way to public attention only by influencing more mainstream artists. The MTV phenomenon in the early 1980s opened a window of opportunity for alternative music styles.

From 1980 to 2006, U2 stayed with Island Records, the largest independent record label. The label allowed the band to maintain both creative control and the legal rights to its albums. Until U2 came along, this business arrangement was nearly unheard of for artists. However, U2 was not alone in its push for independence from the control of the record labels: The band was joined by a group from Athens, Georgia, called REM.

REM toured tirelessly over the course of their first eight years of existence, building a huge underground following by playing colleges and small venues and offering up a jangly, bare-bones, introspective-bordering-on-abstract style of pop rock. As the group's popularity grew, it rejected offers from the major record labels, choosing instead to sign with Miles Copeland III's I.R.S. (International Record Syndicate), an independent label that had a contract with the major record label A&M to assist with album distribution for I.R.S artists. Beginning with *Murmur* in 1983, REM released critically acclaimed albums including *Reckoning* (1984), *Fables of the Reconstruction* (1985) and *Life's Rich Pageant* (1986). Although all of these albums were viewed by critics as exceptional works, none of them broke through into the top 40 charts, despite glowing reviews from *Rolling Stone* magazine. Finally, in 1987, release of the *Document* album allowed the group to chart its first top 40 single, "The One I Love," leading *Rolling Stone* to call REM "America's Best Rock & Roll Band." In 1988, the band left I.R.S. for Warner Bros. Records due to frustration over I.R.S.'s inability to effectively distribute its music overseas, but not before the group had become the poster child for the

U.S. independent music scene. Once again, alternative music, starting as an undercurrent running counter to the mainstream, eventually was adopted and marketed as the next music fad.

The Grunge Alternative

In 1985, two fans of the alternative/underground band the Melvins met while hanging around the band's practice space in the Seattle, Wash., area. After a number of failed attempts to start their own group, Krist Novoselic and Kurt Cobain finally found a drummer, began writing and practicing songs, and settled on a name for the band—Nirvana. Nirvana, with its raw, ragged sonic sound, quickly cultivated a growing fan base through its concert tours, first two albums and several singles released through the independent Sub Pop record label. In addition, the group was played on many college radio stations. The trio broke into the mainstream two years later with the monster hit, *Nevermind*, the first record released on the band's new label, DGC Records. Sales soared, driven by tremendous exposure on radio and the popularity of the video for "Smells Like Teen Spirit" on MTV. By January 1992, *Nevermind* was selling more than 400,000 copies per week and had dethroned Michael Jackson's *Dangerous* as No. 1 on *Billboard*'s charts.

The overnight success of *Nevermind* shocked both the band and the record industry, and the almost instant national and worldwide pressure of superstardom began to take a toll on the group, especially Cobain. Nirvana's second major album, *In Utero*, was—to many alternative music purists—an uncompromising creative achievement, despite having been released by a major label. The band produced a collection of visceral songs that channeled Cobain's own personal demons, songs so abstract and primal that they could not help but offend the casual listener and enthrall underground fans. *In Utero* debuted at No. 1 on the *Billboard* charts. On April 8, 1994, an electrician working at Cobain's Seattle-area home found the group's front man dead from a self-inflicted gunshot wound to the head. With Cobain's death, Nirvana was no more.

5.13

U2 was the first group to achieve mainstream success while maintaining creative control and legal rights to its albums with Island Records—the largest independent record label.

ZUMA Press, Inc./Alamy Stock Photo

5.14

REM, Michael Stipe and Peter Buck playing at Melbourne Park.

Martin Philbey/Contributor

Although Nirvana was part of the music scene for less than half a decade, its influence on U.S. music and the recording industry was deeply felt. Nirvana is viewed as the poster group for the alternative grunge—a musical subgenre characterized by distorted guitars, raw sound and lyrics reminiscent of punk rock. Grunge was also depicted in the fashion choices of the artists: torn jeans, flannel shirts and other thrift-style clothing. Nirvana helped pave the way for several talented groups that managed to enter musical mainstream during the 1990s—the Smashing Pumpkins, Pearl Jam, Hole (fronted by Cobain's wife, Courtney Love) and Nine Inch Nails.

The Hip-Hop Movement

In the early 1970s, black DJs began experimenting with live and recorded mixes. They did so by cutting up and pasting together parts of songs from different genres in a way that accentuated the break—typically the part of a jazz or funk song where the music "breaks" to allow the rhythm section to play unaccompanied—often using two turntables in order to replay the break quickly, creating a unique live-dub sound. Artists with roots in the inner city, such as DJ Kool Herc, began throwing block parties in an effort to bring together rival gangs through the music. A new musical genre emerged, built around improvisational spoken-word poetry, called rap, put to live break-beats, a form that became known as hip-hop for its "hip" (as in "current") rhythmic tempo. Break dancing and graffiti art became synonymous with the new hip-hop culture—all three aspects of the movement reflected a raw urban street vibe; spontaneous, low-tech creativity; and collaboration. Innovation came by way of competition, as scores of gang members found creative outlets for their aggression through impromptu dance-offs and verbal "battling," turning dilapidated public spaces into works of art with spray paint.

This hip-hop movement gave birth to a new brand of popular musical artists, including LL Cool J and Public Enemy, who, through the efforts of newcomer record labels such as Sugar Hill Records and Def Jam (the latter the brainchild of Russell Simmons and Rick Reuben), introduced hip-hop artists to wider audiences and eventually the American mainstream. Hip-hop soon gained footing in nightclubs, on the airwaves and on MTV, replacing disco as the new hot dance music. Other rap artists, including Run-DMC and the Beastie Boys, continued to evolve the genre, increasing hip-hop's influence, particularly among white middle-class young people.

A darker side of rap emerged from racial tensions in Southern California—that would eventually lead to the largest riot in California's history—after a jury acquitted four police officers accused of brutally beating Rodney King, an African-American, in 1992. Gangsta rap, as it would come to be known, was a departure from the relatively lighthearted party hip-hop that originated on the East Coast. It offered a pessimistic, rage-saturated perspective on life that was expressed through foul-mouthed lyrics and swagger, suggesting imminent violence. The parallels between gangsta rap in hip-hop and the early punks in rock 'n' roll are striking, with both subgenres developing as meaner offshoots of their relatively tame parents.

West Coast artists Ice-T, NWA, Snoop Dogg and Tupac Shakur, as well as infamous entrepreneur Suge Knight, who co-founded Death Row Records with Dr. Dre, played central roles in the development of gangsta rap. It was not long before the East Coast responded with its own version of gangsta rap, fronted by rappers such as The Notorious B.I.G., Sean "Puff Daddy" Combs and NAS, who were signed to

5.15

Kurt Cobain and his grunge band Nirvana achieved mainstream and commercial success, despite being on the music scene for a short period of time.

Pictorial Press Ltd/Alamy Stock Photo

The parallels between gangsta rap in hip-hop and the early punks in rock 'n' roll are striking, with both subgenres developing as meaner offshoots of their relatively tame parents.

Combs's Bad Boy Records. The tensions between the two factions received significant attention in the news media, which also helped increase the audiences for gangsta rap, generating huge record sales. The feud eventually turned violent, taking the lives of both The Notorious B.I.G. and Tupac Shakur, regarded as exceptional talents and foundational characters in the history of hip-hop.

After the deaths of The Notorious B.I.G. and Tupac Shakur, hip-hop continued to grow, mature and diversify, adding regional flavors and combining with other genres to produce a variety of subgenres. Many American and international hip-hop artists have made real contributions to the genre throughout its evolution. Although sales of hip-hop records began to steadily decline in 2005, possibly as the result of the increase in illegal peer-to-peer (P2P) file sharing, the genre continues to have a solid presence on the American *Billboard* charts and a large fan base.

MUSIC AND RADIO TRANSITION INTO THE DIGITAL AGE

Advances in technology continued to play an important role in forcing changes in how music was marketed and consumed. For most of the 20th century, the recording industry repeatedly found itself forced to alter its business and marketing methods to react to new technology. In the 1970s, the introduction of cassette tapes made it easy for consumers to copy music at home and share it with friends. This trend made the record labels desperate to find a new technology to deliver high-quality recordings to consumers—better quality than they could record themselves on cassette tape—that would put an end to consumers' copying and distributing of music. The technology that the record labels were looking for was the compact disc (CD). The compact disc format was the product of a cooperative partnership between Philips, which had acquired access to Laserdisc designs from MCA, and Sony around 1981.

5.16

Rapper and Bad Boy Records founder, Sean "Puff Daddy" Combs, played a central role in the establishment of East Coast gangsta rap.

ZUMA Press, Inc./Alamy Stock Photo

CD technology was able to reproduce digital audio with much higher fidelity than previous tape-based systems could achieve. This characteristic immediately made CDs the media of choice for music connoisseurs when they were first released to the general public in the United States in 1983. As with previous audio technologies, early CD systems were quite expensive when compared to cassette recorders, with CD players priced in the range of $2,000 and CDs going for between $12 and $15 each. By 1986, however, the cost of owning a CD player had decreased dramatically, to approximately $200. Although cassettes would remain the leading format for recorded music until 1994, the demise of LPs and eight-track cassettes allowed record labels to build their CD production numbers rapidly during the 1980s and early 1990s.

The shift to CDs gave the record industry a false sense of security, built around the erroneous belief that CD technology would stop the flow of consumer-to-consumer distribution of pirated copies of recorded music, and even stem the

The shift to CDs gave the record industry a false sense of security, built around the erroneous belief that CD technology would stop the flow of consumer-to-consumer distribution of pirated copies of recorded music, and even stem the growing tide of international music piracy. As we all know today, it didn't work.

growing tide of international music piracy. As we all know today, it didn't work. Not only did most consumers continue copying their music CDs using cassette tape recorders, but the growth of the personal computer (PC) industry would soon include CD burning (copying) capabilities as standard equipment on all PCs. These technologies not only led to a boom in music piracy, but also laid the groundwork for the Internet-based, music file-sharing culture that would soon pose an even greater threat to the record industry.[11]

Deregulation and Consolidation Transform 21st-Century Radio

In the transition to the Digital Age, radio, like its sister recording industry, struggled to reposition itself in order to retain its audience base. The U.S. government tried to help the radio industry and stimulate competition through deregulation, culminating in the Telecommunications Act of 1996. This act had a profound effect on radio by eliminating the laws that limited the number of AM and FM stations any one company could own. Rather than encouraging more competition, however, this legislation gave existing radio networks a green light to buy up scores of their smaller competitors. Clear Channel Communications became the largest radio conglomerate in the United States, growing from 46 radio stations before 1996 to more than 1,200 stations in 2002, covering 247 of the 250 top U.S. markets. Clear Channel also bought SFX, a major concert promoter and venue owner. Ultimately, Clear Channel/SFX gained a virtual stranglehold on the live concert market by combining the advertising power of 1,200 radio stations with the largest network of performance venues in the United States. By 2012, Clear Channel owned 850 stations, reaching 237 million listeners each month—making the company still the largest radio station ownership group in the United States.

In addition to consolidating radio stations, deregulation allowed for the restructuring of the recording industry through a number of high-profile mergers. These mergers resulted in three dominant labels, often simply referred to as "the majors": Universal Music Group, Sony Music Entertainment and Warner Music Group. As a consequence of this wave of consolidation, a small group of industry executives gained tremendous influence over which artists got recording contracts and exposure; they exploited this by dumping massive amounts of money into promoting tried-and-true performers, and essentially building a wall to keep out innovative talent.

At the same time, the majors had cultivated an independent promotion racket as a way to get around payola laws. Independent promoters played an overly influential role in creating and selling talent, setting up further roadblocks for independents.

The few dominant radio networks, such as the one operated by Clear Channel, gave top performers such as Madonna, Britney Spears, Dr. Dre, Ricky Martin and 'N Sync enormous amounts of airtime over two decades starting in the early 1990s. Playlists on the country's top radio stations became near mirror images of one another, leaving little room for new talent and innovative sounds. Multigenre artists expressed their views about the state of the music business in the wake of all of the deregulation and consolidation, decrying the need to fit a particular mold in order to get their material played on the radio.[12]

Meanwhile, easier consumer access to music on CDs, combined with the ever-increasing popularity of live concerts, began chipping away at network radio listenership. What was the reason for this significant drop-off? By 2002, both music consumers and many artists began to push back against what consumer advocate groups viewed as the monopolistic practices of the radio conglomerates, especially Clear Channel, that were resulting in the stagnant playlists and subpar music that network radio was offering.

The Recording Industry Association of America (RIAA), along with a coalition of artists, broadcasters and retailers, presented the U.S. Congress with a document that called for the investigation of monopolistic practices in the radio industry and decried the effects of the Telecommunications Act of 1996 as "anti-artist, anti-competition, and anti-consumer." This coalition found a champion in Wisconsin Senator Russell Feingold, who accused the radio industry—and Clear Channel specifically—of "bullying people" and presented tough new legislation that would rewrite payola legislation to include independent promotion and put more checks on the industry's power. However, a number of artists who woke up to find themselves on the same side as the recording industry began to voice apprehension at placing sole blame on the radio networks. Bert

Holman, manager of the legendary southern rock group the Allman Brothers Band, was quoted as saying, "The labels [recording industry] created the system, and now they're trying to cast blame somewhere else. They're certainly capable of that. If it was just the artists getting screwed by payola, they couldn't have cared less."[13]

In 2007, the FCC investigated and eventually disciplined four of the largest radio networks—Clear Channel, CBS Radio, Citadel Broadcasting and Entercom Communications—by assessing them $12.5 million in fines. Former recording industry executive Howie Kline reflected, "Payola corrupts the industr[ies], so we wind up with worse and worse music on the radio, which means worse and worse artists are being signed and developed. It reminds me of American politics, in that money has corrupted the entire process."[14]

Major radio networks are not the only ones being impacted by this growing trend. In the fall of 2012, Universal Music Group (UMG) undertook a major reorganization as a result of its merger with EMI, another major music label. The merger resulted in immediate staff layoffs in an effort by UMG to make its operations more efficient and thus more profitable at a time when the entire music industry, and especially the major music labels, face significant challenges brought about by the growth and popularity of online music sights and the trend of performers sidestepping these formerly dominant major labels to release their work directly to the Web.

Is the Internet Killing Radio?

It would be incorrect to think that the Internet has killed radio. However, the combined forces of deregulation, consolidation, and migration of traditional recording and radio content to the Web have sent the radio industry scrambling to adjust to the new market realities. In recent years, music-only programming has been losing ground to talk radio, a format based on discussions about topical issues of the day. National Public Radio (NPR) member stations, along with independent shortwave stations—the many small, independent stations in North America and throughout the world broadcasting informational, political and religious programming of all stripes—helped lay the foundation for the talk-radio programming model throughout the late 20th century. On U.S. AM and FM commercial stations, conservative political talk-show hosts such as Rush Limbaugh were quicker than their more liberal counterparts to recognize the vast potential of radio to build enormous followings by providing commentary on politics and even pop culture. Numerous other commentators gained popularity during the 1990s and 2000s, including radio and Fox News cable show hosts Sean Hannity and Glenn Beck. Humorist commentator and now-U.S. Senator Al Franken hosted a popular talk show on the now-bankrupt Air America Radio network prior to his election.

In addition to the pressures exerted by politically oriented talk radio, traditional music programming in the 1990s began seeing competition from the morning zoo format—a lifestyle talk-show formula that employs sparse music playlists, zany staged stunts and running pop-culture commentary. The rise of the morning zoo programming format paralleled MTV's shift from a pure music video program lineup to lifestyle programming. The morning zoo format is geared primarily to the 18-and-older male demographic. A few DJs have had enormous success with the morning zoo format, including Howard Stern and Don Imus, who, as shock jocks, have developed their own brand of racy, often controversial, comedic talk shows.

Other styles of radio programming are still attracting niche audience listeners in the 21st century. In addition to the continued popularity of NPR for both its music and news-talk radio programs, other commercial radio programming styles use a music mix formula known as the "four formats": AAA (adult album alternative) music, news-talk, classical and urban. Many of these stations are former NPR stations operated by colleges and universities that have had to reinvent themselves as commercial stations because their parent colleges found it difficult to support them as nonprofit enterprises. These "four formats" stations have struggled to compete for the shrinking pool of advertising dollars, with their foes being the usually better-positioned commercial AM and FM stations. As with many other types of smaller independent radio stations in the 21st century, the migration to Internet radio is helping to assure their survival.

Without question, Internet radio—that is, the migration of traditional radio content to the Web—has had the most significant impact on traditional broadcast radio. Enjoying the same commercial and audience reach as broadcast radio stations, but at a fraction of the operating cost, Internet radio stations have exploded on the Web. They have rapidly emerged as one of the most popular ways for citizens of the Digital Age to consume music in the 21st century. Offering huge music catalogs with minimal commercial interference, Internet radio stations such as Pandora and Slacker allow free access for listeners from anywhere they can connect to the Web, using any Web-enabled device—from PCs to smartphones to tablets. Just as automobile manufacturers jumped into satellite radio by including satellite radio receivers as either standard or optional equipment on new models of cars and trucks, in 2009 automakers began implementing plans to offer wireless Web receiver options as well.

Internet radio sites are on the verge of potentially taking over the traditional radio market. Most talk radio is now available for streaming over the Internet, with a significant amount of popular material also produced for consumption via podcasts—that is, media content produced and released especially for the Web and Web-enabled portable devices. Rather than the death of traditional radio, Internet radio could be merely the logical evolution of existing mass media to better utilize state-of-the-art technology in the age of convergence.

> Rather than the death of traditional radio, Internet radio could be merely the logical evolution of existing mass media to better utilize state-of-the-art technology in the age of convergence.

In the early part of the 21st century, consumers, bored with much of the commercial music being played on the radio and tired of paying exorbitant costs for CDs, were moving to the Internet as their primary source of music, forcing the radio and record industries to reform their business practices. The radio and record industries were being pushed to the brink of extinction by a technological and popular movement that was initially ignored by big business in the lead-up to the dawning of the new millennium.

Much has changed in radio industry since the early days of live broadcasts, studio musicians and the Radio Act of 1927. Technology and legislation have changed, and continue to change, the shape of radio. In the video segment "Radio Today and Tomorrow," veteran radio host Ron Della Chiesa and broadcast historian Bob Thompson share their visions on how the future of radio is being built today. ▶

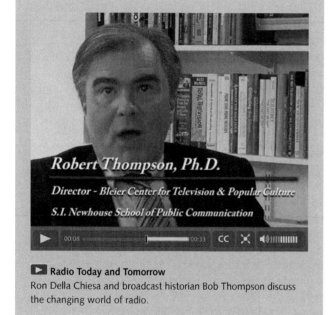

▶ Radio Today and Tomorrow
Ron Della Chiesa and broadcast historian Bob Thompson discuss the changing world of radio.

Commercial Satellite Radio

Commercial satellite radio was developed in the early 2000s in response to the growing number of music consumers, especially young people, who were dissatisfied with traditional music stations and their stale playlists, dominated by a handful of mega-artists, as well as in an effort to expand upon the success of talk radio. Satellite radio hoped to capitalize on the desire of U.S. listeners for greater diversity in radio programming by offering hundreds of channels of commercial-free music and talk in many categories, including channels dedicated to specific subgenres. In 2001 and 2002, respectively, XM Satellite Radio and Sirius Satellite Radio launched as the two main subscription-based competitors in the satellite radio market. For a fee ranging from $2.99 to $12.99 per month, these companies, which merged into the single network Sirius XM Radio, Inc. in 2007, provide listeners with interruption-free, clear-sounding entertainment made available via special satellite radio receivers nearly anywhere around the world. While the concept of satellite radio is appealing to consumers, the growth of Internet radio and the progress and proliferation of multimedia smartphones held back the number of subscriptions to satellite radio. This industry struggled to remain a financially viable business, with indications in early 2009 that Sirius XM was heading toward bankruptcy. By 2011, however, driven by the decreasing costs of satellite radio receivers and the standardization of their installation in new vehicles, Sirius XM began to turn the financial corner toward profitability, with *The Wall Street Journal* reporting the company's earnings and profits jumping.[15]

Peer-to-Peer (P2P) File Sharing Revolutionizes Music

In 1999, Shawn Fanning, a 19-year-old college dropout who had learned to program computers while working summers at his uncle's Internet company, stowed himself away for several weeks in an office in Hull, Massachusetts, to write the source code for a software program that would spark a revolution in the world of music. Fanning's creation, Napster, capitalized on the peer-to-peer (P2P) networking capabilities of the Internet—the ability of many users to allocate a small portion of their personal computer resources for file-sharing networks (see Chapter 7). By itself, Napster was not groundbreaking, because sharing data and files was already at the very foundation of the Internet. However, Napster, aided by advances in MP3 digital audio and CD-R (recordable CDs) technology, launched a revolution in how consumers, especially high school- and college-aged music consumers, acquired music.

Despite its most fervent efforts, the recording industry failed to get Congress to ban or severely restrict MP3 and CD-R technology. With the growing availability of broadband Internet connections by the mid-1990s, Napster was able to introduce its popular Internet service, which allowed the quick and easy transfer of music among its many members. Although music sharing had been going on for almost a decade, Napster represented the first large-scale P2P platform that successfully enabled the widespread free distribution of both original and pre-recorded music. Within a few months of its release, Fanning's Napster, which was available free of charge, had roughly 50 million users.[16]

> Although music sharing had been going on for almost a decade, Napster represented the first large-scale P2P platform that successfully enabled the widespread free distribution of both original and pre-recorded music.

By the late 1990s, the recording industry, seeing this new wave of digital music distribution as an all-out attack, sent its political and legal arm, the RIAA, after companies that were manufacturing and distributing digital recording systems, MP3s, CD-Rs, and recordable DVDs. It also targeted companies that were supplying consumers with the software or Internet-based platforms that enabled users to access music content for free, thereby skirting copyright protections. Of course, its targets included P2P file-sharing sites such as Napster. Congress enacted the Digital Millennium Copyright Act (DMCA) in 1998, aiding RIAA in its battle. The DMCA altered U.S. copyright law to criminalize the production and distribution of technology, devices and services whose intent was to bypass measures that controlled access to copyrighted works.

In 2001, the RIAA won an injunction against Napster in federal court, forcing the company to shut down its P2P file-sharing site. A few months later, Napster settled the case by agreeing to pay music copyright owners $26 million and make an additional advance payment of $10 million against future copyright license fees. These settlement fees were, however, just a fraction of the value of Napster because of its pivotal role in developing an entirely new Internet-based market for music. Less than a year after the settlement, Napster's assets were purchased by the German media giant Bertelsmann for $85 million. In 2008, Napster was sold once again, this time to consumer electronics retail chain Best Buy for a reported $121 million. Napster, while initially working against the record industry, in the end helped pave the way for the vast migration of music sales onto the Web. This migration, while hastening the death of music retailers such as the once-towering national chain Tower Records, also helped establish a Web-based music-consuming culture that forced a partial reinvention of the entire music industry. No company benefited more from this new culture shift than Apple, through its iTunes online music store.

Apple's iTunes online store began operations on April 28, 2003. Within a few years, it had grown to become the single largest seller of music in the world, amounting for approximately 70 percent of all retail music sales worldwide—or more than 9 billion tracks (songs) sold and downloaded by users—which also helped sales of Apple's popular iPods to skyrocket. Like the record and radio industries that came before, the dominance of Apple's iTunes store brought with it mounting complaints from both consumers and artists.

Both claimed that Apple was placing too many market controls on the artists whose music it would accept for sale on iTunes, which meant that the company was exercising far too much influence over popular music. Apple's market dominance was of particular concern to independent artists who felt locked out of the marketplace. Apple's iTunes is not at all an open media platform like YouTube, where anyone can post almost any media content they like as long as it does not violate YouTube's very general membership rules. Rather, iTunes is a controlled-content commercial enterprise where artists must apply to have their works included—a process that can be costly and difficult.

As an alternative to Apple's iTunes, a growing number of artists and small independent music labels are harnessing the power of the Internet, posting music videos on YouTube, launching their own Web-sites, and using popular music blogs and social media sites to undertake viral marketing efforts that can reach audiences in the millions and lead to unprecedented album sales and concert tour success. We read about such efforts—and their successes—at the very beginning of the chapter, as exemplified by Matt & Kim. With the help of their promotions partner Fader, the duo was also able to negotiate with iTunes to host their music—even setting the price below normal album costs. Matt & Kim are among the new wave of up-and-coming artists who have utilized convergent technologies to forge a new path to success—one that avoids the traditional industry-dominated relationship between bands and recording labels. As they discuss in the video segment introduced at the beginning of this chapter, Matt & Kim have built their career as a band on strong live performances, which they promoted via social media, product placement (their single "Daylight" in the Bacardi *Generations* ad) and free distribution of their music and videos through their own Website and YouTube. Although Matt & Kim encourage consumers to pay for the music they download over the Internet, they also believe that getting people out to their shows is much more important to their success than trying to cash in through the traditional record sales approach.

CONCLUSION: MUSIC AND RADIO CONVERGE—AND ENDURE

Following the interconnected history of the music and radio industries, especially through the critical years leading up and into the Digital Age, might lead readers of this chapter to ask the obvious question, "Are these two industries dead, or at least dying?" In other words, have changes in technologies and audience behaviors finally killed the two legacy industries that played such an important role in bringing us music, news and entertainment, essentially rendering them irrelevant as contributors to our culture and society? The answer is a definite no. Music and radio are not dead; they are actually thriving, albeit in new and different ways. In recent years, music has lost much of its edge as an influencer of social and political change. Yet the consumption of music as entertainment has never been stronger. Today the social influence of music also has its downside with, for example, some rap and hip-hop lyrics promoting violence and risky sexual behavior, especially to teenagers.

Music and radio are not dead; they are actually thriving, albeit in new and different ways.

Although it is true that both radio and especially the recording industry failed to adapt quickly to the Digital Age, and in fact attempted (unsuccessfully) to block the migration of music content to the Internet and consumer file sharing, all of the technological and market changes may have actually increased music sales. The advent of digital music and Web-based marketing and distribution mechanisms has breathed new life into the music business. The market for popular music is larger, and the diversity of audiences and artists broader, than ever before. Under the aegis of the Internet, more digital radio stations now offer a greater variety of programming, with the ability to reach vast regional, national and international audiences, and at lower costs, than broadcast radio could dream of just a few years ago. In addition to increasing the accessibility and variety of entertainment and music, the Internet has increased the role and impact of radio-based news reporting in the 21st century. Both radio and popular music—their content as well as the companies and organizations that successfully adapted to the new technological and market realities—are very much alive and thriving.

CHAPTER SUMMARY	KEY TERMS
The Cultural Influence of Music and Sound Recording Explores the historic roots of music and sound recordings and sets the stage on how these have had a profound influence of culture. **Visual Media** **Matt & Kim: Indie Rockers** The indie rock group Matt & Kim go up against the major record labels. 1. Independents Matt & Kim launched their careers on the Internet and leveraged their early exposure into international fame and success as both performance and recording artists. Which up-and-coming artists today have the potential to follow in their footsteps, and what will drive them to success? 2. Compare and contrast the career trajectory of Matt & Kim with that of recent new music stars who were "launched" with the support of major recording labels and TV exposure on popular shows such as *American Idol* and *The Voice*.	sound recording phonograph Nickel-in-the-Slot speakeasies ragtime Tin Pan Alley jazz covers gramophone V-discs
The Birth of the Radio Broadcasting Industry Tells the fascinating story of the birth of radio broadcasting and discusses the major characters and conflicts that made radio possible. **Visual Media** **Evolution of Radio Programs** An encapsulated look at the history and evolution of radio programming with Professor Bob Thompson of Syracuse University. 1. Compare and contrast the radio programs during the "Golden Age" of radio with the structure of popular radio programs of today. 2. How has changing culture and changing audience demand for radio changed the sort of radio programs available today?	radio broadcasting commercial radio Radio Act of 1927 Federal Radio Commission (FRC) amplitude modulation (AM) frequency modulation (FM)
Popular Music: The First Cultural Shift Discusses the evolution of the radio broadcast industry and outlines the connection of technological innovation with corporate interests and governmental regulations.	popular music rock 'n' roll R&B ("rhythm and blues") payola skiffle multitrack recording
The Music of Revolution: The Second Cultural Shift Explains how changes in popular music styles and content helped to drive social and cultural change, especially in America.	folk music psychedelic sound folk rock
Musical Styles Diversify Looks at the radical changes and explosion of popular music through the 1960s and 1970s, which helped launch and grow the careers of international artists that are still very popular today—40 and 50 years later.	arena rock bands hard rock heavy metal punk rock
MTV and the Birth of Music Videos Examines the multiple trends spawned and market segments addressed as the music industry refines its approach to packaging sex, rebellion and social messages to increase profits.	music video alternative music independent (indie) music grunge rap hip-hop gangsta rap

Music and Radio Transition into the Digital Age Demonstrates how the Digital Age and new digital technologies have forever changed how we select and consume music. **Visual Media** **Radio Today and Tomorrow** Ron Della Chiesa and broadcast historian Bob Thompson discuss the changing world of radio. 1. Why do you think broadcast radio will either survive and prosper or become obsolete in the next five to 10 years? 2. What is there that is "special" or unique about broadcast radio that Internet radio will never be able to duplicate?	compact disc (CD) CD technology Telecommunications Act of 1996 the majors talk radio shortwave stations morning zoo format shock jocks four formats Internet radio podcasts commercial satellite radio Digital Millennium Copyright Act (DMCA)

NOTES

1 Scaruffi, P. (2007). *A history of popular music before rock music*. Omniware.
2 Burns, K. (1991). *Empire of the air*. PBS. Retrieved from http://earlyradiohistory.us/sec020.htm
3 Blanchard, M. A. *History of the mass media in the United States*. Retrieved from www.history-of-rock.com/payola.htm
4 The history of African American music writers: Brooks, L., & Young, C. (2003). *Encyclopedia.com*. Retrieved from www.encyclopedia.com/history/news-wires-white-papers-and-books/history-african-american-music; *History: BMI and R&B/hip-hop music*. (2013). BMI (Broadcast Music Incorporated). Retrieved from www.bmi.com/genres/entry/history_bmi_and_rbhip-hop_music; Nero, M. E. (2015, June 29). *The definition of soul music*. Retrieved from http://randb.about.com/od/rb12/p/SoulMusic.htm; Brooks, L., & Young, C. (2003). The history of African American music. *Encyclopedia.com*. Retrieved from www.encyclopedia.com/history/news-wires-white-papers-and-books/history-african-american-music
5 DiMartino, D. (2004). Hitsville USA. In P. Trynka (Ed.), *The beatles: 10 years that shook the world*. London: Dorling Kindersley.
6 Kemp, M. (2001). *The Rolling Stone Encyclopedia of Rock & Roll*. Simon & Schuster. Portions of the Phil Spector biography appeared in this work. Retrieved from www.rollingstone.com/artists/philspector/biography
7 Chaunday, B. (2004, December 3). Brian Wilson, Faces of the Week. *BBC News*. Retrieved from http://news.bbc.co.uk/2/hi/uk_news/magazine/4065193.stm
8 Tiber, E. (1994). How woodstock happened. *The Times Herald-Record* (Middletown, NY).
9 Retrieved from http://vids.myspace.com/index.cfm?fuseaction=vids.individual&VideoID=32304837
10 Lee, M. (2009, June 26). Michael Jackson's thriller: Interview with John Landis. *The Telegraph*.
11 Morton, J. (2004). *Sound recording: The life story of a technology*. Johns Hopkins University Press.
12 Kot, G. (2009). *Ripped: How the wired generation revolutionized music*. Scribner, p. 19.
13 Ibid., p. 22.
14 Ibid., pp. 21–23.
15 Sirius 3Q profit jumps. (2011, November 1). *The Wall Street Journal*.
16 Kot, G. (2009). *Ripped: How the wired generation revolutionized music*. Scribner, p. 25.

6

Film and Television

CHAPTER OUTLINE

Mise-en-Scène An overview of the significance of mise-en-scène in filmic storytelling.

A Trip to the Moon View the special effects—spectacular for their time—of Méliès's *A Trip to the Moon*.

The Great Train Robbery Edwin Porter's crosscutting editing technique made displaying action taking place in multiple locations possible.

The Magic of Special Effects and the Digital Age

The Maltese Falcon John Huston's *The Maltese Falcon* (1941), adopted from the German expressionist style.

Narrative in Television
The Evolution of Television
Television Genres
Conflicting Visions of the Future of Television
Conclusion: The Audience Drives the Future of Film and Television

Special Effects Audiences loved special effects, as depicted in this short video history.

LEARNING OBJECTIVES

1. Explain how Joseph Campbell's "hero's journey" informs the narrative structure of many film and television narratives.
2. Illustrate how the early innovations of both Georges Méliès and Edwin Porter changed the way films represented fantastical environments and action adventure stories.
3. Outline the role the Hollywood studio system played in establishing the movie industry's profit model.
4. Assess the impact the foreign film industry had on the style and narrative of American cinema.
5. Evaluate how the use of special effects such as motion control and animatronics changed the way filmmakers create scenes.
6. Compare and contrast narrative storytelling in television and in film to demonstrate how the two styles have influenced each other.
7. Describe how the Big Four networks came to dominate television broadcasting and how their dominance has affected television programming both now and in the past.
8. Illustrate ways in which cable and satellite television have helped to spur innovation in television programming.
9. Assess the impact advancing media technology access portals such as Internet streaming and DVRs have on the television programming business model.

THE AVENGERS.

released in 2012, was a 3-D action blockbuster film based on *The Avengers* comic books published by Marvel Comics in the early 1960s. The film's storyline pits comic book-style heroes against a stable of evil and powerful villains in a classic battle of good overpowering evil to save the world. The lead character, "Nick Fury," played by Samuel L. Jackson, brings together an alliance of superheroes, each with special powers and portrayed by such leading actors as Robert Downey Jr. as "Iron Man," Scarlett Johansson as "Black Widow," Mark Ruffalo as "The Hulk," Chris Evans as "Captain America," Chris Hemsworth as "Thor" and Jeremy Renner as "Hawkeye." This group of superheroes joins forces in a mission to track down and destroy a powerful "cube" before it can fall into the hands of evil adversaries.

This visually dazzling 3-D action adventure film not only delivers a captivating filmic experience built around compelling characters but also represents a clear example of the basic storytelling structure first outlined by American mythologist Joseph Campbell in his book *The Hero with a Thousand Faces*. Campbell popularized the notion that all stories, especially those told through films and television, engage viewers most effectively when they revolve around characters and stories with which audiences can easily and quickly identify. In other words, the most enthralling stories allow us to vicariously exist in a mythological world populated by recognizable heroes who, guided by mentors, set out on epic quests to save the world.

These stories emphasize a "hero" who is called to adventure and challenged to undertake a difficult journey. An event that forces the hero to leave the comfort of an ordinary life for something greater typically triggers that journey, where the stakes are high and the enemies may not be easily identifiable. A wise character—a guide or mentor—supports the hero along the way, revealing insights about the hero's world, the hero's self and the hero's abilities. The hero eventually faces the ultimate ordeal: a moment in which we await the hero's success or failure, survival or death; when we await the demise of one relationship or the strengthening of another.

Scriptwriters of American film and television have long used this story of the "hero's journey," what Campbell identified as the **monomyth**. In classic filmic or television narrative, the storyline typically ends with some sort of path to success for the hero. Yet, this path does not necessarily mean that the hero is out of the woods. It is enough that the hero is equipped with the skills and understanding needed to defeat the enemy and capture the prize, whether actual or symbolic. These story plot beats, which combine adventure and suspense, all culminate in what Campbell called the resurrection—the moment when the journey and the ordeal forever transform the hero.

Monomythic narratives organize themselves around a main plot, which unfolds in the form of challenges that confront a number of principal characters. A series of subplots then further complicates the primary plot. Secondary characters enter the scene as well, to either support or antagonize the hero. These basic storytelling elements exist in almost all filmic and television narratives and, according to Campbell, in mythic story structures that are common to all cultures.[1] In the purest sense, film and television are in many ways storytelling industries. This chapter explores that idea and begins with an examination of storytelling in film.

6.1

MARVEL Enterprises/Album/Newscom

NARRATIVE IN FILM

Campbell, in addition to being a popular lecturer, served as a script consultant to many celebrated Hollywood films, including George Lucas's *Star Wars* series. Campbell's ideas about narrative storytelling have influenced many contemporary movies, including the *Harry Potter* films, James Cameron's 2009 hit *Avatar* and *The Avengers* (2012). While some storylines are resolved in these films, others are left open to viewers' interpretations; still others suggest the possibility of a sequel. Regardless of such structural variations, narrative storytelling contributes greatly to cinema's effect and power. Audiences consistently gravitate to films that offer familiar narratives, albeit with innovative twists and variations.

Table 6.1 Film Genres

Comedy	*Men in Black 3* (2012)
Drama	*The Hunger Games* (2012)
Action/Adventure/Thriller	*American Assassin* (2013)
Mystery/Suspense	*Atlas Shrugged* (2011)
Romance	*The Vow* (2012)
Western	*Django Unchained* (2012)
Crime/Gangster	*End of Watch* (2012)
Horror	*Underworld Awakening* (2012)
Fantasy/Science Fiction	*John Carter* (2012)
Musical	*Les Misérables* (2012)
Foreign	*A Separation* (2012; Iran)

Genres enable us to organize film types, thereby helping us to determine a film's basic narrative. Categorizing movies within established genres not only allows viewers to identify the story structure of the film, but also helps both producers and distributors to market their products more easily. Major awards programs such as the Academy Awards and the Golden Globe Awards annually reinforce the well-established system of movie genres. Producers who attempt to move too far away from these accepted genres do so at significant economic risk. This does not mean that cross-genre films—films that fall within more than one category—cannot do well. Action-comedy or crime thriller films such as *Inception* (2010) and *The Bourne Legacy* (2012), respectively, and romantic comedies such as *This Means War* (2012) regularly do well at the box office. For such films to succeed, however, regardless of how well the films cleverly straddle multiple genres, audiences must recognize the narrative style. Table 6.1 lists the common film genres and offers an example of each.

Hybrid films have grown popular as well. While still employing established storytelling techniques, these films tend to mix other stylistic components often rooted in other media. Disney was the first major movie studio to produce a string of highly successful hybrid films that combined music and animation—for example, *The Lion King* (1994) and, in partnership with the animation production house Pixar, *Finding Nemo* (2003) and *Monsters University* (2013). In many ways James Cameron's blockbuster *Avatar* (2009) opened new ground for hybrid films, integrating characters and environments produced by computer-generated imagery (CGI) with real actors. This inventive new style is destined to be imitated by future filmmakers.

The environment or mise-en-scène of a film contributes greatly to a viewer's experience of it. A French term meaning "placing on stage," a film's mise-en-scène comprises everything set before a camera: from physical props (e.g., a leafless tree, a half-empty glass, an abandoned house), to the costumes, to where the actual actors stand in place or in motion during a scene. For most films, the mise-en-scène reflects the central themes of the narrative. For example, *The Road* (2009), which is based on the post-apocalyptic novel by Cormac McCarthy, would not have had the same impact on the audience had the film's setting been less bleak and foreboding, or had the characters not been placed as minor elements in the landscape. To better understand how a single image can turn into a powerful scene, view the video "Mise-en-Scène." ▶

▶ *Mise-en-Scène*
An overview on the significance of mise-en-scène in filmic storytelling.

THE EARLY INNOVATORS OF FILM

No single person is responsible for inventing motion pictures. Nevertheless, Thomas Edison in the United States and Auguste and Louis Lumière in France led the building of the industry's foundation. (For more on this topic, see Chapter 2.) Unlike the Lumières, who saw their filmmaking as an extension of art, Edison focused on producing and distributing movies that would entertain mass audiences—and make him lots of money.

The Special Effects of Georges Méliès

In France, a French stage magician-turned-filmmaker named Georges Méliès (1861–1938), inspired by a demonstration of the Lumière brothers' technology, established a rooftop studio where he began pioneering work on special effects and science-fiction films. Méliès's films were nearly devoid of any serious plot but rich with effects, including multiple exposures, as seen in *The One Man Band*, and time-lapse photography, first introduced time in *Carrefour de l'Opera*. Méliès's famous film *A Trip to the Moon* (*Le Voyage dans la Lune*) also pushed the limits of both animation and feature length.[2]

Méliès's pioneering work earned him the distinction of being one of the principal inventors of cinema and founders of movie special effects. He was also one of the first filmmakers to recognize film's potential for delivering fantastical environments, entertaining charac-

A Trip to the Moon
View the special effects—spectacular for its time—of Méliès's *A Trip to the Moon*.

ters and a visual spectacle of events—both real and imaginary. View *A Trip to the Moon* for yourself here and consider how the effects displayed in this film short have inspired the special effects of modern-day films. ▶

The Editing Techniques of Edwin Porter

In the United States, Edison had hired a projectionist named Edwin Porter, who had firsthand experience entertaining audiences with movies. Porter became the head of motion picture production for Edison's New York studio, not only operating the camera but also directing shots and making final edits. Porter's most important work, *The Great Train Robbery* (1903), set new standards for film production through his use of crosscutting, an editing technique that established action taking place in multiple locations. It solidified Porter as one of the most important American filmmakers of the early 20th century.[3] Identify crosscutting in action in this segment from *The Great Train Robbery* and consider how different the film would be without this effect. ▶

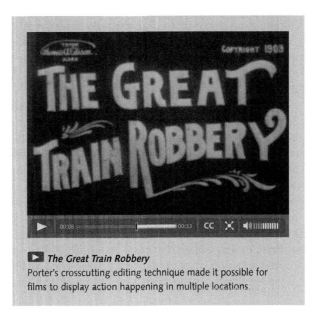

The Great Train Robbery
Porter's crosscutting editing technique made it possible for films to display action happening in multiple locations.

The combined contributions of Méliès and Porter significantly advanced the young movie industry. By introducing strong narrative storytelling and dazzling special effects, these pioneers convinced audiences throughout America and Europe that the cinema was a fantastic new medium offering unimagined entertainment worth paying to see. Due in no small part to Méliès's and Porter's creativity and innovation, scores of nickelodeons—theaters that charged 5 cents for admission—sprang up all over the United States in 1905 and increased the demand for new film content.[4] Nickelodeons were especially popular among European immigrants because the price of admission was low and the films were silent. Title cards containing dialogue to help move the plot along could be changed easily to accommodate any language, essentially providing multilanguage subtitles.[5]

THE HOLLYWOOD STUDIO SYSTEM

In 1908, numerous film companies holding major patents formed an oligopoly (a market dominated by a small number of sellers), which they named the Motion Picture Patents Company (MPPC). The MPPC was the brainchild of Thomas Edison, who was determined to secure an industry dominance for himself and a few other early U.S. companies that held a variety of patents on film, cameras and projectors. By joining the MPPC, companies could pool resources and demand licensing fees from film producers, distributors and exhibitors outside their group. Many of the companies that joined the MPPC did so under the threat that Edison would sue them otherwise.

Members of the broad group that did not belong to the MPPC were referred to as "independents." These independents imported and used equipment that was not licensed by the MPPC to get around the oligopoly's control and, in doing so, created a thriving underground film culture. As a reaction to the upstart independents, the MPPC formed a strong-arm subsidiary known as the General Film Company (GFC) to pressure the independents into compliance. The GFC not only tried to confiscate the nonlicensed equipment from independent filmmakers, but also sought to withhold supplies from exhibitors that played independent films.[6]

The independents soon began building their own film oligopoly. In 1910, the American Mutoscope and Biograph Company sent D. W. Griffith (1875–1948), an aspiring playwright-turned-film-director, to Los Angeles to film a melodrama set in 1800s California, titled *In Old California*. A few miles north of their location, Griffith and his crew discovered a village named Hollywood, whose inhabitants welcomed Griffith and his team. Within a few years, scores of East Coast independents had made their way out west to take up shop in Hollywood. From this base in California, eight film companies went on to turn the industry into the enormous studio-based system that dominated most of the 20th century.

By the time of the Great Depression (1930s), five major studios known as the Big Five and three minor film companies had solidified their hold on the U.S. film industry, with their combined output accounting for 95 percent of the nation's film production. Seventy-five percent of the major film studios' revenues came from their ownership of nearly 3,000 theaters nationwide, a clear sign that *vertical integration*—a system in which a single owner or management group controls all levels and all aspects of the production and distribution supply chain—had become the dominant business model of the industry.[7] Movies had become big business in the United States, and the major studios founded by the so-called independents became the driving force during the movie industry's Golden Age. Table 6.2 offers a brief overview of the founding of these studios and the means by which they came to create America's movie culture.

While silent film dominated the early years of the movie industry, the Golden Age gave birth to the talkies—films with soundtracks that mixed location sounds (real or constructed) with dialogue and background music. A number of technical challenges, however, plagued the pioneers of sound cinema. Although separate devices existed that could record either sound or movement, technology did not yet exist that could synchronize images and sound, amplify sound for the growing audience sizes, or ensure sound quality of the recordings, leaving much to be desired of the new films.

Table 6.2 The Studio System of Hollywood's Golden Age

THE MAJORS	THE MINORS
Paramount Pictures	**United Artists (UA)**
• Founded by Adolf Zukor (1873–1976) in 1912	• Founded in 1919 by actress Mary Pickford, actor Charlie Chaplin, actor/producer/director Douglas Fairbanks and director D. W. Griffith—four well-known film-industry veterans seeking to fight back against attempts by movie companies to control the salaries and creative interests of actors under the studio system
• Merged the Famous Players-Lasky Corporation and the Chicago-based Balaban and Katz theater chain, which was acquired in 1925	
• Two marquee stars during its early period: Bing Crosby and Bob Hope	
• Currently owned by Viacom, one of today's Big Six majors	• Pickford and Chaplin joined forces with Orson Welles, Disney, Goldwyn, Selznick, Korda and Wanger in 1941 to continue the actor-advocate spirit of UA; only when Arthur Krim and Robert Benjamin were given permission by Pickford and Chaplin to attempt to revive UA in 1951 did the company produce anything significant
Loew's/MGM (Metro-Goldwyn-Mayer)	
• Founded by Marcus Loew (1870–1927) in 1924	
• Merged the Metro Pictures Corporation (1916), Goldwyn Pictures (1917) and Louis B. Mayer's Pictures	
• Star system within MGM established by Louis B. Mayer (1884–1957)	• Currently owned by MGM
The Fox Film Corporation	**Universal Pictures**
• Founded by independent film pioneer William Fox (1879–1952) in 1915	• Founded by Carl Laemmle, a clothing store manager in Oshkosh, Wisconsin, in 1912, who left his job at the clothing store to purchase and operate the first of several nickelodeons
• Merged two of his startups: a distribution company called Greater New York Film Rental and a production house called Fox Office Attractions	
• One of the first vertically integrated studios	• When Edison's MPPC began levying greater exhibition fees, Laemmle and a number of other independent nickelodeon owners decided to produce their own films
• Fox was primarily interested in the business side of making movies and set out to corner the theater and exhibition technology markets; filmmaking was only an add-on business endeavor	
	• Started the Yankee Film company in 1909, which quickly developed into the Independent Moving Pictures Company (IMP)
• Following the death of MGM's Marcus Loew in 1927, Fox nearly achieved the purchase of MGM from the Loew family, but Louis B. Mayer convinced the U.S. government that the sale would violate antitrust laws	• Abandoned Edison's practice of withholding billing and screen credits to performers, earning the respect of the actors
	• Credited by many for inventing the star system, because Laemmle had promoted the first movie star
• Currently owned by News Corporation, one of today's Big Six majors	• Merged with eight smaller companies to form the Universal Film Manufacturing Company in 1912
Warner Bros.	• Did not become a vertically integrated film company like most of its competitors, but instead remained focused exclusively on movie production and distribution (not exhibition)
• Founded by Harry (1881–1958), Albert (1884–1957), Sam (1887–1927) and Jack Warner (1892–1978)	
• Opened their first theater in New Castle, Pennsylvania, in 1903	• Currently owned by General Electric and Comcast
• Formed Warner Bros. Pictures in 1904	**The Columbia Pictures Corporation**
• Opened Warner Bros. Studio on Sunset Boulevard in Hollywood in 1918	• Founded by Harry and Jack Cohn in 1919 under the name Cohn-Brandt-Cohn Film Sales
• First successful films: *Where the North Begins* (1923), which featured a French-born German shepherd named Rin Tin Tin; the film saved the Warners from imminent bankruptcy and provided the touchstone for a long line of serials featuring the dog	• In a move spearheaded by the Cohn brothers, Brandt was bought out and the name was changed to Columbia in 1924
	• A horizontally integrated company that did not acquire its own exhibition chain, like Universal Studios

(Continued)

Table 6.2 (Continued)

THE MAJORS	THE MINORS
• Responsible for the *Harry Potter* film series, the highest-grossing film series of all time • Currently owned by Time Warner, one of today's Big Six majors **RKO (Radio-Keith-Orpheum) Pictures** • Founded in 1928 by RCA's David Sarnoff (1891–1971), who needed a way to market RCA's innovative sound-on-film technology, the RCA Photophone • Resulted from the merger and acquisition of the Keith-Albee-Orpheum (KAO) theater chain (which included the U.S. division of Pathé, the world's leading equipment and production company, which itself had merged with the Producers Distributing Company owned by American film director Cecil B. De Mille) and the Film Booking Offices of America (FBO) • Established itself as a film company that would compete with Warner Bros. in the production of all-talking films • Currently co-produce new productions with other companies	• Known for producing mostly low-budget, nearly B-quality films • Persistently encouraged by director Frank Capra between 1927 and 1939 to invest in better material and bigger-budget films, resulting in the Oscar-winning *It Happened One Night* as well as the popular *Lady for a Day* and *Mr. Smith Goes to Washington* • Solidified up-and-comer James Stewart as a star and Columbia as a major studio after the success of *Mr. Smith Goes to Washington* • The last major studio to use Technicolor • Currently owned by Sony

6.2

The studio United Artists was founded in 1919 by D. W. Griffith (left) with stars Mary Pickford, Charlie Chaplin (seated) and Douglas Fairbanks (right).

[D. W. Griffith, Mary Pickford, Charlie Chaplin seated and Douglas Fairbanks at the signing of the contract establishing United Artists motion picture studio]. Courtesy of Library of Congress

New Sound Technologies Herald the Success of Talkies

To address these challenges, numerous European and American inventors created technologies to improve film sound quality. Sound-on-film technology, as developed by Lee De Forest, employed a simple and effective system that imprinted sound into light waves that could be recorded as visual images onto the same continuous film strip. It quickly became the favored technology.

The first enormously successful talkie, although it was not the first ever to be produced, was Al Jolson's *The Jazz Singer* (1927), a film distributed by Warner Bros. Studio.[8] *The Jazz Singer* interspersed a musical score and sound effects with live-recorded musical numbers and two ad-libbed speech scenes; its success proved the potential profit of producing talking films and catapulted the movie industry to a completely new level.

6.3

Scene from Warner Bros, *The Jazz Singer* (1927), the movie industry's first enormously successful "talkie."

Warner Brothers/Album/Newscom

The Star System Maximizes Studio Profits

The success of the studio system depended heavily on the star system—promotion of the 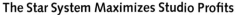 image, rather than the acting, of notable film stars. The studios committed these stars to seven-year contracts, which were intended to maximize studio profits and to prevent them from working outside of their studio. Studios micromanaged every aspect of their stars' careers and personal lives, including loaning them out to other studios, forcing them into roles, and developing scripts solely based on cultivating greater stardom and ticket sales.

Today, remnants of this star system still exist, with fans flocking to the theaters to watch films starring such favorites as Brad Pitt, Cate Blanchett, Jennifer Aniston, Matt Damon, Leonardo DiCaprio and Halle Berry, to name just a few. Unlike their counterparts during the Golden Age of Hollywood, however, today's celebrity actors retain their own managers, agents and publicity firms and are far less controlled by the studios and production companies. In fact, leading actors are often co-owners of their films as opposed to being stuck in compensation deals tightly controlled by the studios during the Golden Age.

The Big Five Start to Lose Power

By the outbreak of World War II, the Big Five studios controlled so much of the film industry that together they became a syndicated monopoly with control over the nation's economy and culture. Toward the end of the 1930s, leading up to the U.S. entrance into World War II, the federal government, at President Roosevelt's behest, began to take aim at the Big Five (Paramount, MGM, Warner Bros., Twentieth Century Fox and RKO) and the industry's abuse of fair trade laws.

In 1938, the U.S. Department of Justice sued the movie industry for violating the Sherman Antitrust Act (part of the American antitrust laws) and indicted the Big Five. The studios claimed that vertical integration and block-booking practices were necessary to make film production and exhibition a financially viable enterprise. The block-booking system typically bundled five films together—a single high-quality A-film along with four lower-quality A- and B-films—and theater operators would then be expected to rent and show the entire package rather than just one film of their choice. The government, using economic data from World War II, clearly showed that the industry had enjoyed a massive windfall during the period. Facing the prospect of forced government regulation, the studios attempted to broker a deal based on the following terms:

1. The Big Five would agree to cease blocking theaters from booking independently produced short films along with feature films.
2. They would no longer force theaters to book movie packages of more than five films.
3. They would no longer force blind purchase of film packages, but would instead allow theater owners or their representatives an opportunity to view films before they were purchased or rented—a practice called trade showing that still continues today.
4. They would agree to the creation of a regulatory administration to ensure that these changes were being carried out.[9]

The federal court trial ended in January 1946, culminating with a ruling that the major studios were guilty of conspiracy in restraint of trade and in violation of the Sherman Antitrust Act. The court order, however, did not force the major studios to break up their holdings until the case reached the Supreme Court. On May 4, 1948, the U.S. Supreme Court upheld the antitrust conviction, but sent the case back to the lower courts to consider a forced and total divestiture of vertical integration. The major studios' antitrust battle with the government hastened the end of their dominance over the movie industry.[10]

The Rise of the Financing-Distribution Model

As U.S. regulation and the film-viewing audience changed, the major studios lost ground to scores of independent production groups. Beginning in the 1950s and into the 1970s, Hollywood would begin its farewell to the original Big Five. RKO became defunct; MGM merged with United Artists; and Walt Disney Productions enjoyed a rise in the ranks.

Following the death of the studio system and the divestiture of the vertical integration structure, a new film industry model emerged: the financing-distribution model. Unlike the studio system, this new system relied on outside financing to create a film. Distribution companies would find theaters to circulate the film and often help with the initial project financing. Additionally, smaller film production companies used talent agents to help find and secure actors rather than developing their own stars.

Although studios could no longer maximize their profits by controlling the entire production to exhibition process, they did find themselves protected from the financial risks that often plagued the industry under the studio system. The financing-distribution model reduced the financial burden on film production companies and allowed for a wider spectrum of film content to make it into the mainstream. Major studios began relying on independent filmmakers to produce movies for distribution, making it feasible for those who could acquire financing and put together a good film to have their movie picked up and distributed by a major studio.

> Major studios began relying on independent filmmakers to produce movies for distribution, making it feasible for those who could acquire financing and put together a good film to have their movie picked up and distributed by a major studio.

Post-Studio System Distribution and Exhibition Practices

Under the post-studio system, separate film distributors and exhibitors negotiate the terms of an exhibition license, which specifies when and where theaters will show a film and the financial agreement between the two parties. To drum up interest, film distributors deliver promotional materials and unfinished copies of films as previews to theater booking agents, focusing on getting as many movies shown on as many screens in as many theaters as possible. Generally, distributors plan a film's release to match up with the peak filmgoing times of the year: summer and the major holidays.

Although distributors usually benefit the most from releasing a film during this time, exhibitors need a steady stream of films to ensure a year-round audience attendance and profit. Distributors are aware of this necessary give-and-take and traditionally develop their release strategies to help theaters maintain steady ticket sales. Meanwhile, booking agents are constantly evaluating movies and deciding which ones will sell the best in their geographical area during any time of year. Negotiating the terms of an exhibition license can be quite complex, covering factors such as the distributor's investment, the exhibitor's operating costs, the period for which the exhibitor will show the film and the percentage of the ticket sales that the exhibitor will pay to the distributor. Film distributors typically receive about 90 percent of box-office sales back from the exhibitor. While the remaining 10 percent might not seem like it would leave theaters with much profit, exhibitors make most of their money from concession sales and not the ticket sales.

Film distributors typically receive about 90 percent of box-office sales back from the exhibitor. While the remaining 10 percent might not seem like it would leave theaters with much profit, exhibitors make most of their money from concession sales and not the ticket sales.

The Film Industry After the Golden Age

The courts' decision to dismantle the Big Five studios may have signaled the end of the Golden Age of American film, but it did not result in the industry's demise. From the 1950s through the 1970s, despite the growing popularity of television and government attempts to censor films, the film industry strengthened via a change in its business model. Studios began focusing their efforts on producing blockbusters—spectacular, huge-budget productions such as *Gone with the Wind* (1939), *Around the World in 80 Days* (1956) and *Ben-Hur* (1959).

These productions not only demonstrated proven profitability (and continue to do so even today), they also attracted huge audiences, making it very difficult for television networks to compete. New mechanical and optical special effects including wide-screen technology such as Cinemascope, Cinerama and studio experimentation with 3-D further increased the draw. In addition, American theaters in the post-studio system were free to display foreign films, a liberty that has continued to contribute to the industry's popularity and survival.

6.4

Following the end of Hollywood's Golden Age, *Gone with the Wind* was one of the earliest blockbusters and reflected a financially successful change in the movie industry's business model.

Moviestore Collection Ltd/Alamy Stock Photo

THE INFLUENCE OF INTERNATIONAL CINEMA STYLES

To appreciate the impact of international cinema on American filmmaking, we must trace the art and industry of filmmaking back to where it all began—Europe. While the contribution of global cinema reaches far beyond the scope of a single chapter, understanding the development of film outside of the United States is critical to understanding cinematic styles today.

European Cinema

Nordisk Films, the oldest film studio in operation, was founded in a suburb of Copenhagen in 1906 by Danish film pioneer Ole Olsen (1863–1943); in 1908, he opened a New York City branch called the Great Northern Film Company. 1910 marked the beginning of the company's venture into feature filmmaking (films made for theatrical distribution). As with most of the films produced in Denmark at the time, Nordisk's

6.5

Scene from the German expressionist film, *Der Student von Prag* (*The Student from Prague*) (1926).

Hulton Archive/Stringer

▶ *The Maltese Falcon*
John Huston's *The Maltese Falcon* (1941), adopted from the German expressionist style.

movies comprised erotic melodrama pieces that had to be toned down for international consumption. Nordisk Films continues to operate today as part of the Egmont Media Group, one of Europe's leading media conglomerates.

German expressionist cinema focused on the darker side of the human experience and revolved around themes of madness, insanity and betrayal. To convey a sense of irrational fear on film, directors relied on dramatic lighting and extreme set and costume designs. Expressionism dominated German cinema through most of the 1920s. Films such as Fritz Lang's *Metropolis* (1927) influenced not only later German and other international cinematic movements, but would eventually cross over into the film sets of later science-fiction films, such as Ridley Scott's *Blade Runner* (1982). German expressionist films also exerted a major influence on the cinematic style that would come to dominate the 1940s and 1950s, first in France and then in the United States—the distinct black-and-white style of film noir.

Popular in the 1940s and early 1950s, the French style known as film noir (or "black film") distinguished itself from other European styles with its overall cynical and menacing overtones. To capture this mood, French directors employed black-and-white visuals, low-key lighting and urban settings to mimic the American crime and mystery novels that inspired the genre. Plots featured stories of entrapment, corruption, betrayal and revenge. Classic American filmmakers who adopted this style included John Huston (*The Maltese Falcon*, 1941) and Alfred Hitchcock (*Strangers on a Train*, 1951). Born in England, Hitchcock worked largely in the United States during his prime filmmaking years. The American film noir style inspired films such as Roman Polanski's *Chinatown* (1974), Ridley Scott's *Blade Runner* (1982), Curtis Hanson's *L.A. Confidential* (1997), Shane Black's *Kiss Kiss Bang Bang* (2005) and Paul McGuigan's *Lucky Number Sleven* (2006). See whether you can identify the realist elements in the film *The Maltese Falcon*. ▶

The next generation of French filmmakers took the film noir to new heights. Independent directors experimented with new cinematic styles that focused on complex character relationships, sexual passions and religious turmoil—such themes characterized the French New Wave. The most notable of these New Wave directors, who dominated the 1960s and 1970s, included François Truffaut (*The Wild Child*, 1970; *Day for Night*, 1973), Jean-Luc Godard (*Breathless*, 1960) and Eric Rohmer (*Chloe in the Afternoon*, 1972).

Italian neorealism featured nonprofessional actors in storylines about the poor and working class. Vittorio De Sica's *The Bicycle Thief* (1952) and Federico Fellini's *La Dolce Vita* (1960) are two popular films produced in this style, and they inspired Giuseppe Tornatore's *Cinema Paradiso* (1988). Each of these films found success among both American and international audiences.

Another subgenre of movies that emerged in Italy during this time (the mid-1960s) was the Spaghetti Western. Spaghetti Westerns were low-budget films shot in southern Italy so as to visually mimic the American Southwest. Cast and crews, except for the leading actors, were primarily Italian. The most famous of these Spaghetti Westerns included the three directed by Sergio Leone, each of which starred the young Clint Eastwood: *A Fistful of Dollars* (1964), *For a Few Dollars More* (1965) and *The Good, the Bad and the Ugly* (1966). These films helped launch Clint Eastwood to international stardom. The combination of strikingly sparse and realistic cinematography with gritty yet limited dialogue

6.6

Barren landscapes, such as this one, characterized the cinematography of the Spaghetti Western—a subgenre of film that was actually inspired by Japanese cinema.

Alan Campbell/Alamy Stock Photo

observed in these films has made a mark on contemporary filmmaking, though the style itself was inspired by Japanese cinema.

Asian Cinema

The history of Asian cinema goes as far back as the 1890s, when filmmakers in Japan and India produced the first short films to come out of the region. By 1912, Japan had already released its first major feature film while most Asian countries were working to develop their own distinct styles, genres and flavors.

The Japanese cinema industry, one of the oldest and most successful in the world, comprises several unique genres. Those most familiar to Western audiences include kaiju (monster films—for example, the *Godzilla* franchise of the 1950s), Samurai cinema (warrior films—for example, Hiroshi Inagaki's acclaimed *Samurai* trilogy of the 1950s), and anime (animation—for example, Hayao Miyazaki's 2002 film, *Spirited Away*). One of the most influential filmmakers to emerge from the postwar Golden Age of Japanese cinema was director, screenwriter and editor Akira Kurosawa (1910–1998).

Kurosawa's body of work, encompassing 30 films over an unparalleled 57-year career, has had a profound influence on not just Japanese and Asian cinema, but on American cinema as well. Kurosawa's style influenced the cinemagraphic and narrative approach to the popular "men on a mission" films, as exemplified and popularized by director Robert Aldrich's *The Dirty Dozen* (1967) and J. Lee Thompson's *The Guns of Navarone* (1961).

6.7

Kaiju, or Japanese monster films, were wildly popular among American audiences.

Photo 12/Alamy Stock Photo

6.8

The stories and characters of Bollywood cinema are largely inspired by the intricate tales of Hindu mythology.

sunsetman/Shutterstock. com

Perhaps one of the most influential of Kurosawa's films is the crime mystery, *Rashomon* (1950), which gave birth to a storytelling style that came to be called the Rashomon effect, which essentially presents mystery-thrillers from the contrasting perspectives of multiple characters. American movies such as *The Usual Suspects* (1995), *Courage Under Fire* (1996) and *Vantage Point* (2008) demonstrate this effect. The innovative cinematography and film editing techniques developed by Kurosawa continue to influence new generations of filmmakers throughout the world, and his work is part of the required curriculum in all major film schools.

While Japan's movie industry is one of the largest in the world, India's Bollywood, based in Mumbai, is *the* largest, producing more than 1,000 films each year—the majority of which are intended for India's domestic market. Stories and characters drawn primarily from the intricate tales of Hindu mythology infuse Bollywood films. The style combines action, comedy and romance, as well as music and singing—filmmaking traditions that are unique to India and Indian audiences. In recent years, however, this distinctive cinematic style has begun to break out of the Indian domestic market to attract worldwide audiences and influence American film production. For example, the director of *The Guru* (2002) relies on the boisterous song and dance of the main character's native cinema to add flavor and energy to the film. Hints of Bollywood are also evident in the musical film *Moulin Rouge* (2001) by Australian director Baz Luhrmann, and in the international hit *Slumdog Millionaire* (2008) by British director Danny Boyle and British screenwriter Simon Beaufoy.[11]

Chinese Cinema offers stories that center around historical events and characters, Chinese folk mythologies and popular Chinese operas. As in Japan, from the 1940s through China's Cultural Revolution (1960s–1980s), Chinese films often featured government-dictated political themes that attempted to combine entertainment with political propaganda. In

6.9

A highly successful film, *The Joy Luck Club*, provides insight into the cultural tensions experienced between first- and second-generation Chinese immigrants.

Hollywood Pictures/Bray, Phil/Album/Newscom

contrast, the late 1980s and the early 1990s saw a new generation of mainland Chinese filmmakers whose works focused on themes that were more personal and more relatable to a new and larger international audience.[12] Wayne Wang's successful 1993 movie adaptation of Amy Tan's best-selling 1989 novel, *The Joy Luck Club*, presents an insightful look into the conflicts affecting older-generation Chinese mothers, who are deeply rooted in Chinese tradition, and their second-generation Chinese American daughters, who are struggling to integrate themselves into American culture.

Two parallel Chinese film industries grew up alongside that of mainland China's in the late 1940s—one based in Hong Kong and the other in Taiwan. Acclaimed Taiwanese film director Ang Lee broke new ground for Chinese films with his Academy Award-winning wuxia (Chinese martial arts film), *Crouching Tiger, Hidden Dragon* (2000). Its striking visuals and fantastical aerobatics earned him critical acclaim, as well as four Academy Awards and two Golden Globe Awards. Lee's work continues to have a significant influence on American moviemaking style; many of producer/director John Woo's films, such as *Reign of Assassins* (2010) shot in China and set during the Ming Dynasty, for example, borrow from wuxia. A new generation of Chinese filmmakers are also following the examples of their predecessors by employing new cinemagraphic and narrative styles.

6.10

Movie poster for director Ang Lee's 2010 action-fantasy film *Reign of Assassins*.

© Weinstein Company/Courtesy Everett Collection

Middle Eastern Cinema

Until recently, Western filmmakers, especially those from France, the United States and Germany, have dominated film depictions of the Middle East. Some well-known examples include *Algiers* (1938), *Casablanca* (1942), *Lawrence of Arabia* (1962) and *Aladdin* (1992). Middle Eastern cinema is both an outgrowth of and a rebellion against the region's long struggle to express, and in many ways control, the stories that define Middle Eastern identity. Middle Eastern identity is very much an amalgamation of cultures, nationalities, politics, religions and aesthetics—each of which battles for fair representation in a Western-dominated movie industry. Historically, Middle East cinema dates back to 1925 in Egypt, although it was not until 1930 that the industry took off. During this time, the country's leading music labels pushed popular Arab-language singers, whom they had under contract, to star in movie musicals. The Golden Age of Egyptian cinema, however, spanned the 1940s through the 1960s and produced such classics as *The Black Waters* (1956) and *The Immortal Song* (1959). Today, Egypt continues to dominate the Arab-language movie industry, with Egyptian production companies turning out original and co-produced (with American and European studios) films. Egypt also hosts one of the major international film festivals each year—the Cairo International Film Festival.

> Middle Eastern cinema is both an outgrowth of and a rebellion against the region's long struggle to express, and in many ways control, the stories that define Middle Eastern identity.

Political crises have played a role in driving filmmaking in this area as well. In response to the first Gulf War in Kuwait and Iraq (August 2, 1990–February 28, 1991), the second Gulf War in Iraq (March 20, 2003–December 15, 2011) and the War in Afghanistan (2001–present), many important films about the regions and the general social and political conflicts that have plagued them have been produced. One such film released during the Afghanistan War was the multiple award-winning film *The Kite Runner* (2007), based on the book by Afghan-born novelist and physician Khaled Hosseini. While not specifically focusing on the current war in Afghanistan, the film follows the lives of two young boys who endured the Soviet invasion of their country, the subsequent mass exodus of their people and the eventual takeover by the fundamentalist Taliban regime.

Latin American Cinema

Latin American cultural traditions, social and political history, indigenous stories and narrative styles infuse this region's cinema production. For the most part, the governments of Central and South America originally funded moviemaking; as such, the cinema served as a vehicle for expressing cultural and political messages steeped in nationalism. In the later decades of

> For the most part, the governments of Central and South America originally funded moviemaking; as such, the cinema served as a vehicle for expressing cultural and political messages steeped in nationalism.

6.11

Rooney Mara as the title character Lisbeth Salander in the 2011 English version of *The Girl with the Dragon Tattoo*, which was based on Stieg Larsson's Swedish-language novel (and film).

Merrick Morton/© Columbia Pictures/Courtesy Everett Collection

the 20th century, moviemaking in Latin America underwent a slow renaissance. One force of change resulted from the immigration of Latinos from Central and South America into the United States. This migration exponentially increased the Spanish-speaking market and, correspondingly, the demand for Spanish-language films. Hollywood responded to this cultural shift by producing films that better portrayed the culture, diversity and character of the countries and their people. Some of the most recent films fitting this description include *Biutiful* (2010; Spain), *Mao's Last Dancer* (2010; China), *Girl with the Dragon Tattoo* (2009; Sweden) and *City of God* (2002; Brazil). All of these films found audiences in America, and many won awards for best foreign film. Together they have opened new doors for the vibrant Latino film industry.

International Films Affect the U.S. Motion Picture Rating System

Many internationally produced films tended to feature adult themes or sexual content that challenged social norms in the United States at the time. Filmmakers worked with such themes in order to expand the cinema beyond commercial and populist boundaries. Box-office sales began to reflect the audience's embrace of such films, and their success eventually led to the abandonment of the strict and censorious Hays Code, established in 1922. In response, the film industry developed its own rating system to avoid provoking government intervention. The new rating system allowed filmmakers to continue pushing boundaries in terms of controversial content while studios maintained the perception that they were indeed concerned with public morality.[13]

Beginning in the mid-1960s, and paralleling the social and cultural revolutions shaking the United States at the time, Hollywood studios began to exploit the deregulation of film content by introducing more sex and violence. To deal with this trend, the Motion Picture Association of America (MPAA) introduced its new Motion Pictures Ratings System in 1968, which allowed studios to test the waters with more controversial content. In turn, films began to feature previously taboo subjects such as drug addiction, prostitution and childbirth. These changes in the ratings system, which reflected the audience's changing tastes, did not hinder box-office sales. In fact, ticket sales increased, demonstrating the American audience's interest in these new trends in film content.

The Rise of the Independent Film Movement

The new legal and creative freedom that flourished after the Hays Code was struck down enabled the film industry to develop new approaches to moviemaking and gave life to a viable independent film movement. Studio heads, recognizing that they could not sustain audience interest with the same formulaic movies, began to borrow from the film noir, neoclassical and New Wave film styles of foreign cinema. At first, increased imports of British and French short and "art" films led the way to the American independent film movement. Italian, Japanese and Chinese films quickly followed.

By the late 1970s, more than 1,000 art house theaters that specialized in showing foreign and lower-budget independent films were in operation in the United States, located mostly in urban centers. Independent films, often referred to as indies, are produced outside the major studio system. However, often studios will come in as the principal distributors after an indie film has been produced—in particular, in cases where the film has received critical acclaim at one of the annual international film festivals. The most famous of these is now the Sundance Film Festival, founded by actor and director Robert Redford and held every January in Park City, Utah. Sometimes well-established producers intentionally choose the independent route over the

Hollywood studio route when they wish to undertake filmmaking projects viewed as highly controversial or in order to avoid the creative controls imposed by large studios. Indie films cost a fraction of the budget of mainstream Hollywood productions, so the risk to producers and investors is less—assuming that a film can gain the audience "buzz" that attracts distribution partners. In other words, for an independent film to succeed, it has to be seen.

THE MAGIC OF SPECIAL EFFECTS AND THE DIGITAL AGE

Moviemaking in the last 60 years has largely been driven by the technical and creative evolution of special effects, or simulations (also called FX or SFX). The success of today's blockbuster films, in particular, hinges on how well the producers can deliver to their audiences movies that represent the next leap forward in characters, environments and action. Consider, for example, whether one of the top sci-fi films in 2012, *The Hunger Games*, would have been as popular among audiences, or whether it would have had the same impact, were it not for the ingenious special effects that kept viewers at the edge of their seats.

Bill Abbott (1908–1985) and Stan Winston (1946–2008) are credited as the key special effects pioneers in 20th-century filmmaking. Abbott, who became the head of the special effects department at Twentieth Century Fox Studios in 1957, spearheaded the use of sophisticated, highly detailed action scale models of everything from World War II ships in battle; to miniature trains, cars, and trucks; to airplanes; to animals and monsters. He combined special lighting and high-speed film cameras to create some of the pre-computer and surprisingly realistic movie FX. Abbott and his teams also invented the use of matte painting and matte shots, which were combined with inserted live action to create highly realistic scenes that would otherwise be impossible to produce. In matte shots, a large painting of an environment, including all elements from trees and roads to buildings, is installed as a background. A small portion of the scene to be shot—either full size or cleverly scaled, perhaps one house on a street where the rest of the village is actually a painting—is then filmed, using special lighting, lenses and camera mounts. Matte paintings can also disguise undesirable real backgrounds—in Abbott's day, that might have included cars on a nearby Hollywood freeway or oil wells in the Hollywood Hills. Abbott's team routinely changed the backgrounds to whatever was called for in the scripts.

6.12

Art house theaters sprang up in urban centers in the late 1970s and primarily featured foreign and independent films. Their popularity reflected changing tastes in films among American audiences.

Naum Chayer/Alamy Stock Photo

6.13

Jennifer Lawrence as Katniss Everdeen in the 2012 blockbuster *The Hunger Games*.

Moviestore Collection Ltd/Alamy Stock Photo

6.14

Special effects artists built animatronics models of dinosaurs for *Jurassic Park* and its sequels.

United Archives GmbH/Alamy Stock Photo

In 1968, Stanley Kubrick's futuristic space epic, *2001: A Space Odyssey*, brought movie viewers an astounding look into a possible distant future of space travel and exploration. The film broke new ground with its use of integrated scale models shot with high-speed cameras and retroreflective matting. This FX technique uses still action photography as well as video, projected through a series of mirrors, to create backgrounds and environments within which actors appear to be moving, but that actually do not exist. Cameras move along specially constructed tracks that allow repeated shooting of scenes from various angles in a process known as motion control. Additionally, for *2001*, specially engineered sets were mechanically manipulated to simulate what it might look like to live and work in a zero-gravity environment.

Sometimes huge, mechanically controlled sets have been constructed to enable filmmakers to create scenes that would otherwise defy the laws of nature or be far too dangerous for human actors—for example, the ships that were built for the films *The Poseidon Adventure* (1972 and 2005) and *Titanic* (1997). The latter actually combined both mechanical/optical effects with computer-generated effects. In both films, actors performed their scenes in specially constructed "ships" that could simulate the capsizing and sinking of huge luxury liners, albeit with none of the gravity-defying positions and massive flooding, and without placing the actors in danger.

Stan Winston, the dean of Hollywood special effects, was the first to use complex animatronics—mechanical and computer-controlled effects—in the film *Jurassic Park* and the film series *Alien* (1979, 1986, 1992, 1997), *Terminator* (1984, 1991, 2003, 2009) and *Prometheus* (2012). In these films, animatronics combined with motion-controlled camera techniques allowed large-scale creatures to move about and interact with actors with astounding realism. This long and rich history of mechanical and optical special effects dazzled and entertained audiences for decades, until greater use of computers moved movie special effects into a new era.

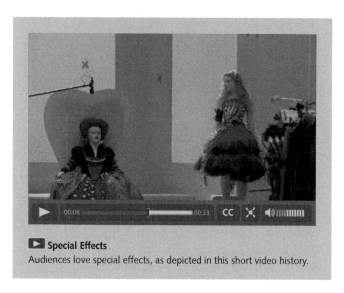

▶ **Special Effects**
Audiences love special effects, as depicted in this short video history.

Producer/director George Lucas led the filmmaking team that took special effects into the Digital Age. He and his Industrial Light and Magic FX shop brought to the screen his epic movie series *Star Wars*. The team of artists, model makers, cinematographers and computer effects specialists combined superrealistic models and animatronic characters with large and intricate matte paintings that set new industry standards, while simultaneously using computer-controlled lighting effects and motion-controlled cameras. This effort required Industrial Light and Magic to virtually invent and build what was, back in 1977 (when the first *Star Wars* film was released), an entirely new generation of computer graphics, 3-D computer animation and image-processing (CGI) hardware and software, along with the creative methodologies and vision to apply all of these SFX systems to cinemagraphic storytelling. Learn more about the history of special effects in the video segment titled "Special Effects." ▶

The film industry in the Digital Age is facing many of the same struggles that other media are encountering in the face of mass media convergence and the explosion of digital technology. Since the development of VHS technology in the 1970s, the film industry has been able to harness the profit potential of home video sell-through and rental outlets, as well as broadcast exhibition through network and cable television. As the technology has developed to allow movies in their own homes, the film industry has been able to expand its market and extend the economic life of its productions. Previously, the studios had relied solely on box-office proceeds to recoup their costs and as the primary source of their profits. The emergence of sell-through products (units that are directly sold to the public) and rental companies created a way for films to enjoy a second economic life after theatrical release. Cable television also provided the film industry with a new source of revenue, including licensing films to premium cable channels such as HBO and Showtime. Pay-per-view distribution opened a potential source of revenue as well. While this service was first test-marketed in the late 1940s, it did not find mass consumer acceptance until the 1990s.[14]

> As the technology has developed to allow consumers to enjoy movies in their own homes, the film industry has been able to expand its market and extend the economic life of its productions.

In recent years, the film industry has experienced a marked decrease in revenue from home video sales and a correspondingly significant reduction in profits. Analysts, scholars and industry representatives attribute this decline to three primary factors: digital piracy, the global economic downturn and new competition. First, piracy via digital distribution over the Internet has accounted for more than 40 percent of the industry's losses between 2004 and 2012, affecting both box-office sales and sell-through revenues. This percentage remains a topic of debate, however, as analysts and congressional investigators have cautioned that the industry has thus far failed to provide hard data to support its claims about piracy's effect on sales. Second, industry officials suggest that the global economic downturn has aggravated film pirating, as many people have more time on their hands and tend to not spend money on entertainment, especially when it can be easily acquired for free. Although evidence clearly points to a large increase in illegal movie download traffic over the Internet, the numbers do not suggest that this activity has replaced what consumers would have otherwise purchased in the past.[15]

> In recent years, the film industry has experienced a marked decrease in revenue from home video sales and a correspondingly significant reduction in profits. Analysts, scholars and industry representatives attribute this decline to three primary factors: digital piracy, the global economic downturn and new competition.

Many experts suggest that the third factor contributing to the decrease in film revenue may simply be new competition. Between relatively inexpensive rental subscription services such as Netflix, Blockbuster Online and the phenomenal rise of the self-service rental kiosk company Redbox, consumers now have even fewer reasons to purchase DVDs. Instead, they can enjoy a constantly updated stream of movies, either delivered right to their doorstep or picked up 24 hours a day at local vending machines, thanks to the size efficiencies of DVDs and Blu-ray technology and most recently via online streaming services vfrom companies such as Netflix, Apple, and Amazon. com. In terms of cost, Netflix and Blockbuster Online charge consumers a flat fee based on the number of rentals, but no late fees. (In 2009, both

6.15

Netflix has taken the lead in direct-to-home distribution of already-released movies, which some critics argue has contributed to the decrease in film revenue.

Ricardo Ramirez Buxeda/MCT

companies charged $19.99 per month; however, by 2012, Netflix's monthly fee had dropped to $7.99, and Blockbuster Online's basic fee had dropped to $9.99 per month.) Both companies now offer portions of their film catalogues streamed over the Internet—a service known as direct-to-home distribution, in which Netflix has taken the early lead. For about the purchase price of one and a half DVDs, consumers can view as many movies as they can watch and return in three-DVD cycles. Redbox has proven to be even more competitive for customers interested in short-term viewing, pricing its rentals at $1.20 per night.

In addition to rental companies competing with DVD sales, competition between retailers has driven the prices of individual DVDs down significantly. Retail leaders Walmart and Amazon have waged a massive price war on this front, driving the average price for many newly released DVDs down to $10 each. Consequently, Blu-ray, which the film industry had counted on to lead the way as its new prestige format, has dropped in price to compete with both rentals and lower DVD costs, further cutting into studio profit margins.[16]

The release of Apple's iPad in early 2010 has presented the movie industry with its latest challenge. This tablet computer makes a wide range of feature-length films and television programs accessible to customers via iTunes—in essence, turning the iPad into a powerful new film distribution channel. Apple— rather than film studios or film and distribution companies—controls this channel, so it is able to claim as much as 30 percent of the film download revenues. As such, the iPad may force a partial revision of the film industry's business model, much in the same way as the iPod and iPhone forced a radical reimagining of the music industry.

NARRATIVE IN TELEVISION

As mentioned earlier in this chapter, mythic story structures are common to all cultures, and to those pervaded by film and television. We just spent several pages discussing storytelling in film; we now examine storytelling in television. Since its heyday in the 1950s, American television has been offering audiences programming content consistent with the narrative content featured in films. Unlike feature films, however, television narratives must face special restrictions—for example, commercial breaks every 10 to 12 minutes and "cliffhangers" at the end of each season to entice the audience back for the next season.

Episodic television dramas have much more storytelling "real estate," comprising 13 hours spread across 13 weeks. These programming structures allow television screenwriters and directors to offer compelling multilevel plots and to include many more lead characters—sometimes referred to as ensemble casts—than is possible in the typical 90- to 120-minute feature film. As prime-time television production budgets have continued to increase, the creators of television series can now enhance their storytelling narratives with action scenes and special effects; just a decade or so earlier, such elements could be found only in higher-budget feature films.

Increased production budgets, which allow for more sophisticated and visual storytelling, have led to the current mainstay of prime-time television drama: crime procedurals, espionage dramas, action/adventure dramas and science fiction. The visual and narrative complexities of today's prime-time dramatic television series often match, and in many cases exceed, what feature films offer audiences. A new level of competition for audiences has evolved between television—including cable and satellite networks—and films that are initially released in theaters or simultaneously released in theaters, on DVDs/Blu-ray and on pay-for-view channels.

Complex television dramas featuring multiple plot lines clearly entice audiences. Consider, for example, the popularity of *Lost*, which aired on ABC from September 2004 to May 2010. The producers of this critically acclaimed sci-fi drama series purposely built into the story highly complex and seldom fully explained narrative elements. These elements ranged from time travel to religion and mythological references to ethical and philosophical questions about the nature of good and evil. *Lost* attracted a huge audience as well as a glut of Websites and fan blogs. Its narrative complexity and constantly open-ended multiple plot lines challenged viewers to "fill in the blanks" and complete the story using their own imaginations.

One way to trace the evolution of television dramas is to look at the developmental stages of narrative storytelling on TV. Narrative storytelling on television started as a natural extension of the popular dramatic serials on the radio (see Chapter 5). By the 1930s, episodic radio dramas had become very popular in

America, attracting vast audiences. Many of these radio dramas made the jump to TV, becoming some of the first prime-time dramas on television. For example, the top-rated radio drama *The Lone Ranger* began in 1933 and migrated to television in 1949. Original TV episodes of the show ran until 1957; reruns are still found on cable channels today. Another good example is *Gunsmoke*, which aired on the radio from 1952 to 1961 and was then a top-rated prime-time TV series from 1955 to 1975. These radio dramas attracted and held large audiences because they utilized narrative storytelling techniques rooted in popular 19th-century literature by writers such as Charles Dickens (1812–1870) and Edgar Allen Poe (1809–1849). Such storytelling styles included strong central characters and regularly appearing supporting characters as well as multipart stories that included plot "cliffhangers" that bridged the story from one episode to the next. This technique established strong audience loyalties—people waited excitedly to see what would happen next, often discussing the stories with their friends, families and co-workers and further strengthening the fan base.[17]

6.16

Poster for the HBO adventure-fantasy series *Game of Thrones*, based on the novels by George R. R. Martin.

Kathy Hutchins/Shutterstock.com/Newscom

Episodic dramas with continuing characters and story arcs, cliffhangers between episodes and long-arc story narratives where storylines stretch over many episodes and even across many seasons took two paths as television matured between the 1950s and 1970s. One path was the daytime soap opera discussed later in this chapter; the other was the production and popularity of the ever-more sophisticated and often complex prime-time drama, starting with examples such as *Dallas*, which broke prime-time audience records during its run from 1978 to 1991 (and returned to television as recently as 2012). Other examples of midevolution dramatic television include the now-classic *L.A. Law* (1986–1994), *St. Elsewhere* (1982–1988) and David Lynch's *Twin Peaks* (1990–1991). These all helped establish the storytelling structural foundations later used in series such as *24* (2001–2010) and *The Closer* (2005–2012).

Popular prime-time police procedural dramas such as Dick Wolf's *Law & Order* series—which began in 1990 and eventually became a multiseries franchise including *Law & Order: Special Victims Unit*; *Law & Order: LA*; *Law & Order: Criminal Intent*; and *Law & Order: Trial by Jury*—help to drive episodic television dramas to the next level. In 1999, writer-producer Aaron Sorkin brought more complex storylines and episodic narratives to prime-time television with his groundbreaking series *The West Wing*. The drama aired on NBC from 1999 through 2006 and had a not insignificant impact on how Americans viewed national politics—so much so that the fictional president in the series, Jed Bartlet, played by actor Martin Sheen, became more popular and "trusted" than the actual presidents during that period.

Today, the narrative storytelling found on dramatic television series has reached new heights of sophistication; popular recent examples that have attracted large, loyal audiences include the award-winning series *The Wire* (2002–2008), *Political Animals* (2012), *Breaking Bad* (2008–2013) and *Boss* (2011–2013). This evolution in narrative storytelling on television has brought American viewers—and through syndication, audiences around the world—an increasing number of high-end dramatic series. These dramas have pushed audiences to demand ever-more sophisticated television stories, thus enriching the contribution to our shared television "literature" and, for the most part, enriching our shared culture.

THE EVOLUTION OF TELEVISION

During the Golden Age of Hollywood, the Big Five Hollywood film studios were too busy battling for control over the film industry to notice that television was starting to draw audiences away from the theaters. The film industry started to lose large chunks of their revenue to this upstart new medium beginning in the late 1940s. More and more Americans began to stay home and crowd around the television, rather than flock to the theater. The programming was free and they could enjoy the entertainment in the comfort of their own living rooms. Certainly, Hollywood had underestimated the appeal and popularity of this new medium. The history of television was covered earlier (see Chapter 2); this chapter will focus on its role in the contemporary media culture that characterizes the United States.

Although television audiences grew rapidly in the late 1940s and early 1950s, media corporations and advertisers were skeptical that the medium would be financially successful; thus they initially hesitated to spend money on its development. Between 1948 and 1958, the number of American homes with television sets grew from 172,000 to more than 42 million. From 1948 to 1952, the FCC attempted to freeze television development to study the problems of interference and the competition between radio and television for the airwaves. In cities where thriving television stations existed, movie theaters and nightclubs began to struggle. Contrary to the perception of industry executives and government officials, however, the American public had already adopted television as the mass medium of the future.[18]

Early Television Programming

It took decades of technological and creative innovations for television storytelling to evolve from its early days of radio-adapted live dramas to the extraordinarily sophisticated programs we are accustomed to today. Early television programmers adapted many of radio's most popular shows to the nascent medium, offering listeners visual versions of previously aired radio content that they could now view. Similarly, television stations employed the same sponsorship model that had been so successful in radio, with many shows named for their corporate partners—for example, the *Philco Television Playhouse* (1948–1955), *Kraft Television Theater* (1947–1955) and the *U.S. Steel Hour* (1953–1963).[19] Corporate sponsorship and funding helped to build the major networks in their early years; it also controlled the programming content. The companies that lent their names and financial backing to these infant networks viewed television as primarily a means for promoting their products.

Corporate sponsorship and funding helped to build the major networks in their early years; it also controlled the programming content.

In 1947, the Columbia Broadcasting System (CBS) and the Radio Corporation of America (RCA)—the two major forces in early television—were vying to have the FCC register their respective proprietary electronic color systems, with RCA winning the first round. RCA's system quickly made older black-and-white sets obsolete and dealt a significant blow to CBS. Both CBS and the American Broadcasting System (ABC) would continue to lag behind RCA in terms of television innovation well into the 1950s. By 1950, television viewership had already eclipsed radio listenership in those cities, with CBS vice president, Hubbell Robinson, Jr., declaring, "Television is about to do to radio what the Sioux did to Custer. There is going to be a massacre."[20] It was clear that television had become a formidable competitor for the movie industry, threatening to usurp the cinema's position as the dominant entertainment medium in the United States. Additionally, television's growing success and popularity opened up new opportunities for production and distribution partnerships.

The Big Three Networks Become the Big Four

In 1926, RCA established the National Broadcasting Corporation (NBC), which would become one of the original Big Three networks (along with ABC and CBS) that would long dominate U.S. television. All three networks offered a multitude of television content, from news, to prime-time and daytime programming, to sports programming. The Fox Broadcasting Company (Fox) came along in 1986, turning the Big Three into the Big Four. The Public Broadcasting Service (PBS), while not considered to be part of the Big Four, is, however, the largest network in the United States. Unlike the Big Four, PBS is a network whose outlets include independent nonprofit television stations as well as numerous new cable and satellite networks; PBS is partially subsidized by federal and state funding and viewer donations.

From a programming standpoint, few differences separate the Big Four television networks. In recent years, all four have faced the challenge of competing not only with one another, but also with cable and satellite networks. As we explore the media industry in later chapters (see Chapter 9), the battle among the networks to attract and retain audiences (measured in audience ratings) and, by extension, advertising revenues has resulted in ever-higher-quality programs. This is especially true during the prime-time

From a programming standpoint, few differences separate the Big Four television networks. In recent years, all four have faced the challenge of competing not only with one another, but also with cable and satellite networks.

television viewing hours of 8 p.m. to 11 p.m. In television, audiences generally determine the success or failure of a series. If a program fails to capture and hold an audience's interest, that program is subsequently canceled, regardless of its production costs or the fame of its cast members.

The competition for audiences among the Big Four television networks, and between the Big Four and the major cable and satellite networks, has been responsible for continued improvement in the quantity and quality of television programs. Competition from PBS has also contributed to this trend, owing to PBS's long history of partnering with such international television networks.

The Nielsen ratings system is the most widely used system for measuring television audience size and composition. It provides programmers with a daily and even hourly snapshot of the viewing audience by monitoring the minute-by-minute viewing habits of a small, yet statistically representative sample of the American (and worldwide) television viewing audience. Nielsen ratings are reported as percentage points or "share" of audience at any given time, where a "share" represents 1 percent of the total number of "U.S. television households" (see Chapter 9). Nielsen Media Research conducts the largest and most influential television audience ratings survey on a daily basis; it does the same thing on a larger scale during the all-important sweeps weeks—seven-day ratings periods held each year in the first weeks of November, March, May and July. Program viewership ratings during the four sweeps weeks greatly determine which television series the networks will retain and which series they might move to different time slots or cancel altogether.

Program viewership ratings during the four sweeps weeks greatly determine which television series the networks will retain and which series they might move to different time slots or cancel altogether.

TELEVISION GENRES

Narrative-based television, like narrative-based film, is organized by genre. Today, the most popular categories include situation comedies, dramas, sports programming, soap operas and reality television.

Television gradually replaced radio as the major electronic window to news, sports and entertainment in the majority of U.S. homes through the 1950s and early 1960s. During the same period, the relationship between the television networks and their corporate advertisers also matured. An American television culture evolved, first built upon the popular sketch comedies (short comedy scenes or vignettes), such as CBS's *I Love Lucy* (1951–1957), which eventually evolved into a regularly recurring series. Viewers loved the show. In fact, during its original airing, it held the title of most frequently watched series throughout four out of six of its seasons. By the time the series ended, it found itself at the top of the Nielsen ratings—the first show ever to earn this achievement.

The Situation Comedy

I Love Lucy, along with *The Red Skelton Show* (1951–1971), and later *The Carol Burnett Show* (1967–1978), gave rise to a rich assortment of situation comedies (or sitcoms—comedies that feature regularly recurring characters in a familiar environment) such as *The Andy Griffith Show* (1960–1968), *Bewitched* (1964–1972), *The Dick Van Dyke Show* (1961–1966) and *M*A*S*H* (1972–1983). Some of the later situation comedies addressed controversial social issues, and in so doing helped pave the way for important social change. *M*A*S*H*, although it was a series set during the Korean War, addressed anti-war sentiments in the last years of the Vietnam War. *The Mary Tyler Moore Show* (1970–1977) helped open the door for more opportunities and equality for women in the workplace. The groundbreaking and often controversial hit series *All in the Family* (1971–1979) dealt very directly with racial, social and gender stereotypes.

6.17

Popular through the 1970s, *All in the Family* dealt with social, racial and gender stereotypes.

AF archive/Alamy Stock Photo

The Drama

Dramas, which generally appear in most of the prime-time slots, include everything from mysteries and action/adventures to political and crime thrillers. Series such as *Alfred Hitchcock Presents* (1955–1965), *Playhouse 90* (1956–1960) and *Rod Serling's Twilight Zone* (1959–1964) were very popular in their day. These programs eventually paved the way for today's popular episodic and anthology drama series such as the multiprogram *CSI* franchise and the *NCIS* franchise, as well as such popular science-fiction adventure series as *Fringe*. Today such episodic dramas make up the mainstay of network television, surpassed in audience popularity only by reality shows such as *Survivor* and *American Idol*, which we will discuss in more detail later.

Sports Programming

Another programming genre tied closely to the history of network television is sports programming. In many ways, professional sports and television established a mutually beneficial relationship. Sports needed television coverage to build its fan base and attract sponsorships, while television networks needed the advertisers and advertising revenues that televised sports attracted. The coverage of sports events for television presented technological challenges that spurred innovative solutions, which have benefited all aspects and genres of programming.

Early television cameras were large and heavy and required extremely bright lighting to produce even minimally acceptable images. The first sports events covered over broadcast television were boxing and wrestling matches—events that took place in smaller, well-lit indoor spaces. Even so, the first televised sports event was a college baseball game between Columbia University and Princeton University in 1939. Despite the technological challenges, sports quickly became a regular fixture on network television and often accounted for as much as a third of a network's prime-time programming. As networks added more varied programming to the prime-time program schedule, sports television migrated to its own niche time slots on the weekends.

As it evolved over the years, sports programming continued to attract loyal audiences and deliver increasingly reliable advertising revenues to the networks.

As it evolved over the years, sports programming continued to attract loyal audiences and deliver increasingly reliable advertising revenues to the networks. Eventually some sports coverage migrated back to prime-time, led by pioneering sports series such as the *Gillette Cavalcade of Sports* (1942–1962) and ABC's *Wide World of Sports* (1961–1998). Today an extraordinarily wide variety of sports television is available, including both network sports coverage and entire cable/satellite channels dedicated to all sports all the time, such as the various ESPN channels. Special-event sports coverage continues to attract some of the largest audiences, and vast amounts of advertising dollars on television, including the highly lucrative Rose Bowl and Super Bowl football games, the World Series baseball games and the NCAA basketball championships. Sports television has, in certain cases, contributed significantly to certain sports becoming part of American cultural phenomena—the best example being NASCAR racing.[21]

The Soap Opera

Another television-driven cultural phenomenon has been daytime soap operas. Soap operas, so named for the household detergent manufacturers that once sponsored these ongoing daily dramas, originally started on radio. The daytime soaps gave their primarily female audiences entertainment outlets, especially during the 1940s through 1960s, when far more women were homemakers and stay-at-home mothers than were in the workplace. Soap operas are types of serial fiction, which cleverly unifies story elements, day after day, for thousands of episodes, into plots that continuously unfold and are never fully resolved. Soap operas developed their own unique storytelling and production styles in part because their screenwriters, producers and actors had to fill so many live screen hours—five days a week, 52 weeks a year.

Some of the most popular soap operas are also among the longest, continually running episodic television in history, including *Guiding Light* (1992–2009), *Days of Our Lives* (1965–present), *As the World Turns* (1956–present) and *General Hospital* (1963–present). What made soap operas so popular and compelling to their audiences was their unique form of storytelling, centered on personal relationships, sexuality and infidelity, emotional and moral conflicts, and "everyday" characters. For many soaps fans, the characters became almost like second families, with their fictional troubles becoming nearly real. Daytime soap operas used the same actors on a long-running basis, the same few sets repeatedly, few off-studio locations, and no stunts or special effects; thus their production costs were low. Large and loyal audiences helped to generate impressive revenues, making it possible for the networks to invest in more costly prime-time programs. The proven popularity of serial fiction first demonstrated with the daytime soap operas has also greatly influenced the story and character structures of prime-time episodic network dramas. Given the many soap operas currently on television, what makes one unique from the other?

Between 1978 and 1993, prime-time television audiences tuned in by the millions to an era of nighttime soap operas. Inspired by the serial narratives and relationship-centered plots of the daytime soaps, the heyday of the nighttime soaps brought viewers in America such popular soap operas as *Dallas* (1978–1991; CBS), *Dynasty* (1981–1989; ABC), *Knots Landing* (1979–1993; CBS) and *Twin Peaks* (1990–1991; ABC). These shows, which had much higher production values than their daytime counterparts, were eventually seen worldwide in syndication (reruns). The strong influence of soap operas can be found in the plot lines, characters, narrative styles and episode-to-episode cliffhanger plot elements found in many of the popular prime-time dramas in recent years. This influence is especially prevalent in a new generation of prime-time soap opera—like series such as *Beverly Hills, 90210* (1990–2000; Fox), *The Sopranos* (1999–2007; HBO), *The L Word* (2004–2009; Showtime), *Six Feet Under* (2001–2005; HBO) and *An American Family* (2012; HBO).

Once in worldwide syndication, the international popularity of many earlier prime-time soaps, such as *Dallas*, which was brought back to prime-time network television in 2012, and *Dynasty*, had an unintended negative impact on international audiences. In the former Soviet Bloc and Middle Eastern countries, especially, the fictional images of Americans as rich, greedy, sexually promiscuous and unethical in business and social dealings were further reinforced through syndication and DVDs.[22]

Reality Television

In 1996, British television producer Charlie Parsons hit on a concept that would change television programming. The concept involved casting a group of real people to participate in a reality game that took place on a remote island. The group would be divided into two "tribes"; each tribe, while stranded on this remote island, would have to compete against the other for survival. First released on the Swedish television network STV as *Expedition Robinson* (a play on the title of Daniel Defoe's novel *Robinson Crusoe*, first published in 1719), the show was an immediate success. By 2000, the concept was being produced worldwide under the series name *Survivor*. The American network version, broadcast on CBS, raked in huge audiences and top ratings in its first season—and has repeated that success every season since. Such would be the beginnings of the new generation of reality television, which consists of low-budget productions built around real people placed in unusual situations. These situations and the bonding experiences and altercations they create play out naturally in front of the camera, on almost a 24/7 basis.

Reality television traces its roots back to real-people shows such as Allen Funt's *Candid Camera* (first aired in 1948), the many popular game shows of the 1950s and 1960s, and Ted Mack's *Original Amateur Hour* (also first aired in 1948). The last program is the historical predecessor to today's overwhelmingly popular *American Idol* series and its many international versions. Today's versions of reality television present a clever combination of drama, romance, sexuality and humor that, in many ways, follows the classic storytelling elements outlined earlier in this chapter. The continued growth in the number and popularity of reality television series (for example, *The Biggest Loser*, *The Amazing Race*, *America's Got Talent* and *The Voice*) is just the most recent trend in a long line of innovative programming efforts.

Some may feel that reality television has damaged society's perception of African-American women. However, there are those that would disagree with that generalization.

Some of the most popular genres can be termed ratchet reality TV, reflecting a somewhat warped version of real life presented as fact but through the creative process is made to look like daytime soaps and prime-time dramas. Bickering housewives, catfights, and an indication of what the stars do for a living outside of being a reality star are dominant themes on many of these shows. Ratchet reality can include anything from women making humiliating choices in life, and violence or aggression or a drink thrown in someone's face. These many times are loud, aggressive black women who feed into the worst of stereotypes. Unfortunately, the shows and the women according to viewers and critics have negatively defined black womanhood.

Usually, a discussion about black women on television focuses on the lack of black women on television. However, showrunner Shonda Rhimes with her Shondaland production company is changing the conversation toward a new Golden Age of TV diversity. Rhimes has been successful in producing two of the most talked about shows with influential black female characters on TV. They include *Scandal*'s Olivia Pope and *How to Get Away with Murder*'s Annalise Keating. Both shows have received acclaim for their diverse casts and portrayal of black women.[23]

Cable Television Innovates Content

Cable television networks have steadily grown in popularity and proliferation since their birth in the 1950s. With its market share increased by the advent of satellite television services, which began in the mid-1960s, cable TV has brought about a sea of change in the number and variety of programming channels available to consumers. The competition for audiences and advertisers by cable and satellite television has seriously challenged the business models of the major networks and caused significant cultural and stylistic changes in television programming. Premium cable networks such as HBO, Showtime and Cinemax have not only profoundly increased the number of program options available to consumers, but have also developed new *forms* of television. Films, series and documentaries that address controversial topics have all become commonplace on cable and satellite television networks. The overwhelming popularity of such programs has resulted in a similar, though less extensive, diversifying of the forms and content of broadcast television programs.

In recent years, the economics of television has driven convergence between broadcast and cable/satellite television, such that programs originally produced for either platform often migrate to the other. This trend makes the production of new and innovative programs, series and made-for-television movies less of a financial risk (see Chapter 9). As a result, audiences are able to enjoy an ever-expanding variety of top-quality television content, including *Boardwalk Empire* (HBO), *Homeland* (SHO) and *True Blood* (HBO).

After over 20 years on the air, HGTV is a top-10 cable network in prime-time in 96 million homes and a multimedia lifestyle brand that includes a magazine and Website.

And while competing networks have seen real estate shows such as *Trading Spaces* grow old and disappear, HGTV has built a consistent lineup of shows, notably, *House Hunters*, which has been around over 15 years. Its arsenal includes *Property Brothers*, *Flip or Flop* and *Fixer Upper*, offering slight variations on the same theme, which is basically people buying, renovating and selling property. HGTV also continues to find still more ways to recycle the inexpensive *House Hunters* formula with shows such as *Living Alaska*, *Beachfront Bargain Hunt* and *Island Hunters* featuring property quests in exotic locales.

HGTV is also the biggest revenue engine for parent company Scripps Networks Interactive, which also owns the majority of the parent of The Times, last year generating nearly $880 million in revenue. The channel provides more than a third of the company's $2.45 billion operating revenue and has shown significant growth, with its 2013 revenue increasing 11.8 percent compared with the previous year. The network ranks No. 1 on cable among women with incomes of $100,000 and higher and performs especially well on the weekends. For the second quarter of 2014, 73 percent of HGTV's prime-time audience was female, 78 percent were homeowners and 67 percent had attended college.[24]

CONFLICTING VISIONS OF THE FUTURE OF TELEVISION

Alternative delivery platforms are changing the television industry in radical ways. Internet television, digital video recorders (DVRs), Internet-linked cable and satellite video-on-demand (VOD) services and mobile media are forcing changes in both programming styles and distribution methods. It seems inevitable that television–Web convergence will lead to equally rapid changes in how consumers select and view television programs and how advertisers try to reach viewers. Indeed, television convergence has already wrought a television revolution.

With this next revolution in television comes important questions: How will the various access portals work together? Which companies will dominate television's new world? The deeply rooted dominance of the four major broadcast networks over both television program production and distribution, as well as the secondary dominance of the major cable and satellite services such as Xfinity (cable) and DirecTV (satellite), has fallen by the wayside. Supremacy in this industry is now up for grabs. There are also conflicting visions of what the future of television will look like.

According to studies and projections by Bobby Tulsiani, senior analyst with Forrester Research; Brad Adgate, senior vice president for research at Horizon Media; and the Interpublic [research] Group:

> Traditional TV viewership is waning, while other kinds of video entertainment consumption rise. . . . Total viewership for the top four broadcast networks in the current season [2009] through mid-November has slumped 42% since the same period in 1994. Including the CW, total viewership for the period is off about 38.5%. In the meantime, other technologies that provide access to video keep growing. More than one in four United States households contained digital video recorders (31 million TV households, or 27% of the total) at the end of the first quarter of 2009. The figure is expected to rise to almost half (51.1 million, or 42%) by 2014. Video on demand was used in 43.1 million TV households, or 42% of 2009 TV households, and is likely to reach 66.6 million, or 64%—nearly two-thirds of households—by 2014. And these are just the TV-viewing experiences that involve the traditional living-room apparatus.[25]

Anyone is now able to select a television episode or movie from hundreds of options, begin watching it at home on TV via a combined Internet and direct satellite connection, get interrupted by a phone call through your television, then pick up where you left off. People can watch a movie on a smart phone or an iPad on their way to school or work, and finish watching on a laptop at home.[26] Additionally, manufacturers of the most popular video game consoles, such as the Xbox, are now including standard features that allow users to view television programs and access Internet sites, further driving the convergent trend toward multiscreen, multiconnection user experiences.

The high cost of these new television access services has been coming down. Competition from similar television delivery services, such as Xfinity (owned by Comcast), Verizon's FiOS and even Apple's Web-based iTunes store, will rapidly increase. Meanwhile, the leading makers of video gaming consoles added Internet television access services with great success. Firms such as Best Buy CinemaNow continue to build the next generation of video downloading technologies. The increasing availability of broadband, along with the U.S. government-mandated switch from analog to digital broadcast television that occurred in June 2009, are combining to make high-definition television programs the norm. The declining costs of all these new television technologies, programming options and access windows are also forcing down the prices paid by consumers. Advertisers continue to develop new ways to reach targeted audiences through these emerging television delivery alternatives, which in turn siphons more advertising dollars away from traditional ad spots on broadcast network television. This trend will continue to decrease costs and increase options for consumers.

What do these trends mean for the future of the Big Four television networks? The competition between two of the Big Four gives us a glimpse into the conflicting visions of what television's future might hold.

CBS and NBC, the two oldest broadcasting networks, with roots dating back to the early years of radio, disagree on what the future of television will be. NBC Universal is investing heavily in its nonbroadcast cable/satellite channels (USA Network, Syfy, Bravo, Trio) and Universal HD channels, its news channels (MSNBC and CNBC), and the production of original series for these outlets. NBC Universal is also a co-owner—along with Fox and Disney/ABC—of the popular Internet television site Hulu. Thus NBC's vision of television's future is clearly focused on convergence with the Web, to such an extent that some analysts have speculated that NBC might close down its legacy broadcast network completely in the not-too-distant future.

CBS plan is to continue to make heavy investments in its popular prime-time program lineup. It holds the view that continuing to deliver award-winning television dramas such as *CSI* and *NCIS*, top-rated reality shows such as *Survivor*, and its highly regarded legacy newsmagazine program *60 Minutes* will enable it to win the rating wars and return to being the dominant broadcast television network. Nevertheless, CBS is still hedging its bet: It is making investments in Web-based television, albeit mostly in the form of strong individual program-tied Websites for its prime-time series, as well as offering most of its programs as streaming video via CBS.com.

It remains to be seen which vision of television's future will turn out to be correct. One thing is certain: Given the speed at which television is changing, it won't take long until we all find out.

CONCLUSION: THE AUDIENCE DRIVES THE FUTURE OF FILM AND TELEVISION

Film and television have traveled closely linked and parallel paths from their earliest days. In many ways, the two industries continue their mutually beneficial, often competitive relationship as both face the extraordinary challenges of the Digital Age, especially the rapid development of new technologies and the inevitable convergence of mass media onto the Internet. Along the way, we, the audience, have greatly benefited from both industries, which have profoundly influenced our lives, culture and society. This evolutionary process continues to progress at an ever-advancing rate, as the television and movie industries innovate to bring us constantly increasing choices in entertainment, sports, news and information. As consumers, we are steering the future of film and television each time we select which movie or television program we want to watch and each time we elect how to view our media. Audience demand has never been stronger for the stories that films and television tell so well. Clearly, the future of movies and television represents a bright spot in the future of mass media.

As consumers, we are steering the future of film and television each time we select which movie or television program we want to watch and each time we elect how to view our media.

CHAPTER SUMMARY	KEY TERMS
Narrative in Film Explains the roots of narrative storytelling found in all movies. **Visual Media** **Mise-en-Scène** An overview of the significance of mise-en-scène in filmic storytelling. 1. How do all the visual elements of a film scene work together to drive the story forward? 2. How does the visual setting of a film establish and support the story?	monomyth genres cross-genre films hybrid films mise-en-scène
The Early Innovators of Film Tells the story of the earliest years of film and shares the contributions of the leading film innovators, whose creativity and technical inventions helped establish the movie industry as we know it today. **Visual Media** ***A Trip to the Moon*** View the special effects—spectacular for their time—of Méliès's *A Trip to the Moon*. 1. What is the most important creative and technical innovation first displayed in Méliès's *A Trip to the Moon*? 2. Name a recent film that utilized a similar, albeit 21st-century, special effect. ***The Great Train Robbery*** Edwin Porter's crosscutting editing technique made it possible for films to display action that was taking place in multiple locations. 1. Why is *The Great Train Robbery* considered such an important early film? 2. What film editing technique was first used in *The Great Train Robbery* and is still commonly used today?	crosscutting nickelodeons
The Hollywood Studio System Explores the historic roots and evolution of the Hollywood studio system and discusses the legacy of the Big Four studios.	Motion Picture Patents Company (MPPC) Big Five Golden Age talkies sound-on-film technology star system block-booking system trade showing financing-distribution model talent agents exhibition license film distributors blockbusters

The Influence of International Cinema Styles Examines the important contributions made by non-American international movie industries and foreign films. **Visual Media** ***The Maltese Falcon*** John Huston's *The Maltese Falcon* (1941), adopted from the German expressionist style. 1. How did the movie *The Maltese Falcon* help establish today's mystery-crime film and TV genre? 2. Name a recent mystery-crime movie whose storytelling style has clear roots in the film *The Maltese Falcon*.	feature filmmaking German expressionist cinema film noir French New Wave Italian neorealism Spaghetti Westerns kaiju Samurai cinema anime Rashomon effect Bollywood wuxia Hays Code Motion Pictures Ratings System art house theaters indies
The Magic of Special Effects and the Digital Age Looks at the history and importance of cinematic special effects and explores how digital special effects have come to dominate 21st-century filmmaking. **Visual Media** **Special Effects** Audiences loved special effects, as depicted in this short video history. 1. Explain how the technique known as "green screen" (or "blue screen") is used to create highly realistic scenes that would otherwise be impossible in films. 2. Name a recent popular film where "green screen" (or "blue screen") FX have been used effectively.	special effects matte shots motion control animatronics sell-through products direct-to-home distribution
Narrative in Television Explores the evolution of narrative storytelling and its impact on television programming.	episodic television dramas ensemble casts
The Evolution of Television Analyzes the multiple genres of television programming and how ratings play a role in the development of content.	Nielsen ratings sweeps week
Television Genres Explains the multiple genres of television shows and reviews the impact audiences have on the creation of content.	sketch comedies situation comedies dramas soap operas serial fiction reality television
Conflicting Visions of the Future of Television Discusses how the often-conflicting forces of new markets and new technologies are driving the creation of future forms of film and television.	

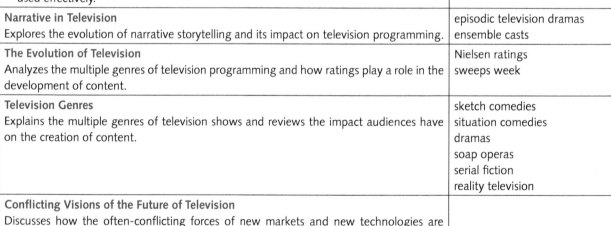

NOTES

1 Campbell, J. (1949/2008). *The hero with a thousand faces*. New World Library.
2 Ezra, E. (2000). *Georges Méliès*. Manchester University Press.
3 Fang, I. (1997). *A history of mass communication: Six information revolutions*. Focal Press.

4   Ibid.

5   Turow, J. (2009). *Media today: An introduction to mass communications*. Routledge, p. 466.

6   Aberdeen, J.A. The Edison Movie Monopoly—The Motion Picture Patents Company vs. the Independent Outlaws, Retrieved from www.cobbles.com/simpp_archive/edison_trust.htm

7   Gomery, D. (2008). *Hollywood studio system: A history*. British Film Institute.

8   Nordin, J. (2009). *The first talkie. All talking! All talking! All talking! A celebration of the early talkies and their times*. Retrieved from http://talkieking.blogspot.com/2009/02/first-talkie.html

9   Aberdeen, J. (2000). *Hollywood renegades: The society of independent motion picture producers*. Cobblestone Enterprises.

10 (1948). The Independent Producers and the *Paramount* Case, 1938–1949. Part 6: The Supreme Court Verdict That Brought an End to the Hollywood Studio System. Retrieved from www.cobbles.com/simpp_archive/paramountcase_6supreme1948.htm

11 Khatami, E. (2009). Is Bollywood coming to Hollywood? *CNN.com*. Retrieved from www.cnn.com/2009/SHOWBIZ/Movies/02/23/bollywood.hollywood/index.html

12 Rose, S. (2002, August 1). The great fall of China. *The Guardian*.

13 Mills, M. (2009). *HUAC & the censorship changes*. Retrieved from www.moderntimes.com/huac/; Georgakas, D. (1992). Hollywood blacklist. In B. Buhle & D. Georgakas (Eds.), *Encyclopedia of the American left*. University of Illinois Press.

14 Moul, C. (2005). *A concise handbook of movie industry economics*. Cambridge University Press.

15 Stetler, B., & Stone, B. (2009, February 4). Digital pirates winning battle with studios. *The New York Times*; Masnick, M. (2009, February 5). NY Times buys bogus movie industry complaint about piracy. *Tech Dirt*. Retrieved from www.techdirt.com/articles/20090205/0319043658.shtml

16 Smith, S. (2009, September 23). DVD sales continue to drop, rentals on the rise. *The Wall Street Journal*; Smith, S. (2009, February 12). Blu-ray prices dropping to DVD levels. *The Tech Herald*; Kaufman, P. B., & Mohan, J. (2008). *The economics of independent and video distribution in the Digital Age*. Tribeca Film Institute; Magiera, M. (2009). DVD threatens film economics. *Video Business*. Retrieved from www.videobusiness.com/blog/1120000312/post/60050006.html

17 Nussbaum, E. (2012, July 30). Tune in next week—the curious staying power of the cliffhanger. *The New Yorker*.

18 Folkerts, J., & Teeter, D. (2002). *Voices of a nation: A history of mass media in the United States*. Allyn & Bacon, p. 442.

19 Briggs, A., & Burke, P. (2007). *A social history of the media: From Gutenberg to the Internet*. Polity Press.

20 Folkerts, J., & Teeter, D. (2002). *Voices of a nation: A history of mass media in the United States*. Allyn & Bacon, p. 442.

21 (2005). *Sports and television*. Museum of Broadcasting. Retrieved from www.museum.tv/eotvsection.php?entrycode=sportsandte

22 Snauffer, S., Reynolds, K. A., & Reynolds, C. (2009). *Prime-time soap operas*. Praeger.

23 Blay, Z. (2015, April 20). Love & hip hop in the Time of Shonda Rhimes. *Cleo'*. Retrieved from http://cleojournal.com/2015/04/20/love-hip-hop-in-the-time-of-shonda-rhimes/

24 Blake, M. (2014, July 18). HGTV builds into a top cable network on foundation of No-Frills shows. *Los Angeles Times*. Retrieved from www.latimes.com/entertainment/tv/la-et-hgtv-cable-network-20th-anniversary-20140720-story.html

25 Steinberg, B. (2009, November 30). The future of television. *Advertising Age*.

26 Ibid.

7

New Media

Wavebreak Media ltd/Alamy Stock Photo

Politics in Cyberspace A look at the impact of new media journalism on politics and democracy.

The History of Video Games A tour of some of the highlights of the evolution of video games.

Firaxis XCOM A fascinating and rare look behind the scenes at the development and production of a hit video game.

LEARNING OBJECTIVES

1. Describe the origins of the Internet and digital media and how each came to be essential in current society.
2. Outline the role that dynamic adaptive learning plays in how we access and apply user-mediated content, recognizing how it has altered the relationship between media users and content creators.
3. Compare and contrast the positive and negative effects of media convergence on the way we learn about the world.
4. Evaluate the social and cultural impact of online social networking on human communication.
5. Explain how new media have contributed to grassroots movements and mainstream politics.
6. Outline the development of multiple forms of gaming and their impact on, and importance to, society and culture.
7. Illustrate how the two parallel yet converging universes of media—one real and one virtual—integrate in today's world.

JOHN PERRY BARLOW.
lyricist for the Grateful Dead rock group and a founding member of the **Electronic Frontier Foundation** (an organization that seeks to defend individual liberties in the digital world), sent an open e-mail to former President Bill Clinton in 1996, calling it "A Cyberspace Independence Declaration." The Declaration was a strongly worded statement criticizing Clinton's signing into law the **Telecom Reform Act**, a bill that attempted to regulate some information and media content on the World Wide Web. Those who supported the Internet's rapid growth, and were convinced that the lack of government regulation was what contributed to it, vociferously protested the bill. Barlow's declaration demonstrated how quickly such protests managed to make their way through the World Wide Web. Within hours of its initial posting via e-mail and Websites, Barlow's declaration had reached millions of Internet users:

> Governments of the industrial world, you weary giants of flesh and steel, I come from Cyberspace, the new home of the mind. On behalf of the future, I ask you of the past to leave us alone. You are not welcome among us. You have no sovereignty where we gather. We have no elected government, nor are we likely to have one, so I address you with no greater authority than that with which liberty itself always speaks. I declare the global social space we are building to be naturally independent of the tyrannies you seek to impose on us.[1]

The rapid evolution of cyberspace has turned the Internet into a platform for the global economy and the operation of national and regional infrastructures. It has built an extraordinarily powerful and far-reaching parallel digital world where the free flow of information, images, ideas and knowledge abounds. Not everyone has been comfortable with the sometimes chaotic, unregulated new media world. With this growth also comes an increase in the potential threats lurking in cyberspace, such as identity theft, child pornography and cyberterrorism. Thus the beginning of the 21st century brought with it new arguments for increased government controls on the basis of **network neutrality**, the view that all service providers and Website owners should allow users equal access at equal speeds to their online content.

Since its inception, the Internet has operated and grown based on this neutrality principle. Many experts, such as leading media law professors (such as Stanford University's Lawrence Lessig) and the members of the Open Internet Coalition, believe that this neutrality has been a key factor enabling the phenomenal national and worldwide use of the Internet in all areas of society, business and government, and that it has served as the basis for the astounding creativity and innovation from which we have all benefited.[2] Net neutrality assures equal access and equal opportunity in cyberspace. Many believe that the government should be allowed to maintain this dictum by regulating Internet traffic, lest the unregulated openness of the Internet invite continued abuses and increased threats to public privacy and security.

The April 6, 2010, ruling by the federal appeals court, however, held that the Federal Communications Commission (FCC) could not impose net neutrality—that is, it could not regulate Internet service to assure equal access. This ruling makes it possible for companies such as Comcast, one of the largest Internet service providers in the United States, to charge higher rates for increased speed and access.

As of 2012, American households with annual incomes of less than $25,000 (43 percent of all homes) still had only the very slow, wired Internet service. The 1996 Telecommunications Act promised to follow the European Union's lead in bringing low-cost broadband to the majority of American consumers. However, the FCC has yet to implement these regulations, and the United States remains 17th among the 34 industrialized countries in delivering low-cost broadband to the majority of its citizens. Clearly, the infighting and political lobbying efforts by American telephone, cable and satellite companies are squarely to blame. In 2012, Google entered the broadband and net neutrality battle with its demonstration project to "wire Kansas City." This may serve as a new model for bringing next-generation wireless broadband to rural areas, but the slow pace of regulatory reform remains the key barrier. One excuse used in the halls of Congress was the growing concerns over Internet privacy.[3]

Congress, as well as international trade organizations, continue to debate this issue. Some voices claim that at least some specifically applied regulation is inevitable—such as laws aimed at reducing the risks of privacy violations and identity theft. This debate over whether the fundamental openness of the Internet will be sacrificed in the end for regulation will likely go on for a number of years.

7.1

hafakot/
Shutterstock.com

WHAT IS NEW MEDIA AND WHERE DID IT ORIGINATE?

A little consideration reveals that the telegraph and then the telephone were the new media of their eras. These inventions revolutionized the flow of information in ways that profoundly influenced culture, society and government, and brought the world closer in ways previously unimagined. Most people accessed the telegraph—the first electronic "Web" of sorts, developed by Samuel Morse, an American inventor and artist—through Western Union. This monopolistic corporation employed operators trained and fluent in Morse code—a character-encoding system that transmitted information via sound and visual signaling (dots and dashes) when sequenced in a particular way, representing specific letters and numbers. Any messages transmitted were charged by the word. As revolutionary as the telegraph was in terms of accelerating the speed of communication, it had its disadvantages. For example, only those people who could afford the per-word fee could use the telegraph to send messages. Also, because telegraphic communication required the presence of cables, no messages or news could be transmitted in areas where there were no cables. These limitations forced a new school of inventors to begin exploring alternative transmission techniques—this time via voice.

In 1876, along came a device that could convert the human voice into electrical impulses of various frequencies and then back again into a human voice via radio waves: the telephone. Although no single individual is credited with actually inventing the telephone, Alexander Graham Bell is considered the first person to have patented it. The telephone allowed, for all intents and purposes, direct user-to-user communication, even though early telephone networks needed operators to route the calls. Central telephone systems (exchanges), located in larger cities and operated by Bell Telephone Company, tied the many local networks into a single national—and eventually international—system. As such, this new instrument vastly improved the speed and distance of communication.

So what is today's "new media," as opposed to yesterday's "old media"? Old media comprise traditional print media—newspapers, magazines and books—and analog broadcast media—TV, radio and films. Starting in the mid-1980s, experts began using the phrase new media to refer to digital media produced using computer-based technologies, distributed via digital platforms and hosted partially or entirely in cyberspace—what was essentially Web 1.0.

Web 1.0 focused primarily on digital publishing and distribution as well as on the introduction of early forms of e-mail communication. Thus the Internet began as a text-dominant alternative to print publishing, starting

7.2

Switchboard operators at work, early 20th century; these central telephone exchanges made it possible to communicate faster and over greater distances.

Everett Historical/Shutterstock.com

with postings of academic and professional journal articles, then expanding to include books, magazines and newspapers that contained pictures. As with traditional print publishing, this medium permitted only one-way communication—from the creator to the consumer. Personal Websites that contained static information and were rarely updated dominated the Internet during this period, due in large part to the complexity of Website design software and the expense inherent in the new technology at that time. Accessing content was also difficult because of the then painfully slow Internet connections, which were a far cry from the exhilarating speeds we now currently enjoy. Over time, as software programs for developing Websites became easier to use, and as the network infrastructure known as the Internet backbone became more robust, static content was replaced with more interactive and dynamic media.[4]

The *New* New Media

By the year 2000, new media had evolved to encompass media content that was both digitally created and digitally distributed as well as interactive. By 2010, new media underwent yet another change: media convergence, the technology-driven fusion of media content (television, radio, print and graphics) into digital communication platforms (the Internet, e-mail and telephone). Web-based social networking and participatory journalism via the blogosphere also grew at astounding rates. Taking advantage of these advances, global Internet companies such as Google, Amazon.com and eBay were able to effectively tap into the expanding new media marketplace. Now, any working definition of new media must also include digital communication devices such as cell phones, smartphones (iPhones, Droids), personal digital assistants (PDAs) and online educational platforms such as Blackboard. From a mass media perspective, these tools have opened up a wider range of options for delivering finely tuned media content to smaller and more clearly targeted audiences.[5]

This ongoing convergence and evolution of new media has merged into an even more robust mass media mosaic called the "*new* new media," a term originally coined by Tim O'Reilly and John Battelle in 2004. The widely accepted term for this latest iteration is Web 2.0. Web 2.0 focuses on greatly enhanced user participation via networked creativity, innovation, information and content sharing, the exchange of intellectual property among users. It is at once both the nucleus and the primary platform of new media,

7.3

Apple's iPhone has quickly become a preferred digital platform for experiencing converged media.

Gary Reyes/San Jose Mercury News/MCT Newscom

built upon enormously improved visual and streaming media—content that is delivered in a constant, continuous manner. Greater Internet bandwidths, much faster and affordable computer-processing and operating systems, Internet service providers (ISPs) and Web-hosting services that are more robust—all have joined forces to turn Web 2.0 into a reality.

So far, these developments have led to the birth of Internet-based social networking, the blogosphere, global user-maintained information archives such as Wikipedia, and innovations in the media-rich delivery of entertainment, educational and business content. They have leveraged the power of the Internet to link tens of millions of users into an expanding, globally networked creativity engine.

The New Media Meme

New media encompasses more than just the media that live in the digital world of cyberspace. The concept itself is also a cultural meme—an idea that spreads rapidly through cultures, exponentially in the same way a virus spreads among living organisms. Indeed, new media represents perhaps the single most important meme of the 21st century.

Ideas that spread on the Internet—even if unreliable or untrue—can also be memes. They can become widely accepted "truths" simply because, like gossip or sensational news, they tend to catch on, attracting large numbers of people as they float around in cyberspace. Snopes.com is a popular Website dedicated to validating or debunking urban legends that, although of uncertain origin and highly questionable credibility, nevertheless seep into popular culture. That many of these legends are disseminated via the Internet is largely due to the viral nature of this forum, which hastens the rumor-spreading process. For example, during the 2012 presidential election, the urban myth that President Obama did not have a valid U.S. birth certificate and thus was not an American citizen and therefore not qualified to be president was being promoted by some conservatives, including well-known figures such as Donald Trump, despite the wealth of facts readily available that debunked such claims.

Although large amounts of unsubstantiated or false information continue to waft along the byways of the Internet, memes can also be used to popularize accurate and balanced ideas and counteract prior false information. For example, in the weeks just after the release of James Cameron's 2009 blockbuster film *Avatar*, widely circulated stories claimed that the film contained hidden messages that were purposely aimed at inciting racism. These Internet memes triggered a mostly positive media discourse that not only corrected the erroneous claims, but also opened up a public discussion about the value of protecting the world's remaining indigenous populations. This phenomenon of spreading memes through viral media—media messages shared through rapid replication via the Internet—has enabled those who have basic Web skills and limited resources to launch effective viral marketing and political movements. These Web denizens have harnessed the power of the World Wide Web, creating competing information that develops into alternative worldviews that are accepted and passed along by large groups of people.[6]

The influence of new media as conduits for cultural memes has exploded with the staggering growth of the Internet. According to the 2011 report *Digital Nation*, issued by the U.S. Department of Commerce's National Telecommunications and Information Administration, more than 483 million Americans go online on any given day.[7] New media and the Internet have radically changed how people communicate, socialize and access information and entertainment—a sea change whose effects we will explore in the course of this chapter. To help us understand how this transformation came about in such an astoundingly short time frame, let us acquaint ourselves with a few of the principal new media pioneers—the people with whom the story of new media begins.

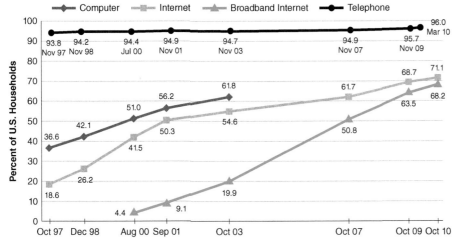

Growth trends in market saturation of media communication technologies in the United States.

Innovators and Visionaries of the Internet

The new media chronicle begins with the Internet, which has an amazingly short history. (Refer to Chapter 2.) The Internet was born in the mid-1970s as a U.S. Department of Defense project called ARPANET. Researchers originally used ARPANET to share work on defense-related research projects, which were based primarily at major universities around the United States. Over the course of just a few years, enormous improvements in computer networking and communication encouraged many more universities to join the ARPANET network. During the next 20 years, computers, application software and networking technologies combined to bring the power of computing to a growing number of users. The increasingly user-friendly software applications and graphical interfaces further spurred on the Digital Age.

In 1991, a young British mathematician named Tim Berners-Lee made a profound decision that would change the history of the world. Working with Robert Cailliau at the European High Energy Physics Center (CERN), Berners-Lee developed a communication language that allowed client computers and servers to communicate with each other, using standardized protocols across a vast network—what would come to be the World Wide Web (WWW), commonly known as the Web, a system of documents (Web pages) that live on the Internet containing text, images and multimedia, all interlinked and easily navigable. Berners-Lee decided to release his World Wide Web program to the world—for free.

7.5

Tim Berners-Lee, also commonly referred to as the "father of the Internet," photographed in his office at the Stata Center at Massachusetts Institute of Technology in Cambridge, MA on October 21, 2013.

Rick Friedman/Contributor

Three acronyms form the foundation of the Internet and represent the heart of Berners-Lee's ingenious innovation:

- URL **(Universal Resource Locator):** a naming system that gives every site in every document on the Internet a unique locatable address that anyone can easily access.
- HTTP **(Hypertext Transfer Protocol):** a collection of communication and software standards that allows many different kinds of computers of different brands, using different operating systems and different programming languages, to communicate with one another over the Web.

- HTML **(Hypertext Markup Language):** a relatively simple programming language that allows Web developers to specify how a document will appear when accessed by a wide variety of Internet browser programs.

While Berners-Lee is commonly called the "father of the Internet," it took two other young visionaries to turn the World Wide Web into the omnipresent digital world that it is today. In 1992, Marc Andreesen and Eric Bina, working at the National Center for Supercomputing Applications at the University of Illinois, developed Mosaic, the first Internet browser—an application whose software allows information on the World Wide Web to be viewed, retrieved and moved. A graphical-based network browser, Mosaic could display both text and pictures, and it let users easily navigate Websites by mouse-clicking URL links.

In 1994, Andreesen joined forces with other innovators including Jim Clark, the founder of Silicon Graphics, and the group collectively debuted Netscape Navigator, the first Internet browser made widely available to the public. Unlike Mosaic, Netscape Navigator offered numerous enhancements to existing interfaces to the Web, including optimization for new modem technology. A modem connects computers via telephone lines, but if communication traffic is congested, this connection can be notoriously slow and cause delays in file downloads. With Netscape came faster download speeds as well as a customizable bookmarks feature and the ability to save viewed files directly to the hard drive of a computer. Such advancements greatly increased the utility and reliability of the World Wide Web.[8]

The Information Superhighway

In 1991, then Senator Al Gore drafted the High Performance Computing and Communications Act of 1991, more commonly known as "the Gore Bill," which allocated $600 million for the creation of the National Research and Education Network (NREN). Gore hailed this network as the foundation for the building of the "information superhighway," which was conceived of by numerous well-known, 20th-century philosophers, scientists and visionaries long before the technology and applications to support it were in place. Philosopher and mass media guru Marshall McLuhan, for instance, envisioned the "global village" back in the 1960s. He saw this global village as enjoying widely accessible digital media and computer-based communications, transmitted over incredibly fast global networks of interconnected computers. He imagined a world where instantaneous communication and the universal sharing of knowledge would bridge national and cultural barriers, time and distance, all of which had separated people throughout history. Today, with the Internet and Web-based new media, one can argue that McLuhan's futuristic "global village" has in many ways been realized.[9]

Today, with the Internet and Web-based new media, one can argue that McLuhan's futuristic "global village" has in many ways been realized.

With government interest and funding playing an important role, what once was considered the innovative Web 1.0 eventually evolved into the more media-rich, easily accessible and interactive Web 2.0. Such U.S. federal government agencies as the National Aeronautics and Space Agency (NASA), the National Oceanic and Atmospheric Agency (NOAA) and the Smithsonian Institution together made sizable investments to help create applications for delivering highly visual content onto the Web, which in practical terms also necessitated the development of faster transfer technology. These and other government agencies continue to lead efforts in the development of the latest advances in Web 2.0. Major corporations including Microsoft, AOL, Netscape, Google and Adobe have also devoted significant research and development (R&D) resources to the creation of new media technologies that are now driving the progress and evolution of Web 2.0.

The Evolution of Web 2.0

Although not often connected in this way, the origin of the Internet is closely related to the development of another staple of new media: video games.[10] Shortly after World War II, the U.S. military recognized the benefits of developing a communications system that would allow researchers around the world to quickly share their work. During the same period, the Department of Defense had been working to develop computer-based simulations to train operators of sophisticated weapons platforms—from fighter plane and helicopter pilots, to air traffic controllers, to ships' officers, to armored vehicle drivers and beyond. This simulation technology would eventually find application in the commercial sector in a form that is omnipresent in U.S. culture today: computer and video games. To enable scientists to collaborate with colleagues and thus facilitate faster and more efficient development of these simulation technologies, the U.S. government invested in the production of what would become the Internet.

In addition to the significant support provided by the U.S. government, the international broadcasting industry has made major contributions to the evolution of Web 2.0 by relying on it to deliver media-rich content. The BBC in the United Kingdom and PBS in the United States were among the earliest broadcast networks to recognize the audience demand for content that users could interactively select and "self-program." Today a good portion of network television programming is also available on the Web—much of it free. Television content on the Web often comes with embedded advertising; much of it is available on Websites that charge one-time or monthly access or download fees.

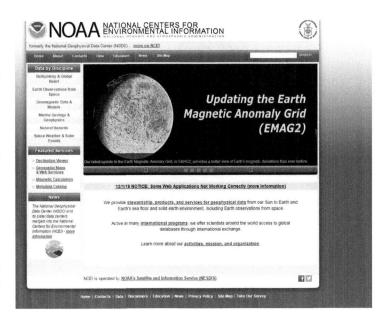

7.6

Together, NOAA and Smithsonian made sizable investments to the development and delivery of highly visual content on the Web.

NOAA

All of these government and commercial players have been driving the extraordinary developments in new media for the last two decades. At the same time, communication over the Internet, including e-mail, text messaging and Voice over Internet Protocol (VoIP)—voice communications that occur over the Internet—is becoming the dominant communication medium around the world.

Today a growing majority of Websites offer Web 2.0 features. These include integrating social media links and applications—which enable user-generated content and the development of virtual communities—and cloud-based applications that mimic desktop applications, interactive video features and even embedded video games.

Rediscovering Text: E-mail and Text Messaging

The emergence of new forms of mass media was accompanied by ever-more powerful and accessible tools for social and commercial networking. Electronic mail, now commonly called e-mail, was initially a digital network-based system for sending and receiving text-only messages. Over time, e-mail technology has evolved to accommodate images, video and audio.

The development of e-mail actually predates the development of the Internet. The precursor to what we know today as e-mail was first developed at the Massachusetts Institute of Technology (MIT) in 1961 and was called the Compatible Time-Sharing System (CTSS). CTSS let users of IBM mainframe computers leave messages for other users within the same system. It also enabled users at remote terminals to access mainframe computers.[11] Then in 1972, a young MIT-trained electrical engineer by the name of Ray Tomlinson (working with a small team) wrote the File Transfer Protocol (FTP), a standard set of procedures used for exchanging and manipulating files across a network of computers, called CPYNET. The popularity of this practical development quickly led to the first standardized e-mail protocol called SMTP (Standard Mail Transfer Protocol), which evolved into the POP (Post Office Protocol) e-mail standard that we all use today. In recognition of his work, Tomlinson is widely credited for having invented e-mail.

7.7

The popularity of texting and social media sites among Japan's youth is so pervasive that the abbreviated language of texting has become adopted into the Japanese language itself.

arek_malang/Shutterstock.com

Today approximately 4 billion people around the world send and receive more than 145 billion e-mails every day.[12] In many ways, e-mail represents a renewal of the popularity and utility of letter writing of past generations, albeit brought into the digital world of cyberspace and expanded to unimaginable levels. In the 21st century, it has become all but impossible to participate effectively in the common social activities of work, school, business and many other aspects of our daily lives without using e-mail.

Communication via digital text took another leap forward with the invention of text messaging ("texting")—that is, of portable digital devices such as cell phones, Web-enabled tablet computers and PDAs to transmit text-only messages.

The popularity of text messaging, also known as SMS (Short Message Service), has grown at an extraordinary rate. While there is no concrete evidence as to who created the first SMS text message, the prevailing view is that it was sent sometime around 1992. In 2000, nearly 20 billion text messages were sent worldwide. By 2005, this number had increased to 500 billion; by the end of 2009, to 1.6 trillion; and by the end of 2012, the number of text messages sent and received had increased to an astounding 9.6 trillion. In just a decade, the number of text messages sent each year has more than tripled.[13]

Text messaging has had, and continues to have, a significant cultural impact around the world. In India, for example, local matchmakers have embraced texting as an efficient means of linking families considering arranged marriages. On a larger scale, trade associations have launched effective texting campaigns to protest new government tax programs—and these campaigns have yielded powerful results.[14] In the United States, during his first presidential campaign, Barack Obama used texting to rally young voters and build a successful grassroots political movement. In Japan, texting became so popular among youth and white-collar workers that it led to changes in the Japanese language itself. Citizens were forced to adopt abbreviated words and word groupings to accommodate the format demanded by texting—in essence, profoundly affecting the Japanese culture.[15]

The exponential growth of texting among the generation of digital natives in Japan, the United States and throughout Europe is drawing a lot of attention. Texting has become so popular among U.S. high school students in particular that it has become a topic of heated debate among parents and experts on culture, linguistics and social psychology. Texting is cheaper, less confrontational and too advanced for the government to censor, so text messaging has also become the most popular form of digital communication in China. By the end of 2012, for example, people living in China sent 44 billion text messages. Texting in that country has continued to increase at an astounding rate, according to the Chinese Ministry of Information and Industry.[16]

THE DYNAMIC NEW MEDIA

Since the Middle Ages, information has been distributed and accessed following the book model. In this model, which remained largely unchanged until the Digital Age, an author creates the content, organizes it according to a specified, typically linear structure and delivers it to the reader, who then follows the author's narrative sequence. The new media model, however, is nonlinear.

Linear Versus Nonlinear Information

How information is organized and accessed is one aspect of new media that sets it apart from the "old media" that came before. The organization of old media was primarily linear. Content in old media, newspapers, magazines, books, music albums and television programs, for example, had clear beginnings and ends. Moreover, users had to make an extra effort to track down any referenced content. For example, an article about life in Key West, Florida, that was published in a print magazine might include a quote from Ernest Hemingway, with a footnote citing the source of the quote. If the reader were interested in reading this quote in the context that Hemingway intended, then it would be up to the reader to conduct the actual research that would lead him to the book. The reader might locate it in a library or bookstore. He would then have to flip through the book to find the section quoted in the article, only then getting a sense of the literary context as Hemingway intended.

New media is far more dynamic, in part because most users access the content in a nonlinear manner. In the new model, users "re-create" or "remix" media content to fit their individual interests and needs. New media lives within an endless, multitiered mosaic of knowledge, the elements of which are always linked in multiple ways.

To see how this works, let's look again at the Ernest Hemingway quote, but this time moving it from an article in a print magazine to a Website. This Website would include many embedded hyperlinks (references or sources that can be accessed by mouse-clicking on a link) to numerous other Web sources and sites—each of which would have its own set of hyperlinks to still more sites. This "linked" knowledge grows exponentially the deeper we delve into it; it is seemingly endless, limited only by how far each individual user chooses to explore. Perhaps the user might click on the Hemingway quote and be presented with an image of the exact page from the book on which the quote appears. This page might show up as a popup window or as a link to another page that automatically opens up. Other links to articles, photographs, video segments and blogs exploring Hemingway's life in Key West might appear as well. These links could then take a user to yet more sites that explore the works of other famous Key West authors, or to sites that display images of Hemingway, or to sites that focus on his polydactyl cats—and on and on it goes, as far as an individual user wishes to click.

User-Mediated Content

As noted earlier, users are not forced to access information in cyberspace sequentially or linearly. Instead, media content is presented in the form or nodes or, in the case of streaming media, podcasts (digital video or audio files that can be downloaded from the Web), which can have multiple associated links to related material within the same site as well as links to related information throughout the World Wide Web. This format represents a radical change from previous dominant forms of media, and it empowers users to create, access and organize information on their own terms.

Recent neuropsychological studies on how human brains acquire, process and store information have demonstrated that, for most people, self-directed selection of knowledge nodes and self-structured organization can vastly increase their ability to absorb and use new information. This approach, which takes advantage of how human learning works best, is called dynamic adaptive learning.[17] Dynamic adaptive learning is the basis for the user-interface design of new generations of Web-based training sites, as well as Web-based knowledge collections such as Wikipedia.

New media-enabled information, when dynamically adaptable to each user's interests,

7.8

Students experience dynamic adaptive learning, which some neuropsychological studies suggest has helped to improve our ability to absorb and apply new information.

Blend Images/Alamy Stock Photo

New media-enabled information, when dynamically adaptable to each user's interests, gives us the power to control how we consume the information found in the new media, including where we get it from and when and how we use it.

gives us the power to control how we consume the information found in the new media, including where we get it from and when and how we use it. Suppose you are a big fan of a particular music group, but you do not like every one of their songs. In the old media world, your only option was to go to a music store and purchase an entire album of that band's music, which most likely included a number of cuts that you didn't want. In today's new media world, you can log on to any one of a number of online music outlets, listen to samples from all the works by your favorite group and select, purchase and download just those songs you like onto your computer. You can then organize these songs to play in whatever order you want to hear them, load them onto your iPod or other portable media player (PMP) and essentially create your own album.

The "re-creation" or "remixing" capabilities of new media content also allow us to take music from one group and sample it with the vocals from another (or our own), thereby creating what is in effect a new work. Anyone with a computer, some inexpensive media editing software and a little skill can make his or her own unique media composition this way. These re-created and remixed works can be easily uploaded and widely distributed through popular content sharing sites such as YouTube as well as peer-to-peer (P2P) user networks such as Rhapsody, Napster, and BitTorrent, where the content is not only shared between peers, but supplied and purchased by them as well. The proliferation of user-mediated content is, in fact, one of the key characteristics of the new media era. There are, of course, controversial copyright issues involved in remixing works from source material created by others. (See Chapter 11.)

Participatory Content Creation

Web 2.0 is, in effect, an ever-growing sphere of collective intelligence that is accessible to an ever-increasing portion of the global population. Think of this new collective intelligence as a shared knowledge base cre-

Think of this new collective intelligence as a shared knowledge base created by the ongoing collaboration.

ated by the ongoing collaboration of hundreds of millions, if not billions, of individuals. New media content is simultaneously born out of this collective collaboration of contributors and serves as the source of emerging ideas and innovations, which in turn provides new tools that empower users to participate in its ongoing expansion.

In a way, the creators of new media content and the developers of the tools that increase the accessibility of, and participation in, the creation of this content share a symbiotic relationship. Part of the power of user-created media content lies in its efficiency and reliable self-correction. The rapid pace of technological change and content availability makes it impossible for anyone to keep up with every single innovation, which in turn forces a dependency on knowledge sharing with vast networks of experts. Participatory content creation is also far more cost-effective and reliable than the creation of the same content by individuals or small isolated groups.

Take, for example, the online global encyclopedia Wikipedia. Launched in 2001, Wikipedia is a non-profit, open-content, Internet-based encyclopedia established by Internet entrepreneur Jimmy Wales and philosopher Larry Sanger. Their goal was to create a self-generating content platform that would eventually summarize all of the knowledge in the world and offer it—for free—to everyone in all of the major languages. Thanks to the denizens of Web 2.0, what started out as a far-fetched dream fast became a reality. Today Wikipedia is the single most used knowledge source in the world, and its accuracy meets and often surpasses its old media rivals, such as the *Encyclopedia Britannica* (which, as a result of Wikipedia's success, started offering user-created content on its own Web-based encyclopedia in 2008).[18]

In the early years of Wikipedia, many scholars and content experts questioned the reliability and potential bias of its articles. Given the enormous size of its pool of contributors, critics expressed concern over its lack of practical controls and fact checking. Over time, however, Wikipedia has proven to be remarkably self-correcting, even to the point of advertising for female contributors to help deal with perceived gender bias in some entries. The accuracy of its content is the result of the work of numerous content experts who have volunteered to police the site's user-generated entries. These thousands of unpaid editors respond quickly to erroneous, biased or malicious entries and correct them swiftly. Malicious or libelous entries are brought to the attention of the Wikipedia staff, who then rapidly remove them. At the same time, volunteer software developers are busy creating tools that will enable the Wikipedia community to rate all articles with regard to their reliability.[19]

Knowledge Sharing: An Open-Source Model

In the new media era, the open-source model has gained prominence as an approach to content production and management that permits easy, widespread access to information in an effort to encourage creative cross-pollination between information sources and information consumers, with the aim of cultivating progress and a more robust knowledge base. Advocates of this model argue that the overall benefit to society gained by releasing traditionally controlled, protected or copyrighted material is much greater than the cost to the individual producer, and that in the end, even the individual producer gains more by contributing to the good of the culture.

While the open-source model has proved a boon to disciplines across the board by making select content that would have otherwise been closed to the general public accessible, this model has served the sciences particularly well. Advances in cyberspace have made the ArXiv possible.

ArXiv (pronounced "archive"), founded in 1991 at the Los Alamos National Laboratory and moved to Cornell University in 2001, is a free online collection of scientific articles from several "hard science" fields—mathematics, physics, biology, computer science and astronomy. This database is open to anyone with an interest in science. A striking aspect of the articles on ArXiv is that they are not peer reviewed, a prerequisite in traditional scientific and academic publishing. Instead, a collection of "expert moderators" reviews the articles, which then receive further scrutiny via a topic-expert endorsement system (similar to that found in Wikipedia).

Consuming New Media: Honing Critical Skills

Distinguishing between high-quality and low-quality information in cyberspace challenges even the most skilled users. Sophisticated search engines (devices designed to search information on the Web) such as Google do some of this work for us; they search Websites using sophisticated algorithms that include both analyzing key search terms usage, also known as Boolean term comparisons, and the number of hits each site receives, then list the results in descending order. The experience of sifting through hundreds and thousands of Websites, social networking sites and blogs helps one to develop familiarity with the keywords and core concepts—information that can then be used to locate credible and reliable sites related to personal or research topics of interest.

Developing critical media consumer skills has always been an important part of the mass media story; the proliferation of new media and the Web has merely heightened the critical nature of that requirement. All of us—both digital natives and digital immigrants—must develop effective selection and filtering skills to avoid being overwhelmed and misinformed. For example, of the thousands of blogs added to the Internet each month, only a fraction attract large numbers of visitors; even fewer become popular or influential over the long term.[20] Why? What do these statistics tell us? The blogs that receive heavy traffic generally do so because of favorable word of mouth. Sites built on poor and unreliable information quickly turn off visitors and often simply disappear.

All of us—both digital natives and digital immigrants—must develop effective selection and filtering skills to avoid being overwhelmed and misinformed.

Of course, media consumers should not blindly accept popular content just because it is popular. Given that other factors may affect the number of visitors to a particular Website—for example, controversial media and even artificially high ratings gained by paid search optimization (increasing site traffic via Internet advertising)—media consumers must stay vigilant and critically evaluate the accuracy of even the most popular sources on the Internet.

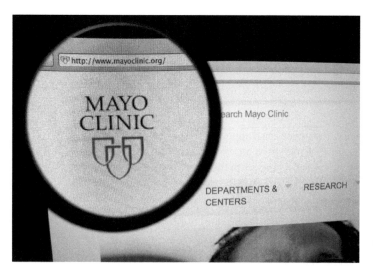

7.9

Failure to develop critical consumer skills can be dangerous, especially when it comes to health or medical topics. Many credible sites are available, such as the Mayo Clinic, but users must be responsible for deciding what's credible and what's not.

Gil C/Shutterstock.com

MEDIA CONVERGENCE

As discussed throughout this book, media convergence is one of the dominant trends transforming both new and traditional media today. Rather than simply replicating the old media equivalents and delivering them via the Internet, this movement actually melds the various types of new media content into an emerging, fully integrated and interactive media format. This practice has stimulated a reformulation of the entire landscape of media content production and distribution, which in turn is forcing a complete redesign of mass media business models. Notably, major media outlets—from newspapers and magazines to radio stations and television networks—are projecting their content into cyberspace and, in the process, adding many levels of user-selectable options and interactive components. (See Chapter 9.)

On the Websites of the major television networks (e.g., ABC, NBC, CBS, FOX) and cable/satellite news networks (e.g., CNN, MSNBC, FNN), fans can immerse themselves in the backstories of their favorite program characters, participate in viewer forums, send suggestions to program writers for future episodes and view special features such as extended scene, graphic novels and interviews with actors. Viewers can also access extended video segments of news stories, participate in the blogs of star news anchors, pitch their own story ideas and even submit their own video segments.

In the new media era, people on the scene of natural disasters such as hurricanes or tornados contribute a significant number of on-the-scene videos that The Weather Channel (owned by NBC) picks up and then sends to the other networks via their Websites. The networks' TV news programs even broadcast the most striking of these user-generated video segments. This convergence is made possible by the previously mentioned migration of all media into digital form and then into cyberspace. It increases the user-participant aspect of new media to such an extent that it often blurs the line between professional and amateur. This transform, in turn, is forcing a reconsideration of the traditional definition of the "journalist" or "professional" media producer. One of the most successful examples of media convergence is the Emmy Award-winning independent media network, Current.

This convergence is made possible by the previously mentioned migration of all media into digital form and then into cyberspace. It increases the user-participant aspect of new media to such an extent that it often blurs the line between professional and amateur.

The Effects of Content Mobility

The transition to all-digital television in the United States, which Congress mandated to be completed by February 2009, provided an added incentive to mass media market leaders to develop technologies and business models that could take advantage of the new all-digital media ecosystem. One of the many benefits of producing and distributing media content in an all-digital environment is content mobility. Sometimes referred to as *three-screen convergence*, content mobility facilitates relatively seamless transferring of video content between digital television, personal computers and mobile devices, thereby giving consumers a wider range of options for accessing video programs, television news, video games and other streaming media material. Increased content mobility is helping to expand the audience base for many software

7.10

Extreme digital mobility on the Huangpu River in the Bund Area of Shanghai, China.

Richard Cummins/Design Pics/ Newscom

programs and is empowering a new generation of content producers, who are able to devise new production techniques to present their video narratives in shorter, more easily portable video pods.

Content mobility is also enabling the convergence of users' "screen experiences." The majority of our day-to-day interface with mass media in the 21st century is our experience and interaction with media screens—from flat-screen TV monitors of all sizes to the screens on our computers, tablets and cell phones. In 2012, Web developers and television broadcasters began to push our common screen experiences to the next level by adding technologies that enable users to enjoy a two-screen experience. For example, imagine watching your favorite television drama on your Web-enabled flat-screen TV at home. Now imagine that three of your friends or relatives, all in different parts of the country, are watching the same TV show at the same time. With a few clicks of your remote, you open a live social networking window that appears as a small popup screen in the corner of your TV screen. Instantly, you and your friends are connected. The viewing of a popular TV program becomes a real-time shared experience no longer limited by geographic barriers. Connect to your friends via a Web video-conferencing service such as Skype, and this real-time shared media experience is further enhanced. In another example of the rapidly developing multiscreen experience, the satellite TV service DirecTV now offers a free iPad app that enables subscribers to access all of their DirecTV channels on their iPad, participate in social media sites or use e-mail services while watching satellite TV channels. They can even control their DirecTV DVR while they're away from home.

Viral Media

Viral media comprises media content—most often video segments—produced by both amateurs and professionals, which gains widespread popularity and distribution through the Internet via content-hosting sites (such as YouTube) and blogs and social networking sites (such as Tumblr and Facebook). Its name was inspired by the way that a biological virus can rapidly spread through a host's body as well as through large segments of the population, as in the case of a flu epidemic. Viral videos can be original productions or captured segments from other videos or television programs. The more clever and successful viral media is, the more quickly it migrates from the Internet into the mainstream media. The videos are sometimes reedited, or "remixed," to express the political, cultural or satirical views of the creators.

Viral videos have a significant influence on culture in the Digital Age. Their effects have been felt in areas ranging from product marketing to entertainment marketing (including creating a market "buzz" for new TV shows, new movies and new music albums) to political campaigns. Viral videos can be used for darker purposes, too: They can easily and effectively be used to spread myths and rumors and to reinforce racial, ethnic and gender stereotyping. Nevertheless, they just as often expand the cultural and political dialogue about hot-button issues and are regularly very entertaining and satirical. For example, on March 3, 2012, a viral video titled "Stop Kony" appeared on YouTube. Its aim was to bring worldwide media attention to atrocities being committed by Ugandan rebel leader Joseph Kony, who has been indicted for war crimes including conscripting children to become child soldiers and child sex slaves. The video went viral with over 55 million views in the first 24 hours and was picked up by major TV news networks around the world. This forced Kony to go underground and caused the African Union to send 5,000 troops into Uganda to join the hunt for the rebel leader. Regardless of the motivation behind viral media, in our new media age, viral media works—in fact, it often attracts millions of viewers. For all these reasons, viral media represents an important element of our 21st-century new media mosaic and is a regular part of the media content that many of us encounter every day.

YouTube and User-Generated Television

The most popular and widely accessed new media platform for video content of every kind, including viral videos, is, without a doubt, YouTube. The YouTube phenomenon has become so influential that it has compelled traditional mainstream media organizations, especially broadcast and cable/satellite television networks, to join in the YouTube revolution.

Launched in 2005, YouTube is a free video-sharing site that hosts an extraordinary variety of user-generated and professionally produced video content, ranging from short video segments to full-length programs. In late 2006, Google acquired YouTube in a stock swap valued at a reported $1.65 billion. Starting in May 2008, YouTube and Google began to release user statistics to the public. According to these publicly released user statistics, Google had more than 100 million daily visitors, making it one of the busiest Websites in the world. In 2012, the number of YouTube visits doubled from the previous year to 800 million. Google searches in 2012 were 1.2 trillion, in 146 languages.[21]

YouTube is widely accepted as one of the flagships of new media and the leader in converging old media television and video in cyberspace. Even so, it has vocal critics. The most frequently voiced criticism of YouTube is that it does not do a good job of assuring that site content complies with U.S. and international copyright laws and treaties. Even though YouTube posts messages warning against copyright violation and makes some effort to police the massive flow of video content, a huge number of copyright-violating videos are posted regularly, resulting in a continual stream of lawsuits being filed against the company. However, the immense size of the YouTube community makes real enforcement of this policy nearly impossible. In the end, YouTube, like so much of the content on the Web, relies on its user community to be self-correcting.

YouTube, along with other social networking sites that allow the posting of videos, can also create instant celebrities with huge online followings.

YouTube, along with other social networking sites that allow the posting of videos, can also create instant celebrities with huge online followings. In 2008, Tennessee State University co-ed Kimber Turner started spending some of her free time posting photos of tattoos that she had pulled mostly from the many body modification Websites on Tumblr. She included her own humorous and often obscene captions with the images. "Within a few weeks, Turner had 300 viewers. She invited others to submit similar images and captions and started receiving over 200 submissions per day. In 2012, Turner had over 695,000 followers. Today she posts about 50 new photos every day, about one every 30 minutes. When Web advertising offers followed, she had a new, full-time career.[22]

While the Internet, including social networking, is undoubtedly the most powerful medium of human communication and mass media in history, it has also enabled the creation of a new meme, where videos of cats jumping into boxes or rabbits balancing pancakes on their heads become overnight media sensations, drawing millions of viewers. Such new, shared experiences often appear to have no real cultural value, but they are nevertheless experienced, every day, thanks to social networking.[23]

YouTube also makes Web narrowcasting economically viable for thousands of content creators and media consumers with special interests in ways that cable and satellite television services offering hundreds of channels cannot match. Internet videocasting, especially YouTube "channels," make it possible for relatively small groups of people with shared interests, say, remote-control model-sailboat racing, to share specialized video content 24 hours a day, seven days a week. Of course, a YouTube channel catering to remote-control model-sailboat racing attracts advertising by companies that manufacture parts and kits and how-to books for model-boat-racing hobbyists—specialty companies whose previous advertising options were limited to specialty magazines.

The governments of some countries, such as Iran and Pakistan, have blocked YouTube, along with other open-source sites, because they consider some of the content to be offensive to Islam. As has been well documented by the international media, China regularly tries to block YouTube content because its free flow of information might enable the exchange of information among anti-government factions, which could threaten the central government's control. At the same time, localized versions of YouTube have sprung up around the world in more than 42 languages.[24]

LINKING UP: 21ST-CENTURY SOCIAL NETWORKING

Online social networking has quickly become a mainstay among members of the millennial generation and represents a new form of social culture that takes place entirely online. Who is actually participating in online social networking, and what are the trends? In a 2008 study to determine social network usage conducted by RapLeaf, then a leading Web 2.0 social networks tracking organization, of the 175 million people in its database, 49.3 million of whom actually participated in the study, approximately 90 percent of the respondents were from the United States. RapLeaf's study also found that while the overall rates of use of and participation in new media and the Internet are roughly equal between young men and young women, young women far outnumber young men as participants on major social networking sites such as Facebook, Twitter and Tumblr. This trend is changing, however, as the percentage of male users is growing rapidly.[25]

Digital natives, the first generation to grow up in a world where digital technologies and the Internet were already in place, stay connected to cyberspace during a large part of their waking hours each day. They create for themselves multiple digital identities that simultaneously "live" in parallel with their real-world identities and with each other. Using the power of the Internet, digital natives are creating their own virtual society and virtual culture populated by online relationships that are largely hidden from their parents and teachers.[26]

By 2007, almost 90 percent of teenagers in the United States were online for a significant portion of each day, seven days a week—and this percentage has grown to just about 100 percent today.[27] Digital natives view their online lives not as separate lives, but rather as a seamless continuation of their real-world lives. They are also heavily involved in and naturally adept at digital multitasking. They often utilize multiple Internet sites for homework, research and entertainment and talk with as many as a dozen online "friends" at the same time. When they are away from their computers, they are on cell phones and tablets, text messaging, accessing the Web and maintaining their online relationships on multiple sites. Some become so good at multitasking that they are uncomfortable being out of the digital loop for even short periods of time.

A 2012 study by the Pew Internet & American Life Project reported that:

> "Teens and young adults brought up from childhood with a continuous connection to each other and to information will be nimble, quick-acting multitaskers who count on the Internet as their external brain and who approach problems in a different way from their elders. . . . Many of the experts surveyed by Elon University's Imagining the Internet Center and the Pew Internet Project said the effects of hyperconnectivity and the always-on lifestyles of young people will be mostly positive between now and 2020. But the experts in this survey also predicted this generation will exhibit a thirst for instant gratification and quick fixes, a loss of patience, and a lack of deep-thinking ability due to what one referred to as "fast-twitch wiring."[28]

Digital Meeting Places

Online social networking allows people to develop and practice social skills in a far less intimidating environment than they might experience in face-to-face interactions. Digital meeting places such as Facebook and Twitter are rapidly melding with, and in some cases replacing, actual physical meeting places where kids hang out after school.[29] As of 2012, these two sites alone had a combined membership of more than 1.5 billion.

Digital environments also offer more focused interactions, such as themed chat rooms and discussion boards. These forums easily connect people with like interests, thereby functioning as online social "icebreakers." Meeting in cyberspace also affords users some anonymity, freedom and, in a counterintuitive way, privacy—all important factors in the development of personal identity. In fact, the ability to experiment with building many different online identities seems to be one of the main reasons why social networking sites are so popular with young users. While most parents would not allow their teenage children to roam freely about the real world, the digital world offers a relatively safe place to experiment with personal relationships and learn to manage them responsibly.[30] Since the digital world has few cultural or spatial barriers, young online social networkers are able to connect with people around the world and experience many different cultures. This interaction can lead to the cross-pollination of ideas, higher cross-cultural awareness and increased tolerance of others. All of these benefits are attractive to many young people.[31]

Online social networking is also highly appealing to those people who may be struggling with learning disabilities or social disorders.[32] For these individuals, online social networking provides the opportunity to foster relationships free from many of the encumbrances that often hold them back from full participation in society. Involvement in digital communities also offers continual exposure to developing technologies and helps young adults cultivate skills that are necessary to adapt to the constantly evolving world of the 21st century. Early awareness of the benefits and dangers present in the digital world can provide younger cybercitizens with the foundational skills needed to navigate effectively the uncertain waters of innovation, while still maintaining control over their own digital identities.[33]

> Early awareness of the benefits and dangers present in the digital world can provide younger cybercitizens with the foundational skills needed to navigate effectively the uncertain waters of innovation, while still maintaining control over their own digital identities.

The Dark Side of Online Social Networking

While the benefits of online social networking are numerous, a darker, more dangerous side of this world also exists. Potential problems such as rumor spreading, fighting and bullying increase exponentially in the digital world, where there are little, if any, means of policing user activity. For example, on September 12, 2010, a Rutgers University student received a tweet (a Twitter message) from his roommate, 18-year-old freshman Tyler Clementi, asking if he could have the room to himself until midnight. Unbeknownst to Clementi, his roommate had set up a hidden Webcam, which captured Clementi "making out with a dude." The roommate posted the clandestine video on the Web. Three days later, Clementi, an accomplished violinist and straight-A student, committed suicide by jumping off the George Washington Bridge into the Hudson River. Prosecutors charged the roommate, Dharun Ravi, with multiple counts of invasion of privacy and using a hidden camera to view and transmit images without Tyler Clementi's knowledge or consent, charges that carry a five-year prison term for each count. The victim's family, supported by leading gay activist groups, considered Clementi's death a hate crime, which could result in federal prosecution and significant civil penalties.[34] In a U.S. Department of Education study conducted between November 2009 and April 2010, nearly 15 percent of teenagers between 12 and 18 years of age reported that they had been the victim of bullying—and a good deal of this harassment had occurred online.[35] The study "Bullying and Adolescent Health," reported by the U.S. Department of Health & Human Services' Office of Adolescent Health at the end of 2011, found that 6.5 percent of all high school students either admitted to cyberbullying or reported having been the victim of cyberbullying themselves.[36]

Most teenagers and young adults participating in online social networking dismiss concerns about personal privacy. As stated earlier, many users often feel that they have more privacy on social networking sites than they experience in real-world social situations. Unfortunately, this widespread perception of anonymity discounts a very real problem: Any content posted on the Web lives forever.

Although users have the freedom to build seemingly secret identities in the cyberuniverse, between the personal information that sites such as Facebook allow users to display and the intimate details that are communicated through the natural development of personal relationships on the Internet, cybercitizens actually leave a nearly indelible trail on the Web. Any personal information or images posted on the Web may become available to unimaginable numbers of people. Such content, especially if it is "inappropriate," can come back to haunt these individuals. This problem is particularly acute for teens or college students seeking to move into more mature environments—for example, graduate school, the workplace or fields in high view of the public such as entertainment or politics.

According to widely prevalent stories in the mainstream media, one of the greatest potential dangers facing adolescents and young adults in cyberspace is the presence of sexual predators. Individuals posing as peers, possible friends or romantic interests are able to exploit the perceived safety of the Internet and lure unsuspecting users into compromising and abusive situations. Although this threat has been popularized through news coverage and television, how real is this danger? If we look back over the course of time, sexual aberrations and sexual predators have been a social problem for centuries. Contrary to some of the more inflammatory stories published in the media, the preponderance of studies show that the percentage of these incidents traceable to Web usage differs little from the percentage occurring in society as a whole. However, when we combine this fact with the ease with which false identities can be created on the Web, it is not surprising that many children's safety organizations and many elected officials remain concerned that social networking sites may allow young victims to be drawn in, manipulated and, in a small percentage of the cases, exposed to very real danger.[37] Such study findings do not mean, however, that there are not real dangers facing young Web users, especially preteens. Children are naturally attracted to the socializing possibilities on sites such as Facebook and enjoy posting photos of themselves and their friends, often along with personal information, without realizing the threat of online predators. Yet predators are not the only dangers in cyberspace. Far more teenagers face the dangers of peer bullying or of being excluded from desired peer groups than encountering adult cyberpredators. This is why parent groups reacted strongly when Facebook publicly announced, in the summer of 2012, its intent to actively recruit members under 13 years of age.[38]

Media coverage of online predators has been increasing for several years. Congress has held a series of hearings on the problem, and police departments routinely send experts on cyberpredators to schools and churches in an effort to inform and rally parents to keep on top of their children's online activities. Despite their good intentions, these efforts have had little or no impact on how young people use social networking sites.[39] High school and college students claim in countless media and polling interviews that they know the danger signs of potential online sexual predators and are very capable—more capable than their parents are, in fact—of easily identifying and avoiding such dangers.[40]

A 2007 study on the threat of online sexual predators, funded by the U.S. Department of Justice, supported this wealth of claims. The research found that one in five children had encountered mild to moderate sexual solicitations online, and that the majority of these children quickly identified and avoided these inappropriate advances. One survey of reported incidents of sexual abuse, where the contacts were initiated online, all apparently involved teenagers who were *actively* seeking such contacts and who followed up by agreeing to meet the adult perpetrators in person.[41]

7.11

Despite having grown up in a digital world, how savvy are young adults when it comes to gauging the dark side of social networking online?

Ian Hooton/Getty Images

Thus it seems that combating this dark side of online social networking with tighter parental controls—most of which teenagers can easily circumvent—is not the ultimate solution. Could promoting media literacy and critical digital consumer skills be the sole key to preventing the majority of crimes committed by sexual predators on the Internet? The counterargument suggests that it is naive to think that media literacy can completely protect young Web users from the potential risks. Nevertheless, as the U.S. Justice Department study suggests, millennials are largely attuned to the dangers of online communities and, therefore, are less likely to fall victim to their pitfalls.[42]

Follow Me on Twitter

Stephanie Sullivan, 46, is the founder of a Web development company in Wilmington, North Carolina. When she was first introduced to microblogging (a much-abbreviated form of blogging), she thought the whole idea of staying connected day by day, hour by hour, with a circle of her friends and acquaintances was a ridiculous concept. Then she started using Twitter to stay close to her boyfriend, Greg Rewis, 44, who was living in Phoenix, Arizona, and working for Adobe Systems. One day she received a tweet from Greg that went like this:

@stefsull: ok. for the rest of the twitter-universe (and this is a first, folks)—WILL YOU MARRY ME?
Her response,
@garazi—OMG—Ummmmm . . . I guess in front of the whole twitter-verse I'll say—
I'd be happy to spend the rest of my geek life with you.[43]

7.12

Twitter's incredible speed allowed it to break the news of the devastating earthquake in China in 2008 before any other media outlet managed to do so.

Gudjon E. Olafsson/Shutterstock.com

Though difficult to substantiate with absolute certainty, Greg's marriage proposal and Stephanie's acceptance were the first engagement to take place over Twitter or any other micro-networking site. These two self-proclaimed "geeks" married and went on to collaboratively write a how-to book about Adobe Dreamweaver.

Greg and Stephanie's marriage proposal highlights the very nature of the Twitter social networking experience—millions of people sharing the everyday happenings of their lives in a public online forum. First launched in 2006 in San Francisco, Twitter is a free social networking site where participants post short text-based updates (maximum 140 characters for each post) called tweets. Many large businesses have begun to use Twitter as an alternative to e-mail and text messaging. Even government agencies have started to use Twitter as an alternative form of communication for emergency first responders during forest fires or other natural disasters.

Social networking sites such as Facebook, LinkedIn and Twitter can also be very valuable for businesses. Advertising and marketing firms, as well as venture capital groups, are flocking to social networking sites

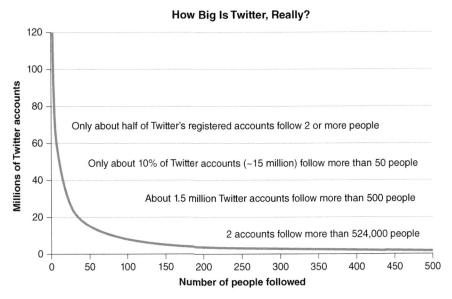

How Big Is Twitter, Really?

Only about half of Twitter's registered accounts follow 2 or more people

Only about 10% of Twitter accounts (~15 million) follow more than 50 people

About 1.5 million Twitter accounts follow more than 500 people

2 accounts follow more than 524,000 people

(y-axis) Millions of Twitter accounts

(x-axis) Number of people followed

7.13

The comparative number of Twitter "followers" per Twitter account shows that not all members follow large numbers of people.

Twitter API

in an effort to identify and target like-minded consumers who share important demographics. Some firms are hiring independent marketing reps—often college students—who apply their social networking skills to promote products and services to the firms' "friends" and "followers," usually without disclosing that they are being paid to make these promotional posts. Other companies are using social networking sites to track employee job performance, monitor employee ethical standards and even predict employee turnover rates. Many corporations use social networking sites more openly. Nike, for example, tracks social networking sites and bloggers to see whose posts most influence the sales of their athletic shoes.[44]

Life-Blogging

Generally, Twitter's major use is life-blogging, wherein millions of individuals share the highlights, and often the minutia, of their daily lives with a circle of online "friends" in a very public forum. Life-bloggers, also called *life-loggers*, use new media technologies—computers and tablets, digital cameras and Internet photo-sharing sites such as Pinterest—to document and openly share their daily lives in an ongoing personal reality show.

Perhaps you remember the main character in director Peter Weir's 1998 dramatic comedy *The Truman Show*. This Academy Award-nominated

7.14

Poster advertisement for *The Truman Show* (1998), about Truman, who attempts to escape the 24/7 public surveillance of life.

D. Trozzo/Alamy Stock Photo

film chronicles the life of Truman Burbank, played by comic actor Jim Carrey. Truman is unaware that he is actually living in a 24/7 televised reality show, where every minute of his life is televised to millions of viewers around the world. When Truman discovers that his life has been on view to a worldwide audience, he tries to escape it. Life-bloggers are doing just the opposite: They *voluntarily* share their lives with thousands of social networking subscribers.

An example of life-blogging is Facebook's Timeline. The Timeline feature allows Facebook users to highlight photos and posts of life events, from important milestones to the miniscule details of one's day-to-day activities. Originally, the Timeline feature was optional, but in 2012, Facebook made it an automatic part of the "walls" of all of Facebook's 800 million users. Timeline aggregates information about each user's Web activities across Websites and tablet apps, not just on Facebook, which raised the alarm of Web privacy advocates and the angst of many Facebook users.

The ability for anyone to build a database clone of his or her life is now more possible than we think—but is it of practical use? One might argue that just because new media technologies allow us to do extraordinary things, it does not always mean that the results have practical value. According to the opposite view, users are regularly finding new and innovative ways to use new media such as Twitter and Pinterest to benefit everyday life or to support political and social causes.

Activism and Citizen Journalism

On both the national and international fronts, activists have effectively used Twitter to organize rallies and coordinate street protests: in China, during the 2008 Summer Olympics; in Moldova, in April 2009 after suspected rigged elections restored the Communist Party to power; and in Iran, during the June 2009 presidential elections.

Closer to home, in March 2008, on the fifth anniversary of the U.S. invasion of Iraq, anti-war protesters used blogging sites and Twitter to coordinate numerous demonstrations around the United States. Additional public support was solicited via text messaging. Potential protesters were able to sign up to receive live updates of the organizers' activities as well as responses from the media and authorities. Videos of aggressive police action against some of the activists, as well as the crowd's reactions, were filmed. These videos quickly found their way onto YouTube and such Web-based video news services as the American News Project (ANP); the ANP then sent out hundreds of thousands of e-mails alerting its viewer base to the story. Within a few hours, the mainstream news media picked up these videos, and they appeared as feature stories on CNN, MSNBC and others.

The level of media coverage and the extensive audience reach of such stories, which start as viral videos and then migrate into the mainstream news cycle, is extraordinary compared to the coverage of similar stories generated by traditional media outlets. Moreover, because mass media often drives the public and government agenda, the story forced responses from Senator Dianne Feinstein (Democrat-California) and then Speaker of the House Nancy Pelosi (Democrat-California), encouraging them to take stronger anti-war positions in their own media appearances.[45]

The rapid evolution of the blogosphere demonstrates how fast technologies and trends can change in the new media world of the 21st century. Since the blogosphere first appeared in 1994, tens of thousands of citizen journalists have come to dominate it. Their presence in the blogosphere was motivated by their desire to bypass paths traditionally open only to professional journalists and the wish for the public to respond to their voices. By the 2004 presidential election, the leading blog-based Internet journalists had gained so much influence in the culture that they were given press credentials for both the Democratic and Republican national conventions and were admitted to the White House pressroom. Yet by 2008, the blogosphere had largely moved away from its roots as a populist free-for-all of public expression, becoming dominated by advertising-supported blogs. These blogs are populated by professional writers, journalists and political pundits—many of them employed by mainstream media organizations. The emergence of such "professional" blog sites has made it difficult, but not impossible, for individual independent bloggers to attract audiences, gain advertiser support and keep their voices being heard in the public debate and the mass media marketplace of ideas.[46]

POLITICS AND NEW MEDIA

Markos Moulitsas Zúniga was born in Chicago on September 11, 1971. His father was a Greek-American and his mother was Salvadoran. Zúniga's family moved to El Salvador during the Salvadoran War (1980–1992), a violent civil war that pitted the Salvadoran government's right-wing security forces against the left-wing rebel forces. Extensive human rights violations were committed by both sides—including the practice of "disappearances," where both civilian and political figures would be kidnapped and "disappeared," their families never to see them again or learn what had happened. Zúniga's experience living amid daily gun-shots and explosions deeply affected his views on war and politics. He learned at a very young age that pol-itics could become a matter of life and death. When his parents received an envelope sent by an anonymous source containing photographs of him and his brother boarding a bus to school, they took it as a clear threat to their lives made by the rebel forces. The Zúniga family soon left El Salvador and returned to Chicago.

At the age of 17, Zúniga joined the U.S. Army, which he cites as a turning point in his life. In the Army, Zúniga gained personal confidence and the nickname "Kos." His military experience radically changed his political views. Before the army, he was an ardent young Republican, but he returned to civilian life as a passionate and outspoken liberal Democrat. In 1992, Zúniga enrolled as a student at Northern Illinois University. There, he became the editor of the school's newspaper, *The Northern Star*, and guided it to become the first college newspaper published on the Internet. He also became a freelance reporter for the *Chicago Tribune* and later attended Boston University School of Law.

The Net Roots Movement

What makes Zúniga's story even more interesting is that he is also the creator of the Daily Kos, one of the most widely read political blogs in the United States—attracting nearly 750,000 visits per day. Through the Daily Kos, Zúniga helped to create a movement to reinvigorate the Democratic Party and to bring it to the forefront of politics in the Internet age. Zúniga's Daily Kos blog has grown to become one of the most influential Websites of the Net Roots Movement (using blogs as a form of political activism), of which he is recognized as the primary founding force. In a 2006 CNBC interview, Zúniga commented:

> What we're saying is that people now are empowered by technology to take an active role in their government, take an active role in the media and not let D.C. dictate what happens and what doesn't happen in this country anymore.[47]

Zúniga's thoughts not only reflect the way that traditional power structures are changing in the Digital Age, but also the growing self-awareness among digital natives that they already have at their fingertips the tools that will shape the future. In addition, Zúniga highlights one of the many world-changing impacts that new media is having on our lives. His story exemplifies how the new media has become a vehicle for creating a new generation of political and social leaders—journalists, politicians, innovators and artists—who in the Digital Age can rise to levels of extraordinary

▶ **Politics in Cyberspace**
New media pioneer Robert Greenwald looks at the impact of new media journalism on politics and democracy.

influence based largely on their creativity and ability to exploit the power of the Internet. Chat rooms, forums and blogs have emerged as some of the most powerful vehicles of 21st-century democracy, especially in the United States. For digital natives, these technologies serve as their primary media for participating in the political process.[48] Further emphasizing this point, in the video segment titled "Politics in Cyberspace," new media pioneer Robert Greenwald explores the astounding impact the Internet has had on how people access news, especially television news, and the resulting effects on politics and participatory democracy.

Technology and Participatory Democracy

During the 2008 presidential campaign, Barack Obama's team took full advantage of the new media, allowing him to dominate the campaign trail. Having carefully studied previous attempts to use the Internet to build grassroots support and raise money, the Obama team recognized the value of attracting the attention of the swiftly growing segment of Americans who participate in the political process via the blogosphere and social networking sites. As such, they placed high priority on building virtual communities for their supporters, where they could congregate online and discuss important issues. The campaign also took advantage of the Internet's viral nature, seeding user-participant Web venues—blogs, YouTube, Twitter, Facebook—with media segments from speeches and rallies as well as video and audio segments produced by devotees. Just two weeks after the election, Obama gave one of his first addresses to the American people via YouTube.

Although all of the candidates in the 2008 presidential election had equal access to Web tools, it has been argued that none applied them as effectively as the Obama team. For example, at the same time that commercials on Obama's plans for bringing health insurance coverage to all Americans aired, the team sent e-mails and text messages to people previously identified as having an immediate need for health insurance assistance. These messages linked to campaign Websites containing additional material on this particular issue, including blogs and forums. Many of those who logged on and participated in these targeted-issue forums received follow-up e-mails and even phone calls from campaign volunteers.

The factors that explain why one candidate was better able to utilize new media more than the other are complex. Nevertheless, it appears that Obama's team demonstrated a familiarity with and an adeptness at using new media technology to microtarget (narrowly define) audiences. This process enabled campaign workers to quickly deliver "packaged" messages geared toward specific audiences, while at the same time feeding broadcast- and Webcast-based campaign ads to the larger national mass media marketplace.

During the 2012 presidential election, the teams of both President Obama and Republican challenger Mitt Romney used the Internet and social networking to an even greater extent than the 2008 campaigns. The Obama team once again demonstrated more advanced and more effective social networking capabilities by tightly scripting messages and combining media hits, a factor that certainly contributed to Obama's re-election.

Donald Trump, the unlikely, often-confrontational populist candidate who became president of the United States in 2017, skillfully utilized new media during his 2016 presidential campaign to an extent even surpassing his predecessor President Barack Obama—whose two successful presidential campaigns revolutionized the use of online and social media. Trump has been heavily criticized for quickly making controversial comments on social media throughout the entire campaign and continuing to do so once ensconced in the White House. His use of social media effectively sidestepped the mainstream media outlets, especially cable news networks such as Fox, CNN and MSNBC, whose reporters and commentators he continues to criticize as being unfair and "horrible people"—usually because they called him on his continued easily fact-checked nonfactual statements and his often-incendiary rhetoric. Trump mentioned at one of his inaugural balls that his usage of Twitter was "a way of bypassing dishonest media." His online dominance was and remains undeniable. Starting in 2011, now-President Trump, based on his close advisers showing him the potential power of social media, rapidly built a remarkably strong social media presence that by 2016 was pulling in 15.3 million followers and eventually propelled him into the White House. Trump's strength at using social media to sidestep traditional media, while extraordinarily effective as a presidential candidate, has become a high-risk strategy term.[49]

THE GAMING GENERATION

Will Wright is not a digital native, but he is one of the pioneers of the video game world. Born in 1960, Wright was raised in the early years of the Digital Age. As a child, he spent much time building scale models of planes, ships, cars and spacecraft. In college, he excelled in subjects such as architecture and engineering, but soon moved into computers and robotics. After five years of college but before he had earned a degree, Wright decided to try developing video games. His first effort resulted in the 1984 release of one of the first successful war-action video games, *Raid on Bungeling Bay*, in which players fly a helicopter through a war zone and earn points by successfully completing a series of bombing missions. Five years later, in 1989, Wright released *SimCity*, the first version of his city-building simulation-game franchise. *SimCity* became the most successful video game franchise ever created, selling more than 100 million copies by the end of 2008, and making Will Wright one of the richest and most famous video game developers of all time.

On September 15, 2008, after six years of development, Wright's company launched its long-awaited revolutionary—and for some, controversial—computer game *Spore*. In *Spore*, players control the evolution of an entire virtual species, from its early single-celled form through its evolution into an advanced species that eventually travels into space. Depending on one's perspective, *Spore* can be seen as a game-based demonstration of Darwinism or as a chance for players to experience a taste of "playing God." *Spore* offers its users a high level of shared creative participation never before seen in computer games, which has established a new model for future games. In an interview with *The Washington Post*, Wright explained that *Spore* is similar to social networking sites such as Facebook in that it allows users to create a good deal of the game's content, characters and environments:

> *Spore* software leaves it largely up to the player whether a species will thrive as a result of befriending neighbors on its home planet—or, alternatively, hunting them down for food . . . As a player's pet species develops the technology to venture into space, *Spore* users can keep exploring the [game's] virtual universe . . .[50]

Video games represent a new form of art or entertainment, and a new culture—some would argue that they are the pinnacle of dynamic storytelling. They can present rich, multilayered entertainment environments that are more complex and more appealing than movies, television or even novels, for unlike these media in which only the directors, producers or writers present their view of a story, video games empower players to participate in the development of the characters and the direction of the story.

Video games represent a new form of art or entertainment, and a new culture—some would argue that they are the pinnacle of dynamic storytelling.

Ongoing advances in computer and display technologies are playing an ever-more powerful role in our digital culture by offering people another mass medium through which they can express their ideas and perspectives on human existence, only in a more interactive fashion than is possible with other forms of media. The full story of the development and growth of video games is rich and fascinating. It is a story of innovation and creativity that could fill the pages of an entire book—but unfortunately one that is far beyond the scope of this discussion. The focus of our discussion here is to understand the impact of video games on 21st-century mass media culture.

War Games Lead to Video Games

Many people do not recognize the modern-day video game industry's historically close ties to the military. Cold War battle simulation programs for the Department of Defense played an important role in building the technology for artificial intelligence programming, a key requirement for today's action-packed video games. Even today, simulation games remain a critical training and risk analysis tool for military and intelligence agencies throughout the world. Video games first migrated from highly secret military environments into the world of public entertainment at the height of the Cold War.

In 1962, while working at MIT, physicist William A. Higinbotham tried to figure out how to create a hands-on exhibit that would assist visitors to his MIT lab in understanding the work going on there. What he came up with was a very basic two-player computer game called *Tennis for Two*, in which users could control the trajectory of little glowing "bouncing ball" blips on a computer screen and, in effect, play a game of virtual tennis. Even though this very early computer game was at the time amazing to anyone who played it, Higinbotham didn't think he had created anything significant in comparison to his previous projects, one of which was designing timing devices for America's earliest bombs during the Manhattan Project. Just one year later, MIT programmer Steve Russell created *Spacewar!*, the first successful third-person shooter computer game. Inspired by Cold War fears, players battled each other's armed spaceships while fighting to avoid colliding with a death star. *Spacewar!* helped push the development of higher-resolution video display technologies during the mid-1970s.

The video game industry had its earliest successes with coin-operated arcade games that were placed in bars, restaurants and gaming parlors, but arcade games did not actually precede home video games. As early as 1967, TV-based tennis and hockey simulation games were being developed for the consumer market. One important pioneer of video games was a German-born American electronics inventor named Ralph Baer. During World War II, Baer served as a U.S. Army military intelligence officer in London. After the war, he founded his own defense electronics company, called Sanders Associates. In 1963, Baer and his colleagues developed the first stand-alone video game system, which he called the *Brown Box*. Baer licensed *Brown Box* to Magnavox, which in 1972 released it as the first consumer video game console, called the *Magnavox Odyssey*. The *Odyssey*, which connected to home television sets, was revolutionary because it used removable circuits built into cartridges—a technology that allowed the same video game console to play many different games. This innovation helped launch video game software development as a separate industry.

The Development of PC and Console Games

The history of video games is marked by the intertwined progress made by both PC software and dedicated console game systems. In 1972, Nolan Bushnell and his colleague Ted Dabney founded Atari, the first large-scale commercial and home computer manufacturer. That same year, Bushnell and Dabney hired University of California–Berkley engineering student Allan Alcorn to develop a coin-operated commercial tennis-type game. In truth, Bushnell had no expectations for Alcorn's first project and really just wanted to see what Alcorn was capable of. The result was a now-legendary game, *Pong*. To test local market interest in *Pong*, Bushnell set up Alcorn's prototype as a coin-operated video game at a nearby tavern, which proved to be a huge hit, collecting more than $300 per week in quarters. When Atari later adapted *Pong* for individual consumer computers, it quickly became an international sensation. Atari grew into the first successful multinational video game company, with Time Warner eventually purchasing the company in 1977 for $28 million—a significant price at the time.[51]

Advances in video game technology were not just being made in the United States. In 1985, a young computer engineer working at the Russian Academy of Science named Alexey Pajitnov invented a simple, yet challenging game that he called *Tetris*. In *Tetris*, players try to manipulate blocks of different shapes falling from the top of the screen. The object of the game is to move the blocks to build a wall without gaps, which eventually fills the entire screen. As the game proceeds, the blocks fall more and more quickly, making the game remarkably difficult. Within one year, versions of *Tetris* that could run on any PC started to appear outside of the Soviet Bloc. By the time the Berlin Wall fell in 1989, *Tetris* could be found on most of the PCs and almost all of the handheld games available around the world. Its success clearly demonstrated the extraordinary power of the shared video game experience to make an easy jump over cultural and political boundaries and contribute to the creation of a global mass media culture.

Also in 1985, Japanese game manufacturer Nintendo introduced to the West the first game console, a computer system designed for interactive entertainment. Nintendo's *Super Mario Brothers*, though populated with simple characters and limited story play, was nevertheless the forerunner of today's highly evolved games, which feature complex characters and storylines that rival or surpass the characters and plot lines of feature films. Within a few years, Nintendo had pushed even further into the realm of multilayered character and narrative with games such as *The Legend of Zelda* (1987). *Zelda* was the first lore-rich video game that focused on the development of each player's game skills as the game progressed, a process known as player progression. At the time, this behavior was considered revolutionary and radical in the video gaming world. The characters implemented classic storytelling elements such as themes of good versus evil, mission quests and tests of bravery. The complex storyline and compelling background music of Zelda—the first video game to offer players a robust fantasy experience—made it extraordinarily popular.

In 1991, less than five years after the release of Nintendo's epic *The Legend of Zelda*, Sony launched the first CD-ROM-based video game system called the Sony PlayStation. The processing speed and storage capability of the Sony PlayStation moved video gaming from the realm of sophisticated toys into the realm of alternative entertainment for older teenagers and adults. This technology allowed Sony to deliver realistic, albeit fantastic, 3-D environments populated by fast-moving characters and dynamic scene changes, further enhanced by stereo-quality background music and sound effects. The range of possibilities for movie-like quality CGI (Common Gateway Interface) effects offered by the new technology revolutionized the video game industry itself. Games such as the *Final Fantasy* series gave players the chance to participate in complex interactive stories, with realistic special effects that successfully rivaled the entertainment experience of a feature film.

7.15

Final Fantasy VII, 1997—one of the first video games to offer realistic film-like effects and interactive story development.

Entertainment Pictures/Alamy Stock Photo

Video Games Converge With Hollywood Movies

Video game companies such as Sony and Nintendo grew even more competitive as video game technology advanced from 2-D to 3-D displays and interactivity became quicker and more dynamic in the 21st century. A variety of companies introduced radical new gaming platforms that highlighted the best capabilities of their technologies—Sony's PlayStation 3, Microsoft's Xbox 360 and Nintendo's Wii, for example. Initially, these companies released racing, flight simulation or battle games that allowed players to operate rapidly moving vehicles through realistic 3-D environments as a way to demonstrate their console's capabilities and attract higher sales than their competitors.

Back in the early 1990s, the growing speed of computer processors and video cards enabled game developers to create characters that were more dynamic. These characters responded in real time to players' manipulation of buttons and joysticks, which in turn allowed for the introduction of fighting games such as *Street Fighter* (1990) and *Mortal Kombat* (1992). *Mortal Kombat* was particularly advanced for its

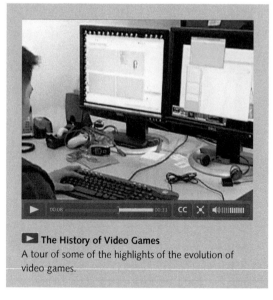

▶ **The History of Video Games**
A tour of some of the highlights of the evolution of video games.

time, employing digitized sprites of live actors as opposed to *Street Fighter*'s traditional animated characters. Many of these fighting games also contained unprecedented amounts of violence. Game characters had the ability to perform gory, horrific actions such as dismembering their opponents' bodies and triumphantly holding up body parts dripping with blood.

The violence of these games raised an outcry from parents' groups and governments, especially in the United States and the United Kingdom, which resulted in growing demands for greater government control over video game content. The controversy expanded with the increase in graphic and action realism and the popularity of first-person shooter games such as *Doom* (1993) and third-person shooter games such as *Grand Theft Auto 3* (2001). *Grand Theft Auto 3* was especially controversial because players had the ability to kill any game characters, including authorities such as police and even innocent bystanders. *Grand Theft Auto 3* also introduced a new trend toward increasingly explicit sexual content in video games.

Action and violence were not the only notable trends in video games that took great leaps forward in the late 1990s and early 2000s. Between 1995 and 2005, interactive sports video games, such as the football game *Madden* (1989–2008) and the soccer game *FIFA* (1993–2008), as well as image-rich multilayered fantasy games such as *Final Fantasy VII* (1997), *EverQuest* (1999) and *World of Warcraft* (2004), increased in popularity. In recent years, the fantasy world of video games has been converging with the fantasy world of Hollywood films. Popular film franchises such as George Lucas's *Star Wars* have been transformed and extended into video games, while popular games such as *Resident Evil*, *Resident Evil Apocalypse*, *Final Fantasy*: *The Spirits Within* and *Tomb Raiders* have successfully migrated to the film screen. For a preview of some of the genre's most formidable franchises, view the video segment titled "The History of Video Games."

While this movement signals a large step forward in the advancement of media technology, the convergence of video game and film media is just one of the first phases of new media advancements. The next stage, the convergence of the digital and physical environments, is the hallmark of the emergence of virtual reality.

Virtual Worlds: Playing in Alternate Realities

In the 21st century, virtual reality (a computer-simulated environment) has become part of our everyday lives. The idea of participating in virtual worlds is an integral facet of any discussion of new media. It can be fairly stated that most of us effectively live, work and play in two parallel realities—one in the real world and one in the virtual world. Most of us comfortably jump back and forth between the two realms with little or no conscious thought about the implications of simultaneously living in two worlds.

> It can be fairly stated that most of us effectively live, work and play in two parallel realities—one in the real world and one in the virtual world. Most of us comfortably jump back and forth between the two realms with little or no conscious thought about the implications of simultaneously living in two worlds.

New media technologies continue to advance at an astounding rate, with convergence playing a central role in the production and delivery of new media content, and cultivating our ability to manage our experiences in the virtual world. Two basic categories of virtual reality (VR) are distinguished, although they have rather loose boundaries and are slowly merging.

The first category we will call immersive virtual reality (IVR)—the purist form of VR. Digital VR technologies combine sophisticated interactive devices—most often 3-D stereoscopic goggles, stereo headphones and hand and foot movement sensors—with realistic computer-generated environments, thereby engaging most of our human senses. They deliver shocking and convincingly realistic simulations. The user experiences full immersion and high-level inter-activity with the computer-simulated environment. Full immersion VR requires costly computer power and technology, so these systems are mostly found in advanced training facilities, such as those used by the military to train pilots or by medical schools to train surgeons.

Some of this type of VR technology has filtered down to the consumer market. For example, in recent years, Disney has added VR or VR-enhanced attractions to its theme parks. Video game manufacturers such as Sony and Nintendo have come out with partial-immersion game systems. Some of these consumer systems use visors and sensors that users strap to their wrists and ankles to create a partial-VR player expe-rience. Nintendo's Wii system was first launched in late 2006 and immediately became popular, selling more than 13 million units just in the United States within its first two years. Wii uses a large-screen LCD or flat-screen plasma display and comes with a set of handheld controllers, called nunchuks, and a sensor platform that players stand on, depending on the particular game being played.

The second category of VR is participatory virtual reality (PVR), also referred to as *participatory explo-ration*. This new media technology, which is accessed online or via digital storage devices such as DVDs or Blu-ray, enables users to move through, explore and interact with computer-generated environments. PVR, while not immersive, still delivers a captivating user experience and is the foundation of popular participa-tory content platforms such as *SimCity* and *Second Life*.

SimCity

Back in 2000, Will Wright, the genius video game designer of *Spore* (discussed earlier in this section), released one of the first strategic life-simulation computer games, called *SimCity*. *SimCity* was inspired by a personal crisis: Wright lost his home and most of his possessions in a firestorm that hit the hills above Oak-land, California, on October 20, 1991. The devastating fire strained emergency personnel and resources; even equipment and personnel from a nearby U.S. Naval Air Station were called into service on the fire lines. This disaster scenario, which called into question building codes and development planning, forced many victims to rebuild their lives—literally from the ground up. *SimCity* was the first entrant in the *SimCity* game franchise, which has since included numerous expansions and the popular spin-off, *The Sims*. It remains one of the best-selling video games in history.

The objective of the *SimCity* games is to successfully build and run a virtual city. Players must establish a city development plan with zoning for residential, commercial and industrial areas; create a tax structure; develop power and transportation systems; and create other buildings and infrastructure common to an average city. Along the way, players must respond to natural disasters as well as attacks from a number of other zany threats such as monsters and alien intruders. In the virtual reality of the *SimCity* world, the play-ers must make decisions, deal with their consequences and otherwise make a multitude of choices that build the virtual environment. In *The Sims*, players create an avatar family (a player's alter ego)—the Sims—and control the choices that their avatar family makes, but only up to a point.

One of the many clever aspects of *The Sims* game design is that the characters have a certain amount of free will and often behave independently from the player. As with decisions about city design and infrastructure in the original game, players must make choices about the careers, health, work and leisure activities of the avatar family. In game theory, this approach yields an agent-based artificial life program. The game technically has an open-ended unlimited progression: It never ends as long as the player wants to keep the game going, whether that's for days, weeks, months or even years.

From social networking sites to blogging to online game worlds, today's new media society is popu-lated with people who create multiple virtual representations of themselves. Digital natives can establish and creatively express themselves through alternate identities by way of an astounding array of online sites and services. Perhaps the ultimate expression of our fascination with building and interacting with others via multiple identities in cyberspace is the online participatory virtual reality found in *Second Life*.

Second Life

Second Life is the largest Internet-based, interactive 3-D simulation in the world. Launched in June 2003, it was created and is operated by Linden Labs, a San Francisco-based new media company, which offers *Second Life* as a free downloadable program. *Second Life* lets users create individual avatars, or residents in the vast *Second Life* alternative world, navigate through the virtual metaverse; communicate with other residents; purchase property, goods and services using *Second Life*'s internal currency called "Linden Dollars"; and participate in most human activities usually associated with the real world. You can make your avatar tall or short, fat or thin, human or not. It doesn't have to be anything like your real self.

These participatory exploration environments are so effective that even government agencies such as NASA use *Second Life* as an alternative method of internal networking and communication as well as a novel way of promoting space exploration.[52] Other cutting-edge companies are staking out their own space in *Second Life*, recognizing it as an inexpensive, yet effective training or sales platform. Organizations such as Intel, IBM, and Cisco use it to conduct virtual meetings and convene virtual sales conventions.

In 2007, HBO aired a feature documentary by American documentary filmmaker Douglas Gayeton that was produced entirely inside *Second Life*. *Molotov Alva and His Search for the Creator: A Second Life Odyssey* follows the story of an avatar who decides to live his live entirely inside the *Second Life* virtual world. The film is a video diary of Molotov's adventures as he builds a virtual life. He struggles with losing memories of his real life as well as the possibility that his real life might cease to exist altogether and that he might be trapped forever in a virtual reality. As Gayeton has described in press interviews, this captivating story either reflects a new media Marco Polo story or a sobering critique on the dangers awaiting those who allow themselves to become so immersed in virtual worlds that they endanger their existence in the real world.

Just as in real life, not all is perfect in *Second Life*. Pornographic content and solicitations abound. Legal cases are on the increase as residents of *Second Life* take to actual courts to file complaints about Linden Labs' handling of monetary issues. In the summer of 2007, Linden Labs was forced to remove all gambling activities from *Second Life*, which at the time amounted to more than 5 percent of the virtual economy transactions.[53] That same year, *Second Life*'s largest virtual banks collapsed. Despite all the financial transactions taking place within this virtual world—from the buying and selling of virtual goods and services, to

7.16

Avatars from the online game, *Second Life*.

360b/Shutterstock.com

virtual business deals for the sale of virtual land, and the construction of virtual buildings—there is no real-world legal oversight of the very real commerce in *Second Life*.[54]

The Anatomy of Video Game Production

Firaxis Games, now a division of Take-Two Interactive, is one of America's leading video game developers. Founded in 1996 by the renowned Canadian-American game developer Sid Meier, Firaxis has specialized in creating highly popular strategy and simulation games, including *Civilization*, *Gettysburg!*, *Sid Meier's Antietam!*, *Alpha Centauri*, *Sid Meier's SimGolf*, *Civilization III*, *Civilization IV*, *Sid Meier's Pirates!*, *Civilization V* and, most recently, the new space strategy game *XCOM*. This video segment tells the inside story of *XCOM*'s final development in 2012 and highlights the key stages and team members required to produce today's most sophisticated and visually complex video games.

The video segment demonstrates that the development and production of dynamic video games require a large team of creative specialists, state-of-the-art supercomputing resources and a significantly long schedule. The entire process mimics the complexities of producing a feature film with a million-dollar budget. Unlike a feature film's storyline and character arcs, however, video game story elements and characters are player interactive. This means that the Firaxis team must not only produce many user-responsive alternatives for every scene, but they must also engineer highly sophisticated user-interface components that are essential to delivering a compelling player experience. Additionally, similar to most popular video games today, *XCOM* is "staged" in a series of real-world-like dynamic 3-D environments that enable players' characters to walk, drive or fly through seemingly endless layers of strikingly real surroundings. As demonstrated in the video segments, each 3-D environment requires hundreds of hours of computer animation and programming to construct, display and perform seamlessly as players move within and through scenes. Add multiple layers of sound effects and music, and the result is a popular video game that quickly draws players into an alternative world, allowing them direct participation in stories that rival the best action movies.

XCOM is a good example of the trend in combining complex 3-D virtual world strategy gaming with exciting—and indeed at times violent—action characters and stories that are allowing video gaming's popularity to rival Hollywood blockbuster films. In fact, many Hollywood films released today are either rooted in popular video games or give birth to new ones.

▶ **Firaxis XCOM**
A fascinating and rare look behind the scenes at the development and production of a hit video game.

Massively Multiplayer Online Role-Playing Games

Another genre of virtual reality gaming that has become enormously popular worldwide is the massively multiplayer online role-playing games (MMORPGs). MMOPRGs—or, as players often refer to them, MMOs—combine the virtual reality and online networking features of games like *Second Life* with compelling, user-driven fantasy adventure stories. One of the most popular of these online multiplayer games is *World of Warcraft* (*WoW*), which expands the fictional universe of Blizzard Entertainment's legendary *Warcraft* real-time strategy games. Released in 2004, the original game is set in a fantasy 3-D world called Azeroth, where players use their characters to explore territories, battle hostile creatures and villains and, in true storytelling tradition, undertake grand quests.

Through questing, which occurs when a game spans across a particular place or geographical area, characters gain experience points that accumulate and allow them to increase their level, along the way gaining new customizable combat abilities, trade skills, armor and weaponry. Many of the more difficult quests and villains require players to team up in groups or raids to defeat epic enemies threatening Azeroth. This aspect of *WoW*'s gameplay is referred to as player-versus-environment (PvE). Players can also pit themselves against droves of other players of the opposing faction through the game's player-versus-player (PvP) online networking.

The story dynamic of the game is constantly evolving, driven by the designers who create new plot lines, crises and challenges. From time to time, the game developer, Blizzard Entertainment, introduces a game update (often referred to as a patch) that adds new story elements and challenges to the game. In September 2005, for example, the company released a patch that introduced a virtual epidemic into the *WoW* called "Corrupted Blood." Brought on by a major villain in the *WoW* universe, this epidemic spread throughout the game's virtual worlds within just a few days, killing tens of thousands of online players' characters, much like the Black Plague that spread throughout Europe in the Middle Ages. The spread of this virtual plague, and players' reactions when faced with it, so closely modeled what could happen in a real-world epidemic that epidemiologists have used it as a model to study the threats from outbreaks of diseases such as influenza and to project how communities and governments might react to major outbreaks around the world.

The "Corrupted Blood" outbreak in *WoW* is just one illustration of the way reality and virtual reality overlap in the Digital Age. In addition to its recreational benefits, this scenario has helpful applications in such areas as predictive science and human behavioral study. Yet, despite the game's popularity, numerous questions remain about how the emergence of virtual reality and its integration into the real world affects human life and society. It used to be a relatively straightforward, albeit difficult, process to establish our identities—everything that makes up who we are and how we view ourselves. Virtual reality offers users the opportunity to create alternate identities and escape everyday life. Yet at the same time, aspects of virtual reality can easily creep back into real life when people try to bring their experiences and relationships back with them. The traditional view—that throughout our adult lives, it is unlikely that most people will make radical changes to who they are—is undergoing an evolutionary change. As citizens of the parallel worlds of reality and virtual reality, we now have the power to frequently and even radically change our identities. This raises important questions about the very nature of what we call "reality."

CONCLUSION: *NEW* NEW MEDIA AND THE IMPACT ON SOCIETY AND CULTURE

In this chapter we explored some of the highlights of the evolution of new media, noting how it compares with the old media that came before. More importantly, this chapter has examined the impact of new media on society and culture—on all of our lives—in the 21st century. New media is so foundational to how we experience mass media today that the term is already becoming extinct—that is, new media is being so seamlessly woven into our lives that we no longer perceive it as being *new*. As technology and innovation continue to drive the richness of Web 2.0 toward the coming era of Web 3.0, perhaps the cutting edge should be more appropriately termed "the *new* new media." Video games are having such a profound effect on other forms of media content, from television programs to movies, to educational media, to the way we interact with content on the Web, that sometimes we experience aspects of media rooted in video games without even being aware of it. Meanwhile, online social networking, in forums ranging from Facebook and Pinterest to Twitter, is becoming a part of the normal day-to-day social tapestry for the majority of us.

Regardless of the collective name that we bestow on the many aspects of new media, the 21st century seems destined to progress in two parallel yet converging universes—one real and one virtual—with each of us searching for the most satisfying, and healthy, way to integrate these worlds. For digital natives and the generations that will follow, the convergence of mass media in these two parallel worlds will continue to enrich our lives, contribute to our knowledge and present us with new challenges.

CHAPTER SUMMARY	KEY TERMS
What Is New Media and Where Did It Originate? Explores the fascinating story of the history and evolution of new media and lays the foundation for the exploration of media in the 21st century.	Electronic Frontier Foundation Telecom Reform Act network neutrality telegraph Morse code telephone new media Web 1.0 Internet backbone media convergence Web 2.0 content sharing streaming media meme viral media World Wide Web (WWW) URL HTTP HTML Internet browser Netscape Navigator modem High Performance Computing and Communications Act of 1991 Voice over Internet Protocol (VoIP) cloud electronic mail Compatible Time-Sharing System (CTSS) File Transfer Protocol (FTP) SMTP POP text messaging SMS
The Dynamic New Media Explains the process and dynamics of new media, including its key aspects of underlying nonlinearity and user-mediated adaptive content and how these dynamics influence communications and information sharing.	hyperlinks podcasts dynamic adaptive learning peer-to-peer (P2P) Wikipedia open-source model search engines paid search optimization
Media Convergence Revisits the key concept of mass media convergence and explores some of the more important implications of mass media convergence both for today and the future.	content mobility

Linking Up: 21st-Century Social Networking Delves into the evolution of social networking and discusses many of the controversies surrounding the phenomenal impact of social networking on today's society and culture.	digital natives online social networking microblogging Twitter tweets life-blogging
Politics and New Media Looks at the impact of new media on how 21st-century political campaigns and elections are conducted and on the exercise of American democracy today. **Visual Media** **Politics in Cyberspace** A look at the impact of new media journalism on politics and democracy. 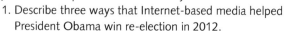 1. Describe three ways that Internet-based media helped President Obama win re-election in 2012. 2. How did Internet media, including Webcasts and blog sites, contribute to the level of partisanship and the lack of political compromise that led up to the 2012 presidential election and that continues today?	Net Roots Movement
The Gaming Generation Examines the evolution of state-of-the-art of video games and considers their impact on popular culture. **Visual Media** **The History of Video Games** A tour of some of the highlights of the evolution of video games. 1. What are some of the key links between today's popular video games and the popular board games of the early to mid-20th century? 2. What is it about some popular video game characters and stories that enables them to migrate successfully to blockbuster Hollywood movies?	console player progression virtual reality immersive virtual reality (IVR) participatory virtual reality (PVR) avatar agent-based artificial life program massively multiplayer online role-playing game (MMORPG) questing
Firaxis XCOM A fascinating and rare look behind the scenes at the development and production of a hit video game. 1. Describe three aspects of today's 3-D video-game visual dynamics that contribute to making the virtual reality of games like XCOM so realistic. 2. Explain how interactive character features in 3-D action video games help enrich the stories and quickly engage players.	

NOTES

1 The full text of this famous e-mail can be read at www.homes.eff.org/~barlow/Declaration-Final.html
2 Schonfeld, E. (2008, August 31). The net neutrality debate all on one page. *TechCrunch*. Retrieved from http://techcrunch.com/2008/08/31/the-net-neutrality-debate-all-on-one-page/
3 Porter, E. (2012, May 8). Keeping the Internet neutral. *The New York Times*.
4 Flew, T. (2008). *New media: An introduction*. Oxford University Press.
5 Cotton, B., & Oliver, R. (1997). *Understanding Hypermedia 2000*. Phaiden.

6 Alvarez-Hamelin, I., et al. (2007, June 19). Mapping the Internet: Lanet-vi program. *MIT Technology Review*.

7 U.S. Department of Commerce, National Telecommunications and Information Administration. (2011, February). Digital nation: Expanding Internet usage. *NTIA Research Preview*.

8 Graham, I. (1995). *The HTML sourcebook: The complete guide to HTML*. John Wiley & Sons.

9 McLuhan, M. (1962). *The Gutenberg galaxy: The making of the typographic man*. University of Toronto Press.

10 Moschovitis, C. J. P. (1999). *The history of the Internet*. ABC–CLIO.

11 VanVleck, T. (2004). *The IBM 7094 and CTSS*. Retrieved from www.multicians.org/thvv/7094.html

12 Naughton, J. (2012, May 12). Now 4 billion people know the joy of texting. *The Guardian/Observer*.

13 *mobiThinking.com*. (2012). Global mobile statistics Part C: Mobile marketing, advertising, and messaging.

14 Birla, P. (2003). VAT a way 2 protest: Traders turn to SMS. *DELHI Newsline*. Retrieved from www.cities.expressindia.com/fullstory.php?newsid=46606

15 Okada, T. (2005). Youth culture and shaping of Japanese mobile media: Personalization and the keitain Internet as multimedia. In M. Ito, D. Okabe, & M. Matsuda (Eds.), *Personal, portable, pedestrian: Mobile phones in Japanese life*. MIT Press.

16 Hongé, M. (2008). Chinese expected to send 17 billion text messages during Spring Festival. *China View*. Retrieved from www.news.xinhuanet.com/english/2008-02/08/content_7581868.htm

17 From author's work with Robert Goddard et al., Adaptive Learning Technologies, Inc. and Cognitive Path Systems, LLC.

18 Terdiman, D. (2005, December 15). Study: Wikipedia as accurate as Britannica. *CNET News*.

19 Giles, J. (2005, December 14). Internet encyclopedias go head to head. *Nature*.

20 Caslon Analytics. *Blog statistics and analytics*. Retrieved from www.caslon.com.au/weblogprofile1.htm

21 Helft, M. (2009, March 24). YouTube blocked in China, Google says. *The New York Times*. Retrieved from www.nytimes.com/2009/03/25/technology/internet/25youtube.html?_r=1

22 Leckhart, S. (2012, September 26). Finding fame, and sometimes fortune, in social media. *The New York Times*.

23 Leith, S. (2011, October 16). What does it all meme? *Financial Times*.

24 Helft, M. (2009, March 24). YouTube blocked in China, Google says. *The New York Times*. Retrieved from www.nytimes.com/2009/03/25/technology/internet/25youtube.html?_r=1

25 (2008, July 29). *Rapleaf study reveals gender and age data of social network users*. Retrieved from www.rapleaf.com/business/press_release/age

26 Palfrey, J. G., & Gasser, U. (2008). *Born digital: Understanding the first generation of digital natives*. Perseus.

27 Pew Internet & American Life Project. (2010, February 3). *Social media and young adults*. Retrieved from www.pewinternet.org/Reports/2010/Social-Media-and-Young-Adults.aspx

28 Anderson, J., & Rainie, L. (2012, February 29). *Future of the Internet—Millennials will benefit and suffer due to their hyperconnected lives*. Pew Internet & American Life Project. Retrieved from www.pewinternet.org/Reports/2012/Hyperconnected-lives.aspx

29 Nielsen Company. (2008). *Nielsen online provides fastest-growing social networks for September 2008*. Retrieved from www.blog.nielsen.com/nielsenwire/wp-content/uploads/2008/10/press_release24.pdf

30 McCarthy, C. (2009, January 13). ComScore: In U.S., MySpace Facebook race goes on. *CNET News*.

31 Lewin, T. (2008, November 19). Teenagers' Internet socializing not a bad thing. *The New York Times*. Retrieved from www.nytimes.com/2008/11/20/us/20internet.html

32 Ibid.

33 Ibid.

34 Foderaro, L. W. (2010, September 29). Private moment made public, then a fatal jump. *The New York Times*. Retrieved from www.nytimes.com/2010/09/30/nyregion/30suicide.html?_r=3&

35 Krasny, R. (2010, April 9). Teen suicide puts spotlight on high-tech bullying. *The Washington Post* and *Reuters*. Retrieved from www.washingtonpost.com/wp-dyn/content/article/2010/04/09/AR2010040903193.html

36 Retrieved from www.hhs.gov/ash/oah/news/e-updates/eupdate-7.html

37 Standberry, K. (2006). *When kids with LD network online: The benefits and risks*. Retrieved from www.greatschools.net/cgi-bin/showarticle/3120

38 Seigel, L. (2012, October 15). The kids aren't alright—the perils of parenting in the Digital Age. *Newsweek*.

39 Standberry, K. (2006). *When kids with LD network online: The benefits and risks*. Retrieved from www.greatschools.net/cgi-bin/showarticle/3120

40 Wolak, J., Finkelhor, D., Mitchell, K. J., & Ybarra, M. L. (2008). Online "predators" and their victims. *American Psychologist, 63*(2), 111–128.

41 U.S. Department of Justice, Internet Crimes Against Children Task Force.

42 Ibid.

43 Wallace, L. (2008, March 23). True story of a Twitter marriage proposal. *Wired*.

44 Broughton, P. D. (2011, July 19). Brave new networked world—social networking sites can be useful for business. *Financial Times*.

45 Boutin, P. (2008, October 20). Twitter, Flickr, Facebook make blogs look so 2004. *Wired*. Retrieved from www.wired.com/entertainment/theweb/magazine/16-11/st_essay

46 Moulitsas, M. Retrieved from www.dailykos.com/special/about

47 Ibid.

48 Musgrove, M. (2008, September 6). In the beginning, finally: Much-delayed game lets you play God. *The Washington Post*.

49 Snibbe, K. (2017, January 30). *Where President Trump and Twitter rank in social media*. Southern California Group; Barbarooct, M. (2015, October 5). Pithy, mean and powerful: How Donald Trump mastered Twitter for 2016. *New York Times*. Retrieved from www.nytimes.com/2015/10/06/us/politics/donald-trump-twitter-use-campaign-2016.html

50 Sanger, D. E. (1984, July 3). Warner sells Atari to Tramiel. *The New York Times*.

51 Foust, J. (2007, June 25). Virtual reality and participatory exploration. *The Space Review*.

52 Talbot, D. (2008, January/February). The fleecing of the avatars. *Technology Review*.

53 Naone, E. (2007, November/December). Financial woes in second life. *Technology Review*.

54 Ibid.

Section III

Media Business Economics

8

Advertising and Public Relations

Yaacov Dagan/Alamy Stock Photo

CHAPTER OUTLINE

Tracing the History of American Advertising

Mini-Stories A video montage of Mobius award-winning commercials.

Mobius Awards

Product Affinity: Making Us Want It

Ejector Pew Provocative commercials can use trendy, humorous imagery to relay religious messages.

Mobius Awards

Breaking the Rules: Advertising in the 21st Century

Suspend Reality Commercial advertising asks us to accept that we can be part of the story.
Mobius Awards

Humor Humor is an effective way of engaging audience attention or "capturing eyeballs."
Mobius Awards

Dove Evolution A series of Dove commercials that encouraged women to embrace their beauty and self-esteem.
Mobius Awards

Johnson, *Daisy Girl* **Ad** Negative messages can be far from subtle, as depicted in this (in)famous 1964 Lyndon Johnson ad.

Tracing the History of American Public Relations: Building and Managing Image
Today's Strategic Public Relations: 360-Degree Campaigning

Clinton's *Role Models* **TV Ad** A very effective negative campaign ad focused on negative impact of then-presidential candidate Donald Trump's own words on impressionable young children.

Conclusion: Selling Ideas, Framing Perceptions

Sample PSAs Anti-drinking and anti-smoking reinforce health and safety.

LEARNING OBJECTIVES

1. Define advertising and explain how it influences mass media content.
2. Illustrate how narrowcasting helps advertisers target specific audience groups in order to maximize audience and advertiser influence.
3. Compare and contrast commercial and political advertising and the way in which they each use images to reach their audience.
4. Explain how public relations campaigns differ from advertising.
5. Outline public relations' expansion from politics, to entertainment, to social-awareness issues, demonstrating the approaches used to impact political, consumer and social agendas.
6. Evaluate how advertising and public relations work together to cultivate the public's perception of the client, its image and brand.

IN HIS NOVEL

1984, British writer and social critic George Orwell presents a frightening view of life under the ultimate dictatorship—in a country called Oceania, where a totalitarian government watches everyone and controls all information. In this fictional society, personal privacy is sacrificed in the name of national security, and the Ministry of Truth monitors all media and speech. The government restricts freedom of expression, mass media and even the thoughts and ideas of its citizens by manipulating all information, determining what is "fact" and what is "truth." People live under patriotic slogans of submission such as "Big Brother Is Watching" and with doublespeak such as "Freedom Is Slavery" and "Ignorance Is Strength." The story follows the lead character, Winston Smith, an "intellectual worker" at the Ministry of Truth, as he struggles to break free of the government's authoritarian yoke, risking his life in the process. Although the novel was first published in 1949, its popularity grew as the year 1984 approached.

In fact, during the 1984 Super Bowl, millions of viewers witnessed a disturbing Orwellian commercial featuring futuristic throngs of gray-uniformed people, obediently marching into a huge auditorium where they watch a big screen and listen hypnotically to a Big Brother figure spewing dogmatic slogans. Suddenly, helmeted shock troops appear, chasing a lone woman, who is clad not in the official gray worker's uniform, but rather in colorful running shorts and athletic T-shirt. The heroic woman runs up to the giant screen and hurls a sledgehammer at it, breaking the screen and, ostensibly, the hypnotic hold of Big Brother on her fellow

citizens. This now-famous television commercial, conceived by a creative team at the advertising agency Chiat-Day, was not a political message, but a clever and controversial advertisement announcing Apple's launch of its new Macintosh computer.

The Apple commercial was directed by Ridley Scott, who had just completed his science-fiction masterpiece, *Blade Runner* (1982). While Scott's movie has become a classic, Apple's 1984 commercial never ran again. The A. C. Nielsen Group estimated that the commercial reached 46.4 percent of American households, and its one-time airing garnered astronomical and unprecedented viewer recall ratings, unmatched by any other commercial before or since its broadcast. It generated millions of dollars in free editorial exposure for Apple as media critics and pundits argued for weeks over the message and impact of the commercial. Of course, all of

this controversy increased demand for Apple's new Macintosh computer far beyond initial estimates.[1]

The legendary Apple 1984 commercial has the reputation of being one of the most influential television ads in history, not only surviving on Websites such as YouTube, but also shaping futurist-styled advertisements for technology and communication products. Why has the impact of this controversial commercial lived on, three decades after its one airing? We might argue that the creators of the Apple 1984 ad were not directly trying to sell their new Macintosh computer, but rather were trying to sell the "idea" of the Macintosh computer. That is, they were selling the idea that to own a new Mac was to make a statement. Buying a Mac, they suggested, was a way to combat conformity, to exert independence and freedom of thought. Their aim was to establish the Macintosh brand

8.1

Terry Shmitt/UPI Newscom

name as a symbol of assertive, free thinking. Whether the Macintosh was a better personal computer than its competitors—and whether it was worth the extra cost—was beside the point.

The message in Apple's 1984 TV commercial made an extraordinary impact, exemplifying the power of mass media advertising and dramatically illustrating its ability to sell ideas and create cultural movements via persuasion. Many marketing experts argue that advertising can influence the ideas, beliefs and behaviors of large audiences just as much as major breaking news stories. At the same time, many critics warn that the power of advertising poses a growing danger. Advertising underwrites—that is, finances—American mass media, so its voice tends to dominate content production. This debate over the positive and negative influences of advertising on society and culture remains ongoing and unavoidable.

TRACING THE HISTORY OF AMERICAN ADVERTISING

The United States is the most media-rich country in history. We now have more media choices and far more avenues of access than could be imagined just 20 years ago, all either free or available at relatively low cost. Advertising is what makes this wealth of content possible. Advertising is a type of communication that attempts to persuade individuals to take some form of action (buy, believe, consume) toward a product, idea or service.

In the early years of the 18th century, newspapers were the dominant mass media in the United States. Colonial publishers supported their enterprises through revenues from advertising-paid announcements posted by local merchants. As the country grew, advertising became more sophisticated. The Industrial Revolution gave birth to consumerism, a system that creates and encourages the purchase of goods and services in increasing amounts. With this sea change in society, advertising evolved into a cultural force, linking the tremendous growth in products and services with a market built on growing consumer demands. Mass production, supported by advertising, formed the core of this modernization process. It helped to create a lasting marriage between advertising and media in modern America. As the mass media have grown exponentially, so has the advertising industry that supports them.

By the late 20th century, competition in the advertising industry had grown rapidly as entrepreneurs attempted to secure for themselves a portion of the huge revenue streams that the industry generated. Not only did advertising professionals have to compete with one another for a slice of the marketing pie, but they also faced the challenge of competing with other media producers for the attention of the American public. As the programming content grew and expanded, marketers had to find new and creative ways to hold on to the public's focus, even by waging a competition with noncommercial media.

Despite these new challenges, advertising continues to play an important role in mass media into the 21st century. To better identify their markets and to test the impact they have on their targeted audiences, advertisers often run sophisticated demographic studies (studies that examine basic human characteristics such as individuals' age, gender, race and income) and psychographic studies (studies that look at individuals' lifestyles, values, attitudes and personalities), carefully analyzing the results to help them better focus their advertising dollars and resources. As an unknown advertising executive once quipped, "I know I'm wasting half my advertising dollars—I just don't know which half." Advertisers must face the Herculean task of getting consumers to pay attention to their commercials, which fund large portions of the content that is driving this media-rich Digital Age. To fall off consumers' radar screens means to jeopardize an advertiser's ability to tell good stories or to inform the public about its products and services in clever ways that can produce the revenue necessary for the firm's ongoing survival.

> Advertisers must face the Herculean task of getting consumers to pay attention to their commercials, which fund large portions of the content that is driving this media-rich Digital Age.

In the 1950s, the renowned American social psychologist Solomon Eliot Asch, in an attempt to scientifically explain group conformity and the effects of Nazi propaganda during World War II, conducted a series of important studies to demonstrate that propaganda was most effective when it played to an audience's ignorance and fears.[2]

Based on his research, Asch postulated that our need to conform to the group is so ingrained in us psychologically that we will often accept information that we know to be untrue if we hear the false messages often enough and no one questions them. Asch's research has been replicated in numerous contemporary studies that confirm his conclusion that our need to conform to the group, to what we view as the community-accepted norms, still exerts significantly strong influence today. Advertisers know this well and skillfully apply this knowledge of social psychology when creating their ads.

Advertising is everywhere. Everyday ads bombard us, competing for our attention and requiring us to work at finding meaning in the images, sounds and motions that compose 21st-century media. In the United States, advertising revenues—as they do in much of the world—make possible the variety of mass media content that we all enjoy. (We will explore this point further in Chapter 9.) At its best, advertising entertains and even educates us, while striving to alter our attitudes, beliefs and behavior to get us to buy and consume certain products, use particular services or form certain opinions. According to Kevin Roberts, CEO of Saatchi & Saatchi Ideas Company, one of the world's leading advertising agencies, it is exactly this combination of sights, sounds and motions that makes good advertising so engaging and successful. From this compelling combination, Roberts coined his own term, *sisomo* (sight, sound and motion), which he now believes majorly influences all 21st-century mass media.[3]

▶ 00:08 ——————————— 00:33 CC ✕ ◀))▮▮▮▮▮

▶ **Mini-Stories**
This video montage of Mobius Award-winning commercials illustrates how successful advertising draws us into the story, despite how impractical or unreasonable it may be.

Mobius Awards

Like Roberts, creators of advertising spots view and use such advances in media technologies as HDTV, video-capable cell phones, enhanced color and image clarity in print ads and the expansion of satellite and digital radio to capture buyers' attention. Once they do, advertisers then hope they can attract an audience to a product or brand. As noted earlier, a good deal of advertising tells mini-stories that stimulate the imagination. These ads draw us in with their dynamic images; they entertain or move us; and they engage us by emotionally connecting us to the product. They inspire us to participate in the experience, to be a part of the culture or part of the "in-group" established by the message. As the video montage of Mobius Award-winning commercials illustrates, successful advertising pulls us into the story, despite how impractical or unreasonable it may be. ▶

Consider the Starbucks experience. Starbucks has been phenomenally successful in creating demand for a product that far outpaces the practical behavior of purchasing a cup of coffee. We do not go to Starbucks just to buy a cup of specialty coffee. After all, we can buy a cup of coffee at a fast-food restaurant or local quick mart far more easily, quickly and cheaply. In many cases, that cup of $1.00 coffee will be just as good as the $4.50 cup at Starbucks. Starbucks is able to get us to wait in lines, choose from complex menu options and spend three or four times the amount its competitors charge for a normal cup of coffee because the company is, in fact, selling us more than coffee. That is, Starbucks is selling us a shared idea, a shared emotional and cultural experience. Starbucks is a treat, a splurge, a little bit of luxury in a day largely devoid of treats and luxuries. At its core, the Starbucks "product" is the emotional payoff that results from a manufactured cultural experience; people the world over have come to value it—thus a cup of specialty coffee is often the least of what Starbucks is selling us.

PRODUCT AFFINITY: MAKING US WANT IT

Regardless of how advertisements are presented in the media, most try to accomplish the same thing: to persuade us to accept a product's message or brand and to create a strong emotional relationship with it,

If an ad campaign creates cultural momentum, it will encourage larger segments of the target audience to feel that they are part of the story, to believe that they belong to the "in-group" that has discovered the life-changing brand or product.

or product affinity, even if this affinity is irrational. If the ad succeeds in doing this, the audience is more likely to alter its opinion and take action by buying the product. If an ad campaign creates cultural momentum, it will encourage larger segments of the target audience to feel that they are part of the story, to believe that they belong to the "in-group" that has discovered the life-changing brand or product. Thus the message is not just that Apple's Macintosh computer might be a good personal computer, but rather that by owning a Mac, one becomes part of the Mac-owning "in-crowd" and part of the Mac "culture." Likewise, Starbucks is not just a place to buy a good cup of coffee, but rather a gateway to a specific cultural and social identity.

While certain ads, such as Google's text ads, do strictly aim to *inform* more than *persuade*, much of commercial advertising at its most effective asks us to suspend reality and accept that we can be part of the story it is presenting: Just buy these shoes, take this pill, drink this brand of beer, drive this car and you're on your way to being one of the beautiful, happy people in the story. The fact that the shoes are uncomfortable, the pill has serious side effects, the beer tastes just like other beers matters little as you lose yourself to the fantasy.

Unlocking the Code to Our Desires

What makes us want a product? Which persuasive strategies do advertisers employ? Dr. Clotaire Rapaille, a leading consultant to many of the world's top advertising and marketing executives, offers his theory. At first glance, Rapaille appears to be a character right out of an espionage novel. He is a man of many hats: a trained psychoanalyst who studied at the Sorbonne in Paris; the founder of a tremendously lucrative consulting practice called Archetype Discoveries Worldwide; and the author of numerous books on advertising and marketing, including the most popular and influential, *The Culture Code: An Ingenious Way to Understand Why People Around the World Live and Buy as They Do*. He is also famous for decoding "why people do what they do." It is no wonder, then, that members of the industry flock to his seminars in the United States and Europe. For more than three decades, Rapaille and his team have developed techniques to train creative advertising minds, helping them to unmask human behavior beyond what they can find out in surveys or focus groups. Rapaille's firm, Archetype Discoveries, "digs under our 'rational' reasoning, to uncover the true emotional and biological roots of our opinions and behaviors. Understanding this unconscious foundation gives us the tools to better motivate consumers, design new products, and improve communications strategies.[4]

8.2

According to Rapaille, effective advertisements tap into individuals' innermost desires and fantasies.

Mobius Awards

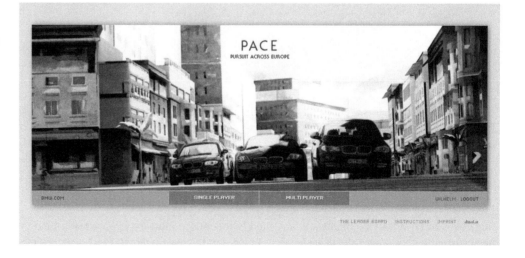

Rapaille believes that advertising works best when it is able to speak directly to the individual's inner desires. He asserts that certain cultural imperatives dictate how individual consumers project themselves into an advertisement's story. People tend to build their identities and their world around the products they purchase. To uncover what consumers really want from a particular product—how they subconsciously relate to its name, what its physical characteristics should be and how they envision themselves owning the product—advertisers must unlock a "code." Once unlocked, they must then structure their ads to speak directly to consumers' inner desire—even when these inner desires fly in the face of practicality or rationality.

Rapaille's approach to advertising might appear extreme to some. Nevertheless, his theory helps explain why certain commercial advertising is successful as well as how such advertising creates a cultural shift from desirable, to perhaps necessary, lifestyle changes. Consider, for instance, the soaring increase in gas prices in 2012 and the effects this price hike had on automobile culture. That year, advertisers moved to promoting smaller, more fuel-efficient, "cleaner" cars (such as the Smart car and the Tesla Model S), thus turning the tide away from an American automotive culture that once embraced large, fast cars and SUVs. In general, for this to occur, advertisers need to feature more than just relatable characters or remarkable and dynamic images—they must also deliver a strong message that touches on the significant issues of the day—in the case of the Smart car or the Tesla, the price of gas, the reliance on foreign oil, the environment and global warming.

Relying on Universal Appeal

As much as advertisers rely on consumers' desires or their sense of social responsibility to facilitate cultural change or to sell a product, they also rely on universal appeal—and sex is one of those appeals. Sexual imagery in advertising often pushes cultural limits by presenting evocative situations. Generally, the more sexually provocative an ad is, the more it appears to garner lasting audience attention.[5] Advertisers' reliance on social and psychological relationships is drawn in part from social learning theory (outlined in Chapter 1). Simply stated, "We all have a strong tendency to copy what we see others do, especially if they appear powerful, rich, and attractive."

Not all sexually themed advertisements seek to "sell sex" and not all such ads are necessarily pornographic. Some effectively mix humor and sex to attract its audiences. Consider, for instance, the Old Spice commercial, "The Man Your Man Could Smell Like," which premiered in early 2010. With tongue-in-cheek sexuality, the ad suggests that while the men who use Old Spice may not end up looking like the handsome, baritone-voiced, well-built man in the commercial, they can at least *smell* like that man— and that can be just as good.[6] Although the Old Spice commercial is campy and fun, others, such as the Victoria's Secret's alluring "Angel" ads, are overtly sexual. But are women necessarily objectified in these ads? Or are they invited to feel pride in their womanhood and in their sexuality? Sexual imagery is also used to promote value messages that actually have very little to do with sex: In the artful "Go Naked" ads put forth by People for the Ethical Treatment of Animals (PETA), for instance, celebrities are photographed in sensual poses claiming they would rather "go naked" than wear fur.

Advertisers also rely on the universal appeal of popular culture. As the examples discussed earlier in this chapter demonstrate, advertisers contribute to the creation and the maintenance of popular culture. In this way, advertising serves as a vehicle for establishing cultural norms. For instance,

8.3

Rylan Clark attends a photocall to launch his new anti-fur advert in support of PETA at Marble Arch on June 12, 2013 in London, England.

Ben Pruchnie/Contributor

Advertisers contribute to the creation and the maintenance of popular culture. In this way, advertising serves as a vehicle for establishing cultural norms.

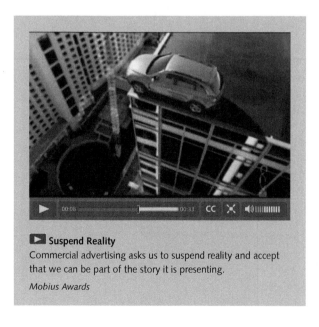

▶ **Ejector Pew**

Provocative religious commercials, such as this one, can cast religious messages using trendy and even humorous imagery.

Mobius Awards

▶ **Suspend Reality**

Commercial advertising asks us to suspend reality and accept that we can be part of the story it is presenting.

Mobius Awards

would we see as many people plugged into iPods, reading on Kindles or lovin' McDonald's were it not for the influence of advertisers? Even our common parlance is embedded with speech from advertising slogans: "Can you hear me now?"; "Just do it!"; "Friends don't let friends drive drunk."; "Milk: It does a body good."; "A diamond is forever." Advertising images have also made their way into our popular culture: We see a gecko, and we immediately think of the talking gecko from the Geico Insurance commercials; we see an Apple symbol, and we immediately conjure up visions of Macbooks and iPhones; we see golden arches, and we may (or may not) crave McDonald's.

Additionally, advertisers touch upon individuals' sense of values: health and beauty; friends and family; success and happiness; hope and faith. Religious organizations, broadcasters and megachurches have used advertising to attract hundreds of thousands of converts/consumers, many of whom send in donations as well as purchase paraphernalia, books, tapes, CDs and DVDs. Viewed purely from a mass-communication perspective, the promotion of religion through advertising is a viable option for churches and religious movements because it works—in the same way it does for any other product, political platform or social cause. View one of these provocative religious commercials in the segment titled "Ejector Pew," and note how it employs humor and entertainment to promote its message. ▶

Audiences generally need to be entertained. Visual action ads that offer a glimpse of adventure will typically draw attention, as will humor and surprising story outcomes. Regardless of the techniques used or the object of universal appeal, the conclusion of an advertisement must present the promise of a reward, real or imagined. We envision ourselves solving the case, getting the beautiful woman or handsome man, riding off to adventure in that new SUV or just having a wonderful time with our friends—with that brand of beer or soda clutched in hand. To see samples of such advertising, view the video segment titled "Suspend Reality," and consider how effectively these commercials manage to suck you into their fantasies: Are you left in a state of suspended reality after watching them? ▶

Teaching and Informing

Advertisers primarily rely on persuasion to reel in consumers and hold their interest, but they also entice and attract them through product education and information. Commercial ads can teach us about which technology trends are happening, about what is fashionable, about what is the next "hot" product to reach the marketplace. Furthermore, they can inform us about a multitude of products and developments—for example, new medical treatments and pharmaceuticals; advancements in vehicle safety and fuel efficiency; the availability of new environmentally friendly products. Ads also provide valuable data about schools, vacation destinations and worthwhile charities.

The onslaught of advertising we face on a daily basis—especially on television and the Internet—can also bring about information overload, overwhelming our ability to thoughtfully examine the ideas we are exposed to and making us more pliable and prone toward adopting the view of content producers. Information overload, which challenges our ability to think selectively and critically about that information, suggests that more than ever we must be aware of the goals and means of advertisers; we must prepare ourselves to be responsible media consumers. We need to train ourselves to ask critical questions, such as "How do we evaluate all the information with which we are bombarded?" and "How can we identify the misleading or risky information from the factual?" Moreover, we need to train ourselves to answer those questions by scrutinizing the content we encounter.

> Information overload, which challenges our ability to think selectively and critically about that information, suggests that more than ever we must be aware of the goals and means of advertisers; we must prepare ourselves to be responsible media consumers.

Advertisements not only teach us about products, but also teach us about being literate media consumers. For example, how often do we hear narrators in pharmaceutical commercials announce, "One out of every three doctors recommends. . . ." When we hear such statements, we should immediately apply some set of critical criteria to help us determine the validity of such statements. We might ask ourselves, what are these doctors' areas of expertise? What, exactly, were they asked? What specifically did they say? Where are the studies that prove the advertiser's point? Inevitably, these ads are followed by a postscript disclaimer noting that the product has "serious side effects." We might well wonder, would "one out of every three doctors" truly recommend a drug with such a seemingly endless list of side effects? Generally, advertisers will give consumers enough details that they can draw their own conclusions about the products being advertised—but then consumers must decide for themselves whether that product will help them live more informed, satisfying lives.

Narrowcasting: Connecting Consumers and Products

As alluded to earlier, the increase in the number of advertising groups and the proliferation of ad content have made it more challenging for advertisers to identify their target audiences. As a result, it has become more difficult to provide consumers with relevant and attractive content. Since measuring the success of a campaign accurately and effectively is such a complex process, advertisers have found it more difficult to allocate their campaign resources wisely. Given that the mass media landscape of the early 21st century is ever-changing, advertisers have recognized that they must change along with it. Specifically, more and more have been moving away from audience broadcasting, which seeks the widest reach and the largest number of "eyes" or "ears" for an ad, to narrowcasting, which creates narrowly directed messages that are targeted to smaller, more clearly defined audience segments. Narrowcasting is foundational to marketing in the Digital Age because it heightens awareness of key needs in consumers, both real and felt, and provides marketers with important feedback that better gauges the relevancy and effectiveness of their advertising campaigns. This shift from broadcasting to narrowcasting emphasizes the importance of forging a relevant connection between products and consumers, and the challenge of doing so in a media-saturated environment.

> This shift from broadcasting to narrowcasting emphasizes the importance of forging a relevant connection between products and consumers, and the challenge of doing so in a media-saturated environment.

Advertisers also rely on the Internet—the fastest-growing venue for commercial advertising. Internet advertising focuses on keyword search behaviors, rather than demographics. Google has developed the world's largest Internet-ad placement services, also known as long-tail advertising, called AdWords and AdSense. With these services, advertisers pay for ad placements that match keyword searches that appear next to search results. The fees for these ads are based on the number of clicks that redirect people to advertisers' Websites. For example, a search that includes such keywords as "skiing," "vacation" or "Colorado" would return advertiser-paid links to ski lodges and resorts in Vail, Colorado, as well as links to travel agencies offering ski vacation packages and Websites selling ski equipment and clothing. Recently, this type of narrowcasting has faced the growing problem of click fraud, where Website owners hire services to create large runs of repetitive automated link clicks—giving a false representation of the number of real-page views. These false views, which are run by programs called clickbots, increase the cost of the ads.

Customized ad viewing has proven to be a much more effective form of Internet-based advertising that also relies on narrowcasting. Consider, for instance, the success of Hulu.com. Hulu offers Internet users professionally produced streaming and licensed media content. Like its major competitor YouTube, Hulu makes money by selling Internet advertising. Instead of forcing consumers to view certain ads or interrupting entertainment content with advertising, Hulu allows users to select which ads they will watch and when they will watch them. Someone who visits Hulu to view a recent episode of the popular TV series *Modern Family*, for example, might be given the option of watching an ad for a new SUV or snack product. Visitors can also decide which ad they prefer to watch at the beginning of the video. Through customized ad viewing, viewers not only have the opportunity to learn about new products in which they might have already been interested, but Hulu, and the companies that advertise with it, gain valuable information about the interests of their viewers, which can then be used to make narrowcasting even more effective.

The success of narrowcasting has, in large part, been made possible through the progress of technology. The advent of new media technologies—cell phones, PDAs, smartphones, tablets, iPod and the continuing growth of the Internet—has created opportunities for advertisers to reach new audiences. For example, Apple's iADs service allows advertisers to directly embed advertisements in applications running on iPads, iPhones and iTouch devices. Learning to reliably track the effects, and thus calculate the cost–benefit ratios, of advertising expenditures in a narrowcasting world is one example of the challenges facing the advertising industry in the Digital Age. How do advertisers, who spend millions of dollars on multiple-venue advertising campaigns (e.g., TV spots, magazine ads and long-tail Internet ads), determine which elements yield the best results? How do they determine which combination of mass media venues will eventually result in increased sales?

The ability to focus advertising on smaller, more clearly defined audiences has spawned an entire industry that seeks to collect and sell vast databases of information about consumers. Consider, for example, Acxiom Corporation, the largest U.S. data-mining company. Most people have never heard of it—and Acxiom would like to keep it that way.

Acxiom collects publicly available information on almost everyone in the United States who shops with a credit card; uses a grocery or drugstore discount card; mails in a consumer registration form; buys or rents a car, a house or apartment; joins a health club; subscribes to a magazine or newspaper; or fills a prescription. Every time we use a credit card, swipe a discount card at the supermarket or have a prescription filled, we are leaving an information trail about ourselves, our lifestyles and consumer behavior. This valuable information is constantly fed into Acxiom's huge server farms. Acxiom's clients include advertisers, manufacturers, publishers and politicians, all of whom pay Acxiom to identify narrowly targeted audiences and consumers. Without such highly focused and reliable data-mining services, narrowcasting would not be possible, and advertising campaigns would be far more costly and less efficient.[7]

Product Placement: Advertising Without Advertising

Product placement is a highly effective way of creating audience affinity with a product or message without direct commercial advertising. Also referred to as *product integration*, it comprises the mixing of identifiable products and brands into entertainment programming. Product placement is the Snapple iced tea you see in front of the judges on every episode of *America's Got Talent*. Product placement is when a character in a film or TV drama opens a laptop with its Apple or Microsoft logo facing the camera. When the lead characters all drive Cadillacs, or when the hero in a car chase drives a BMW while the bad guys all drive more generic vehicles, that is also product placement. Try to count the number of product placements during a normal night of TV viewing—a Starbucks coffee cup in a character's hand, a bottle of Smirnoff vodka on the bar, a VW Bug parked in a driveway—and you will see how thoroughly commercial messages have been integrated into entertainment media.

The growth of product integration in television programs and movies is commonly referred to as Madison-meets-Vine. The center of the advertising industry is located around Madison Avenue in New York City; the center of the TV and movie industry surrounds Vine Street in Hollywood. Together, they drive product integration. The reasons driving this marriage are twofold.

First, the costs of producing more visually sophisticated entertainment continue to rise, even as the increasing number of channels that compete for audience attention claim more narrowly defined shares of the revenues earned by entertainment media. To cover their costs in the face of a highly splintered audience and potentially smaller share of the overall revenue stream, production companies must find alternate revenue sources early in the project—and product integration is becoming a more important source of this funding.

The second force driving the trend toward increased product integration is the large number of media technologies that enable viewers to avoid television advertising altogether. For example, the omnipresent remote control allows us to "mute" the commercials we do not wish to watch. In addition, the proliferation of DVRs and services such as TiVo enable viewers to self-program television content, usually avoiding all of the commercials. Commercial-free pay-per-view movies and video-on-demand (VOD) services are further cutting into advertising reach and revenues.

8.4

Logo-clad cups in front of the celebrity judges' panel of America's Got Talent illustrate product placements in reality TV shows.

Photofest

According to Doug Scott, senior partner and executive director of Ogilvy Entertainment, product integration has become a better advertising investment than the traditional 30-second television commercial:

> When you look at what the traditional marketer spends, the average 30-second spot in the industry is probably pushing $1 million or more. But the shelf life of that is roughly six months . . . The shelf life of short-form branded content, however, can be several years. The ownership of that content allows you to really mold the message you're looking to carry out there.[8]

Product integration has proven so successful as an alternative advertising approach that it is creeping into all types of television content, not just entertainment programs, and is showing up more frequently in music videos and video games. For example, in 2009, EA Black Box released *Skate 2*, a multiplayer video game that features dynamic billboards in the game's fantasy environment that carry real-world advertising. This evolving trend proves the staying power of the historic marriage between advertising and mass media content, which makes available free or inexpensive superior and multifarious mass media content, paid for in large part by the advertising industry.

BREAKING THE RULES: ADVERTISING IN THE 21ST CENTURY

Just as mass media have evolved since the dawning of the Digital Age, so has the advertising industry. In the past, an advertising agency has been a services company that creates, plans and produces advertising—as well as associated promotions and public relations campaigns—for a wide range of companies, brands and products. In recent years, however, the traditional Big 10 agencies, including Ogilvy & Mather and Saatchi & Saatchi, are being forced to transform their business models to remain competitive with agencies

8.5

CP+B's innovative campaign for the Mini Cooper made small cars cool again for American drivers.

Mobius Awards

that are directly rooted in the experiences, culture and lifestyles of the millennial market—a much sought-after consumer base. Consider Crispin Porter + Bogusky (CP+B), a Miami-based agency renowned for its extremely successful Mini Cooper campaign, which helped to introduce the car to the U.S. market.

CP+B was founded by Sam Crispin, who recruited two other unlikely advertising freelancers: Alex Bogusky, a graphic designer and dirt-bike enthusiast, and Chuck Porter, a copywriter and avid windsurfer. The young trio set out to create an ad agency that differed as much as possible from the mainstream ad agency mindset. They staffed their new agency primarily with young, highly innovative people whose backgrounds were unrelated to advertising. They were extreme sports enthusiasts, musicians and artists deeply immersed in various aspects of the new millennial culture, and who approached advertising challenges the same way they approached their own lives—with an outlook that contained little or no separation between work and play.

At first, the agency attracted smaller clients that shared their outlook and cultural values, and that sold such products as video games, surfing gear, racing bikes, skateboards and extreme sports clothing lines. These clients did not have the time or resources to engage in traditional advertising and marketing approaches, so instead they took extraordinary risks with their relatively small advertising budgets. The unique combination of risk-taking clients and a rule-breaking creative team allowed CP+B to experiment with new ideas on how to develop ad campaigns. CP+B team members built advertising geared toward the way its market lived—that is, by combining TV and print advertising with Websites, online minifilms and interactive media, live events, point-of-sale promotions, podcasts and posters, T-shirts, guerrilla theater stunts and anything else they could come up with. Taken together, these activities created "cultural movements" built around their clients' products and brands.

CP+B's goal was to get its clients noticed and their products identified with the millennial culture. Company leaders soon discovered that the more they broke the traditional advertising rules, the better the outcomes were. As a result, CP+B's fame grew. The agency dubbed its approach "Creating Hoopla," and it published a coffee table-style book titled *Hoopla* as yet another break-the-rules way to promote its marketing method. Before long, CP+B was stealing major accounts from the Big 10 New York- and London-based agencies. These accounts included Burger King, Virgin Atlantic Airlines, Miller Lite, IKEA, Gap, Volkswagen, and, as the subject of one of the agency's most famous campaigns, Mini Cooper.

The Mini Cooper USA campaign was quintessential CP+B. This totally integrated mass media promotion aimed to create a new lifestyle icon and a new anti-SUV cultural movement by pulling audiences into the "Mini story" and selling the idea that "the SUV backlash officially starts now." From placement in popular films such as *The Italian Job*—where the Minis became characters in the story—to TV commercials, Web media, posters and billboards, the campaign carried the evolving humorous Mini story everywhere.

Minis appeared being driven down the streets of major cities or on the roof racks of SUVs, sporting the slogan "What are you doing for fun this weekend?" Disassembled Minis showed up atop billboards, as if they were Transformer toys. CP+B also created Websites and backstories that made these Mini-robots seem "alive." The agency even created ads that resembled bizarre tabloid "news" stories featuring the Mini: "Mutant steals Mini Cooper car for joy ride" and "Counterfeit Mini Coopers: A big problem that's growing bigger." These tabloid headlines all referred readers to Mini Cooper Websites. The Websites, in turn, featured photos showing "how to identify a genuine Mini" and asking the public to report counterfeit Minis to the "Counter Counterfeit Commission" (CCC), whose goal was to help the public "protect itself from the humiliation of owning a fake!" Highly amusing stories tracked the exploits of CCC agents as they scoured the countryside and prowled the Web, tracking down the fakes.

As a single dynamic advertising package, CP+B's Mini Cooper campaign was very successful in capturing public attention and creating brand recognition. It quickly and effectively raised the image of the Mini Cooper to iconic stature by capitalizing on the power of integrated mass media, which use all of the available mass media technologies to connect effectively with an audience. Furthermore, the campaign revealed how the use of clever advertising can establish perceived high value and generate a "buzz" around a product. The product then becomes a symbol that, for many consumers, is as desirable and fulfilling as the product itself. Proof of this can be found in the significant number of Mini Cooper purchases that resulted from this campaign as well as Americans' embrace of the Mini Cooper idea and ethos.

In addition, the Mini Cooper campaign demonstrated that effective imagery is integral to an advertisement's success. When imagery attracts a viewer and holds his or her attention, the result is known in the industry as "capturing eyeballs"—whether those images are startling, unexpected or built around characters engaged in action, adventure, fantasy, romance or comedy. Experience how the video segment "Humor" "captures eyeballs" through effective use of humor and imagery. ▶

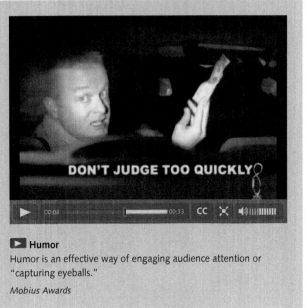

▶ **Humor**
Humor is an effective way of engaging audience attention or "capturing eyeballs."
Mobius Awards

The Influence of Commercial Advertising

American culture is a consumer culture, and commercial advertising is seen as one of the major influences that contribute to its formation. At its most overt, images encourage viewers to project themselves into a fantasy world, full of sexually attractive people who live interesting, adventurous lives. By selling these images and ideas, advertisers manipulate the goals and expectations of the audience. Unfortunately, this impact can have significantly negative effects on younger children and teenagers. Children, critics of advertising argue, are highly susceptible to the manipulative nature of advertising because they are more likely to believe that the images presented in ads are real. Children have more difficulty than adults do in determining the value of commercials. Indeed, some national parents' groups have lobbied Congress to control advertising content because of their belief that children must be protected from any sort of suggestive media content. On the opposing side, the advertising industries have successfully argued that advertising qualifies as commercial free speech. This debate is far from settled. (See Chapter 11 for further discussion.)

The concerns with commercial advertising go beyond how its messages and images affect children and young adults to include how they affect young women. In a compilation of studies published in 2010 by the *Journal of Consumer Research* titled "The Effects of Thin and Heavy Media Images on Overweight and Underweight Consumers: Social Comparison Processes and Behavioral Implications," it was reported that young people, especially girls, are highly influenced by what they see in ads while older consumers are far less influenced:

> While it's well established that seeing images of underweight women make normal or overweight women feel bad about themselves, some recent research has found that the conventional wisdom in the fashion and advertising worlds is wrong, and that consumers are less interested in buying products that make them feel insecure. (The same research, though, found that exposure to overweight models had a similar negative effect on women's self-esteem.)[9]

8.6

Do advertisements depict unrealistic images of the "ideal woman"?

Mobius Awards

These advertising images of the "perfect woman" have caused a worrisome number of women to take extreme measures in an attempt to meet this industry-created standard. Studies have identified, for example, a significant increase in both elective plastic surgery and eating disorders among increasingly younger women. In a study reported in the *Journal of American College Health* in 1998, followed up with a study reported 10 years later in the *Journal of Behavior Modification*, 20 out of every 100 female undergraduates in the United States were found to be suffering from mild to moderate symptoms of anorexia or bulimia.

According to statistics collected by the American Society of Plastic Surgeons, women younger than age 25 underwent 8.5 million elective plastic surgery procedures in 2001. In 2003, nearly 100,000 of these procedures were performed in girls younger than the age of 18. Today's numbers are virtually the same as those of the original study. In a trend paralleling the growth of advertising-supported new media, especially Internet sites, the number of women younger than 20 years of age in both the United States and Western Europe electing to undergo plastic surgery is increasing.[10] In response to this disturbing trend, the Dove brand produced a series of commercials that, rather than promote artificial beauty, encouraged young women to embrace and nurture their natural beauty, body and self-esteem. To view one of the commercials from this campaign, click on "Dove Evolution." ▶

The actual number of people who are negatively influenced by images of ideal men and women in commercial advertising, however, represent only a small fraction of the total viewing audience. Advertisers have also relied on these images of healthy, active men and women—at every age—to serve as a more positive influence—that is, as role models for healthy living, good nutrition and regular exercise. Encouraging viewers to strive to be like the characters depicted in ads is exactly how advertisers persuade viewers to accept their stories, build audience affinity for the ads' underlying messages and encourage consumers to purchase the products or service. More than 50 years ago, mass media theorist Marshall McLuhan identified the positive message of advertising as a counterbalance to the somber stories covered by the news media:

8.7

Frequent TV ads including images of the "perfect woman" help drive the popularity of elective cosmetic surgery.

Image Source/Alamy Stock Photo

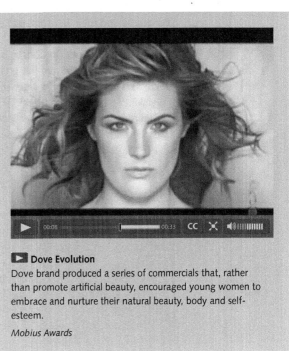

▶ **Dove Evolution**
Dove brand produced a series of commercials that, rather than promote artificial beauty, encouraged young women to embrace and nurture their natural beauty, body and self-esteem.

Mobius Awards

The ads are by far the best part of any magazine or newspaper. More pain and thought, more wit and art, go into the making of an ad than into any prose feature of press or magazine. Ads are news. What is wrong with them is that they are always good news. In order to balance off the effect and to sell good news, it is necessary to have a lot of bad news. [Newspapers and news magazines] have bad news for the sake of intensity and reader participation. Real news is bad news . . . and as any newspaper from the beginning of print can testify, floods, fires and other communal disasters by land and sea and air outrank any kind of private horror or villainy as news. Ads, in contrast, have to shrill their happy message loud and clear in order to match the penetrating power of bad news.[11]

Political Advertising: Making Us Vote for It

Knowing how to determine the positive or negative influence of a product or service message is required as much in commercial advertising as it is in political advertising. Political advertising has always been a vital aspect of American politics, but presidential campaign expenditures on advertising have now reached astronomical levels. During the 2012 presidential election cycle, the two leading candidates raised and spent just over $2 billion. President Obama, on the Democratic side, raised $1,072 million and spent $985 million; Mitt Romney, on the Republican side, raised and spent $992 million.[12] That amount does not include the money spent by the other candidates before dropping out of the race. The largest portion of these funds goes to paid television advertising, which represents the single highest expenditure in national political campaigns.

While the Obama camp expertly garnered support through effective application of social media, when the race came down to just the single Democratic and Republican candidates, both used narrowcasting to address audiences as small as specific neighborhoods. Campaign organizers also sent supporters door-to-door armed with tablets, which they used to play short video ads on issues of high interest to people living in these precincts. A neighborhood predominantly populated by factory workers might have been shown a video about the risk of jobs being moved overseas, for example, whereas people living in a riverfront community might have been shown a video on the need to increase federal spending on improving levees and other flood control infrastructure.

Politicians and their advisors, pollsters, fundraisers and assorted experts all make the obvious assumption that political advertising must be a significant element of any campaign, whether national, state or local. In reality, experts continue to debate both how effective political advertisements are and whether positive or negative campaign ads have the greatest impact. What is widely agreed upon is that political advertising on television has a significant influence on the electorate, or voting public, and that the most memorable, controversial and infamous political TV ads of the last four decades featured negative messages.

Sometimes these negative messages are far from subtle. Such was the case in the 1964 Lyndon Johnson *Daisy Girl* ad, which showed a little girl in a meadow playing with a daisy. She is pulling off daisy petals, counting, "1, 2, 3, . . ." When she gets to nine, a threatening male voice starts a launch countdown: "10, 9, 8, . . ." The camera zooms in on the little girl's frightened face and focuses on her eye, which reflects the mushroom cloud of a nuclear explosion. As viewers watch the devastating explosion, Lyndon Johnson's voice announces over the loud rumble: "These are the stakes: to make a world in which all of God's children can live, or to go into the dark. We must either love each other, or we must die." The ad simply ends with a black screen and voice-over "Vote for President Johnson on November 3rd." Johnson's ad was clearly and directly negative, playing on the Cold War fears of most Americans at the time. That November, Lyndon Johnson defeated his Republican opponent Barry Goldwater in a landslide election. Johnson's campaign was widely criticized for suggesting that the election of Barry Goldwater as president would inevitably lead to a nuclear World War III and the potential annihilation of the United States. Although the *Daisy Girl* ad aired only once, on September 7, 1964, during the NBC Monday Night Movie, it is credited for having contributed to Johnson's landslide victory. ▶

▶ Johnson, *Daisy Girl* Ad

Sometimes negative messages are far from subtle, as depicted in this 1964 Lyndon Johnson ad, which played on the Cold War fears of most Americans at the time.

During the 2004 presidential campaign, a Republican political action group called the Swift Boat Veterans for Truth created a series of television ads questioning the actions of Democratic presidential candidate and sitting U.S. Senator John Kerry. They strongly suggested that Kerry had not only lied about his experiences as the skipper of a river swift boat during his tour of duty in Vietnam, but that he was a traitor and therefore unfit to serve as president. The firestorm of investigative media coverage that followed revealed the truth about Kerry's service and courageousness—that he did, in fact, place himself before enemy fire to save the lives of the men serving under him. Yet, despite evidence vindicating Kerry, the *Swift Boat* ads still managed to significantly damage his campaign; some say they contributed to the re-election of George W. Bush, who, unlike Kerry, had avoided service in Vietnam.

A more recent example of negative political advertising took place in during the recent 2016 presidential campaign. One of the most divisive and negative presidential campaigns in modern history was hard fought between two equally flawed presidential candidates—former First Lady, New York senator, and Secretary of State Hillary Clinton, the Democratic candidate, against the Republican candidate billionaire real estate mogul and reality TV star Donald J. Trump. Although Hillary Clinton won the popular vote by more than a 3-million-vote margin, Donald Trump won enough Electoral College votes to become the 45th president of the United Sates—shocking most major polling organizations and the majority of mainstream media commentators. Both candidates were easy media targets; Clinton because of an endless stream of revelations and accusations of mishandling allegedly classified e-mails as well as false claims about the activities of the Clinton Foundation, and Trump because of his many incendiary, racist, misogynistic, and fact-less comments on the campaign trail and in the media, and his refusal to release his tax returns or divest himself of his international business holding to comply with the historic and constitutionally mandated ethical standards for presidents.

Both campaigns spent tens of millions of dollars producing negative TV ads against the other. The most effective of these negative ads was produced by the Clinton campaign. Called *Role Models* the ad showed a series of vulnerable looking multi-ethnic young children with shocked looks on their faces watching Trump say outrageous, offensive, racist and inflammatory comments. The voice of Trump is the only narration very effectively using his own words against him. Even though Trump became president by Electoral College votes, this Hillary Clinton ad has become a model for effective negative political advertising. But does even very effective negative advertising actually work? Think about this question as you view the Clinton *Role Models* TV ad. ▶️

▶️ **Clinton's *Role Models* TV Ad**
A very effective negative campaign ad focused on negative impact of then-presidential candidate Donald Trump's own words on impressionable young children.

Political advertising generates considerable debate among commentators, campaign representatives, pundits, bloggers, Twitterers and Facebook users. The problem is that these ads too often divert the public's attention from the important issues facing the nation and redirect it to what they perceive as more interesting for the public—namely, the clash of political personalities. The convergence of political campaigning onto the Internet has also had an obvious impact on the life cycles and influence of political advertising. Today every candidate must have his or her own Website, and in the case of national campaigns, multiple Websites. Social media, online organizations and participants in the blogosphere who support one candidate or another all maintain multiple sites devoted to promoting their views. These Websites serve as platforms for streaming media that extend the reach of political TV ads; popular media portals such as YouTube help to increase their shelf life. As such, controversial or negative ads remain especially enduring.

The effects and influence of political advertising, especially negative political advertising, and the role of highly funded political action committees called PACs (or "third-party groups"), became all the more controversial during the run-up to the 2012 presidential election, due in large part to the U.S. Supreme

Court decision in the landmark case known as *Citizens United*.[13] In this case, the court held that the First Amendment prohibited the government from restricting independent political donations by corporations or unions, unleashing an onslaught of political advertising funded by wealthy individuals and organizations that had been previously limited in the amounts they could donate to political campaigns. In the wake of the ruling, political advertising no longer needs to be endorsed by the candidate and the approach and content of PAC-funded ads are not in candidates' direct control. Political advertising has increased significantly since the ruling, yet preliminary research suggests that many people are just tuning out the barrage of negative political ads, especially those on television. This is not only bad news for PACs, but also bad news for local TV stations that receive a large chunk of their revenues during election years from political advertising. In a 2012 study, the Pew Research Center for the People & the Press found that 54 percent of voters had heard about *Citizens United*, and of these, 78 percent reported that these new campaign finance rules and their resulting increase in negative political advertising were having a negative effect on the 2012 presidential campaign.[14]

As we explore throughout this book, convergent mass media technologies in the Digital Age are having a significant impact on the U.S. electoral process and, by extension, American democracy. More mass media channels and increased interactivity on the Internet are ensuring that a multitude of political voices can be heard, thereby extending the quantity and quality of the national debate. Moreover, at a time when negative and misleading political advertising is reaching new heights, the widespread growth of political Websites, social media and the blogosphere has created a population of avid fact checkers. These serve as an effective counterbalance to the political "spin doctors," misinformation and disinformation that have always been a part of political advertising.

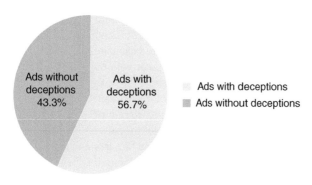

8.8

Well over 50 percent of the money spent by the third-party groups on TV ads either attacking or supporting Republican presidential contenders in 2012 included deceptions.

TRACING THE HISTORY OF AMERICAN PUBLIC RELATIONS: BUILDING AND MANAGING IMAGE

In mid-2008, the public relations (PR) department at Verizon flooded the inboxes of technology reporters with articles about problems with iPhones, which are sold through a partnership between Apple and AT&T. Verizon's PR team distributed these e-mails under headings such as "Another negative iPhone/AT&T story," "iPhone down the drain," "iPhone dropping calls like flies" and "iPhone hating." Tech reporters and the blogosphere picked up many of these stories, which breathed new life into the stories about iPhone problems and forced Apple and AT&T to launch an extensive counter-PR effort. Their joint campaign, in turn, contributed to keeping the original stories alive and circulating, especially in cyberspace. In utilizing a public-relations rather than an advertising or marketing approach, Verizon succeeded, albeit for a short time, in increasing the competitiveness of its cell phones and services against a sexy new product. The company's campaign influenced the content of the stories that journalists and bloggers were writing and kept the spotlight on the purported problems with the iPhone 3G for as long as possible.

Modern public relations developed in part out of journalism; both fields are rooted in the communication of messages and information delivered to the public in the form of stories. In the case of PR, these stories are intended to generate good will, understanding and support for the individual or organization represented, or to improve the image of a client in the public's eye. Successful PR agents make the transition from journalism to public relations rather seamlessly by applying best journalistic practices. In fact, early job descriptions for public relations agents often seemed like journalist-in-residence positions, with the most common tasks of the practitioner being to generate news releases, edit internal publications, give speeches and press conferences and organize marketing displays. Today such in-house media specialists are known as communication managers. The key distinguishing characteristic between in-house communications managers and PR agents is most often their level of working autonomy. Communication managers generally do not make their own decisions, but rather implement the decision of higher-level company officers, and they are seldom asked for advice on policy or overall campaigns. Public relations specialists are given a seat at the executive table and can influence the direction of a client's message.

This expanded role of PR agents evolved as modern technological developments enabled the influence of mass media on public opinion and consumer behavior to grow exponentially. The public relations industry continues to flourish as companies, nonprofit organizations, politicians and celebrities have an ever-increasing need for multitalented PR professionals whose public opinion organizational skills reach beyond the mere dissemination of information.

While public relations professionals have no direct power to persuade journalists and editors to tell a story a certain way, they can be very effective at pointing out to journalists something new and different about a product, service or company. In doing so, they can help to reframe a story and move it in a new direction—one more positive toward the clients that they represent. PR in the Digital Age has evolved into a media enterprise that, along with advertising, fashions and drives the mass media presence and message of corporations, cultural associations and government agencies. The closing gap between PR and marketing suggests that public relations is becoming a more integrated sector of advertising, although it can still be identified as an industry that focuses on building and managing clients' brand and perception. While the seemingly increased integration of advertising and PR has caused some debate among academics and practitioners who view this blending of skills with skepticism, others welcome the trend as a way to better respond to the challenges and opportunities of mass media convergence.

In the United States, the roots of modern public relations can be traced back to the time of the American Revolution. During the months and years leading up to this conflict, pro-independence supporters used staged events such as the Boston Tea Party, drawings of the Boston Massacre and leaflets such as Thomas Paine's *Common Sense* to increase the public's political awareness of the British Crown's abuses, both real and imagined. These attempts at swaying public opinion in favor of independence were far from what today's audiences would consider fair or balanced journalism (see the discussion in Chapter 13). Pro-independence advocates embellished the events of the day, adding fictionalized elements to make a more compelling case for rebellion.[15]

When a former newspaper reporter, Ivy Ledbetter Lee, took on the job of cleaning up the public image of large American companies in the early 1900s, he simultaneously established public relations as a separate profession. During this time, public relations served as a political and entertaining voice for such media producers as Charles Dickens, P. T. Barnum and two infamous rival newspaper moguls, William Randolph Hearst and Joseph Pulitzer.

Lee's foundational work included the development of the first ethical standards for public relations, which he published in his Declaration of Principles. In reality, Lee himself broke many of these principles during his professional career. He became the target of numerous critics owing to his attempts to whitewash the reputations of many giants of U.S. business, despite all his claims to be an advocate of reform. Lee argued that these businesses operated on behalf of public interests at a time when consumer protection laws were nonexistent and when the government was taking a primarily "Let the buyer beware" approach toward consumer protection.[16] At the end of his life, Lee was under investigation by the U.S. Congress for pro-Nazi PR work he had done on behalf of I. G. Farben, the fourth largest international corporation of the early 20th century, and one of the largest industrial operations under Hitler's Third Reich.[17]

Public relations could be said to have begun with Austrian-American author-practitioner Edward L. Bernays (1891–1995). Bernays believed in both the power and the dangers of message manipulation in the media. While working for President Woodrow Wilson as a member of the Committee on Public Information during World War I, Bernays helped to bring the term "public relations" into common use to counteract the negative implications of propaganda. He strongly doubted the reliability of public agenda setting as an important aspect of democracy. He also believed that the public's judgment on important issues was not to be trusted; he feared the dangers of an easily led public, which might support the wrong candidates or political agendas. Bernays was an ardent follower of Sigmund Freud and used his public relations techniques to help popularize Freudian psychology in America. This effort led directly to Bernays's pioneering work in the use of psychological models and methodologies in public relations, especially to analyze and understand public opinion. In 1919, he opened one of the first PR agencies, based in New York City. He subsequently taught PR courses at New York University and authored the book *Crystallizing Public Opinion* (1923), followed by *Propaganda* (1928). Both of these are considered foundational works of the field.

During and after World War II, the U.S. government used public relations professionals to create campaigns to help keep the American public's morale up and the domestic war efforts on track. In some cases, the government turned to leading war correspondents, asking them to disseminate stories that would help the war effort. One good example was Edward R. Murrow. During the war, and in the years following, Murrow was the preeminent American newsman. As a reporter on the radio, and later as a TV newscaster for CBS, Murrow built a reputation as an ethical professional, willing to take a moral stand on controversial issues. During the German bombardment of London, known as the Blitz, Morrow's radio reporting, with the sounds of nearby bombs falling in the background, moved the American public to support the war effort at the cost of extraordinary levels of sacrifice at home. By the late 1950s, however, Murrow was ready to leave broadcast journalism and readily accepted President John F. Kennedy's invitation in 1961 to become director of the U.S. Information Agency (USIA), which was from 1953–1999 the "public relations" arm of the U.S. government.

Murrow accepted the position with guarantees that he would be present at policy meetings, such as those surrounding the U.S. response to the building of the Berlin Wall and the Cuban missile crisis. His job was to make sure the American perspective was given to news organizations and governments around the world. In response to Kennedy's interest, the USIA also conducted a number of surveys of public opinion in foreign countries about U.S. policies towards its racial minorities. In June 1963, when President Kennedy gave a speech strongly in support of civil rights legislation, Murrow and the USIA were prepared to disseminate the speech and positive commentary about it to news organizations around the world. Because he knew the importance of good relations with journalists, governments and worldwide media organizations, Murrow was able to project effectively the aims and goals of the Kennedy administration. Murrow's story is a classic early example of the skillful bridging of journalism and public relations professionals.

Although the "spin doctor" image describes most of what was called public relations throughout much of the 20th century, PR has been reinvented in the 21st century. For the purposes of our discussion here, we refer to this reinvented PR as "new PR." We discuss how this new PR distinguishes itself from old PR in the pages that follow.

Given that 21st-century technology now offers the public nearly unlimited and instantly accessible information, an army of fact checkers has made spin unprofitable and unwise in most situations. Take, for example, the public relations campaigns undertaken by the tobacco industry to try to convince the public, as well as the U.S. Congress, that tobacco use does not cause cancer and other health problems. The overwhelming evidence of the multiple health dangers of smoking eventually became so compelling that the tobacco industry was forced to make the largest consumer product safety liability settlement in history. This Tobacco Master Settlement Agreement between the leading tobacco products companies and the attorney generals of 46 states happened in no small part because of decades of false advertising and PR disinformation campaigns.[18]

Fair Advocacy

While it might be argued that today it is just as easy to spread misinformation over the Internet as it is to disseminate facts, the ready accessibility of Internet technology prevents competing and minority perspectives from being shunted from the public's view, as was sometimes the case before this technology emerged. Public relations professionals in large part realize the necessity of honest and fair advocacy. Manipulating facts could destroy a professional's career, or significantly damage a client's interests, should the public learn that a PR campaign intentionally hid information about a product or failed to tell the whole truth about the background of a political candidate. When PR campaigns intentionally present false information to the public, the ramifications can be serious, as, for example, in the case of a pharmaceutical company misleading its consumers to believe that an over-the-counter drug is safe, when in fact it may cause serious and even life-threatening side effects for some users. In the mass media environment of the 21st century, facts and truth surface quickly. Lies and disinformation campaigns are undertaken at a clear risk to the perpetrators. This more conscientious and direct approach to strategic communication is a major characteristic that differentiates the old practice from contemporary public relations.

While it might be argued that today it is just as easy to spread misinformation over the Internet as it is to disseminate facts, the ready accessibility of Internet technology prevents competing and minority perspectives from being shunted from the public's view, as was sometimes the case before this technology emerged.

Content Creation

In his book *The New PR*, author Phil Hall describes how the PR team for Freddie Mac—more formally known as the Federal Home Loan Mortgage Corporation—created its own TV show to attract potential Hispanic homebuyers. The show's producers patterned *Nuestro Barrio* after the telenovela format, popular for its melodramatic storylines. *Nuestro Barrio* chronicled the lives of two married, Hispanic nightclub owners as they began the process of buying a home. By 2008, a number of independent television stations had picked up the 13-episode series and it was still being aired. *Nuestro Barrio* and similar projects illustrate the second way in which new PR distinguishes itself from its predecessor: New PR has become a major player in the production and distribution of media.

Historically, PR professionals used their influence to entice traditional media producers, such as print journalists, to investigate and create favorable content about their clients, or their clients' products, so as to generate positive media attention. New PR, however, proactively creates its own content and delivers it to the mass media-consuming public. *Nuestro Barrio*, for example, not only was broadcast by TV stations, but was also made available directly over the Internet, offering audiences a multiple-venue media experience in which they can engage with interesting stories, powerful images, popular music and other opportunities for personal interaction.

TODAY'S STRATEGIC PUBLIC RELATIONS: 360-DEGREE CAMPAIGNING

While there are many, often innovative, approaches to the practice of public relations today, they all use a similar four-phase approach commonly described by leading PR authors and practitioners. In the first phase, PR professionals conduct a detailed analysis of their clients' current situation: its organizational strengths, weaknesses and opportunities and the prevailing public attitudes about the client. In the second phase, they work with key members of the client's management team to establish the goals and objectives of the campaign—formulating a detailed strategic action plan that includes establishing the client's message and how best to successfully convey that message to the public. During the third phase, PR professionals carefully select the most appropriate media platforms and communication tactics and then implement and manage the strategic media campaign. The fourth and final stage is focused on evaluating the results and presenting them

8.9

The launch of Coca-Cola's 2012 London Olympics PR campaign is more about establishing a relationship between the brand and the 2012 Olympics than selling product.

Ben Pruchnie/Stringer

to the client, along with ideas to help the client maintain a more positive image and higher ranking in public opinion. Of course, this well-established public relations formula varies depending upon who the client is—individual celebrity, organization, company or political candidate—and if the campaign is proactive, working to establish or improve the client's public image; or reactive, working to repair damage to a client's public image due to a crisis such as product safety failure, environmental damage, or media attacks from a political rival, just to name a few examples. (See the video segment in Chapter 16 with Marcus Bass of the large Hollywood-based PR firm Spelling Communications.)

In today's media-dominated environment, public relations agents are being given regular high-level access to the top management of companies and national associations, and their advice and guidance is being included in major management decisions at unprecedented levels. Research conducted recently by the International Association of Business Communicators (IABC) Research Foundation surveyed from 1,827 IABC members worldwide (Bowen and Heath, 2006). The study revealed that PR practitioners around the world reported that 65 percent have regular access with the "dominant coalition," or the decision-making executives or chief officers of their organizations. This finding demonstrates that, in recent years, public relations managers are involved in decision-making about advising and public relations campaigns at the highest levels and often are commonly involved in the strategic management and planning process. Of that 65 percent who said they had access to the dominant coalition, 30 percent said that they report directly to the CEO of their (or their client) organization, with the remaining 35 percent reporting to senior-level executive managers.[19]

New media and Web 2.0 have made viral public relations—a new form of PR that did not exist a decade earlier—possible. (See Chapter 7 for further discussion.) The simplest method of "viralizing" a message and tapping into previously inaccessible venues is to start a blog, stimulate consumer interest on social networking sites such as Facebook and Twitter, or post short promotional video segments on YouTube. A blog will get picked up by multiple links in cyberspace, spreading the message like a virus. For PR people in the 21st century, the viral nature of mass media is really the profession's core challenge. The focus of PR campaigns is to synchronize public relation efforts with the fluid nature of Web 2.0.

PR firms and their clients now use the Internet as a social networking resource to build identification with clients and to attract new interest in their products, much in the same way we use Facebook or Instagram to connect with friends and family. Their goal is to create a large virtual community surrounding the clients' products and services.

PR firms and their clients now use the Internet as a social networking resource to build identification with clients and to attract new interest in their products, much in the same way we use Facebook or Instagram to connect with friends and family. Their goal is to create a large virtual community surrounding the clients' products and services. To do this, PR firms often employ 360-degree campaigns, which present a client's message across a wide range of media platforms, including the Internet, television and radio, print and mobile devices. These campaigns create the sense of a "special community" among consumers (or supporters of a political candidate). Editorial news stories and, in some cases, paid advertising then reinforce identification with this virtual community. For example, consider the eventual success of Apple's iPhone 3G, despite the negative PR campaign staged by its competitor Verizon. This success is in part a testament to Apple's long history of engendering a feeling of community and status among its loyal customers—even though Apple products are consistently more expensive than their competitors and are often plagued by technological glitches after their initial launch. In mid-2008, Verizon's PR department began distributing waves of reports highlighting problems with iPhone service to tech publications. Although the resulting negative coverage cast a shadow over iPhone's shiny image, the vast majority of Apple customers remained loyal due in large part to the Apple ethos. Apple cleverly continues to help its customer base feel that they are members of an elite community of technology adapters and users.

Developing Public Interest: Paparazzi and Promoters

Prior to the mid-19th century, PR in the United States served primarily to publicize and support political issues and campaigns. In 1842, however, the promotional activities surrounding Charles Dickens first visit to and tour of the United States changed that aim. Dickens's books were hugely popular in the United States and, everywhere the author traveled, he was greeted by large crowds. American newspapers covered Dickens travels throughout the country in a manner similar to today's paparazzi.

Nineteenth-century America was in love with Charles Dickens, but it was a one-sided love affair—Dickens was not equally enamored with the young nation. When the popular British author and social critic returned home to England, he published an account of his trip in a book titled *American Notes*. In the book, he harshly criticized American slavery, voiced dismay at the widespread abuses in dismal American prisons and mental institutions, and mocked what he viewed as the uneducated country-bumpkin lifestyles and manners of the American populace. Dickens was particularly angered by the nation's lack of copyright laws and protections at that time, which he viewed as having cheated him of the sizable publishing royalties that should have resulted from his enormous fame and popularity. Dickens *American Notes* caused a PR crisis for America and American publishers in Europe.

Eight years later, public relations took a different turn with the arrival of P. T. Barnum (1810–1891), a pioneering entertainment promoter and co-founder of the Barnum & Bailey Circus. Barnum's circus eventually merged with the Ringling Brothers Circus in 1919, creating the Ringling Brothers and Barnum & Bailey Circus, which continues to tour throughout North America today. Barnum masterfully produced national PR campaigns to promote his entertainment businesses; he created widespread press coverage and public interest in the celebrities he managed and toured. His efforts brought such European music stars as Jenny Lind (the "Swedish Nightingale") on national concert tours. Barnum also founded popular museums based on the circus sideshow attractions of the famous "Siamese twins" Chang and Eng and the "midget" Tom Thumb. He convinced the public to believe in such outright hoaxes as "mermaids" and counterfeit archeological treasures and zoological specimens.

P. T. Barnum's PR intentions were far from honorable, however. In fact, they can be best summed up in the famous words often attributed to him: "There's a sucker born every minute." Barnum's overt manipulation of the public's faith in what was true and what wasn't led to PR's unethical "huckster" image—a view that stuck with the profession for many decades. Many PR practitioners who followed in Barnum's footsteps made their fortunes through similar PR stunts, hiding the wrongdoings of their clients and manipulating the public's trust.

Developing Public Trust: PR Ethics

In response to this manipulation of the public trust, Ivy Lee (introduced earlier as the founding father of modern PR) authored the Declaration of Principles—an established framework for ethical practices for public relations professionals. Lee was a true pioneer: He established one of the first modern PR agencies, invented the concept of the PR-initiated press release and introduced the role of PR professionals in media crisis management. Lee believed in what he called the "two-way street" principle of PR, which articulated the idea that the PR professional was a communications facilitator between clients and the public. However, even Lee's own agency more often than not promoted propaganda—a type of communication that concentrates on persuading clients to support a very specific issue, such as a cause or a social movement, and most commonly a government's decision to go to war.[20]

As the industry expanded into the mid-20th century, PR agencies and PR professionals found themselves serving their corporate, political and government clients very much in the Lee model—in essence, endorsing propaganda and protecting the clients' interests at all costs, usually at the sacrifice of facts and truth.[21] By the 1960s and into the 1970s, however, public relations began a transition toward more ethical and professional practices. Its role focused on helping clients not only promote positive aspects of their business in the press and sway public opinion in a favorable direction, but also respond effectively to media crises—as in the famous Johnson & Johnson Tylenol case, which also illustrates how PR can be either pro-active or reactive.

Reactive PR attempts to rescue companies when crises occur. The case of the tainted Tylenol is a classic example of effective reactive PR. Beginning in late September 1982, seven residents in and around Chicago between the ages of 12 and 35 died of mysterious causes. Investigators discovered that each of the victims had taken Tylenol Extra Strength capsules right before their deaths, and that the products, all purchased from different stores, had been laced with lethal amounts of cyanide. Law enforcement agencies imme-diately issued warnings to the public, even driving through Chicago neighborhoods with loudspeakers to alert citizens of the danger. Fear quickly spread throughout the Chicago community and then throughout the nation, with Tylenol, which had been an industry-leading product, now suspected of being an agent of death. PR professionals at McNeil Consumer Products, along with its parent company, Johnson and Johnson (J&J), swiftly took action to alert the public of the danger and issued a massive recall of more than 31 million bottles of Tylenol capsules, valued at more than $100 million. They also convinced company executives to order their factories to cease production.

The company immediately undertook a thorough and very transparent investigation to determine whether the tampering had taken place during production or at some other point before the capsules reached the consumer. Investigators discovered that someone had tampered with the capsules at stores and cleared the manufacturer of any wrongdoing. The damage to the product's reputation had already been done, however, and it sent the company's stock value plummeting.

J&J quickly began to rebuild Tylenol's reputation by developing new tamper-proof packaging and offering free replacements of Tylenol tablets. These changes, along with a massive media campaign to examine the Chicago incident and inform the public of the steps the manufacturer had taken to ensure the safety of its customers, were enormously successful. Within just a few years, Tylenol was again one of the top-selling pain medications on the market.

How a company handles PR in a crisis can make the difference between life and, as in the case of Tylenol, death. This point highlights the third difference between the old and new PR: scope—or in other words, the goal of PR and the tools PR professionals had to accomplish it.

Raising Social Awareness: The PSA

Paul David Hewson was born and raised in Dublin, Ireland, in a family deeply involved in the Anglican Church of Ireland. His wife, Alison, and their four children live much of the time in Killiney, located in the southern part of County Dublin—that is, when they're not traveling the world with their husband and father. Hewson is better known by his stage name, Bono, which he uses in his role as lead singer and song-writer for the rock band U2.

Bono is much more than a rich rock star, however: He has won arguably greater fame as a humanitarian activist. His activism has brought him worldwide acclaim, friendships with presidents and world leaders, and three nominations for the Nobel Peace Prize. In 2005, *Time* magazine named Bono its Person of the Year. In 2007, he was knighted. Bono has created one of the most successful political and social issue media cam-paigns in recent history. This campaign targets debt relief for the developing world and raises international awareness about the plight of Africa and the AIDS pandemic.

With an intimate knowledge of how to use TV advertising to advance social and political causes, and as co-founder of the ONE campaign, Bono was a principal creative force behind an extraordinarily powerful public service announcement (PSA). The aim of this TV spot was to raise the visibility of African poverty and AIDS and place these issues higher on the public agenda and to encourage the U.S. Congress to increase its level of humanitarian aid for these causes from a mere $495 million of the 2012 U.S. budget. In 2010, that number remained unchanged.[22]

Joining creative forces with several producers, the ONE television campaign was launched with the global premiere of the ONE Declaration television spot, featuring cameo appearances by two dozen entertainment celebrities. At the height of the spot's run in the weeks prior to the 2005 G8 Conference, it generated an unprecedented 1.5 billion viewer impressions worldwide and made AIDS in Africa a significant issue at the summit that year. The genius of the spot is that it asked for no money, but simply asked viewers to "add their voices" to the humanitarian outcry.

The narrative of the 30-second spot is spoken by the two dozen unnamed but recognizable celebrities in unison, as if by one voice:

> One by one they step forward. A nurse. A teacher. A homemaker. And lives are saved. But the problem is enormous. Every three seconds, one person dies. Another three seconds, one more. The situation is so desperate in parts of Africa, Asia, even America, that aid groups, like they did for the [2004 Indian Ocean] tsunami, are uniting as one, acting as one. We can beat extreme poverty, starvation, AIDS. But we need your help. One more person, letter, voice, will mean the difference between life and death for millions of people. So please join together. By working together, Americans have an unprecedented opportunity. We can make history. We can start to make poverty history. One, by one, by one. Please visit us at www.one.org. We're not asking for your money, we're asking for your voice.[23]

Bono's ONE Declaration exemplifies proactive PR, a type of public relations that engages with the public and seeks to demonstrate good will. It also demonstrates the power and influence of social cause promotion—the overall goal of which is to persuade the audience to accept an organization's views on a particular issue. One aspect of social cause promotion is expressed in the form of public service announcements (PSAs)—noncommercial and presumably nonpolitical advertising. PSAs have been around since the earliest days of the broadcast advertising industry. Indeed, throughout much of the late 20th century, government regulation required both television and radio broadcasters to air a certain number of nonpaid PSAs. For these media, airing PSAs was an easy way to demonstrate that a station was operating "in the public interest."

In the early 1980s, the Federal Communications Commission (FCC) began an effort to deregulate television and radio by eliminating some of the complex rules governing broadcast stations and networks. The FCC embarked on this course on the premise that the advertising-supported media marketplace would naturally ensure that broadcasters provided programming of value and interest to their audiences. Broadcasters continued to air PSAs even after the deregulation of the broadcast industry in the 1980s, and into the 21st century. PSAs are even aired on cable and satellite radio

8.10

Bono's ONE Campaign is one of the most popular and effective social-awareness PR campaigns that emerged within the last decade.

UPPA/ZUMA/Newscom

Most of Budget Goes Toward Defense, Social Security, and Major Health Programs

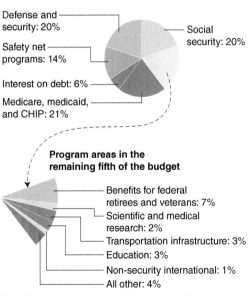

Defense and security: 20%
Safety net programs: 14%
Interest on debt: 6%
Medicare, medicaid, and CHIP: 21%
Social security: 20%

Program areas in the remaining fifth of the budget

Benefits for federal retirees and veterans: 7%
Scientific and medical research: 2%
Transportation infrastructure: 3%
Education: 3%
Non-security international: 1%
All other: 4%

Note: Percentages may not total 100 due to rounding.
Source: Congressional budget office, 2010.

8.11

According to the Center on Budget and Policy Priorities, funding allocated toward humanitarian aid makes up less than 1 percent of the federal budget.

▶ Sample PSAs

Anti-drinking and anti-smoking ads, such as the ones shown in this video, reinforce the health and safety risks of alcohol and tobacco use, especially to younger audiences.

and television channels, which have never been subject to such legal requirements. Large media trade groups contribute generously to many PSA campaigns that promote a wide range of social, education, health and safety issues. They also encourage their members to air PSAs. These trade groups include the Advertising Council (AC), the National Associations of Broadcasters (NAB) and the National Cable and Telecommunications Association (NCTA). In fact, the Advertising Council, a private nonprofit organization supported by the advertising industry, is the largest single producer of PSAs in the United States.

Some PSAs attempt to target a specific demographic. The Truth anti-smoking campaign, for instance, is developed especially for young audiences and emphasizes the health risks of tobacco use. Whether scientifically grounded or audience focused, these PSAs have the same primary focus: to persuade viewers to accept a specific viewpoint—to create viewer or reader affinity for a cause. Just as in commercial and political advertising, the secondary goal is to convince the viewer to take some action based on that viewpoint. An anti-marijuana ad, for example, might suggest that the public monitor children for evidence of marijuana use and contact state legislators to protest the legalization of marijuana use. To view some sample PSAs, click on "Sample PSAs." ▶

Facilitating Communication: Diversity in New PR

Today the field of public relations has become even more closely linked to the field of advertising, as companies, government agencies, political parties and nonprofit organizations alike strive to build integrated campaigns to change the attitudes and affinities of ever-more targeted audiences. PR professionals play an important role in facilitating communication between diverse media professionals—brand and product managers, writers, media producers, audience survey and analysis experts, lobbyists, product placement specialists and others—who, while coming from different disciplines, all seek to create and manage effective media campaigns aimed at influencing public opinion, attitudes and actions.

In the old method of public relations, PR professionals often silently served corporate executives who had very little understanding of how PR worked. It was the job of PR professionals to stimulate interest in a product after a product line was developed, or to reform the image of a company in the wake of an emergency, often referred to as crisis communications. Most of this work consisted of damage control, with PR professionals having little influence in cultivating future growth or policy. In the Digital Age, PR experts have come to understand that successful public relations begins in the initial stages of product development and policy creation, long before PR problems could arise. In the example of the Tylenol scare, J&J had not previously established any internal procedures for dealing with such an emergency. Instead, the firm's leaders had to rely on quick-thinking PR professionals to salvage the company's reputation. While J&J managed to bounce back from the crisis, too many institutions fail to react effectively to major public relations problems—a failing that can easily result in their untimely demise.

In the Digital Age, PR experts have come to understand that successful public relations begins in the initial stages of product development and policy creation, long before PR problems could arise.

While PR as a profession is transitioning from its traditional model to this more expansive, convergent approach with numerous subspecialties, it is still helpful for those interested in seeking a career in PR to be familiar with the traditional categories within PR profession. One of the largest of these categories within PR is lobbying, which focuses on communicating the interests, concerns and issues pertinent to particular individuals and organizations to local, state and national legislatures. The flip side of lobbying is political consulting, which involves advising politicians about how to best engage their constituencies. Image consulting seeks to groom the client's image in ways that promote positive public perceptions of the client. Professionals in the field of financial PR are able to accurately and persuasively communicate events in the business world to other institutions as well as to consumers.

Many organizations depend on PR professionals who specialize in fundraising to help facilitate capital drive campaigns, whether through organizational training or actually implementing such campaigns. Contingency planning deals primarily with the development of action plans that address problems that are likely to confront organizations in the future; it includes crisis management, discussed earlier in this chapter. Public relations polling is an important means of acquiring data for companies and other branches of PR to help inform their approaches to cultivating public opinion.

While not an exhaustive list of PR subspecialties, these categories of traditional PR professional practices portray the broad sweep of interests that have dominated the profession up to the Digital Age. New PR not only addresses the needs of today, but also prepares clients to meet the challenges of tomorrow. It does so by studying cultural, political and economic conditions and by influencing policies that will protect and bolster the interests—and particularly the image—of its clients in the future. New PR professionals map out current trends, plot projections, train company executives so that they can effectively interact with the media, develop strategies for crisis management, create engaging image-bolstering media and build public trust.

CONCLUSION: SELLING IDEAS, FRAMING PERCEPTIONS

Whether we are discussing how advertising utilizes narrowcasting to sell cars and political candidates or how public relations employs the media to convince people to take up a particular social cause, a central theme of both advertising and public relations is the project of building affinity between things— whether ideas, people, groups, businesses or products—and an audience. The complexity of this project is underscored by the success of convergent media campaigns and, at the same time, the continual struggle on the part of advertisers and public relations professionals to come up with a universally effective approach.

The most effective ads are the ones that present us with captivating alternative realities that draw us into their stories and encourage us to project ourselves into the narratives. Effective advertising engages audiences and helps redefine attitudes, incorporate new ideas and establish affinities that benefit the individuals and groups represented by advertising campaigns. As an integral part of advertising, public relations works to cultivate the public's perceptions of its clientele and directly address issues that affect the public's perception of the client and its image and brand. New PR takes a more hands-on approach than its predecessor, not merely working behind the scenes to attract traditional media producers to generate positive content focused on their clients or clients' products, but also filling a key role in the proactive management of media campaigns.

While addressing the needs illustrated in the numerous specialized subcategories within the traditional field of PR, new PR reflects a more holistic approach, helping to create and manage long-term media goals as well as guide the media aspects of crisis management when and if needed. In other words, new PR addresses the media image and message management needs of today while preparing clients to effectively navigate the unknown waters of tomorrow. Although advertising and public relations have come a long way as our understanding of media and culture has matured, the future is wide open. The look and success of these two highly linked fields in the Digital Age will greatly depend on their ability to persistently engage audiences and create and change attitudes working within the growing global media culture.

CHAPTER SUMMARY	KEY TERMS
Tracing the History of American Advertising Explores the historic roots of advertising and explains the theoretical foundations and practices on which modern advertising is built. **Visual Media** **Mini-Stories** A video montage of Mobius Award-winning commercials illustrates how successful advertising draws us into the story, despite how impractical or unreasonable it may be. 1. Describe how the underlying stories and characters used in some ads make them more effective than storytelling ads that do not tell a story.	advertising consumerism demographic studies psychographic studies
Product Affinity: Making Us Want it Explains the role and dynamics of product affinity and how advertising campaigns seek to create and exploit the wants and needs of consumers. **Visual Media** **Ejector Pew** Provocative religious commercials can use trendy and even humorous imagery to relay religious messages. 1. Does the increasing trend in religious advertising, especially on television, result in more positive or more negative public image of religion and religious organizations? Why? **Suspend Reality** Commercial advertising asks us to suspend reality and accept that we can be part of the story it is presenting. 1. How does the suspension of reality, fantasy and special effects combine to make some ads so compelling?	product affinity audience broadcasting narrowcasting long-tail advertising AdWords AdSense click fraud clickbots customized ad viewing product placement Madison-meets-Vine
Breaking the Rules: Advertising in the 21st Century Discusses the trend and dynamics of the shift from "broadcasting" to "narrowcasting" and how much more effective narrowcasting ad campaigns have become. **Visual Media** **Humor** Humor is an effective way of engaging audience attention or "capturing eyeballs." 1. Why are the majority of Super Bowl television ads based on humorous stories? **Dove Evolution** Dove brand produced a series of commercials that encouraged young women to embrace and nurture their natural beauty, body and self-esteem. 1. In your view, are recent television and magazine ads having a positive or negative influence on the self-image and self-esteem of women? Why do you think this is the case?	

Johnson, *Daisy Girl* Ad Sometimes negative messages are far from subtle, as depicted in this famous (or infamous) 1964 Lyndon Johnson ad. 1. Describe a negative TV political ad from the most recent presidential election cycle and compare its impact to this classic and infamous 1964 Lyndon Johnson ad. **Clinton's *Role Models* TV Ad** A very effective negative campaign ad focused on the negative impact of then-presidential candidate Donald Trump's own words on impressionable young children. 1. What real impact did this negative ad have on the presidential campaign in 2016?	 	
Tracing the History of American Public Relations: Building and Managing Image Examines the history, evolution, practices and ethics of the public relations industry and considers its increasingly convergent ties with advertising.		public relations (PR) Declaration of Principles
Today's Strategic Public Relations: 360-Degree Campaigning Looks at the rationale and dynamics of today's 360-degree campaigns, which can effectively integrate the work of advertising and public relations professionals and serve as a representative model of strategic media convergence. **Visual Media** **Sample PSAs** Anti-drinking and anti-smoking ads reinforce the health and safety risks of alcohol and tobacco use. 1. Explain why television PSAs either have or do not have a significant impact on your own attitudes and behaviors and on those of your peers.		360-degree campaigns "two-way street" principle of PR propaganda reactive PR proactive PR social cause promotion public service announcements (PSAs) crisis communications lobbying political consulting image consulting financial PR fundraising contingency planning public relations polling

NOTES

1　Linzmayer, O. (2004). *Apple confidential 2.0: The definitive history of the world's most colorful company*. No Starch Press.

2　Asch, S. (1955). Opinions and social pressures, "What I tell you three times is true." *Scientific American*, *193*(5).

3　Roberts, K. (2005). *Sisomo: The future on the screen*. PowerHouse Books.

4　Rapaille, C. (2006). *The culture code: An ingenious way to understand why people around the world live and buy as they do*. Broadway Publishing, Crown Publishing Group.

5　Ewen, S. (1988). *All consuming images*. Basic Books.

6　To view this commercial, go to www.youtube.com/watch?v=owGykVbfgUE

7　Behar, R. (2004, February 23). Never heard of Acxiom? Chances are it's heard of you. How a little-known Little Rock company—the world's largest processor of consumer data—found itself at the center of a very big national security debate. *Fortune*. Retrieved from http://money.cnn.com/magazines/fortune/fortune_archive/2004/02/23/362182/index.htm

8   Hampp, A. (2008). Branded content has a longer shelf life than a 30-second spot. *Advertising Age*.

9   Smeesters, D., Mussweiler, T., & Mandel, N. (2010, April). The effects of thin and heavy media images on overweight and underweight consumers: Social comparison processes and behavioral implications. *Journal of Consumer Research*.

10   American Society of Plastic Surgeons. (2016). Plastic Surgery Report. Retrieved from www.plasticsurgery.org/news/plastic-surgery-statistics

11   McLuhan, M. (2003). *Understanding media: The extensions of man*. Gingko Press.

12   The 2012 money race—compare the candidates. (2012, November 15). *The New York Times*.

13   *Citizens United v. Federal Election Commission*, 558 U.S. 50 (2010).

14   Pew Research Center for the People & the Press. (2012, January 17). *Super PACs having negative impact, say voters aware of "Citizens United" ruling*.

15   Ross, J. (1975). Paul Revere—patriot engraver: Early American life. *Early American Society*, VI(1–6).

16   Hiebert, R. E. (1966). *Courtier to the crowd: The story of Ivy Lee and the development of public relations*. Iowa State University Press.

17   Ibid.

18   King, C. III, & Siegel, M. (2001, August 16). The master settlement agreement with the tobacco industry and cigarette advertising in magazines. *New England Journal of Medicine*, *345*(7), 504–511.

19   Bowen & Heath (2006). IABC Research Foundation Reports, 2015. Retrieved from www.iabc.com/rf/

20   Gale, T. (1999). *Gale encyclopedia of U.S. economic history*. Thomson Gale.

21   Ibid.

22   Center on Budget and Policy Priorities. (2010). Retrieved from www.cbpp.org/cms/index.cfm?fa=view&id=1258

23   *ONE.org*. (2005). Declaration spot: ONE: The campaign to make poverty history.

9
Media Industry

dailin/Shutterstock.com

Corporate Influence on the News An excerpt from *Outfoxed: Rupert Murdoch's War on Journalism*, highlighting public concerns over corporate control over news.

Brave New Films

Arianna Huffington *The Huffington Post*'s successful business model is helping to drive the migration of newspapers and news organizations onto the Web.

LEARNING OBJECTIVES

1. Explain vertical integration and understand how it has contributed to the evolution and control of the mass media industry.
2. Distinguish between the major business models of mass media.
3. Evaluate how early regulation and more recent deregulation has impacted how the U.S. government regulates the business practices of media conglomerates.
4. Describe the evolution of music and sound recording from 1750 to the birth of radio in the 1920s.
5. Compare and contrast both the positive and negative roles technology played in the evolution of the consumer radio industry.
6. Explain the major stages in the process of creating a film or television show.
7. Illustrate the significant role the audience plays in the development, production and distribution of mass media content.
8. Outline the ways in which the Internet is forcing media industries to adjust their traditional methods of content distribution to ensure a profitable return on investment.
9. Describe the challenges facing the various U.S. mass media industries as they compete in the globalized media marketplace.
10. Illustrate how today's media businesses are responding to evolving technologies and a changing consumer market.

ORSON WELLES'S

future looked bright in 1941. Only 26 years old, he was already an ambitious and brilliant film director, writer and actor. Then he released a movie, *Citizen Kane*, that became the center of buzz and speculation for months. Many film historians still consider Welles's masterpiece to be one of the best films ever made. It starred Welles as the lead fictional character, Charles Foster Kane, a thinly veiled, hostile portrait of American media tycoon William Randolph Hearst. At the time, Hearst was the most powerful media magnate in the United States and one of the wealthiest men in the world. The Kane character likewise was a ruthless newspaper owner who used his near monopoly over media outlets, along with his immense political and financial power, to manipulate news stories and influence government officials ranging from members of Congress to presidents of the United States.

Hearst, aware of the unflattering portrait, tried to block the release of *Citizen Kane*, first by attempting to buy the film, and then by trying to destroy all the copies before the film's release. When those efforts failed, he began a campaign of intimidation and harassment against theater owners whose venues showed the film. He also launched a national media blitz in his newspapers, threatening to expose scandals involving Hollywood celebrities and Washington political figures and hoping to ruin the reputations of Orson Welles and everyone else involved in the production of the film. When those threats also failed, Hearst tried to blackmail government officials into closing down any theaters showing *Citizen Kane*. He even coerced J. Edgar Hoover's FBI to launch investigations in an attempt to stop the film. *Citizen Kane* received nine Academy Award nominations in 1942, but thanks to

Hearst's behind-the-scenes threatening of Academy members, Welles won only one award—the Oscar for best screenplay, which he shared with screenwriter Herman Mankiewicz.[1]

Welles's masterpiece, and his powerful portrayal of Kane, realistically depict the unchecked power of those seeking to control mass media in the United States and the havoc such single-handed control can wreak. The story of the real William Randolph Hearst perfectly exemplifies how the ownership of too many big media companies by one individual or group can influence the course of history—and financially enrich media moguls and family dynasties.

Already born into a wealthy family, Hearst learned early in life that to gain control of the media meant to accumulate vast power. After attending Harvard University, he became the owner and publisher of *The San Francisco Examiner* in 1887 as payment for a gambling debt. Hearst soon built the foundation of his national publishing empire by acquiring *The New York Morning Journal*. By sensationalizing the news—that is, all too often having his reporters and editors make up events and characters and report them as if they were facts—and thus establishing the era of yellow journalism in America, Hearst further advanced his own fortunes.[2] (Recall "The Newsmakers" discussion in Chapter 2.)

Much like modern media moguls with strong political views—such as Rupert Murdoch, Robert Maxwell, Silvio Berlusconi and Ted Turner—Hearst's primary goal was to build and manage a media empire—and, of course, to accumulate vast wealth in the process. This media ownership-based wealth brought with it unprecedented national and global influence. Hearst, along with his rivals Joseph Pulitzer and E. W. Scripps, effectively invented the phenomenon of the **mass media conglomerate**, a single entity that owns the majority of the media industries. At that time, this media empire comprised national newspaper chains, magazines and news wire services (agencies that charge for news distribution). Throughout the 20th century, however, book publishing, movie studios and radio and television networks became part of these industrial giants.

9.1

Pictorial Press Ltd/Alamy Stock Photo

TRACING AMERICAN MEDIA OWNERSHIP

Media conglomerates wield enormous power and accumulate great wealth, which can result in extraordinary abuses of the media. Single individuals or dynastic families who gain control over the media compromise the media's role as fair and reliable informants for the public. Instead, such owners may use the media to pressure governments, push their own agendas and influence the course of history. Such abuses are what Orson Welles depicted so artfully in his movie *Citizen Kane* and what William Randolph Hearst's exploits exemplified. In one of his bolder manipulations of facts and attempts at controlling the media message, Hearst contributed to the start of the Spanish-American War (1898). He inflamed the American public and incited Congress and President William McKinley with largely fabricated stories of Spanish atrocities in Cuba and the Caribbean. These stories, along with his editorial commentary, directly sought to agitate Congress into going to war with Spain.

> Single individuals or dynastic families who gain control over the media compromise the media's role as fair and reliable informants for the public. Instead, such owners may use the media to pressure governments, push their own agendas and influence the course of history.

Sacrificing the truth to gain financial profit and political influence is always dangerous, but it becomes even more worrisome when a single individual or family has amassed so much control over the media that they have the power to manipulate governments and change the course of world events. In this chapter, we explore how the business of mass media works, and how the ownership and control of media conglomerates—both American and international—have evolved. We also explore a key question: What role does media ownership play in influencing national and global events in the 21st century?

9.2

Media ads dominate New York City's famous Times Square—the traditional hub of America's media industries.

Alexey Malashkevich/Shutterstock.com

The period between the late 19th and early 20th centuries was the era of the media monopoly—when the production and distribution of a specific media industry were dominated by a single group. During this time, newspapers were the dominant mass media in the United States. Thus, by buying up the largest papers and forcing out the competition, individuals like Hearst were able to amass huge personal fortunes. Hearst, Pulitzer and Scripps each managed to build a nationwide mass media empire by attempting to run all aspects of the media, from production to distribution, and to own and control the dominant media outlets in every major city in the country.

When the Hollywood movie industry started to take off in the 1920s, Hearst and other media tycoons, including Louis B. Mayer, Adolph Zukor, the Warner brothers (Albert, Harry, Sam and Jack) and Markus Loew (of Loews Theaters fame), created what came to be called the Hollywood Studio System. This handful of enormous movie studios virtually ruled the entire film industry, controlling everything from screenwriters' and actors' contracts, to production facilities and financing, to distribution, to the ownership of movie theaters. (Refer to the table "The Studio System of Hollywood's Golden Age" found in Chapter 6.) During the Golden Age of Hollywood between the late 1920s and into the 1960s, the five dominant mega-studios were Metro-Goldwyn-Mayer (MGM), Paramount, Warner Brothers, 20th Century Fox and RKO. These studio giants sometimes collaborated and sometimes competed. At the time, they were largely able to avoid Congress' antitrust laws—federal efforts to break up industry monopolies that prevented healthy competition in such as areas as steel, tobacco and oil. These legislative efforts, which spanned 60 years, ranged from the Sherman Antitrust Act (1890), which allows the government to investigate companies it suspects might have violated antitrust regulations, through the Celler–Kefauver Act (1950; also known as the Antimerger Act), which seeks to close loopholes that might result in conglomeration of businesses (for example, when one company attempts to purchase or merge with all the assets of another).

9.3

Vertical integration made it possible for single media companies to not only control entire industries, but the labor practices of everyone involved—from typesetters in publishing to production crews in film.

iStock © bjones27

Vertical Integration: Process and Impact

Before we explore how media conglomerates have evolved and changed—and how they contributed to making the United States the leading media-producing country in the world—we should first look at the basic business model that these early media barons created, especially as it applied to the newspaper and film industries. If one company can operate and control all of the means of production, distribution and exhibition for a large segment of the news publishing or movie industry—a practice known as vertical integration—then it can also attract the majority of national advertising dollars or ticket revenues. This dominance places that company in the position of ultimately and solely owning an entire industry as well as all the revenue it produces.

By following the principle of economies of scale—increasing cost advantages by increasing production levels and sometimes expanding the business—the dominant, vertically integrated company makes competing extremely difficult for smaller, less integrated business. The smaller competitor is left with limited choices: keep fighting a financially losing battle with the integrated media giants, join forces with other smaller operators to form a cooperative syndicate (collective) that might be able to better compete, allow itself to be purchased and absorbed into one of the giants or simply go out of business. Another option that might better ensure a smaller company's survival, and one that we will explore later in the chapter, is to reinvent and refocus the company's goals on filling a clearly localized niche (as in the case of newspapers and magazines) or catering to special topics and audiences (as in the case of smaller independent film production companies).

Beyond the perhaps unfair competitive advantages that monopolies hold over their smaller competitors, the existence of these mass media conglomerates had other troubling effects. Since they owned and controlled so many aspects of their industry, media barons were able to dictate labor practices: They could determine the contract terms and the wage levels for various trades personnel, such as printers and typesetters for the publishing industry, and electricians, camera operators, carpenters and costumers for the movie industry. Even more troubling, these industry leaders had the power to advance the careers of writers, editors, actors, directors and producers whom *they* liked, and virtually blacklist (deny privileges to) and ruin the careers of those professionals whom they did not like. This controlling authority was what the Charles Foster Kane character in *Citizen Kane* dramatized so well; it was also one of the reasons why William Randolph Hearst reacted so aggressively to the film.

The Value Chain of Multimedia Companies

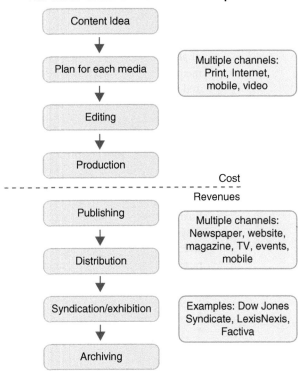

Source: World Association of Newspapers

9.4

This figure charts the cost investment and revenue yield of a typical multimedia company.

Even more troubling, these industry leaders had the power to advance the careers of writers, editors, actors, directors and producers whom *they* liked, and virtually blacklist (deny privileges to) and ruin the careers of those professionals whom they did not like.

Public Corporations and Private Ownership

Not all media ownership is the same. Some media corporations are publicly traded companies with their equity (ownership shares in the corporation) bought and sold daily on the New York Stock Exchange, the NASDAQ (National Association of Securities Dealers Automated Quotations) stock exchange or other major exchanges throughout the world. The shareholders of publicly traded media corporations are the actual legal "owners" of these companies and are represented by elected officers on each company's board of directors. Sometimes one or more voting board members might include agents for the surviving members of the original families who once controlled the company before it became publicly traded—as was the case with the Washington Post Company, for example.

Regardless of their historical ties to private ownership, all board members of publicly traded corporations are required by law to make their best efforts to manage their firms so as to protect the interests of all of shareholders. The legal term for this primary accountability is called fiduciary responsibility. Board members of media companies have the responsibility to maintain or increase their company's market value, and if possible to create profits that filter down to the company's owners, the shareholders, as dividends on their investments. Thus the board members and upper management of large publicly traded media corporations are not likely to have anything except a very general input into the news or programming content of the media outlets they manage. Such influence might violate their fiduciary roles and lead to significant personal legal liability. Instead, these individuals' jobs focus on leading their companies in directions that are most responsive to the marketplace, that attract the largest audiences for their media services and that attract the highest advertising and subscriber revenues.

Some notable exceptions do exist, however. Sometimes one or two powerful individuals or families hold significant ownership of a media conglomerate where, because of their level of ownership control, they do influence news and media content. Perhaps the most notable example involves Fox News Network, which is owned by the international media conglomerate News Corporation (News Corp.). News Corp. is a publicly traded worldwide media conglomerate headquartered in New York City, with significant holdings in the following areas:

- Book publishing: HarperCollins and others
- Newspaper publishing: *The Wall Street Journal*, *The New York Post*, *The Sun* (United Kingdom), *The Sunday Times* (United Kingdom) and many others worldwide
- Magazines: *Weekly Standard*, *Vogue* (Australia), *GQ* (Australia) and more than two dozen others
- Twentieth Century Fox (also known as 20th Century Fox) and Fox Television Studios
- Fox Television Networks, including the Fox News Network
- The largest collection of satellite television services in the world, including being the largest single shareholder of stock in DirecTV in the United States, BSkyB in the United Kingdom, Sky Latin America and many others worldwide
- On the Web: Fox Interactive, MySpace, IGN Entertainment, Hulu (jointly with NBC Universal) and dozens of other Web content providers throughout the world

Today, the top 10 multinational media conglomerates control an extraordinary share of worldwide media production and distribution. These companies exert significant influence on societies and cultures—influence that is not always welcome. (See Chapter 9 on media bias and Chapter 14 on global media.)

Examples of Modern Media Mergers Creating Mega-Media Companies
1990   Warner Communications enters into a $14.1 billion merger with Time Inc. creating Time Warner.

1991   Matsushita Electric Industrial Company buys film studio MCA for $6.9 billion.

1993   The New York Times Company buys *The Boston Globe* for $1.1 billion.

1994   Viacom Inc. buys movie studio Paramount Communications for $10 billion.

1995   Walt Disney Company buys Capital Cities ABC for $19 billion.

1996   Time Warner enters into a $7.6 billion merger with Turner Broadcasting System.

1996   International publisher Penguin Group buys Putnam Berkley Group from MCS for $336 million.

1997   Radio broadcasting conglomerate Chancellor Media Corp. consolidates ownership of 103 radio stations.

1997   Infinity Broadcasting merges with CBS Radio Broadcasting, consolidating ownership of 1,000 radio stations.

1997   CBS Corp buys leading TV program syndicator King World Productions for $2.5 billion.

1999 Viacom merges with CBS for $38 billion.

1999 American Media Inc. consolidates the major tabloid newspapers *National Enquirer*, *Star*, *Globe* and *Sun* under single ownership.

2000 AOL buys Time Warner for $136 billion.

2000 Chicago Tribune Company buys Time Mirror Company (publisher of *Los Angeles Times*) for $6.3 billion, making Chicago Tribune Company the third largest newspaper group in the United States, with 11 newspapers (and Internet sites) and 22 TV stations.

2006 Time Warner splits up its unsuccessful merger with AOL.

2006 News Corp. sells its satellite TV system DirecTV to Liberty Media Corp.

2007 News Corp. buys *The Wall Street Journal*.

2008 Time Warner sells its Warner Cable division.

2010 *The Washington Post* puts *Newsweek* magazine up for sale.

2011 Microsoft buys Skype for $8.5 million.

2011 Recording giant EMI is sold and split up to Universal Music Group and Sony.

2012 Facebook goes public with initial value of $104 billion then slips from this high point in the following weeks of trading.

2012 Walt Disney Company buys Lucasfilm for $4 billion.

2013 Amazon.com Jeff Bezos buy The Washington Post Company.

2013 Comcast merges with NBC Universal.

2014 Time Warner spins off its publishing division Time Inc. which becomes its own publicly traded company.

2015 AT&T buys DirecTV for $48.5 billion.

2016 AT&T attempts to buy Time Warner, which would create the world's largest media conglomerate, but is stalled by regulators.

Localism: A Model Alternative

The counterforces to the trend that emerged in the early and mid-20th century and created a few large consolidated media conglomerates came from two directions: localism and government regulation (which will be discussed later in this chapter). When the big national media companies found that it was not practical to cover every single topic of interest to local and regional audiences, print and broadcast news producers saw an opportunity to fill this gap by tending to this localized demographic. Because so much of people's daily lives center on neighborhood issues—where they live, work, go to school, attend church or community centers and shop—newspapers and magazines realized that covering these local stories would enable them to build a market demand against which national media outlets could not directly compete. Thus, publications and broadcast stations figured out how to harvest local market share and did so in ways that allowed for a thriving independent newspaper and broadcasting industry throughout most of the 20th century.

This industry was further strengthened by consumers who prefer to get their national news, international news and entertainment from large national media outlets, and their local and regional news from community-based outlets, which they view as more reliable and tuned into a community's issues and stories.

The erosion of localized media actually began with the move from predominant local ownership to absentee ownership—a characteristic of national media conglomerates. With this shift came the loss of local roots and local voices. Although newspapers have especially strived to maintain local relevance and interest by publishing regional sections and catering to local advertisers, from an operational and financial perspective, trying to serve national audiences and advertisers while simultaneously serving multiple local areas most often works at cross purposes. With national and international ownership comes greater interest in national and international news; thus, to maintain cost-effectiveness and maximize profits, the content that amasses the farthest reach takes precedence.

> With national and international ownership comes greater interest in national and international news; thus, to maintain cost-effectiveness and maximize profits, the content that amasses the farthest reach takes precedence.

This conflict between the localized media business model and the more national and international business model remains a source of struggle for many media companies. Also, as the Internet continues to flatten the world and stamp out borders, countless local companies are finding they must either seek acquisition by deep-pocketed suitors or go out of business. This trend does not mean that the audience for local media content has diminished; rather, it means that this audience has migrated to new Web-based media platforms and business models.

Content Control from the Boardroom

A key question explored in this chapter is just how much influence the owners of media corporations actually have on the content their audiences consume and on the actual programming decisions of their individual media outlets—whether those outlets deliver news, television, radio or film. In addition, we look at how they actually apply this influence, if it exists.

Consider, for instance, the case of News Corp. Easily included in every listing of the top five or 10 global media conglomerates today, it was founded in 1980 by Australian media entrepreneur Rupert Murdoch. While publicly traded, the company is effectively controlled by Murdoch and his two sons, Lachlan and James (although Lachlan resigned from his executive roles in 2005). The next largest shareholder of News Corp. is John Malone's Liberty Media, another (albeit smaller) media conglomerate.

Although Murdoch and his representatives frequently deny these claims, as the accompanying media clip makes clear, Murdoch has historically wielded intense and quite controversial influence over the news and programming content of the media organizations that News Corp. owns. Given that in 2010 Murdoch personally donated $1 million to the Republican Party, the influence of his political agenda on media content must come into question. Large corporate equity ownership held by an outspoken individual creates a media bias, as the video segment titled "Corporate Influence on the News" shows. This video contains excerpts from documentary filmmaker Robert Greenwald's award-winning film *Outfoxed: Rupert Murdoch's War on Journalism*. In this documentary, Greenwald attempts to convey the consumer backlash and heightened public concerns that can result when large media corporations gain too much power over government agendas—what most view as an evident threat to democracy. ▶

▶ **Corporate Influence on the News**
An excerpt from *Outfoxed: Rupert Murdoch's War on Journalism*, highlighting public concerns over corporate control over news.

The decades-long pattern of using his newspapers and television networks to influence and manipulate government in the United Kingdom, and possibly the United States, became very public in July 2011 when Murdoch, his son James and other top News Corp. managers were forced to testify before a committee of Parliament. In front of the world's media, they responded to allegations of phone hacking, police bribery and improper influence over elected officials by reporters and editors of Murdoch's flagship newspaper, *News of the World*. The result was the closing of the paper after 168 years of continuous publication. In the weeks that followed, many of Murdoch's international media organizations came under similar intense scrutiny, including investigations by the FBI. In May 2012, the Parliament committee released its report, concluding that Murdoch "exhibited a willful blindness to what was going on in his companies and publications [making him] not a fit person to exercise the stewardship of a major international [media] company. . . ."[3]

Whether or not one agrees with Murdoch's political and social views, the important issue in the context of this discussion is how media ownership can have an undue influence on media content, especially news coverage. In reality, the case of Rupert Murdoch's News Corp. may be the exception and not the rule. The ownership of the majority of today's global media conglomerates is diverse, with the managers and directors focused on influencing operational decisions to ensure profits rather than to promote any particular agendas. Even in the case of News Corp., and as he has made clear during his many news conferences and interviews, Murdoch's primary motive is profit.

Catering to the Local Audiences

For much of the history of modern mass media, local ownership of media companies was the norm. Long before the Internet came onto the scene, newspapers afforded citizens the opportunity to participate in the discourse about issues that affected their lives and gave politicians a vehicle for interacting with their constituents. Typically, these open dialogues would take place in editorials and letters to the editor. Community newspapers considered this engagement not only part of their role, but their responsibility.

Neighborhood businesses wanting to target local customers paid for the ads that maintained the financial stability of locally owned newspapers, radio and, to a lesser extent, television outlets. Under this business model, the publisher of the local newspaper or the owners of the local radio or TV station were expected to use their media companies to endorse certain political candidates and to influence public opinion on important issues. The owners of these media outlets were often prominent families and respected members of the community, and at times holders of elected leadership roles themselves. Similar to today's blogs (and as we will explore in Chapter 10), producing and publishing content meant to persuade the people to move in one direction or another is considered media bias *by intent*. For the most part, readers and viewers accepted and applauded this bias.

The trend toward national media conglomeration dramatically altered the influence that local ownership had on media content. No longer was the control held by the community, and no longer did content strictly deal with topics that mattered to local audiences. Covering neighborhood news became less of a financial benefit and more of a financial cost. In response, content coverage gradually shifted to more national and global issues of debate. Further challenging the economic viability of local media ownership was the borderless nature of the Internet. While the desire for information and news about regional issues has not diminished, surely the platform that delivers that content has. This leaves us with a question: Even if local news blogs and hyperlocal news sites can find homes online, can they survive the continued conglomeration of the media industries?

While the desire for information and news about regional issues has not diminished, surely the platform that delivers that content has. This leaves us with a question: Even if local news blogs and hyperlocal news sites can find homes online, can they survive the continued conglomeration of the media industries?

9.5

Topix.com is a Web-based news community that connects individuals in every U.S. city to important discussions and news about their town. For more on how Topix works, go to www.topix.com

Toppix.com

THE ECONOMICS OF MEDIA: THREE MODELS

Mass media—historically referred to as "the press"—serve a critical role in the establishment and health of a democracy by keeping the public informed of the actions of their government and by maintaining platforms for the exercise of free speech and free expression. (For more on this topic, see Chapter 11.) This does not mean that the media needs to be government funded. The American Founding Fathers, many of whom were publishers of and/or contributors to colonial newspapers, believed that government should not be the primary owners of the nation's media. Rather, they considered that democracy and the public interest is better served when the press is commercially owned and supported by the marketplace (see Chapters 2 and 11).

THE
9/11
COMMISSION
REPORT

FINAL REPORT OF THE NATIONAL COMMISSION ON TERRORIST ATTACKS UPON THE UNITED STATES

AUTHORIZED EDITION

9.6

Founded by an act of Congress in 1869, the U.S. Government Printing Office is one of the largest publishing operations in the United States, publishing such texts as the 9/11 Commission Report.

Reuters/Alamy Stock Photo

The American Commercial Model

The American-style media business model, also known as the market model, funds the majority of its media through a combination of advertising revenue and subscription fees, with advertising sales remaining the dominant of the two revenue streams. When it comes to media content produced under this model, federal, state and local governments all lend to its creation and distribution through the U.S. Government Printing Office, the Corporation for Public Broadcasting (CPB, which supports PBS and NPR programming) or individual and organizational grants from such agencies as the National Endowment for the Arts and quasi-government organizations such as the Smithsonian Institution. Support also comes through the Websites of various government agencies such as NASA and NOAA.

Despite government support, these media content producers must still compete for audiences in an open marketplace dominated by commercial media content producers. In other words, to be successful, a PBS program, even when it is partially supported by government funding, still has to attract audiences, make distribution deals, purchase advertising in popular magazines and Websites, sell DVDs and sign up subscribers to its companion Website in the same way it would if it were a program broadcast on one of the commercial networks. The popularity and financial success of U.S.-style media—especially American-produced music, television programs and movies—are an enduring testament to the strength of the commercial model of media ownership, production and distribution. Indeed, this model has been frequently copied throughout the world.

To judge the success of a media company, we can look at several factors: the popularity of the content it produces; the size and makeup of the audiences its media content reaches; the number and relative prestige of the awards that its media products garner each year. Economists and business analysts like to look at the strength of each media company's revenues, both direct and indirect. Direct media revenues come from selling media products and content directly to the consumer through a combination of sales—books, movie tickets, DVDs and paid subscriptions. Indirect media revenues come primarily from advertisers and advertising-related sales such as product placements (see the discussion of product placements in Chapter 8).

Other indirect media revenues come from licensing and syndication of media products, or portions of media products, for reuse by other content distribution companies, including outlets around the world. For example, a television series initially released through a television network owned by NBC Universal might quickly be sold into worldwide syndication to networks throughout the European Union (EU), creating additional licensing revenue for NBC Universal. In another example, a portion of a feature article with photography originally produced and published by *Vanity Fair* magazine, which is owned by Advance Publications, might be licensed to be included in a book to be published by HarperCollins, which is owned by News Corp., thereby generating licensing revenue from both the text and the photography reused by HarperCollins. When repeated hundreds or thousands of times for any given media property, this process can generate significant revenues. In fact, in some cases, the licensing/syndication revenues might surpass the revenues generated from the original publication or broadcasting of the property.

Media business analysts try to predict the total eventual revenues from both direct and indirect sources during the shelf life of a particular media property, using this revenue stream as a basis for projecting a property's value. The total projected value, sometimes referred to as media asset value, of all of the media properties produced and owned by a company in any given year is then compared to the total cost that the company expended to create or acquire these assets. The more high-valued media assets a company can economically produce by the efficient use of its production resources (called economies of scale), the higher the combined value of its media assets, the higher its revenues and thus the higher the return on investment (ROI) to the company's shareholders. Obviously, to be successful, a media company must be able to create consistently high-quality media products that will attract large audiences, which then will attract advertising dollars from firms wishing to reach those same audiences. At the same time, the successful media company must be able to use ingenuity and innovation to achieve the following goals:

- Produce the most popular media properties using cost-effective methods.
- Maintain effective marketing and distribution operations that take full advantage of today's convergent multiplatform opportunities made possible by the migration to digital media and the Internet.
- Create and market viable licensing and syndication capabilities with a worldwide market focus.

Today's successful media companies are able to work within a complex and counterintuitive business environment that requires aggressive competition but also strategic partnering—a good example of which is the highly popular and successful Web-TV site Hulu, a joint venture between competitors Fox Television, NBC Universal and ABC Disney.[4]

The Public Sphere Model
The public sphere model of mass media is the counterargument to the profit-driven market model. The former "for-profit" or commercial model serves as the dominant economic structure of U.S. mass media as well as of most mass media in the world today. In contrast, under the public sphere model, the various media serve as the central environment or "space" in which ideas and views circulate and act as primary vehicles for information sharing and

9.7

Launched as a joint venture between NBC, FOX and ABC television networks, Hulu.com is one of the first sites to develop a profitable model of advertiser-supported network-level television for the Web.

M4OS Photos/Alamy Stock Photo

storytelling. An example of the public sphere model is CSPAN TV and Radio. In this way, media become the hub of democratic processes and societal advancement. Under the public sphere model, media companies should not be judged solely on their market presence and ability to generate profits for their shareholders, but must also be judged on how well they perform in the public interest. Moreover, this model assumes that it is the responsibility of the owners of media companies to ensure that information and media content flow to the public freely and without limitations placed upon them by either government or owners.

To be well-informed citizens, media consumers need full and equal access to all available information. In other words, the broadest possible audiences should have easy access to the broadest spectrum of knowledge, ideas, and political, cultural and religious views. Finally, under the public sphere model, media should educate audiences about how they can become more engaged citizens who participate meaningfully in the political and social arenas of life.

From an economic perspective, the public sphere model assumes that the more a media company or media conglomerate operates in the public interest, the more people it will be able to serve and thus the more profitable it will be. Moreover, market-driven media ownership contributes to the public good by ensuring the greatest possible variety of media content and thus voices and views, by creating and distributing media content that is highly responsive to what the public wants and by supporting the maximum levels of creativity and innovation.

As the business of mass media has evolved through the 20th century and now into the 21st century, the market model has remained dominant—yet the public sphere model endures. Both radio and television broadcasting—both now and, especially, in the decades before cable and satellite—require the allocation of frequencies by federal governments. These broadcast frequencies are viewed as being owned and controlled as a public trust. It is in the allocation, licensing and monitoring of the use of broadcast frequencies where the government, through the Federal Communications Commission (FCC), exercises a counterbalancing force to the dominant commercial market-driven interests of companies owning and operating broadcast stations. With the vast migration of television and radio broadcasting away from publicly controlled airways in favor of corporately owned and controlled cable and satellite services in recent years, the power of the FCC as a counterbalancing force has been greatly diminished. However, this has not been the only force promoting media in the public interest.

In 1970, the Public Broadcasting System (PBS) and its sister organization, National Public Radio (NPR), were established as a network of partially government-funded nonprofit television and radio stations, respectively. They were intended to serve as a balance to commercial broadcasting and as a home for programming that was solidly in the public interest. In reality, the federal government has never fully funded public broadcasting. The actual level of funding from government sources is greatly dwarfed by a variety of other funding sources for PBS and NPR. Today, funding comes from a combination of grants from foundations, membership donations "from viewers like you" and corporate underwriting. This corporate underwriting has morphed into thinly veiled advertising, as anyone who watches PBS or listens to NPR quickly discovers. While the general tone, style and programming on both PBS and NPR networks and stations remain clearly more aligned with the public sphere model, and ownership of PBS and NPR stations remains nonprofit, these public stations must compete for audiences and revenues on a more or less level playing field with commercial for-profit stations and networks. In fact, the larger program-producing stations on both PBS and NPR networks do a good job of competing with their commercial counterparts.[5]

Once again, the benefits of the market-driven model appear to win out over the public sphere model. In the postmodern media world of the 21st century, it appears that the convergence of both media models offers the best way to remain viable and to continue serving the public's diverse wants and needs. With Congress mandating full conversion to digital television (DTV) in June 2009, along with the growth of cable and satellite-delivered television and radio programming and the migration of media onto the Internet, it would seem that not only have the media companies benefited, but we all have—as media consumers. What we have won is a tremendous range of programming choices.

The New Media Model: The Internet Alternative

The Internet has brought about major challenges to the business and operational models of book, magazine and newspaper publishers. In the early years of the Internet (see Chapter 7), a widely held belief posited that as media content migrated into the digital realm, the creators of media content—authors, filmmakers, composers, photographers, artists and the like—would benefit the most because they could sidestep the conglomerates who controlled the media production and distribution companies that dominated the analog media world. Many independent media creators are trying to use this new media model, or Internet alternative, to reach and sell to their audiences directly. Some of these entrepreneurs are very successful, as we will see in the "Business of Music" section later in this chapter.

The Impact on Newspapers

It may surprise many readers to learn that through most of the history of the newspaper business, classified advertising accounted for between one-third and one-half of all revenues for a given newspaper.[6] With the advent of online classified ad services such as Craigslist, Monster.com and Careerbuilder.com, along with auction sites including eBay and eBayMotors, most of this locally sourced revenue has migrated to the Web. The cost in lost ad sales to print newspapers especially has been tremendous—one of a number of economic factors contributing to many papers either downsizing, converting to Web-only publishing or going out of business entirely. According to the trade publication *Information Week*, Web-based classified ad services now capture more than 50 percent of the market annually, forcing newspapers into the difficult position of having to make up this significant loss by attracting more advertisers—a growing challenge.[7]

9.8

More than one-half of all classified advertising has migrated to the Web, and the trend appears to continue to increase annually.

NetPhotos3/Alamy Stock Photo

In 2009, the international accounting and consulting firm PricewaterhouseCoopers, in cooperation with the World Association of Newspapers (WAN), issued a report on the challenging future faced by the newspaper industry, titled *Moving into Multiple Business Models: Outlook for Newspaper Publishing in the Digital Age*. The report concluded that newspaper publishers must change their business model to remain profitable in the convergent media environment of the 21st century:

- Newspaper publishers have a competitive advantage in creating content. Consumer research reveals that they would benefit from leveraging this competitive advantage online by creating compelling content for specific niche markets and distributing it across multiple platforms.
- Newspaper publishers could also engage in strategic partnerships with other content providers to strengthen their position. Constant dialogue with readers is crucial for newspapers to stay up-to-date with readers' radically changing media preferences. Readers must be able to give feedback on the current media mix and to express their needs and preferences with regard to media consumption.

- Technological developments such as directories, e-commerce and 2-D barcodes offer newspaper publishers the potential for developing value-added service offerings and reinforcing partnerships with advertisers. In their online venues, they need to offer unique, premium service concepts, as banner display advertising is relatively ineffective, and players such as Google dominate the more successful search advertising market.
- As content production is a publisher's core competence, the traditional organizational structure is moving away from a channel-oriented structure and toward a content production structure. This shift challenges the traditionally perceive need for vertical integration, where newspapers not only create content but also print and distribute it.
- Given that the advertising market is dominated increasingly by multiplatform campaigns, newspaper publishers need to rethink their marketing and sales efforts. Partnering more closely with advertisers will help them to anticipate these developments and optimize their position within custom-tailored campaigns.
- Newspaper publishers need to become more flexible and innovative in their product offerings and be prepared to negotiate alternative, flexible, contingency fees with advertisers.
- The disaggregation of classified advertisements has dramatically affected newspapers' profitability. Although consumer-to-consumer classified advertising has largely been lost, business-to-consumer advertising remains an opportunity for newspaper publishers, at least in some countries.
- Offering flexible solutions such as template-based self-service options can both facilitate cost savings and attract advertisers.[8]

▶ Arianna Huffington
The Huffington Post's successful business model is helping to drive the migration of newspapers and news organizations onto the Web.

The transition to this new convergent media business model is difficult and costly for newspapers. It involves retasking resources, providing training and, in many cases, eliminating personnel. Given that the newspaper industry is highly unionized, making these changes often requires difficult renegotiations of union contracts. It also requires recruiting "new media"—trained and tech-savvy employees, ranging from editors and journalists to photographers and Website developers.

One of the most successful independent news organizations following the new media model is *The Huffington Post*, launched in 2005 by Greek-American author, syndicated columnist and frequent television news pundit Arianna Huffington. After only four years of existence, *The Huffington Post* garnered numerous journalism awards. By early 2009, it was attracting nearly 9 million unique visitors each month—making it one of the largest Internet-based news organization in the world. The success of *The Huffington Post* came at a time when traditional newspapers were struggling to survive and being forced to restructure and migrate to the Web. Some critics have accused Huffington of contributing to the downfall of the old media newspaper publishing industry—an accusation that she easily defends herself against in a media segment taken from an ABC *Nightline* special report. ▶

The Impact on Book Publishers

While newspaper and magazine publishers appear to be the hardest hit by these new media marketplace and business model changes, book publishers are also struggling to adapt and thrive in these chaotic media times. In Chapter 6, we looked at some of the changes facing the book publishing industry, which we suggested have implications for the life and possible death of books. Of course, it is unlikely that the book publishing industry will disappear. Nevertheless, just like the newspaper publishers that are scrambling to reinvent their business models, book publishers and distributors are equally challenged to find a new path to financial stability.

A small number of authors have been able to amass significant sales by self-publishing and distributing their work through Amazon.com—although the company retains a hefty percentage of all such sales. Vanity presses and subsidy publishers such as XLibris and Dorrance Publishing offer authors low-cost alternatives to the commercial publishing houses, at which getting signed is a challenge. These presses require their writers to partially contribute to the publication and promotional costs of their works, taking advantage of publishing-on-demand operations and Internet-based marketing and distribution.

The growth and success of online booksellers show that the way we purchase and use books is changing. As such, we now have a new, dominant breed of media conglomerates: Google, Amazon.com, Apple iTunes. For all practical purposes, these three online giants control much of the access to media content on the Web, overshadowing the independent efforts of vanity and subsidy presses. For example, Amazon's Kindle e-book reader, which allows users to download a huge array of books, magazines and newspapers, is dominating the digital publication industry. Amazon has not released actual e-book sales numbers, but the company's CEO, Jeff Bezos, announced they were up 70 percent in 2012.[9] In the words of *Newsweek* magazine's tech editor Daniel Lyons, "that would be like Sony going to HBO and saying that they want 70% of what people pay for HBO because people watch it on Sony televisions."[10]

The Impact on Music and Video Distribution

Apple's iTunes store has become the largest legal supplier of downloadable music on the Internet. As a result, it dominates the music industry, significantly influencing which artists become popular, which tours sell the most tickets and, owing to its tie-ins to television programs such as *American Idol*, which new artists will be financially successful. This is much the same role that the major music labels played in the analog world. Apple's iTunes store earns 30 cents for every music track that a user downloads. For 2012, Apple reported 30 billion downloads, resulting in $7.13 billion in revenue.

Daniel Lyons, *Newsweek's* tech editor, points out that the great myth of the Digital Age is that once we fully transition away from old analog media distribution, we will encounter few barriers to content distribution in the digital world.[11] The reality has turned out to be much different: a digital world dominated by a new breed of content providers. Companies such as Google, Amazon and Apple are among the few businesses in the world with the technical resources to build and operate media content delivery and distribution juggernauts. In October 2006, Google bought YouTube. YouTube is a huge platform for the viral launching of independent artists and content creators (see the story about the indie music group Matt & Kim in Chapter 5) as well as one of the leading platforms for launching and marketing new works offered by traditional music labels, film studios, television networks and even publishers.

THE FEDERAL COMMUNICATION COMMISSION

A longstanding debate in the United States and worldwide focuses on how well government regulates the business practices of conglomerates. Is it mindful of when these businesses are exploiting consumers? Does it carefully limit their monopolistic practices or alliances to ensure that the market remains healthy and competitive? Government and political trends toward greater regulatory control over media companies are perhaps even stronger because media companies control both the access to communication platforms and the flow of information itself, which can potentially promote media bias. (See Chapter 10.)

> Government and political trends toward greater regulatory control over media companies are perhaps even stronger because media companies control both the access to communication platforms and the flow of information itself, which can potentially promote media bias.

This built-in source of friction in the media industry model rouses dual forces: (1) those that drive media companies along the path of mergers and acquisitions, typically vertical integration, wherein the means of media production, distribution and exhibition are controlled by a single, common owner; and (2) those that cause government concern about the unbalanced power held by the resultant single corporation.[12] Such

9.9

The Economics of Media: Three Models

The public sphere model suggests that a media company be responsible for ensuring that information reaches its citizens without federal or corporate interference. How well would such a model work in our contemporary society?

kurhan/Shutterstock.com

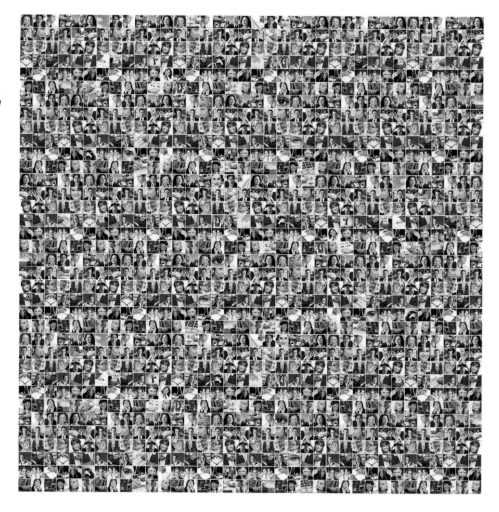

concerns are rooted in the yellow journalism era, as depicted in the video excerpt from Orson Welles's *Citizen Kane* linked earlier in this chapter. Media tycoons such as Hearst taught Congress valuable lessons about the problems with unchecked power over the media: It can lead to disastrous consequences and even endanger democracy itself. To prevent this from happening in the future, Congress attempted to regulate media monopolization by a single firm. While it had no way of stopping the consolidation of newspapers and magazines, it did have the power to regulate the ownership of radio and television stations, because the federal government controlled the licensing of all broadcast stations through the authority vested in the Federal Communications Commission.

Regulation

The Federal Communication Commission (FCC), which was originally established by Congress in 1934 through the *Communications Act*, empowered the federal government to regulate the licensing and use of the broadcast spectrum by all nongovernmental organizations, companies or individuals. Part of the FCC's regulatory mandate, through its licensing authority, is to monitor and limit the ownership of radio and television stations in an effort to maintain a viable competitive broadcast marketplace that is not dominated by any single media company. To fulfill this mandate, the FCC created regulations that restricted the number of

9.10

Clerks fulfilling product orders at one of Amazon.com's giant warehouses.

Apex News and Pictures Agency/ Alamy Stock Photo

television stations that any one company could own in a given geographical market. These regulations were effective in encouraging competition and limiting the potential dominance of any one media company, at least in television station ownership, for much of the late 20th century. Eventually the FCC limited the number of broadcast television stations that a single company could own, the number of television stations that it could own within each individual broadcasting region and the number and geographic spread of television stations owned by companies that also owned newspapers.

In 1996, when it became clear that cable and satellite television would soon overwhelm over-air broadcasting as the principal delivery system for television channels, Congress deregulated the broadcast industry and removed the long-running restrictions on multistation ownership (MSO). The Telecommunications Act of 1996 is partially responsible for the reemergence of the dominant media conglomerates of today.[13] This deregulation came at the height of a major movement to create a new generation of multinational mega-media conglomerates through an unprecedented move toward mergers and acquisitions in the media industry.

Starting in the late 1980s, media companies, with some acknowledgment of the economies of scale that their media baron predecessors enjoyed, began a process of high-stakes mergers and acquisitions that created the major consolidated media conglomerates that we know today. Meanwhile, U.S. copyright laws have continued to support the commercial success of the media industry by maintaining a complicated system of copyright laws and regulations that benefit corporate copyright holders. (For more coverage of copyright law, see Chapter 11.) Copyright laws do this in part by making it very difficult, especially for individuals and small business-based media content creators, to legally reuse, repackage or remix media content without obtaining permission from the copyright holder—often a very expensive proposition.[14]

Deregulation

Given that the federal government appears to support and protect the interests of the commercial advertiser-based media model through legislation, it can be credited—at least to some extent—for driving the current trend toward multinational mega-media conglomeration. It achieved this feat through a cycle beginning first with the absence of regulation of the media industry, followed by a period of anti-monopoly regulation and strict management of broadcast ownerships and licensing, followed by the more recent period of

9.11

Devices such as handheld video cameras are making it easier for the everyday citizen to become media content producers—another sign that technology is changing our mass media culture, experience and interactions.

Radharc Images/Alamy Stock Photo

deregulation. The current trend toward deregulation reflects a lessening in the concern of federal government and FCC regulators to block media-ownership monopolies.

Support for deregulation in the media industry stems from the idea that vertically integrated U.S. media conglomerates can better compete with non-U.S.-owned media conglomerates, which challenge the United States as the leader in seducing media audiences and gaining sales worldwide. Having the world's media industries dominated by fewer than a dozen major conglomerates may have a 21st-century downside, but it presents us with another argument for deregulation. With the increased accessibility to content-producing technology (such as the Flip video camera, for example), a broader range of independent media producers will emerge. The ability for more individuals to produce media content, combined with the growth in Internet-based or linked media channels, should make it easier for smaller, independent content producers to reach larger audiences and succeed financially.

While the Internet has enabled a wider range and a greater number of media content producers to attract audiences, the potential revenue to be gained from attracting these audiences has not kept pace with the number of content producers. There are exceptions, of course. Sales of video and computer games continue to skyrocket, while the music industry is reinventing itself to cater to Web-based music buying trends. The theatrical-released movie industry—that is, films released initially in theaters as opposed to being released directly to DVD, Blu-ray or cable/satellite—also continues to see positive revenue growth in the United States and worldwide. In contrast, viewership and the associated advertising revenues for television are continuing their decade-long slippage. The migration of television and movies to the Internet represents a change so significant that third-party distributors such as Netflix have capitalized on it; movie studios have yet to establish a business model that will deliver consistent profits to them from this source.

THE BUSINESS OF MUSIC AND SOUND RECORDING

Music as a business began to emerge in the Classical period (approximately 1750 through 1825).[15] During this era, composers such as Wolfgang Amadeus Mozart and Ludwig von Beethoven developed a growing interest in bringing their music to mass audiences through widespread public performance. Most of these concerts were held in impressive concert and opera halls or in smaller chamber music venues. Such performances required ticket sales, which of course generated revenue. In this sense, the classical composers were the first music industry entrepreneurs. By the 18th and early 19th centuries, composers were for the first time able to make a living off their work, especially as popular demand for sheet music grew. Gutenberg's printing press, invented 200 years earlier in 1440, made it possible for composers to mass-produce and sell their compositions to musicians throughout Europe.[16] In effect, this era marked the emergence of a new music publishing industry.

Technology Turns the Tide: Music Makes Money

Advances in music technology further revolutionized this concept of music as a business. In the early years of the 19th century, a French scientist and mathematician named Jean-Marie Constant Duhamel (1797–1852) began experimenting with acoustics, an interdisciplinary study dealing with the science of sound. Working with centuries of research on sound theory, Duhamel attached a pen to a tuning fork that, when tapped, would sketch the shape of sound waves. This little experiment led to one of the first music recording devices. Building on Duhamel's theory, his successors working in this field, including English physicist Thomas Young, French printer Leon Scott de Martinville, American scientist Alexander Graham Bell and ultimately the first inventor to present the phonograph to the masses, Thomas Edison, contributed to the technology that would drive the early sound recording industry.

A key figure in the history of the recording industry, Thomas Edison not only refined and implemented earlier designs for copying music onto recording cylinders—the earliest record players—but also had a keen eye for promotion. As soon as Edison completed work on his first tinfoil phonograph in December 1887, he and two associates took a train from their laboratory in Menlo Park, New Jersey, to Manhattan, where they surprised the staff at the highly respected magazine *Scientific American* with an impromptu demonstration of the device. The editor of the magazine, amazed and delighted by Edison's invention, wrote a glowing article about it for the magazine, which resulted in a nationwide buzz. More than a decade would pass before the recording industry really took off, however. By then, both Edison's first phonograph and Bell's competing gramophone were introduced to a mass market. Edison, a far better promoter and entrepreneur than Bell, recognized the vast business potential of the recording industry for popular entertainment.

In 1889, an important event occurred that gave Edison the opportunity to pursue his vision. Louis Glass, an early adopter of phonograph technology and the president of a small phonograph distribution company in California, installed the first coin-operated phonograph, the nickelodeon, at the Royal Palace Saloon in San Francisco. Glass had been experimenting with ways to keep his struggling business afloat. The unit that he set up at the Saloon consisted of one of Edison's machines outfitted with a custom coin-collecting device and four sets of rubber ear tubes. Even though the unit still had significant design issues and could play only one relatively poor-quality musical recording at a time, it was an instant hit. Within the year, Glass had begun selling kits to convert Edison's machines for commercial use in addition to installing more of his own units in public places. The immense popularity and financial success of these coin-operated units kept Glass in business and immediately drew Edison's attention.[17]

9.12

Thomas Edison is considered an essential figure as well as a sharp promoter in the early recording industry.

Thomas Edison. Courtesy of Library of Congress

The Recording Industry

Initially, serious music composers and performers questioned the legitimacy of records as true forms of music; they criticized the poor quality of the early recordings and intimated that the recording industry threatened not only to taint audiences' tastes, but also to destroy the livelihoods of the composers, singers and musicians who depended on live performances for their income. In 1902, this resistant attitude began to subside when Italian opera star Enrico Caruso (1873–1921) agreed to record his performance. The records sold widely and were marketed by a commercial enterprise, the new Victor music label established in 1904. (Eventually, this company would become RCA Victor.) In response to criticism from artists, Victor engineered a high-fidelity premium record (a record containing sound produced at advanced levels) that it marketed under the name Red Seal. These records sold for approximately $2 each—a steep price increase over the basic record format of the time, which retailed between $.25 and $.50.

Caruso's star power, coupled with the higher production quality of these new records, proved a huge boon to the nascent recording industry, drawing in scores of top artists. With the improved quality of recorded music and the cost of both the records and the machines to play them on low enough, a huge market for recorded music was created, and a comprehensive music industry—beyond just music publishing—was born. Companies created back then that continue to dominate the industry today include Columbia Records, RCA and Universal Music Group.

Race Music: The Precursor to Rhythm and Blues

As the number of record companies drastically increased from 1900 to 1920, over-competition slowly began to cause a deterioration of the record market. Smaller record companies attempted to carve out niche markets among American minority groups, often focusing on music that catered to racial stereotypes—known as race music. Though it goes against our 21st-century sensibilities, this kind of racially charged banter between different ethnicities was very popular and socially accepted in the first half of the 20th century. Eventually, the term "rhythm and blues" replaced the term "race music" in the 1950s.[18]

One of the most important subgenres of this new musical niche was African-American music. Although very few blacks were able to record their music before the 1920s, white artists were paid to record watered-down versions of jazz and blues tunes, known for their provocative lyrics and sexy sound, specifically for consumption by white audiences. Record companies feared that the sensual nature of these musical genres would offend white listeners when, in fact, that sensuality was a large part of the draw. The combination of the alluring subject matter and danceable, percussive tunes made jazz extremely popular among white urbanites who were trying to break free of the moral strictures of previous generations.[19] Herein we see early examples of music as a form of social revolution—albeit, through a business strategy that drives sales and caters to niche markets. Historically, this strategy has amassed audiences and driven up revenues, and it continues to do so today.

By the 1920s, with the birth of radio, U.S. consumers essentially stopped buying records because they could get higher-quality music over their radios for free. This decline in record sales brought about the dissolution of such recording industry leaders as Columbia and Victor, which, by the early 1930s, were eventually absorbed by the new radio-based Columbia Broadcasting System (CBS) and the Radio Corporation of America (RCA). While the transition to radio marked the death of many of the early recording industry giants, it also breathed new life into a reinvented record industry, pushing recording technology and music itself into the age of broadcasting—a radical new era in American media history.

9.13

Despite the growing interest in jazz, before the 1920s, very few blacks were able to record their music. Here we see jazz legends Ella Fitzgerald, Dizzy Gillespie, Ray Brown, Milt (Milton) Jackson and Timmie Rosenkrantz at a New York club in 1947.

Gottlieb, William P. [Portrait of Ella Fitzgerald, Dizzy Gillespie, Ray Brown, Milt Milton Jackson, and Timmie Rosenkrantz, Downbeat, New York, N.Y., circa September 1947] Courtesy of Library of Congress

THE BUSINESS OF RADIO

The radio era of the early to mid-20th century represented the next great leap in the evolution of American media industries. Originally, radio as a revenue-generating industry was viewed as a failed technology, because its earliest business owners and inventors envisioned it as primarily being a wireless replacement for the telephone. The problem with this technology from a business model perspective was that anyone with a radio receiver could pick up all radio signals, making private communications far too challenging of a technological hurdle to overcome at the time. Early broadcast visionaries who began to "think outside the box" quickly recognized the business opportunities that the new broadcasting technology offered: radio signals represented an unprecedented marketable resource.

Commercial Radio: Beginnings

The extraordinary market reach of broadcasting, spreading media content through telecommunications, made radio an attractive medium for advertisers in the economic boom following World War I. Commercial radio was in many ways impossible before this time due to the rudimentary technology and the relatively high costs associated with it. Major refinements of radio technology from military development during the war made radio a profitable new media business for large companies to operate; investments in this business soon followed. The war also allowed amateur radio enthusiasts to use their technological savvy to help push broadcasting technologies forward throughout the second half of the 20th century. The open nature of this development initially caused significant problems because amateur radio had always been about experimentation and innovation, not commercial exploitation.[20]

After World War I, radio technology became relatively inexpensive. Considerable competition ensued as amateur outfits sprang up all over the country to compete with major networks. One of the main differences between these smaller stations and those associated with major networks was the programming. Large corporations such as Westinghouse and General Electric/RCA began setting up chains of radio stations throughout the United States that were able to pool funds to pay for better-quality live content. Such programs drew in more advertising revenue, which provided even more money for investment in talent, broadcasting facilities and equipment. The content offered by these large networks was extremely popular with American audiences and sent smaller radio networks and unaffiliated stations scrambling to find a way to get a piece of the U.S. market.

Smaller commercial radio stations could not afford to hire live performers and had to resort primarily to playing records. A number of record companies, such as Victor, tried to cash in early on radio by selling licenses that allowed network radio stations to play recordings from the record label's star performers. Smaller stations began pooling their own resources to purchase new content—such as the syndicated *Amos 'n' Andy* show—which was then distributed via hardcopy recordings to affiliates. The introduction of Western Electric's 331/3

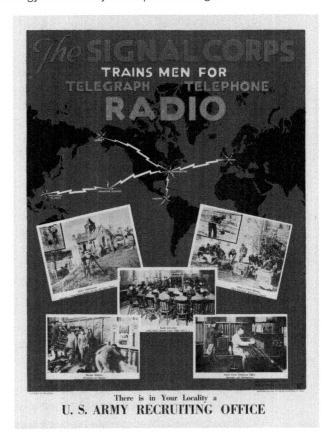

9.14

Although it took some time for the radio industry to catch on as a commercial success, it eventually did, thanks to amateur radio enthusiasts during World War I.

The Signal Corps Trains Men for Telegraph, Telephone, Radio by Mueller, Harry S. (http://digital.ncdcr.gov/cdm/ref/collection/p15012coll10/id/2166) Courtesy of Library of Congress

rpm long-play disc in the 1930s made the syndication of full radio programs an affordable alternative for smaller radio stations.

The U.S. government, through the Radio Act of 1927, took greater control of the emerging U.S. radio market. (See Chapter 11 for more on this topic.) Specifically, it began requiring licensing for all radio stations, took control over all frequency allocations and established limits to station power. To some extent, it also set limits on the content that stations could broadcast. These regulations favored the larger stations and networks owned by wealthy broadcasting companies, eventually driving out the competition from the smaller, low-power stations.

This biased regulatory environment changed with the establishment of the FCC in 1934. By this time, Congress had grown fearful of the economic and political implications of a few large broadcasting conglomerates controlling radio commercial broadcasting. So it had the FCC, in a groundbreaking move, order the National Broadcasting Company (NBC)—which was jointly owned by RCA, General Electric and Westinghouse—to divest itself of one of its two radio networks. NBC was forced to sell NBC Blue, its non-sponsored cultural and news programming branch, to industrialist Edward J. Noble. In 1945, Noble acquired the rights to the name the American Broadcasting Company (ABC), which the network has used ever since. Although this breakup did not completely level the playing field in the radio industry, it did stimulate competition.[21]

Recording Technologies Drive Radio Content

By the late 1930s, radio broadcasts of recorded music started making a comeback, thanks in part to stricter copyright and licensing laws passed to ensure that artists were able to receive royalties on their work. The reemergence of a popular music market can also be attributed to other economic and technical developments in both the music recording and radio broadcasting industries. These developments included the advent of high-fidelity (hi-fi) recordings and the availability of hi-fi record players, improvements in the sound quality of radio and the invention of stereo by Bell Laboratories in 1932.

In 1934, a Brooklyn, New York, firm called the Presto Recording Company introduced a new acetate blank recording disc onto which radio stations could record on the spot—earning it the name the "instantaneous" record. The ability to make inexpensive recordings on the fly resulted in a drastic increase in the types of content that radio stations could record, from auditions of potential performers to air checks (recordings of commercials sent back to advertisers to prove they had received the airtime they purchased). This improved technology increased the viability of radio stations as commercial advertising alternatives to newspapers and magazines, generating significantly increased advertising revenues for station owners.

The United States' entrance into World War II nearly stopped this new wave of record popularity dead in its tracks in the 1940s. The materials used to produce records (primarily shellac) were needed to produce war goods, especially once the Japanese blockaded shipments of the materials from Asia. Americans were asked to turn in their records to be recycled for the war effort. In addition to the lack of materials to produce records, a strike by the American Federation of Musicians in 1942, brought on by disputes over royalties, meant that few new recordings were available. But while commercial radio and recording in the United States essentially went into hibernation during the war, the U.S. military continued making progress in the technology that would affect the course of both industries after the war. Military demand for recorded material throughout the war kept record companies in business during this stagnant period. It also encouraged musicians such as the members of the American Federation of Musicians to drop their ban on producing new recordings that could be used by radio stations—without paying royalties to the artists—so that music could be distributed to the troops.

The influence of the magnetic-tape-based, multitrack recording had a profound impact on the business dynamic between the recording industry labels and composers, musicians and performers. Previously, the recording industry sought to capture the unique quality of live performances—quality that either rose or fell depending on the performer. Especially with classical recordings, which helped to sustain the recording industry through the economic challenges between the two world wars, the demand for better-quality and longer recordings came from consumers who appreciated exceptional compositions and musicianship. In this way, the music drove technological innovations in recording.

In the 1950s and 1960s, this model began shifting in the opposite direction. Multitrack recorders allowed studio engineers to cut out and replace errors in performances as well as to create compositions so complex that they were difficult, if not impossible, to reproduce outside the studio environment. Audiences failed to notice any difference between the traditional live and the new mixed recordings. In fact, consumer interest in hi-fi, a thriving economy and changing tastes resulted in an explosion in record sales in the 1950s and 1960s. This significantly increased market demand, which in turn drove up the revenues from the sale of quality music recordings. Although the public was purchasing records with the names of popular musicians on the label, little did they know that often the real geniuses behind the music were the engineers and producers who were essentially using editing technologies to "compose" new music.

> Although the public was purchasing records with the names of popular musicians on the label, little did they know that often the real geniuses behind the music were the engineers and producers who were essentially using editing technologies to "compose" new music.

While musicians still provided the marketable face of music and were to a greater or lesser degree responsible for their own sounds, the recording industry had the final say as to what would end up on retailers' shelves and on the radio. This production and distribution dominance over the music industry remained firmly rooted in place until the advent of consumer-accessible digital recording and remixing technologies and the emergence of Internet-based music distribution channels—from Napster to iTunes—that challenged this business model and forced the industry to reinvent itself.

Going Digital: The Demise of Music on the Radio

The advent and rapid consumer market saturation of digital recording technologies resulted in a rapid decline in retail music sales and forced the music industry to reinvent itself quickly. First came the CD-R and CD-RW formats, which both the recording and radio industries were unsuccessful in getting either Congress or the courts to block. MPEG-3 (MP3) and P2P file-sharing software quickly followed from companies such as Napster; these programs allowed millions of music consumers to capture and share whatever music they wished without paying royalties to the music labels. Despite fervent attempts to regain control over the market, the recording industry continued to see a drastic drop-off in CD sales in the late 1990s and early 2000s. Industry executives simply failed to prevent this market catastrophe. Stepping into the void left by the struggling record companies, Apple began selling MP4s (Apple's replacement for MP3s) over the Internet through its revolutionary iTunes store in 2003—the same year that the record labels, through their trade association (the Recording Industry Association of America [RIAA]), unleashed a torrent of copyright infringement lawsuits against individual music file sharers.[22]

By the mid-1990s, radio had migrated to the Internet and satellite services, with news-talk radio being the only format still attracting large audiences and reliable revenues. Music retail outlets had disappeared; the bastion of music marketing, MTV, seldom aired music videos any longer; and sales of music albums on CDs were quickly following record albums into market oblivion. Where only a decade ago the music labels controlled the industry by selecting and "creating" the new music stars, maintaining the popular market for established ones, controlling music tours and promotions and, as a result, dictating popular

9.15

In the Digital Age, families no longer gather around a radio to listen to programs such as Roosevelt's "fireside chats." These days, people plug in to listen to podcasts, playlists and other media downloads.

Vitchanan Photography/Shutterstock.com

tastes and trends, the power of the music labels was disappearing and the companies were being all but marginalized.

When Columbia Records (now owned by Sony) brought Ric Rubin, founder of Def Jam Records, on to co-direct the company in 2007, it realized that the old business strategies, though once the paths to success, were now leading to certain failure. Using young music buyers as its primary focus group, Columbia Records easily determined that its target audience no long listens to radio. Rather, potential buyers download the music they want either legally from sites such as iTunes or illegally from file-sharing sites. Columbia also learned that the most powerful form of music marketing is viral "word of mouth" through social networking sites. Columbia executives confirmed for themselves that the market is mostly interested in creating individual digital music libraries one track at a time, and that their company brand no longer had much impact on sales.

To encourage music sales, some companies now promote music soundtracks from popular movies and televisions series. Rubin, however, seeks to take matters a step further. He and the heads of other major music labels hope to pave the way to a new digital subscription model similar to the content-on-demand models emerging in Web-based television and movies.[23]

THE BUSINESS OF TELEVISION AND FILM

We are daily bombarded with advertisements for the latest new cable and television series or the next blockbuster film—but do any of us ever really stop to wonder how any of the media we consume is made possible? This process begins with the acquisition and development stage. During acquisition, a film or television producer acquires the film rights to a story by purchasing the book rights, script or story concept—usually developed and presented in abbreviated form, called a treatment, by a screenwriter. These treatments might be already written on speculation, known as a spec script (which is written for the open market), or be commissioned by the producer or the studio or production company. During development, the producer invests a significant amount of time and resources to shape the screenplay and characters, researches the story background and potential shoot locations and builds a detailed production budget to estimate project costs. Often, the producer contracts with a well-known director or leading actor during development to make the project more bankable with investors. Such early signed bankable talents are known as show runners, because they can often make a project happen on the strength of their previous projects.

In some cases, a major studio or distributor will invest early in a project and help fund the acquisition and development stages in return for a percentage ownership in the project and the exclusive rights to distribute it once it is produced. In other cases, especially when independent producers are involved, it is the producers who must bear the costs associated with the acquisition and development stages to get the project to the point that they can pitch it to studios, networks and distributors in an effort to acquire full financing. A major studio, television networker or distributor will then put up additional development funding. Nevertheless, this early success does not assure that a project will be produced: media companies fund the development of many projects, the vast majority of which are never produced.[24]

Next comes the production financing stage. In this stage, the producer lines up the lion's share of the funding for the project. Media production financing is a complex topic that, while often overlooked, is at the heart of making each movie and television program possible. In the golden years of Hollywood (discussed in Chapter 6), the major studios were also single-source financers of the movies they produced. Today, this is no longer the case, although major studios may still play multiple roles in project financing by supplying soft-cost resources. These resources include production crews and equipment, postproduction facilities, marketing and promotions expertise and a willingness to play a lead role in the distribution of the program. The usual film or television project financing comes from a combination of studio and/or network participation, international co-production deals as part of distributor presales, product placement deals (see Chapter 8), independent investors, bank loans and the sale of ancillary rights to product tie-ins (e.g., T-shirts, books, toys). Through these combined financing sources, the project budget is funded, but the ownership rights of the producers are usually reduced to small percentages. These slivers can still prove very valuable if the project meets with even moderate market success.

With full funding in place, the project goes into the preproduction, production and postproduction stages. During the preproduction stage, the many details of production are put in place, including the casting of the actors, hiring of the crew, contracting with locations, designing and building sets or special effects, costuming and arrangements for transportation, lodging and catering for the cast and crew.

The production stage, known traditionally as the principal photography stage, is when all of the story scenes are filmed (or shot in high-definition video). Productions are always shot in a nonlinear sequence, and sometimes by more than one production unit working simultaneously to take advantage of location, cost and scheduling efficiencies. This is usually the most costly and resource-intensive stage of a project, where any delays or changes can quickly

9.16

Sales of product tie-ins such as the ones shown here from the *Twilight* movies often supplement the financing of film and television projects.

Eric Engman/Zuma Press/Newscom

add to the costs and thus the risks associated with the project. Today's sophisticated digital technologies enable most film and television projects to be in both the production and postproduction stages at the same time, which is essential for projects that involve digital special effects.

During the postproduction stage, all of the material that has been shot is edited into a linear story. Music, special effects and even recolorization may be added. To many, it is in the postproduction stage that the story of a film or television program is actually created out of the raw material produced in the production stage.

During the distribution stage, the final project is released to theaters, or it premieres in the lead television network's programming schedule. If the movie is based on a popular book, the publisher shares in the marketing and promotions for the film, helping to create more market buzz and more media coverage, which leads to larger audiences and ultimately higher sales revenues for the various participants. In today's global media marketplace, theatrical release films move into cable and satellite TV pay-per-view (literally, "pay as you view") sometimes in a matter of weeks, while home DVD and Blu-ray sales and international distribution and syndication quickly follow.

Media production and distribution is first and foremost a business, requiring infrastructure and financial backing as well as solid marketing plans, a good understanding of what audiences will want and a lot of pure luck. Ultimately, whether it is a made-for-TV movie, television series, magazine or newspaper, radio program or Internet media site, at the core of the media business, the audience is king.

> Media production and distribution is first and foremost a business, requiring infrastructure and financial backing as well as solid marketing plans, a good understanding of what audiences will want and a lot of pure luck.

THE AUDIENCE IS "KING"

Both media companies and advertisers today are far more interested in reaching smaller and more clearly defined targeted audiences, sometimes referred to as niche audiences (see Chapter 8). There is a strong link between an industry's ability to determine what audiences want and how to deliver that desired product and its ability to generate profits through advertising. For these companies, knowing how to identify the audiences that they wish to reach and effectively gaining and holding the audience's attention long enough to deliver the numbers and demographics that advertisers are willing to pay to reach remain ongoing challenges. If, for example, the audience turns out not to be the proper size or the right age for the product an industry is trying to sell, then logically revenues will drop. Even with all the free media content available on television, radio and the Internet, the revenue streams of media companies are entirely and ultimately dependent on audiences as media consumers. A number of factors play into the process of identifying and targeting audience segments with the media content that they want.

Finding the Right Audience: Targeting Factors

Audiences are identified by geographic region, age group, gender, income levels, educational levels, race or ethnicity, social class and lifestyle (sometimes referred to as psychographics). While you might think these determinants would be sufficient to narrow down mass media audiences into easily targeted segments, in today's complex media marketplace these basic demographic factors are not nearly fine-tuned enough to be of value to many media content providers and their advertising clientele. The more fine-tuned audience targeting gets, the more value each resultant audience segments represents. In the years between the 1950s and 1980s, the dominant approach to audience targeting was a "shotgun" approach. The theory was that if a media product reached several million people, as in the case of a television program, and 1 to 2 percent of that large audience responded to the advertising messages, then the value of that audience was delivered; diffusion of the message over the remaining 98 to 99 percent of the audience was considered unimportant collateral. That method of targeting mass media audiences worked well when the number of media outlets was relatively small, only a fraction of the number available today.

To help visualize this difference, think about a television series about fly-fishing. In the past, this topic would have had to attract only a small portion of the total potential audience to make it commercially viable. It was certainly not a topic that would attract millions of loyal viewers—which is why we did not see many TV programs about fly-fishing. Today, however, the sophisticated methods of identifying and communicating with the audiences via various advertising, publications and promotions in print, online and on TV make it possible to deliver a commercially successful fly-fishing television series targeting just a small audience. Such a series would be highly attractive to advertisers of fishing gear, sailboats, fishing lodges and guides and outdoor clothing that want to target that very specific viewing audience. The more focused the niche audience for a program or publication, the more valuable to advertisers that audience becomes. In other words, today's audience value lies in the *quality* of the audience targeting as much as—or even more than—the *size* of the audience reached.

The more focused the niche audience for a program or publication, the more valuable to advertisers that audience becomes. In other words, today's audience value lies in the *quality* of the audience targeting as much as—or even more than—the *size* of the audience reached.

Audiences Under the Influence: Media Effects

The mass media industry, which for the purposes of this discussion includes media content producers, media content providers, advertisers and advertising agencies, is concerned with capturing and holding the attention of narrowly targeted audiences. At the same time, the industry is concerned with how both media content and advertising will influence audience views, attitudes and actions. We introduced some of the leading theories about media influence, also known as media effects, in Chapter 1. Here we expand on one of these theories to help us better understand the role and importance of audiences for the business side of mass media.

University of Amsterdam communication theorist Denis McQuail is one of the leading mass communication theorists today. He has looked at how media influence audiences and has put forward a widely recognized model that he calls the uses and gratifications model. McQuail's model, which is drawn from wide-ranging mass media research studies conducted over the last 50 years, focuses on why media consumers select and use media in an effort to gain specific gratifications of their individual needs. Working with McQuail, theorists Elihu Katz, Jay G. Blumler and Michael Gurevitch (1974) attempted to present a comprehensive view of the role of audience members in the mass communication process. Their theory suggested that people actively seek out specific media and media content that will give them particular gratifications and or results. In other words, when each of us seeks out specific media content, we are seeking—either consciously or unconsciously—to fulfill a need or a collection of needs. When we make a selection from the many content options and venues with which we are presented every day, we are in effect fulfilling one or more of our needs, or at least we feel that we are. According to this model, there are four primary reasons why we select and use media:

- Our media selection fulfills a self-identity need by helping us reinforce our own attitudes and behaviors through identifying with role models and the values they exemplify, from political and religious to social and even sexual.
- Our media selection and usage fulfill a social need by helping us feel that we are interacting with and knowledgeable of other people, even if indirectly, through the characters in TV, films, radio, the Internet, magazines and newspapers. Today, more than at any other time in history, media play a big role in helping us feel socially and culturally connected.
- The media that we select and use help us fulfill our need for security by giving us informational windows through which we educate ourselves about what is going on in the world.
- The media we select and use, taken together, have evolved into the major vehicle through which most of fulfill our need to be entertained and to gain the release that entertainment media provides.

This set of theories, often referred to as "uses and gratifications," view media consumers through an active lens of evaluating how specific media deliver on these goals. Thus, these four basic reasons for consuming media, it is argued, explain why mass media are the best way to sell us things—from products to entertainment options to ideas. This model is also the foundation of the work of advertising guru Dr. Clotaire Rapaille, famous for uncoding "why people do what they do" to uncover the unconscious foundation for consumer behavior.[25] (See Chapter 8.)

Let's consider the uses and gratifications model from the broader perspective of the mass media industry. In the media-rich world of the 21st century, we have an ever-increasing need for media specifically because such content fulfills many of our personal and social needs, and we tend to stay with those outlets that satisfy such needs. If we were to identify this model as the core of the entire media industry, then one could argue that media business models are built around audience identification, targeting and need fulfillment—which collectively equate to revenues and profits for those involved in the industry. The more effectively focused media content is, the more money it directly or indirectly generates.[26]

> In the media-rich world of the 21st century, we have an ever-increasing need for media specifically because such content fulfills many of our personal and social needs, and we tend to stay with those outlets that satisfy such needs.

Researching the Audience: Identifying Trends

Media companies are constantly analyzing which forms of and approaches to their content are attracting the targeted audiences they wish to reach. They often do this through audience research tracking and reporting services, such as those offered by Nielsen Media Research (NMR). NMR is the largest and best-known research company that measures television viewership across all platforms as well as online and mobile reach. Since 1950, its ratings system has been used to rank television programs, and its results significantly influence which programs are canceled or which are renewed each season.

The Nielsen group also studies media content that has already attracted the desired audiences and tracks the outlets that are attempting to imitate the most seemingly successful approaches. Competing companies vie for these niche audiences through advertising, hoping to persuade them to cross over. This is why when a new television reality show, sitcom or drama is successful, other shows that copy the style of the original appear very quickly (consider, for example, the spate of reality cooking shows). By watching shows that we like, we participate in the audience segments that not only help the program providers increase their revenues, but also help to determine which other shows will soon appear. This process works in reverse as well. When a television series start to lose significant audience share, not only might it be cut from the programmer's schedule, but similar shows in development or in production might also be terminated.

A similar process is underway all the time in all forms of media content—television, movies, magazines, newspapers, music, radio, Internet sites. All of these varied media content producers and providers continually face the challenge of the Rule of Three: targeted audience capture = increased revenues from sales and/or advertising = content control. The audience has the ultimate control over which media content gets produced and distributed because, by selecting the television shows, movies and music that it wants to enjoy and thus satisfying certain needs, the audience determines where the money flows and, therefore, which new media content will be produced.[27]

Targeting the Children's Audience

Children, particularly those younger than 12 years of age, are a very special and lucrative media audience, especially for television and now the Internet. Targeting media content and advertising to young children remains a controversial topic, however. This debate arises in large part because younger children, as a niche audience, are viewed by both the public and the government as significantly more vulnerable to the influences and even manipulations of the media because they have not yet developed a personal foundation of emotional and moral self-awareness and maturity. In this traditional view, young children have little understanding of their need gratification process and can easily be manipulated into believing that they need things that they do not need, and that may even be harmful or dangerous. According to the National Institute on Media and the Family:

> With children either spending or influencing $500 billion worth of purchases, marketing techniques have been turned upside down. In the past, the most effective way to sell children's products was through mom and dad. Now the opposite is true: children are the focal point for intense advertising pressure seeking to influence billions of dollars of family spending. Advertisers are aware that children influence the purchase of not just kids' products anymore, but everything in the household from cars to toothpaste. Thus, these "adult" products are being paired with kid-oriented logos and images.

With children's increased access to new communication technologies being combined with the fast pace and busy schedules of today's families, parents are less able to filter out the messages from the advertising world. Children themselves have been asked to assume more purchasing decisions than ever before.[28]

The ongoing academic and social debate about media effects and children will likely continue for years to come and into future generations of digital natives. It is possible that children who grow up today in media-rich environments could develop critical media consumption skills sooner than their predecessors with early guidance and education, but one can only speculate as to how the media and advertising industries will adapt and modify their strategic messaging to target the next generation of young consumers.[29]

9.17

Young children today are surrounded by media content, challenging the ability of parents and government agencies to completely control the media content that children consume.

Marka/Contributor

EMPOWERING THE PASSIVE MEDIA CONSUMER

New media technologies challenge the old media business models and force media companies to reinvent themselves to be profitable in the Digital Age. Such reinvention must be built around several new realities: media of all kinds are migrating to and converging in cyberspace. This trend is simultaneously providing media consumers with vastly more content options and content delivery channels than were imaginable just a decade or so before. These same advances in technology, coupled with the exponential increase in content choices, are empowering us to move from being passive media consumers to active media self-programmers. Audiences that take active roles in programming their content consumption make it much more difficult for media companies to build reliable revenue models because such audiences are constantly changing the content they consume.

For example, how can a television network or advertising agency establish value and pricing levels for program ads when consumers using DVR services such as TiVo can avoid television ads entirely? How does a television network bring in reliable advertising revenue for episodes of the same program available on its Website or through multinetwork Websites such as Hulu.com? How can record labels sell entire "album" collections on CDs priced at $20 when the majority of music consumers today prefer to self-program their own music collections by purchasing and downloading only the specific tracks that they want—for example, at $0.99 to $1.29 per track on Apple's iTunes online store?

The combination of greatly increased content choices, expanding number of delivery platforms through which we access the media content we need and the ability to self-program when and in which size slices we want presents today's media content producers and distributors with unprecedented challenges. How can they provide the media content that target audiences want in a way that generates profits at levels that make the process viable from a business perspective? How does a producer of a new television series construct a business model that allows enough of a budget to produce a high-end media product and that includes distribution channels for cable/satellite television, the Web, portable media player devises, DVD/Blu-ray sales and international syndications—yet still assure enough return on investment to warrant project funding? Does the continued expansion of digital technologies and the Internet offer media businesses enough new opportunities to counterbalance all of the new costs and risks inherent in providing new content? No longer do we question *if* a media business should enter a convergent media world; rather, the question is *how* it will survive and thrive once it does.

Audiences that take active roles in programming their content consumption make it much more difficult for media companies to build reliable revenue models because such audiences are constantly changing the content they consume.

Does the continued expansion of digital technologies and the Internet offer media businesses enough new opportunities to counterbalance all of the new costs and risks inherent in providing new content? No longer do we question *if* a media business should enter a convergent media world; rather, the question is *how* it will survive and thrive once it does.

9.18

A typical low-cost PC-based home recording studio—available technologies are empowering passive media consumers and turning them into media content producers.

Tadamasa Taniguchi/Getty Images

THE EFFECTS OF MEDIA GLOBALIZATION

Starting in the 1980s and increasing through the 1990s, many countries established bilateral and multilateral international media co-production treaties in an effort to respond to the economic challenges facing their respective native media production companies. Advances in media technologies brought about these challenges, as did the convergence of media content and delivery and the desire to counter the continued dominance of U.S. media companies and its resultant cultural and political ramifications (see Chapter 14). These treaties aim to support the collaboration of media production companies and the sharing of financial and production recourses, thereby reducing the financial risk and increasing the market competitiveness to media producers.

Today, the largest media co-production treaties are found within the EU, with France being the largest participant. Both Canada and the United Kingdom are also very active in the framework of international co-production treaties. Although the United States is not a signatory to any of these treaties, U.S. media companies frequently partner with treaty-participating media companies in Canada, Europe and Asia in an effort to take advantage of the government-backed financial incentives available to such co-production partners.

International co-productions can provide important creative "local content" benefits for films and television programs requiring extensive overseas locations and built around multinational or cross-cultural stories. While financial incentives to producing media through international co-productions exist, and such international partnerships can increase international distribution potential for a given project, the disadvantages and trade-offs from these liaisons can be substantial.[30]

Trade-Offs

The trade-offs for partnering with media companies participating under international media co-production treaties are often difficult for U.S. media companies to accommodate. Co-production treaties aim to level the media business playing field and support participant countries' cultural heritage by requiring that key production personnel such as writers, editors, actors, producers and directors be citizens of the treaty countries. They often require that a large percentage of production resources come from participating countries. Under these treaties, percentage formulas have been negotiated and agreed to that help support the media industries, and the culture, of participating countries.

For example, a feature film produced under the international co-production structure with EU partners—say, France and Germany—might be produced under the auspices of a U.S.-based film studio. Under the terms of the treaty, the majority of its shooting locations would need to be split equally between France and Germany, have an American screenwriter but a French director and employ a collection of both French and German key crewmembers. The lead characters might be well-known American actors, but either French or German actors would have to play all of the supporting roles, with perhaps some filled by actors from other EU countries. The postproduction editing of the film would take place primarily in France or Germany, as would the music scoring and special effects work. The French and German co-production

9.19

As the media marketplace continues to globalize, as shown in this example from India's Bollywood, how will it affect American media influence at home and abroad?

Dinodia Photos/Alamy Stock Photo

partner companies, as well as their respective governments and financing banks, would most likely require the film to premier and launch simultaneously in Europe.

All of these treaty-based requirements can add to the creativity and multicultural, multimarket appeal of the film—but they also add many layers of business and logistical complexities to the project. In addition, adhering to the treaty terms limits the amount of work contracted to U.S. companies using American creative talent.

Only a small portion of the feature films and television programs that U.S. companies produce each year are created under the international co-production treaties structure. Many of these programs are produced in Canada. As a result of its strong relationships with the media production industry in the United States and its ability to serve as a "bridge" into the EU treaty system, Canada has become the United States' largest co-production partner, followed closely by the United Kingdom. Due to the increasing importance of international markets along with the increasing costs of production and distribution, the trend is toward more international co-productions. Nevertheless, primarily American companies and crews produce far more American media projects with international topics, stories and locales each year outside of the international co-production system. The growth of new media technologies that allow easier and less costly access to international markets is contributing to the trend toward more international co-production partnerships, both within and outside of the treaty system. The next time you watch a feature film in a theater or on television, pay close attention to the titles and credits; see if you can determine whether the film was produced as an international co-production or as a solely American production.

Distribution

In the 21st century, with the astounding growth and omnipresent nature of the Internet and the convergence of media content from traditional media platforms—print, music, television, movies—much of the mass media business has become global, both by choice and by necessity. From a business and financial perspective, globalization requires content producers and distributors alike to operate in the worldwide business environment. There they must meet the simultaneous business challenges of remaining relevant to a local, regional or national audience while at the same time catering to international audiences with often-conflicting cultures, politics, sensitivities and needs related to the media they consume. In the latter part of the 20th century, U.S. media companies were able to dominate their international competition based on the sheer size and scope of the U.S. media industry, with little or no regard given to the cultural sensitivities of its international markets. In other words, the history of the U.S. media industry has been guided by the business attitude that "American media are better than everyone else's, so other societies and cultures will just have to adapt to U.S. preferences." This American media dominance has caused cultural, political and diplomatic backlashes (see Chapter 14).

More recently, American media industries have been compelled to make considerable changes geared toward making them more internationally sensitive. This does not mean that U.S. media industries have lost their dominant position in the global market; they have not. American media content—movies, television programs, music, magazines, video games and some news organizations (e.g., CNN, Bloomberg, *The Washington Post, The New York Times* and *Time* magazine)—still attracts robust and growing global audiences. Today, however, that means operating in a globalized mass media marketplace and competing head-to-head with British, French, German, Italian, Indian, Japanese, Australian and Middle Eastern media companies. Not all American media companies have been equally well prepared to address the challenges of a globalized media marketplace with viable international competitors: mistakes have been made, and businesses lost or acquired by non-American media conglomerates with stronger records of successfully doing business on a culturally sensitive international stage.

CONCLUSION: MASS MEDIA COMPANIES ADJUST AND THRIVE IN THE DIGITAL AGE

The mass media in the Digital Age operate as a business, just as they have throughout history, especially in the United States. Media businesses now face economic challenges that demand they reinvent their business models to respond to evolving technologies for producing and distributing media content, and to a changing consumer market. The Digital Age, and especially the proliferation of the Internet, has increased the rate and scope of these changes so profoundly that they have forced entire media industry segments to make radical revisions in how they operate just to stay competitive. In the end, media industries will survive based in large part on their ability to predict economic and market changes early on and adapt their operations accordingly.

It is tremendously difficult for company owners and managers, investors, financial institutions and, of course, consumers to keep up with these changes. As is the case with all economic upheavals regardless of the industries involved, some innovative and nimble companies will survive and many slow-to-adapt companies will be absorbed or simply go out of business. As media consumers, we ultimately benefit from the innovation and corporate reinvention that result from this battle for survival. In the case of mass media industries, reinvention is resulting in better technologies, better content and vastly expanded consumer choices.

CHAPTER SUMMARY	KEY TERMS
Tracing American Media Ownership Explores the historic roots of media ownership in America, including coverage of the establishment of early media monopolies and the eventual antitrust battles against them. **Visual Media** **Corporate Influence on the News** Excerpt from *Outfoxed: Rupert Murdoch's War on Journalism*.  1. In the wake of the recent wiretap scandals and resulting Parliamentary hearings in the United Kingdom, do you think Rupert Murdoch's direct influence and ideologically based manipulations of news reporting by his News Corp. outlets worldwide have significantly lessoned or now merely become more covert? 2. Is corporate influence of new reporting, with the exception of Fox News, commonplace, or are corporate owners and boards of directors primarily focused on costs and profits and not directly interested in influencing news coverage decisions?	mass media conglomerate media monopoly Hollywood Studio System antitrust laws Celler–Kefauver Act vertical integration economies of scale syndicate blacklist fiduciary responsibility
The Economics of Media: Three Models Explains the American market-driven commercial model of mass media and its economic underpinnings and discusses the resulting approaches to media content and delivery used worldwide. **Visual Media** **Arianna Huffington** *The Huffington Post*'s successful business model is helping to drive the migration of newspapers and news organizations onto the Web. 1. Why has *The Huffington Post* become one of the most successful and influential of all Internet news services? 2. Do you think *The Huffington Post* is a model that other major media organizations must move toward in order to survive in the 21st century? If so, why, and if not, why not?	market model direct media revenues indirect media revenues media asset value return on investment (ROI) public sphere model new media model vanity presses subsidy publishers
The Federal Communication Commission Looks at both the historic roots and current role of the FCC in regulating mass media and examines the debate surrounding federal government control of broadcast media.	Federal Communication Commission (FCC) broadcasting region Telecommunications Act of 1996

The Business of Music and Sound Recording Describes the history of the economics of the music industry and how changing technologies have forced changes in the music industry's business models.	high-fidelity premium record race music
The Business of Radio Examines the history of commercial radio and looks at how radio became a primary commercial platform for news, entertainment and information in the 20th century and how it has adapted to the technological and audience demands of the early 21st century.	broadcasting commercial radio 33 1/3 rpm long-play disc acetate blank recording disc air checks studio engineers digital subscription model
The Business of Television and Film Reviews the business and economics of televisions and movies and explains the stages of how TV programs and movies are financed and produced.	acquisition treatment spec script development show runners production financing stage soft-cost resources product tie-ins preproduction stage production stage postproduction stage distribution stage pay-per-view
The Audience Is "King" Analyzes the significant role of audience demand and trends in determining what television and films get funded, produced and released—along with the media effects analysis used to try to predict audience trends.	niche audiences psychographics uses and gratifications model audience share Rule of Three
Empowering the Passive Media Consumer Illustrates the changing dynamics of audience participation that, driven by rapidly changing media technologies, are moving toward greater audience participation in media content creation and delivery.	
The Effects of Media Globalization Explains how the globalization of various media is impacting the changing business and economic models of what media content is produced and how and where it is produced.	international media co-production treaties

NOTES

1 Epstein, M. (1996). *The battle over Citizen Kane*. PBS.
2 Filler, L. (1994). *The muckrakers*. Stanford University Press.
3 *New York Times*. (2012, May 1).
4 Croteau, D., & Hoynes, W. (2006). *The business of media*. Pine Forge Press.
5 Adelson, A. (1999, April 5). The business of National Public Radio. *The New York Times*.
6 Nikbakht, E., & Goppelli, A. A. (2000). *Barron's finance*. Barron's Educational Series.
7 *InformationWeek*.
8 Price Waterhouse Cooper, in cooperation with the World Association of Newspapers. (2009). *Moving into multiple business models: Outlook for newspaper publishing in the Digital Age*.
9 Lyons, D. (2009, June 6). Don't "i-Tune" us. *Newsweek*.

10 Ibid.

11 Ibid.

12 Blevins, J., & Brown, D. (2008). Broadcast ownership regulation in a border era: An analysis of how the U.S. Federal Communications Commission is shaping the debate on broadcast ownership limits. *All Academic Research*.

13 Ibid.

14 Croteau, D., & Hoynes, W. (2006). *The business of media*. Pine Forge Press.

15 Bekker, P., & Herter Norton, M. D. (2007). *The story of music: An historical sketch of the changes in musical form*. Kessinger Publishing.

16 Ibid.

17 Morton, D. L. (2004). *Sound recording: The life story of a technology*. Johns Hopkins University Press.

18 du Noyer, P. (2003). *The Billboard illustrated encyclopedia of music*. Watson-Guptill.

19 Vogel, S. (2009). *The scene of Harlem cabaret: Race, sexuality and performance*. Chicago: University of Chicago Press.

20 Balk, A. (2005). *The rise of radio: From Marconi through the Golden Age*. McFarland & Company.

21 Morton, D. L. (2004). *Sound recording: The life story of a technology*. Johns Hopkins University Press.

22 Ibid.

23 *Digital music report*. (2012). Retrieved from www.ifpi.org/content/library/DMR2012.pdf

24 Cones, J. W. (2009). *Introduction to the motion picture industry: A guide for filmmakers, students and scholars*. Marquette Books.

25 West, R., & Turner, L. H. (2010). *Introducing communication theory: Analysis and application* (4th ed.). McGraw-Hill Higher Education.

26 McQuail, D. (2000). *McQuail's mass communication theory* (4th ed.). Sage.

27 The Rule of Three is a simple formula to describe the interrelationships between audience targeting, direct and advertising revenues, and the new content creation decisions of media content producers. It is based on the author's 30-plus years of experience as a television producer and used by the author in his lectures and seminars. It is not original, in that many authors and experts have created similar illustrative explanations of this dynamic relationship.

28 Chen, N. (2009). Parents should limit children's exposure to advertising. University of Missouri Extension. Retrieved from www.mediafamily.org/facts/facts_childadv.shtml

29 Jordan, A. (2011). Special Issue: Children's media policy: International perspectives. *Journal of Children and Media*, 5(1).

30 Baltruschat, D. (2002). *Globalization and international TV and film co-productions: Search for new narratives*. Paper presented at Media in Transition-2: Globalization and Convergence, Massachusetts Institute of Technology, Cambridge, MA.

10
Media Bias

Scott J. Ferrell/Congressional Quarterly/Alamy Stock Photo

CHAPTER OUTLINE

Catherine Crier on Media Bias A former state Supreme Court judge, author and TV host discusses media bias.

Perspectives on Media Bias Multiple perspectives on bias in the media from top personalities in the field.

LEARNING OBJECTIVES

1. Explain the differences between natural bias and intentional bias in news reporting.
2. Evaluate the key aspects of the three primary types of mass media bias and their impact on news reporting.
3. Analyze the role advertising sales plays in shaping media messages and its impact on media balance.
4. Assess media critically in order to recognize underlying social, cultural and political biases in entertainment programming, such as movies and television.
5. Describe how intentional bias in both news and entertainment media attracts audiences and can serve as a viable media business strategy.
6. Evaluate multiple sources on issues and separate fact from opinion in news reports and expert analysis of news stories to form independent conclusions of what is truth.

ONE OF THE MAJOR MEDIA EVENTS of the 2012 presidential election campaign was the early September release by newsmagazine Website *Mother Jones* of a viral video of Republican presidential candidate Mitt Romney speaking to a small group of wealthy contributors. The secretly shot video was brought to light by researcher James Carter IV, a self-described partisan Democrat and grandson of former President Jimmy Carter. The video showed Mitt Romney doing what political candidates do when they appear at supposedly private fundraisers: speaking candidly about their views on political issues. In this case, candidate Romney, in response to a question about people who pay little or no federal taxes, replied that:

". . . There are 47 percent of the people who will vote for the president no matter what. All right, there are 47 percent who are with him, who are dependent upon government, who believe that they are victims, who believe the government has a responsibility to care for them, who believe that they are entitled to health care, to food, to housing, to you-name-it. That, that's

an entitlement. And the government should give it to them. And they will vote for this president no matter what . . . These are people who pay no income tax. . . . My job is not to worry about those people. I'll never convince them they should take personal responsibility and care for their lives."[1]

These negative comments about what amounts to nearly 50 percent of the American electorate became the lead story throughout the media, generating endless commentaries from both Democratic and Republican pundits. The story remained center stage in the campaign coverage leading up to the presidential debates and contributed to Mitt Romney losing the election. Democratic commentators jumped on Romney's statements as a clear demonstration of his disregard for "average Americans." Republican commentators defended the candidate by insisting that he was simply offering his straightforward, unscripted views to inform contributors about who they were supporting with their large

campaign donations, while at the same time loudly complaining that the biased "liberal media" was driving the story in a collaborative effort to defeat Romney and help re-elect President Barack Obama to a second term.

Conservatives are constantly accusing the media of a liberal bias, and liberals just as often disparage the loud voices and large audiences of media outlets such as Fox News. Studies have indeed demonstrated the consistently liberal-leaning beliefs of those individuals working in the news media. However, these liberal-leaning findings are by and large centered on social issues. Many other empirical studies, including numerous studies reported in the *Quarterly Journal of Economics*, have demonstrated that the core of media bias is primarily economic, with media outlets striving to attract and retain specific audiences— Fox News thus catering to conservative Republicans, MSNBC catering to liberal Democrats and most news outlets (broadcast, print and Web-based) falling somewhere along this continuum. Bias sells. Bias attracts audiences and advertiser dollars. But how does one identify bias and separate fact from opinion?

THE BUILDING BLOCKS OF BIAS

While there is a good deal of debate about how to define the term, at a basic level, media bias is simply the intentional or unintentional slanting of news reporting toward one side due to the political views or cultural beliefs of journalists, producers or owners of a media outlet. Bias is always built upon a foundation of facts manipulated to skew the meaning and the message of a story in a direction that supports the particular views of the outlet and the audience. Even undisputed "facts," including statistical studies and poll results, can easily be presented to *appear* to support any point of view on an issue.

Let's consider the case of Catherine Crier—one of the youngest judges ever elected as a state judge in Texas. Although she was a Republican in a historically Republican state, Judge Crier soon became an outspoken critic of the ultraconservative movement, which she saw as attempting to remove "activist" judges from the federal bench and to replace them with conservative judges. Seeing her as a traitor to the Republican cause, conservative politicians criticized Crier—but the attacks on her Republican credentials backfired. In her book *Contempt: How the Right Is Wronging American Justice*, she debunked the urban myth that liberal judges bent on destroying the United States' religious and family values have taken over the federal judiciary. Crier's well-documented work rebuts the message of the conservative media by supplying easily confirmable facts: Most sitting federal judges today are Republican appointees, who are highly motivated to do a good job and to support the Constitution.

Crier's story shows how, armed with facts and the courage to risk career and peer acceptance, a skilled storyteller can turn the tables on skewed messages in the media. For Crier, removing bias from the media involves more than just merely balancing arguments between the Left and the Right: It involves truth telling. It involves healthy debate about the issues from voices across the political spectrum. In the following video segment, "Catherine Crier on Media Bias," Crier entertains the notion of engaging in an issues-based dialogue without having to resort to the labels that typically invite bias—that is liberal, conservative, Democratic, Republican. ▶

Standing in contrast to Crier is Mark Levin, a prominent conservative commentator and constitutional scholar who served as an advisor to President Ronald Reagan and top members of the Reagan administration. Like Crier, Levin moved from practicing law to becoming a nationally recognized media pundit, with a top-rated radio program and a contributing editor position with the *National Review*. In his well-researched book *Men in Black: How the Supreme Court Is Destroying America*, which relied on much of the same factual evidence as Crier's work, Levin argues that the federal court—and especially the Supreme Court—"imperiously strikes down laws and imposes new ones purely on its own arbitrary whims."[2] Levin presents the argument that the Supreme Court practices a form of "judicial tyranny" that favors liberal policies and results in American society continually drifting to the left. From his perspective, federal judges have a long history of practicing judicial activism, which in the case of the majority of Supreme Court justices has the effect of undermining democracy in favor of their own liberal agendas.[3]

> Bias is always built upon a foundation of facts manipulated to skew the meaning and the message of a story in a direction that supports the particular views of the outlet and the audience.

> For Crier, removing bias from the media involves more than just merely balancing arguments between the Left and the Right: It involves truth telling. It involves healthy debate about the issues from voices across the political spectrum.

Catherine Crier
Author, TV Anchor & Correspondent

▶ **Catherine Crier on Media Bias**
Catherine Crier, former state Supreme Court judge, author and TV host, discusses media bias.

Are the Media Always Biased?

Many people see the media as biased, often against whatever political, social or religious beliefs they themselves hold. Media watch organizations, most of which have their own agendas, all claim that the media are biased in one direction or the other. The organization Accuracy in Media (www.aim.org) claims that its research demonstrates that the mainstream media has a liberal slant, while Fairness & Accuracy in Reporting (www.fair.org) asserts that its research shows that the mainstream media has a conservative bias. Studies by the Gallup polling organization and the Pew Research Center have found that the public views the media as "generally" balanced and reasonably accurate. Nevertheless, when polled about specific hot-topic issues, the majority of the people criticized media outlets that highlighted stories skewed toward whatever side of a debate they opposed.

The fact is that media outlets tend to attract and hire people who share their general political leanings and worldview. For example, NBC and its cable news channel MSNBC, which has a deeply entrenched liberal-leaning organizational culture, tends to attract journalists who share that point of view. In contrast, more conservative-leaning television networks such as FOX and, to a lesser extent, ABC tend to attract journalists who share a more conservative outlook.[4] Meanwhile, the views and bias of newly minted media professionals also follow the swings of society as a whole. Surveys taken at journalism graduate schools in the 1980s and 1990s showed a consistent majority of journalists entering the profession to be liberal-leaning, by a margin of nearly 8 to 1. This tendency shifted for a number of years until 2006, when it appeared that the pendulum had swung back toward the liberal side.[5]

> the extreme voices and views on both sides of a given issue offer the media consumer the opportunity to make up his or her own mind—assuming that we each make the effort and take the responsibility to do so.

Commonly held views suggest that all media bias is bad and all-encompassing. Of course, the reality is far more complicated—and far more interesting. Moreover, in the rich mosaic that is mass media today, with so many venues presenting multiple voices and views, a natural process of checks and balances prevails much of the time. In other words, the extreme voices and views on both sides of a given issue offer the media consumer the opportunity to make up his or her own mind—assuming that we each make the effort and take the responsibility to do so.

In 2012, Mihee Kim, Ph.D. candidate at the University of Maryland, undertook an extensive study comparing how political partisans—politically active individuals—perceived bias and credibility in controversial news stories about politically charged stories produced online by both professional journalists and nonprofessional "citizen journalists." For her study, Kim used the same-sex marriage bill, which was working its way through the Maryland legislative and electoral processes to become a state law. She defined media "perceived bias" as distortion of facts as conceptualized by each individual's subjective perception of a story's content, the sources allegedly providing the story and the author and/or media outlet reporting the story. Simply stated, Kim's study asked two core questions: How do politically partisan individuals' opinions influence their evaluation of news stories produced by professional journalists in terms of bias and credibility? And how do politically partisan individuals' opinions influence their evaluation of news stories produced by nonprofessional "citizen" journalists via blog postings (which often get picked up by mainstream news media outlets) in terms of bias and credibility)? The study clearly demonstrated that the audience-perceived bias of a reporter, whether professional or "citizen journalist," equally determined the credibility of both the reporter and the stories being reported.

Packaging Media Bias

Most people want to believe that the news they consume is accurate, especially from media outlets with which they are already comfortable. Once viewers are comfortable with a particular media outlet, many find it easy to accept as factual whatever that media source feeds them, even when a critical review might suggest that "their" TV network or favorite talk-radio commentator is misrepresenting important facts. Having such a high level of audience trust can have momentous consequences when a star journalist or commentator gets the story wrong.

In September 2004, while the U.S. media were fully focused on a highly negative, divisive presidential campaign, CBS's popular prime-time news anchor Dan Rather presented a story on the network's *60 Minutes* program that turned out to be false and strongly slanted against sitting President George W. Bush. Rather and his producers initially claimed they had documents "proving" that President Bush had avoided his duties as a National Guard pilot during the Vietnam War. They suggested that Bush used his family's money and political influence to avoid training and to assure that he remained stateside. Rather's report presented "experts" to confirm that the documents were authentic.

Bush and his staff quickly challenged the documents. In doing so, they accused CBS and Rather of making up the story in an effort to push their biased political agenda in support of Democratic presidential candidate John Kerry. CBS denied the charge of intentional bias and appointed an independent panel to investigate Rather and his producer, Mary Mapes. Rather continued to defend the story and the investigative reporting behind it, while CBS management, at least initially, stood behind their star anchor and accused the Bush campaign of trying to mislead public opinion with its attacks on Rather and the network.

Growing evidence, including opinions from independent document experts, indicated that Rather and his producer had been duped and that the documents were forged. CBS started to pull back from its defense of both the story and Rather, reporting on the controversy in a more even-handed manner, in an attempt to counter the accusations of blatant anti-Bush bias. Eventually Rather was forced to admit that he had done a poor job of vetting the source material and instead had relied on his producer's word that the story was factual and the source documents were authentic. CBS apologized to its viewers; Rather announced his "early retirement."

Television news producers play an important role behind the scenes and often, as was the case for CBS's Mary Mapes, take the fall when something goes wrong. Dan Rather, in his role as both news anchor and CBS News managing editor, also shared in the fallout from this misreported story. In her 2005 book *Truth and Duty: The Press, the President, and the Privilege of Power*, Mapes defended her record and put forward her defense that she was sacrificed when CBS submitted to Bush administration pressure and right-wing attacks on the network—attacks that were both clearly biased and factually suspect.

10.1

Former *60 Minutes* news anchor Dan Rather, who reported during the 2004 presidential elections that George W. Bush had avoided National Guard duties during the Vietnam War, announced his early retirement after evidence to the contrary surfaced.

Ezip Peterson/UPI/Newscom

When a partisan group sees another individual's news evaluation to be favorable to the group, the group members do not judge the news to be hostile to their point of view. On the other hand, when a partisan group views another's news evaluation to be unfavorable to the group, partisans in the group evaluate the news as unfavorable relative to the other group.

The theory of hostile media effect hypothesizes that politically partisan individuals perceive seemingly "balanced news" as biased against their own opinions and worldviews. Kim's study confirmed that overall, partisans with opinions agreeing with mainstream news stories evaluated them as less biased and higher in author and content credibility than individuals holding opposing opinions. Meanwhile, the level of agreement between politically partisan individuals' opinions and similar stories presented on popular blog sites appeared to significantly influence the perceptions of whether the blog is a believable and trustworthy news source.

In other words, and as we will discover through the examples presented throughout this chapter, news bias very much exists in the minds of the beholders. If we agree with the views of a particular news author and outlet, we perceive the story as being balanced and factual. Yet if we generally do not agree with the views of the stories, author or the news outlet, we generally perceive the story as being biased and less credible—whether in fact the story and the reporting in question are *actually* biased or not.[6]

It is interesting to note that Dr. Kim's study, along with many others in recent years, actually postdated far earlier research done by Cooper and Jahoda in 1947. In their groundbreaking studies, Cooper and

10.2

Media commentator Ann Coulter, like many others, packages her own truth for her audiences.

CD1 WENN Photos/Newscom

Jahoda looked at how racially and ethnically prejudiced people responded to cartoons that made fun of prejudice. They demonstrated that people look for mental defenses to keep from understanding the message that contradicts their views. They also try to avoid messages that cause them to feel cognitive dissonance as a result of conflict with their own well-established values and beliefs. They called this process "evasion." They found that evasion is used with astoundingly high frequency when people are confronted with realities that conflict with their deeply rooted beliefs. This causes them to see opposing views, even those well grounded in fact, as propaganda and a threat to their own and their families' well-being.[7]

It remains unclear whether Rather intentionally set up the story in an effort to support his own political bias or fell into it through careless journalism. The lesson learned from the Dan Rather story is that a large audience can easily accept a compelling story, told by an effective storyteller and skillfully packaged by a media outlet, even when the message contains easily identifiable lies. It is human nature to believe what we want to believe, even when it conflicts with the facts. Media commentators such as Bill O'Reilly, Rush Limbaugh and Ann Coulter on the right, or Bill Maher, Rachel Maddow the Reverend Al Sharpton and Chris Matthews on the left, are able to create their own truths and package them for their eager and loyal audiences, regardless of facts, precisely because that is what their audiences want them to do. They are highly skilled suppliers of what their audiences already want to believe.

Media bias sells in large part because we want to buy it. The results of packaging bias can be far-reaching and historic. Noam Chomsky, a renowned professor of linguistics at Massachusetts Institute of Technology (MIT), philosopher and political activist, coined the term manufacturing consent to help describe how media can be used to set the public agenda—the list of policy issues that affect the people of a town, a city or a nation.[8] One of Chomsky's favorite examples of manipulation of mass media to manufacture public consent occurred during the presidency of Woodrow Wilson.

> Media bias sells in large part because we want to buy it.

In 1916, Woodrow Wilson was elected U.S. president on a "peace through isolation" platform, as most Americans were against any involvement in a European war against Germany's rising power. In reality, the Wilson administration was secretly committed to taking America to war, "to make the world safe for democracy." To gain support for this position, it had to change the attitude of the American public from isolationist to patriotic and pro-war. Wilson established a propaganda organization called the Creel Commission, which in less than one year slandered everything German. It convinced the majority of Americans that the United States was in imminent danger from an aggressive and evil enemy. In fact, Germany had no plans to attack and was doing its utmost to avoid bringing the United States into the conflict.

Fast forward 85 years and history appears to have repeated itself. During the George W. Bush administration, Americans saw manufactured consent in action when, after the terrorist attacks on the United States on September 11, 2001, the Bush administration used Americans' fear and heightened patriotism to win support for a preemptive, second war in Iraq. The Bush administration worked hard to link the 9/11 attacks on America to Saddam Hussein in order to justify attacking Iraq. The administration claimed that Hussein posed an imminent threat to the free world, due to the nation's possession, use and acquisition of weapons of mass destruction (WMDs). In advocating for attacking Iraq, Bush emphasized the dire need to oust Hussein from power and to confiscate these so-called WMDs. Almost a decade later, the public generally believes that Bush's claims regarding WMDs in Iraq were merely attempts at manipulating the U.S. Congress, the American public and the world so as to garner global support to strike against Iraq.

Initially, in the media race to appear patriotic after the 9/11 terrorist attacks, mainstream media and pundits and commentators from both sides of the political spectrum supported what turned out to be disinformation from the administration. This caused most Americans, and many people around the world, to believe that Iraq was part of the 9/11 attacks. The administration's PR campaign became a more powerful influence on the American public than most all other reporting and editorials at the time. The administration's campaign included paid ads sponsored by an activist conservative group allied with the Bush administration called Freedom's Watch. This group produced four "public service" spots that aired multiple times in 60 congressional districts across the country that urged Congress to continue to back the president's war in Iraq. Eventually, journalistic fact checking caught up with the public relations campaign and exposed the misrepresentations, but by then it was too late—America was once again at war with Iraq.[9]

10.3

The media captures former President George W. Bush in a defensive moment.

Kristoffer Tripplaar/Alamy Stock Photo

The real difference between President Woodrow Wilson in 1916 and President George W. Bush in 2002 lies not so much in how *they* responded in their respective situations, but in how the *media* reacted. Today, the media are far more likely to question the truth of such sweeping accusations—especially those made by the leader of the free world—and are far more aggressive in their fact checking. In time, in response to the overwhelming evidence against the Bush administration's handling of the supposed Iraqi threat and its rationale for committing American troops to war in the region, even several pro-Bush media outlets were forced to change their positions. Notably, a major turnaround happened in early 2010, after former Bush White House senior advisor Karl Rove published his memoir *Courage and Consequence: My Life as a Conservative in the Fight*. In his book, Rove offered firsthand accounts of how the Bush administration mishandled the lead-up to the Iraq War. Rove's well-established credibility and insider perspective forced conservative commentators such as Fox News's Bill O'Reilly to modify their previously unshaken support for the handling of the war by President Bush and Vice President Cheney.

TYPES OF MEDIA BIAS

Media bias can come in many forms and can be either intentional or unintentional, as John Street, professor of political science at University of East Anglia, outlines in his book *Mass Media, Politics and Democracy*:

> Partisan bias is where a cause is deliberately promoted. . . . This can take the form of explicit recommendations to vote for one party or another, or it can be identified in the blatant endorsement of a cause.
>
> Propaganda bias is where a story is reported with a deliberate intention of making the case for a particular party, policy or point of view, without explicitly stating this.
>
> Unwitting bias occurs when hard choices have to be made about what [stories] to include and what to exclude . . . [because of limitations in the number of pages in a publication, or the number of airtime minutes in a news broadcast.] The same [unwitting bias] is carried by the ordering of the broadcast news: the main stories are dealt with first and at length. These [editorial] judgments constitute a form of unwitting bias, and though the bias is explicit . . . it is not conscious or deliberate.[10]

The preconceived views and beliefs that are held by media consumers play a significant role in how we perceive the bias or nonbias of a particular news story or media outlet. Thus media bias is, in large part, in the mind of the beholder.

Consider, for instance, the ongoing conflict between Israelis and Palestinians. Media outlets from both sides continually attempt to elicit sympathy and support from the outside world for their side's struggles and cause. One news broadcast may show chilling images of Palestinians waiting in long lines at food relief stations; severely wounded children being treated in poorly equipped hospitals; or families cold, hungry and huddled around a small camp stove to stay warm. Another media outlet may broadcast interviews with Israeli victims of suicide bombings, anguished because they have lost a loved one, their home or oftentimes both; it may also show harrowing images of the carnage and bloodshed resulting from a roadside bombing of a bus filled with Israeli women and children.

All such imagery attempts to sway public opinion toward or against the Palestinian or the Israeli cause. Yet, while we naturally react empathetically and sympathetically to such reports of human suffering, ultimately the media *bias* we experience as consumers is guided largely by our *own* political perspectives on the issue. This is not to say that the media outlets themselves do not strategically think about how or when they will broadcast or print a specific story, or how or when they will actually cover the specific details of a story. In other words, bias can occur as the natural result of the editorial decision-making process.

10.4

Boutique/Getty Images

Bias by Selection

The editorial decision-making process involves making choices. These choices include figuring out which stories to cover, how much coverage to actually give each story and where in the news lineup each story should occur. By settling on which stories will appear at the beginning of a nightly news program, which will come after the first commercial break and which will run at the end of the broadcast, the program producers communicate the relative importance of those stories. This bias by selection process is even easier to see in the stories that the producers decide *not* to run that night or that the newspaper editors decide *not* to print that day. Of course, something has to be the *lead* story. Because there are always far more stories than can be covered in a single, 23-minute nightly news segment or printed in a limited-page newspaper, some stories must be cut every day. Thus, the very nature of the editorial process makes the resultant bias that occurs intentional.

10.5

In what ways do these images of the Israeli-Palestinian conflict depict or not depict bias?

Jack Guez/Stringer

As modern news audiences migrate away from traditional evening news broadcasts toward 24/7 cable news channels the process of media bias by selection also shifts. What was traditionally the role of the news editors and producers has now largely become the role of the audience. With so many news outlets available all the time, most of us naturally gravitate toward those sources whose apparent bias—intentional or not—most closely aligns with our own views and beliefs. Of course, accessing only those outlets with which we agree means that we are biasing the news we select. Not only does this tendency blind us from other views and deafen us to other voices, but it also leaves us with just *half* the media story and thus vulnerable to *uninformed* bias. As a result, we fail to invest the effort required to become critical media consumers.

Bias by Extraordinary Experiences

Most media reporters, editors and commentators show unintentional bias some of the time. For instance, their natural reactions to such extraordinary events as war, terrorism, genocide, natural disasters and negative political campaigns can lead to some degree of biased reporting, however unintentional. Reporters are only human: They cannot help but be moved by stories of tragedy or the human experience. Ted Turner, the founder of CNN and the inventor of the 24/7 news phenomenon, has said that the experiences of frontline journalists covering human suffering tend to push them toward biased reporting. When faced with the horrors of the battlefield or the devastation of a natural disaster, it is hard for media professionals to stay objective. Human nature pushes most reporters to try to use the power of the media to motivate their audiences and their governments to take action—to do something, anything, to lessen or cease the devastation.[11]

But no matter how much such experiences might provoke a journalist to abandon objective reporting, the direction in which that journalist personally leans will depend solely on that journalist's own experience and political stance. We do not know whether the photojournalist who witnesses the death of a child by a sniper will support calls for an end to war. In fact, he may encourage continuation of the battle and claim it is up to the free world to help defend those who cannot defend themselves. Alternatively, the photojournalist may return from the modern battlefield and feel more committed to in his beliefs that war should be condemned. The point is this: Regardless of the bias that the media intentionally or unintentionally express, we, as consumers of the media's stories, are once again responsible for deciding how to read and interpret the media message. This brings us to yet another point of discussion: Is media bias solely dependent upon the market's demand for it?

Bias by Market Demand

American mainstream media companies are businesses whose market success is driven by audience ratings and supported by advertisers. Opinion and controversy are what sell in 21st-century America—which is to say that biased voices and views sell. Like bullies on the playground, biased voices are often the loudest voices; they are able to push and shove their extreme opinions to the foreground of the consumer's attention. Today, in attempts to cater to the many segments of the splintered American media audience, a glut of intentionally slanted news/talk radio and television programs has emerged. Each segment of the audience gravitates to those media outlets that reinforce what it wants to believe and what it already believes. Fox News, for example, caters to a decidedly conservative audience segment. Driven to compete with the success of Fox News in attracting a very large conservative audience, MSNBC has taken a strategic shift toward a left bias in its attempt to attract and hold a liberal audience. Meanwhile, CNN struggles to capture the middle ground and thus appears to be more politically neutral. But CNN is paying the price for

accessing only those outlets with which we agree means that we are biasing the news we select. Not only does this tendency blind us from other views and deafen us to other voices, but it also leaves us with just *half* the media story and thus vulnerable to *uninformed* bias. As a result, we fail to invest the effort required to become critical media consumers.

10.6

Images of damage and human involvement can stir up feelings of unintentional bias in both the media reporter and the consumer. How does seeing this image of an oil spill cleanup impact you as the viewer?

ZUMA Press, Inc./Alamy Stock Photo

▶ Perspectives on Media Bias Multiple perspectives on bias in the media from top personalities in the field.

its efforts at balanced journalism with decreasing audience and reduced advertising revenues. Yet despite its efforts, CNN's lack of advocacy can make its coverage appear bland, or even more biased, to those with strong leanings one way or the other. One theoretical explanation of why CNN's efforts at journalistic balance is costing its audience share can be found in social judgment theory. This theory attempts to classify audience attitudes along a continuum between acceptance and rejection. The "acceptance" side of the continuum represents positions that people find acceptable. By contrast, the "rejection" side is where individuals judge the messages as being mostly counter to their own positions on issues. As a result, the theory suggests that a message that runs counter to one's already well-established views will only change attitudes when the message falls within a tight range of already accepted positions. The further away from this tight range in latitude of acceptance, the less likely persuasion is to occur.[12]

Furthermore, as the media voices in the video segment "Perspectives on Media Bias" suggest, the personalities that entertain *as* they push the envelope also tend to attract the most viewers—even if the content of that entertainment offers little in the way of factual information. ▶

According to studies conducted by the National Association of Broadcasters, the Pew Research Center for the Media and the Kennedy School of Government at Harvard University, *intentionally* biased radio and television broadcasts in the United States tend in the direction of conservatism. In fact, intentional *conservative* bias outnumbers intentional *liberal* bias at a consistent rate of approximately 3 to 1—as evidenced by the extraordinary success of conservative talk radio.[13] The entertaining and popular voices of Glenn Beck, Rush Limbaugh, Sean Hannity, Lars Larson and Laura Ingraham would agree. Also popular among conservatives is the Salem Radio Network, the Christian-oriented, full-service satellite radio network based in Dallas, Texas. Salem owns and operates 95 radio stations, with 60 stations in the nation's top 25 markets and 29 in the top 10.[14]

10.7

Salem Radio Network is one of the more intentionally biased, full-service, satellite radio networks on the air today, catering specifically to a conservative, Christian audience.

Salem Radio Network

Free Talk Live, a radio call-in show that caters to the sometimes left-leaning, sometimes right-leaning Libertarians (depending on individuals' view on property rights) aired its premier broadcast in November 2002. It currently airs seven days a week on 109 radio stations and four television stations across the United States, as well as through live and archive program streaming on the Web.[15] In 2004, to counter the conservative dominance of talk radio and to capture their own audience share, entrepreneurial brothers Stephen and Mark Green launched Air America Radio, home to such liberal hosts as Marc Maron, Al Franken (now U.S. Senator for Minnesota) and Randi Rhodes. Unfortunately, despite initial success that sustained the station for six years and led it to be carried by approximately 100 outlets across the country, Air America declared bankruptcy in January 2010 and announced its closure.[16]

With more than 1,300 stations nationwide, Clear Channel, the largest corporate owner of radio stations in the United States and the world's leading radio network, at first featured a somewhat politically balanced stable of both conservative and liberal commentators and talk-radio hosts. As the company struggled with cash flow and creditors, however, it transitioned to more conservative programming. Notably, in March 2010, Clear Channel fired popular liberal talk-show host Al Roney and replaced him with the syndicated conservative talk-show host Glenn Beck. Beck has been both criticized and lauded for his polarizing views, but he has also become popular and well known as a result. In deciding to swap Roney for Beck, Clear Channel demonstrated that, at least in the talk-radio business, conservative programs and commentators sell while liberal commentators struggle to attract audiences. During the 2012 presidential election, Clear Channel took advantage of the *Citizens United* decision by the Supreme Court to use its radio stations and billboard signs division to try to influence voters in support of extreme conservative political positions. The reasons for this disparity are a matter of heated debate in the blogosphere. What *is* apparent is that rather than be drawn to broadcast talk radio, liberal audiences either tend more toward programs on National Public Radio or seek out what they need from the Internet radio versions of CNN and MSNBC.

THE ECONOMICS OF MEDIA BIAS

Noam Chomsky believes that media are biased mainly because of economics. He considers corporate ownership of the mainstream media and the use of advertising to fund media as the root of media bias.[17] In 1987, the economics of media bias played out in public in the form of talk radio, which flourished when the FCC repealed the Fairness Doctrine. This doctrine, which is also known as the *equal time law*, required radio stations to provide free airtime for all opposing views to assure that all sides of important issues had a fair chance of being heard on the broadcast airwaves, regardless of position or economic resources. However, problems emerged when fringe groups and individuals began demanding equal time to present views that mainstream America found extreme or that promoted violence or aberrant sexual behavior (see Chapter 11).

The notion of equal time also ran contrary to the advertiser-supported, economic foundations of the broadcasting system in the United States. That is, because broadcasting revenue depends so heavily on advertising sales, the economics of media bias means that the advertisers sometimes play a crucial role in shaping the media message. This relationship, of course, puts editors and reporters in direct conflict with those who sponsor them financially and those who control the flow of revenue. The economics of media bias is such that the demands of advertising sales can sometimes play a disproportionately influential role in shaping the message that is sent out. Such economic pressures of retaining advertising revenue can at times put editors and reporters in direct conflict with the realities of keeping sponsors happy and ad revenues flowing. (Experience how one newspaper managing editor handled such conflict in one of the "Day in the Life" videos in Chapter 16.)

Corporate Control of the Media Message

Media balance often depends on the degree of independence a particular news operation has from the influence of its corporate owners and management. Does corporate ownership equate to corporate control of media message? There is a tendency for news operations to reflect the views of their owners, especially in editorials and when covering political stories. Certainly Rupert Murdoch's ownership of Fox News Network and *The Wall Street Journal* makes these outlets' conservative tilt effective stages for Murdoch's own conservative views. Nevertheless, Murdoch's stated mission for his network is to enhance profit rather than to promote a political agenda. Does Disney Corporation's ownership of ABC have any real impact on ABC News reporting?

A Harvard University study authored by Sendhil Mullainathan and Andrei Shleifer and published in *American Economic Review* demonstrated a positive link between media content that panders to audience-shared beliefs and the maximizing of advertising revenue-based profits.[18] In other words, Fox News's conservative angle is well rewarded by audience members' response to Fox advertisers. From a purely economic perspective, Fox News Network's clear and intentional conservative media bias makes very good business sense.

Federal Control of the Media Message

Media corporations are not the only sources of management-based media bias. The federal government also influences the bias of broadcast media networks that receive federal tax dollars as a portion—albeit a small portion—of their operating and program budgets. In 1968, Congress established the Public Broadcasting Service (PBS), whose initial mandate was to be the United States' noncommercial educational broadcasting service modeled after the BBC in the United Kingdom. The same act of Congress also established a quasi-governmental agency, the Corporation for Public Broadcasting (CPB), to serve as the federal government's conduit for passing taxpayer funding into the public broadcasting system through station and programming grants. At their inception, PBS and the National Public Radio Service (NPR—PBS's sister radio network) were modeled after the BBC with one difference: Because the British taxpayer funds the BBC, British law prohibits the U.K. government from attempting to influence its content.

As a result of this separation of powers, the BBC World Service—both television and radio—has a long tradition of "fair and balanced" reporting. NPR and PBS, by comparison, have never been able to maintain a similar complete independence from government influence. While CPB denies having a partisan agenda, the CPB board members are all political appointees. The president of the United States appoints each member, who, after confirmation by the Senate, serves a six-year term. The CPB's control over a portion of the operating budgets of PBS and NPR puts the government in a position to attempt to direct program content. In reality, achieving influence over programming and editorial decisions has proven difficult, in large part because more than 80 percent of public broadcasting's funding comes from corporate underwriting, member donations and academic institutions. These members and donors continue to be successful for the most part in protecting a long-enjoyed programming independence from government oversight.[19]

BIAS IN FILMS, TELEVISION AND ONLINE

American private enterprise and innovation have built American media dominance and success around the world. From Hollywood films, to popular network dramas and sitcoms, to the 24/7 TV news invented by CNN, the world is bombarded with an explosion of U.S.-originated media. The dominance of American media is so profound that cultures from the Middle East to Western Europe often see themselves as under siege from U.S. social forces. Although non-U.S. media counterforces have arisen, they often seem to emulate American media style rather than fight it. For example, the largest Arabic-speaking media network in the world, Al Jazeera, does not try to hide the fact that its model is CNN, even though its message is often strongly anti-American. Al Jazeera claims that it is simply speaking to the views of its audience, as does CNN. As mass media, American television and film reach far greater audiences than all other mass media vehicles combined. Therefore, while recognizing that similar examples abound in radio, print media and the World Wide Web, the following examples of embedded biases focus on television and film content.

Much of the media content we consume—documentaries, investigative reports, reality shows, dramas and comedies—presents skewed messages and political agendas. Often the underlying agendas of the program producers are obvious. At other times, the slanted messages can be deceivingly subtle. Following

10.8

Broadcast around the globe, the FIFA World Cup 2010 and media coverage brought together an international community of viewers (as seen here in a pub in Munich, Germany).

dpa picture alliance archive/ Alamy Stock Photo

are discussions of examples from recent documentaries, prime-time dramas and news-based comedies that contain embedded biases. Depending on your own beliefs, the impact of the clear biases presented in these examples can be either positive or negative. What is undeniable is that all of them have had a significant influence on audiences and the public agenda.

The Liberal Rebel

There are no doubts or subtleties about the liberal position of the Academy award-winning film-maker Michael Moore. From his investigation of General Motors in *Roger & Me* (1989); to his anti-gun exposé in *Bowling for Columbine* (2002); to his confrontational anti-George W. Bush stance in

Fahrenheit 9/11 (2004); to his critiques of the money-making machine of the American health care system in *Sicko* (2007); to his look at college student's voting and political activism during the 2004 election in *Slacker Uprising* (2008); to his scathing documentary about wall Street and current economic policies in the United States in *Capitalism: A Love Story (2009)*, Moore's successful documentaries have served as blatant platforms for his liberal positions and political beliefs. Critics on both sides of the political fence consider Moore's filmmaking style as self-aggrandizing and his approach to documentary storytelling as manipulative. Like him or not, Moore has consistently and effectively helped to keep hot-button issues such as the controversial Iraq War, the struggle of blue-collar workers in declining industries, the state of health care in United States and the failures of the federal government to effectively regulate the financial industry at the top of the public agenda and in the forefront of

10.9

Moviestore collection Ltd/Alamy Stock Photo

Media pundits love to criticize Moore's slanted messages but admit that he has spurred productive discourse among partisan groups. One can certainly suggest that Moore is successful in garnering considerable media attention for the issues he takes on *because* of his clear biases, not *in spite* of them.

10.10

Al Gore.

Allstar Picture Library/Alamy Stock Photo

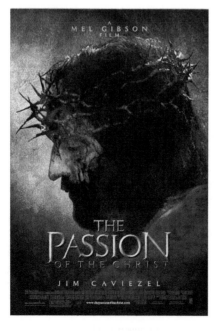

10.11

Movie poster of *The Passion of the Christ*.

Moviestore collection Ltd/ Alamy Stock Photo

public debate. Media pundits love to criticize Moore's slanted messages but admit that he has spurred productive discourse among partisan groups. One can certainly suggest that Moore is successful in garnering considerable media attention for the issues he takes on *because* of his clear biases, not *in spite* of them.

The Global Evangelist

Al Gore, a former U.S. senator from Tennessee and U.S. vice president as well as a Nobel Prize Winner, is also a powerful, world-respected voice on global warming and ecological issues. His Oscar-winning film *An Inconvenient Truth* (2006) is one of the most influential documentaries in recent years. Regardless of his bold topic partiality, and what some claim to be clear bias regarding the reality and causes of global warming, the entire range of the political spectrum has embraced his message. Since it first aired at the Sundance Film Festival in 2006, *An Inconvenient Truth* has reinvigorated global discussions about how to handle the environmental crisis. In the fall of 2009, Gore produced *Our Choice: A Plan to Solve the Climate Crisis*, the sequel to the film. Recognizing that "laying out the facts" would not be enough to address the climate issues that continue to plague the planet, he also wrote a book and developed a new set of slide shows that decidedly target a very specific audience—the religious and the righteous. According to Suzanne Goldberg, U.S. environmental correspondent for *The Guardian*, Gore's book is an "appeal to those who believe there is a moral or religious duty to protect the planet."[20]

The Missionary Filmmaker

Mel Gibson's award-winning film *The Passion of the Christ* (2004) is one of the most controversial feature films in the last decade—largely due to allegations that the movie is highly anti-Semitic and gratuitously violent. In an interview with Diane Sawyer in the year the film was released, Gibson claimed that he had produced and directed a movie that was faithful to the narratives depicted in the four Gospels and asserted that anyone who might object to the film was doing so because "They have a problem with the four Gospels."[21] In making this statement, Gibson absolved himself of any form of intentional bias, claiming also that anti-Semitism was "against the tenets of his faith."[22]

Members of the Anti-Defamation League found otherwise: "At every single opportunity," they said,

"Mr. Gibson's film reinforce[d] the notion that the Jewish authorities and the Jewish mob [were] the ones ultimately responsible for the Crucifixion."[23] Biblical scholar and Rutgers University Professor Emeritus of Religion M. H. Smith asserted that Gibson did not even honor the *contradictions* present in the Gospels, but instead "concocted a drama out of arbitrarily selected details from various texts."[24] For many, the root cause for the criticisms against *Passion* was less its depiction of violence—however brutal and gratuitous it was—but more its strongly anti-Semitic message and lack of historical accuracy. The controversy surrounding the film filled the news media, from prime-time newscasts to talk radio, for weeks when the film was first released—which contributed greatly to the film's financial success. Proof of the old adage "Any publicity is good publicity" is the fact that criticism of unbalanced messages in entertainment media appears to have a positive impact on audience demand and thus financial success.

The Civics Lesson

For five years starting in 1999, NBC writer Aaron Sorkin brought U.S. television viewers into the world of a fictitious Democratic president and his West Wing staff, as they battled a fictitious Republican Congress to solve challenges facing present-day America. *The West Wing* series, which was a prime-time television hit from 1999 through 2006, used drama to deliver a weekly civics lesson on American government. It appealed to a broad audience—both liberal and conservative, Democrat and Republican—precisely because it was solidly produced entertainment. Through effective storytelling and compelling characters, the series depicted a liberal and effective Democratic presidency to highlight what the series' creators viewed as the failings of the then-Republican administration. Martin Sheen's character, President Jed Bartlet, was such a captivatingly human, honest and effectual president that television polls showed a substantial segment of the public wished the United States had a president "just like him." His character influenced the public view of both the actual president at the time, George W. Bush, and future presidential candidates.

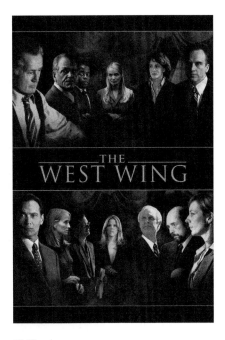

10.12

The television show *The West Wing* impacted how we view the presidency.

Photo 12/Alamy Stock Photo

As television drama and as entertainment, *The West Wing* has had an impact on how Americans view the presidency. Here we have an example of how dramatic entertainment programming can deliver effective, biased, political messages to very large audiences at home and abroad. Due to its international syndication, worldwide audiences are now able to see *The West Wing* series as a model of how the U.S. government should work.

The Newsman-Comic

The popular series *The Daily Show with Jon Stewart* on the Comedy Central Network uses comedy and parody to deliver a liberal perspective on top stories. Stewart's parody of a trustworthy network news anchor is so entertaining and successful that, according to the Pew Center for the People & the Press, 21 percent of television viewers younger than age 29 cite *The Daily Show* as one of their primary sources of news.[25] In addition, the show has become a must-appear-on venue for national politicians and presidential hopefuls. Jon Stewart, meanwhile, has emerged as a highly sought-after political pundit and media critic in his own right, appearing on CNN and in documentaries about the role of American media in the political process. Using humor, Stewart skillfully satirizes conservatives and their positions while offering liberal-leaning viewers confirmation that the Democrats, while sometimes as laughable as the Republicans, are on the right track.

10.13

The Daily Show.

*Brian Cahn/ZUMA/
Newscom*

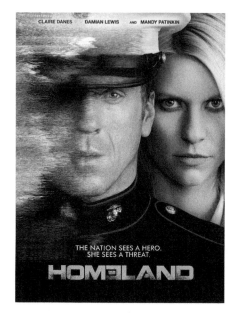

10.14

Homeland offers a sophisticated look at both sides
of major political, cultural and religious conflicts.

AF Archive/Alamy Stock Photo

The Protector

In 2011, Showtime network launched its dramatic thriller *Homeland*, which
quickly won critical acclaim and major awards recognition. *Homeland*,
based on the popular Israeli TV series *Hatufum*, follows the story of a troubled female CIA officer. After she is discredited due to her personal struggle with manic-depressive disorder, the officer discovers that a former U.S.
Marine sergeant, captured by Islamic extremists during the Iraq War and
held for eight years before returning home as a national hero, was actually recruited by his captors and is in fact now a terrorist himself. Moreover, he has been elected to Congress and is under consideration as a
vice presidential candidate. *Homeland* was changed significantly from the
Israeli version that inspired its production; the storyline and characters are
strongly pro-American, and in the view of some critics, highly biased against
Islam.

Fox Network's popular series *24*, whose 192 episodes ran for eight consecutive seasons in worldwide syndication, drew similar anti-Muslim and anti-Islam
criticism. But where *24*'s biases were clearer, the bias of *Homeland* is far more
subtle and may be in the eyes of the beholder. The producers of *Homeland*
went the distance to present both sides of what has become the major political,
cultural and religious conflict of the early 21st century. While certainly pro-
American in that the terrorist is exposed in the end and the CIA operatives protect America, the bias of *Homeland* may be more of a bias toward presenting
the reality of our times.

Bias in Blogs

One of the growing online venues for publishing intentionally biased views and opinions is the blogosphere—the interconnected community of blogs. Blogs allow individuals to share their views, beliefs and opinions with readers; readers, in turn, are encouraged to post their own responses to these blog posts, thereby creating wide-ranging virtual dialogues and debates on a wealth of topics from the hopelessly mundane to the highly controversial. The use of blogs as platforms for individual opinion rather than as examples of balanced journalism is precisely what makes blogs so effective—as well as inherently biased. Whatever your interests; whatever your views on local, national and world events; whichever sports or celebrity gossip and entertainment news is of interest to you, large groups of like-minded people in cyberspace are awaiting your opinion. With a little creativity and decent writing, blogging can attract amazingly large audiences.[26]

Blogs are sometimes sponsored by mainstream media organizations but are most often independent. Blogging began in 1994 as a form of online journaling; essentially, bloggers posted running accounts of their lives and interests (see Chapter 7). These early online journals quickly evolved into a rapidly growing segment of the World Wide Web. By 1999, blogs had become a powerful and influential cyberspace stage for both professional and citizen journalists (see Chapter 13). These bloggers included politicians, religious groups, artists, economists, scientists, authors, environmental activists and filmmakers—a seemingly endless list of independent voices. The influence of blogs grew so much that by the 2004 presidential election cycle, blogs had changed the landscape of the political and election process. Some argue that blogs have altered the course of presidential elections and campaign fundraising forever. During the 2008 presidential race, blogs converged with mainstream media to such an extent that the blogosphere, along with such social networking sites as Facebook and Twitter, became a major portal through which America experienced a rebirth of participatory democracy. This trend continued through the 2012 presidential campaign, which saw social networking services fully integrated into both Republican and Democrat candidates' election strategies as well as the mainstream media coverage.

Political bloggers are usually upfront about their biases. They frequently see themselves as a counterforce to mainstream media, which they often view as unreliable and even dishonest by hiding its bias. This counterforce leads to some interesting mixtures of backgrounds and viewpoints. Consider British-born Andrew Sullivan, one of the more popular and successful conservative political bloggers. Sullivan started his popular blog, *The Daily Dish*, in 2006.[27] In its first year, it reported more than 40 million page views; since then it has served as Sullivan's voice and presence in cyberspace. Originally a writer for *Time* magazine and *The New Republic*, Sullivan is a frequent conservative guest commentator on liberal-leaning talk shows. Like all blogs, *The Daily Dish* is slanted to the individual views and beliefs of the blogger. Sullivan, a self-described gay Catholic conservative who is pro same-sex marriage, anti-abortion and against the war on drugs, is famous for taking on controversial topics with a mixture of conservative and libertarian bias. He has loudly criticized conservative Christian celebrities such as Mel Gibson, and in 2008, he endorsed both Libertarian presidential candidate Ron Paul and Democratic presidential candidate Barack Obama. During the 2012 presidential campaign, many leading bloggers became regular commentators on mainstream television news networks, especially Fox News and MSNBC, as well as frequent guests on popular news commentary programs like Jon Stewart's *The Daily Show* on Comedy Central and Bill Maher's *Real Time with Bill Maher* on HBO. One effect of this acceptance of leading political bloggers as cable news network commentators is the recognition by the networks, and by the viewing public, that political blogs have become a significant and irreversible force in influencing American politics.

Bloggers like Sullivan, for example, are not trying to be balanced journalists. Opinionated commentary has a long tradition as an important aspect of the media. Just look through the editorial section of any major newspaper in the country. Throughout the history of media and journalism, reporting has coexisted side-by-side with editorial commentary. The problem arises when reporting and editorializing—expressing an opinion as if it were objective fact or an opinion about an otherwise objective account—become intertwined, making it difficult for media consumers to distinguish between the two. In today's rich media environment, with so many channels, so many voices and now the convergence of leading blogs with mainstream news reporting, much perceived media bias is the result of this comingling of reporting and opinion. Moreover, the dominance of the 24/7 news cycle contributes to making it even more difficult to sort out news from opinion.

In their 2010 *Citizens United v. Federal Election Commission* ruling, the Supreme Court attempted to address concerns by conservative political factions who alleged that that there is something wrong with the way elections are funded in the United States. *Citizens United* struck down longstanding campaign spending limits on corporations, ruling such limitations were intrusions on free speech. The majority opinion stated that the First Amendment rights of corporations may not be abridged simply because they are corporations, and not individuals. Yet while corporations may be deemed to have some of the legal rights of people, the court has never held that corporations have any of the political rights of citizens. The core of the issue has been the use of dark money—contributions to political campaigns from undisclosed hidden sources—to unduly influence American elections.

The Washington Post reported that through the end of January 2016, 680 corporations gave nearly $68 million to "super PACs" in this election cycle, which amounts to 12 percent of the $549 million raised by such groups. The figure does not include undocumented amounts of "dark money" contributions to other groups that are not disclosed by the donor or recipient.[28]

ARE MAINSTREAM MEDIA LIBERALLY BIASED?

A 2005 national study conducted by the Gannett First Amendment Center and published in the *American Journalism Review* found that nearly two-thirds of those surveyed rejected the idea that "the news media try to report the news without bias." Further, two-thirds of respondents agreed that "falsifying or making up stories in the American news media is a widespread problem." As in similar prior studies, the direction of the perceived bias of the study's respondents was split between conservative and liberal, but with a leaning toward perceived liberal bias.[29] Does this mean that the mainstream media tilts liberal, or does it mean that conservative voices are just more vocal in making such claims?

10.15

2005 Gannett First Amendment Center Media Bias Study.

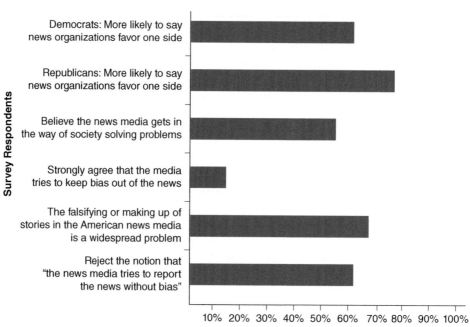

2005 Gannett First Amendment Center Media Bias Study

In its 2005 survey *Public More Critical of Press—But Goodwill Persists*, The Pew Research Center for the People & the Press found that despite continued perceptions that the media is biased on both sides of the political spectrum, most Americans reported that they like mainstream news outlets. The Pew study found that the majority of Americans view their local print and TV news media favorably (80 percent) and only slightly fewer people view network and cable news programs favorably (75 percent). Of course, these favorable numbers are directed toward outlets that appear to share survey participants' established views and reverse to unfavorable (21 percent and 25 percent respectively) for news outlets that they perceive do not share their political and social biases.[30]

Journalists have a responsibility to challenge the political agendas of government officials and the actions of big business. At the same time, reporters rely heavily on government agencies and press contacts for the raw material from which they build their news stories. As a consequence, the media are at once suspicious of and yet work with the government. This situation often causes media stories to seem imbalanced. As the experiences of this author attest, these factors combined make the media *appear* liberally inclined much of the time. Yet, because of the many voices and views that play such integral roles in the U.S. mainstream media, it makes sense to assume that the media coverage should end up balanced as a result. But does it? Your own experience with the media and what you learn from reading this text should help you determine that for yourself.

> Yet, because of the many voices and views that play such integral roles in the U.S. mainstream media, it makes sense to assume that the media coverage should end up balanced as a result. But does it?

Drawing the Line Between Fact and Opinion

Being an informed and critical media consumer in the United States today is like being a well-informed voter—and the U.S. record on both fronts is discouraging. It takes work to carve out the truth from the morass of nicely packaged half-truths and massaged facts that we routinely encounter in today's mass media. Because most media consumers want strong, attractive and entertaining media personalities to confirm their views of the truth, vocal and entertaining commentators seem to overpopulate the news media.

The vast audience of radio and television broadcast news expects both an array of opinion and entertainment. Indeed, this delicate mixture is one of the things that makes news programs entertaining and helps to attract and hold viewers and listeners. Because of audience demand, the media deliver a constant stream of "experts" who are paid to captivate and demonstrate the core of their story—what they claim is their real "truth." But whose truth is it?

In print media, the line between news reporting and editorial opinion is usually easy to identify. For news, we turn to the news section; for opinions and editorial views, we read the op-ed page. Traditionally, most major newspapers in the United States have established their political voices, and thereby their biases, by endorsing candidates for local, state and national offices. By clearly identifying editorial content, print media have a way to share their editorial views with their readers. When newspapers and news magazines tackle major investigative stories, they usually approach their reporting by clearly distinguishing the "facts" and determining the origins and sources of those facts.

10.16

Example of social and political satire from *The Onion*, a satirical newspaper founded at the University of Wisconsin–Madison in 1988. *The Onion* has grown in audience and stature into a national publication and popular Website.

NetPhotos/Alamy Stock Photo

Humor and satire can facilitate the process of sorting out facts and truth. Print media have a long tradition of using satire to cut through the blaring voices with their competing perspectives, from political cartoons to satirical essays and editorials. Many high school- and college-aged people today gravitate away from the mainstream news media and form their views on critical issues using satirical publications such as *The Onion*.

The Onion began in 1988 as a student newspaper at the University of Wisconsin–Madison and has grown into a national phenomenon. It operates today as a national satirical news organization with a national print circulation of over 400,000 and a popular Website (launched in 1996) with an estimated 7.5 million visitors each month. *The Onion* also produces and syndicates prepackaged satirical radio and video news segments through its "Onion News Network"—itself an ongoing satire of mainstream and cable broadcast news. *Onion* editorial staff members and regular contributors are frequent guests on usually liberal-leaning radio and television talk shows. The *Onion* has also published its satirical articles via partnerships with numerous mainstream newspapers, both in the United States and Canada, but retains total editorial and creative control over its material.

In broadcast media, making the distinction between news reports and editorials has become far more difficult because the line between reporting and editorial commentary is often far less clear-cut. Sometimes this line is intentionally blurred to support a broadcast network's political and social biases. Consider *The Colbert Report*, a spin-off of Jon Stewart's *The Daily Show. The Colbert Report* is actually a satirical spoof of the conservative show *The O'Reilly Factor* on Fox News, but because the style of "reporting" is so akin to that of a true news program, the boundaries between reality and farce are not always distinct. While *The Daily Show* does cover important news stories, Stewart is the first to argue that his program is entertainment and not news, even though viewers use it to learn about important issues and controversies.

No big media story escapes editorializing on television, radio and the Web. The major networks and the cable/satellite news channels often link hot stories with comments and analysis from so-called experts, who are actually paid consultants for the network. For example, retired U.S. Army Four-Star General Barry McCaffrey has often appeared as a paid expert on NBC even though he maintains close ties to both the Pentagon and major military contractors. General McCaffrey has been criticized for his advocacy for continuing the war in Iraq and expanding the war in Afghanistan, even though he was an early critic of the U.S. war policies under former President George W. Bush. Media critics, such as *Columbia Journalism Review*'s Charles Kaiser, have argued that McCaffrey's

10.17

The abundance of 24/7 news broadcasts have created the need to fill airtime with analysis and commentary; media consumers need to carefully evaluate the editorializing of news stories.

J.R. Bale/Alamy Stock Photo

commentaries are biased because of his financial interests insofar as his consulting services are related to military equipment sales. Kaiser claims that NBC News executives, aware of such interests, act irresponsibly by using McCaffrey as an expert commentator. NBC has countered this argument by noting that, despite the seeming conflicts of interest, the general performs his role as a highly knowledgeable military expert appropriately.[31] News organizations must learn to manage the perception of bias that might come across when they rely on the expertise of paid analysts: Some will come with the appearance of bias, or actual bias, and controlling that image has been the primary challenge for the broadcast media.

The rapid increase in the amount of commentary and editorializing stems from the 24/7 news culture. With so many hours of airtime to fill seven days a week, the news networks are forced to rely on commentators to load these hours by analyzing the importance and implications of each story. Straight reporting on a story could never fill all those hours, thus making it all the more important for media consumers to remain vigilant and cognizant of when straight reporting slips over the line into editorial commentary. The danger is that the analysis and commentary often morph into the substance of the story. Whether with stories about politicians or celebrities, crime victims or scandalous affairs, the beast of the 24/7 news cycle must be continually fed, even when there is no new aspect of the story to report.

CONCLUSION: WHAT IS THE IMPACT OF BIAS IN AMERICAN MEDIA?

All media can be viewed as biased in some way, and some media outlets deliberately gravitate in a specific direction so as to attract and control market share. As such, we, the audience, in many ways, drive media content and media bias. Clearly slanted media succeed because there are large segments of the audience who want slanted content, who seek it out and who remain loyal consumers of those outlets expressing positions with which they agree. Given that advertising supports the vast majority of U.S. media—including, for all practical purposes, public broadcasting—the owners and managers of media organizations are highly motivated to give their audiences exactly what they want. Since audience demand and audience demographics drive the content, the market creates and supports bias in the media.

The good news is that this system works quite well, with liberal voices countering and balancing conservative voices, and vice versa. Thus, this ongoing balancing of voices and views causes the American media overall to be generally balanced. For every conservative media voice out there, an equally strong liberal voice strives to win consumers' hearts and minds. So who is responsible for determining the facts and finding the truth? Who is responsible, in the end, for balance in the media? We are—all of us. The responsibility for creating a balance of voices lies not just with the media creators, but with media consumers. The rapid evolution of media technologies through the late 20th century and now in the dawning years of the 21st century has brought an abundance of media outlets. Just as we deliberately select our preferred media delivery channels—television, radio, print, Web, podcasts—for our individual needs, so we must take responsibility for becoming smart media consumers. Skilled and critical media consumers consider many voices and multiple sources on important issues, and form independent conclusions as to what is real, what is factual, what is the truth.

> The responsibility for creating a balance of voices lies not just with the media creators, but with media consumers.

As the examples in this chapter aim to demonstrate, some media bias is intentional, but not all media bias is bad. Both the public and politicians use the term "media bias" in a critical sense. In reality, media bias is not the enemy of truth; rather, it is a function of how we gather truth from the sea of information available to us every day. As our media world continues to evolve, it is important for media consumers to recognize bias and understand its dynamics. Moreover, it is up to each of us to take responsibility for extracting facts and truths for ourselves and to recognize the role that our own views and our own biases play in forming our worldview.

CHAPTER SUMMARY	KEY TERMS
The Building Blocks of Bias Introduces the issue of bias in the media and explains the important differences between and implications of intentional and unintentional media bias. **Visual Media** **Catherine Crier on Media Bias** A former state Supreme Court judge, author and TV host discusses media bias. 1. In what ways does former judge Catherine Crier's perspective on media bias change your own understanding of how bias can mislead audiences? 2. Based upon your viewing of this video segment, which are the most and least biased news outlets that you commonly encounter? Describe why you have chosen each as an example on the media bias continuum.	media bias theory of hostile media effect manufacturing consent public agenda
Types of Media Bias Describes and illustrates the principle types of media bias. **Visual Media** **Perspectives on Media Bias** Multiple perspectives on bias in the media from top personalities in the field. 1. How do economic factors and competition for audience drive the level of bias found in cable television news? 2. What criteria can be used to differentiate between intentionally biased news media "entertainers" and professional journalists who are striving to make their reporting as unbiased as possible?	partisan bias propaganda bias unwitting bias bias by selection social judgment theory *Citizens United*
The Economics of Media Bias Explores the close relationship between media bias and the economics of running successful news organizations, including how the economics of attracting and holding audience share drives the level of news bias in the United States.	Noam Chomsky Fairness Doctrine Public Broadcasting Service (PBS) Corporation for Public Broadcasting (CPB)
Bias in Films, Television and Online Compares and contrasts media bias as commonly found in movies, on television and on the Web.	political bloggers editorializing
Are the Mainstream Media Liberally Biased? Presents a realistic look at the often-heard criticism and claim that the American media have a liberal bias.	op-ed page

NOTES

1. Quote from 2012 Republican presidential candidate Mitt Romney recorded during a fundraising event and first posted on YouTube.
2. Levin, M. (2005). *Men in black: How the Supreme Court is destroying America*. Regnery.
3. Ibid. Author's summary of Levin's commentary.
4. Groseclose, T., & Milyo, J. (2004, December). *A measure of media bias*. Retrieved from www.sscnet. ucla.edu/polisci/faculty/groseclose/Media.Bias.8.htm

5 *Frontline: News wars*. Part II. (2007). PBS.

6 Kim, M. (2012). *Partisans and controversial news online: Comparing perceptions of bias and credibility in news from blogs versus mainstream media*. Ph.D., University of Maryland.

7 Kris, E. (1948). The evasion of propaganda: How prejudiced people respond to anti-prejudice propaganda. *Psychoanalytic Quarterly, 17*.

8 Chomsky, N. (2002). *Distorted morality: A 55-minute talk by Noam Chomsky*. Harvard University. Video recording by N. Chomsky & Epitaph/Plug Music.

9 Baker, P. (2007, September 12). 9/11 linked to Iraq, in politics if not in fact. *The Washington Post*.

10 Abstracted from Street, J. (2010). *Mass media, politics and democracy* (2nd ed.). Palgrave McMillan.

11 CNN founder Ted Turner, during an interview for the documentary special, Ellerbee, L. (2004). *Feeding the beast: The 24-hour news revolution*. Producer/commentator.

12 Baldwin, J. R., Perry, S. D., & Moffit, M. A. (2004). *Communication theories for everyday life*. Pearson.

13 Pew Center for the People & the Press. (2009, September). *Press accuracy ratings hit two decades low: Public evaluations of the news media: 1985–2009*; Pew Center for the People & the Press. (2009, August). *Internet news audience highly critical of news organizations: Views of press values and performance: 1985–2007*; Groseclose, T., & Milyo, J. (2004, December). *A measure of media bias*. Retrieved from www.sscnet.ucla.edu/polisci/faculty/groseclose/Media.Bias.8.htm; Media Research Center. (2005). *Media bias 101: What journalists really think—and what the public thinks about the media*. Retrieved from www.mediaresearch.org/static/biasbasics/MediaBias101.aspx; Media Research Center. (2010). *Exhibit 2–21: Trust and satisfaction with the national media*. Retrieved from www.mediaresearch.org/static/biasbasics/Exhibit221TrustandSatisfactionwiththeNationalMedia.aspx

14 (2017). *Salem Communications*. Retrieved from www.salem.cc/Overview.aspx

15 (2017). *Free Talk Live*. Retrieved from www.freetalklive.com/

16 Nessen, S. (2010, January 21). *Air America Radio closes, will file for bankruptcy*. Retrieved from www.wnyc.org/news/articles/148722

17 Noam Chomsky's theory on economics of media bias is abstracted from Harman, E. S., & Chomsky, N. (2002). *Manufacturing consent: The political economy of the mass media*. Pantheon.

18 Mullainathan, S., & Shleifer, A. (2005). The market for news. *American Economic Review, 75*(6), 1071–1082.

19 Media Matters for American. (2005, July 27). *CPB chairman Tomlinson failed to refute NY Times' "false" charges against him*. Retrieved from http://mediamatters.org/research/200507270004; www.npr.org/templates/story/story.php?storyId=4724317; www.yuricareport.com/Media/BattleForControlOfThePress.html

20 Goldenberg, S. (2009, November 2). Al Gore's *Inconvenient Truth* sequel stresses spiritual argument on climate. Retrieved from www.guardian.co.uk/world/2009/nov/02/al-gore-our-choice-environment-climate

21 Smith, M. H. (2004). *Gibson Agonistes: Anatomy of a neo-Manichean vision of Jesus*. Retrieved from http://virtualreligion.net/forum/passion.html

22 Ibid.

23 (2004). ADL and Mel Gibson's "The Passion of the Christ." *Frequently asked questions*. Retrieved from www.adl.org/interfaith/gibson_qa.asp

24 Ibid.

25 Pew Center for the People & the Press. (2007, April 15). *Public knowledge of current affairs little changed by news and information revolutions: What Americans know: 1989–2007*.

26 *Newsweek*. (2008, February 18).

27 (2015). *The Daily Dish*. Retrieved from http://dish.andrewsullivan.theatlantic.com/

28 Weintraub, E. L. (2016, March 30). Taking on citizens united. *New York Times*. Retrieved from www.nytimes.com/2016/03/30/opinion/taking-n-citizens-united.html

29 Gannett First Amendment Center. (2005, September/August). *American Journalism Review*.

30 Pew Research Center for the People & the Press. (2005, June 26). *Public more critical of press—but goodwill persists*.

31 The flog of war. (2008, December 12). *NPR: On the Media*. Retrieved from www.onthemedia.org/transcripts/2008/12/12/04

11
Mass Media Law and Ethics

trekandshoot/Shutterstock.com

CHAPTER OUTLINE

Brief History of Mass Media Law
Defamation: Libel and Slander
Media and Privacy

Mass Media Law and National Security
Historical Roots of Copyright Law

Privacy in Public Places The widespread use of security monitoring technology in public places is challenging the protection of individual privacy.

Lawrence Lessig on Copyright History Stanford University Law Professor Lawrence Lessig explores the challenges of U.S. copyright law.

Copyright Basics An animated quick tutorial on how copyright works.

Confidentiality in Newsgathering
Pornography: Free Expression of Obscenity?
Ethics and Mass Media

Creative Commons Introduction to the Creative Commons alternative to traditional copyright law.

The Ethical Challenges of a Converged World
Conclusion: Are We Legally and Ethically
Responsible?

Journalistic Ethics Former White House correspondent Lee Thornton on journalistic ethics and the Jayson Blair case.

LEARNING OBJECTIVES

1. Analyze the First Amendment's role in the evolution of American mass media law and its impact on governmental attempts at media censorship.
2. Explain the media's legal responsibilities regarding defamation.
3. Compare and contrast individual privacy rights and the freedom of the press.
4. Illustrate the ways in which the Freedom of Information Act (FOIA) helps the media to monitor and report on the actions of government.
5. Outline the historical roots of copyright law as well as the new alternatives to the traditional copyright process.
6. Describe the challenges of using confidential sources.
7. Evaluate the standards of "public morality" used to distinguish free expression from pornography.
8. Assess the media's professional code of ethics and its application in today's world.
9. Outline the ethical challenges that the media, the government, and media consumers face in this age of media convergence.
10. Explain how the changing role of the public as media producers has impacted mass media ethics and media law.

THE *NEW ENGLAND*

Courant was the first American newspaper to establish itself as a successful business enterprise and the first to use a staff of reporters, although they were unpaid volunteers. The *Courant's* founder and publisher was James Franklin, Benjamin Franklin's older brother. Early on, James Franklin realized that the press could serve as a powerful voice for the people. At the time, around 1722, New England was suffering from a scourge of pirates who were regularly attacking ships sailing to and from England, looting the cargos

and often killing the crews. This activity made for bad business in the British colonies. Franklin believed colonial authorities were not taking the problem seriously—a controversial claim. Realizing that controversy was good for selling newspapers, he began to publish articles that attacked the leaders of the British colonial government. In these articles, Franklin criticized the lack of official action and portrayed the leaders as ineffectual, caring more about fashion and dinner parties than New England's economic well-being.

Franklin also refused to pay the required licensing taxes for his newspaper.

The Massachusetts General Court declared James Franklin a scofflaw and threw him in jail for publishing libelous and seditious statements about the British Crown and its colonial government. Undaunted by his imprisonment, Franklin instructed his younger brother Benjamin to continue using the *Courant* to attack British authorities. A few weeks later, James Franklin was released from jail, but only after agreeing to apologize to the Court and the colonial governor. Yet, in his next series of articles, he retracted his apology, chastising the English government for its indifference to the welfare of the colonies. By 1723, Franklin was regularly publishing editorials that criticized the conduct and aptitude of the Crown-appointed governor of colonial Massachusetts.[1]

In response to Franklin's ongoing provocation, the General Court acted again, charging Franklin with disrespecting the Crown officials' authority. It forbade Franklin from publishing the *New England Courant* or any other publication until he paid all taxes and submitted each edition of the paper for prior approval. Franklin refused to obey the Court's ruling. At one point, he published the entire text of the Magna Carta to remind the Court and the colonial governor of the rights of free men. Unfortunately, rather than eliciting sympathy from the Court through this historical rejoinder, Franklin's actions had the opposite effect. The Court ordered the sheriff of Boston to shut down the *Courant* and to escort its publisher back to jail. Luckily, Franklin's inside sources warned him of the arrest warrant in time for him to go into hiding. The *Courant* continued to publish under the direction of its new owner—James Franklin's more diplomatic younger brother, Benjamin Franklin. Eventually, Benjamin moved on to Philadelphia, where he used his publishing enterprises to help launch the American Revolution.

BRIEF HISTORY OF MASS MEDIA LAW

Media law, which regulates print, radio and television broadcasting as well as much of the content and platform of the Internet, in an attempt to ensure that its content is in the interest of the public, is rooted in the ongoing struggle between citizens' rights to free speech and the government's efforts at limiting such freedoms for the "greater good." The mass media's primary mission is to inform the public of the actions taken by the government and to act as venues for the people to express their opinions, concerns and even outrage about those actions. As James Franklin's story illustrates, when governments try to regulate information freedom, media producers must develop effective means of skirting those regulations.

The Printing Press Challenges Early Regulation

Gutenberg's printing press, invented in approximately 1450, and its subsequent rapid mass production and proliferation, made it very difficult for the British Crown to control and manipulate the media. In the pre-printing press world, it was relatively easy to hunt down the sources of anti-government writings and put them out of business. But the spread of the printing press ushered in an entirely new age that made it very difficult for the Crown's censors to do their jobs. In the face of this new technology, the British Parliament acknowledged that it was nearly impossible to control the ideas themselves. Instead, the government decided to control the medium responsible for spreading those ideas. This regulatory concept remains the basis of American mass media law today. Parliament essentially determined that to most effectively maintain a system of censorship, it would have to enact laws to control the mass media technology. In other words, if one can control the means of distribution of troublesome ideas, then one can effectively control the ideas themselves.

With this point in mind, in 1556 Parliament authorized the Stationers Guild to regulate and enforce licensing fees on printing presses and printed documents of all kinds—by force, if necessary. To print anything on a printing press in England, one had to pay a fee to the Guild. To obtain licenses from the Guild, printers had to post sizable bonds of money and title to their property, which assured their compliance with established rules of approved content. The Guild was also responsible for prohibiting the printing of any libelous or seditious content against the Crown or Parliament. Officials were empowered to arrest violators and drag them before a secret tribunal called the Star Chamber for prosecution and punishment, while confiscating their printing press and other property—ink, paper, shop and house.

Despite Parliament's attempt at controlling the technology and thus regulating the media, technology continued to march ceaselessly onward—in this case, in the form of smaller, more efficient and affordable printing presses. By the 1680s, these devices were widespread. Even today, the relationship between lawmakers and law enforcement and the media reporting on them is constantly affected by advancing media technologies. As media technology within a society evolves through innovation, legislatures in turn pass new laws aimed at balancing the media's increasing power and influence that result from such advancements. Even in democracies, government continually attempts to control and limit the influence of the media.

Benjamin Franklin and the Fourth Estate

England's extensive system of censorship and control of the publication of ideas worked well for decades, albeit at the cost of slowing down intellectual debate and scientific innovation. Eventually, members of Parliament found themselves being charged with violations of the censorship laws after printing pamphlets of their own speeches or political positions that differed from those of the King's. Not surprisingly then, in 1649, Parliament recognized the right of "certain individuals" to "initiate discussion on any subject" and ruled that members of Parliament, and their printers, could not be prosecuted for seditious statements. This ruling gave birth to the laws that would guarantee freedom of speech.[2] By the early 1700s, the British Crown and Parliament abolished the Stationers Guild's printing license—but not, however, in the American colonies. This disparity fueled dissent among the American people, and many began to voice their discontent. One of these dissenting voices belonged to Benjamin Franklin.

By the late 1720s, Franklin was publishing and distributing passionate arguments for the protection of free speech and a free press from his print shop in Philadelphia. Franklin asserted that these freedoms were the "God-given right of every man." He was one of the first of the group that we now refer to as America's Founding Fathers to write on the fundamental doctrines of freedom of speech and freedom of the press. Franklin held that these were not only the rights of every citizen, but also the *ethical* responsibility of every just and effective democratic government. These ideals would later lay the groundwork for what would become the Fourth Estate of America's democracy—the guaranteed role of the free press, enshrined in the U.S. Constitution's First Amendment. It is no surprise, then, how threats of censorship played a role in sparking the American Revolution.[3]

The First Amendment

With the birth of the United States of America, freedom of the press immediately blossomed. In the years following the Revolutionary War, pioneers launched nearly 500 independent newspapers. This number is extraordinary, considering how small the new nation was. Through the growing and free mass media, the United States waged a new battle of ideas: how to build a nation. The Articles of Confederation, under which the newly found country had operated following its initial independence, represented the first attempt at a national government. The Articles, however, made no mention of freedom of speech or freedom of the press.

11.1

Basic tenets of the U.S. Constitution, and the core of American democracy, include three essential freedoms: of speech, of the press and of expression.

Rich Koele/Shutterstock.com

Between May and September 1787, delegates of the Constitutional Convention (known also as the Philadelphia Convention) congregated in Philadelphia to write a constitution that would form the core of a new democratic nation. Freedoms of speech and the press became essential components of the U.S. Constitution in no small part because of the active role of the free press. Even today, freedom of speech, freedom of the press and freedom of expression remain basic tenets in U.S. constitutional law, as evidenced and strengthened by the First Amendment:

> Congress shall make no law respecting an establishment of religion, or prohibiting the free exercise thereof; or abridging the freedom of speech, or of the press; or the right of the people peaceably to assemble, and to petition the government for a redress of grievances.[4]

In his popular HBO series *Assume the Position*, actor and humorist Robert Wuhl—who is well known for his fascination with and study of American history—offers his college audience an entertaining window on how the mass media have played a pivotal role in the survival of free speech and free expression, as guaranteed in the Bill of Rights.

Early Attempts at Censorship

While the First Amendment to the U.S. Constitution guarantees a free press, many U.S. presidents, sometimes with the support of Congress, have attempted to circumvent these basic freedoms by evoking the need "to protect the American way of life." In 1917, for example, on the heels of World War I, Congress in cooperation with President Woodrow Wilson enacted the Espionage Act, which made it a federal crime to publish anything that "attempted to cause insubordination, disloyalty, mutiny, or refusal of duty in the U.S. Armed Forces." In 1918, Congress amended the Espionage Act with the Sedition Act, which made it a crime to attempt to stop or publicly protest recruitment by the Armed Forces, or to cause "contempt for the Constitution, the flag, or the uniform of the armed forces." Under this law, U.S. citizens could be fined, imprisoned or executed for voicing dissent—a clear violation of the Constitutional stipulation of freedom of speech in the First Amendment. The Espionage and Sedition Acts were not successfully challenged and reversed until the mid-1930s.

In 1940, Congress passed the Smith Act. This law attempted to control the "danger and menace" of the American Communist Party and made it a federal crime to "advocate the violent overthrow of the government, or to conspire to advocate the violent overthrow of the government, or to be a member of any organization advocating the violent overthrow of the government."[5] Prosecutions and persecutions under the Smith Act continued for almost 20 years, through what is known as the McCarthy era— named after the now-infamous Wisconsin Senator Joseph McCarthy. In 1957, the U.S. Supreme Court began to overturn prosecutions under these acts as unconstitutional, ruling that they violated freedom of speech and freedom of the press.[6]

In effect, these acts represented early attempts at government censorship, the

11.2

Censorship continues to occur in America today, with public school libraries the usual target.

Steve Skjold/Alamy Stock Photo

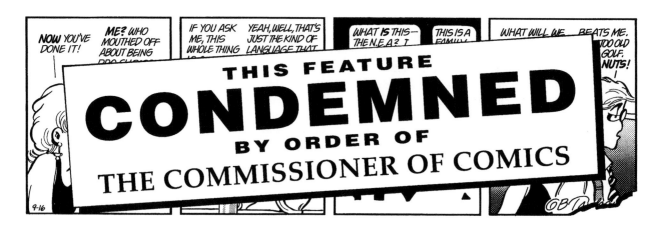

11.3

Doonesbury © 1992 G. B. Trudeau

effort to control or ban the flow of information. By its very nature, censorship suppresses free speech and limits the ability of the media to report on government actions. Censorship takes many forms, from the direct enforcement of regulations limiting the media's ability to publish or broadcast information (usually in the name of national security), to the less formal but often equally effective blocking of expression and access for "moral" considerations—for example, the censorship of pornographic content or racial slurs. Censorship also typically prevents access to sensitive information such as details of military operations during wartime. Publishing information about military planning, deployment of ships or troops, weapons or defensive technologies and so forth is considered to pose a national security risk. The problem arises when governments abuse this national security rationale and try to cover up unlawful activities by censoring the media or media access. Determining when the government's argument for censorship is truly valid in the name of national security, and when it violates the rights and responsibilities of a free press, remains an ongoing challenge for the courts. We will further discuss this debate later in this chapter.

Regulatory Censorship in the 21st Century

Censorship has also been used as a way for powerful groups to force their views and beliefs onto others. Consider, for instance, the case of *Kitzmiller v. Dover Area School District*. In 2005 in Pennsylvania, Tammy Kitzmiller et al. took the Dover Area School Board to federal court on the grounds that its mandatory inclusion of "intelligent design" in science textbooks as an alternative to Darwin's theory of evolution violated the Establishment Clause, which states that "Congress shall make no law respecting the establishment of religion." The plaintiffs—the American Civil Liberties Union (ACLU) and Americans United for the Separation of Church and State—won the case by successfully arguing that "intelligent design" was a thinly masked form of religious creationism and thus a violation of the U.S. Constitution. This case highlights the ongoing challenge that the courts must face: determining whether regulatory censorship is being used to push ideological, religious or political agendas.[7]

> Censorship has also been used as a way for powerful groups to force their views and beliefs onto others.

In another recent case that actually crossed international borders, in September 2005, a major Danish newspaper, *Jyllands-Posten*, published a series of satirical, less-than-flattering depictions of the Prophet Muhammad. Knowing that the cartoons would most likely spur some controversy, the paper also published an editorial stating that the cartoon series represented an attempt to "contribute to the [public] debate regarding the important issues of censorship and criticism of Islam in the post-9/11 world."[8] The response was widespread protests, many violent, across the Muslim world. In Syria, Iran and Lebanon, angry mobs set fire to the Danish Embassies. In Europe and North America, protesters set fire to the flags of those countries whose media had reported on, and in many cases reprinted, the offending cartoons; these countries included Denmark, the Netherlands, Norway, Germany, the United Kingdom and the United States. Some Middle Eastern countries banned the sale of Danish goods. In response, the Danish government created an international campaign urging consumers to "Buy Danish"—as a show of support for Denmark's long tradition of freedom of the press and freedom of expression.

Despite the decrial of Muslim leaders and commentators that the cartoons were racist and blasphemous against the Muslim faith, many Western politicians and commentators nevertheless supported the publishing of the cartoons. They claimed the act proved timely, for it not only highlighted the continued threat of Islamic terrorism, but also served as a legitimate demonstration of the importance of freedom of speech. In an open letter to ambassadors from 11 Muslim countries, Danish Prime Minister Anders Fogh Rasmussen wrote, "The freedom of expression has a wide scope and the Danish government has no means of influencing the press."[9] He went on to point out that in a democracy, those parties who feel that they have been defamed or discriminated against have the legal recourse to file suit in the courts. Several Muslim organizations took the Danish prime minister's suggestion and filed a criminal complaint against the publisher, *Jyllands-Posten*. Less than a year later, the Danish public prosecutor's office ended its investigation by determining that the publication of the cartoons did not constitute a criminal offense and that the publication of the cartoons was well within the arena of free press and the public interest.[10]

Challenges to free speech in the West—enabled by the proliferation of Web-based mass media and triggering mass protests and violence in the Middle East—continue. In early September 2012, a low-budget and rather amateurish film called *The Innocence of Muslims* that mocked the Prophet Muhammad was produced and released virally on the Web by a Coptic Christian extremist living in Southern California. The film's characterization of Muslims as immoral and violent and its claims that the Prophet Muhammad was a homosexual triggered violent protests and riots throughout the Islamic world—especially in Egypt and Libya, where some believe organized terrorists used the riots as an excuse to launch a strike against the U.S. consulate in Bengasi, killing four Americans, including U.S. Ambassador to Libya Christopher Stevens. The media coverage of these events highlighted the ongoing cultural gulf between the American (and more generally Western) protection of free expression and free speech—even when the content is considered abhorrent to most people—and the Muslim world's insistence that such anti-Muslim speech be halted and the producer punished (in this case the American government).

DEFAMATION: LIBEL AND SLANDER

Defamation is any form of implied or explicit communication that damages a person's, organization's or product's reputation or standing in the community. Spoken defamation is called slander. Written defamation is called libel. Libel is one of the legal problems most often faced by people working in the media. Anyone who writes or speaks about others in the public arena can find himself or herself becoming the target of a libel action or defamation suit. People who work as reporters or editors of news media, whether public (e.g., newspapers, magazines, radio and television) or private (e.g., corporate newsletters, association journals, corporate Websites and e-mail), are all vulnerable to libel suits.

When taken to court for libel, news media defendants usually lose if the case is tried by a jury whose members are skeptical about the practices of the media.[11] This risk explains why premiums for "errors and omissions" insurance (i.e., libel protection) continue to climb. Insurance companies are often eager to push their media clients into out-of-court settlements. For this reason, relatively few media libel cases actually make it to trial. In those cases that do go to trial, plaintiffs can win substantial monetary judgments. Since a wronged plaintiff cannot get injunctive relief (a form of court-ordered prior restraint), his or her only remedy is to seek defamation action *after* the alleged defamation has occurred. A journalist's *reckless disregard for the truth*—that is, knowledge that what one is about to publish something is not true—is considered defamation with malice. When you have knowingly committed a wrongful action with the intention of harming another person, you have acted out of malice or spite. A defendant can also be found guilty of negligent libel and ordered to pay damages. This outcome happens when defamation of or damage to the plaintiff is

313

unintended; it results when one simply fails to exercise reasonable care in the creation and dissemination of material that could be deemed potentially defaming.

Perhaps the most famous libel case in U.S. history is *New York Times v. Sullivan*, which established the key precedent for how courts rule in subsequent libel cases brought against the media. In March 1960, at the height of the civil rights movement, *The New York Times* ran an editorial advertisement that was sponsored by a civil rights organization called the Committee to Defend Martin Luther King and the Struggle for Freedom in the South. The ad featured a scathing editorial statement about police treatment of civil rights demonstrators at Alabama State College. It made numerous allegations that turned out to be false. L. B. Sullivan, the commissioner of police for Montgomery, Alabama—who was not directly named in the ad—believed that he and his police department had been defamed. Sullivan, along with Alabama's governor and a number of other Montgomery officials, filed a lawsuit against *The New York Times*, arguing that the paper was liable for damages because of its negligence in not checking the accuracy of the ad's statements. An Alabama court awarded Sullivan and his co-plaintiffs a half-million dollars, and the Alabama Supreme Court upheld the defamation award against *The New York Times*. The *Times* appealed to the U.S. Supreme Court, which in 1964 overturned the judgments of the Alabama courts.[12]

The Supreme Court's ruling in *New York Times v. Sullivan* set the legal bar for determining defamation cases against media organizations and remains unchanged today. Writing for the Court, Justice William Brennan stated that to be held liable for defamation, a media organization or individual reporter must be proven to have acted in actual malice "with knowledge that the information being published (or broadcast) was false" and to have published anyway with "reckless disregard for the truth."[13]

MEDIA AND PRIVACY

In 2003, an enterprising blogger in Florida named Tucker Max was operating a self-promoting Website that brought him national media attention—and a court order from a Florida judge to "cease and desist." On his Website, Max posted pictures and critical commentaries about his former girlfriends, including Katy Johnson, whom he described as "vapid, promiscuous, and an unlikely candidate for membership in the Sobriety Society."[14] Johnson, a former Miss Vermont, had been publishing her own Website since 2001. Her Website, which promoted sexual abstinence, had brought her national media attention and was the subject of a feature article in *Teen* magazine. Johnson filed an invasion of privacy lawsuit against Max and won a court order that, according to court documents, "forbids Mr. Max to write about Ms. Johnson" and "[prohibits] Mr. Max from 'disclosing any stories, facts or information, notwithstanding its truth, about any intimate or sexual acts engaged in by Ms. Johnson.'"[15] The story of the legal battle between Tucker Max and Katy Johnson highlights the challenge that judges face in determining the right to individual privacy, especially in a mass media world dominated by the Internet.

Privacy on the Internet

Privacy, according to attorney Robert Standler, "is the expectation that confidential personal information . . . will not be disclosed to third parties, when that disclosure would cause either embarrassment or emotional distress to a person of reasonable sensitivities."[16] Technology is far outpacing the government's ability to protect private information, which comprises "facts, images (e.g., photographs, videotapes), and disparaging opinions."[17] Given this trend, it falls to each of us to protect information about our finances, lifestyles and medical records when we use the Internet.

In early 2007, a high school student named Allison Chang was shocked when she discovered that a photo of her, taken by her church youth counselor and posted on the Website Flickr.com, had resurfaced a few months later in a Virgin Mobile Australia ad campaign. Chang never authorized the use of her image for commercial purposes, nor did she receive any compensation for its use. Chang's parents filed a suit against the company for violation of her privacy.[18]

Does the mere posting of a photo without express permission on a popular website—a very common activity in the Digital Age—qualify as a violation of privacy? Given that we are all the "owners" of our name, likeness and personal data, we also have the right to disallow their use for commercial purposes by others, including advertisers. Consent, sometimes also called a release, is a written authorization agreeing to allow someone else to access and use your name, likeness and private information for commercial purposes. To be legally valid, consent should be in writing, and some kind of consideration must be given—that could come in the form of money, or other things of "value," including goods and services, discounts (such as airline frequent-flyer accounts), free professional subscriptions, discounted Internet access and the like.

The rapid growth of Internet-based consumer services—health, financial, educational, shopping, travel and much more—has brought with it a blurring of what the courts have previously considered as legal release and consent. We all frequently encounter Websites that ask us for personal information and often ask us to click an "Agree to Terms" button. How many of us actually read the terms to which we claim to agree? Most of us just click these buttons and move on. In reality, each time we click the "Agree" button, we are giving up some of our privacy rights. Congress and the courts are struggling to build an information-privacy safety net of laws and regulations, but it is an uphill battle against technology and the cyberspace-based world economy.

> Congress and the courts are struggling to build an information-privacy safety net of laws and regulations, but it is an uphill battle against technology and the cyberspace-based world economy.

Privacy concerns also affect social media. In early 2010, Mark Zuckerberg, CEO of Facebook, rolled out a new policy dealing with the site's privacy settings in response to protests about its earlier policies lodged by critics and privacy advocates. Critics alleged that the settings were not only not intuitive, but also outright deceptive. Privacy advocates expressed their concerns with Facebook's Open Graph initiative, which allowed users to comment on things they like on the Web—from a blog they have read, to a YouTube video they have watched, to a product they have noticed on Amazon.com. Zuckerberg's stated goal in rolling out this feature was to "build a Web where the default is social."[19] In the real world, this "social default" setting had critics and users alike up in arms. While Facebook's default settings had always called for maximum exposure to *other* Facebook users, this change enabled even *non*-Facebook members to see users' personal profiles and interests. Going back to reject this feature would not have caused such an uproar had Facebook not made it so difficult to change the settings in the first place. In May of 2010, Guilbert Gates, business writer for *The New York Times* commented, "To manage your privacy on Facebook, you will need to navigate through 50 settings with more than 170 options."[20] Despite the criticisms, the fact remained: The options for privacy are there.

Invasion of Privacy Laws

Initially, privacy was a minor if recognizable concern of American governance and the American people. Only recently did it become an arguable constitutional right—and laws to protect it are still in their infancy stages. At first, citizens considered invasion of privacy to consist of activities such as trespass, assault or eavesdropping. Over time, however, advanced technologies have altered individuals' experience with privacy. Until the invention and proliferation of modern mass media technologies (for example, wiretaps, microphones, still cameras, video cameras, the Internet), people lived in relative security. Generally, it was impossible for someone to gain access to private conversations, and personal documents were reasonably easy to secure. When the technological means for recording and mass-transmitting various types of information became a reality, privacy started becoming a legal issue in the United States.[21]

Currently, the single fastest-growing and most pervasive criminal activity in the United States and Europe is identity theft, according to the U.S. Federal Trade Commission. The law is struggling to catch up with and control the ability of third parties to collect information about unsuspecting individuals. To prohibit this unauthorized appropriation or use of an individual's name, likeness and certain private data (e.g., employment records, medical records, financial records) for commercial purposes without the prior consent of the individual, Congress commissioned an appropriation tort. This tort protects individuals against the theft of any element that makes up an individual's private identity and personal history and against the use of this information for the benefit of anyone other than the individual who "owns" it.

Working journalists often find themselves bumping up against these new privacy protection and anti-intrusion laws. Bona fide journalists can collect any information they wish for a story, but only if they do not break any laws in the process.

Taking a picture with a telephoto lens of the victim of a sexual assault would certainly be judged differently than taking a picture with a telephoto lens of the wife of a celebrity arguing with her famous husband. In the former example, the individual, a private citizen, has the right to expect a significant degree of privacy. In contrast, in the latter example, the public celebrity status of the actor-husband would most likely overshadow the privacy limits of his wife. With few exceptions, the courts have taken the position that there is no privacy in public places. The "reasonable enjoyment of privacy" that you can expect in your backyard is not at all comparable to the level of privacy you can expect walking on campus, sunbathing on a public beach or strolling through your local shopping mall. Moreover, if you voluntarily elect to talk to a journalist, or call in to a talk-radio program, you should assume that you have effectively given up some of your right to privacy.

The Privacy of Public Figures

The courts have consistently ruled that the reasonable privacy of celebrities, politicians and other public figures is to be judged on a far different scale than that of the noncelebrity private individual. But what exactly constitutes a public figure? Simply put, a public figure is an individual who has chosen to place himself or herself in the public arena and benefits from the media exposure. The courts have held that this definition also depends on a number of interrelated issues:

- *Job description:* The Supreme Court has held that the position being held or sought, whether by election or appointment, "invites public scrutiny of the person holding [the position] entirely apart from the scrutiny and discussion occasioned by the particular charges in the controversy."
- *Nature of the story or statements:* The first criterion is whether the content of the statement or story directly relates to the public responsibilities that the individual is seeking or holds. The courts have held that public figures still have the right to personal privacy, albeit a far more limited right than a private citizen has. The second criterion relates to the question of if and how the individual's (seeking or holding public position) private life, habits or personal traits might put into question the fitness of the individual to hold a public position.

11.4

Entertainment, sports and political celebrities are considered public figures, which means they have far less right to media privacy than non-celebrities.

Andrea Raffin/Shutterstock.com

- *All-purpose public figure:* The law considers certain individuals, by the nature of their careers and the level of their public persona, to be all-purpose public figures. These persons include individuals seeking or holding high-level public office (senators, the president and cabinet members, for example) and entertainment and sports personalities. The law sees these all-purpose public figures as automatically and permanently having very limited rights to personal privacy because of the very nature of their voluntary exposure to public scrutiny and criticism.[22]

A special area in media law focuses on when an individual's right to privacy is effectively waived in the service of the democratic political process. An individual surrenders much of his or her right to privacy by voluntarily entering the political arena to run for elected office or to become a candidate for a political appointment. In today's media-dominated political environment, this standard can mean allowing the opposition extraordinary freedom to investigate, publish or broadcast anything it likes about one's private life, regardless of its basis in fact or its defamatory effect. The law leaves few recourse rights for political figures, other than their own ability to use the media to counterattack when they are targeted by media scrutiny. Legal recourse—that is, the ability to file libel and slander lawsuits—does not apply to those persons whom the law and the courts consider to be public figures, especially political figures.

To publish or broadcast private information about any individual, regardless of his or her public-figure status, may leave the media source open to a defamation lawsuit if the potentially damaging statement or information meets the following criteria:

- It is knowingly false.
- It demonstrates a reckless disregard for the truth.
- It is the result of clear negligence in reporting.
- It is based principally on malice toward the individual or group being defamed.[23]

Most people assume that the right to privacy is a simple concept, basic to all democracies and guaranteed by the U.S. Constitution. In fact, that is not the case. The concept of privacy is actually a complex legal issue comprising many challenges to defined social and cultural values. In today's world, we must constantly weigh the right to individual privacy against the needs of governments to prevent crime, protect security and "domestic tranquility" and "assure a common defense" against those who wish to harm the country or its citizens. One fundamental question continues to arise: Where does the government's authority end, and individual privacy rights begin? This question has been the root of increasing controversy in the post-September 11 world, where many people feel they are being asked to sacrifice their privacy on a daily basis in exchange for security.

Over the last few years, for example, as an additional measure against terrorist threats and in response to public mandates for better crime prevention, law enforcement authorities in London, New York, Washington, D.C. and many other large cities have installed extensive video surveillance networks. Almost every corner of every downtown area is covered by 24/7 surveillance cameras. These cameras sometimes appear in plain sight, but more often are concealed, leaving people unaware that they are being watched and recorded.[24] Although these surveillance networks have proven extremely successful in both preventing crime and apprehending lawbreakers, how have they affected citizens' right to privacy? Given the underlying motivations for these networks' installation, can the free press continue to practice its traditional role of informing citizens of the government's actions? To better understand how surveillance networks have altered the right to privacy in public places, and how the media have responded to them, view the video segment titled "Privacy in Public Places." ▶

▶ **Privacy in Public Places**
The widespread use of security monitoring technology in public places is challenging previous legal limitations on the protection of individual privacy.

MASS MEDIA LAW AND NATIONAL SECURITY

Throughout the history of the United States, Congress and the courts have held that the federal government, especially during times of war, has the right to limit freedom of speech and the press for the protection of the nation. Some dramatic

The American Founding Fathers identified the free press as one of the four checks and balances needed to maintain an effective democracy. They also acknowledged the key role played by the federal government, whose job it is to ensure the safety and security of the nation.

confrontations between the press and the federal government have occurred as a result of these actions. At stake in each of these cases is the role of a free press or, to use the terminology introduced earlier, the Fourth Estate. The American Founding Fathers identified the free press as one of the four checks and balances needed to maintain an effective democracy. They also acknowledged the key role played by the federal government, whose job it is to ensure the safety and security of the nation. The free press, then, informs the public about the actions of the government, in war and peace. Of course, the government needs to keep some details of its operations secret, lest the information fall into enemy hands. Such was the U.S. government's very argument before the Supreme Court in the precedent-setting case known as the Pentagon Papers, discussed in greater detail in this section.

Prior restraint occurs when the government tries to stop someone from publishing or airing a story that it fears will damage the government. Since the Vietnam War (1963–1975) and throughout the late 20th century, conflicts between the media and the government in the area of prior restraint have often brought freedom of the press issues before the Supreme Court, thereby keeping these issues high on the public agenda. One of the most famous cases in this area relates to the Pentagon Papers. In the Pentagon Papers case, the federal government attempted to prevent *The Washington Post* and *The New York Times* from publishing material supplied by Daniel Ellsberg, a Defense Department analyst. Ellsberg provided the newspapers with a classified, 7,000-page collection of top-secret documentation of the government's internal planning and strategies for the Vietnam War. These documents clearly revealed ongoing efforts to deceive both Congress and the American people—right before the presidential election—about unpopular decisions to expand the war and about what was actually taking place during the war.

The Court ruled that to carry out prior restraint, the government had to prove that the press was doing more than merely reporting on governmental planning and military strategies for conducting the war. It had to demonstrate that the actions of the press were resulting in a real and compelling risk to national security—for example, by proving that the media had intentions of publishing timely and specific information that would clearly place U.S. troops, ships or aircraft in danger. "Thus, [the Government] carries a heavy burden of showing justification for the imposition of such a restraint [of the freedom of the Press]."[25] Despite the ruling in this case, however, the Supreme Court has continued to uphold the right of the executive and judiciary branches of the U.S. government and Congress to block the publication or broadcast of current news in the name of national security, even when, by doing so, the government restrains the media. Critics argue that this restraint of the media conflicts with the First Amendment's guarantee of the freedom of the press. During times of war, we assume that this debate becomes easier—but does it?

Today's confrontational environment finds the media competing head-to-head with the keepers of national security. While the government tries hard to keep much of its activities secret, the media tries equally hard to investigate and report on them in the name of the people's right to know.

The Freedom of Information Act

While the news media continue to fight government efforts to limit access to secrets, these efforts are also putting war correspondents in harm's way. The technology of newsgathering and reporting may have changed, but this modern conflict persists largely unchanged. One of the legal tools that media organizations have used to try to stay ahead of this curve in recent times is the Freedom of Information Act (FOIA).

In 1966, Congress established an important information-gathering tool for journalists with FOIA. In principle, FOIA opens government records that were previously closed to public scrutiny. Journalists have effectively used FOIA to uncover government activities, both past and present. Private citizens have also successfully used this legislation to access public records collected by government agencies that have directly affected their lives. Every year more than 600,000 FOIA requests are filed with the federal government. Although FOIA has had some success in opening government records, it has also resulted in ongoing government efforts to block its impact. Unofficial government policies such as failing to hire enough workers to process FOIA requests, establishing convoluted record-identification systems and effectively "misplacing" sensitive records can combine to make many people feel that the federal government is, in fact, more closed than open to public scrutiny.

In addition, the rapid advancement of information technology has challenged both the protection of truly sensitive information and the application of FOIA. When this legislation became law in 1966, government files and records comprised hard copies of documents, plus some audio, video, film and photographic records. By the late 20th century, federal officials argued that any information created and held in digital form is beyond the definitions of "files" and "records" under FOIA and, therefore, is exempt from forced disclosure. The courts are catching up with legal definitions of what constitutes a "file" or a "record" under FOIA, but the rapid rate of technological change will continue to outpace the courts' ability to adapt its legal definitions. Meanwhile, this same onrush of technological change has challenged the government to protect an ever-increasing body of information that could legitimately endanger national security, or simply violate the right to privacy of individuals. These competing challenges present important legal questions that the courts will have to address in coming years.

HISTORICAL ROOTS OF COPYRIGHT LAW

While the right to privacy has only fairly recently come to the forefront of mass media law and has become a heated subject of debate among Constitutional scholars, the protection of individually created content has a much longer history. To better define copyright law and the processes for enforcing copyright in the United States, it is important to understand its roots. Copyright protects the intellectual properties (original works) and the rights of the individual creators and owners—artists, writers, photographers, composers—from unauthorized and uncompensated appropriation. In other words, copyright law protects the creators of intellectual properties by controlling the unauthorized "copying" and distribution of their works.

In England, starting in the mid-16th century, the ruling powers of the Crown and Parliament enacted legislation to establish intellectual property rights. This legislation launched a fascinating and important period in the development of American copyright law. Until the American Revolution, the Crown's colonial governors in the American colonies applied British copyright law. After the United States of America won its independence, the American Founding Fathers relied heavily upon their experiences with the British system in framing the foundation for U.S. copyright law, starting with Article I, Section 8, of the U.S. Constitution: "The Congress shall have Power . . . To promote the Progress of Science and useful Arts, by securing for limited Times to Authors and Inventors the exclusive Right to their respective Writings and Discoveries. . . ."[26] In 1790, Congress acted on this power by adopting copyright and patent statutes quite similar to England's Statute of Anne. Enacted in 1710, the Statute of Anne was the first piece of European legislation to vest the rights to a work to the author instead of to the printer.

In the history of international copyright law (the challenges of which will be discussed in greater depth later in this chapter), the United States started out as a major copyright pirate's haven. The wording of America's first copyright laws all but encouraged the practice of copyright piracy (also known as *copyright infringement*):

> . . . nothing in this act shall be construed to extend to prohibit the importation or vending, reprinting or publishing within the United States, of any map, chart, book or books, written, printed, or published by any person not a citizen of the United States, in foreign parts or places without the jurisdiction of the United States.[27]

In other words, the law protected American authors and American publishers; everyone else was fair game. From this history came the establishment of the Copyright Law of the United States, which Congress enacted in Title 17 of the U.S. Code in 1976. The law states that original works of authorship are those that can be perceived, reproduced or otherwise communicated, either directly or with the aid of a machine

Copyright law does *not* protect ideas, procedures, processes, systems, methods of operation, concepts, principles or discoveries, regardless of how they are described or illustrated. It *does*, however, protect compilations and derivative works, as long as the use of such selections is lawful.

Lawrence Lessig on Copyright History
Stanford University Law Professor Lawrence Lessig explores the historic roots and present 21st-century challenges of U.S. copyright law.

or device, including works of literature, music, drama, choreography, art, sculpture, architecture, sound recordings and audiovisual.

Copyright law does *not* protect ideas, procedures, processes, systems, methods of operation, concepts, principles or discoveries, regardless of how they are described or illustrated. It *does*, however, protect compilations and derivative works, as long as the use of such selections is lawful. Also, the copyright protection in the case of compilations and derivative works extends *only* to *new material*, but *not* to components already copyrighted by their original authors. Note that in copyright law, the term author means any creator of an original work, regardless of the form of the work. For more on the history of American copyright law and its challenges, view the video segment titled "Lawrence Lessig on Copyright History."

Fair Use Doctrine

The legal construct of fair use, often referred to as the "fair use doctrine," has been a part of U.S. copyright law since its inception. Even if a work contains a proper copyright notification and is protected under copyright laws, *it can still be used within limited parameters without the user seeking permission to do so*. Fair use doctrine is the term assigned to the category of copyright law covering certain cases of limited lawful use without license or release. The fair use of copyrighted work includes limited reproduction by means of photocopies, audio/video copies and digital copies (CDs, tapes, discs); it is directed toward the support of education and research.

Also included within the fair use doctrine are such activities as criticism, news reporting and all forms of scholarship. Under its provisions, individuals and institutions can employ portions of a copyright-protected work without the permission of or compensation to the original author or publisher, as long as they comply with the following fair use "tests":

1. Is the intended use for nonprofit educational purposes?
2. What is the nature of the work that the material will be used in—teaching, research, criticism commentary, news reporting?
3. How much of the original work is to be used under the fair use claim—both as a percentage of the original work to be used and in terms of the size of the anticipated distribution?
4. Will the unauthorized use of the copyright-protected work have a demonstrable negative impact on the potential market value of the original work?
5. Will the unauthorized use result in significant revenue to the user that should rightfully be going to the legal owner?

Under the fair use doctrine, your instructor can take small portions of this textbook and its companion multimedia offerings and copy them into his or her own course-related website. As long as the intended use falls well within the accepted legal limitations, it is not necessary to ask permission from the author or the publisher before reusing the materials in this way.

Copyright and Ownership of Digital Properties

How does the basic copyright process work today? Earlier, we read about the story of Allison Chang, whose photo was downloaded from Flickr by Virgin Atlantic, which then used it in one of the company's advertisements. Chang did not give Virgin Atlantic permission to do this, and Chang's parents sued the airline for violation of privacy as a result. What we should also wonder is this: How was Virgin Atlantic even able to download the photo from the Flickr site in the first place? Did they locate the photographer, Allison's church youth counselor, and ask for his consent? In fact, when the counselor posted his photos onto the site, he had agreed to a licensing agreement that allowed others to reuse his content without risk of copyright violation—a Creative Commons alternative, which we will discuss later in this section.[28] This brings up yet another question: Who now owns the photo—Virgin Atlantic or the photographer who took it? Also, is the photo, once used in this new context, now considered a "new work"?

On October 19, 2007, *The Washington Post* published a story that illustrates just how easily and innocently an average person can run afoul of copyright laws in the Digital Age. In February of that year, a young mother, Stephanie Lenz, proud of her 13-month-old son Holden, decided to make a home video of him and post it on YouTube to show her family and friends. She played Prince's "Let's Go Crazy" on the stereo, shot a 30-second video of Holden smiling and bobbing to the music and posted it on YouTube. A harmless action taken by a proud mother, right? Wrong—at least according to Universal Music Publishing Group, the record label that owns the rights to Prince's song. The company threatened to file a copyright infringement suit against Lenz a few months after her video first appeared and demanded that YouTube remove the video.

"The idea that putting a little video of your kid up on YouTube can mean you have to go to court, and maybe declare bankruptcy and lose your house, is just wrong," Lenz told the *Post*'s reporter. "I don't like being made to feel afraid, and I don't like being bullied."[29] Lenz counter-sued Universal Music—taking bold action to fight what many see as the ongoing abuses of copyright enforcement by large multinational media companies against individual media users in cyberspace. Her decision made Lenz an overnight celebrity. She quickly gained legal and financial support from organizations such as the Electronic Frontier Foundation, a nonprofit advocacy group made up of lawyers, policy analysts and activists working on behalf of media consumers. In the end, Universal Music backed down in the face of the negative media exposure for the company that Lenz generated, and YouTube put the video of Holden back up on its site.

The impact of technology and the rapid evolution of mass media continue to challenge the application of copyright laws and precedents. Mass media technology is growing at an increasing rate, resulting in an ever-increasing communication capability that is both affordable and accessible to a highly diverse population. Directly related to this trend are the new demands that this growth places on our system of protecting intellectual property created and/or published (distributed) in digital form.

Enforcing Copyright Law in a Digital World

Legal jurisdiction, or the geographical area over which law can be applied, is one of the core challenges for applying mass media law to the World Wide Web. The Internet, by its very nature, exists everywhere in the world at the same time. Cyberspace has no national boundaries. A Website that is available to anyone in the world who has access to a computer and a modem might have been created in Israel, be managed through a contracted server-farm in the Philippines and have its major content contributors located in Australia. Meanwhile, the Internet service provider (ISP) that enables you to access this Website could be an U.S. company whose technical operations are maintained in Canada. In this very typical scenario, where does the Website actually "live"? And if the Website is operating in violation of the law, which legal jurisdiction would rule—that is, whose laws apply?

In the same vein, where does the identification of an original work begin and end? Consider the following example. While searching the Web, you come across a photograph that you would like to use in a brochure you are creating to promote your freelance business. You select the photograph, copy it to your hard drive, do a little resizing and color adjustment, copy it into the brochure file in your desktop publishing software and then print out a master copy of the new brochure with this photo on the cover. In this scenario, where is the "original work"? And who is the "owner" of the new photo on your brochure? Is it the photographer who shot the image you captured? Is it the Website that "published" the image? Is it the software company that sold you a license for the image-processing software? Given that you manipulated the image, is it now a new "original" work of which you are the author? This is an oversimplified scenario, but the questions and issues are certainly valid and cut right to the heart of the problem of protecting and enforcing copyright laws on the Internet.

What blurs the boundaries between content owned and content borrowed even further is the fact that everything on the Internet and communicated over the World Wide Web is digital. It is split up into packets by the "sender's" ISP, with the packets speeding separately through the Web to be reassembled by the "receiver's" ISP. Do nationally and internationally recognized copyright laws have any real meaning when material is digitally created and distributed over the Internet? Who is the "author" of digital material—the creator who encodes the digital material or the receiver who decodes it? These questions are just a small sample of the intimidating legal challenges presented by the World Wide Web.

Even as these questions continue to perplex legal scholars, advances in regulation and enforcement are emerging within the realm of digital publishing. In digital publishing, content—magazines, newsletters, books and even video and television programming—is created digitally off-line and distributed via the Internet, usually to registered subscribers, like you or me. Those subscribers have supplied certain information about themselves in return for password-controlled access to the digital publications they wish to view, much like the online elements of this textbook. This model solves many copyright-related problems because the users voluntarily identify themselves, agree to basic terms of use and allow the owners/distributors of the digital publications to track their access. It is similar to the approach that has proved highly effective in pay-per-view television.

The possibility of developing workable, enforceable international systems of law for the Internet depends on the foundation of the Internet itself—technology. Internet encryption and other security systems are among the fastest-growing areas being driven by technological innovation. These technologies allow content producers and distributors to encrypt their content and even embed hidden identification mechanisms within digitally published material. The next stage will be to develop reliable systems for identifying—without the user's knowledge—who is accessing specific Web-based and Web-distributed content, and then tracking the use of the accessed material. These technologies offer reliable solutions for the protection and enforcement of copyright laws, but also pose challenges to the protection of personal privacy. The conflict is simple: To enforce copyright, one has to be able to identify reliably who is accessing and using copyright material—but how can this be accomplished without placing undue burdens on individual privacy?

> To enforce copyright, one has to be able to identify reliably who is accessing and using copyright material—but how can this be accomplished without placing undue burdens on individual privacy?

Using existing technologies, content owners can block most unauthorized use and identify situations where someone is attempting copyright infringement—that is, violating copyright law through the unlawful use of another's intellectual property. But, despite these advances in security, Internet content pirates are still ahead of the curve. Those parties wanting to establish workable legal controls for the Internet remain in the difficult position of using their efforts and resources to play catch-up to the masses of technological buccaneers who continue to invent new ways to work around copyright protections and enforcement efforts. No one knows how soon the marriage of laws and technology will occur. In the meantime, it is the responsibility and ethical obligation of every professional working in the field of media and communication to contribute to the solution, not the problem. Respecting the copyright established for others' work and seeking permission to use that work appropriately should remain a priority, as the video segment "Copyright Basics" explains. ▶️

Further complicating the copyright landscape is the soaring increase in peer-to-peer (P2P) file sharing in the last decade. According to industry-sponsored studies, P2P file sharing of music in violation of copyrights has been increasing more than 8 percent per year; in the period between 2000 and 2007, it cost the music industry more than $5 billion annually in lost revenues. A study by Digital Life America reported that an astounding 80 percent of movie downloads were done illegally, with only 20 percent of Americans (in 2006–2007) utilizing legal movie download services.[30] This 2007 study concluded that the use of the inconvenient DRM (Digital Rights Management) format by popular online media sources such as iTunes Store, Xbox Live Video and Amazon Unbox made a greater contribution to the large number of illegal media downloads than the cost of legal downloads. In other words, the DRM technologies that were put in place to protect against unauthorized downloads of copyright-protected media have had the opposite effect—namely, encouraging more users to illegally download videos and music.

While the market drives the use of copyright protection technologies, it can also drive the market leaders to change their approaches to copyright issues. In late 2007, after years of fighting an aggressive copyright enforcement battle, Universal Music Group announced that it had agreed to allow online

▶ 00:08 ━━━━━━━━━ 00:33 CC ✕ ◀))|||||||||

▶ **Copyright Basics**
An animated, quick tutorial on how copyright works.

retailers such as Amazon.com and iTunes to sell Universal-owned music tracks without DRM protections. The music company EMI also began selling DRM-free music tracks. In today's highly competitive environment, where film studios, television networks and music labels alike are struggling to reinvent their business models for the Digital Age, most copyright infringement cases do not have such happy conclusions. Digital technology and the Internet have combined to make it extremely easy to violate copyright and extraordinarily difficult to define and protect ownership of creative content, challenging the very definition of copyright. Furthermore, to create and publish any work is to enter into the convoluted and sometimes risky world of copyright protection and enforcement.

Alternative Approaches to Copyright Protection

Copyright law has always evolved in reaction to the social and political value placed on intellectual property, and on the artists and writers who create intellectual properties. With the advent of the Digital Age, identifying what constitutes a "new and original work" has become much more challenging, and the unauthorized use of copyright-protected works has become much more widespread. Some copyright experts now advocate an overhaul of the entire copyright system to reflect the realities of the Digital Age's creative culture.

Stanford University Law Professor Lawrence Lessig is leading the charge in developing an alternative approach to copyright protection. Lessig and his followers have created Creative Commons, a copyright system that exists in parallel to the U.S. government's existing structure. This organization enables authors and owners of works to allow a range of usages of those works without prior authorization or licensing.

It is costly and time-consuming to chase down and confirm the rights of every single image, every graphic, every line of text or every minute of music that could be copyright protected. Often such source material, which is widely available on the Web, includes clear copyright notifications, or even the new Creative Commons notifications, with links to information on what rights are available and how to license them. Unfortunately, all too often this information is not included or is incorrect. As Lessig proclaims in the video segment titled "Creative Commons," "Creative Commons was created to set culture free."[31] Lessig is not alone in this view: Many experts join him in arguing that it is the costliness, time consumption and lack of clear copyright notices that demonstrate the need for and effectiveness of the Creative Commons

▶ **Creative Commons**
An introduction to the Creative Commons alternative to traditional copyright law.

11.5

International copyright piracy has become as lucrative a business as drug trafficking and illegal-arms dealing. As pictured here, Chinese authorities destroy masses of pirated DVDs on a regular basis.

Peter Parks/Staff

alternative. Adding to the challenge of enforcing copyright law in the Digital Age is the fact that this issue is now being addressed on a global scale. ▶

Enforcing Copyright Law Globally

Borders blur when it comes to the international distribution of media content in cyberspace. This problem makes it challenging for content creators—from large organizations to individual authors and artists—to legally manage and protect media content. Under which national jurisdiction does the work fall when an author writes a book, when a photographer publishes a photograph, when a songwriter releases a new album or when a documentary producer releases a new film? Do these media creators have to secure their legal rights under every jurisdiction on earth? If an author or artist, or an employer, fails to protect intellectual property rights in one country, can it jeopardize those rights in every other country? Digital technology, especially the Internet, makes protection of intellectual property an extremely difficult undertaking. These new media copyright issues are even more challenging as the convergence of broadcast media and the Internet (discussed in Chapter 7) continues to increase in scope and in pace.

In 1902, an international treaty was ratified in an effort to reconcile copyright law conflicts and bring much of international copyright law into a cooperative treaty structure. This treaty was called the Berne Convention (after Berne, Switzerland, where the treaty talks were first held). It was not until 1988—a full 96 years after the first Berne Convention—that the United States finally ratified this international copyright treaty. In so doing, the country officially ended its more than two centuries' refusal to join the community of nations in the area of copyright protection. Since 1988, the United States has become an international copyright champion, due in large part to the technology-driven globalization of media and the economic incentives of enforcing international intellectual property rights (IPR) laws.

In terms of its scope, international copyright piracy rivals other large-scale international crime such as drug trafficking and illegal-arms dealing. The estimated revenue from international copyright piracy is a staggering $250 billion per year, according to government and industry figures, and this illegal revenue stream only continues to grow. The challenges facing today's international copyright enforcement community are equally staggering. Intellectual property has become one of the most valuable commodities in world trade. Similarly, enforcement of copyright compliance and identification and prosecution of organized copyright piracy are becoming essential components in ensuring the health of the global economy. Still, copyright theft and illegal trade in forged art and manuscripts continue to bring handsome profits to criminal organizations around the globe. Fortunately, international copyright enforcement is championed by two strong groups: Both the United Nations and the World Trade Organization (WTO) have established entire departments and allocated significant financial resources toward fulfilling this mission, in recognition of the fact that nations view protecting intellectual and artistic assets as important to international trade.

International Models of Intellectual Property Law

While British and American copyright law traditions have become an important part of global trade, they are not the only copyright traditions. Some countries model their intellectual property laws on the French-Napoleonic legal system, which bases the protection of intellectual property on the idea of author's rights. In the late 20th and early 21st centuries, the conflicts between the copyright legal tradition and the author's rights legal tradition have presented a major challenge in the negotiation of international trade agreements. The basic differences between the two approaches are outlined here.

Laws and treaties based on copyright legal tradition, like those established in the United States and the United Kingdom, view intellectual creations as another form of "property." As property, the title (ownership) of intellectual property can be bought and sold, licensed, transferred and inherited, quite similar to buying, selling or otherwise holding or transferring ownership in "real" property such as land, buildings, cars and so forth. For example, as the author of this textbook, I am the original creator of this work. Because I live and work in the United States, U.S. copyright law automatically protects my work. However, I am writing this book under contract with the publisher to which I have licensed the work. In doing so, I transferred its ownership to the publisher in return for the agreed-upon compensation and royalties. The publisher is now the legal owner of the work, just as if it had created it. It can sell and license all or portions of the work as it sees fit, as long as it honors its contract with me (the author).

If I were living and working in France, this textbook would come under the author's rights system, which states that the value of the created product can never be separated from the original author. Thus I would always remain the sole owner of the textbook, and this ownership right would automatically pass to my surviving heirs. If I license the book to a publisher, the publisher's rights would be limited. It could not alter or sell any portion of my work to another publisher without my (or my heirs') express permission every time.

The internationalization of different intellectual property traditions in the face of new technologies has proved difficult for U.S. lawmakers to accept. The European concept of authors having *natural rights* (another term for author's rights) does not work well within the realm of digitally produced intellectual properties such as photographs, video and sound recordings and computer programs. The civil law approach to copyright already well established in the United States better protects such technology-based reproductions.

International Broadcast Law and Regulation

International media law covers more than copyright laws and treaties. All countries have laws regulating the ownership, operation and content of broadcast media. Broadcast media law is a major subcategory of media and communication law, and a detailed discussion of this area is beyond the scope of this book. Following is just a brief overview of some key concepts in this area.

In the United States, the Federal Communications Commission (FCC) has authority over the licensing of broadcast stations. The Communications Act of 1934 essentially empowered the FCC to regulate communication media, including radio and television (both cable and satellite), the allocation of frequency bands and some of the content. It also gave the FCC the authority to decide whether the

11.6

Weary of battles with the FCC over its accusations of indecent broadcasting, shock jock radio personality Howard Stern eventually signed on with the uncensored, Sirius XM satellite service in 2006.

Corey Sipkin/KRT/Newscom

content being broadcasted was in the public interest as well as for which purposes and by which users. While the FCC charter technically does not establish this federal agency's power to directly censor program content, the courts have given the FCC the ability to fine broadcasters and withhold license renewal—powers that it sometimes wields in an attempt to influence content.

The FCC's authority to regulate broadcast program has hit home as part of the public and political debate over obscenity, political programming and children's programming. The concept that the broadcast airways belong to the public and are held by the federal government as a "public trust" forms the legal theory behind the FCC's regulatory and enforcement authority. In the United States, there is no federal government ownership of broadcast networks, as is the case in other countries—for example, as evidenced by the British Broadcasting Corporation (BBC) and the Canadian Broadcasting Corporation (CBC). Even so, Congress has created and partially funded two quasi-government broadcast networks—the Public Broadcasting Service (PBS) and National Public Radio (NPR). There is also the government/private-sector hybrid of C-Span TV and C-Span radio, both of which are funded and operated by the cable/satellite broadcast industry as a "public-service trust."

These noncommercial broadcast networks, and their member stations, are subjected to far more regulatory scrutiny than are their commercial counterparts. Because all governments claim ownership or control over their broadcast airways and the content transmitted over them, international treaties have evolved to try to regulate the cross-border reach of broadcast programming. Once again, the rapid evolution of technology is making such treaties highly difficult to enforce. From shortwave and AM radio through FM radio and television and up to satellite broadcasting, there is now extensive "spillover" of broadcast programming between countries and regions worldwide. Governments that previously blocked broadcast transmissions they considered threatening are finding this feat to be an impossible task in the Digital Age.

CONFIDENTIALITY IN NEWSGATHERING

Journalism schools have long taught aspiring reporters the importance of protecting their sources. Many states have enacted shield laws in an effort to clarify and solidify the protection accorded to reporters, unless the government can present reasonable and compelling arguments in asking a court to force reporters to reveal their sources. These shield laws are state laws that have been enacted in reaction to the lack of specific language covering this issue in the federal Constitution. The courts must determine, on a case-by-case basis, when these state-level shield laws should be overruled in favor of the more flexible, albeit less clear, federal laws. Many believe that without the use and protection of confidential sources, the press would be unable to perform its important Fourth Estate role in helping to maintain the checks and balances essential to the functioning of a democracy. This is especially true for investigative journalists who report on government officials and government agencies.

Reporting on Government Officials and Agencies

Journalists have been refusing to disclose their sources since at least 1848, when John Nugent, a reporter for the *New York Herald*, refused to reveal who provided to the paper the draft treaty that the United States was using to try to end the Mexican-American War. Nugent was later jailed for contempt of Congress.[32] The courts have held that reporters and their news media employers can challenge such subpoenas only if they can make a compelling argument along one or more of the following lines:

- The demand of the government does not reach the standards established by a state's shield law.
- The reporter and his or her news media employer have a constitutional right to withhold their sources.
- The government has reasonable access to the information being demanded via other sources.
- The demanded revealing of confidential sources does not have compelling relevance to the specific case.
- The language of the subpoena is too broad.[33]

The Supreme Court has ruled that constitutional protection of news sources has no basis in the First Amendment. In *Branzburg v. Hayes*, a precedent-setting case on this issue, Justice Byron White stated the following as the majority opinion of the court:

> The sole issue before us is the obligation of reporters to respond to grand jury subpoenas as other citizens do and answer questions relevant to an investigation into the commission of a crime. Citizens generally are not constitutionally immune from grand jury subpoenas; and neither the First Amendment nor other constitutional provisions protect the average citizen [and by extension a reporter] from disclosing to a grand jury [or other judicial body] information that he has received in confidence.[34]

As a result of this ruling, journalists must recognize that their "right" to protect their confidential sources is far from legally assured. Therefore, ethical journalists should never promise absolute confidentiality to their sources, beyond the assurance that they will make a reasonable effort to maintain confidentiality. The reality is that in practice, confidential sources want guarantees from reporters, and reporters proffer such promises of confidentiality to be able to get the story. In doing so, a reporter is taking a significant individual risk that might put such "guarantees" to the test when the journalist later confronts the choice between disclosure and jail.

ethical journalists should never promise absolute confidentiality to their sources, beyond the assurance that they will make a reasonable effort to maintain confidentiality.

Meanwhile, investigative journalists who take on controversial stories, especially concerning the activities of government and political figures, often face harassment. The parties who find themselves to be the focus of investigative stories will sometimes pressure the journalists by trying to subpoena them and force them to disclose sources. For example, during the Senate confirmation hearings for Supreme Court Justice Clarence Thomas, pro-Thomas factions grilled NPR reporter Nina Totenberg to try to force her to reveal the names of confidential informants who had leaked statements made by Anita Hill (who had accused Thomas of sexual harassment during the hearings). Totenberg held her ground.

Reporting on the Judiciary

A parallel and ongoing legal debate exists regarding the right of the press to inform the public about the activities and potential abuses of the criminal justice system, especially by the criminal courts. Civil rights advocates such as the American Civil Liberties Union (ACLU) have long argued that it is the responsibility of the press to gain access to information on police investigations so as to keep the public apprised of law enforcement activities and potential abuses. Congress and the courts, acting on concerns about the misuse of and unauthorized access to information collected by law enforcement agencies, established a Code of Federal Regulation for the criminal justice system. This code limits the disclosure of nonconviction information. To obtain the hidden information, journalists must identify the information sought and convince the law enforcement agencies to release it, even though most still manage to get much of the information they seek by following police activities and developing long-term contacts with inside sources.

Congress and the courts have long struggled to balance the electorate's constitutional right to information and the accused person's constitutional right to a fair trial with impartial judge and jury. In an effort to assure fair trials in criminal courts, judges often issue severe limitations—restrictive orders also called gag orders—on the press and media. Through a gag order, a judge commands all of the participants in a trial to have no contact with the news media. In especially high-profile cases, judges have also issued gag orders to the press, limiting or even blocking press coverage during a trial. Violations of such restrictive orders amount to contempt of court, for which the offending reporter can be fined and even jailed. Such gag orders on the media are usually appealed to a higher court, in hopes that it will overrule the edict in favor of enforcing the constitutional guarantees of freedom of the press.

The struggle of Congress and the courts to establish a balance between the government's responsibility to control information, the media's responsibility to monitor and report on the activities of government and the impact both have on individual privacy remains a formidable challenge. Further complicating this issue is the ongoing advances of media technology, which make it all the more essential to refine and define mass media law in the Digital Age.

PORNOGRAPHY: FREE EXPRESSION OR OBSCENITY?

One of the most emotionally charged debates in United States involves pornography. Efforts to limit pornography come down to distinguishing between obscene and pornographic and between pornographic and erotic. This is a difficult task for lawmakers in a society that values and protects free expression. What is pornographic? Is pornography art? Who should decide?

Robert Hurt, a 54-year-old rancher from Kerrville, Texas, was shocked and offended by what he viewed as the "blatant and prolific nudity openly displayed in the nation's capitol" and appointed himself the leading advocate for removing all of these statues and paintings from public areas of Washington, D.C. Hurt even lobbied, albeit unsuccessfully, to have his cause, nudity in art as part of the moral decline of the country, included in the national platform of the Republican Party, according to a story first appearing in the Dallas *Daily News* and then in *The Washington Post* (June 16, 2008).

Hurt represents just one of the many voices who seek to limit free expression and free speech based upon their interpretations of "public morality." When is nudity considered art and when is it pornography? And perhaps more important, does this distinction really matter in a democracy that values an individual's right to free expression? While there are no easy answers to these questions, the critical reader will notice that Hurt himself is utilizing the right to freedom of speech, even if his own moral critique suggests that free expression should be regulated.

11.7

Fountains at the Library of Congress in Washington, D.C., to which Robert Hurt took offense.

robertharding/Alamy Stock Photo

Distinguishing Between Obscenity and Pornography

To better understand this debate, we must define obscenity and pornography. Obscenity is any behavior considered lewd, offensive or indecent. Pornography is any form of media that depicts sexual behavior for the purposes of arousing an audience. Thus obscenity and pornography are not the same things, although pornography can be considered *obscene*. It is when the latter surfaces that we most often experience the social, cultural and constitutional clashes over free expression.

Where does the right to freedom of expression begin and end? Do communities have the right to determine what is considered "pornographic" and "obscene"? Doesn't the First Amendment guarantee the right of every individual to create and distribute whatever he or she wishes, regardless of who might be offended by it? Why are certain types of erotic or pornographic material legal in Nevada or California and illegal in South Carolina or Montana? Why aren't the laws regulating pornography standard from community to community, and from state to state? The courts have long struggled with these issues and have long attempted to quell communities' concerns over what they can deem obscene without violating individuals' First Amendment rights.

In the late 1950s and early 1960s, Lenny Bruce, an outspoken comedian and social critic, took it upon himself to confront these issues head-on. We focus here on Lenny Bruce because he was the first popular entertainment artist to dedicate his life and career to solidifying the practice of freedom of speech in contemporary media. One can argue that because of Bruce, contemporary and often controversial pop-culture figures such as Lady Gaga, Bill Maher, Howard Stern and Madonna now have their own platforms from which they can freely speak. In one of his many court trials for violating obscenity laws, which prohibit behavior deemed by a culture as socially unacceptable, Bruce's argument cut to the core of the debate over what is obscene or pornographic:

Where does the right to freedom of expression begin and end? Do communities have the right to determine what is considered "pornographic" and "obscene"?

11.8

Should images such as the one shown in this ad be considered free expression or obscene and indecent? Who should be the one to make this decision?

Whittle/Splash News/Newscom

> Your Honor, how the hell can I, or any citizen, know what the [expletive] is obscene? . . . Pornography? Pornography, the book jacket told me it was art! . . . How do I, or any citizen, know that it is legal for me to say [expletive] in California, but when I say it in Georgia I can get my [expletive] thrown in jail! Where are the signs at the border that tell me that it's OK to say [expletive] in one state but not in another? . . . And, more importantly, who the [expletive] has the right to determine what is or is not obscene? If certain people are offended by what I say on stage, then let them stay home! Nobody is forcing anyone to come to hear my gigs.[35]

The Miller Test

In the *Miller v. California* case in 1973, the U.S. Supreme Court attempted to define the standards that regulation of obscenity and pornography must meet. While the courts have ruled on numerous other cases over the three decades since *Miller v. California*, this ruling remains an important "test" for all obscenity-versus-freedom-of-speech cases. The Miller decision articulates the following standards, which have become commonly referred to as the Miller test:

- An average person, applying contemporary local community standards, finds that the work, taken as a whole, appeals to prurient interests.
- The work depicts in a patently offensive way sexual conduct specifically defined by applicable state law.
- The work in question lacks serious literary, artistic, political or scientific value.[36]

11.9

Lenny Bruce was the first popular entertainer to dedicate his life and career to promoting the freedom of speech in mass media.

Everett Collection/Newscom

11.10

What are the different ways one can interpret Lady Gaga's work? Is she visually obscene or is there a deeper meaning to her performance art?

Anton_Ivanov/Shutterstock.com

More recently, the FCC has renewed its efforts to regulate what it considers obscene language and images in radio and television by significantly increasing fines for violations—with the repercussions of Janet Jackson's and Justin Timberlake's now-infamous "wardrobe malfunction" at the 2004 Super Bowl being a vivid example. The overall impact of the FCC's more aggressive regulatory efforts in this area is negligible, however, because the agency has legal jurisdiction only over broadcasted content: The majority of media consumers in the United States now get their TV and radio programming via cable and satellite services, which fall outside of the FCC's regulatory jurisdiction. Meanwhile, major media industry associations have undertaken voluntary regulation in an effort to avoid costly confrontations on obscenity and pornography issues. These associations include the National Association of Broadcasters (NAB), the Record Industry Association of America (RIAA), the Motion Picture Association of America (MPAA) and others. Their regulatory efforts have largely focused on establishing rating systems, such as the MPAA film-rating system: G (general audiences), PG (parental guidance), PG-13 (parents strongly cautioned), R (restricted audiences) and NC-17 (no one 17 and under admitted). While conservative and religious organizations have continued to challenge this self-regulation, so far both Congress and the courts have viewed the rating categories as adequate, market-driven protections that do not violate the First Amendment.

What about pornography on the Internet? The ready availability of pornographic content over the Internet has been a source of social and legal controversy since the Web's earliest

days. In fact, Internet pornography producers and distributors have well-rooted legal rights to freedom of speech and freedom of expression. The ongoing challenge for Congress and the courts is to balance these constitutional rights with the need to protect young children. Websites catering to child pornographers clearly violate U.S. law—but if the site originates from outside U.S. jurisdiction, who has the authority to prosecute the site's developers? Perhaps the country of origin has signed one of the international agreements to locate and stop child pornography on the Web. It is just as likely, however, that the country is one of many "Internet haven" countries that make no effort at enforcement and instead encourage scofflaw Web operations to locate in their territory.

ETHICS AND MASS MEDIA

Issues concerning explicit pornography and obscenity raise concerns about sexual exploitation. Thus, while the topic brings to the fore debates about freedom of expression, it also touches on the topic of ethics in mass media, as the saga of Britney Spears illustrates.

Spears's charismatic personality and sexy schoolgirl image won her an enormous fan base and contributed to her meteoric rise as an icon of pop culture. At the same time, Spears became a staple of the tabloid media and often the 24/7 TV news cycle, becoming increasingly more controversial as her music videos and stage performances evolved to become more adult oriented. Her infamous girl-on-girl kiss with Madonna at the 2003 MTV Video Music Awards ceremony made international headlines.

Spears's personal life also became fodder for media attention and overshadowed her professional career. By 2006, the relentless media spotlight had clearly become a contributing factor to her personal life's downward spiral. Spears underwent several stints of substance rehabilitation, fought a gritty custody battle for her children, was charged with a misdemeanor hit-and-run and then failed to launch a professional comeback as evidenced by a humiliating performance of her single "Gimme More" at the 2007 MTV Video Music Awards. Throughout her unraveling, the press closely followed and analyzed every incident, including the removal of her children from her custody and her psychological diagnosis. In October 2008, the court extended this conservatorship indefinitely.[37]

11.11

Was the media responsible for accelerating Britney Spears's personal downward spiral?

ZUMA Press, Inc./Alamy Stock Photo

The Britney Spears story, though not unlike other stories of troubled celebrities, illustrates a number of important mass media ethical issues. As discussed earlier in this chapter, celebrities are unlike private persons and by law have the right to far less privacy from the media. These cases nonetheless raise important questions: Did the media contribute to Spears's psychological problems, and if so, is the media responsible? Are journalists ethically responsible if their coverage of a celebrity actually contributes to the celebrity's mental and emotional decline? In this age of media convergence, 24/7 news coverage and the Internet, what are our ethical responsibilities as mass media consumers?

In the Digital Age, technology gives all of us easy access to powerful tools that enable us to be both media content consumers and media content creators. Does that mean that all individuals who employ these tools—even an internationally famous pop star—should conduct themselves by the ethical standards of traditional media producers? In our rapidly evolving, global culture, what can we point to as media ethics standards?

To address such questions, we must first look at the way media ethics has developed along with mass media. Media can influence individuals, groups and entire cultures in radical ways. As in Britney Spears's case, the mass media can become so dominant a social force that they can sometimes produce significant and unintended effects. With this enormous influence comes equally enormous responsibility. The role of media ethics is to tell us what that responsibility means for all those involved, and to help individuals and cultures safely navigate the uncertain waters of rapid progress.

The Philosophy Behind Mass Media Ethics

Socrates (469–399 b.c.), one of the first great thinkers of Western philosophy and ethics, warned his listeners of the power of media in his critique of poets. Poets were the storytellers and powerful media channels of his day. Socrates believed these ancient media producers were guilty of morally corrupting young people by telling stories about the immoral activities of the ancient gods and goddesses, and by explaining the real world with stories that had no basis in fact.

> Applying Aristotle's thinking today, an ethical journalist would give an unbiased, balanced portrayal of his or her subject, instead of focusing only on positive or negative elements. This is the ideal of ethical fairness.

Countless philosophers since Socrates's time have tried to come up with ethical principles to direct personal and social life. Aristotle (384–322 b.c.) suggested that being ethical is a balance between possible extremes, which is often referred to as the golden mean. The word "mean" expresses the idea of an average, or middle path between two opposites. Applying Aristotle's thinking today, an ethical journalist would give an unbiased, balanced portrayal of his or her subject, instead of focusing only on positive or negative elements. This is the ideal of ethical fairness.

Within a few hundred years after Aristotle identified the golden mean, early Christians (circa 33 a.d.) had begun teaching and practicing an ethical principle known as the golden rule: Do to others as you would have them do to you. Under this ethical guideline, the interest of the individual was seen as always being connected to the interests of the community as a whole.

Still other philosophers, such as the 18th-century German Immanuel Kant (1724–1804), thought differently. Kant taught that categorical imperatives govern thoughts and actions. These imperatives are principles that people are obligated to observe, regardless of the outcome, because they are intrinsically right. Consider, for instance, the tragic terrorist bombing of the Taj Mahal Hotel in Mumbai, India, in late 2008. Local and international media outlets broadcasted up-to-the-minute media coverage of the attacks on the heart of the city—reports that disclosed both the location of government forces and their knowledge of the terrorists' communication channels. The terrorists, by simply turning on their television sets, were able to change their strategy and evade the government's countermeasures.[38] This example roughly illustrates the difficulty inherent in Kant's philosophy. Kant argued that it is an ethical responsibility to reveal truthfully your knowledge of an individual's whereabouts to someone who is seeking to do that person harm, regardless of what the first person does with that information. For Kant, what is right or ethical is always ethical, no matter what the circumstances or eventual outcome might be.[39]

> The biggest temptation for many journalists is to sacrifice all other competing interests in pursuit of the truth.

Kant's theory presents a basic dilemma for journalists: To what should the media ultimately pledge their allegiance? Truth? Subject? Audience? Employer? Or is the ethical path to try to balance all of these things? The biggest temptation for many journalists is to sacrifice all other competing interests in pursuit of the truth. Would the media be justified, for example, if their coverage of terrorist attacks actually helped the terrorists to carry out further violence, as in the Mumbai example?

Benjamin Constant (1767–1830), a French philosopher, politician and contemporary of Kant, countered that taking Kant's system literally would make society impossible. In the 19th century, British philosopher John Stuart Mill (1806–1873) came up with an ethical system based on what he called the "greatest-happiness principle"; it states that the right course of action is the one that leads to the greatest happiness for the greatest number of people *within certain reason*. "Certain reason" means that a common logical and ethical boundary stops people from doing whatever they want and using their collective happiness to justify their actions. When investigative reporters use false names and backgrounds to convince people or organizations to give them access to insider information, for example, their behavior would demonstrate Mill's principle. Reporters might justify this approach by saying it allows them to do a better job of informing the public—in other words, it is dishonesty in service of a greater good. Mill's view is part of a tradition of ethics called utilitarianism.

If a newspaper reporter found out that one of the paper's major advertisers was doing something unsafe or illegal, the editor might hesitate to publish that information. This scenario roughly illustrates the problem that 20th-century American philosopher John Rawls (1921–2002) addressed. Rawls added the idea of a veil of ignorance to the philosophical discussion of ethics. It suggests that being ethical requires a sort of ignorance of any individual characteristics that might influence someone's decisions. Rawls argued that certain people or groups could use personal distinctions to bend ethical standards. According to Rawls, no one should be exempt from the media's scrutiny, regardless of wealth, power, position, ethnicity, sexuality and so forth. This type of ethical challenge becomes a factor in any situation where media producers accept payment from outside sources, such as advertisers or sponsors, which might tempt them to "spin" their coverage so as to benefit their business relationship.

Although these thinkers' theories are examples of the major philosophical perspectives in the Western tradition, their ideas on ethics are far from the final words on ethics in mass media. More than ever, voices of dissent in the West, such as that of Benjamin Constant, along with postmodern and Eastern philosophers, are renewing the global debate over ethical standards for mass media in the 21st century. It is important that we recognize that while there is no single accepted model of ethics, ethical decision-making in the media is critical to the well-being of everyone involved in using mass media content, from the individual consumer to the global community.

The evolution of the Internet, new media and Web 2.0 has blurred the lines between the traditional roles of media producers and media consumers such that all of us who encounter media must develop greater awareness of our roles and ethical responsibilities. (See Chapter 10 for further discussion of this topic.) Like pioneers in the American Old West, those who are blazing the trails on the technological frontier and are concerned about the potential dangers of mass media in the Digital Age often ask, "Who's the law in these here parts?" The answer to this question is, in part, the changing legal and regulatory systems discussed throughout this chapter; to a large degree, however, the answer is "all of us." We all must take more responsibility for our individual roles as cyber-media citizens.

11.12

Did categorical imperatives guide the media coverage during the tragic Taj Mahal Hotel terrorist attack in Mumbai on November 22, 2008?

India Today/SIPA/Newscom

It is important that we recognize that while there is no single accepted model of ethics, ethical decision-making in the media is critical to the well-being of everyone involved in using mass media content, from the individual consumer to the global community.

Self-Regulation in the Media

In addition to heeding the external constraints applied by government, the media have developed a keen self-awareness of their own ethical responsibilities. This awareness includes both a sense of duty to all the parties involved and the ethical principles involved in the process of producing media content. How does the final product affect one's audience, employer, profession, society and self? These are all important considerations for ethical media producers. At the same time, they must decide which ethical principles should guide their decisions in creating content, such as fairness, timeliness, truthfulness, accuracy and the protection of privacy. In the constantly evolving mass media world of the Digital Age, it can be incredibly challenging for any one person to wrestle with all the current ethical concerns, let alone balance them in practice.

One of the important efforts at self-regulation within the media is the establishment of professional codes of ethics. A code of ethics is a clear statement of ethical guidelines developed to help individuals make decisions. It typically addresses issues that are relevant to the interests of a particular group—in this case, media producers. The greatest drawbacks to professional codes of ethics are that they are often not specific enough to help with individual ethical problems, and they can quickly lose relevance as society and technology evolve. Three examples of codes of ethics tailored to address the broad ethical issues facing professional media producers are the Society of Professional Journalists' Code of Ethics, the American Society of Newspaper Editors' Statement of Principles and the Radio-Television News Directors Association's Code of Broadcast News Ethics. Of course, with the rapid rise of bloggers and other citizen journalists who neither belong to mainstream professional organizations nor subscribe to these established codes of ethics, the challenge of maintaining basic ethical standards for media content producers has become far more challenging.

A second method of self-regulation that media producers have historically employed is the development of institutional policies for conduct. Unlike codes of conduct, these standards are enforceable within an organization. Policy books in broadcasting, along with operating and editorial policies in print media, comprise collections of prescriptive standards that govern the conduct of media producers on ethical issues.

Even though these broad forms of self-regulation at the professional and organizational levels can be helpful, ultimately the burden of responsibility for ethical conduct rests primarily on every individual who creates media content. The importance of this principle becomes painfully clear in the story of one former *New York Times* reporter, Jayson Blair.

Jayson Blair was a hungry young reporter who, despite questionable ethical practices early in his career, managed to work his way up through the ranks at *The New York Times*. He became one of the lead reporters at the paper's national desk and was a prolific contributor to the *Times* during his four-year career there. Documented complaints about serious errors in Blair's reporting stretched as far back as his college days, when he was editor-in-chief of the University of Maryland's school paper, *The Diamondback*. Managers at *The New York Times* either missed or ignored these red flags when they accepted Blair as a summer intern in 1998, and subsequently offered him an extended position in 1999 upon completion of his degree. In actuality, Blair did not finish his degree before returning to the *Times*, but claimed that he had.

In 2001, Blair was promoted to full-time staff reporter and in 2002, advanced to the national desk. His coverage of the Beltway sniper attacks in Washington, D.C. drew harsh criticism from prosecutors and law enforcement officials involved in the case, who regularly cited huge errors in Blair's reporting. In April 2003, questions about Blair's journalistic practices came to a head as hard evidence surfaced that he had plagiarized an article written by a former intern at the *Times*. Blair resigned from *The New York Times* a month later. An internal investigation revealed that almost half of the 73 stories he had written for the national desk from late 2002 onward contained serious fabrications and, in some cases, outright plagiarism.[40]

In the aftermath of the Blair fiasco, management at *The New York Times* acknowledged failures within the organization that allowed Blair to keep practicing journalism despite his unethical conduct. Although the paper was partially responsible for Blair's abuses, it would be nearly impossible even for a media outlet with the immense resources of the *Times* to check every detail of every story written by every journalist on its staff. The story of Jayson Blair illustrates the difficulty of policing media ethics, and it highlights the critical need for individual media producers to strive to practice their craft in an ethical manner. Lee Thornton, former White House correspondent, talks about journalistic ethics and the Jayson Blair case in the following segment, "Journalistic Ethics." ▶

THE ETHICAL CHALLENGES OF A CONVERGED WORLD

The convergence of media forms has led to the blurring and even disappearance of the traditional roles of producers and consumers. To fully understand how convergence affects media ethics, we need to return to the three major players behind the story of mass media: the media, the government and the media consumers. The media, as both content producers and government critics, struggle to maintain the balance between observing legal constraints and honoring the ethical principles of journalism—namely, monitoring the actions of government and freely disseminating ideas across society.

Ethical Responsibilities of Public Media Producers

The growing accessibility of technology allows nearly everyone to directly access and consume mass media content. Armed with a personal computer, cell phone, digital camera, video or voice recorder and access to the Internet, anyone can easily produce media content and distribute it around the globe with just a few keystrokes. The potential to produce and distribute content places a new and enormous power in the hands of the public. Along with this sweeping mass media power, however, comes a new level of individual responsibility. The all-too clear and present danger is that, without an awareness of and commitment to media ethics, these new consumer/producers could compromise the very freedoms that mass media must strongly protect.

▶ Journalistic Ethics

Former White House correspondent Lee Thornton on journalistic ethics and the Jayson Blair case.

Along with this sweeping mass media power, however, comes a new level of individual responsibility.

Consider, for instance, the tragic case of Megan Meier. Meier, a resident of the small town of Dardenne Prairie, Missouri, committed suicide in October 2006 after being rejected by a boy named Josh Evans, who had been courting her on a social networking site, MySpace. She was only 13 years old. Investigators later discovered that Josh Evans was a fictional character created by Lori Drew, the mother of a former friend of Meier's. Drew created "Josh" to get back at Meier for allegedly spreading rumors about her daughter. Over the course of several weeks, Drew used this character to romance Meier. After successfully winning the girl's affections, Drew then used "Josh" to verbally attack her, regularly posting notes implying that Meier was a gossip and that Josh didn't want to be friends with such a person. On the morning before her death, Meier received a heartbreaking MySpace message from "Josh": "The world would be a better place without you."[41] According to an employee of Drew's at the time, Meier's last posting to Josh was "You're the kind of boy a girl would kill herself over."[42] Twenty minutes later, Meier's parents found her hanged to death in her closet.

In May 2008, Drew was indicted by a federal grand jury in Los Angeles, where MySpace's servers are located, on four computer-related charges: She was found guilty of three. One of the major problems facing prosecutors was that there were very few laws and even fewer legal precedents in effect that had any significant bearing on the case. Technology had progressed past the established jurisdiction of the law, which in turn had no way of dealing with the more serious ethical implications of Lori Drew's actions.

Especially in the absence of the law, ethics is vital to protecting the liberties and privacy of every individual and group. The Meier case illustrates how essential it is for us all to learn to be both media and ethically literate in the new digital community.[43] But how do we do that? Let's consider the case of Ken Silverstein.

Critical Models for Mass Media Ethics

Ken Silverstein and his colleague sat across a conference table from several representatives of the power-house lobbying firm Cassidy and Associates. Silverstein had contacted the firm, one of the most influential in Washington, D.C., to enlist its help in launching a public relations campaign to bolster the troubled image of the country of Turkmenistan, where Silverstein's employer, the Maldon Group, had significant business interests. What Cassidy and Associates didn't know was that Silverstein, who had been interacting with the firm under the name "Ken Case," was not really a consultant for the Maldon Group. The Maldon Group itself was fictional. Rather, Silverstein was a journalist and the Washington editor of *Harper's Magazine*.

Silverstein had gone undercover to try to expose the corruption and the utter lack of ethical concern in the Washington lobbying machine. His report, published in *Harper's* July 2007 issue, was called, "Foreign Agents . . . What U.S. Lobbyists Do for Dictators: An Undercover Report by Ken Silverstein." Silverstein not only exposed the corruption, but he also boldly revealed how he used deception to obtain the information he needed for the report. His actions rekindled a robust discussion about the ethics of undercover journalism. Silverstein's critics, such as Howard Kurtz of *The Washington Post*, condemned his methods as unethical and stated that no story is worth lying to get. In his own defense, Silverstein claimed that the wrongs done by Washington lobbyists, revealed through his investigation, far outweighed his ethical transgressions because they affected the lives and security of the nation. But if a journalist like Silverstein is willing to lie to get information from an unwilling subject, what stops him from also lying to the reader? On the other side of the coin, if lying is the only way to get important information that might affect the public good, is lying the lesser of two evils?[44]

Media participants face such difficult questions like this every day, and their number and complexity will only grow as advances in technology continue to push past established laws and ethical systems. Ethicists have developed critical thinking models in an effort to help decision makers tackle these difficult issues. For example, philosopher Ralph Potter created "Potter's Box," a four-step system arranged spatially in a square, as a sequential outline for ethical decision-making. Finding out what happened, analyzing values, identifying loyalties and looking at the principles involved constitute the four corners of this box and present a logical path for decision makers to follow.

Sissela Bok has suggested another framework for making ethical decisions using three steps: (1) consulting one's conscience, (2) consulting others to learn if there is a way to achieve the same goal without facing an ethical problem and (3) considering how an action will affect others.[45] Also, to help journalists in ethical decision-making, Roy Peter Clark of the Poynter Institute for Media Studies offers the following questions, which serve as guidelines in the decision-making process:

1. Is the story, photo or graphic complete and accurate to the best of my knowledge?
2. Am I missing an important point of view?
3. How would I feel if this story or photo were about me?
4. What good will publication do?
5. What does my reader or viewer need to know?

Although differing somewhat in their details, all of these models share the common goal of showing what critical thinking in an ethical context looks like in practical terms. Wading through the sea of competing views to arrive at a paradigm that is both helpful and satisfying can seem overwhelming. However, those who have adopted critical thinking as a way of life will have the clear advantage in safely navigating through the uncharted waters of change. At the end of the day, it will be these critical thinkers of the world who will serve as ethical guiding lights—as did Su Shi and James Franklin in their generations—and for generations to come.

CONCLUSION: ARE WE LEGALLY AND ETHICALLY RESPONSIBLE?

Having a basic understanding of the key aspects of mass media law is more important in the 21st century than it has ever been. Mass media law is no longer merely the purview of lawyers and MBAs working in the various media production and distribution industries that collectively make up the field of mass media. As discussed throughout this book, mass media in the Digital Age—with its easily accessible and low-cost technologies—are blurring many of the previously clear lines between media content producers and media content owners. With this new power comes greater responsibility, requiring all of us as participatory media consumers to cultivate our understanding of the core areas of mass media law and ethics. With the rapid growth of consumer-created media on the Internet, from YouTube to blogs and other forms of citizen journalism, to such social media sites as Facebook and MySpace, we all have a vested interest in arming ourselves with a sound knowledge of mass media law and ethics so as to better prepare ourselves and our fellow digital denizens to be able to identify and address potential legal pitfalls and dangers. When we grasp the essential workings of law and ethics, we will be much better equipped to not only prevent liabilities for ourselves, but also to explore and enjoy the ever-expanding reaches of the digital universe in responsible, ethical ways.

CHAPTER SUMMARY	KEY TERMS
Brief History of Mass Media Law A brief overview of the fascinating history of mass media law—from Gutenberg's printing press to present day—provides context for the discussion of current mass media law.	media law Stationers Guild Star Chamber Founding Fathers Fourth Estate Articles of Confederation Constitutional Convention Espionage Act Sedition Act Smith Act censorship
Defamation: Libel and Slander Investigates the basic forms of defamation: libel and slander	defamation slander libel defamation with malice negligent libel
Media and Privacy Looks at the issue of privacy in the media, including the Internet, and invasion of privacy laws and explains individual rights to privacy and circumstances that are exceptions to our rights to privacy. Visual Media **Privacy in Public Places** The widespread use of security monitoring technology in public places is challenging previous legal limitations on the protection of individual privacy. 1. Do you perceive the trend in heavy use of video surveillance in the United States as a disturbing violation of our personal privacy or as a fair trade for the added security? Why? 2. Do you feel that the federal government should have more or less authority to regulate the use of video surveillance technologies? Why?	privacy release appropriation tort public figure
Mass Media Law and National Security The special and often-conflicting issues of national security and the media's right and responsibility to monitor the activities of government are explained.	prior restraint Freedom of Information Act (FOIA)

Historical Roots of Copyright Law The historical foundation for studying the fascinating and often complex work of copyright law is explored. **Visual Media** **Lawrence Lessig on Copyright History** Stanford University Law Professor Lawrence Lessig explores the historic roots and 21st-century challenges of U.S. copyright law. 1. Explain the primary difference between U.S. copyright laws and author's rights laws found throughout the European Union. **Copyright Basics** An animated, quick tutorial on how copyright works. 1. Based upon your viewing of this animated explanation of copyright, what are the basic steps you would undertake to protect a written, musical or artistic work? **Creative Commons** Introduction to the Creative Commons alternative to traditional copyright law. 1. Explain why you do or don't feel that the Creative Commons system is as good as, or perhaps better than, the traditional copyright registration system administered through the Library of Congress.	copyright intellectual properties Statute of Anne copyright piracy Copyright Law of the United States authorship author fair use doctrine legal jurisdiction copyright infringement Berne Convention international intellectual property rights (IPR) copyright legal tradition author's rights system Communications Act of 1934
Confidentiality in Newsgathering The often controversial and contentious issue and conflicting interests of news reporters and news organizations protecting confidential sources from exposure during court trials and legislative hearings is analyzed.	shield laws Code of Federal Regulation gag orders contempt of court
Pornography: Free Expression or Obscenity? Explores the ongoing and contentious conflict over pornography and obscenity in the media and looks at how Congress and the courts have struggled to set and enforce "community standards" in a rapidly evolving society driven by ever-changing mass media technologies.	obscenity pornography obscenity laws Miller test "Internet haven"
Ethics and Mass Media The historic foundations and contemporary challenges of journalism and mass media ethics are examined. **Visual Media** **Journalistic Ethics** Former White House correspondent Lee Thornton on journalistic ethics and the Jayson Blair case. 1. Based upon this video segment, what is your view of the current state of journalistic ethics in America? 2. Can journalistic ethics ever be effectively adopted by the rapidly expanding world of Internet news, where the very definition of who is and isn't a journalist has become blurred?	media ethics golden mean golden rule categorical imperatives "greatest-happiness principle" Utilitarianism veil of ignorance code of ethics
The Ethical Challenges of a Converged World Investigates the special challenges presented when establishing and enforcing ethical standards to rapidly changing media in a news environment driven by the converging mass media platforms of broadcast, print and the Internet.	"Potter's Box"

NOTES

1   The Cambridge history of English and American literature in 18 volumes: Colonial and revolutionary literature: Early national literature, Part I. XV. (1907–1921). Retrieved from www.bartleby.com/225/0702.html

2   Extensive portions of this chapter are drawn from the author's Mass Media Law course lectures, University of Maryland, University College.

3   Ibid.

4   Bill of Rights, First Amendment to the U.S. Constitution.

5   The Alien Registration Act or Smith Act (18 U.S.C.§ 2385).

6   Extensive portions of this chapter are drawn from the author's Mass Media Law course lectures, University of Maryland, University College.

7   *Tammy Kitzmiller, et al. v. Dover Area School District, et al.* (400 F. Supp. 2d 707, Docket no. 4cv 2688).

8   Rasmussen, A. F. (2005). *Danish Prime Minister's official response.* Retrieved from http://gfx-master.tv2.dk/images/Nyhederne/Pdf/side3.pdf

9   Ibid.

10 Ibid.

11 Jurkowitz, M. (2005, January 9). Media distrust may be libel-case key. *Boston Globe.*

12 Burnett, N. (2003). New York Times v. Sullivan. In R. A. Parker (Ed.), *Free speech on trial: Communication perspectives on landmark Supreme Court decisions.* University of Alabama Press.

13 *New York Times v. Sullivan, U.S. Supreme Court,* March 9, 1964 (376 U.S. 254).

14 Liptak, A. (2003, June 2). Internet battle raises questions about the First Amendment. *New York Times.*

15 Ibid.

16 Standler, R. (1998). *Privacy law in the USA.* Retrieved from www.rbs2.com/privacy.htm

17 Ibid.

18 Associated Press. (2007, September 21). Virgin sued for using teen's photo. *The Age.* Retrieved from www.theage.com.au/news/technology/virgin-sued-for-using-teensphoto/2007/09/21/1189881735928.html

19 Fletcher, D. (2010, May 20). How Facebook is redefining privacy. *Time.* Retrieved from www.time.com/time/business/article/0,8599,1990582,00.html

20 Gates, G. (2010, May 12). Facebook privacy: A bewildering tangle of options. *The New York Times.* Retrieved from www.nytimes.com/interactive/2010/05/12/business/facebook-privacy.html

21 Standler, R. (1998). *Privacy law in the USA.* Retrieved from www.rbs2.com/privacy.htm

22 Ibid.

23 Ibid.

24 Vlahos, J. (2009, October 1). Surveillance society: New high-tech cameras are watching you. *Popular Mechanics.*

25 *New York Times Co. (and the Washington Post) v. United States* (1971: 403 U.S. 713, 91 S.Ct. 2140, 29 L.Ed.2d 822, 1 Med.L.Rptr. 1031).

26 The Constitution gives Congress the power to enact laws establishing a system of copyright in the United States. Congress enacted the first federal copyright law in May 1790 (which included this language), and the first work was registered within two weeks. Originally claims were recorded by clerks of U.S. district courts. Not until 1870 were copyright functions centralized in the Library of Congress under the direction of then-Librarian of Congress Ainsworth Rand Spofford. The Copyright Office became a separate department of the Library of Congress in 1897, and Thorvald Solberg was appointed the first register of copyrights. [U.S. Copyright Office. (n.d.). *A brief introduction and history.* Retrieved from www.copyright.gov/circs/circ1a.html]

27 Patterson, L. R. (1968). *Copyright in historical perspective.* Vanderbilt University Press.

28 Associated Press. (2007, September 21). Virgin sued for using teen's photo. *The Age*. Retrieved from www.theage.com.au/news/technology/virgin-sued-for-using-teensphoto/2007/09/21/1189881735928.html

29 Rampell, C. (2007, October 19). Standing up to take down notices: Web users turn the tables on copyright holders. *Washington Post*. Retrieved from www.washingtonpost.com/wp-dyn/content/article/2007/10/18/AR2007101802453.html

30 (2007). Digital Life America. *2007 survey*.

31 See the author's "Creative Commons" video segment in this chapter.

32 MLRC Institute. (n.d.). *The reporter's privilege: A historical overview*. Retrieved from www.gsspa.org/conferences/fall/10051964_1%20-%20Historical%20Overiview%20of%20the%20Reporter_s%20Privilege.PDF

33 *Branzburg v. Hayes*, 408 U.S. 665 (1972).

34 Ibid.

35 Abstracted from live recordings of Lenny Bruce in concert describing his court battles over obscenity and pornography charges.

36 *Miller v. California* (1973).

37 Greenwood, P. (2007, September 19). The decline and fall of Britney Spears. *The Times*. Retrieved from http://entertainment.timesonline.co.uk/tol/arts_and_entertainment/music/article2484550.ece

38 Veena. (2008, December 5). *Media coverage 24/7: Mumbai strikes did more harm than good*. Retrieved from http://aware.instablogs.com/entry/media-coverage-24x7-mumbaistrikes-did-more-harm-than-good/

39 Kant, I. (1785). *Kant's critique of practical reason and other works on the theory of ethics*.

40 Nwazota, K. (2004, December 10). Jayson Blair: A case study of what went wrong at *The New York Times*. Retrieved from www.pbs.org/newshour/media/media_ethics/casestudy_blair.php

41 Steinhauer, J. (2008, November 26). Verdict in MySpace suicide case. *The New York Times*. Retrieved from www.nytimes.com/2008/11/27/us/27myspace.html?ref=todayspaper

42 Ibid.

43 Ibid.

44 Lisheron, M. (2007, October/November). Lying to get the truth. *American Journalism Review*.

45 Bok, S. (1999). *Lying: Moral choice in public and private life*. Vintage.

The Media Experience, Culture and You

12

The Power of Photography in Mass Media

aaltair/Shutterstock.com

CHAPTER OUTLINE
Visual Communication in Mass Media
Finding Meaning in Visual Media
Photography and Modern Culture
Photojournalism: The Image as a Mass Medium
Photography in the Digital Age
Conclusion: The Mass Media Effects of the Photographic Image

LEARNING OBJECTIVES

1. Explain what visual culture is and how it has indelibly informed our interactions with and understanding of mass media.
2. Illustrate why visual literacy is so important to becoming a skilled mass media consumer.
3. Characterize the role of images, especially photographic ones, in the creation and expression of modern media culture.
4. Outline the role of photojournalism in newsgathering and reporting.

5. Describe how digital photography and digital-image processing have revolutionized the mass media.
6. Evaluate how advances in digital photography and photographic technologies have altered the ways in which media uses images.

AMERICAN PHOTOGRAPHER

Alfred Stieglitz (1864–1946) is considered to be one of the most influential figures in the history of visual arts. Through his photography and writing, and in his efforts to advance photography and art in the United States, Stieglitz contributed enormously toward establishing the role of visual images across modern media platforms. In 1887, he wrote his first article about photography, titled "A Word or Two about Amateur Photography in Germany" and published in *The American Amateur Photographer* magazine. By the time he returned to the United States in 1891, Stieglitz had emerged as a prize-winning professional photographer. In 1893, he became co-editor of *The American Amateur Photographer*, the leading photography-focused publication at the time. In 1902, Stieglitz launched his third major photography publication, called *Camera Works*, through which he advanced his ideas of the high technical and artistic standards required to support photography as a legitimate art form and predicted the foundational role photography would play in the evolution of mass media. Stieglitz saw well-composed and well-published photographs as powerful windows on the world that allow the viewer to ponder the human experience. In the July 1918 edition of *The Photographic Journal of America*, he wrote:

As I travel and study what art has accomplished in various countries and what nature really means and is, photography's possibilities assume gigantic proportions. It is to [those] who understand nature and love it, and who love photography, that the future will bring the revelations little dream of today.[1]

Alfred Stieglitz remained a leading figure in the evolution of photography until his death in 1946 at the age of 82. His powerful works reveal a prophetic sense of how photography would evolve through the 20th and now into the 21st century. Recent advanced technologies have made it possible for anyone to become a photographer, and this technological trend parallels the trend toward a read–write culture, in which we are all as much media producers as we are consumers (see Chapter 3). Photography plays a pivotal role in culture and society and, as such, this chapter focuses largely on how images convey and reinforce mass media messages.

Recent advanced technologies have made it possible for anyone to become a photographer, and this technological trend parallels the trend toward a read–write culture, in which we are all as much media producers as we are consumers.

12.1

Käsebier, Gertrude, photographer. Blessed Art Thou Among Women. Courtesy of Library of Congress

VISUAL COMMUNICATION IN MASS MEDIA

Today, most of us interact with mass media primarily though images, sometimes supported by text or audio, depending on the content and the medium. Research psychologists working in the area of human perception have demonstrated that for the great majority of people, regardless of their cultural context, the visual image is by far the dominant source of information. Therefore, it is not surprising that modern mass media are, to a large extent, built around visual images.

Numerous psychological and neurological processes help explain how we interpret and extract meaning from images. Nevertheless, knowledge of how visual communication functions in a mass media context is what drives our *understanding* of visual culture—those aspects of our day-to-day lives that rely on some form of imagery to convey meaning. According to researchers, even when we receive information

12.2

Images dominate the way cultures communicate, see themselves and interact with each other.

J Marshall—Tribaleye Images/Alamy Stock Photo

through senses other than sight, our minds automatically convert this information into "mental images" of what is being communicated. In other words, we automatically "visualize" the message to identify meaning, to understand and to learn. The ability to evaluate, apply or create visual representations and to understand how they communicate meaning is known as visual literacy.

In this Digital Age, it would be rare to go through an entire day without being bombarded by some form of visual media or media technology. This daily interaction, some would argue, has forced us to grow more sophisticated at digesting, analyzing and interpreting visual messages. In his book *Visual Culture*, Richard Howells of the University of Leeds (England) describes visual culture as the dynamic process in which visual meaning is both created and communicated throughout our visual world. Visual literacy, by extension, is the understanding of how all forms of visual media—including drawings, graphs, paintings, photographs, films, advertisements and television programs communicate meaning in a *mass media* world.[2]

FINDING MEANING IN VISUAL MEDIA

While this chapter focuses primarily on the media impact of photographs, visual media can comprise any form of physical media, such as fine art, drawings, graphic illustrations, sculptures, visual icons and so forth. Our ability to interpret visual media is affected by several factors—the form of the visual medium, the subject matter of the medium and the environment in which that medium is delivered.

The Visual Form

Iconic images, or visual representations, are common in the larger visual language of mass media. Their meanings are culturally determined and widely shared. Icons may come in the form of abstract symbols that represent a system of beliefs, such as the Christian cross or the Muslim crescent moon. These symbols may appear either alone or embedded in more contextualized images. Imagine, for example, a photograph of a white building resting amidst a rural setting, where a cloudy and ominous sky

12.3

Visual media come in all forms, and thus convey multiple meanings. What do you think of when you see this image?

ImageZoo/Alamy Stock Photo

12.4

The iconic symbol (the cross) on the roof of this building indicates that it is a church, thus limiting the extent to which we may interpret this photo.

Alexander Gayuk/Stringer

12.5

Since the mid-20th century, yellow ribbons have represented solidarity and support for soldiers—both loved ones and strangers—who are facing dangers in war zones around the world.

Karin Hildebrand Lau/Shutterstock.com

indicates a threatening storm. We see the building, its door, windows and roofline. People are absent from the scene and the viewer is left to project his or her own meaning or story onto the image. Now imagine the same scene, the same building, on the same stormy day. This time, against the dark storm clouds at the peak of the building's roof, we see a cross. This iconic symbol immediately reveals that the building is not just a random, nondescript structure, but rather a country church. Such knowledge determines how much meaning we can project onto the image. The photographer has chosen to draw the viewer's attention to this iconic symbol—in essence, communicating a visual story that relates to our shared, cultural conceptions of a "church." While we will look at the photograph and certainly develop our own individual interpretations about what it means, by introducing the cross, the photographer has influenced that process toward a particular direction.

Iconic images are sometimes quite visually literal: a flag-draped coffin, an American flag waving in the breeze. These images convey meaning and facilitate the communication of a story, whether or not those stories actually represent the central theme of the image. The quick recognition evoked by an iconic image—whether a memorial sculpture (the Marine Corps Memorial representing the raising of the flag on Iwo Jima during World War II), a light installation (the blue lights representing the World Trade Center towers) or a video (footage of the landing of US Airways Flight 1549 on the Hudson River)—serves as a useful storytelling tool for visual media artists. Some logos, such as the familiar Nike swoosh, are immediately recognized around the world in all their forms; the same is true of the pink ribbon for breast cancer awareness.

The Subject Matter

Visual media that effectively establish a strong creator–viewer interaction are highly valued and can have a profound impact on society, reaching across geographical and cultural barriers. Often, what creates this strong connection is the subject matter. For example, at 8:00 a.m. on May 12, 2008, a massive earthquake that measured an astounding 8.0 on the Richter scale hit Sichuan Province, China, killing a reported 68,636 people and more than 12.5 million animals and destroying many towns and villages. The earthquake left 12.5 million Chinese homeless and caused an estimated $20 billion in property damage. Chinese authorities, who are usually highly averse to negative publicity, allowed the international press, including photojournalists and TV journalists from around the world, unprecedented access to the scenes of devastation. Images such as those captured by Reuters photojournalist Jason Lee showed the world the human tragedy of the Great Sichuan Earthquake, causing many who viewed the images to feel an emotional connection with the victims. Textual descriptions of the Great Sichuan Earthquake, along with radio and TV news reporters' narratives, supplied us with the facts and statistics of the story, but powerful images brought the emotional story to world audiences. Lee's iconic images of the tragedy have entered the visual history of modern China. Although such images convey a heartbreaking human story, they are, in their own way, quite beautiful.

12.6

Images such as this one brought the real story of the massive destruction caused by the May 12, 2008 Sichuan earthquake to the world despites the Chinese government's initial attempts to limit the story.

Aurora Photos/Alamy Stock Photo

The Media Environment

The environment in which we experience visual media can also directly affect our ability to find meaning in them. For example, consider the experience you might have while looking at an image-rich magazine article in *National Geographic* magazine, and then consider how that experience would change if you viewed the same article on the *National Geographic* Website. The text, images, and story might be the same, but the Website's interactive options and links to related articles and features would enable you to resize each photograph for closer viewing. It might even contain a link to a companion documentary film from the National Geographic Channel.

Essentially, the impact that the visual media have and the meaning and stories that they convey have changed with the change in medium. Both versions offer the same images but in different ways that change your experience with the content. Much like the creative people at *National Geographic*, the author and publisher of this book offer you options for mixed content by incorporating closely linked media through which you can experience photographs as well as videos. In both of these examples, and in many other examples we encounter regularly, the idea is to combine compelling visual and textual information to create a captivating and memorable story.

The creators of visual images *encode* the images with meaning that we, the viewers of the images, then *decode* (see the discussion of the transactional model of communication included in the Mass Communication Models, Theories and Research chart in Chapter 1). However, as with all mass media and

12.7

Devastating images of the aftermath of the earthquake in Sichuan Province, China. This photo, and many others like it, were shot in May 2008 by photographer Jason Lee and have become part of the visual history of modern China.

Aurora Photos/Alamy Stock Photo

The photographer or artist uses the visual medium to communicate a story, but the story we experience is a combination of what the creator has brought to the image and what we have projected into it.

communication, the meaning that we decode from any image can never be exactly what the creator of the image intended, simply because we all bring a unique set of skills, experiences, cultural biases and personal tastes to the process. The photographer or artist uses the visual medium to communicate a story, but the story we experience is a combination of what the creator has brought to the image and what we have projected into it. The most celebrated artists and photographers not only recognize this collaboration between creator and viewer, but actually strive to compose each work so that it delivers the most visual content—thereby enabling a wide range of viewers to build their own story and extract their own meaning from the image. Creators of the images we experience in print, in films, on television and on the Web work with viewers in the same way, relying on the synergistic and interdependent relationship between the creator and the viewer to establish a meaningful narrative.[3]

The physical and technological platforms through which we view images are elemental to our media environment. In the mid-20th century, media futurist Marshall McLuhan posited, "The media is the message." He was partially on the right track. We know today that the

We know today that the medium through which we access and experience any form of media content—whether visual or textual—is not the message per se, but it certainly exerts a great deal of influence over our media experience and our understanding of the message.

medium through which we access and experience any form of media content—whether visual or textual—is not the message per se, but it certainly exerts a great deal of influence over our media experience and our understanding of the message. For example, our experience viewing photographs in a book or magazine is quite different from our experience viewing photographs on the Internet. The technologies through which we view images—the types of visual windows we use—influence our ability to extract meaning from the thousands of images that we encounter every day. It is not by accident that Microsoft for many years named its industry-dominating operating system "Windows."

In her fascinating 2006 book *The Virtual Window: From Alberti to Microsoft*, author Anne Friedberg offers a thought-provoking definition of visual windows as frames that contain and portray the content of our experience within a "two-dimensional surface" and which "dramatically alter our conception of space and, even more radically, of time."[4] In other words, the multiplicity of image screens, both physical and virtual, through which we experience and interact with images greatly contributes to our understanding of limitless environments and endless stories, both real and virtual. From books and magazines, to movies and televisions, to computers and smartphones, the boundaries between the real world and the virtual world are fading each day. Our ability to understand how we interact with images, and to use our relationship with images to enrich our lives, has never been more important.

PHOTOGRAPHY AND MODERN CULTURE

Storytelling through mass media is a central theme of this book. Today, more than at any time in human history, images, especially photographic images (including from film and video) have become the primary means by which we meaningfully consume and communicate stories. A brief history of photography demonstrates how the photographic image evolves into an important cultural tool for understanding reality. (See Chapter 2 for more on the history of photography.) In fact, as American author and political activist Susan Sontag explored in her influential book *On Photography*, culture in the 20th century was created by the widespread production and viewing of photographs, which she deemed one of society's most important activities, claiming how "a photograph is never less than . . . a material vestige of its subject in a way that no painting can be."[5]

Photography can also alter reality and present a dreamlike, irrational vision, far removed from the documentary representation of people, places and events. As described at the beginning of this chapter, Alfred Stieglitz established photography as an inseparable combination of technological process and artistic expression that could hold its own with paintings and illustrations, often surpassing painting and illustration in its ability to communicate emotions. Stieglitz saw photographs as visual metaphors built around their ability to elicit emotional reactions in the viewer, which he termed equivalence.

This equivalent experience helps explain how some images can capture and expand our imaginations, while others open disturbing windows onto previously unimaginable realities of poverty, war, genocide, and natural and human-made catastrophes.

Through photographic images, we are able to see the unbelievable; often, we are forced to confront hard-learned and painful truths. Today, some people fear that society has developed an overreliance on images, preferring them over direct experience. Others are convinced that both photographic images and moving images from film and television have infinitely enriched our lives and served as extraordinary catalysts for uniting peoples and cultures—to an extent that Stieglitz himself could not have imagined. Films' and television's image-based storytelling relies on a series of individual images, called frames, that speed before our eyes at a rate of 24 frames per second for films and 30 frames per second for television. In other words, our mind no longer perceives individual images; rather, we experience continuous photographic scenes that tell a story.

Manufactured Realities

In 2006, a photograph taken by Chinese photographer Liu Weiqing received international attention. Liu claimed that he waited hidden in a ditch to capture a shot of wild antelope walking across the Tibetan countryside, apparently unfazed as a high-speed train sped by along the recently opened Qinghai–Tibet railway. The Chinese state-run news service released the image to promote the controversial new train system, hoping it would persuade critics that the train system was environmentally safe and nonthreatening to the fragile Tibetan wildlife and ecosystem. This compelling image, which was deemed one of the top 10 photographs of 2006, even won the photographer a national award. In less than two years, however, both the image and its photographer went from famous to infamous.

By 2008, a number of photographers familiar with digital-image manipulation techniques found a microscopic line near the lower segment of the railway bridge in Liu's photograph. Its presence indicated that the image was actually a composite—that is, a clever fusing of two separate photographs. Around the same time, animal behavior experts voiced their concerns about the image, asserting that wild antelope are highly sensitive to noise and vibrations; thus, the animal would be unlikely to calmly trot next to a passing high-speed train, but would instead disperse in utter panic at the disturbance. The photographer eventually admitted that the image was a government-sponsored hoax, but the desired effect had already been achieved. His manipulated image managed to garner national and international acceptance of the new rail system, which most agreed both respected the ecological infrastructure of the region and benefitted the Chinese and Tibetan peoples.

The manipulation of photographs as visual "proof" has a long and checkered history that parallels the history of photography itself. For much of this history, the percentage of manipulated photographs was small, principally because accomplishing this feat required great skill and the clever use of chemicals and darkroom equipment. By the later decades of the 20th century, however, photographic manipulation techniques had become much more sophisticated. In areas such as fashion and glamour photography, they were seen as acceptable and completely ethical—as long as they were not used to intentionally and directly mislead the public. This all changed with the advent of powerful, relatively easy-to-use, and inexpensive digital photography software programs, the most famous of which are Adobe's Photoshop and Lightroom programs. Today's digital darkroom programs enable anyone—professional and amateur alike—to alter photographs in ways that are often difficult or impossible to detect.

> By the later decades of the 20th century, however, photographic manipulation techniques had become much more sophisticated. In areas such as fashion and glamour photography, they were seen as acceptable and completely ethical—as long as they were not used to intentionally and directly mislead the public.

Manufacturing realities via photography is not just a characteristic of modern culture. For example, American Civil War photographer Mathew Brady (first introduced in Chapter 2) staged some of the most

12.8

Manufactured realities in fashion shots such as this are just one of the many techniques photographers employ to capture and persuade the media consumer.

RazoomGame/Shutterstock.com

famous images of the war. Photo-historians and photojournalism ethicists generally agree that Brady—unlike Liu Weiqing—was not intentionally trying to manipulate the public. Instead, he was merely coming up with creative solutions to overcome the challenges he faced—the size and technological requirements of the cameras and mobile darkrooms, safety concerns related to both the darkroom chemicals and the potential threats posed by snipers. Though staged, Mathew Brady's frontlines Civil War images made a tremendous impact on his contemporaries' experience and understanding of this very important period in U.S. history—and they still do the same for 21st-century audiences. At the end of the 20th century, his photos inspired and served as the foundation for the award-winning documentary television series *The Civil War* (1990) by Ken Burns. Images have such an enormous influence on what we believe, or what we accept as truth, that the proliferation of image manipulation technologies must factor into what we accept or reject as physical evidence for our own views and beliefs.

Advertisers hope that the old adage, "Seeing is believing," is true enough to persuade the public to believe in their products or services—but is that enough? (See Chapter 8.) Does our acceptance of the 21st-century visual age make us more easily manipulated than our predecessors at any time in human history? These questions arise when we explore the role and impact of images in our daily lives. In venues ranging from advertising and fashion photography to public relations and political campaigns, from movie special effects to the photographic and video coverage of sporting events, we routinely encounter manipulated images. And in many ways, we benefit from the efforts and the technologies. Think about your favorite movie, sci-fi fantasy or adventure series. Would entertainment film franchises such as *Star Wars* or *Harry Potter*, or TV series such as *Lost, Fringe* or *Flash Forward*, even be possible to bring to the screen without the liberal use of image-manipulating special effects? Generally, society as a whole, and each of us as an individual media consumer, have our own criteria for what and when we find manipulated images acceptable—in films and television programs, for example. Creative, manufactured realities in film, television, art and fashion magazines and in advertising all serve to entertain us and enhance our viewing experience.

Framed Realities

Because of the very nature of the photographic process, photographs can be far more powerful and effective at influencing our attitudes and beliefs than films or videos of the same subjects. All photographs are, to a varying degree, the framing of reality; that is, as soon as photographers press the shutter, they capture moments and freeze time and space. Photography affords us *controlled* slices of reality rather than—as many people assume—*unbiased* representations of reality. With each photograph, the photographer is selecting that slice of reality that she or he wants to capture. Pressing the shutter button a few seconds before or a few seconds after might yield an entirely different freeze-frame. Decisions about what exactly to capture can be rooted in years of artistic or journalistic experience as a photographic storyteller or can simply reflect the luck of happenstance. Regardless of the level of intention and forethought, part of the power of photographs derives from their ability to capture and communicate these segments of time in a way that no other art form can equal.

Artist and author Susan Sontag suggests, however, that the power and the meaning of photographs derives greatly from the intent, skills, and decisions made by the photographer before and after the shoot.

For example, we can look at the path that photographs take in the construction of a photo essay in *National Geographic* magazine (see Chapter 16 and the "Photo Editor" video segment accompanying that chapter). The typical *National Geographic* photographer, after attending meetings with the magazine's editors to get their vision of a story, will go out into the field and shoot an astounding 20,000 to 30,000 frames. The photographer delivers these images via satellite uplink to a photo editor at *National Geographic* headquarters in Washington, D.C., and receives immediate feedback and suggestions while still in the field. Upon the photographer's return from the field, he or she sits with the photo editors and sifts through thousands of image frames to select the 15 or 20 photographs that they, working as a creative team, feel best represent the story they wish to tell. Next, this group presents their selections to a larger group of editors for their feedback. After making the final selections, magazine staff then use a digital darkroom computer program to enhance, crop, size and manipulate the lighting and color balance of each image. Finally, the photo editor works with the author of the supporting text to arrange each photograph for maximum effect.

At each step in this process, the editors manipulate and "re-create" the message and meaning of each image beyond the slice of reality that was captured when the photographer first pressed the shutter button. The meaning of each image, as Sontag suggests, has changed through this process from initial capture through the levels of creative decision-making through publications. How we then view the resulting images also changes their meaning and impact. As explained earlier, the experience of the images, and thus the story they are telling, differs depending on the medium in which the audience views them—whether in the *National Geographic* magazine, via the magazine's Website, as part of a documentary film or in a book. All of these media deliver a unique experience of the same photos and thus have a different impact on the viewer. The story that they enable viewers to "see" significantly contributes to what each viewer comes to understand and believe about the people, places and issues depicted in the content. If "seeing is believing," then we are all vulnerable to images' ability to profoundly influence what we believe.

12.9

Chiang Mai Taxi (1993) by J. Charles Sterin. In what way is this photograph intentionally framed to tell a story?

12.10

Photojournalist takes a photo during the Europa League match between Shakhtar Donetsk and Istanbul Basaksehir, July 25, 2016, Arena Lviv, Ukraine.

Vlad1988/Shutterstock

All of these media deliver a unique experience of the same photos and thus have a different impact on the viewer.

Edward Curtis, an American photographer, is most well known for his 20-volume publication *The North American Indian*. Curtis created more than 2,000 photographic images of approximately 80 different Native American tribes in the hopes of preserving cultures he feared would ultimately disappear. His goal was to create an idealized portrayal of the Native American peoples, even if that meant having to occasionally stage a photograph to achieve this goal. As Rayna Green of the Smithsonian Institution describes in the video "Photography and Society," "Edward Curtis made it his enterprise to photograph a people he believed would disappear. . . . Curtis gave non-Indians an image of a world they wanted in tact; Indians as beautiful . . . Indians as romantic."[6] She continues to assert that despite Curtis's staged efforts, his work became a legacy, a preservation of a people and a time that "we all wish were true."[7]

Sexuality as Subject

The more effectively an image stimulates our imaginations, the more powerful it is in inspiring us to create our own meanings. Many of the mass media images that most effectively captivate our imaginations are those that focus on human sexuality. The seeming modern reality in advertising is that "sex sells." (See Chapter 8.) Historically, however, sexual imagery is neither new nor especially modern. Explore any art history book, visit any large art museum in the world, watch any movie—and you will find works displaying the nude human form. Human sexuality has long been celebrated as a form of visual and cultural expression in the media. Even in societies where cultural norms and practices tend to suppress sexuality, the visual art of these cultures still express it in abundance.

The experience of images depicting nudity or other forms of an implied or explicit sexual nature arises from a two-way relationship between the image creator and the image viewer, whether the images are photographs, drawings, paintings or scenes in films and video. This dynamic relationship has deep roots that span the history of art. In his book *The Nude: A Study in Ideal Form*, British art historian Kenneth Clark describes nudity in art and photography as a traditional visual storytelling tool to express the full range of human emotions. The creator of works with sexual content uses a wide range of image techniques—from light and shadow, staging, the style and staging of clothing and draping, to the degree of explicitness of the human body, to the depiction of physical interactions between characters—to communicate sexually loaded stories that range from subtle to overtly erotic. As image consumers, we all learn from a rather young age to notice and be attracted to the depiction of human sexuality, whether symbolic or explicit, and use these images to influence and sometimes enhance our own sexual identities.[8]

While the style might differ, both Eastern and Western cultures have consistently focused on human sexuality in their art and media. Erotic art, for example, goes back several millennia. Even religious art—Judaic-Christian, Islamic, Buddhist, Hindu and other—is often liberally salted with explicit sexual depictions. Some great civilizations are well known for their sexually explicit texts: the Indian *Kama Sutra*, which dates back more than 2,000 years, is a good example; another is the classic Japanese text *The Pillow Book* by Sei Shōnagon, which inspired the 1996 visually erotic film of the same name by British director Peter Greenaway.

To assert that sexual images persist in contemporary media because people are naturally attracted to such content oversimplifies their appeal and influence. Sexual imagery also symbolizes a common human experience that can be easily communicated across culture, class, language and religious differences. Philosophers and psychologists such as Sigmund Freud, Carl Jung and many others dedicated long careers of research and writing to attempts to explain this widespread multicultural phenomenon. Writers, poets and filmmakers have relied on the universal power of sexual images as material for their stories, while art historians and critics continue to push the discussion forward today. Expressions of sexuality in visual images create powerful affinities between image creators and image viewers, and thus emphasize commonalities in the human experience. Since this shared connection is so strong and so universal, sexual imagery is perhaps the most powerful tool we have to sell beliefs, ideas, services and products to mass audiences.

> Expressions of sexuality in visual images create powerful affinities between image creators and image viewers, and thus emphasize commonalities in the human experience.

PHOTOJOURNALISM: THE IMAGE AS A MASS MEDIUM

Photojournalists, also referred to as documentary photographers, are reporters who use primarily images—and also videography—to report on news and stories. They use the power of visual narratives to comment on people, places and events for news media consumers.

One of the first practitioners of photojournalism as we know it was a Danish-born newspaper reporter named Jacob Riis (1849–1914). In 1870, at the age of 21, Riis immigrated to America. He disembarked onto the teaming streets of late 19th-century New York City at a time when millions of immigrants were flooding into the city, creating unprecedented diversity, rapid and unregulated urban growth, and social and cultural turmoil. Riis, a keen observer and natural reporter, eventually landed a job as a police reporter for the *New York Tribune* newspaper, in part because the paper's city editor needed a reporter who could work in the infamous Five Points neighborhood of New York's Lower East Side. At the time, this area was the most dangerous, crime-ridden part of the city. Riis drew from his own experiences of living in a boarding house and witnessing the day-to-day struggles of poor immigrants with no political voice. Prowling the bleak streets and alleyways, he wrote often overly dramatic stories for the *Times* and the *New York Sun*. He tried to convey the misery and violence he witnessed in the hopes of engaging the attention of the well-off and politically powerful. Soon, however, he came to feel that words alone could not effectively communicate the turmoil that characterized this underbelly of the city.

In desperation, and with the help of a friend who was an amateur photographer, Riis bought a camera and learned how to

12.11

Jacob Riis, one of the first photojournalists, documented the immigrant experience in New York City's Lower East Side. Here he captures men gathered in Bandit's Roost, 1890.

Library of Congress/Contributor

take photographs. Through the window of his camera lens, he showed New Yorkers and Americans from all over the country the poverty and brutality of life in the city's slums. He captured the human tragedy of the immigrant poor. With the help of two other photographers, Henry Piffard and Richard Hoe Lawrence, Riis's photojournalistic exposés made journalistic history and played a major role in establishing the credibility of the field of photojournalism. His work also brought the social and economic problems of inner-city poverty, especially in immigrant neighborhoods, to the attention of lawmakers at city, state and national levels.[9]

Another pioneer of photojournalism was Frank Leslie (1821–1880). Born in Ipswich, England, Leslie began his career as a sketch artist for the *Illustrated London News* at a time when hand-drawn illustrations were the only images found in newspapers and magazines. In 1853, he immigrated to the United States. Two years later, he founded his own publication, *Frank Leslie's Illustrated Weekly*, which remained successful decades after his death and into the 20th century. This periodical offered a mix of news and short fiction articles richly illustrated with drawings, many done by Leslie himself. In an 1859 article, Leslie accurately predicted the future importance of photography and photojournalism as the principal tools by which news publications would be able to provide absolute realism to the public. In his words, "Nothing was beyond the capacity of the camera." Leslie, along with other photojournalism pioneers of the mid- to late 19th century such as Mathew Brady (see Chapter 2) and Alexander Gardner (originally one of Brady's assistants), revolutionized the news industry and established the foundation for the seminal role photojournalism would play in the mass media of the 20th and 21st centuries.[10]

Covering Major Events

The popularity of photojournalism and documentary photography-based magazines, including *Life* (1883), *National Geographic* (1888) and *Look* (1937), helped to solidify the popularity of photojournalism's

12.12

Until the great
San Francisco
earthquake in 1906,
war photography
dominated
photojournalism.
Soon thereafter,
photojournalists
would cover other
major events, from
natural disasters to
presidential elections.

*Genthe, Arnold, pho-
tographer. San Francisco
earthquake and fire
of 1906. Courtesy of
Library of Congress*

image/narrative storytelling. These publications served as models for many of today's news and documentary magazines, such as *Newsweek* (started in 1923), *Time* (1935) and *People* (1974), along with most of
the image-rich publications populating the magazine stands today. The topics covered by these magazines
certainly vary, as does the balance of photography and text across any given publication or story; however,
the central fact that images drive storytelling and audience is well established. It is common to find photojournalism essays even in text-driven magazines such as *The New Yorker*.

In the early 20th century, war photography remained at the forefront of photojournalism; however,
that dominance changed in 1906. In that year, California suffered one of the greatest natural disasters in
American history—the San Francisco earthquake and fire, which photojournalist Arthur Genthe brought
home to the nation and the world through dramatic images. Other photographers of this era were capturing interesting events, too, including the first flights of the Wright Brothers, mine explosions and the lives
of immigrants, gangsters, sports figures and politicians. Early entertainment celebrities such as the internationally renowned dancer and spy Mata Hari, artists and authors, heroes and rogues—all were brought to
the public limelight through the power of photography. Then came World War I.

During the First World War, the U.S. government limited access by reporters and photographers to the
frontlines and restricted war reporting, particularly photojournalism, in an effort to keep key information out
of the hands of the enemy. For that reason, news photography tended toward local stories. The only images
that made it past the censors were, for the most part, simple and uninformative. While on a full war footing,
the U.S. government became very thorough at censorship in the cause of national security—informing the
public was not a high priority.

After the war, the evolution of documentary photography and photojournalism picked up momentum
again. In fact, during the Great Depression, even the federal government went into the photojournalism
business.

Profiling the Faces of the Great Depression

President Franklin D. Roosevelt established the Farm Security Administration (FSA) as part of his New
Deal program (see Chapter 2). The FSA hired many of the leading photographers of the time—including

Dorothea Lange, Walker Evans, Marion Post Wolcott, and Gordon Parks—sending them to document on film the human and natural devastation brought about by the simultaneous national crises of the Great Depression and the Dust Bowl, the years of drought and dust storms that plagued Middle America. The FSA distributed (free of charge) thousands of striking photographs to newspapers, magazines and book publishers throughout America in an effort to build support for the Roosevelt administration's New Deal agricultural and social welfare programs—many of which remain part of the federal government today.

In her 2009 biography of Lange, titled *Dorothea Lange: A Life Beyond Limits*, Linda Gordon describes how Lange's photos of the poor and homeless in rural California and the Midwest helped to influence the public's concern and galvanize the government to launch rural aid programs. When Lange's *Migrant Mother* photograph was first published in the *San Francisco News*, it prompted an outpouring of donations to help migrant families; the federal government under the Roosevelt administration quickly established emergency migrant worker camps in California. Lange's images, and those captured by her fellow FSA photographers, were a powerful social and political force that pushed the politicians in Washington, D.C., to take actions that they might not otherwise have taken.[11]

Defining Images of World War II

Between the two world wars, photojournalism experienced a rapid resurgence. Cameras such as the 35-millimeter Leica became smaller and more portable, and were made compatible with the latest advances in rolled film and interchangeable lenses; such progress allowed photographers to work quickly, unobtrusively and even in poor lighting conditions. These technological improvements, when applied by visionary and creative artists, brought photojournalism of age—both as a mass media style and as a profession. The combined photographic and filmic coverage of the battlefields of World War II brought Americans together, turning both the tragedies and the triumphs of the war years into a mutual, shared experience. In the United States as well as throughout Europe, the popularity of photography abounded both in reporting and artistic expression. This popularity launched the careers of some of the icons of the field, including Robert Capa, Henri Cartier-Bresson and Alfred Eisenstaedt.

> These technological improvements, when applied by visionary and creative artists, brought photojournalism of age—both as a mass media style and as a profession.

In the years leading up to World War II and throughout the war's duration, photojournalism played a major role in the war effort, from training to public relations, to domestic and international propaganda and to intelligence gathering and analysis, while reporting on the progress of the war and on the devastation experienced by cities in England, throughout Europe, across the Soviet Union and in the Pacific, China and South East Asia. Both the Allies and the Axis powers of Germany and Japan used photography to inform—and often mislead—their respective peoples. Thousands of books, films and television documentaries have been produced in the decades since the end of this conflict, all utilizing the vast photographic archives created during World War II.

Perhaps the most well-known World War II photographer was Robert Capa (1913–1954). When the war began, Capa was already an internationally known war photographer, having covered both the Spanish Civil War (1936–1939) and the Japanese invasion of China (1937–1945). His images include some of the most famous war photographs of all time. Capa landed on Omaha Beach with the allied forces on D-Day (June 6, 1944), photographed the liberation of Paris from Nazi occupation and shot astounding frontlines images during the Battle of the Bulge and the liberation of the concentration camps, which served as documentary evidence of the Holocaust. He went on to cover the founding of the state of Israel and the early years of the Indochina war (the precursor of the Vietnam War). Capa's extensive body of work exemplifies how photojournalists' visual stories can become important elements in the historical record, chronicling important people and events for future generations.

> Capa's extensive body of work exemplifies how photojournalists' visual stories can become important elements in the historical record, chronicling important people and events for future generations.

12.13

Henri Cartier-Bresson is most famous for photographing images that evoke candid, "real-life" drama, as shown in this image, Srinagar, Kashmir, 1948.

Henri Cartier-Bresson

Capa's friend and co-founder of the prestigious Magnum Photographers Agency, Henri Cartier-Bresson (1908–2004), is another photographer whose work helped to preserve and inform our understanding of history.[12] In 1947, Cartier-Bresson traveled to India to cover the partition of the longtime British colony into two new countries, India and Pakistan. The resultant violent flight of more than 10 million Hindus, Sikhs and Muslims in both directions across the new borders amounted to the greatest religious and ethnic mass migration in history, which also sadly resulted in more than 1 million deaths and countless injuries. Hundreds of thousands of people became homeless on both sides of the newly drawn border. Cartier-Bresson photographed Indian leader Mahatma Gandhi on the very day Gandhi was assassinated by a Hindu extremist. His images of the fallen spiritual leader on his deathbed, and the thousands of followers who gathered in desperation trying to get near him, made shocking headlines worldwide and turned Gandhi's assassination into an internationally shared experience. His captivating photographs provide a significant record of the violent history of the founding of India and continue to reaffirm the contributions made by Gandhi, an icon of peace and nonviolence. Cartier-Bresson's "real-life" or "street photography" style of capturing images made him a master of candid, straightforward photography. His style would influence subsequent generations of photographers and photojournalists alike.[13]

Iconic photographs play a critical role in anchoring our shared experiences of public celebration or public grief. Alfred Eisenstaedt's *V-J Day in Times Square* photograph communicated for a war-weary nation the joy and relief at the ending of World War II. The image so succinctly captured the shared emotions of the American people that it required no explanation or caption. We don't even need to know the story behind the sailor and the woman's celebratory kiss; in fact, any more information than the photo itself conveys would lessen its universal impact.

12.14

Iconic images such as Eisenstadt's V-J Day in Times Square (August 14, 1945) helped to cheer a weary and war-worn United States.

Andrea Izzotti/ Shutterstock.com

Shaping the Post-World War II Years

In the post-World War II years, during the Korean and Vietnam wars and the cultural revolutions of the 1960s and 1970s, several generations learned to accept documentary photography and photojournalism as ordinary and irreplaceable vehicles for learning about local, national and world events. Photographers became respected professionals and, in some cases, media celebrities. Professional associations promoted high standards, along with increasingly high compensation, for their members' work. These organizations included the National Press Photographers Association (NPPA) and the American Society of Magazine Photographers (ASMP) as well as photographers' agencies and cooperatives such as Magnum Photographers and the Aperture Foundation (founded in 1952 by Ansel Adams, Dorothea Lange and others).

As audiences turned to news and documentary images delivered through television, many photojournalism magazines died. Others, like *National Geographic* magazine, *Smithsonian* magazine, *Paris Match* and *Stern*, remained centers of documentary photojournalism. In the later years of the 20th century, newspapers moved along an inevitable path of ever-increasing images, first black and white, and eventually color, to anchor their news stories and better compete with television, and then the Internet, in an attempt to remain popular and financially viable (See Chapter 3).

Because much of news reporting and documentary narratives aim to give audiences a window into people, places and events not immediately or practically available to them otherwise, we have come to rely on photojournalists to bring the realities of the world to us. We want to "see" things for ourselves and build our individual understanding of events and the world. The work of photojournalists and their close cousins, news and documentary videographers, supplies us with a never-ending stream of image building blocks that we use to establish and broaden our under-standing and our viewpoints. Sometimes these photographic windows show us parts of the world that we would rather not see, yet must see to be a part of a shared experience.

> The work of photojournalists and their close cousins, news and documentary videographers, supplies us with a never-ending stream of image building blocks that we use to establish and broaden our understanding and our viewpoints.

Many historians believe that the relentless media coverage of the human toll of the Vietnam War—the stateside arrivals of coffins of soldiers killed during the war, specifically—helped to fuel the widespread anti-war protests that eventually led to U.S. forces pulling out of that conflict. For more than 20 years after the start of the first Gulf War, the military banned the media from covering, in photography or video, the caskets of those who lost their lives in combat as they arrived at Dover Air Force Base, the nation's receiving station for uniformed service men and women killed in the line of duty. President Barack Obama lifted this ban early in the first year of his administration. Now families of fallen soldiers can elect to allow media coverage of the solemn "dignified transfer" ceremony or, alternatively, have it photographed and filmed

12.15

Concerned that seeing images of fallen soldiers would negatively affect public opinion about the First Gulf War, the administration of then-President George H. W. Bush banned the media from photographing images such as this one. When the Obama administration took office in January 2009, they lifted this ban.

Paul J Richards/AFP/Getty Images

by a military camera crew. Since the new rules went into effect, media turnout for the ceremonies has been inconsistent and underwhelming, so the military itself—posting the images on the Web—have become the source of these moving images of honor guards unloading flag-draped caskets from transport planes. In the middle of an October night in 2009, President Obama himself attended one of the solemn transfer ceremonies at Dover. The images of the president honoring the fallen made headline news around the world.

In a story by *Washington Post* staff writer Christian Davenport about the conflict between freedom of speech and the public's actual desire to view or not to view troubling images, University of Delaware journalism professor Ralph Begleiter postulated that such images are "a measure of the human costs of war" and encouraged the public's consideration of whether the government should or should not "ultimately have control over what we see or not see," thus impacting perception of the event.[14]

12.16

How have images of 9/11 influenced your own memory and perception of the event and contributed to "shared" memory of the event among Americans?

Jeff Kowalsky/Stringer

Families of the fallen, the military and elected officials may disagree about this issue. Even so, the ongoing debate highlights the power of photos and their ability to evoke mutual feelings of patriotism—as did images captured on September 11, 2001.

Many photographs and hours of video were shot of the September 11 terrorist attacks on the World Trade Towers in New York City as well as of the two other terrorist-targeted sites—the Pentagon in Washington, D.C., and the field in which United Flight 93 crashed in rural Pennsylvania. Together these images and videos form the visual record of the largest assault on the United States since the Japanese attack on Pearl Harbor that brought America into World War II. A few of the thousands of images were immediately elevated to iconic stature, such as Thomas Franklin's *Three Firefighters Raising the American Flag*. This powerful image of three New York City firefighters raising an American flag in the midst of the unfathomable destruction of Ground Zero speaks volumes about the combined grief, resiliency and determination of the American public far more succinctly than any written commentary or speeches from elected officials could. In the purest sense, the responsibility of journalists is to record and represent important events, but an effective photojournalist will also evoke understanding of and sympathy for her or his subject.

Impacting Science and Nature

The visual image has played a critical role in the advancement of science throughout history, especially during the Renaissance. Consider, for instance, the visually rich journals of Leonardo da Vinci, which were responsible for helping to launch a new age of scientific discovery. Da Vinci attempted to explain the natural phenomena he observed through his illustrations; he also relied on his drawings to explain his engineering inventions. Other early pioneers of science, including German mathematician and astronomer Johannes Kepler (1571–1630), French mathematician and physicist René Descartes (1596–1650) and English natural scientist and architect Robert Hooke (1635–1703), produced astoundingly intricate drawings of scientific and natural phenomena as a means of widely communicating their ideas to colleagues and to the public. Many still survive and remain highly prized pieces by art collectors and science historians. For the generations of scientists and engineers who were to follow these early "men of science," the advent of photography in the early

For the generations of scientists and engineers who were to follow these early "men of science," the advent of photography in the early decades of the 19th century meant that scientists no longer had to be accomplished artists to effectively communicate their ideas.

decades of the 19th century meant that scientists no longer had to be accomplished artists to effectively communicate their ideas.

Beginning in the early 20th century, some photojournalists began specializing in stories of science and innovation. The inclusion of science stories in such magazines as *Look* and *Life*, the continued demand for science articles in *National Geographic*, and the addition of photography to magazines such as *Popular Science* (first published in 1872) all contributed to the evolution of this specialty. As photographs became more widely used in both newspapers and magazines, science reporting likewise became more prevalent. Photographs of scientific phenomena can have a striking impact on our understanding of earth's relationship to an endless universe—an impact that would be impossible without photographs.

NASA's phenomenal images taken by the Hubble Space Telescope are a wonderful example of this capacity to inspire wonder. Put into orbit by the space shuttle in April 1990, the Hubble space telescope is perhaps the most widely known of all of NASA's space exploration projects since the moon landings in the late 1960s. More than any single scientific instrument, Hubble has opened a visual window on the cosmology of the universe for global audiences. One of the legacies of two-plus the decades of accomplishments since the Hubble Space Telescope project first began—beyond its scientific achievements—is its mass communication achievements; its photographs have animated what were previously just theories about the universe and the interaction of astronomical bodies in the vastness of space. They have also contributed enormously to humankind's joint understanding of the universe.

In the same vein as the Hubble Space Telescope, Ansel Adams (1902–1984), who many art and photography historians consider one of the greatest nature photographers of the modern age, helped to expand our understanding of the natural world. Born in San Francisco at the dawning of the 20th century, he was expelled from a series of schools because, possessing both a photographic memory and a high level of creative energy, the young Adams had little tolerance for the no-nonsense regimentation of early 20th-century

12.17

The advent of science reporting and scientific photojournalism coincided with the increased use of photographs in newspapers and magazines. Here is one of the many astounding images taken by NASA's Hubble Space Telescope.

NASA Earth Observing System

schools. Ultimately, he took charge of his own education. Adams turned to his father and an aunt as regular tutors and spent most of 1915 exploring the Panama-Pacific International Exposition held in San Francisco from February to December of that year. He received his first camera, a Kodak 31 Box Brownie, from his father in 1916, when photography was already nearly 100 years old. In that same year, young Adams made his first visit to Yosemite National Park, where he became enthralled with taking photographs of the valley's pristine wilderness and natural wonders. Destined to become a lifelong environmentalist and internationally recognized proponent for the establishment and preservation of national parks, Adams returned many times to photograph Yosemite. Over his lifetime, his work resulted in 40,000 images, 500 exhibitions and sales of more than 1 million copies of his books.

Throughout his career, Adams remained committed to teaching other photographers his techniques. He created the Zone System of photographic composition, which separates ranges of light into 11 zones; it is still used by many professional and amateur photographers and photojournalists today. In addition, Adams led a variety of photography workshops and supported numerous photography organizations, such as *The Friends of Photography*, which he co-founded in 1966.[15] Adams became not only a celebrated photographer, creating images that opened a window on natural wonders throughout North America for millions of people, but also a prolific author of photography books. His many photography books published in the last decades of his career—which continue to rack up sales today, decades after his death—set the standard for photography publishing. His books and exhibits also brought the natural wonders of America to international audiences. One example of the profound impact of his work was an exhibition held in Shanghai, China, in 1983. More than 5,000 people stood in long lines every day of the exhibit to get a look at the famous American photographer's work. The exhibit, which was later moved to the Museum of Art in Beijing, served as a subtle yet powerful cultural bridge at a time when Cold War tensions between China and the United States were at their highest levels.[16]

Photographic images of the natural world enable each of us to—in a virtual sense—visit places that are not otherwise accessible due to barriers of time, geography and financial resources. Today the popularity of nature photography, along with nature documentaries such as the Discovery Channel's *Life* (2010) and *Planet Earth* (2006) series, are more popular than ever. Books, magazines, Internet sites, documentary television networks and programs and documentary feature films about explorations in unexplored natural places attract huge audiences and generate consistently sizable revenues. Ansel Adams would be proud that his work and career helped to establish such a major division of mass media content.

PHOTOGRAPHY IN THE DIGITAL AGE

As we describe in many sections of this book, the Digital Age has transformed every level and aspect of mass media, including photography. The ability to take, store, manipulate and share photographic images has never been more accessible. This capability has come about thanks to small and relatively inexpensive digital cameras, image-capturing capabilities now commonly available on cell phones and smartphones, and a variety of plug-and-play interface-enabled digital photo devices and personal computers. Image-processing software has made digital-image processing equally commonplace, with scaled-down versions of professional digital darkroom programs such as Adobe's *Photoshop*, Google's *Picasa* and many others made available for free. As a result of these revolutionary developments in the technologies for taking and processing photographs, the lines between the professional and citizen photographer and photojournalist have been irreversibly blurred.

The advent of digital photography and digital videography made much of this revolution possible. The effects on the practice of photojournalism have been profound, from both methodological and creative standpoints, and can be summed up in a single word—immediacy. Today, a photojournalist working in the field—even in highly remote locations—can immediately download the images he has just shot onto his notebook computer and have virtually all of the sophisticated image-processing capabilities available to enhance, modify and otherwise manipulate the images. Then, using broadband communication links to the Internet via cell phone or satellite phone, the photographer can rapidly upload the finished images to his editor. Communication with the editor can occur either through e-mail, text messaging or real-time cell phone or video conferencing, made possible by popular services such as Skype. Editorial adjustments can be agreed upon and additional photos requested and planned—all while the photojournalist is still in the field and his editor perhaps thousands of miles away. (For more on digital technologies and their effects on the quality and speed of photographic imagery and reporting, view the video and discussion with the *National Geographic* photo editor and one of her photographers in Chapter 16.)

> The effects on the practice of photojournalism have been profound, from both methodological and creative standpoints, and can be summed up in a single word—immediacy.

Digital-image technologies are not only blurring the lines between professional photojournalist and citizen photojournalist, they are also forcing media outlets that commission, purchase and or display photography to confront new challenges in the areas of legal and ethical editorial considerations. With the immediacy of image availability and the increasing vagueness as to who is to be accepted as a qualified photojournalist, editors are often required to make on-the-fly determinations about the legal and ethical viability and the associated risks of the photos that they accept. As we saw earlier in this chapter in the example of the widely distributed Tibet railway photos taken by Chinese photographer Liu Weiqing, the doctoring of images is becoming increasingly difficult for even the most experienced editor to detect. Meanwhile, the ability of photos to spread globally and rapidly through viral distribution via YouTube, Twitter and Facebook, reaching audiences numbering in the millions in mere hours or days, makes the job of the photo editor all the more difficult.

The move to digital photography and the rise of social media has changed the way photographs are not only taken, but also how they are stored, curated, circulated, and shared. Smartphones have built-in cameras and photo apps. The majority of social media platforms offer photo sharing. Taken together these easy to access and easy to use photo-sharing tools have led to a reemergence of photography not seen since the launch of the early Kodak cameras made the taking and sharing of photographs a popular leisure pursuit. Social media is once again reasserting the social significance of the photographic image. Perhaps one of the most noticeable aspects of the convergence of digital photography and social media is the "everydayness" of the many millions of images created, uploaded, tagged, and shared every day. This increasing emphasis on "the visual" in social media and the ways in which new emergent forms of "visuality," along with new modes of cultural expression, blur the traditionally understood boundaries and categories of media production, distribution and reception.

The converging capabilities of digital technologies; the rapid increase of innovative Web applications, services, and platforms; and the tremendous volume of images currently in social circulation is staggering. Estimates in a 2014 study indicated that 5 million pictures were uploaded to the photo-sharing site Flickr every day, and Instagram (Facebook's photo-sharing service) was at 200 million users sharing 60 million photographs a day. As a result, everyday creativity and visual forms of cultural expression have become an integral part of social networking. Digital photography is possibly the most visible manifestation of this phenomenon. This trend for amateur forms of photography has exponentially grown to the point where mundane and formerly private forms of creativity have now become part of a globally shared public culture.[17]

CONCLUSION: THE MASS MEDIA EFFECTS OF THE PHOTOGRAPHIC IMAGE

Photography is an essential component of 21st-century mass media. It has become so commonplace that it is easy to overlook the often-complex elements and skills required to create a photograph effective enough to influence one's understanding of the world and one's interpretation of mass media messages. Photography, since its early years in the mid-19th century, has played an increasingly important role in mass media, especially in journalism and documentary storytelling. This trend continues in the 21st century, with photography becoming a dominant visual mass medium. For this reason, each of us must in general hone our visual literacy skills and become more critical photography consumers. At the same time, advances in digital photography and photographic technologies are profoundly altering the nature of contemporary photojournalism—citizens have become not only consumers, but also creators, of the photographic image as a mass medium.

CHAPTER SUMMARY	KEY TERMS
Visual Communication in Mass Media Visual literacy is defined and the important role of photography in our highly visual culture is discussed.	visual culture visual literacy
Finding Meaning in Visual Media Explains how we view photographic images, how we interpret visual media, and how images have a powerful influence on our understanding of media content, stories and overall visual culture.	visual media iconic images visual windows

Photography and Modern Culture Explores how photographic images drive our understanding of both historic and current events.	equivalence composite
Photojournalism: The Image as a Mass Medium Outlines the history and role of photojournalism and documentary photographers from the late 19th through the 20th century, explaining the major impact photojournalism has had on setting both the public and political agendas.	photojournalists documentary photographers Jacob Riis Zone System
Photography in the Digital Age Looks at photography as a critically important aspect of mass media in the Digital Age and how we've moved from a primarily visual media-consuming society to a visual media-participatory society.	

NOTES

1 Whelan, R., & Greenough, S. (2000). *Stieglitz on photography*. Aperture Foundation.
2 From the author's "Photography and Visual Aesthetics" lectures.
3 Hall, S. (1993). *Encoding, decoding: The cultural studies reader*. Routledge.
4 Sontag, S. (1973). *On photography*. Picador.
5 Sontag, S. (1977). *On photography* (3rd ed.). Picador.
6 Quoted from an interview with Rayna Green on the video segment "Photography and Society," from *American Photography*, Twin Cities Public Television & PBS, 1999.
7 Ibid.
8 Clark, K. (1972). *The nude: A study in ideal form*. Princeton University Press.
9 Yapp, N., & Hopkinson, A. (2006). *Photojournalism*. Konemann-Getty Images.
10 Blanchard, M. A. (1998). *History of the mass media in the United States*. Fitzroy Dearborn.
11 Gordon, L. (2009). *Dorothea Lange: A life beyond limits*. W. W. Norton.
12 Kobre, K. (2008). *Photojournalism: The professional's approach*. Focal Press.
13 Magnum is a professional photographers' and photojournalists' cooperative founded in 1947 by Robert Capa, David Seymour, Henri Cartier-Bresson and George Rodger. It has grown to become one of the preeminent photographers' agencies in the world, with headquarters in New York City and offices in Paris, London and Tokyo.
14 Davenport, C. (2009, October 24). With ban over, who should cover the fallen at Dover? *Washington Post*.
15 Pritzker, B. (2004). *Ansel Adams*. JG Press World Publishing Group.
16 Ibid.
17 Woodfield, K. (2014, November). *Researching social media and visual culture*. National Centre for Social Research/Sage. Retrieved from www.researchgate.net/publication/289497516_Researching_Social_Media_and_Visual_Culture

13

Journalism in the Digital Millennium

Bill Gentile

CHAPTER OUTLINE

Reinventing Journalism for the Digital Millennium
Journalism Online
The New World of Reporting, Writing and Editing the News

Backpack Journalism: Delivering More with Fewer Resources

Hyperlocal Journalism at TownDock. net A successful hyperlocal journalism site based in the coastal village of Oriental, North Carolina that serves both a local and national audience.

Penniman on Backpack Journalism See how the American News Project applies backpack-style journalism to muckrake (investigative) reporting.

Gentile on Backpack Journalism Backpack journalism pioneer Bill Gentile shares his experiences working as an embedded journalist on the frontlines.

Unique Ethical Challenges of New Journalism
Conclusion: The Mission of Journalism Remains
the Same

Yaros on Training Journalists for the 21st Century Popular lecture on what skills are required and what challenges this new generation of journalists face.

LEARNING OBJECTIVES

1. Assess the industry changes and challenges facing journalists today and identify the skills needed to be successful in 21st-century journalism.
2. Outline the alternative forms and methodologies of online journalism.
3. Explain the growing trends in hyperlocal news sites and the opportunities they afford entry-level and citizen journalists.
4. Characterize the techniques and special ethical challenges associated with backpack journalism.
5. Illustrate the unique ethical challenges presented by the new journalism—24/7 news cycle, the blogosphere, social media, citizen journalists.
6. Describe the mission of journalism in the 21st century.

IT HAD NOT ALWAYS BEEN EASY being the eldest daughter of U.S. senator and former presidential candidate John McCain. It was even harder to be one of the rising stars and moderate voices of the Republican Party in an era of intractable partisanship, and at a time when the party was struggling to reinvent itself. Yet, Meghan McCain began making her mark as a blogger, columnist, media pundit and author. It all started with a blog she wrote while on the campaign trail with her father in 2007. Shortly before the 2008 presidential election, McCain penned an illustrated children's book about her father's life and his heroic military career. In 2009, she became a contributing journalist for the news Website *The Daily Beast*. In 2010, McCain wrote a book on politics for Hyperion; by 2011, she was appearing regularly as a Republican commentator on MSNBC. McCain is also active on Twitter, often using social media to call into question conservative Republican positions on social issues. These tweets have at times elicited harsh responses from her detractors.

Meghan McCain's skill at developing a successful career grounded in Web-based journalism serves as a model for aspiring Internet journalists of all political stripes.

Far from the usual follow-the-party-line conservative, she has used her rising media profile to challenge conservatives on many political hot topics. McCain has openly confronted such conservative media stars as Anne Coulter, Laura Ingraham, Rush Limbaugh and Glenn Beck on issues such as contraception and gay marriage and the impact their brand of conservatism is

13.1

Rena Schild/Shutterstock.com

having on the future of the Republican Party. Arguing that labeling socially liberal or moderately conservative Republicans as RINOs (Republican in name only) only hurts the party and is out of step with the world today, McCain continues to use multiple media outlets to share her views.

Although her father lost his bid for the presidency, McCain emerged as a media winner who may be a model for the Republican Party's emergence from its struggle between old-school moderate conservatives and Tea Party radical conservativism.

She has enjoyed national media appearances on such shows as *The Colbert Report* and *The View* and on NPR and MSNBC. In 2012, after undertaking a cross-country road trip with humorist Michael Ian Black, the two collaborated on the satirical and popular book *America, You Sexy Bitch: Love It or Leave It*. From blogger to media pundit to respected journalist and author—McCain has clearly evolved as a model of political journalism for the Digital Age, whether one agrees with her political views or not.

Time will tell if McCain and other young digital-savvy Republicans will have a significant impact on the direction and agenda of their party. In the wake of the 2012 presidential election, it is clear that the Democrats repeated and built upon their Internet successes and thus led their Republican rivals in Internet aspects of the race. Will the Democrats, with their far more sophisticated Web campaign methods, continue to dominate politics on the Internet the way Republicans continue to dominate politics on talk radio?

REINVENTING JOURNALISM FOR THE DIGITAL MILLENNIUM

The journalism profession and journalists' practices are undergoing tumultuous changes. Convergence of news media platforms and the Internet, related changes in the business models of news organizations, and the new technological, practical and professional ethics discussed throughout this book have all contributed to these changes. In this chapter, we look at the new roles and challenges facing journalists today from the perspective of the practitioner. We also explore how the closely linked media components are partly serving as a gateway to the profession for aspiring new media journalists.

It is a gross understatement to say that journalism today is undergoing a transition. In fact, journalism in the 21st century is experiencing radical shifts both as a profession and as a business. The news business is a business after all, and one that is grappling with the need to reinvent itself as a viable industry that fulfills a key role as a critically important public service. Journalists in the 21st century can no longer focus on a single medium that reaches an easily identifiable audience. In the past, media students trained to be newspaper reporters, magazine reporters, photojournalists or broadcast journalists for radio or television, for example. For today's journalists, such specializations are becoming increasingly more infrequent, if not outright rare. In the Digital Age, due to the convergence of all news media onto the Web, a reporter must often write each story so that it appears in either a newspaper or a magazine, on that publication's Website, and possibly integrated into a media segment with images, audio and video that might be simultaneously Webcasted and broadcasted.

Today's journalists are also no longer reporting their stories for a primarily passive audience. In the past, members of this audience would read, listen to or watch whatever stories the media industry made available to them. Only a small fraction of this audience would take the time to send feedback by writing a letter to the editor. In contrast, modern-day reader and viewer feedback and criticism—from competing news outlets, Websites, blogs, e-mails, social networking sites and tweets—are almost immediate and continual for every story journalists produce. This kind of response demonstrates how the practice of journalism has become an extraordinarily public endeavor.

The advent of cell phone still and video cameras, Flip cameras, iPhones and increased access to the Internet are just a handful of the technological advances that have helped give rise to this new form of public journalism. News stories reported by citizen journalists and enormous numbers of minority media outlets have found their way into mainstream media, exposing media consumers to news events from around the

13.2

In January 2012 the world witnessed the Cairo, Egypt, demonstrations in which thousands took to the streets to demand a faster transfer to civilian rule of the country; footage was primarily shot by citizen journalists using cell phone cameras.

Megapress/Alamy Stock Photo

world. In the wake of the Iranian elections in the summer of 2009 and again during the winter of 2010, for example, Iranian citizen journalists armed with cell-phone cameras reported on the widespread street protests against what many viewed as electoral fraud as well as on the violent government crackdown that occurred in response to these activities. "The regime does repression very well," said Karim Sadjadpour, an Iran expert at the Carnegie Endowment for International Peace in Washington, in a 2009 interview with the PBS program NewsHour.[1] Yet, despite the Iranian government's concerted efforts at limiting the media's access, it failed to successfully suppress the voice of the people or the growing concern of the watchful global audience. In large part because the world continues to stay on top of the internal civil struggles in Iran, and in other nations around the world seeking similar democratic reform, citizen and minority journalists have grown in power and influence. Their roles are making a significant impact on world public opinion and the diplomatic agendas of the global community. Increased access to advanced media technologies around the world promises to keep this movement rolling, much to some governments' dismay.

The New Wave of "New Journalism"

Many journalists find both the rapid convergence of news media and the increasingly interactive nature of their field both exciting and rewarding. These trends offer journalists unprecedented opportunities for their stories to be seen, heard and viewed by large and diverse audiences. Also compelling are the multimedia aspects of the Web and the new modes for researching and reporting stories. Furthermore, the nonlinear nature of the Internet enables reporters to move out of the strict linear structure of traditional journalistic writing by linking their audiences to stories that can be more individually and interactively experienced. Throughout this chapter, we will refer to the combination of convergent multiple news platforms, immediate audience feedback and criticism and required proficiency in multimedia technologies as new journalism.

The term "new journalism" was first used in the 1960s and 1970s by such authors as Tom Wolfe, Truman Capote and Norman Mailer, although Tom Wolfe is credited for formally defining it. This sobriquet refers to a literary style of newswriting typically found in magazines such as *The New Yorker* and *Rolling Stone*. When it first emerged, this new journalism style tended to be much more intensive and truth telling, as well as subjective, allowing the writer to interject his or her opinion about the subject matter—a technique deemed unconventional for news writers at the time. In this book, "new journalism" has been extended to also include all of the technology-driven news styles and outlets of news reporting not previously seen or considered possible until the advent and proliferation of the Internet.

Some journalists—especially those whose careers are rooted in more traditional "old media" methods—may find it difficult to transition to the convergent new journalism of the 21st century. In an era when so much of news reporting seems to be rushing headlong onto the Internet, some journalists are voicing valid concerns about the possible loss of journalistic ethics—the set of ethical responsibilities expected of journalists when reporting and writing a story. Such responsibilities include the assurance of the accuracy, attribution and acknowledgment of sources—aspects of journalism that some critics of "new media" methods suggest are slipping away under the digital onslaught. A number of experienced journalists fear that in today's Internet- and 24/7-dominated news cycles, factual reporting is too often losing ground to loud, splashy and fast sensational reporting. In other words, the viral nature of 21st-century news may be winning out over foundational journalistic practices: good fact checking and multiple-source confirmation (the requirement of reporters to confirm a story's facts with at least three sources, so as to ensure the reliability and credibility of those facts). There is also concern that multilayered news content and multiplatform delivery options—described as "short-tail journalism giving way to long-tail journalism"—make it difficult for professional editors and broadcast news producers to mediate news coverage and focus audiences on the essentials of each story.

From Short-Tail to Long-Tail Journalism

Short-tail journalism and long-tail journalism are concepts borrowed from the field of economics. These terms refer to how businesses analyze and graphically illustrate consumer sales on charts. Short-tail retailers focus on large-volume sales of small quantities of many different products, such as purchases made in supermarkets or department stores. Long-tail retailers focus on large-volume sales of a small number of specialty items, such as purchases made in clothing boutiques or in specialty electronics stores such as those now operated by Apple. Traditional news organizations operate on the short-tail journalism model, in which news is commonly packaged and delivered via newspapers or broadcast programs with limited pages and airtime. This model attempts to attract a large audience via daily offerings of a broad selection of short, focused stories that the editors or producers have decided are the most important or most interesting. Internet news organizations follow a long-tail journalism model, delivering their products through a medium where space or airtime is virtually unlimited. Such illimitability allows online news outlets to deliver news stories in detail with many different links and a high level of user interactivity.[2]

CNN, for example, successfully operates in both the short-tail and long-tail journalism environments. Founded by media entrepreneur Ted Turner in 1980, CNN has blazed the trail for a new form of broadcast journalism that has influenced all forms of journalism since. On an hour-by-hour basis, its news producers select which stories will fill their 24/7 news broadcasts. They make ongoing editorial decisions on how they will deliver these stories in small program bites, each only a few minutes in length. The exception to this pattern occurs with major breaking stories—stories that occur in the moment and call for more airtime and commentaries.

These same stories are reported on CNN Radio, the network's Internet-based 24/7 radio "broadcasts." Many are video-streamed on CNN. com. On both the CNN Radio site and CNN.com, greater detail on every story is available through links to archives and related stories. Users are also able to track which stories other users find interesting. Individuals can submit their responses to stories via embedded blog pages and post questions, commentary and even amateur news videos that they think will contribute to the reporting process. CNN calls these user-generated news segments I-Reports. Each hour, an editor selects a few of

13.3

Ted Turner foresaw the business of the news when he founded CNN, which has since become a mainstay of mass media culture.

Ben Rose/Contributor

them to air as part of CNN's television news broadcasts. In this way, CNN has evolved its news organization to operate simultaneously in traditional short-tail and new media long-tail modes, successfully integrating the two to offer the most choices to its audience.

The 24/7 News Cycle: All the News, All the Time

CNN made another historic contribution to the reinvention of journalism in the 21st century—one that we all take for granted today, but which has brought a wealth of opportunities to the profession along with a good deal of controversy. Specifically, it created a new time element for news reporting: the 24-hour news cycle. Under this model, reporting simultaneously expands and contracts. It expands because the network has so much airtime to fill, 24 hours a day, 7 days a week, 365 days a year. CNN broadcasts stories that are sometimes breaking and important, and sometimes unimportant and repetitive, because there can be no downtime during which no news or information is being aired or released (what is known as dead air).

With so much airtime to fill, journalism is frequently transformed into commentary: The network brings forth a parade of pundits (experts) to dissect and debate the most minute details of the story. Such a long-tail reporting environment is driven by two factors: the fear of missing a development that the competition might report first and the constant demand for material imposed by the prospect of having to fill the 1,440 minutes of the 24/7 news cycle even when there is nothing new to report.

Breaking the Story in the 24/7 News Cycle

Under the challenges of today's new journalism, reporting becomes limited in the 24-hour news cycle. When important breaking news stories occur, coverage is so immediate that little or no time is available for traditional mediation of the stories. Reporters have little time to check facts thoroughly. Editors have little time to select and focus the stories before they get on air. As a result, reported "facts" sometimes turn out to be wrong and must be refuted. Also, because few opportunities exist for checking that a story's coverage is fair and balanced, natural reporting bias can slip in more easily.

In an interview for Linda Ellerbee's 2004 influential documentary film, *Feeding the Beast: The 24-Hour News Revolution*, Ted Turner explains why such bias among journalists might naturally occur. He asserts that the nature of 24/7 news has given rise to embedded journalism, wherein more reporters and photojournalists find themselves in the trenches with the people on whom they are reporting; thus, they tend to write stories from their subjects' point of view—and that point of view can either be liberal or conservative.[3] (For a more detailed discussion of reporting bias, see Chapter 10.) This embedded nature of new journalism has become even more prominent now that journalists are individually taking on many roles that were traditionally filled by a whole team of people: researcher, writer, photographer or videographer, even editor.

> This embedded nature of new journalism has become even more prominent now that journalists are individually taking on many roles that were traditionally filled by a whole team of people: researcher, writer, photographer or videographer, even editor.

To illustrate how traditional journalism and 24/7 new journalism differ in terms of reporting and editorial oversight, let's look at how the same breaking story might be covered by each type of news organization. Imagine that you are a reporter working in the metro section of a major newspaper. Late on a Friday evening, you get a message from your editor assigning you to a breaking story. A neighbor at a home in an exclusive section of the city was alarmed at the escalating noise of a party next door. He called the police, claiming he saw two young men acting drunk and driving away from the party. Four squad cars arrived on the scene a few minutes later. When police entered the premises, they observed alcohol and illegal drugs, including the date rape drug Rohypnol. Based on this discovery, the police searched the entire home. In one bedroom, they found two couples actively engaged in sex; a third young woman was also in the bedroom, but fully clothed and yelling at one of the couples. All of the partygoers were clearly underage. Their IDs were checked over the police radio. Soon thereafter, the media circus began, in large part because the third young woman—the one yelling at the couple having sex in the bedroom—turned out to be the daughter of a prominent U.S. congresswoman who is currently under consideration for a U.S. Cabinet appointment.

Let's dig a bit further into this situation from the perspective of you in the role of a real reporter. When you arrive on the scene, you find a growing swarm of TV news vans, remote units from local radio stations and a gaggle of reporters and photographers. Within another 10 minutes, breaking news reports are appearing on cable news channels, and local television stations are interrupting their programming to return to their late-night news teams for updates. Soon the story is all over the Internet, from Twitter and Facebook to YouTube. These reports are liberally salted with speculation as to the impact the story will have on the congresswoman's pending Cabinet appointment because the broadcast and cable news airways reported the story virtually as it was happening.

Your paper has a few hours rather than a few minutes to research the story before publishing anything, so you start your reporting process carefully. You interview police officers, talk to a few of the kids who were at the party and interview the neighbor who called the police. While you are not yet able to interview the congresswoman's daughter, you are able to interview one of her close friends, who was also at the party. From these interviews you are able to begin to piece together what really happened, and what you come up with is far different from the stories that are currently capturing the public attention on the 24/7 television and Internet news outlets.

You text your editor, alerting her that there is more to the story than has been reported so far. Through careful checking of multiple sources, you are able to confirm that the congresswoman's daughter was not initially at the party, but rather had rushed over in response to a cell-phone call from one of her friends, who pleaded with her for help after she had been sexually assaulted. While it might be argued that the daughter should have called the police immediately rather than rushing to the party to help her friend, the facts strongly suggest that the congresswoman's daughter was neither a participant nor a victim, but rather an innocent bystander who had gotten caught up in the police raid. By the time your detailed story appears as a feature article in your paper's Sunday edition approximately 30 hours later, the cable news networks and Internet news sites are scrambling to correct their facts after hours of covering the story—and many are now using your article as their primary source.[4]

In this scenario, the reason why you are able to report the story more accurately than the competing 24/7 news networks and Internet news sites is not just because you are a good journalist—after all, the 24/7 cable channel reporters and the local TV news reporters are good journalists, too. Rather, you are able to get the story right thanks to paper's editorial to publication cycle, which affords you the benefit of time and editorial oversight. You have time to research and double-check multiple sources before reporting anything and time to follow the well-established path of the five W's (and one H) of journalism (the who, what, when, where, why and how of a story). Your editor also had the opportunity to review your story at a number of stages and offer guidance as to where you needed to tighten up or clarify. While the 24/7 news outlets struggled to match their competitors' coverage of the story—which meant filling some of their airtime with partial facts, suppositions and opinion—you had the luxury of focusing on fact checking and sorting out real events from politically motivated speculation.

13.4

Late CBS News Anchor, Walter Cronkite (1916–2009), remained a conscientious journalist, despite the breaking pace, and at times unmediated nature, of 24/7 news.

Allstar Picture Library/Alamy Stock Photo

These differing approaches and time demands do not just distinguish print journalism from 24/7 and Internet news; they also characterize old-time television news reporting. The day after America's iconic TV news anchor Walter Cronkite died (he died July 17, 2009), *The Washington Post* featured an article written by media critic David Shaw. In his article, Shaw described his experiences watching Cronkite supervise the preparation of stories for one of his *CBS Evening News* broadcasts in 1979—an era before the Internet and 24/7 cable news stations emerged, and a time when three major networks (CBS, NBC and ABC) dominated the television landscape:

> . . . he was a hard-driving, fiercely competitive newsman off camera . . . Throughout the day he was calling sources, prodding subordinates, asking questions, editing copy, deciding how stories would be played on that night's [news] broadcast . . . At one point, when someone handed him a statement that had come in earlier from the Iranian Embassy, answering several questions that [Cronkite] had been pursuing, he exploded . . . [and] he continued to fume and fret and drive and demand through the day, right up to until 6:28, when he combed his hair, put on his jacket and—two minutes later—began the broadcast with his calm and customary "Good evening" . . . [5]

What Shaw describes in this passage is not just Walter Cronkite operating in his role as America's most respected newsman, but Cronkite performing in the role of a conscientious news editor, using the hours before a story is reported to do anything possible to assure that the facts are correct and the story is well told. The operative concept here is being able to take the time. The reality is that editors and news directors have only minutes to assure the reliability of stories and mandate adherence to the most basic journalistic standards because so much of the 24/7 news cycle is motivated by getting stories out at the same instant as the competition, if not before. While new journalism is increasing the numbers and types of sources used, the coverage provided and the access to news, it also faces special challenges that traditional journalism did not face in the same way or to the same degree. Whether new journalism will be able to thrive given today's 24/7 Internet-convergent news industry is a story whose ending has yet to be written.

> While new journalism is increasing the numbers and types of sources used, the coverage provided and the access to news, it also faces special challenges that traditional journalism did not face in the same way or to the same degree.

Pioneers of the 24/7 News Cycle

Throughout the 1980s, cable news channels—led by CNN and joined quickly by MSNBC, Fox News Network and others—were the primary sources of 24/7 news. Then came the 1990s and the first Gulf War. This conflict drove broadcast news on both television and radio to imitate the compressed 24-hour news cycle, with CNN receiving numerous awards for its coverage of the war. Internet news blogs began to emerge, as did the transfer of television and radio news to the Internet, driving the 24/7 news trend further and faster. Similar trends in newspaper journalism occurred almost in parallel.

In 1982, Al Neuharth launched a national newspaper that in its style and approach was the print equivalent of CNN. Eventually, *USA Today* became the most widely read newspaper in the country. What CNN did for broadcast news, *USA Today* did for print news: It forced radical changes on the entire newspaper industry, ushering in a trend toward more stories of condensed length supported by many more color images. Reporters working for *USA Today* quickly learned to deliver their stories faster by taking on more of the roles that were traditionally fulfilled by a team of professionals. The *USA Today* phenomenon, much like CNN, was made possible by advances in computer technologies that revolutionized the entire production process, from reporting and editing, to layout, to printing, to a hub-and-nodes distribution model—a conceptual model used to illustrate how multiple related links can work together to achieve a common goal for mass benefit (see Chapter 4 on print media).

Also launched in 1982 was Michael Bloomberg's Bloomberg News Service, another pioneer of new journalism. Bloomberg, who is one of the wealthiest entrepreneurs in the United States and the mayor of

New York City from 2002 through 2013, began Bloomberg News as a computer terminal-based financial news reporting service. By 1987, it had approximately 5,000 subscribers, all of whom paid sizable annual subscriptions for the service's exclusive feeds. By the late 1990s, taking full advantage of the growth of cable and satellite television and the Internet—and with a pioneering understanding of the future of media convergence—Bloomberg had grown his company into a news media conglomerate that included 10 24/7 television and news channels. They were available in seven languages and reached more than 200 million homes and offices worldwide. Bloomberg's efficient application of new journalism to news production models is partially responsible for its success.

For example, in its New York City headquarters, a Bloomberg news radio reporter might use Internet-based resources to research a story, write the broadcast script, send it to the editor for changes and then log into the system, swing a broadcast radio microphone over to her desk and go on air with her report—all without ever leaving her workstation. On another floor, one of Bloomberg's television news anchors might host a news segment in a studio without any crew, supported by robotic cameras and systems. Upstairs, the same story might be fed to one of Bloomberg's Websites and international outlets from another automated studio, this time in Japanese, German, French or Chinese. Although Bloomberg News Service employs nearly 10,000 people in 135 offices worldwide, it delivers an extraordinary array of news reporting and analysis, produced by a relatively small number of journalists, editors, radio and television technicians and Web specialists.[6]

13.5

Before he was the mayor of New York City, Michael Bloomberg was one of new journalism's early pioneers. With his launch of the computer-terminal based Bloomberg News, he saw the future and the power of media convergence.

ZUMA Press, Inc./Alamy Stock Photo

JOURNALISM ONLINE

The convergence of traditional news media forms and the migration of much of today's news reporting onto the Web is radically changing and expanding the traditional definition of journalism—as exemplified by CNN, *USA Today*, and Bloomberg News Service. Of course, large news media companies are not the only leaders in this reinvention of journalism and the news business. There are three other important contributors to this story: blogs, online news aggregators and hyperlocal news sites.

Blogging

Blogs, originally called Web logs, are Websites launched and maintained by individuals who have strong interests in—and usually strong views about—the topics on which they focus. Examples of news blogs include *The Drudge Report* and *The Huffington Post*, founded in 2005 by liberal columnist Arianna Huffington. Among the five largest news and commentary Websites in the world, *The Huffington Post* attracted 50 million unique U.S. visitors each month and 20 million overseas in 2012 alone. These interactive news platforms not only deliver news to sizable audiences and allow consumers to respond to them immediately, but also influence the type of reporting that broadcast and print news organizations conduct during any given news cycle. In many respects, blogging is both a new form of journalism and a fresh news culture, where the line separating journalism from rumor and opinion is often blurred.

13.6

Blogging began in the early 1990s and was initially dominated by individual journals that focused on the interests, concerns and opinions of each blog operator. Less than 10 years later, the blogosphere—the interconnected community of blogs—has evolved so that it has become dominated by "professional" online commentators and online journalists, often associated with the Websites of mainstream news media companies, both broadcast and print. In short, this medium is now a major contributor to the tapestry of 21st-century news reporting. For example, each of CNN's regular reporters and commentators maintains a blog that can be accessed through the various CNN Websites, and some of the content and discourse occurring on these blogs form the building blocks of the stories on which CNN reports. Blogs deliver both direct content and content derived from user participation. Just as importantly, they supply links to other blogs and news sites, forming a Web of links. These links influence which stories are reported on, and for how long, and to what depth, during any given 24-hour news cycle or any given news publication cycle.

The impact of these links cannot be overstated. A story posted on *The Drudge Report* or *The Huffington Post* can result in hundreds of thousands of visits to other sites via links posted within the story. This Web of links can drive a story forward and keep it in the forefront of the public agenda and therefore part of the news media agenda. Blogs can drive up audience sizes for mainstream news organizations as well, by excerpting and commenting on stories from the companion Websites of newspapers, news magazines and radio and television news. Blogging has expanded the definition of journalism and made reporting accessible to a range of diverse writers. Many experts view blogs as positive contributions to the democratization of news and journalism and as a counterbalance to what some critics view as elitism asserted by the traditional journalism profession.[7] (For an in-depth discussion of blogs, see Chapter 10 on media bias and Chapter 7 on new media.)

In November 2016, CNN made a strategic move aimed at cultivating a millennial audience by hiring the technology and talent behind the social media app, Beme. Casey Neistat and Matt Hackett are the builders and starters of Beme. Neistat has attracted millions of millennials daily to his YouTube video blogs, and Hackett, a former vice president of engineering at Tumblr, is a seasoned pro in the online technology arena. Beme's 12 employees joined CNN as part of the deal.

CNN's goal was to bring that "authenticity" idea to a news and media environment, and to attract a largely untapped younger audience to CNN. CNN shut down the Beme app, which had 1.2 million downloads before losing users. Beme benefitted from Neistat's followers, but failed to capture a sizeable portion of the social media market against competition such as Facebook, Instagram, and others. Snapchat's video- and photo-sharing app was more successful in engaging users as Neistat had planned for Beme users. The purchase of Beme was a positive step toward fulfilling CNN president Jeff Zucker's goal of transforming CNN into a "digital company."[8]

News Aggregator Sites

Also original to online journalism are news aggregator sites, the next journalism form on our list. A news aggregator site does not produce its own stories or perform its own journalism, but rather compiles and presents news stories from other sites. Some news aggregator sites pull stories from many other news-producing sites with few editorial changes, other than to select and cluster stories around topics of interest to the site operator. In other cases, the stories may be edited and have commentary added to support the interests—and the biases—of the site operator.

Some news aggregator sites, such as *The Political Simpleton*, *Google News*, *News-Burst*, *Pluck* and *InForm*, just to name a few, are very popular and offer value to audiences because they do the work of finding and clustering stories on particular topics of interest to target audiences. For example, by regularly visiting a health sciences news aggregator site focused on breast cancer, users can easily view a large amount of updated information in one place without having to do hours of online research themselves. Many news sites, including very large and popular sites such as *Google News* and *Breitbart*, are a hybrid of originally produced content and aggregated content drawn from other sites. The common practice of salting stories with many links to other sites means that most news blogs are also news aggregators to some extent.

> Additionally, the growing trend in news aggregation supports a shift in how people obtain news information—namely, away from seeking detailed coverage and toward consuming news headlines and information bites.

News aggregation on the Web presents some controversial issues. With rare exceptions, these sites provide no compensation to the news-producing source. Instead, such sites typically provide attribution—that is, acknowledgment—but show little inclination to respect copyrights or offer compensation to the original source. Additionally, the growing trend in news aggregation supports a shift in how people obtain news information—namely, away from seeking detailed coverage and toward consuming news headlines and information bites.

Online Local News

The New Voices Mission was an initiative of the Institute for Interactive Journalism (J-Lab) that took advantage of the steady move toward online localized news. Part of the American University's School of Communication in Washington, D.C., the initiative's goal was to promote community-building media projects throughout the United States. Jan Schaffer, who was the executive director, stated "New Voices projects are training citizen journalists and helping to provide local news and information in communities where there is little available news."[9] With the support of the John S. and James L. Knight Foundation, a grant institute that promotes worldwide excellence in journalism, New Voices invested in a total of 48 hyperlocal media projects since 2005 and contributed to the startup of 48 more by the end of 2010.[10]

The New Voices initiative opened doors not only for citizen journalists, but for minority media groups as well—an indication that diversity in the news remains an enduring issue. For example, the eight new sites that received grant funding in 2009 included one spearheaded by the Annenberg School at the University of Southern California called Intersections: The South Los Angeles Reporting Project. This project's primary mission is to serve "African-Americans, Latinos, Asians and immigrants. [It] will use multimedia reporting by journalism students, community residents and community leaders and will focus on education, economic development, housing and immigration."[11]

> The New Voices initiative opened doors not only for citizen journalists, but for minority media groups as well—an indication that diversity in the news remains an enduring issue.

Another project that was geared toward diversifying the mainstream media with an emphasis on avoiding "personal attacks" and "attacks on race, religion, national origin, gender and sexual orientation" was MyMissourian.com.[12] A local news site launched in 2004, it was originally sponsored by the Columbia Missourian, a community news organization directed by professional journalists and staffed by students of the Missouri School of Journalism in Columbia, Missouri. All of the content came directly from the community.

Yvette Walker, who was a University of Missouri–Columbia graduate student when *MyMissourian* was launched in 2004 and served as the editor of the site's civic life section then, stated at the time, "It's easy to forget to seek out these voices. . . . In some cases, the media tends to feature minority communities only when there's a bad news story to be told."[13] Walker's contributors included stories that featured an African-American student who described how she felt other black students from larger cities perceived her; a lawyer who, despite negative public opinion, chose to represent the lesbian, bisexual, gay and transgendered communities of Columbia, Missouri; and a disabled reporter who covered the daily activities of an apartment complex that catered specifically to elderly and disabled persons.[14] Today, Yvette Walker is Director of Presentation and Custom Publishing at *The Oklahoman*. She still has a strong interest in diversity in the newsroom, training and minority affairs coverage in the mainstream media, stating, "Diversity [is] an area of expertise for me, not only because I am a black female in the media industry, but also because I understand that all people do not look alike, think alike, work alike or consume news and information alike."[15]

Much has changed since the early conflicts between established media and citizen journalist blogs. In 2012, *MyMissourian* transferred its content to "My Readers," a new section at ColumbiaMissourian.com that serves as its participatory journalism forum. The goal of the initiative had been reached—citizens can be and are now an active part of daily journalism.

Although hyperlocal sites such as *EveryBlock*, *Bluffton Today*, *The Spring Street Project*, *InBerkeley* and *MyBallard* are geared toward local audiences, they often attract consumers from around the country and around the world. Using such a site, parents in the military who are deployed overseas can keep up with their child's high school sports team. The young professional who is starting her career in a big city hundreds of miles away from the small town where she grew up can stay abreast of hometown events and friends. Hyperlocal sites also attract people exploring relocation or retirement to a new out-of-state community. These individuals can get a flavor of what the new community is like, track new homes for rent or sale, find information on recreation opportunities or link to menus and reviews of local restaurants.[16]

Although most hyperlocal sites are independent local ventures started by part-time journalists residing within their focus areas, their financial potential has not been lost on larger media companies. Newspapers, including those of such large metropolitan regions as Baltimore (*The Baltimore Sun*), Los Angeles (*Los Angeles Times*), Chicago (*Chicago Tribune*) and New York (*The New York Times*), are using hyperlocal sites within their distribution footprint as they transition from print publishing to Web publishing. This approach does, however, increase competition for the dollars spent by local advertisers. On the other hand, it also increases the opportunities for new journalists, part-time journalists and freelancers to gain valuable experience. Such small online venues often help journalists launch their careers.

THE NEW WORLD OF REPORTING, WRITING AND EDITING THE NEWS

Collectively, all of these trends and changes in the practice of journalism are influencing how the process of reporting—the writing and editing of news stories—is done in the era of new journalism. Viewed from one angle, the trend toward multilevel, nonlinear long-tail journalism means that in theory, there is no limit to the length of stories. Nor is there a limit to the capability to combine text with photos or with companion audio and video segments. As a consequence, today's practicing journalist is far less often a print journalist or Web journalist or television journalist and far more often a multimedia journalist—a reporting professional who has some skills in all of the media and is able to operate comfortably regardless of the desired mix. Depending on the focus of the news outlet, a reporter may choose to lead with combinations of these integrated elements—text, images, audio or video segments—with other storytelling media serving supportive roles. Of course, regardless of which of these media might start out as the lead, the dominant ones may be repositioned as the coverage evolves.

That said, and even as journalism struggles to reinvent itself and adapt to the Digital Age, all journalism is, at its core, storytelling—and almost all storytelling begins with writing. The challenge today is that practicing journalists must learn to write stories that can be easily adapted to whatever mix of media the audience demands. For example, writing to time for a radio or television news broadcast (writing to

13.7

Still photographers cover Judge Samuel A. Alito Jr., U.S. Supreme Court nominee, during confirmation hearing, Senate Judiciary Committee in 2006.

Rob Crandall/Shutterstock.com

befit the airtime that has been allocated for a given story) and writing for column length for a newspaper or magazine (writing to befit the physical space and layout) are rooted in different structural rules. As another example, when writing an article for print, the author has one set of considerations depending on how image-focused versus text-focused a particular publication is. By comparison, when writing a piece for television or video Webcasting, the author writes to support the images, which are the primary storytelling mechanism. Today's new journalists typically write stories that must work effectively in both worlds. Unfortunately, this practice can sometimes require a compromise in terms of journalistic ethics, as discussed earlier. Journalists must consider all potential venues and all potential audiences and structure their stories accordingly so as to capture and retain the interest of the audience in all its variations.

Recognizing this trend, CNN announced in 2008 that it would start hiring "all-platform journalists" (APJs) to meet the needs of the rapidly changing industry. Criteria for these APJs include not only demonstrated proficiency in

13.8

Kami Yitzhakyan, who was born in Iran and moved to Israel 25 years ago, hosts a radio show at the "Radisin" radio station in Holon, south of Tel Aviv, on March 2, 2012.

Jack Guez/Staff

digital technologies and the instruments making up the CNN-designed multimedia toolkit (which includes Flip cameras, MacBook Pro laptops and Canon still cameras), but also editorial strength, on-air presence and an exceptional mindset.[17] According to CNN Director of Coverage Victor Hernandez, "I want them to look at storytelling content and not be beholden to precedent and the way things have always been done . . . It's the ability to look at each story and figure out the best platform."[18] And, unlike journalists who must satisfy the standard fast turnaround times characteristic of 24/7 news, these APJs will have several days to flesh out and refine a single story. Hernandez emphasizes that CNN wants reporters who can write with a distinct style: "It's really the 'anti-TV' reporter in terms of look. We want someone free-spirited, off-the-cuff, interactive."[19] Unfortunately, and perhaps because the criteria have proved so demanding, CNN has been able to fill only four of the 10 slots reserved for APJs. Even so, CNN's lofty goals for APJs suggest that today's new journalists are expected to demonstrate not just technological aptitude, but also continued and proven editorial integrity, style and strength when working with newly emerging technology.

Mediated Content in the Digital World Still Needs Editors

Editors and news directors face similar challenges in selecting and steering stories developed by the reporters working for them. An editor at *The Washington Post*, for example, looks to see that stories developed by staff reporters can:

- be published in an upcoming edition of the paper;
- perhaps be repackaged for *Newsweek* magazine, which is owned by *The Washington Post*;
- appear effectively on the washingtonpost.com Website; and
- possibly feed the news programs at the television stations owned by The Washington Post Company.

While this example might be extreme, it nonetheless illustrates the expanded role of the news editor in the 21st century.

More than ever, today's news editors have to consider an expanding range of technical issues, resources limitations, both the short-tail and long-tail life of every story and ethical and legal considerations: Have the sources been confirmed and vetted—that is, evaluated for reliability and credibility? Are the reported facts accurate and able to withstand the unprecedented consumer fact checking of the blogosphere? Editors must continuously consider the various media that they can use effectively to reach and hold the attention of a changing news audience.

Furthermore, editors and news directors must concern themselves both with what a story says and with how it will look. Editors must constantly judge all graphical considerations—even the color backgrounds—and think about how well each story can deliver the most compelling experience to the consumer. In this regard, the saying "A picture is worth a thousand words" has never been truer. We live in a journalistic era where images—specifically, photography, video, animation and graphics—drive rather than merely support storytelling. (See Chapter 12 for more on the impact of photography and other visual images on today's mass media.)

Mediated news content is an important aspect of the 21st-century definition of a journalist, and a challenge we all share as consumers of journalism products. Mediated news content refers to information that a professional news editor has selected and reviewed, and to which he or she has applied the editorial oversight necessary to assure that the story is factual, focused and appropriately presented. In addition, the author's reporting and writing practices are checked for adherence to generally accepted journalistic ethics. At *The Huffington Post* and *The Drudge Report*, Arianna Huffington and Matthew Drudge, respectively, have a direct hand in providing strong editorial oversight; they also employ staffs of professional news editors for this purpose.

13.9

In television news, directors and producers perform a role similar to newspaper and magazine editors—mediating the content that viewers see.

Tom Carter

Differentiating between mediated and unmediated news content can be quite a challenge, however, because such distinctions are not always readily apparent. Citizen journalists, for example, often post on YouTube video news segments that they have personally produced, but that have not been subjected to any editorial oversight. Text and video postings to political, news or public interest blogs may or may not undergo any editorial scrutiny, depending on the individual operating procedures of that site. Most traditional news outlets offer blogs hosted by their leading reporters and commentators. Unlike with most blogs, teams of professional editors and news directors supervise these media-tied news blogs in the same way they supervise stories on the parent news outlets.

There is no easy way to determine whether any given story has gone through editorial mediation, which presents an ongoing dilemma for the news-consuming public. Without question, the Internet and the increased access to the tools of production have empowered enormous numbers of people to create news reports. At the same time, this increased access and the vastly increased number of journalistic voices are contributing to a certain level of information chaos. Taking all of these factors into account, editors and news directors clearly have a reinvigorated, reinvented and expanded role to play in 21st-century journalism.

The Rise of Hyperlocal Journalism

The town of Oriental, North Carolina, sits at the confluence of the Neuse River and the Pamlico Sound on North Carolina's Inner Banks. It is known as both the sailing capitol of North Carolina and a favorite East Coast boating destination. In fact, there are more boats in and around Oriental than there are year-round residents, by a 3–1 ratio. From April through September, the town's population increases even further with the arrival of tourists—some by coastal cruise ships, some by car—as well as hundreds of boaters making annual cruises up and down the Intracoastal Waterway. Many of these visitors, boaters and retirees or both, consider moving to Oriental permanently to take advantage of the milder climate and benefits of coastal living. This means that there are many people around the country and even overseas who have a stake in what is happening in Oriental, but do not live there full time. It also means that the town of Oriental is the perfect place for a well-written and visually rich Web-based news site to take root and blossom—enter TownDock.net.

In the mid-1980s, then NPR host Melinda Penkava and her boyfriend Keith Smith, a broadcast and IT engineer, discovered Oriental. They visited many times and even got married there in 1992. The couple moved to the village permanently in 2002 and launched their successful hyperlocal news Website, TownDock.net. TownDock.net offers an array of local news and information geared not only to full-time residents, but also to the many thousands of visitors who have a part-time interest in people and events around the village. The site attracts a wide local, national and even international audience, in part because it is so well written and—with the help of local photographers and artists—superbly illustrated. Of course, large loyal audiences result in solid advertising revenues.

The term hyperlocal journalism denotes news and information focused on a well-defined, consistent community. The value of a well-run hyperlocal news site is that its daily content is tightly focused on its audience in both time and space. Since almost all hyperlocal news operations today are primarily Internet based, they can offer text-based stories that are well integrated with still photography and videos at a cost that is far lower than daily printed newspapers or weekly magazines. They are able to deliver this integrated, audience-focused content so rapidly that it feels almost instantaneous for the consumer. A popular feature on the TownDock.net site is its live Webcams, which during storms and hurricanes enable property and boat owners real-time views of the changing conditions—even if they happen to be thousands of miles away.

Hyperlocal news sites offer great reporting opportunities for small communities. Their exceedingly low startup and operating costs and their ability to build content through local citizen journalists (nonprofessional, untrained journalists who write stories and share information via the Internet or mainstream news services such as CNN's "I-Reports" program) make them even more attractive. Small businesses operating in the same neighborhoods find advertising on hyperlocal news sites to be a bargain: the advertising costs are low, and the audience is narrowly focused.

▶ **Hyperlocal Journalism at TownDock.net**

TownDock.net is a successful hyperlocal journalism site based in the coastal village of Oriental, NC, and it serves both a local and national audience.

Hyperlocal news sites can now be found in towns and big city neighborhoods throughout the country. They offer an effective alternative to larger regional news organizations that could not cover the many local stories throughout their subscriber areas as efficiently and rapidly. Hyperlocal news sites also offer experience and employment for freshly minted journalism school graduates at a time when traditional news outlets are cutting their staffs. In this video segment, TownDock.net founders Melinda Penkava and Keith Smith give us a look behind the scenes at their successful news operation. ▶

For example, a Web-based news organization developing a story on global warming will find that its open alignment with environmental public interest groups is more accepted. This open alignment between the reporting group and its information source implies a level of trust and an attitude of "nothing to hide," creating an environment in which true investigative reporting can happen. The reporting organization will see how much easier it is to take advantage of the environmental groups' topical expertise—and certainly easier than the same task might be for a mainstream broadcast news organization. Why? Because the Web-based organization is practicing a model of journalism intended for the public interest. Financial support for this "journalism in the public interest" model relies on nonprofit funding rather than advertising. Also, because it is not advertising driven (which in turn eliminates its need to appeal to a broad audience), the organization, much like the ANP, can make its own decisions about what stories to highlight on any given day. Additionally, it is far less costly to produce direct-to-Web video news stories than it is to produce video news segments for mainstream television news programs. Therefore, direct-to-Web news organizations, especially public interest-focused ones such as the ANP, do not have to be concerned with capturing and holding audience numbers or advertisers when making decisions about the stories on which they opt to report.

BACKPACK JOURNALISM: DELIVERING MORE WITH FEWER RESOURCES

Rapid technological advances, the continued migration of news to the Web, and the economic limitations that these changes have brought to the industry in recent years have forced broadcast news organizations, much like their sister print news organizations, to reinvent their operational models (see Chapter 9 on the media industry). One outcome of this reinvention process is the emergence of backpack journalism. Backpack journalism requires the individual journalist in the field to perform all the roles of newsgathering, photojournalism and reporting that traditionally have been spread among a team of professionals. Refinements in journalistic training and the development of new methodologies enable backpack journalists to work either on their own or in teams of two. When working alone, a backpack journalist is fully capable of serving as the on-camera reporter, the field producer, the researcher and writer, the camera and sound person and often the video editor.

The news departments of local stations, and even national news networks, no longer send large and costly teams of people supported by remote news vans and satellite uplink booms into the field to cover every story. Remote news vans are self-contained television news field production units—usually built into a small- to medium-sized van—comprising cameras, lights, audio equipment, video postproduction equipment and satellite uplink booms (built-in retractable satellites or microwave-transmitting antennas that can be elevated above natural obstructions such as buildings and trees). While personnel-heavy media still show up to cover some major stories—for example, the devastating earthquake that killed thousands and

13.10

Here, a fully equipped news crew shoots on site as a reporter relays the details of a breaking news story.

iStock/Lisa-Blue

displaced more than a million people in Haiti in January 2010 and the failed terrorist bombing of Northwest Flight 253 on Christmas Day in 2009—these traditional approaches to broadcast news coverage are extremely costly.

Backpack journalism offers a cost-effective alternative to traditional newsgathering teams. It is much easier and less expensive to send a single individual or team of two to follow a complex story on location for extended periods of time than it is to send a whole crew. In this second video segment titled "Penniman on Backpack Journalism," Nick Penniman, head of video production for the online news site *The Huffington Post*, offers a frontline perspective on how backpack journalism has altered the way investigative news stories are covered today. ▶️

Backpack journalism is becoming a standard for longer-form investigative reports. For this reason, it is not surprising to learn that this style of journalism has its roots in long-form investigative documentary filmmaking, as Bill Gentile, an award-winning documentary filmmaker and one of the pioneers of backpack journalism, would agree. As a reporter and photographer, Gentile built a career working for mainstream news organizations, including *Newsweek* magazine, *The New York Times* and United Press International (UPI). He has also produced investigative news documentaries for the Discovery Channel, The Learning Channel, National Geographic Television, ABC's Nightline program and Bill Moyer's NOW program on PBS.

To date, Gentile's body of work includes reports filmed while traveling with Sandinista fighters during Nicaragua's Contra War (1979–1990), from the frontlines of the Salvadoran Civil War (1980–1992), during the U.S. invasions of Panama (December 1989–January 1990) and Haiti (2004), from the Persian Gulf

▶️ **Penniman on Backpack Journalism**
View how the American News Project applies backpack-style journalism to muckrake (investigative) reporting.

▶ Gentile on Backpack Journalism

Backpack journalism pioneer Bill Gentile shares his experiences working as an embedded journalist on the frontlines.

War (August 1990–February 1991) and from the Iraq War (2003–present) and the War in Afghanistan (2001–present). While serving literally under fire as an embedded journalist in these frontline locations, Gentile not only demonstrated how backpack journalism must occasionally be conducted under hostile and dangerous conditions, but also repeatedly proved the effectiveness and efficiency of this emerging approach to new media journalism. Today he is an artist in residence at American University in Washington, D.C., helping to teach his unique approach—while also focusing on the special ethical challenges that accompany it—to the next generation of journalists. To view his experience and hear his thoughts about backpack reporting on the frontlines, watch the video segment titled "Gentile on Backpack Journalism." ▶

In addition to changing the face of frontline reporting, backpack journalism is revolutionizing documentary reporting in geographically remote areas, making isolated peoples and cultures more accessible. Stories may be immediately distributed to worldwide broadcast and Web audiences, a feat that was impossible only a few years ago. The experience of *Voice of America*'s (VOA) video journalist Bart Childs exemplifies this new level of cultural and scientific reporting that backpack journalism makes possible.

Working on assignment for *VOA*, Bart Childs accompanied his brother, Tucker Childs, a professor of linguistics at Portland State University, on his final trip to remote areas of Sierra Leone and Guinea in Africa. Tucker Childs was wrapping up a three-year study of isolated tribes speaking the dying languages known as Kim, Bom and Mani. Joining his brother, Bart Childs explains his assignment in the following way: "The idea [was] to shoot and produce reports in the most inaccessible areas, yet manage to get the stories out onto the Web in minutes."

13.11

Today TV reporters often use highly mobile computer-based technologies to report and even edit stories in the field.

Eddie Gerald/Alamy Stock Photo

The regions to which the Childs brothers traveled lacked electricity and phone service. As a consequence, they had to carry in everything they would need to shoot and edit the reports and then uplink them to satellite for immediate broadcast on the *VOA* networks and over the Web. Bart Childs's entire equipment package included two high-definition video cameras and related equipment for shooting, a notebook computer for editing the reports, a BGAN satellite terminal (a Hughes Company satellite-based phone and Internet service that allows full phone and Internet access from anywhere in the world), batteries and solar recharging panels. All of this equipment fit into a single waterproof case weighing less than 75 pounds, which was easily carried into the bush.

Each day, Bart and Tucker Childs interviewed the last native speakers of these soon-to-be-lost languages and shot background footage of village life. In the evenings, Bart Childs edited the material into mini-documentary reports using editing software on his notebook computer. Next, he connected to *VOA* headquarters, located thousands of miles away in Washington, D.C., via his portable satellite terminal and uploaded the completed video segments. In less than 30 minutes, Child's reports were available on the Web and used as "live link" segments for *VOA*'s Washington Forum television program, which is broadcast worldwide.[20]

VOA is a U.S. federal government service, but leading commercial networks with long histories of producing such programs in remote areas of the world are quickly adopting similar reporting approaches. Not only does this intimate investigative style extend the reach of cultural and scientific documentary reporting, but it also brings us closer to the diverse peoples of the world, making deeper understanding possible. Television networks now following the *VOA*'s example include National Geographic Television, Discovery Networks, A&E Networks, The Smithsonian Channel and networks operated by the British Broadcasting Corporation (BBC).

Trade-offs and Risks of Backpack Journalism

On March 17, 2009, journalists Laura Ling and Euna Lee, working on a version of backpack journalism on assignment for Current TV, apparently walked a short distance over the border between China and North Korea. North Korean border guards captured Ling and Lee, although their cameraman and guide were able to escape. Despite an international outcry, the North Korean regime charged the two young reporters with spying for the United States.

After weeks of what South Korea's Joong Ang Libo newspaper described as most likely intense interrogations, the two reporters were convicted in a show trial in Pyongyang and sentenced on June 8, 2009, to 12 years of hard labor at one of North Korea's infamous labor camps. Pleas for Ling's and Lee's release by their families and international media organizations such as the Committee to Protect Journalists were ignored, and experts predicted it would take months if not years for diplomatic efforts to succeed in freeing the two women. Yet, these predictions did little to dissuade the Obama administration from continuing such efforts. Two months after their sentencing, former President Bill Clinton traveled to North Korea for a private meeting with President Kim Jong-il to negotiate and secure the release of Ling and Lee. Following Clinton's earnest apologies and requests for leniency on the journalists' behalf, Kim agreed to issue Ling and Lee a "special pardon." On August 4, 2009, they were set free.

According to statistics compiled by the Committee to Protect Journalists, 742 journalists were killed worldwide while practicing their craft between January 1, 1992, and

13.12

One of the many protest rallies that were held in 2009 demanding that the North Korean government free imprisoned journalists Euna Lee and Laura Ling.

Jung Yeon-Je/Staff

July 8, 2009. Meanwhile, more online journalists were jailed worldwide than journalists working in any other medium, with 56 online journalists reported to be serving sentences in 2009.[21] The international organization Reporters Without Borders reported that in 2009 alone, 26 journalists were killed and 177 were imprisoned worldwide.[22]

The trade-offs and risks in engaging in backpack journalism are clear. It makes sense that backpack journalists, whether working alone or in small teams in dangerous locations, face greater risks of arrest, kidnapping and even death than those working in traditionally configured large news crews. Larger news crews are more difficult to isolate and harass than are one, two or even three reporters working on their own with small cameras and little or no institutional backup. This problem, however, is not unique to 21st-century new journalism.[23]

13.13

Ismail Khader, a video cameraman for the Reuters News Agency, recoils as a concussion grenade explodes at his feet April 5, 2002 in the West Bank city of Ramallah.

Reuters

Talk with any seasoned news or documentary crew with experience working in similarly precarious locations and such "war stories" will quickly surface. They are usually as fun in the telling as they were frightening when they occurred. One of the things that makes new journalism in the 21st century different and at times more dangerous is the fact that many more freelance journalists, who often have only limited training and experience, are placing themselves in harm's way with minimal institutional backup. The evolution in the technologies of news reporting and the economics of the news industry have combined to make such mishaps increasingly more commonplace. This trend poses very real risks to the growing ranks of up-and-coming and eager reporters.

Certainly, backpack journalism is one of the new waves in 21st-century reporting. Not surprisingly, those multiple-skilled people coming out of journalism schools who are able to excel at some variation of this new wave are the ones who are finding the best job opportunities. Those capable and innovative practitioners who are retraining themselves to work within this model are also finding more welcoming paths to career advancement. It is no longer a question of whether new journalism is coming, but rather a matter of how quickly each news organization is able to adapt to these new industry trends. As news teams grow smaller, cheaper and more mobile, and as techniques for populating multiple outlets with immediate story content grow more flexible, so does the demand for higher-quality control and ethical standards.

▶ **Yaros on Training Journalists for the 21st Century**
In excerpts from his popular lecture series, Professor Ron Yaros, Philip Merrill School of Journalism at the University of Maryland, discusses what skills are required and what challenges this new generation of journalists face.

Training New Journalists for the Demands of 21st-Century Digital Journalism

The training of the new generation of 21st-century digital journalists is driving radical changes in journalism and mass media curriculums at colleges and universities throughout the United States and around the world. As we have seen throughout this chapter, today's journalists can no longer succeed simply by becoming good reporters and writers. Along with reporting and writing skills, journalists now need significant capability in computer and Web content technologies, online researching, photography and videography, whether they're working for a large national news organization or a hyperlocal site. In the video "Yaros on Training Journalists for the 21st Century," Professor Ron Yaros of the University of Maryland Philip Merrill School of Journalism, a nationally recognized expert in the training of journalists, shares excerpts from his popular J-school graduate lectures and offers his view on what it takes to train the successful journalists of today and tomorrow. ▶

UNIQUE ETHICAL CHALLENGES OF NEW JOURNALISM

The 24/7 news cycle, the blogosphere, Twitter and YouTube in general and backpack journalism specifically—all bring unique kinds of ethical challenges. Given that so many new avenues for reporting on news stories are available today, it is not surprising that certain traditional journalism practices are undergoing revolutionary changes. These sea changes are partly rooted in the fact that in this Digital Age, anyone can decide that he or she is a journalist and start reporting stories. Of course, not all of these stories are mediated, which means that they are not always reliable—even if they do wend their way through blogs, Websites or even mainstream news outlets and into the public consciousness. This ease of distribution and infiltration into various news media further increases ethical concerns.

Additionally, critics question how truly unbiased backpack journalists are, given that they are reporting directly from the trenches, typically working solo alongside frontline troops in a war zone. It is obviously easier for a team of professionals to guard against this kind of bias and to implement checks-and-balances practices during the process of reporting a story. Checking one's own biases when working as a solo journalist, in contrast, is highly challenging.

> Even though the ethical standards traditionally taught by journalism schools have become increasingly difficult to practice, they remain the ethical foundation in the Digital Age's brand of new journalism.

Even though the ethical standards traditionally taught by journalism schools have become increasingly difficult to practice, they remain the ethical foundation in the Digital Age's brand of new journalism. The basic principles of journalistic ethics are:

- *Truth, honesty and impartiality*. While absolute honesty or complete nonbias is a nearly impossible goal to achieve, society assumes that professional journalists are committed to reporting their stories as honestly and impartially as possible.
- *Privacy*. Despite the controversies surrounding tabloid journalism, the confrontational practices of the paparazzi and the debates about who qualifies as a public figure, the public expects professional journalists to fairly weigh the importance of a story and the public's right to know against the equally important right to individual privacy.
- *Confidentiality*. While there continues to be a push for federal shield laws giving reporters some means of protection against forced disclosure of confidential information or sources, it is a generally accepted journalistic practice to protect the identity of sources when asked to do so—unless ordered otherwise by a judge or by Congress.
- *Profit and conflict of interest*. While the news business is primarily a commercially funded industry, the public expects professional journalists to refuse to accept bribes that would influence their reporting and to go out of their way to avoid even the appearance of a conflict of interest in what they report on and how they present their stories.
- *Social responsibility*. Professional journalists are viewed as people working in the general public interest; as such, they should strive to do their work in such a way as to not intentionally harm others.

Our experience with today's media coverage, which some critics argue has grown increasingly biased and others purport has abandoned its muckraking traditions for more viral, sensational news, makes it is easy for us to recognize regular violations of one or more of these ethical standards. As we have discussed throughout this book, the history of mass media, and by extension the history of journalism, is influenced at least in part by the ongoing debate as to what constitutes appropriate journalistic practices. Of course, the profession of journalism is for the most part self-regulating. Unlike lawyers, doctors, accountants, plumbers or beauticians, a journalist does not need to pass an exam or apply for certification or licensing in order to practice in the field. In the attempt to fill this gap in professional certification, the leading national and regional professional associations of journalism schools, reporters and editors have all established their own codes of ethics and standards. These organizations include the American Society of Professional Journalists, the American Society of Newspaper Editors and the Radio and Television News Directors Association.

Clearly, thanks to the emergence of the Internet, the Digital Age has afforded unprecedented consumer-participant opportunities to join the world of journalism this has greatly blurred the lines of what constitutes journalism—and ethical journalistic practices—as a result.

CONCLUSION: THE MISSION OF JOURNALISM REMAINS THE SAME

Despite the radical changes in the technology, organization and economics of journalism that have occurred since the new millennium, the mission of journalism remains very much the same as it was before the Digital Age: fact finding and storytelling. Additionally, journalists face the same core challenges today that they faced in the past: how to identify and get to the heart of the stories that people need to hear, how to capture an audience's attention and how to tell a story in a compelling but truthful way.

More than ever before, people are aspiring to become journalists, and the technological developments of the last two decades have made it much more feasible and accessible to do so. As a result, journalism schools are struggling to effectively turn out graduates with the skills required to succeed in this industry, which is itself undergoing radical reinvention. People entering or already in the profession are finding that multiple skill sets are vital and that the specialized "writing" role is rapidly being replaced by the specialized "multimedia" role. In addition to writing skills, jobs now require computer knowledge, Internet savvy and photography and videography proficiency.

> Despite the radical changes in the technology, organization and economics of journalism that have occurred since the new millennium, the mission of journalism remains very much the same as it was before the Digital Age: fact finding and storytelling.

The trends reshaping 21st-century journalism are many. On the economic front, the news as a business is being driven by the convergence of news media onto the Internet, which means that fewer people will be employed to report on a story and more news content will be produced in shorter and shorter periods. The number of platforms for distributing news has also increased exponentially, although this particular trend has not automatically resulted in better news coverage. As journalism focuses on developing innovative techniques for the effective use of the many new platforms and methods of producing and distributing news stories, it must simultaneously present new ethical and operational standards, especially for those already in the profession and for those trying to build new careers there. Ultimately, these news industry changes have allowed the everyday citizen to become his or her own journalist, thus placing greater responsibility on each of us to be not just critical media consumers, but also critical media creators.

CHAPTER SUMMARY	KEY TERMS
Reinventing Journalism for the Digital Millennium A look at the changing face of journalism in the 21st century and the challenges facing journalists and news organizations as the industry struggles to reinvent itself.	new journalism journalistic ethics multiple-source confirmation short-tail journalism long-tail journalism breaking stories I-Reports dead air embedded journalism editorial to publication cycle five W's (and one H) of journalism hub-and-nodes distribution model
Journalism Online Explores the varied and changing aspects and practice of journalism on the Web.	blogs blogosphere news aggregator site

The New World of Reporting, Writing and Editing the News Explains today's digital technologies-driven reporting and editing process in the context of converging news media platforms and presents an overview of the work of today's reporters, writers and editors—in print, in broadcasting and on the Web. **Visual Media** **Hyperlocal Journalism at TownDock.net** A successful site based in the coastal village of Oriental, North Carolina, that serves both a local and national audience. 1. Find a hyperlocal news site in your area and describe how it compares to the TownDock.net operation featured in this video segment. 2. What are the three or four primary features that, taken together, help hyperlocal journalism sites become successful?	multimedia journalist writing to time writing for column length mediated news content hyperlocal journalism citizen journalists
Backpack Journalism: Delivering More with Fewer Resources Analyzes how rapid advances in technologies, reduced operating budgets and the continued migration of news reporting onto the Internet have created a new category of multiskilled journalists who alone do the work once performed by numerous specialized professionals. **Visual Media** **Penniman on Backpack Journalism** View how the American News Project applies backpack-style journalism to muckrake (investigative) reporting. 1. Describe the special demands and rewards journalists face every day working for national Internet news operations. 2. What are the two or three primary reasons why some stories first appearing on national Internet news sites are picked up by the major TV and cable news networks? **Gentile on Backpack Journalism** Backpack journalism pioneer Bill Gentile shares his experiences working as an embedded journalist on the frontlines. 1. How has frontline war reporting changed since World War II, the Korean and Vietnam Wars and up through the more recent wars in the Middle East? 2. Why do the backpack journalism methods featured in this video segment make frontline war correspondents more effective and allow them to easily integrate with fighting troops? **Yaros on Training Journalists for the 21st Century** In excerpts from his popular lecture series, Professor Ron Yaros of the University of Maryland discusses what skills are required and what challenges this new generation of journalists face. 1. Looking at the journalism and/or mass media programs at your own college, what efforts are underway to teach the skills graduates need to enter the real-world profession of journalism? 2. What skills does an integrated media journalist most need before entering today's job market as a new reporter?	backpack journalism remote news vans satellite uplink booms BGAN satellite terminal Committee to Protect Journalists
Unique Ethical Challenges of New Journalism Investigates the new and unique ethical challenges facing journalists working in today's convergent, multiplatform news industry.	shield laws

NOTES

1 Sajadpour, K. (2009, December 28). New clashes test Iranian regime's grip on Tehran. *PBS News-Hour; Carnegie endowment for international peace*. Retrieved from www.carnegieendowment.org/publications/index.cfm?fa=view&id=24411

2 Faust, J. (2009). *Online journalism: Principles of news for the Web*. Holcomb Hathaway Publishers.

3 Ellerbee, L. (Executive producer). (2004). *Feeding the beast: The 24-hour news revolution*; Trio Network Special.

4 Fictionalized story based on an actual incident covered by the author while he was serving as one of the lead video journalists for TBS's investigative series *America at Risk*. The author worked on this television documentary special in the summer of 1990 as one of the lead cinematographers and has changed the names, locations and other minor details to protect the privacy of those involved. Other than these small changes, this is a true story.

5 Barnes, B. (2009, July 18). American's iconic TV news anchor shaped the medium and the nation. *Washington Post*. Retrieved from www.washingtonpost.com/wp-dyn/content/article/2009/07/17/AR2009071703345.html

6 Information from Bloomberg L. P., publications and websites as well as the author's visits to Bloomberg News headquarters operation in New York City in 2008. See Retrieved from http://about.bloomberg.com/company.html

7 For more on this issue, see the following sources: Touri, M. (2009). News blogs: Strengthen democracy through conflict prevention. *Aslib Proceedings, 61*, 170–184; Shes, D. (2008, October 5). Are blogs good for democracy? A debate featuring the Yale Political Union. *Huffington Post*; Reyes, F. (2008, October 5). Blogging towards a digital democracy. *Huffington Post*.

8 Isaac, M. (2016, November 28). CNN brings in the social app beme to cultivate a millennial audience. *New York Times*. Retrieved from www.nytimes.com/2016/11/28/technology/cnn-brings-in-the-social-app-beme-to-cultivate-a-millennial-audience.html

9 New Voices home page: www.j-newvoices.org/

10 Ibid.

11 See April 21, 2009, press release, New Voices invests in eight hyperlocal news sites, on the New Voices website: Retrieved from www.j-newvoices.org/site/story/nv09_grantees_release/

12 For more about *MyMissourian.com*, see Retrieved from http://mymissourian.com/about/

13 Alderman, N. (n.d.). Written by the community; edited by journalists. *J-Lab Online*. Retrieved from www.j-newvoices.org/site/story_spotlight/written_by_the_community_edited_by_journalists/

14 Ibid.

15 See Yvette Walker's professional profile on *LinkedIn.com*: Retrieved from www.linkedin.com/in/yvettebwalker

16 An easy-to-use portal to start exploring the online world of hyperlocal websites is *WikiCity.com*.

17 Wenger, D. (n.d.). All-platform journalism at CNN. *NewsLab*. Retrieved from www.newslab.org/2009/10/14/all-platform-journalism-at-cnn/

18 Ibid.

19 Ibid.

20 Childs, B. (July 2009). Live from Africa, Using the barest of video tools. *Government Video Magazine*, pp. 10–12. *Governmentvideo.com*. Retrieved from www.voanews.com/english/LostVoices.cfm

21 Committee to Protect Journalists. (2009). *Journalists killed*. Retrieved from www.cpj.org/deadly

22 Reporters Without Borders. (2009). *Press freedom barometer 2009*. Retrieved from www.rsf.org/index.php?page=rubrique&id_rubrique=2

23 In early 1990, barely six months after the Ukraine declared its independence from the Soviet Union, and before such customary government services as police were fully established, I was working with a three-person crew from Reuters News Agency on a documentary film in Ukraine's capitol city, Kiev. While en route to shoot an interview with a government minister, approximately a dozen well-armed

soldiers working for the local mafia chief surrounded the team. They first tried to extort money to "assure safe passage." When it became clear there was little cash to be had, the mafia soldiers grew more aggressive. They appeared ready to steal the camera and possibly kidnap the team for ransom. Just as the situation was escalating, the team made a run for it. We were chased for blocks through downtown Kiev before we finally made it to the newly opened American Embassy. There, phone negotiations ensued and resulted in an arrangement with the local mafia leader, a Chinese-Ukrainian calling himself Uncle Lee. The deal involved our paying a "licensing fee"; in exchange, Uncle Lee and his men became our guides, drivers and bodyguards for the remainder of the visit.

14

Media Impact on the Global Stage

Boro1/Shutterstock.com

CHAPTER OUTLINE

The Role of Mass Media
Global Mass Media Systems
Mass Media Systems in Development

Women on the Frontlines Jeanine Nahigombeye, director of Radio Isanganiro, explains her sometimes risky efforts, and the efforts of other women like her, to present fair and balanced journalism promoting peace in civil war-torn Burundi.

Mass Media and Cultural Context
Media Cultures Compete for Survival
Media Dominance and the Global Marketplace
Mass Media and Global Diplomacy
Equalizing the Global Community Through Media Technology
Conclusion: The Transformative Power of Mass Media

Arthur C. Clarke Clarke's groundbreaking work in satellite television continues to serve as a model for the important role mass media technology plays in social and cultural development.

LEARNING OBJECTIVES

1. Characterize the ways in which the mass media can direct the public agenda on both the national and international stages.
2. Distinguish between the different mass media systems around the world and explain the model upon which American media are based.
3. Explain the development of emerging mass media systems in developing regions of the world.
4. Compare and contrast the ways in which cultural context drives media content and how it affects the way audiences react to the stories covered.
5. Evaluate how American mass media both attract and inflame audiences in the Middle East.
6. Illustrate the ways in which American media have dominated the world stage and the ways in which access to the technologies of media production and distribution is empowering other countries.
7. Outline the critical role played by mass media in terms of international diplomacy. Identify the limits of mass media in nondemocratic countries and explain how those limits affect government power and control.
8. Assess the causes and implications of the Digital Divide and the Digital Divide 2.0.
9. Explain how mass media are affecting how individuals identify with cultures and nations and their impact on the global village.

IN 2012, THE ISRAEL DEFENSE FORCES (IDF)

launched its largest assault on Hamas in the Gaza Strip in over four years. This IDF offensive included an unprecedented use of social media sites (such as Facebook, YouTube and Twitter) to publicize the offensive and to create pro-Israeli media coverage. The IDF's use of social media was an attempt to defend its actions and explain the threat posed by Hamas's ongoing rocket attacks. It was also an appeal to Israeli and international public opinion, in Europe and particularly in the United States. But the use of social media to influence public opinion in the 21st century is rather egalitarian and, as a result, can have both a positive and a negative impact on the message being conveyed.

Enter Harry Fear, a young British documentary filmmaker who, with no organizational support, entered Gaza one week before the Israeli offensive. He had in his possession his camera and his laptop computer as well as a commitment to film "the real story"

to post on YouTube and share with the world. Broadcasting both live and pre-recorded footage from his apartment in Gaza City, Fear reported from the receiving end of the IDF assault. He

reported on the locations of air strikes, the number of persons killed and injured, and sent audio of the buzzing of unmanned drones overhead and the blasts when the rockets hit their

14.1

ChameleonsEye/Shutterstock.com

targets. His YouTube segments featured his on-camera reports from the ruins of the Gaza Airport, in front of bombed-out apartment buildings and while facing off with IDF forces on the Gaza border.

Over a half a million viewers tuned into his live feeds, and his Twitter followers jumped overnight from a hundred to nearly 30,000. Fear's independent social media-based reporting of the Israeli offensive countered the social media efforts by the IDF, making Fear an overnight, independent Web-journalism celebrity. Within a few weeks, he was on an international speaking tour that included the United States, the Netherlands, Australia, Canada, Malaysia and New Zealand. In an interview for *The New Yorker* magazine in early February 2013, Fear explained that his social media reporting adventures from the frontlines were just beginning—next stop, Afghanistan.[1]

The popularity and impact of such independent reporting via social media sites from troubled areas around the world speak volumes about the growing sophistication of the use of digital media by all sides in international conflicts. It also speaks to how these media messages and audiences' responses to them can be easily manipulated. The endless search for answers to the question of *Why* begins with a study of global media. Studying how attempts to turn mass media into an international stage for regional conflicts—conflicts with inevitable global implications.

THE ROLE OF MASS MEDIA

Hamas and other pro-Palestinian groups reinforced the messages of wreckage and ruin at the hands of Israelis on blogs and social networking sites such as Facebook and Twitter. Like Israel, Hamas also posted video segments on YouTube. Meanwhile, Israel's effort to control media access to the Gaza battlefield, even after the Israeli Supreme Court had ordered its military to allow access to a "limited pool" of journalists, quickly proved ineffectual. This failure to fully control media access was due to the in-place resources of the Arab media as well as the effectiveness of citizen journalists who, using cameras, cell phones and the Internet, managed to capture their own stories and get them out to the world.

For many years, the Western media, especially the American media, have been accused of siding with Israel in its religious and territorial struggle with Palestine—even when Israel appears to commit unprovoked acts of violence or terrorism. Support for Israel in the United States, especially among the large conservative Jewish and Christian populations and their like-minded representatives in Congress, simply solidified with each new round of confrontations. However, the images and stories of the horrific suffering endured by Palestinians in Gaza appeared to generate previously unseen sympathy for their plight even from longtime supporters of Israel. Does this significant turn of events mean that the media tactics of Hamas and its Arab supporters won the media battle, even if they lost the military campaign? Does it mean that the Arab media were able to outperform the Western media in capturing the hearts and minds of the world audience? Did the success of the Palestinian media message so overwhelm that of the Israelis that the long-term political, diplomatic and economic fortunes of the Palestinian people will now be altered?

These questions are not easily answered, but certainly the Israeli and Palestinian media campaigns demonstrate the power of mass media and emphasize how converged media systems, in particular, can more effectively and rapidly change the political tide and the common political opinion about long-enduring international conflict. Mass media's impact on the global stage is undeniable. To understand mass media's social, cultural and political roles throughout the world in the 21st century, we need to look first at how mass media systems contribute to the public agenda, and then follow these systems' development from the mid- to late-20th century.

Setting the Public Agenda

Throughout the 20th century, and now in the 21st century, mass media have had profound impacts on the sociopolitical environment locally, nationally and internationally. Twenty-first-century mass media support a previously unheard-of amount of information and cover public debates on issues large and small, turning mass media into the principal means for setting the national and global public agendas. Intense media coverage strongly influences how the public views select issues and events, despite the filtering and interpretation provided by culture-colored lenses. Who sets the public agenda for the media in the United States?

By its nature, a democracy partially allows the public to determine which issues are important and what the government should do about them. In the United States, however, many people, including most political experts and pundits, believe that because of his position, it is the president who sets the media agenda. The president's importance as a national and global political leader—his statements, actions and program naturally take center stage in the media—makes him one of the prime newsmakers in the world. While the president cannot control *how* the media portray him or his ideas, his actions influence *what* the media will cover on a daily basis.

Countering the argument about presidential influence over the media have been several former White House press secretaries, including Dee Dee Myers (President Bill Clinton), George Stephanopoulos (President Clinton) and Ari Fleischer (President George W. Bush), who have written about their administrations' struggles to control the media. Although the extent of the president's power over the media is debatable, the relationship between politics and media and the way in which that relationship helps set the public agenda is undeniably complex. All presidents and their White House staff must know how to artfully frame the president's message in a way that invites and maintains public support. The twofold challenge is to do so while countering media attacks by the political opposition and avoiding the manipulation of facts or the direct feeding of information to the media—media analysts would suggest that the latter is an attempt to force a disingenuous perception of the administration onto the public. Thus, as a result of the relationship between politics and media, the media do not simply determine what is important by focusing the audience's attention on an issue. They also influence how we think about what they determine *is* important.

Inspiring Democracy

One of the primary goals of 17th-century English philosopher Thomas Hobbes (1588–1679) was to establish a theory of how human societies come together to form nations and governments based on shared cultural histories, values and artifacts. In his famous work *Leviathan* (1651), Hobbes argued that when these elements are taken together, they form the basis of a social contract between rulers and citizens. The purpose of this social contract is to maintain and protect these parties' mutual culture. That contract legitimizes national identity and, in Hobbes's view, strong authoritarian or "Big Brother"-type centralized governments. According to Hobbes, the human condition is naturally violent, materialistic and competitive. Thus, while all people may desire peace, human beings are fundamentally unable to create and maintain peace on their own. As a consequence, it is necessary for those being governed to hand over all of their natural rights to their leaders, and it is their leaders' responsibility to use any means necessary to ensure the safety and continuation of society. Essentially, Hobbesian law empowers governments to use any means they see fit to maintain the security of the people, including censorship, control over education and rule over religious practices. Although Hobbes's ideas sparked and continue to inspire heated debate, his work made significant contributions to Western political philosophy, including contemporary thought about representative governments, sovereignty and democracy.

Historians generally consider the period between the mid-18th century and today as the "age of democracies": It is during this period, and to a large degree through mass media, that democracies were born and upheld.[2] The media can influence the public and political agendas by making the process of government transparent to the people. As such, closed societies, which discourage freedom of thought and expression, are forced to become more open—that is, to expand access to information that the political, economic and information elite had previously controlled. This immediate and almost limitless access to the political process can certainly wreak havoc upon authoritarian governments. The more freedoms granted to the constituent populations, the less effectively closed-society, militaristic governments are able to perform information filtering—the weeding out of what they deem unwanted or irrelevant information—to keep people in the dark and to maintain their power over them.

In contrast, open societies (characteristic of democracies), allow significant opportunities for the media to monitor and report on the operations of governments, the courts, corporations, financial institutions and the like—in effect, "opening" their actions to the light of public scrutiny. The more information available to the people, the more opportunity there is for freedom and democracy to take root and grow. Aiding this growth is the exponential increase of mass media technology (for example, the Internet), which has also helped to transition the world into an extraordinary era of participatory democracy. Such a system permits and encourages a greater number of people to participate in the larger political process. This growing participatory system can be seen in even the more mature democracies, such as the United States, as demonstrated by the 2012 presidential campaigns.

U.S. Presidential Elections: 2008 and 2012

Recognizing early on that the Internet could be a powerful tool for closing the gap between the citizens and the politicians—the "us" and the "them"—both in 2008 and 2012, Obama's team used the Internet to gather supporters, to raise funds for his campaign and to spread the word about his stance on election issues; the campaign also took advantage of free advertising courtesy of YouTube for Obama's political ads. In effect, Obama's Internet and converged media campaigning changed *political* campaigning forever, and paved the way for more citizen coverage of and opining about an election.[3] As such, the election of President Obama in 2008 may go down in history as the event that brought U.S. politics and media into a new age of technology-enabled participatory democracy. The use of the Internet and especially social media via blog sites, Facebook, Twitter and YouTube increased significantly during the 2012 presidential election. This added a new media aspect to American politics that has both become a permanent feature and has had an unprecedented influence on the outcome of national elections and the shifting attitudes of the American electorate.

We saw this participatory model at work in China during the 1989 Tiananmen Square pro-democracy movement (and again on a new, technology-enabled level on its 20th anniversary in June 2009), and in Burma in late 2007 during the Saffron Revolution—what was considered the largest anti-government protest since 1988, when the country's first pro-democracy movement took place.

Tiananmen Square

On April 15, 1989, hundreds of Chinese university students, intellectuals and other patriots gathered in Tiananmen Square—at the front of the Forbidden City in China's capital city of Beijing—to mourn the death of former Secretary General Hu Yaobang. A strong advocate for pro-market and pro-democracy reform, and therefore a threat to the Communist regime, Hu was forced to resign from his position. Many Chinese citizens had hoped for reforms similar to those engendered by the former Soviet Union's 1985 glasnost policy. Initiated by then General Secretary Mikhail Gorbachev, this policy advocated transparency in government and a less regulated flow of information to the people. The institution of this policy was the beginning of the movement that would eventually dissolve the former Soviet Union, bringing down the Iron Curtain—the post—World War II symbolic divide between Eastern and Western Europe—and ending the ideological Cold War in 1991. While Hu's forced resignation weakened hope for such reforms in China, it did not discourage thousands of students from assembling and forming a pro-democracy movement in Hu's honor.

By the eve of Hu's funeral on April 21, 1989 the number of gathering mourners had grown to nearly 100,000. The atmosphere in Tiananmen Square quickly changed from that of a funeral to a charged political rally, where demands included free speech and a free press. Government officials scrambled to squelch the protests. On June 3, 1989, military forces equipped with live ammunition, armored personnel carriers and tanks marched into Tiananmen Square and began firing on the unarmed protestors. The assault resulted in hundreds of civilian deaths and thousands more wounded. Through the eyes of the global media, the world watched in real time as the Chinese military violently subdued the pro-democracy rally. International outcry immediately rang out.

Those demonstrators who had survived the crackdown were so threatened by the leadership's response that they almost immediately ceased speaking with the press. State-run media groups attempted to deliver the message that the military were sent in to quell violent student protestors who were allegedly attacking innocent government officials. The Western media believed and revealed otherwise. U.S. news stations kept a close lens on the events, broadcasting the crackdown as it was occurring—it would be their first-ever attempt at devoting nonstop, live coverage of a breaking international news event as it was unfolding. China endured three years of economic sanctions for its government's brutal response to the demonstration and suffered the scorn of the rest of the international community.[4]

Twenty years later, on the anniversary of the Tiananmen Square protests, old authoritarian systems reemerged. Officials censored, shut down, blocked and expelled all foreign media outlets. Their actions included tearing out articles about the events from such news sources as *The Economist* and the *Financial Times*; prohibiting Western media from entering Tiananmen Square; blocking such popular sites as Twitter, YouTube and Flickr; and blacking out computer screens at any mention of Tiananmen.[5] A number of Chinese Internet users and Website managers did not respond to these shutdowns without protest. Rather than explicitly object to the government's actions, however, they instead took down their sites for "maintenance" in honor of "Chinese Internet Maintenance Day." Browsers—whether ordinary citizens or government censors—encountered this message each time they attempted to access the home page of one of these sites. It is thought that this announcement, which reportedly appeared on several Websites that day, was a veiled attempt at protesting state censorship.[6]

Today, Chinese authorities continue to limit media access to the inner workings of the government and to arrest those who push the limits of freedom of expression in that country. As the Website "maintenance" story demonstrates, however, many have learned to work around these government restrictions—relying on veiled ways of participating in and pushing the message of democracy, while still avoiding punishment. In an article about the government's attempts at online censoring on the anniversary of Tiananmen Square, the U.K.-based news source *The Guardian* reported, "Internet users in China often deploy subtle methods to criticize the government without falling foul of the law. Among the favored techniques is repurposing Internet slang to make fun of leading political figures or mock their policies."[7] In the first decade of the 21st century, the global news media have given the world a new window into China's movement toward democracy, even though it still has a long way to go.[8]

14.2

This 2012 image of growing citizen participation in Tiananmen Square, China, differs greatly from those of the protests in 1989.

Mark Ralston/Staff

The Saffron Revolution

A series of events horribly reminiscent of the Tiananmen Square massacre took place in Burma in late 2007. On August 15, 2007, the military government of Burma unilaterally and without warning removed all fuel subsidies, resulting in a 100 percent spike in the cost of natural gas—drastically affecting a country that was already ranked as one of the poorest in the world. In response, scores of students, political activists and

14.3

The Saffron Revolution was the largest pro-democracy movement to occur in Burma since the late 1980s. Images of government brutality, captured by citizen journalists, made its way into the global media and outraged the world.

Thierry Falise/Contributor

ordinary citizens initiated small anti-government protests in Yangon (Rangoon) and other nearby cities. The government managed to detain most of the protesters and break up most of these demonstrations by gradually increasing force. By late September, thousands upon thousands of saffron-robed Buddhist monks began to gather and march through Yangon and into Mandalay in peaceful protest—what would come to be known as the Saffron Revolution—against the country's military dictatorship and on behalf of imprisoned pro-democracy leader Aung San Suu Kyi. The march continued to gather more participants until the military police eventually resorted to violence to suppress the protesters, beating, tear-gassing and arresting the monks, as well as the nuns and civilians who stood with them in support. At the same time, the regime attempted, but failed, to block all Websites enabling advocates of Suu Kyi to bring the plight of the Burmese people to the eyes and ears of the international community.

Images of the government's atrocities against its peaceful citizenry were captured and reported by citizen journalists and eventually made their way into the global media, seizing the attention and gaining the support of both ordinary and powerful people as well as human rights organizations worldwide. The world was so appalled by Burma's clear violation of the tenets put forth by The Universal Declaration of Human Rights that the ruling military was forced to temper its response to the demonstrations and to suffer economic sanctions imposed against Burma by the United States, the European Union and Canada. This empowering of the people and the participating citizenry continues to spur the growth of democracies around the world and challenge the survival of authoritarian regimes.

Jump to 2012. The Burmese people and the international community have witnessed a series of previously unimaginable political and economic reforms undertaken by the military-dominated government. The Burmese government accepted the reforms in an effort to retain its position in the face of uncontrollable international media coverage, supported by social media, of how it governed in the context of its long history of abuses against its people. Nobel laureate and pro-democracy leader Aung San Suu Kyi, finally released from her many decades of house arrest, is now a member of the Myanmar (Burmese) Parliament; she regularly travels internationally and meets with world leaders to gain support for her country. Meanwhile, in the 2012 parliamentary elections, Suu Kyi's National League for Democracy Party won a landslide 41 of the 44 contested seats.

14.4

Aung San Suu Kyi, Nobel laureate and Myanmar (Burma) member of Parliament, on stage after receiving the 2012 Global Citizen Award in New York on September 21, 2012.

Ramin Talaie/Contributor

GLOBAL MASS MEDIA SYSTEMS

How have mass media become involved in political and cultural dynamics around the world? The answer to that question involves the development of tightly overlapping networks of media resources called mass media systems. By the 1930s and 1940s, technologically advanced countries such as the United States, Great Britain, Canada and the Scandinavian countries had started building the foundations of current regional mass media systems. It was not until the mid-20th and early-21st centuries that this regional trend was reversed, allowing mass media to merge into a more or less global system. Such systems, especially those involving radio and television broadcast media, developed along different technological paths depending on where they were located. The basic systems we see in action today can be broken down into four models, each of which is based on the mass media theories espoused by Fred S. Siebert, Theodore Peterson and Wilbur Schramm: libertarian, social responsibility, authoritarian and Soviet-Communist.[9]

The Libertarian (Free Press) System

Of these four, we are most familiar with the U.S. mass media system, which some media pundits refer to as a libertarian-based system built on a commitment to present all views and cultural tastes of its audience. It remains the dominant media system in the world, albeit not without conflict and controversy. In the United States, the media system has primarily been rooted in strong constitutionally guaranteed freedoms of speech and expression (as discussed in Chapter 11). This is a reliable principle because under the American media system, corporations—not government agencies—own the majority of media outlets. These corporations are totally dependent upon the continued financial support of the marketplace, relying on advertising revenues, ticket sales, subscription purchases and cable and satellite service fees to ensure their survival.

The exception to this corporate model is the *Voice of America* (VOA), which was launched during World War II. Run by the Broadcasting Board of Governors (BBG), an independent federal agency comprising nine presidentially appointed bipartisan members, the *VOA* aired its premiere broadcast in 1942. Its goals: to spread the word of democracy, to quell enemy propaganda and "to get reliable news to people living in closed and war-torn societies."[10] Today, these goals remain largely intact, and the *VOA* remains a leading voice in international multimedia broadcasting, broadcasting in 45 languages and reaching audiences of as many as 125 million listeners weekly.

The Social-Responsibility System

In other Western media systems, the government plays a much stronger role in operating or controlling mass media outlets, especially broadcast media. In the British model, as exemplified by the long-running British Broadcasting Corporation (BBC), the government establishes and maintains mass media as part of its social responsibility (thus following a social-responsibility system). In turn, the press acts as a Fourth Estate—an eye that ensures that the government is not abusing its powers.

Despite government ownership of such groups as the BBC, British law prohibits the government from influencing the content of the media in any way. In 1972, the British Parliament enacted the Sound Broadcasting Act, which made it possible for privately funded companies to begin broadcasting regionally, so as to encourage the development of an independent and commercially funded broadcast media. Its vision was to allow for the introduction of media sources similar to the American model. These new companies grew rapidly and now compete with the government-owned BBC.

The Authoritarian System

Under the authoritarian system, found in monarchical and emperor rule in Western Europe, the government totally controls all media content. The media function as the political and propaganda arms of the state and their primary role is to spread information to favor the government's authority. Such systems can be found today in such nations as Burma, Iran and Libya. Initially, both the British and American media systems began as authoritarian systems in which the government controlled media content through burdensome licensing and censorship. These authoritarian media systems eventually gave way to—first in the United States and eventually in Great Britain—highly independent social-responsibility and libertarian models. It is important to note that elements of both models actually exist in the U.S. and British press systems.

The press system of the United States, for instance, is actually *both* libertarian and social responsibility based, depending on the news source and the journalist. For example, NPR is an example of a system that follows the social-responsibility principle of the press. By comparison, news outlets such as Fox, MSNBC and CNN, which are backed by corporate agendas and advertising and present sensationalistic content, are theoretically more akin to the libertarian (or free press) models. Consider, for instance, Nancy Grace, a former prosecutor turned television commentator. Although she claims to speak out on behalf of victims and victims' rights on her justice-themed CNN television show, in the vein of Maury Povich and Jerry Springer, Grace has also been accused of exploitation, network pandering and reporting on stories that have little bearing on the lives of most Americans. Essentially, both the United States and the United Kingdom defend freedom of expression vehemently—whether that expression is for the greater good or not.

> Essentially, both the United States and the United Kingdom defend freedom of expression vehemently—whether that expression is for the greater good or not.

The Soviet-Communist System

A close relative of the authoritarian model of the press is the Soviet-Communist system, which was developed in the former Soviet Union. The basic tenets of this system reflect the ideologies of Karl Marx and Friedrich Engels, both of whom believed that "the ideas of the ruling classes are the ruling ideas." Under this system, mass media are to be publicly owned, unmotivated by profit, and used solely to educate the masses so as to promote socialization and conformity. Such systems remain in place in the former Soviet Bloc countries of the Czech Republic and Romania as well as in North Korea, China and Cuba.

Like its former Soviet Union counterpart, mainland China maintains a Soviet-Communist mass media system that borders on being authoritarian. This system began with the then Communist Party leader Mao

Zedong following his triumph over the Chinese Nationalists in 1949; the system reached its pinnacle during the disastrous years of the Cultural Revolution (1965–1968), the effects of which did not start to ease until the 1990s, with social and market reforms. While the Chinese government still closely guards its authority over all mass media, the globalization and convergence of mass media in the 21st century have made maintaining an authoritarian system highly impractical and politically untenable, especially as China moves toward becoming a major economic world power. Ever since the Tiananmen Square massacre, pressures on China to support basic democratic rights—including free speech and a free press—and to address unlawful arrests or "disappearances" (or other similar abuses of human rights) of any individuals who attempt to practice such rights, have intensified. The Chinese government's stranglehold on the media that could expose such infringements would only encourage additional economic sanctions.

14.5

Media critics saw the 2008 Summer Olympics as an opportunity for China to relax its stranglehold over the media—but did that occur? What kind of coverage (images, new stories, events) of the Chinese Olympics do you recall seeing and how did that coverage reflect contemporary realities in China?

Sergiu Turcanu/Alamy Stock Photo

It was not until 2008, when China hosted the Summer Olympics in Beijing, that some loosening of the noose around the necks of both the Chinese and foreign media seemed possible. Despite worldwide attempts at boycotting the Beijing Olympics in protest of the country's long record of human rights abuses—against political dissidents, spiritual groups (such as the Falun Gong) and advocates of a Free Tibet—many China experts in the West saw the games as an opportunity for China to relax its authoritarian rule over the media.

As China continues to experience significant reforms, it has also felt the pressure of its elevating status on the global economic landscape. As such, government officials recognize the practical need to reconsider their stance on media access and information control—but this move is not without its complications. What this ultimately means is that the media situation is China is very complex and this complexity goes beyond simply direct censorship by the authorities.

MASS MEDIA SYSTEMS IN DEVELOPMENT

In August 2004, Radio Rutomorangingo—a pirate radio station equipped by Rwandan militants—began broadcasting into the neighboring country of Burundi, a small landlocked country in central Africa. With programming driven by catchy music and Western-style talk programs, Radio Rutomorangingo droned a singular message: "Rise up against your oppressors!" In this case, the so-called oppressors were the Tutsi minority, an ethnic group that held the lion's share of political power in the country. The majority, the Hutus, had long struggled to assert their voice in government, which resulted in constant turmoil between the two groups. This conflict had erupted in violence on several occasions over the course of Burundi's history, but this time the tensions had destroyed all civility between the Hutus and the Tutsis, resulting in civil war.

Hutu guerrillas were trying to incite Burundian Hutus to take up arms against their Tutsi neighbors, using propaganda broadcast over the radio to portray the Tutsis as subhuman and capable of horrific acts of violence. This campaign proved incredibly effective in Rwanda, ultimately resulting in the brutal extermination of nearly 1 million Tutsis by their Hutu co-workers, teachers, politicians and religious leaders who had been won over by these messages. Thankfully, the international community quickly stepped in and aided the Burundian government in jamming such hate radio. While approximately 300,000 Hutu and Tutsi Burundians had died in the struggle as of 2009, the number of casualties would have been much greater were it not for the help from the outside.

Throughout Burundi's civil war, guerilla commandos constantly plagued the country with random acts of violence, threatening the tenuous stability and peace of a nation in the process of rebuilding. While international aid has helped to thwart the mainstream broadcasting of hate radio, ethnic propaganda still has a presence in Burundi. International civil rights activists and Burundians from both the Tutsi and Hutu ethnic groups have been working to take back control of the airwaves and to use them as tools to encourage constructive public dialogue, education and hope in the struggling region. Radio Isanganiro, spearheaded by such international coalitions as the United Nations, is one such broadcasting effort that reaches out to both Tutsis and Hutus in Burundi, offering thorough and balanced journalism that addresses the issues facing all Burundians.[11] Jeanine Nahigombeye, director of Radio Isanganiro, elaborates on this goal and comments on the role of women in this effort—undertaken even at the risk of their own lives—in the Peace X Peace video segment, "Women on the Frontlines." ▶

14.6

Olinchuk/Shutterstock.com

▶ Women on the Frontlines

Jeanine Nahigombeye, director of Radio Isanganiro, explains her sometimes risky efforts, and the efforts of other women like her, to present fair and balanced journalism promoting peace in civil war-torn Burundi.

Radio Paves the Way

Burundi's story highlights a subcategory of media systems present in developing countries: systems in development. While it may seem surprising in this age of converged media, globalized television and the World Wide Web, radio remains the largest and most effective mass medium in the developing world. Its popularity persists in large part because of the high percentage of illiteracy that continues to plague such nations, despite major infrastructure programs that seek to build schools and promote literacy.[12] Such programs are often supported by nongovernmental organizations (NGOs), groups created by nonparticipating and nonrepresentative individuals of a ruling administration or regime. UNESCO (United Nations Educational, Scientific and Cultural Organization) is one such NGO that promotes peace and universal respect through collaboration, education and unfettered sharing of knowledge and ideas.

In addition, radios are inexpensive to set up and operate. Shortwave radio has a tremendously long transmission range and individual radio receivers have become one of the least costly of all modern media technologies to manufacture and to own. By comparison, print media is expensive and resource intensive, requiring not just the work of the content producers, but also the availability of industrial presses, paper mills, distribution hubs and the personnel to run them. Television requires significant investments in studio production facilities and transmission infrastructure, and individual ownership of televisions is beyond the economic reach of the tens of millions of poor rural citizens. Unlike Radio Isanganiro, the vast majority of radio and television stations in the developing world are government owned; typically they are used to promote a government's political and social agendas. As in the case of Burundi, militants have used radio and television—especially radio—to deliver propaganda that incites violent religious and tribal conflicts. More often than not, these conflicts have resulted in bloody civil war and genocide. In a 2008 study, Gallup found that radio remains the main source of news and information in sub-Saharan Africa. Its research, spanning 23 African countries, found that six in 10 people there reported that national and international radio broadcasts were the most important mass media for them and for their communities.[13]

Fortunately, because radio receivers are so inexpensive and pervasive in the developing world, and because shortwave radio broadcasts can travel so easily across borders and over long distances, information that challenges militant propaganda can be made readily available to the masses. Radio broadcasts have long been proven difficult to jam and impossible to completely block; consider, for instance, the attempts made on this front by Germany's Third Reich during World War II, the Soviet regime during the Cold War, the Chinese Communist regime during its Cultural Revolution and the repressive regimes in North Korea and Iran today. Indeed, radio has played a pivotal role in the emergence of democracies and the convergence of cultures throughout the 20th century. It will certainly continue to play a significant role in the formation of mass media systems around the world in the 21st century, although technological advancements and innovations, as well as the gradual elimination of energy and cost factors, will also strengthen the influence of television and the Internet.

The Influence of Satellite Television

The story of television's rise as a contributor to global mass media systems, and thus to global politics, parallels the shift from analog-based terrestrial broadcasts (where broadcast signals are transmitted and received via antennas through radio waves) to satellite-based digital broadcasts (where broadcast signals are transmitted and received via microwave radio relay technology). One of the early visionaries of satellite communication and satellite-delivered radio and television was futurist and best-selling author Arthur C. Clarke. Clarke, who died in 2008, served in the British Royal Air Force as a radar engineer during World War II. After the war, he became a pioneer in the development of geostationary satellites (satellites that orbit the equator) and related ground-based relay systems. Early on, Clarke imagined the social and cultural impact that the network of communication satellites would have. That network today is an indispensable communications Web that circles the globe.

Clarke believed that satellite television would generally bring about improved education and literacy levels and better agricultural and health practices among citizens of the developing world as well as populations in other countries that were forced to live in virtual isolation—at the time, those behind the Soviet-dominated Iron Curtain. His rationale was that satellite television would broadcast general and practical knowledge—for example, how to better plant and irrigate crops, how to more safely handle food, how to purify water for drinking, how to practice basic hygiene, and how to practice safe birth control.

Using his own resources and in cooperation with UNESCO and the BBC, Clarke undertook a pilot project to bring satellite television to poor rural villages in Sri Lanka, where he lived and worked in his later years. This work won Clarke international praise and humanitarian honors, including a nomination for the Nobel Peace Prize in 1994. Clarke's groundbreaking work demonstrates the positive impact of satellite-delivered television on poor villages in the developing world. It continues to exemplify the importance of mass media technology on social and cultural development and to inspire humanitarian projects throughout the world today. For more on Clarke's pioneering efforts, view the video "Arthur C. Clarke." ▶

Clarke's groundbreaking work demonstrates the positive impact of satellite-delivered television on poor villages in the developing world. It continues to exemplify the importance of mass media technology on social and cultural development and to inspire humanitarian projects throughout the world today.

▶ **Arthur C. Clarke**
Clarke's groundbreaking work continues to serve as a model for the important role mass media technology plays in social and cultural development.

The Role of the Internet

The Internet—thanks to its ability to expose in viral fashion the issues that would otherwise remain hidden from the eyes of the international community—has proved a saving grace in many ways. It has pushed the cause of democracy in many countries onto the global media landscape and given voice to dissidents and all their supporters.

A good example of the power of social media to bring about social and democratic change is Esraa Abdel Fatah, an Egyptian Internet activist and blogger also known as "Facebook Girl." An Egyptian human resources administrator by profession, Esraa co-founded the April 6 Youth Movement in 2008 and was shortly thereafter arrested by President Hosni Mubarak's secret police. She was released after two weeks. Although her arrest and treatment was virtually ignored by Egypt's heavily censored mainstream media, her postings on Facebook and her blog site went viral, turning her into an overnight national and international symbol of resistance against the corruption and authoritarian practices of the Mubarak regime. In January 2011, Esraa once again gained a huge Internet following both in Egypt and around the world when she reappeared on Facebook and in blogs as a major voice of the nationwide protests in Egypt as part of the Arab Spring. She helped broadcast the Egyptian revolution throughout the Middle East and beyond via her appearances on the Arab-language news network Al Jazeera, and she contributed to the fall of the Mubarak regime. Esraa continues her social networking-based reporting about the Muslim Brotherhood, which came to power in post-revolution Egypt, and has been put forward as a candidate for the Nobel Peace Prize.

Since then, activists, politicians and numerous celebrities have spoken out in support of revolutionary voices like Esraa Abdel Fatah, often using social media such as Twitter, Facebook and YouTube; in this way, they reach audiences otherwise unaware of the reality of situations on the ground as new voices of democracy battle established authoritarian governments in the Middle East, Africa, and Central Asia and China.[14]

MASS MEDIA AND CULTURAL CONTEXT

Earlier in this chapter, we credited Thomas Hobbes for making major contributions to Western political philosophy. Even more importantly, Hobbes was one of the earliest Western thinkers to identify the role of culture in structuring societies and maintaining social order. He developed the terminology we now use for speaking about cultural relationships. An understanding of Hobbes's philosophy, which promotes independent libertarian ideas and argues against irrelevant morality and irrelevant cultural standards, helps us recognize the importance of cultural context—that is, the social, religious and political rules that govern how people are expected to behave and respond toward one another. The dynamics of this principle, which applies to all intercultural and intracultural interactions (outside of and within the same culture, respectively), is essential to understanding why cultural conflict can occur between individuals, among groups and within the media.

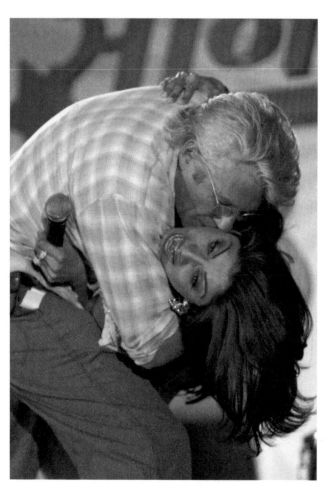

14.7

The Indian media repeatedly aired images of American actor Richard Gere kissing Bollywood actress Shilpa Shetty on the cheek at an AIDS benefit, despite outcries that the action was considered culturally offensive. Why would the Indian media do this?

STRDEL/AFP/Newscom

Take, for instance, the story of Richard Gere and Shilpa Shetty. In 2007, Hollywood leading man Richard Gere found himself wanted by the police—the police in New Delhi, India, that is. Gere, a passionate advocate of HIV/AIDS awareness, was in New Delhi to appear at an anti-AIDS rally when he spontaneously planted a long, passionate kiss on the cheek of Bollywood star and fellow activist Shilpa Shetty. In Indian culture, public displays of affection—even those that would seem innocent to Americans, such as a kiss on the cheek—are considered offensive. Within hours, the Indian media captured images of the embrace and distributed them to outlets throughout the globe, resulting in public outrage, mostly in India. In response to formal complaints filed by Indian citizens, authorities in New Delhi issued warrants for the arrests of both Gere and Shetty, on the tenuous grounds that they had violated public obscenity laws. The charges were eventually dropped because they reflected a breach in cultural mores and well-established social norms, rather than violations of Indian law.[15]

Indian television networks, newspapers and magazines focused on the story for days, supplying the public with repeated photos and video images of the cultural offense. Why would they do this? It's possible that the intent of the continued media spotlight was in part to draw attention to how the globalization of mass media has aided in the softening of traditionally rooted limitations on public behaviors. Whatever the reason underlying the Indian media's intent, Gere's blunder and the attention it drew demonstrate the importance of respecting not only the *audience* in a communication situation, but also the *cultural context*.

The Influence of High- and Low-Context Cultures

Throughout this book, we have emphasized how mass media allow everyday citizens to participate and share in the making of cultural and social histories. Whether in the form of newspapers, radio broadcasts, videos or blogs, each medium has played some pivotal part in the continuance, conflict and convergence of distinctive cultures. As we move toward a more global culture and experience the myriad mass media systems at work in the development and sustenance of this culture, we must first define culture in general terms to understand how these shifts are playing out. Culture shapes a people; it comprises the unique mixture of language, symbols, beliefs, traditions, ideologies, artifacts and history that make one group distinct from another. Historically, geography has strongly influenced culture. People who were geographically connected develop shared language, lifestyles and belief systems, which were generally distinct from those of the people who, say, lived over a mountain range or across an ocean from them. One example of this is regional pronunciation—a Southern drawl versus the Brooklyn accent, for instance.

The greater the differences between cultural groups, the more critical and challenging communication between them becomes. As such, culture can act as either the principal bridge that brings groups together or the barrier that rends them apart. For this reason, it is especially crucial for mass media, which operate in some ways as the face and the voice of a culture, to be viewed within the cultural context in which they operate. In his influential book *Beyond Culture*, cultural theorist Edward T. Hall identifies two distinct categories of cultures that have influenced the way mass media behave within and across their borders: high-context cultures and low-context cultures.

> culture can act as either the principal bridge that brings groups together or the barrier that rends them apart. For this reason, it is especially crucial for mass media, which operate in some ways as the face and the voice of a culture, to be viewed within the cultural context in which they operate.

In high-context cultures, such as those in Japan, China and Saudi Arabia, both the producers and the consumers (the audience) of media content—the actual words, images and stories—heavily depend on a shared understanding of the context within which that media content is presented. High-context cultures rely on symbolism and implied meaning and demand a certain degree of "reading between the lines" from their audiences.[16] For example, the color "red" in a high-context culture such as China can communicate Communist Party loyalty, patriotism and country in a national context (such as a political event); it may also signal auspiciousness, wealth and happiness in a celebratory context (such as a wedding).

In low-context cultures, such as those in the United States, Canada, the United Kingdom and much of Western Europe, the media content that is produced and consumed is generally more straightforward, although a few media creators may include subtle messages in their content. Yet even this more direct media-message style varies from culture to culture.[17]

The Cultural Divide Plays Out in the Media

It should come as no surprise that the cultural differences that deeply divide high- and low-context cultures are the same differences that are played out in the global media. Western culture, which is highly committed to secular democracy (not determined by religion) and modernism, is often depicted as materialistic, self-promoting and oversexed. Consider, for instance, the cable and television programs that are popular among the media-consuming public in the United States today: *The Real Housewives*, *Grey's Anatomy* and *Family Guy*. Since the United States dominates the world's film and television industries, many religious, more conservative nations—especially those of the Islamic world—believe that the American media intentionally target and threaten Muslims and the very fabric of their culture and traditions.

In response to these perceived threats, Islamic television networks based in Lebanon, Saudi Arabia and Egypt, for example, combine religious, political and entertainment programs as alternatives to Western media. At the same time, other television networks in these same countries try hard to imitate American- and British-style programming. For instance, Al Jazeera, the international news network based in Doha, Qatar, is modeled closely on the U.S.-based CNN. In addition, stations throughout the Middle East air entertainment programs ranging from dramas to situation comedies, as well as feature films, purchased from Western television networks.

14.8

Understanding cultural customs in any communication situation
is important, but this is especially true in a media context. Here,
United Nations Goodwill Ambassador Angelina Jolie listens to
Somali refugees describe their experience and overcrowding in the
refugee camp.

SIPA USA/Newscom

Cyberspace Globalizes Media and Culture

In the 21st century, advances in communication and mass media technologies have broken down barriers and contributed to the creation of an international marketplace. In turn, the birth of the global marketplace has led to the growth of a common global culture. As a consequence, it is not unusual for a high school student living in Gaborone, Botswana, to model her or his language, dress, career aspirations and entertainment interests on what the student sees on television or in the movies. Likewise, an American interested in world music may find selections of traditional Botswanian music at a local street festival. Furthering this exposure and commingling of distinct cultures is the Internet.

Today, communication and mass media technologies are rapidly changing traditional geographic and cultural boundaries, and bringing disparate cultures together in an emerging globalized cyberculture. As such, today's media consumers and Internet participants are far more aware of and sensitive to diverse cultures and peoples than their parents' and grandparents' generations. This convergence begs a question: Are the 21st-century mass media primarily a conduit of cross-cultural understanding and increased tolerance for diverse worldviews, ideas and beliefs? Or are they contributing to the destruction of cultural diversity as the world moves inexorably toward a single mass media system driven by a globalizing culture? Bringing the peoples of the world together into Marshall McLuhan's global village, while at the same time recognizing and maintaining the value of diverse cultures, may be one of the greatest challenges of the 21st century.

While the extensive benefits associated with this globalization of culture through mass media and the Internet are undeniable—increased education and literacy levels; new economic and business opportunities; greater availability of information about local, regional and international developments—some cultural anthropologists and social psychologists fear that the less structured cyberculture is contributing to the breakdown and devaluation of localized cultures. In their opinion, this perceived threat could result in the loss of diverse heritages in many culturally rich areas of the world—especially among younger generations.[18]

MEDIA CULTURES COMPETE FOR SURVIVAL

The survival of cultural diversity in the Digital Age is a great concern, but not only for academics. From the moment people first appeared on the scene, human culture has been in a constant state of upheaval. Fractionalization and competition have dominated our story ever since. Why? According to Thomas Hobbes, cultural competition came about for two reasons: (1) humans are inherently selfish creatures and (2) the world contains limited resources. The desire for survival and, to an even greater extent, the desire to attain the highest good lie at the heart of all conflict. Hobbes's view is one of many theories that have been used to explain the presence of competition and to suggest a solution for conflict. For Hobbes, the solution to humankind's problem involves the total conveyance of power to an iron-fisted, god-like government. Although this idea is somewhat helpful in that it explains in concrete terms the nature of cultural competition, Hobbes's view of humankind is overly grim and fails to account for the positive strides humans have exhibited over the course of history to deal with the problem.

Cultures seldom allow themselves to be driven into extinction without a fight. Traditionalist leaders, from militaristic politicians to religious authorities, react forcefully when they see their beliefs, their cultural norms and their own authority being threatened by a competing culture. Consider, once again, the current cultural conflict between the Islamic and the Western worlds. Islamic fundamentalists view Western culture, predominantly represented by American mass media, as anti-religious, overly liberal and irreverent. Such dominance exists in part because mass media in the United States have the longest history of financial success, and in part because they express the views and values of a democratic culture—that is, independence, individualism, secularism, capitalism. Many people throughout the world, who have long suffered the abuses of their oppressive regimes, desire such ideals. To quell the influence of such media, some countries make a concerted regulatory effort to limit the number of U.S.-made films and television programs that are allowed to be legally imported. Such efforts are almost impossible to enforce effectively because of the insatiable demand for—and therefore the thriving black market in—American mass media.

In his groundbreaking documentary film *Hollywood and the Muslim World* (2003), filmmaker Charles C. Stuart interviewed college students, television producers and journalists and academics throughout the Middle East in an effort to present Americans with a better understanding of how their mass media both attract and inflame audiences in the Middle East. One consistent theme throughout these interviews is the notion that young Muslims are highly attracted to American films, television and music, paired with the fear that such media are quickly destroying Muslim culture, such that within just a few more generations, Muslim traditions will disappear. Some interviewees also express the belief that Americans are engaged in a conspiracy to destroy Muslim culture, rewrite its history and subvert Islam with Christianity. To paraphrase the words of a Kurdish professor interviewed in this documentary, that which is valuable and adaptable in one culture and one religion will be valued and become part of the dominant culture. Conversely, that which is not of value and which is inflexible in the face of inevitable change will disappear—as it should.[19]

14.9

The international dominance and demand for American movies and television shows can cause a cultural and political backlash in countries where strong conservative religious factions see them as an intentional assault on the morality of their societies.

Ajaree Meenapha/EyeEm

While history testifies to the reality of this ongoing struggle for cultural dominance, the advances of technology and mass communication have been instrumental in the rise of a global community that transcends these deep-rooted patterns of competition and conflict. In the Digital Age, many people throughout the world have seen that the free exchange of ideas can take place without violence or political agendas; people from different cultures can identify themselves as members of a greater human culture.

MEDIA DOMINANCE AND THE GLOBAL MARKETPLACE

In reality, 21st-century cultural imperialism—the spread of a culture into the society of another, generally without that society's consent—can be viewed as a side effect of economic and market prominence.

Time Warner, News Corp., Disney, Viacom, Bertelsman (German), Sony (Japanese), General Electric (NBC Universal) and Vivendi (Italian), to name a few of the largest multimedia corporations, reflect a cultural hegemony of media ownership—that is, they control the lion's share of media throughout the world. As a result, these powerful media corporations can exert an enormous influence on the content of global media, indirectly influencing the globalization of culture. The majority of these leading global media conglomerates are American owned.[20]

These principal mass media conglomerates share a common mission of making ever-increasing profits from the sale and licensing of media content along with the sale of advertising. From this perspective, one can argue that their aim in influencing government agendas is simply to affect the regulation of their businesses. These dominant media corporations are not joined in some grand conspiracy to corrupt cultures; rather, they are out to make money for their investors. They compete against one another, and this healthy competition benefits consumers. American mass media industries have, from their onset, been built around a market-driven commercial model, such that the development of revenue-producing media content is their primary goal. What dictates the style, content and message of the media, therefore, is the desires of the market.

While the ever-growing global demand for such content can act as a counterforce to authoritarian governments, the role of bringing to public awareness humanitarian abuses that might result from these governments' actions generally falls under the auspices of the news divisions of these mass media giants—not, in fact, the media company overall. While the conglomerate certainly has the prerogative to fill this role, such an action will not make it profitable. The major percentage of revenue for mass media conglomerates typically comes from entertainment media; this revenue, in turn, helps pay for the less profitable news divisions. For example, CNN is the leader and model for 24/7 television news throughout the world, but CNN's global news operations are made possible in part because they are owned by Time Warner, a conglomerate largely sustained by its profitable entertainment divisions.

The production and distribution of U.S. films and television programs is a hugely profitable global industry. American blockbuster movies attract the largest international audiences, generating huge profits for the studios and distributors, which they invest in creating the next round of blockbusters. Given the great diversity of audiences throughout the world, the consistent success of U.S. movies and television is undeniable proof of the hunger for American-style entertainment. Does the global demand for American media content have an impact—positive and negative—on other cultures? Without question, yes. Is this a demonstration of an *intentional* effort to subvert and destroy non-American cultures? Absolutely not.

American media are the dominant media in today's world because they offer the products and services that the global market wants to buy. In the video segment from *Hollywood and the Muslim World*, Taiseer Alouni, a correspondent for Al Jazeera television, admits that his network deliberately patterned its own format after that of American media because of the latter's wide appeal. There is no grand conspiracy, just simple straightforward economics. More importantly, Al Jazeera broke the lock on government control when it established itself as the first Arab-based and -oriented 24-hour news service station, modeled after the success of CNN.

Technology has played a big role in extending the influence of American mass media. As the cost of consumer media technologies has decreased over the last two decades—VCRs, CD and DVD players, satellite television, digital music players, smartphones and tablets—the proliferation of Western media, especially U.S.-created media, has increased. Low-cost media technologies have made low-cost media content available to larger global audiences, cutting across both cultural and economic barriers. As we have explored in other chapters throughout this book, the rapid growth and global spread of the Internet have greatly contributed to the onrush of global mass media.

A decade into the 21st century, American dominance of mass media, especially entertainment media, is starting to show signs of diminishing as the technologies of media production and distribution have become more accessible. The digital revolution has made the tools of mass media easier to adopt and to exploit. For example, for decades, the largest number of theatrical films produced each year did not come out of

Hollywood, but rather were created by the equivalent movie industry in India, known as Bollywood. Yet Indian films and television series found few audiences outside of India and the Indian expatriate community. Then, in 2008, along came a relatively low-budget film called *Slumdog Millionaire*, produced entirely in Mumbai, India. It featured an all-Indian cast and a storyline uniquely rooted in the culture and environment of Mumbai. It stormed the American and Western European media establishment, winning Best Picture at major film festivals and awards programs, including the Golden Globes and an astounding eight Academy Awards. *Slumdog Millionaire*, beyond being a compelling story well told, demonstrated that the tide of American dominance over global mass media might indeed be starting to turn.

MASS MEDIA AND GLOBAL DIPLOMACY

The evolution of mass media, especially the proliferation of 24/7 television news and the Internet, can potentially promote global diplomacy and the growth of common understanding among people and among governments around the world. Marshall McLuhan's vision of a mass media-enabled global village in many ways has become a reality, bringing with it the ability of governments and their diplomatic representatives to more easily join forces to address shared global challenges. Nevertheless, although the immediacy and global reach of news coverage can support diplomatic efforts to defuse regional crises, it can also complicate diplomatic efforts. Governments now find that they must compete with a wide range of media voices when trying to sway public opinion in their own countries and abroad. The marshalling of public opinion across national and international borders via the global media is all the more difficult for diplomats in the 21st century because they have lost control over two elements—time and secrecy—that were once so vital a part of the professional diplomat's stock in trade.

> Marshall McLuhan's vision of a mass media-enabled global village in many ways has become a reality, bringing with it the ability of governments and their diplomatic representatives to more easily join forces to address shared global challenges.

Information Immediacy and Its Effects on Diplomacy

As long as citizens the world over have computer and Web access, the immediacy of information in cyberspace and the ability to interact directly with people in other nations will continue influencing international relations both positively and negatively. Both top leaders and their citizens now witness world events as they unfold in real time. Acts of genocide in Rwanda, anti-government riots in Thailand, a volcanic eruption in Iceland or an oil spill in the Gulf of Mexico—all have instantaneous impact on media audiences throughout the world, almost as if the events were happening in the next town or village. We all unavoidably share in the information about humanitarian, economic, environmental or political crises as they happen across traditional boundaries of culture, language and nation. This media-driven shared experience gives world leaders and their diplomatic representatives little time to analyze intelligence reports, form well-considered policy decisions and set these

14.10

No matter where in the world a disaster might strike, the speed of advanced media technologies has made it possible for virtually everyone to witness the event unfold in real time. Images such as this one, which was taken in the aftermath of the catastrophic earthquake that struck Haiti in early 2010, helped to compel several countries to contribute humanitarian aid.

Jessica Brandi Lifland/ZUMA/Newscom

decisions into action. Sometimes the extremely short time between the joint experience and the taking of action can exacerbate a crisis. At other times, the global sharing of images of humanitarian suffering can drive governments to action when they might have otherwise stayed on the sidelines.

A good example of a shared media experience causing positive government actions occurred in 1992, during the civil war in the former Yugoslavia that essentially tore the nation apart through ethnic genocide. The West and especially the United States had been slow to come to the aid of Serbian Muslims during the 22-month conflict between Bosnia's Serbs, Muslims and Croats. That all changed when a mortar bomb slammed into a crowded market in Sarajevo, killing 68 people and seriously wounding 200 others. CNN happened to have a camera crew very near the market at the time of the bomb attack. As a result, the world witnessed images of the carnage and human suffering in nearly real time.

Among the world audience watching the crisis unfold was President Bill Clinton and a number of his close aides, who were working that Saturday at the White House. These presidential aides reported later that President Clinton was so shocked and angered by what he was watching that he immediately made moves towards changing U.S. policy toward the conflict. Within hours, he ordered U.S. military action against the Bosnian Serb army and government, leading the way to a rapid American, NATO and United Nations military response that would eventually end the war. Had President Clinton not witnessed the real-time sounds and images of death and destruction in that far-away open-air market, the atrocities in the former Yugoslavia might have dragged on for many more months and with far less shared diplomatic will to intervene.[21] This single incident serves as a shining example of the potential influence of journalism in the Digital Age and how mass media has helped change the role and process of international diplomacy influence of CNN and new sources like it. Besides representing one of the news network's finest hours, it was an event that helped change the role and process of international diplomacy.

National Security and the World Wide Web

History has demonstrated that leadership is often judged by its ability to embrace changing media technologies and skillfully sell public policy through the mass media.

History has demonstrated that leadership is often judged by its ability to embrace changing media technologies and skillfully sell public policy through the mass media. Global mass media, from the shared experiences of 24/7 satellite news to the cultural barrier-busting Internet, is a 21st-century force that national leaders ignore at their own peril. Yet the same World Wide Web that can bring people and nations together also brings its own potential threats to national security.

Al-Qaida, perhaps the most prominent terrorist group in the world in the wake of its attacks on the United States on September 11, 2001, maintains a significant presence on the Web. During his first term in office, President Obama increased the attacks on al-Qaida and its splinter groups. On May 2, 2011 a Delta Force successfully attacked Osama bin Laden's longtime hiding place in Pakistan and killed him. Yet, while these attacks have significantly hurt al-Qaida's ability to plan and execute acts of terrorism, the threat posed by its various offshoots remains. These organization use sophisticated Internet and new media technologies to spread their propaganda and recruit new members. Some experts believe that al-Qaida also uses the Internet to secretly communicate with its widely dispersed cells through encoded messages embedded within some of its Web pages, thereby enabling its operatives to evade monitoring by U.S., British and other intelligence agencies. In its report, the United States Institute of Peace (USIP)[22] summarizes the reasons why terrorist groups use the Internet as their core communication platform:

- Easy access
- Little or no regulation, censorship, or other forms of government control
- Potentially huge audiences spread throughout the world
- Anonymity of communication
- Fast flow of information
- Inexpensive development and maintenance of a Web presence

- A multimedia environment (the ability to combine text, graphics, audio and video and to allow users to download films, songs, books, posters and so forth)
- The ability to shape coverage in the traditional mass media, which increasingly use the Internet as a source for stories[23]

It is at once striking and troubling that the reasons why the Internet is of such value to terrorist groups are the same reasons why the Internet is of such high value to individuals, businesses, nonprofit organizations and governments around the world. Much like "mainstream" Websites, terrorist sites attempt to use engaging images and streaming audio and video clips, along with narrative text, to tell stories about their history and mission and to promote their causes.

The Websites serve as fundraising vehicles, encouraging donations and marketing promotional items such as T-shirts, flags and DVDs—the latter to further reinforce their extremist messages and recruit new followers. Terrorist groups such as al-Qaida are also very good at using the Internet and other media technologies to sway public opinion. The overall effect is to help make these extremist groups appear to be far more influential and powerful than they actually are. Since the goals of terrorism are generally to create fear and uncertainty among the general public and to divert government and economic resources and attention, terrorist groups can accomplish some of their mission without actually having to organize, fund or launch actual attacks, thanks to their skillful use of the Internet and ability to produce and distribute unregulated content to a mass audience.

14.11

This Internet posting by al-Qaida's media arm shows one of the 9/11 terrorists speaking from an unknown location.

AFP/Getty Images

EQUALIZING THE GLOBAL COMMUNITY THROUGH MEDIA TECHNOLOGY

In February 2009, the U.S. House of Representatives passed a measure to push back the elimination of analog television broadcasts to June of the same year. The switch from analog to digital television (DTV) was the result of legislation passed in 1996 to free up broadcast bandwidth, which could then be used for such public services as police, fire and rescue communication networks as well as the development of new technologies by the private sector. Although this transition would ultimately benefit the public, a majority in Congress agreed that too many Americans, especially among the poor and elderly, lacked easy access to the technology that would let them convert their analog sets to digital. Implementing the conversion to all DTV in the United States on schedule would deprive such citizens of vital information and culture.

The concern of Congress in ensuring equal access to basic media for all Americans illustrates the problem of the Digital Divide, which a percentage of the population in countries throughout the world encounters. Although scholars continue to debate how to define the problem, many agree that the issue centers on how economic, social and political factors affect and are affected by access to the technologies that form the information distribution pathways in 21st-century society.

Since technology and media are central to the way we live, learn and do business in the Digital Age, the opportunity to use technology directly correlates with many aspects of the quality of everyday life. This is an issue not only for Westerners, but (as we saw earlier in this chapter) for all cultures around the world.

Who should have access to technology? Who decides who should have access and who should not? Who is responsible for providing access to technologies, including paying for it? How can societies bear the economic burden and facilitate the distribution, user education and maintenance of technology and media for the public good? These are significant challenges that governments, NGOs and the private sector must address to limit the growing negative social and cultural consequences of the Digital Divide.

These questions are at the heart of a number of projects spearheaded by cooperatives of humanitarians, inventors, academics and politicians, a few of which we have already explored, such as Arthur C. Clarke's satellite-based digital television broadcasts. The experts and organizations currently involved in the global effort to bring technological equality to all cultures are convinced that if all people have access to the vital information that media provide, the world will make radical progress toward solutions to the problems facing most societies—health care, poverty, stability. Education is a powerful tool that brings about change, and mass media constitute a formidable global delivery system.

The world's governments, innovators, entrepreneurs and philanthropists are already making significant contributions toward closing the Digital Divide. In one noteworthy example, in 2008, the *Bangkok Post* reported that under the patronage of Princess Maha Chakri Sirindhorn, permanently disabled children in Thailand are using media technology to overcome learning and communication impediments.[24] In another example, the proliferation of computer and Internet technology in distant and previously disconnected portions of Tibet is improving the quality of education, while at the same time helping to preserve Tibetan culture. In the past, northern Tibetans would record their history on dried palm leaves that were then kept in wooden cases in an attempt to preserve them. The natural disintegration of the leaves meant that these histories were seldom read. Now, with the aid of media technology, these histories are being digitally recorded and distributed throughout Tibet and the world, further broadening Tibetan cultural awareness.[25]

While advances in technology and lower manufacturing costs have made it possible for more societies around the world to afford greater access to the Internet and other vital mass media content, new problems are arising for the poor and other disadvantaged subgroups that could signal a second iteration of the Digital Divide—a Digital Divide 2.0. Now that many developing nations have built a basic technological infrastructure, there is an enormous need for content relevant to and desired by users in these diverse cultures. Media content must not only address the specific life conditions of the consumers, but also help maintain the delicate balance between the preservation and convergence of cultures.

Since a majority of the technology and content on the Internet has been produced in the West, American English is the dominant language for an enormous portion of the media content available to global audiences. As a consequence, this content primarily reflects American cultural perspectives. Nevertheless, users in Korea, for example, do not face the same issues as Americans and would not address those issues in the same way. Overcoming language and relevancy barriers to meet the diverse needs of peoples throughout the global community poses an extraordinary challenge in terms of both technological resources and content creativity. Although the need is great and the obstacles are numerous, recent history is demonstrating a relatively rapid bridging of the original Digital Divide. This progress suggests that even these new problems can be solved through innovation and understanding made possible by our mass media-driven burgeoning global culture.

During the last decade, we have seen progressive social movements powered by the web surface across the world. There was the Green Revolution in Iran and the Arab Spring in the Middle East and North Africa. In the United States, we saw the Occupy Wall Street movement and the Black Lives Matter protests. Video, social and visual content defined coverage of the most dramatic news stories of the year including in the terrorist attacks in Paris. LaMonde journalist Daniel Psenny captured graphic scenes as crowds fled the Bataclan concert hall in Paris on his iPhone. Twitter user Stephane Hannache was one of many using live streaming app Periscope hosting more than 10,000 viewers. A Vine video from the Stade de France with clearly audible explosions was one of the first verified accounts of the attacks. BBC correspondent Matthew Price filmed an immersive 360° video at the Place de la République using a cheap simple consumer mobile device.[26]

CONCLUSION: THE TRANSFORMATIVE POWER OF MASS MEDIA

American media content certainly is the most sought after and valued internationally. Even so, some countries, such as France, make a concerted effort to limit the amount of American-produced film and television content allowed in, thereby decreasing the perceived cultural threat from this source. Cultural traditionalists in France believe that this effort is one way to

14.12

In what ways can we bridge the Digital Divide in the 21st century to ensure true globalization of mass media and mass media technologies?

Tim Gainey/Alamy Stock Photo

protect the French language and French culture. Nevertheless, with the globalization of international trade, of which mass media are a component, government efforts to erect protectionist cultural barriers seem to be fighting a losing battle. In his book *Understanding Media: The Extensions of Man*, McLuhan wrote: "The effects of technology do not occur at the levels of opinions or concepts, but alter the sense ratios (balance of our senses) and patterns of perception steadily and without resistance."[27]

McLuhan's premise is that the most important impact of mass media is how it affects ideas and individuals' understanding of how they see the world. The global reach of television, radio, the Internet and such major print publications as *Newsweek*, *Time* and *People* magazines ensures that these sources have a profound influence on how people in different parts of the world perceive and understand other cultures and how other cultures view themselves. McLuhan believed that the evolving growth and proliferation of mass media, especially television and the Internet, would continue to result in a reduction of how individuals identify with cultures and nations, and would be the primary driving force of a profound cultural convergence. McLuhan called this the trend toward creating a "global village."

McLuhan believed, and a majority of today's mass media experts accept, that in our media-dominated "information age," the success, continued evolution and even survival of the human species are predicated on our understanding of how mass media are transforming cultures and societies. The continued and exponential growth of electronic media is producing a revolutionary transformation in how people around the globe view and participate in our world. The powers and influence brought by the ever-expanding mass media in the 21st century are increasing demands on the participants of the global village for more flexibility in the application of their own cultural norms and values as well as a greater acceptance of and willingness to merge with the cultural norms and values of others. Moreover, as has always been the case, the media produced by the more popular and dominant culture will certainly overwhelm and eventually replace much of the media produced by less dominant and less flexible cultures. For some, this reality is a difficult vision to accept—one that requires inciting the populace to fight against it, even to the level of violence and civil unrest.

> McLuhan believed, and a majority of today's mass media experts accept, that in our media-dominated "information age," the success, continued evolution and even survival of the human species are predicated on our understanding of how mass media are transforming cultures and societies.

CHAPTER SUMMARY	KEY TERMS
The Role of Mass Media Briefs the overview of the impact and importance of mass media on international relations as well as the contacts between and confrontations among nations and cultures around the world.	social contract closed societies information filtering open societies participatory democracy glasnost policy
Global Mass Media Systems Describes the historic and current differences between mass media systems throughout the world and how these systems have evolved along differing paths.	mass media systems libertarian-based system social-responsibility system Fourth Estate Sound Broadcasting Act authoritarian system Soviet-Communist system
Mass Media Systems in Development Explores the state of mass media in the developing world and looks at how different forms of mass media become dominant in developing nations. Visual Media **Women on the Frontlines** Jeanine Nahigombeye, director of Radio Isanganiro, explains her sometimes risky efforts, and the efforts of other women like her, to present fair and balanced journalism promoting peace in civil war-torn Burundi. 1. Research and describe a recent example in which radio had an important impact on the course of world events. 2. Compare and contrast this example of the influence of radio during a civil war with a recent example of the use of the Internet and social networking sites during civil conflicts or revolution. **Arthur C. Clarke** Clarke's groundbreaking work in satellite television continues to serve as a model for the important role mass media technology plays in social and cultural development. 1. Describe how one of Arthur C. Clarke's futurist predictions has now become a commonplace reality. 2. Describe a recent instance where the introduction of Internet and networking technologies has had an impact on a poor, rural population similar to the impact of satellite TV on rural Sri Lankan villages as described in this video segment.	hate radio systems in development nongovernmental organizations (NGOs) UNESCO analog-based terrestrial broadcasts satellite-based digital broadcasts
Mass Media and Cultural Context Illustrates the dynamics of cultural context and how mass media influence high-context and low-context cultures.	cultural context culture high-context culture low-context culture
Media Cultures Compete for Survival Looks at some of the major dynamics and historic roots of cultural conflicts and the role mass media plays in both global cultural confrontations and the survival of dominant cultures.	

Media Dominance and the Global Marketplace Investigates the role mass media plays in the conduct of international diplomacy and the influences of the growing immediacy of news and information on national security and international relations.	cultural imperialism cultural hegemony
Mass Media and Global Diplomacy Studies the impact of the globalization of mass media, especially the World Wide Web, on the emergence and futures of new democracies around the world.	Digital Divide Digital Divide 2.0
Equalizing the Global Community Through Media Technology Explores the implications of the global Digital Divide—the widening separation between the technology haves and the technology have-nots—and how this Digital Divide can be manipulated by rogue governments and terrorist organizations.	

NOTES

1   Mead, R. (2013, February 4). Brave new world—live from Gaza. *The New Yorker*.

2   Wilentz, S. (2008). *The rise of American democracy: Jefferson to Lincoln*. W. W. Norton. See also Fischer, D. H. (2005). *Liberty and freedom: A visual history of America's founding ideas*. Oxford University Press.

3   For more on Obama's 2008 Internet campaign, see Miller, C. C. (n.d.). How Obama's Internet campaign changed politics. *Technology Bits*. Retrieved from http://bits.blogs.nytimes.com/2008/11/07/how-obamasinternetcampaign-changed-politics/

4   Read a brief history of the impact of Tiananmen Square on global media on the Museum of Broadcast Communications website: www.museum.tv/archives/etv/T/htmlT/tiananmensqu/tinananmensqu.htm

5   For more about the Chinese government's preemptive response to media coverage of the 20th anniversary of the Tiananmen Square protests, see Zetter, K. (2009, June 2). China censors: The Tiananmen Square anniversary will not be tweeted. *Wired*. Retrieved from www.wired.com/threatlevel/2009/06/china-censorsinternet-before-tiananmen-square-anniversary/

6   Johnson, B. (2009, June 4). Chinese websites mark Tiananmen Square anniversary with veiled protest. *The Guardian*. Retrieved from www.guardian.co.uk/technology/2009/jun/04/chinese-websites-tiananmen-squareanniversary

7   Ibid.

8   For more on the Tiananmen Square movement, see Richelson, J. T., & Evans, M. L. (1999, June 1). *Tiananmen Square, 1989: The declassified history*. National Security Archive Electronic Briefing Book No. 16. Retrieved from www.gwu.edu/~nsarchiv/NSAEBB/NSAEBB16/

9   Siebert, F. S., Peterson, T., & Schramm, W. (1956/1963). *Four theories of the press: The authoritarian libertarian, social responsibility and Soviet-Communist concepts of what the press should be and do*. University of Illinois Press.

10 *Voice of America online*. Retrieved from http://author.voanews.com/english/About/FastFacts.cfm

11 For a military background on the Burundi civil war, go to GlobalSecurity.org: www.globalsecurity.org/military/world/war/burundi.htm. GlobalSecurity.org is a Washington, D. C.-based website devoted to exploring innovative solutions to security challenges in the Digital Age.

12 UNESCO international literacy statistics: Projected number of total illiterates by region and age group, for the years 2005, 2010 and 2015.

13 English, C. (23 June, 2008). Radio the chief medium for news in Sub-Saharan Africa. *Gallup World*. Retrieved from www.gallup.com/poll/108235/radio-chief-mediumnews-subsaharan-africa.aspx

14 Fouche, G. (2011, September 27). Nobel Peace Prize may recognize Arab Spring. *Reuters*; *The Arab Spring: A revolution*. (2011, December 17). NPR.

15 Hammel, S. (2007, April 18). Complaints filed in India over Richard Gere kiss. *People Magazine*; Gere kiss sparks India protests. (2007, April 16). *BBC News*.

16 Hall, E. T. (1976). *Beyond culture*. Anchor Press.

17 Ibid.

18 Biggs, S. (2000). *Global village or urban jungle: Culture, self-construal, and the Internet*. Media Ecology Association. Retrieved from www.media-ecology.org/publications/MEA_proceedings/v1/global Village.html

19 See Charles C. Stuart's 2003 documentary, *Hollywood and the Muslim World*.

20 Bagdikian, B. H. (2000). *The media monopoly*. Beacon Press.

21 Former Clinton Press secretary Dee Dee Myers in an interview about the Clinton administration's response to the Yugoslavia civil war images coming in via CNN: Ellerbee, L. (Executive producer). (2004). *Feeding the beast: The 24-hour news revolution*; Trio Network Special.

22 United States Institute of Peace. (2004). Retrieved from www.usip.org/resources/wwwterrornet-how-modernterrorism-uses-internet

23 Ibid.

24 HRH Princess Maha Chakri Sirindhorn, the brightest guiding light for the disabled. (2007, May 21). Thailand illustrated. *Bangkok Post*.

25 (2017). *Tibetan Village Project*. Retrieved from www.tibetanvillageproject.org/; *Welcome to Tibet*. Retrieved from www.cbw.com/tibet/culture.html; *Internet Links to Tibet Information*. Retrieved from http://tibet.dharmakara.net/TibetLinks.html

26 *Journalism, media and technology predictions 2016*. (2016, January 10). Nic Newman, Reuters Institute for Politics. Retrieved from https://reutersinstitute.politics.ox.ac.uk/sites/default/files/Journalism,%20 media%20and%20technology%20predictions%202016.pdf; Manjoo, F. (2016, November 16). Social media's globe-shaking power. *New York Times*. Retrieved from www.nytimes.com/2016/11/17/technology/social-medias-globe-shaking-power.html

27 McLuhan, M., & Lapham, L. H. (1994). *Understanding media: The extensions of man*. MIT Press, p. 18.

15

Stories of Diversity in American Media

Mangostock/stock.adobe.com

CHAPTER OUTLINE

Pioneers of Latino Media in America

The Emergence of Latino TV Univision's Mariá Elena Salinas explores the impact of Univision and Latino television on today's Latin American Communities.

Pioneers of Black Media in America

John Sengstacke and the *Chicago Defender* Groundbreaking black newspaper publisher John Sengstacke tells the story of the role of the *Chicago Defender* in the Great Migration to the North.

Pioneering Women in American Media

Women Stereotypes A critical look at historical and contemporary portrayals of women in the media, particularly through film.

Pioneers of Asian-American Media
Pioneers of Gay and Lesbian American Media
Conclusion: On the Path Toward Greater Future
Diversity

**The Impact of Women in
Media** Filmmaker and author Patricia
Melton explores the global impact of
women on television.

LEARNING OBJECTIVES

1. Illustrate the ways in which the pioneers of Latino-American media helped to establish the group's representation in the mainstream media.
2. Assess the significance of the African-American press in opening doors to other areas of the mainstream media.
3. Outline the parallels between the American women's liberation movement and women's rise to prominence in American media and worldwide.
4. Evaluate the ways in which Asian-Americans have managed, and in many ways are still struggling, to overcome media-driven stereotyping.
5. Explain how the struggle of gays and lesbians to enter the mainstream media has both hindered and hastened their crusade for equal rights.
6. Compare and contrast the stories of the many diverse groups who have struggled for, achieved and are still hoping for equal, fair and accurate representation in and acceptance by the American mainstream media.

JAY SILVERHEELS

(1912–1980), whose original name was Harold J. Smith, was born on the Six Nations of the Grand River First Nations Indian Reserve in Ontario, Canada, in 1912. Using his skills as a lacrosse player, the young Silverheels left the reservation to travel around North America. After a number of years as an amateur and semi-pro athlete, he made the jump to being a motion picture and television actor. Starting in 1937—still using the name Harry J. Smith to help him get into auditions and land parts—Silverheels landed supporting roles in movies, especially the westerns that were growing in popularity at the time. His early film credits included *Broken Arrow* (1950), *War Arrow* (1953), *Drums Across the River* (1954) and *Walk the Proud Land* (1956). Native

American actors had been working in the movies since the early silent film era, starting around 1910. Typically, they were cast in minor supporting roles, with the major Native American roles going to white actors. The few Native American actors cast in larger supporting roles almost without exception played savage "bad guy" characters, who attacked the more civilized white "good guys" and were always killed or defeated by the end of the movie. Through derogatory and distorted portraits of Native peoples, Hollywood helped perpetuate longstanding stereotypes about native peoples and tribal cultures.[1]

Jay Silverheels led the way for a major, albeit slow, change in the portrayal of Native Americans in the mass media when in 1956 he landed

the role in *The Lone Ranger* that he is famous for to this day—the Lone Ranger's faithful friend, Tonto. He played the sidekick first in two feature films, *The Lone Ranger* (1956) and *The Lone Ranger and the Lost City of Gold*, and then in the very popular *Lone Ranger* television series.

For much of his life, activists in the Native American rights community accused Silverheels of selling out. They claimed that the Tonto character contributed to anti-Native stereotyping of the "good Indian" as opposed to the "bad Indian" in popular media of the time. Yet Silverheels unquestionably helped to change the dynamic of how mainstream media audiences viewed Native Americans as individuals and a culture. He accomplished this feat through his well-remembered Tonto character—the popular, sometimes heroic, sometimes humorous and always compelling character. In fact, American writer and mythologist Joseph Campbell (1904–1987) identified him as the epitome of the wise and loyal mentor.

Did Silverheels's Tonto character bring down the longstanding racial barriers and negative stereotyping of Native Americans? Unfortunately, no, but he unquestionably paved the way for other Native American actors, along with a growing number of Native American film producers, directors, technicians, and stunt men and women, who continued on the path of using media to change how they and their people were viewed. Together they helped usher in more realistic depictions of Native American characters, history and culture in Hollywood movies and television. Some Native American actors who have followed in Silverheels's path include Chief Dan George, Floyd Red Crow Westerman, Lois Red Elk, Graham Greene, Elaine Miles, Lou Diamond Philips and Benjamin Bratt.[2]

In July 2013, Disney Studios released the long-anticipated next iteration of the Lone Ranger. In this latest film, the role of Tonto is played by Johnny Depp as a Native American spirit warrior—bringing audiences a stronger character steeped in traditional Native American culture and mythologies. Depp brings his unique background as a popular interpretative actor and musician to his Tonto—but Depp, unlike Silverheels, is not himself a Native American. While the film's cultural roots are well presented, it is left up to audiences to decide if Depp's intriguing and at times humorous interpretation of a traditional Native American holy man trumps the fact that he is not a Native American actor. In fact, in 2012, Depp was adopted as the honorary son of LaDonna Harris, a tribal leader of the Comanche Nation, even though his portrayal of Tonto in this latest Lone Ranger movie remains controversial for many tribal members.

The idea that mass media can serve as both the gateway to and the catalyst for social and cultural change is one of the core themes woven throughout this book. This chapter explores three ways—sometimes conflicting—in which ethnic, racial, cultural and sexual diversity is represented in the media.

- The media can give voice to minority groups who are or have been wronged and held back by racism, collective segregation, ethnic isolation, stereotyping and related forms of social and economic inequality.
- The media can highlight the role models who have contributed to the dismantling of stereotypes—for example, civil rights leader Martin Luther King, Jr., Supreme Court Justice Sonia Sotomayor, broadcaster Ann Curry and political activist Harvey Milk. As a result of these depictions, society revises its perception of minority groups; negative images and stories that tend to reinforce cultural typecasting dissipate, and lines of communication among diverse populations open.
- The media can help minority groups—especially immigrant communities—celebrate and perpetuate their rich and unique heritages as they struggle to assimilate with mainstream society; the media help to teach future generations how to embrace, rather than reject, their roots.

Certainly, the struggle for social equality is not limited to the American experience; it is a worldwide phenomenon. However, because the messages sent by U.S. media tend to dominate throughout the world, this chapter focuses largely on how diversity is portrayed in American media, and how different cultural groups have attempted to push beyond the mainstream to ensure that every voice be heard, and every face be equally and accurately represented, among all media outlets.

15.1

Silver Screen Collection/Contributor

PIONEERS OF LATINO MEDIA IN AMERICA

The story of Latinos in America, and by extension the evolution of the Latino media, is a complicated story, and a detailed exploration of these peoples' struggles and triumphs is beyond the scope of this chapter. As with all of the minority groups studied in this chapter, the relationship of the Spanish-speaking population in the United States with the mass media has progressed along two parallel paths. One path has led toward the establishment of a separate Latino press and media. The other has focused on making inroads into mainstream media, as a means of breaking down racial and ethnic barriers and bringing about a greater level of acceptance of Latinos by the majority American society.

The Spanish-Language Press Offers Voice to the Exiled

The establishment of a Spanish-language press in America began through the founding of three distinct yet interconnected movements. We should remember that there were Spanish-speaking settlements in the American Southwest and Gulf Coast regions prior to the early 1800s, starting in the 1500s, even before there were English-speaking settlements in North America. Spanish was commonly spoken in Maine, Louisiana, Florida and the Southwest. Early immigrants from Spain and the Spanish-American colonies of Central and South America established the Spanish press in exile. Centered in the Spanish-speaking quarter of early 19th-century New Orleans, this exile press largely comprised political and social protesters who flocked to the United States to take advantage of the constitutionally guaranteed protections of the press. *El Misisipi*, the first Latino newspaper in the United States and the fountainhead of the press in exile, was established in 1808. This four-page, biweekly publication reprinted news concerning Spain from other larger metropolitan newspapers, along with local advertisements. News was printed exclusively in Spanish, but

15.2

Despite cultural differences, immigrants from South America and the Caribbean shared a common language (Caribbean celebration shown here). It was this common language upon which the Spanish immigrant press was founded.

Megapress/Alamy Stock Photo

ads were printed in English as well. While *El Misisipi* and other early Latino papers were typically used to drum up support for Spain among both Spanish-speaking transplants and English-speaking Americans, later newspaper publishers, such as Cubans Félix Varela and José Martí as well as Mexican Ricardo Flores Magón, utilized the Fourth Estate as a safe haven from which they could continue to lead revolutionary movements in their home countries.[3]

Shortly after the birth of the Spanish press in exile in the early 1800s, Spanish speakers from South America and the Caribbean began immigrating to the United States in great numbers—this time for economic rather than political reasons. While their cultural roots differed, all of these new Americans shared Spanish as a common language, which helped make possible the introduction and ongoing success of the Spanish immigrant press. This press served the needs of Spanish-speaking immigrants, offering them a sense of community and security in their adopted country, as well as publishing stories of local community interest. It also served as a venue for Latino art and literature.

A particularly popular genre and an early staple of the Latino immigrant press was the *crónica*, or "chronicle." The crónica was a short, weekly column that provided readers with satirical commentary on current events, issues and trends, often through fictional characters and stories. Crónica writers, called *cronistas*, used humor to encourage Latinos to remain faithful to their own culture. By masking its stark criticisms in comedic characters, the crónica highlighted the surrendering of cultural values and norms that Latinos faced every day. The crónica vehicle was used by Mexican-American traditionalists to promote their México de afuera ("Mexico outside") ideology. This ideology sought not only to protect immigrants against the perceived loss of the Spanish language, but also to maintain Latino culture's close links to the Catholic Church.[4]

Unlike the Latino immigrant press, which sought to maintain Spanish culture as a distinct culture-within-a-culture, the Latino native press viewed itself as an integral part of American culture. Conscious of the minority status of Latinos, the native press focused on securing the rights and voices of these individuals as guaranteed under the U.S. Constitution.

To protect Latino rights, the Latino native press identified itself and its constituents as participants in American culture. The readership enjoyed by these publications was due in part to the high levels of literacy among the Spanish population around the time when printing presses were introduced into California and New Mexico in the early 1830s. White newspaper publishers in Southwestern towns recognized the importance of engaging the Latino population in their areas as a viable market. Thus, many of the publications in the American Southwest at this time were bilingual, with a smaller group of Latino writers translating into Spanish news stories and other content originally written by white journalists. By the time New Mexico was admitted to the United States as a state in 1912, for example, it was home to more than 90 Spanish-language publications and had its own Latino newspaper association, *La Prensa Asociada Hispano-Americana*.[5]

The Latino native press also flourished in other areas around the West and along the Eastern Seaboard, especially in New York and Florida, which were home to sizable Cuban and Puerto Rican populations. The more moderate, integrationist approach of the native press helped Latinos to celebrate and maintain their unique cultural identity and laid a foundation for the modern Latino media of today. Empowered by its growing independence, the Latino native press began to advocate more assertively for Latino-American interests, including better education and employment opportunities, and provided a media voice for American life from the Latino perspective. Today, there are many Spanish-language newspapers and magazines published in the United States, some dating back to the early decades of the 20th century. For example, a popular weekly is *La Gaceta*, which is the nation's only trilingual newspaper, published in Spanish, English and Italian. It has been published in Tampa, Florida, since 1922 and was founded by a former "reader" who had been hired to read to the Cuban workers at a local Tampa cigar factory. *La Gaceta* continues to help to integrate minority populations in the Tampa Bay area and teach them English.

> Empowered by its growing independence, the Latino native press began to advocate more assertively for Latino-American interests, including better education and employment opportunities, and provided a media voice for American life from the Latino perspective.

Latino Radio Attracts Business

In the late 1920s and early 1930s, owners of mainstream radio stations realized that it was not financially practical to produce content for off-peak hours—late at night and early in the mornings. Hoping to bring at least some revenue from these "wasted hours," many station owners allowed enterprising Latino radio program producers to purchase these time slots at nominal cost. Early Latino radio personalities such as Rodolfo Hoyos were able to attract Latino businesses as advertisers because of the wide audience reach of their Spanish-language programs. Pedro J. González, one of the pioneers of Latino radio, started broadcasting from KELW in California in 1927 with his show *Los Madrugadores*, which combined live musical performances with public-interest programming and promotions of community events.

González was popular with listeners, so the station owners generated a significant amount of advertising revenue from the Latino business community. However, González began to use his popularity to advocate for immigrant rights and criticize the deportation of Mexicans during the United States' Operation Wetback—an effort by the Dwight D. Eisenhower administration in 1954 to deport 3 million undocumented immigrant living in the Southwest United States. Soon after, KELW owners fired him and canceled the station's Spanish-language programming, citing González's arrest on trumped-up charges of rape—for which he was later exonerated—as their reason.

15.3

Pedro J. González, pioneer of Latino radio, used the airwaves to criticize the Eisenhower administration's decision to deport millions of undocumented Mexican immigrants residing in the Southwest. This photo of a Mexican citizen crossing into the United States was taken near the Southern California/Mexico border.

Tom Pennington/MCT/Newscom

As a result of stricter licensing regulations, intended to limit minority access to the airwaves and the lack of support from mainstream U.S. stations, many Latino radio producers of Mexican descent moved to Mexico, to continue their broadcasting ventures from a friendlier environment. The most prominent of these Mexico-based radio pioneers was Emilio Azcárraga Vidaurreta. Azcárraga first positioned himself to capitalize on the growing demand for Spanish-language radio during the 1930s by forming a partnership between the Mexican government and the National Broadcasting Company (NBC) in the United States. Through this partnership, he was able to build his powerful station XEW, based in Mexico City, which became the anchor station for the first Latino radio network in North America. The network's financial success forced American radio stations to reconsider Latino programming: By the 1960s, largely due to the groundbreaking efforts by Azcárraga, Spanish-language radio was once again a strong force on U.S. radio airwaves, with entire programming schedules and stations devoted to it.[6]

Latino Television Unites, Educates and Empowers

The first official Latino radio station in the United States was KCOR-AM in San Antonio, Texas, founded by media pioneer Raoúl A. Cortez in 1946. In 1955, only nine years after the birth of KCOR-AM, Cortez helped usher Latinos into the television age with the inaugural broadcast of KCOR-TV, the first Spanish-language television station in the United States. In 1961, Cortez sold the station to an investment group led by Emilio Azcárraga Vidaurreta.

Spanish-language television had taken off a few years earlier in Mexico, and Azcárraga had organized the first Mexican television network, *Telesistema Mexicano*, in 1955—the forerunner to today's Mexican media conglomerate *Televisa*. The group formed the Spanish International Network (SIN) in 1962. Over the next two decades, SIN expanded its viewership by acquiring emerging Spanish-language television stations all over the United States. The company offered television programming aimed at a general pan-Hispanic audience with program lineups filled with Spanish-language variety shows, sports broadcasts and telenovelas. SIN programming was highly profitable because it was packaged for a much wider pan-Hispanic audience during a period when Latinos had few other local alternatives.

In 1967, President Lyndon B. Johnson appointed the Kerner Commission to investigate the increase in race-related violence in the United States. The Commission found that a lack of minority representation in the mainstream media significantly contributed to inaccurate coverage of race relations and race-related violence, specifically among blacks and whites. The Commission completely failed to acknowledge the absence and effects of Latino-Americans in the mainstream media. While the Kerner Commission's efforts encouraged the inclusion of black journalists in the mainstream media, Latinos remained virtually excluded. This exclusion of Latinos from mainstream media coupled with the increasing flow of Spanish-speaking people into the United States led to a parallel, but separate, evolution of the Latino media.[7]

A pivotal moment in the history of the Latino media came in 1986, when Mexican media giant Televisa and the American greeting card company Hallmark formed a partnership to purchase SIN. They renamed the new television network Univision. Univision went on to become the largest Spanish-language television network in the world. It broke out of its own traditional programming model in 1987 by signing Cuban journalist Cristina Saralegui to launch the Spanish-language talk show *El Show de Cristina*, which earned its host the title of "the Spanish Oprah." Univision also launched a national nightly newscast, Noticiero Univision, co-anchored by Jorge Ramos and the critically acclaimed journalist Mariá Elena Salinas.

Like their mainstream network counterparts, while Latino media corporations such as Univision see entertainment as central to their success, they also demonstrate keen commitment to social responsibility. In 2007, Univision, in cooperation with the University of Miami in Florida, hosted the first ever presidential debates formatted specifically to address Latino-American concerns and issues. This historic television event marked the public ascension of Latinos as a significant political interest group and voting bloc in the United States. At the same time, it also highlighted the commitment of the Latino media to the education, integration and advocacy of Spanish speakers in 21st-century United States. In the video segment "The Emergence of Latino TV," Mariá Elena Salinas of Univision explains why and how the media should be held responsible for informing and empowering the diverse Latino populations of the United States. ▶

> This exclusion of Latinos from mainstream media coupled with the increasing flow of Spanish-speaking people into the United States led to a parallel, but separate, evolution of the Latino media.

▶ **The Emergence of Latino TV**
Univision's Mariá Elena Salinas explores the impact of Univision and Latino television on today's Latino-American communities.

Latino Entertainment Enters the Mainstream

Numerous Latino-Americans have in fact risen to stardom in the mainstream film, television and music industries of the 20th and 21st centuries. Early Latino film stars such as Dolores Del Río and José Ferrer (the first Latino awarded the Oscar for best actor) gained both popular and critical acclaim in Hollywood from the early 1920s through 1960s. Their fame and popularity paved the way for future Latino actors and actresses, including Rita Moreno (the first Latina to win Emmy, Grammy, Tony and Academy Awards), Raquel Welch (born Jo Raquel Tejada), Anthony Quinn, Richard "Cheech" Marin, Andy Garcia, Jimmy Smits, Martin Sheen and his sons Charlie Sheen and Emilio Estevez, and Salma Hayek, to name a few. Latino filmmakers such as George Romero (*Dawn of the Dead, Night of the Living Dead*), Guillermo del Toro (*Hellboy, Hellboy 2, Pan's Labyrinth*), and Robert Rodriguez (*Desperado, Sin City, Spy Kids*) have made a significant impact on the U.S. film industry. Desi Arnaz, Linda Carter (born Linda Jean Córdova Carter), Ricardo Montalban, Erik Estrada, Geraldo Rivera, John Leguizamo, Eva Longoria and Sofia Vergara are just a small sampling of Latino stars who have enjoyed successful careers in mainstream U.S. television. American television has also drawn influence from popular Latin American telenovelas. For example, ABC's *Ugly Betty* television series (2006–2010), starring America Ferrara and produced by Salma Hayek, was based on the Colombian telenovela *Yo Soy Betty La Fea*.

Latino singers and musicians have become stars of the American music industry as well, including rock 'n' roll pioneer Ritchie Valens, Vicki Carr (born Florencia Bisenta de Casillas Martinez Cardona), Celia "the Queen of Salsa" Cruz, Joan Baez, Carlos Santana, Gloria Estefan, Mariah Carey, Jennifer Lopez and Christina Aguilera.

Although it might be tempting to conclude that Latinos as a group have become fully integrated into American culture, it is important to recognize that mainstream media still often misrepresent authentic

Latino culture and values. However, the explosion of the Latino population in the United States and the strength of the Latino market are beginning to change the balance of power in the media, with Latinos having vastly greater influence and representation. The American Latino population's social, political and economic sway continues to grow. Digital natives among the bilingual youth embrace the convergence of traditional media and the Internet; in turn, this trend is encouraging the Spanish-language and Latino media to become more fully integrated into mainstream American media.

PIONEERS OF BLACK MEDIA IN AMERICA

Early in 1839, a subscription agent for the abolitionist newspaper *The Liberator*, edited by prominent abolitionist William Lloyd Garrison, approached a fugitive slave on the streets of New Bedford, Massachusetts, about subscribing to the paper. The young black man, who had been taught to read by the wife of one of his white owners (an illegal act on both his and her part), and had in turn taught other slaves to read, told the agent that he was too poor to be able to pay for the paper. The agent signed him up for the paper anyway. This subscription agent did not suspect the enormous effect his act of trust would have on the history of African-American media. By putting *The Liberator* into the hands of that struggling former slave, this now-unknown subscription agent had set the mind of the young black man ablaze—a fire that would burn throughout his life and power the struggle for civil rights in America for the next 150 years.[8]

Born Frederick Bailey, that 21-year-old would later write in his autobiography, "*The Liberator* became my meat and my drink. My soul was set all on fire." Bailey, who began calling himself Frederick Douglass after his escape from slavery in an attempt to avoid recapture, quickly learned the principles of the abolition movement by reading *The Liberator* and by attending local anti-slavery meetings. He became such a powerful orator that audiences questioned his claim that he had become a free man only a few years before, thereby disproving the popular stereotypes of the time that caricaturized freed blacks as uneducated and happier in their roles as servants and slaves.

To help defend the authenticity of his stories, Douglass wrote his autobiography, titled *Narrative of the Life of Frederick Douglass: An American Slave*. His autobiography earned him prominence in both the United States and Europe. Douglass was committed to telling his story as accurately as possible and used actual (rather than fictitious) names, places and dates to depict the events he had directly experienced. Unfortunately, as much as his story garnered him support and tremendous publicity, it also revealed his whereabouts.

U.S. law at the time granted former masters and slave hunters the right to reclaim runaway slaves as property—including Douglass. With the help of some of his fellow abolitionists, Douglass fled to England, which had already abolished slavery, and where he would continue lecturing to foster international support for the abolition movement. While in Europe, Douglass supporters raised $700 and purchased his freedom.

Upon his arrival back in the United States, Douglass moved his family to Rochester, New York, to start his own abolitionist paper. In his book *My Bondage*, he recounted his motivation for going into the newspaper business:

15.4

Frederick Douglass's (1817–1895) founding of a black abolitionist newspaper was one of the first steps toward helping African-Americans reclaim their identities and culture.

Schreiber, George Francis, photographer. [Frederick Douglass, head-and-shoulders portrait, facing right]

> I further stated, that, in my judgment, a tolerably well conducted press, in the hands of persons of the despised race, by calling out the mental energies of the race itself; by making them acquainted with their own latent powers; by enkindling among them the hope that for them there is a future;

by developing their moral power; by combining and reflecting their talents—would prove a most powerful means of removing prejudice, and of awakening an interest in them.[9]

Although some white abolitionists—particularly William Lloyd Garrison—believed that a black-owned and -published newspaper would create unnecessary competition for the other white-owned abolitionist papers, Douglass was convinced that the establishment of the black media was an essential step in the struggle for emancipation.

The Black Press Restores Black Identity

Objectification, the practice of reducing peoples and cultures to mere objects, is one of the many horrendous dynamics of slavery. White owners seldom allowed their slaves to practice any African traditions that might enable them to maintain some semblance of a culture in an effort to thwart insurrection among the slaves. Slave owners tore apart families, prohibited community building and severely punished anyone caught gathering for meetings of any kind without their owners' consent. The building and the communication of a black American identity became the mission of the emerging black media. Douglass newspaper, which he first called *The Northern Star* and later renamed *The Frederick Douglass Paper*, became the voice and vehicle for that mission. In his role as a spokesperson for equality and as a media pioneer, Douglass helped establish the legacy of the black media as a primary educator, advocate and organizer of black Americans—a legacy that remains evident even today.

> In his role as a spokesperson for equality and as a media pioneer, Douglass helped establish the legacy of the black media as a primary educator, advocate and organizer of black Americans—a legacy that remains evident even today.

Despite its historical significance, *The Northern Star* was not actually the first black publication in the United States. That distinction belonged to *Freedom's Journal*, which was founded in 1827 by the Reverend Samuel Cornish and John Russwurm. In the early 1800s, the mainstream media consistently portrayed negative depictions of blacks and questioned the truthfulness of abolitionists' claims about the atrocious living conditions of Southern black slaves. In response to this unceasingly ugly portrayal of blacks, Russwurm and Cornish published the *Freedom Journal* to condemn the racist stereotypes perpetuated by the white media as well as to document the daily lives of black Americans.

This commitment to confront the social and political issues of the day has historically been one of the primary objectives of the black media; it has also contributed to today's persistent tension between the black and mainstream media. As discussed in Chapter 1, by recording events and distributing ideas, the media not only document a culture, but also codify, interpret, project and legitimize it.[10]

The Black Press Exposes Inequality

While white abolitionists fervently fought for the emancipation of black slaves, they often failed to address the issue of equality. Rather, some proposed that freed blacks be sent back to Africa or perhaps confined in segregated communities within the United States. In contrast, most blacks saw themselves as Americans who had helped to build the country and wanted to be integrated fully and equally into U.S. society. Even in states where slavery was illegal, such as Massachusetts, racial prejudice ran rampant. Freed blacks in the North could not get good-paying, skilled work because whites refused to hire them for such positions; as a result, most ended up in low-paying, manual-labor positions.

After the Civil War and emancipation of all slaves in the United States, the black media continued its dual function of defending black Americans against social abuse and advocating on behalf of black American culture. While slavery was no longer a legal issue, there existed a huge gap in civil rights between blacks and whites in this country, and this inequality persisted on both sides of the Mason–Dixon Line. During Reconstruction (1865–1877), the period wherein all freed slaves were granted federally protected civil rights, as well as in the early Jim Crow era, African-American journalists such as Ida B. Wells (1862–1931)— an early leader in both the civil rights and women's rights movements—doggedly exposed the rampant problems facing blacks in America. These issues included not just discrimination, but also such heinous crimes as beatings, rape, murder and lynching. Wells's investigation of the lynching problem made her the target of hate threats, especially after she wrote an editorial for her paper, *The Free Speech*, in which she suggested that white women and black men might genuinely be attracted to each other—a scandalous claim in an age when racist ideologues portrayed blacks as genetically inferior to whites.

The black media faced several challenges during the Jim Crow era (1867–1965)—the period that deemed blacks "separate but equal" and in effect formalized segregation in the United States for nearly a century. The first challenge involved a question of ideology: What role should the black media play in the greater scope of American mass media? In other words, should the black media become integrated into a resistant white culture? If so, how? Moreover, how could the black media become integrated with the nonblack media and simultaneously meet the needs of their black constituency?

The *Chicago Defender* (1905), one of the largest and most influential national black-published newspapers in history, led the way for many black publishers during the Jim Crow and civil rights eras. The *Defender*'s founder, Robert Sengstacke Abbott, financed the first issues of his newspaper with a $25 credit line from Western Union. An additional loan through a friend allowed him access to the *Chicago Tribune*'s printing presses. Abbott sought a wide readership for the *Defender* and wanted the paper to promote civil rights. To achieve this goal, he produced entertainment reporting on Bronzeville (the nickname for the black neighborhoods of Chicago) balanced by more serious, advocacy-focused stories.

Abbott's blending of sensationalist journalism with advocacy was a huge success. The *Defender*'s circulation eventually expanded from Chicago into black communities in the South and throughout America, earning it the distinction of being the first national black newspaper.[11] Abbott used the popularity of the *Defender*, and the respect he had earned from the black community, to encourage a migration of Southern blacks toward the more racially tolerant northern Midwest. Abbott's lobbying contributed to the Great Migration, in which approximately 1.3 million blacks emigrated from the South between 1916 and 1930. Since the *Defender* exposed the abuse of black civil rights in the South and advocated black migration, a number of Southern cities banned it. Individuals caught possessing or distributing copies of the paper were subject to stiff penalties.

15.5

During the Jim Crow era, black Americans were free, but they were not equal. The influential *Chicago Defender*, still in publication today, advocated for the end of segregation, among other civil rights.

Wolcott, Marion Post, photographer. Negro going in colored entrance of movie house on Saturday afternoon, Belzoni, Mississippi Delta, Mississippi. Courtesy of Library of Congress

To get around this ban, Abbott enlisted the help of an extensive network of black Pullman porters to smuggle the paper into Southern black communities. During the late 19th and early 20th centuries, when trains were the primary means of transportation, George Pullman's (1831–1897) Pullman Sleeping Cars provided relatively comfortable and private travel, offering a vast improvement over the uncomfortable bench seats used prior to his innovation. Pullman hired black men as uniformed porters to serve in each of his sleeper cars. Traveling throughout the United States, these porters secretly distributed the *Defender* to the black community and, in effect, contributed to the diversification of American culture.

After Abbott's death in 1940, his nephew John Sengstacke inherited the company. For more on the impact the *Chicago Defender* made on racial relations in the United States, view the video segment "John Sengstacke and the *Chicago Defender*." ▶

Another important contributor to the progress of minorities working in news media is veteran journalist John C. Quinn, who dedicated his life to bringing diversity to the newsroom. His generosity afforded opportunities to thousands of minority journalists. He was a former deputy chairman of the Freedom Forum, the founding editor of *USA Today* and a former president of Gannett News Service. Quinn was executive vice president/news of Gannett Co. Inc., when he retired in 1990. With his late wife, Loie, he founded the Chips Quinn Scholars program as a memorial to their son John "Chips" Quinn, also a journalist, who was killed in an automobile accident.

The Chips Quinn Scholarship program provides minority journalists with hands-on training and mentoring by caring news veterans. Alums of the Chips Quinn Scholarship Program are affectionately referred to as "chipsters." More than 1,300 men and women have been named Chips Quinn Scholars since 1991, making it the largest and most enduring diversity initiative of the Newseum Institute. The program provides training and support that will open doors to news and information careers and bring greater diversity to the newsrooms of the United States.

Although the mainstream media began to recruit black journalists in the late 1940s, the number of African-Americans in the mass media remained proportionately small in the two decades that followed. Although black Americans favored civil equality, they also took pride in their culture and wanted to preserve the black American perspective. This tension between integration and preservation—a tension shared by all minority media—became even more vivid during the Civil Rights era. The Black Power movement, which represented a subcurrent within the larger civil rights movement, encouraged Afro-centrism and black autonomy along with a more violent approach toward civil rights activism. Advocates of the Black Power movement formed competing media outlets to get their message out, such as Malcolm X's *Muhammad Speaks* and Bobby Seale's and Huey Newton's *The Black Panther*. Both newspapers were popular with the black American community and clearly outlined their sponsoring organizations' civil rights platforms. John H. Johnson (1918–2005) was another influential black publisher and the founder of *Jet* and *Ebony* magazines. Johnson helped bring positive portrayals of blacks into the mainstream media, encouraging advertisers to use attractive black models and target the rising middle-class black consumer audience. Johnson also succeeded in attracting major corporations to advertise in black publications, which helped Johnson build his publishing empire into one of the largest black-owned corporations in the United States.

▶ John Sengstacke and the *Chicago Defender*
Groundbreaking black newspaper publisher, John Sengstacke, tells the story of the role of the *Chicago Defender* in the Great Migration of blacks to the North.

Black Radio—The Voice of the People

In 1957, a young minister and civil rights activist named Martin Luther King, Jr., along with other civil rights leaders including fellow minister Ralph Abernathy, founded the Southern Christian Leadership Conference (SCLC). SCLC set up its headquarters in the Masonic building on Auburn Avenue in an affluent black neighborhood in Atlanta, one floor below the radio station WERD. WERD was owned and operated by Jesse B. Blayton, a professor at Atlanta University. Jack "Jockey Jack" Gibson, one of the original DJs at WERD and a popular black radio celebrity and political voice during that period, recounted years later that King had a close relationship with the station, both on and off the air. WERD's studio was located directly above the SCLC offices, and when King wanted to make an announcement over the air, he would tap the ceiling with a broom. Gibson would immediately interrupt his broadcast and lower a microphone through a hole cut through the floor of the broadcast booth into King's office, and King would make his announcement.

when King wanted to make an announcement over the air, he would tap the ceiling with a broom. Gibson would immediately interrupt his broadcast and lower a microphone through a hole cut through the floor of the broadcast booth into King's office, and King would make his announcement.

In addition to playing popular music, Gibson would report on civil rights news and events in a personalized, persuasive style that frequently impelled his listeners to action. Gibson, like his fellow black DJs around the United States, also exposed his audiences to prominent voices in the civil rights movement.

The lack of representation in local and national government was one of the great difficulties facing black Americans during the 20th century. The lack of elected representatives in government made African-American media producers, and especially black radio DJs and commentators, the most effective representatives of their communities. During the height of the civil rights movement in the late 1950s through the 1960s, black radio DJs played a pivotal role in advancing black politics and culture. Specifically, they helped organize the concerns of black citizens into a unified voice that forced civil rights onto the agendas of white politicians and gave this movement greater coverage in the white-dominated mainstream media, especially radio and television news.

Black Entertainers Dismantle Stereotypes

African-American actors and actresses gradually began to take their places as stars of the movie and television industries. In 1963, Sidney Poitier became the first black man to win the Academy Award for best actor for his role in *Lilies of the Field*. Two years after Poitier received his Oscar, Bill Cosby became the first African-American lead on the popular prime-time television show *I Spy*. From the early 1970s through the early 1990s, sitcoms such as *Good Times*, *Benson* and *The Cosby Show* gained widespread acceptance among mainstream audiences, garnering critical acclaim for their portrayals of black American life. Blacks on television and in the movies helped to chip away at racial stereotypes. *The Cosby Show*, for example, portrayed blacks as successful, intelligent professionals. The show featured Cosby's character, Dr. Heathcliff Huxtable, a practicing obstetrician, along with his attorney wife and their college-bound children, living in an affluent section of Brooklyn. The Huxtable family in many ways brought to life the traditional white American dream, but applied to an African-American model, challenging the popular view that blacks were unsophisticated and lacked stable home lives.[12]

The 1980s and 1990s saw the rise of prominent black television talk-show hosts. In 1984, Oprah Winfrey took the struggling *AM Chicago* morning talk show and turned it, nearly overnight, into the highest-rated talk show in Chicago. The show was renamed *The Oprah Winfrey Show* in 1986 and began broadcasting nationally. The incredible popularity and critical success of *The Oprah Winfrey Show* made it the highest-rated talk show in the history of television, established Winfrey as an international media mogul, and, by many accounts, made her one of the wealthiest women in the world. Winfrey's success opened the door for other black hosts on daytime television, with programs such as *The Montel Williams Show* and *The Tyra Banks Show* enjoying success with audiences across all racial and ethnic lines.

The commercial and critical success of black Americans in mainstream movies and television, unfortunately, does not suggest that all racial barriers in America have disappeared. After Sidney Poitier won his Oscar in 1963, it would not be until 2002 that a black actor would win the award again; in that year, Halle Berry became the first black woman to win the Oscar for best actress for her work in *Monster's Ball* (2002). Berry's emotional acceptance speech has been seared into our memories not just because it touched all of those who watched her that night, but also because it took nearly 40 years—after desegregation, after the civil rights movement—for an African-American to be so publicly recognized again.

15.6

Sidney Poitier, the first African-American to win an Oscar for his leading role in the film Lilies of the Field (1963), is shown here in They Call Me Mister Tibbs (1970).

Photo 12/Alamy Stock Photo

The struggle for integration and equality has and continues to be a long journey for many minority groups, and many people—black women, for example—have been forced to fight a two-front battle. This brings us to the story of the media's role and influence in the fight toward equality for women.

PIONEERING WOMEN IN AMERICAN MEDIA

Historically, women fought their own battles for representation in the mass media as well. In film and in television, depictions of female characters mirrored the social, stereotypical view of women at the time—that they were frail, naive and best suited for domestic work and child rearing. Fortunately, several pioneering individuals attempted to dispel these stereotypes as well as make inroads into the mass media. In fact, one of these figures, Mary Ann Shadd Cary, was not only a woman, but a black woman. For a closer look at how stereotypes about women have carried into contemporary media, albeit in more subtle ways, view the video clip, "Women Stereotypes." ▶

The First Black Woman Newspaper Editor

The story of women in the media is in many cases closely linked to the struggle for equal rights for African-Americans. Consider the trail blazed by Mary Ann Shadd Cary, who was born in Wilmington, Delaware, in 1823. Cary's father was the son of a free black woman and a German soldier. In addition to working as a shoemaker, Cary's father played a key role in the success of the Underground Railroad, serving as a subscription agent for the abolitionist newspaper, *The Liberator*. Cary was in her own right a civil rights activist; she staunchly believed in educating black children and taking strong action to amend the injustices of discrimination. In 1848, she volunteered to become one of the organizers for the Seneca Falls Convention, the first major national event of the American women's suffrage movement. This movement, led by Elizabeth Cady Stanton and Lucretia Mott, marked the start of a 70-year-long struggle for women to secure the right to vote in the United States.

By 1852, Cary had moved to Canada—a nation that had abolished slavery in 1833—and settled in Toronto to teach. There, she founded the *Provincial Freeman* to voice opposition to the Fugitive Slave Act, which legally permitted slave owners to reclaim their runaway slaves. She also used the paper to encourage migration to Canada, where she felt that blacks could live in relative safety and freedom. Since women were considered second-class citizens at the time, Cary enlisted the Reverend Alexander McArthur and Samuel Ringgold Ward to serve as the editorial figureheads for the newspaper; Cary billed herself as a publishing agent. She further disguised her gender by using only her first two initials on her editorial byline. When Cary eventually dropped the paper's two male figureheads from the paper's masthead, and the public discovered that it was actually run by a woman, they were outraged and

15.7

The first Oscar awarded to a black female actor would not happen until 2002, when Halle Berry won for best actress in the film *Monster's Ball* (2001).

Everett Collection/Shutterstock

▶ **Women Stereotypes**
A critical look at historical and contemporary portrayals of women in the media, particularly through film.

15.8

Women traditionally did not have a face in the media, but their battle for equal representation began in Seneca Falls, New York—the site of the first convention of the women's suffrage movement. This battle for women's right to vote would endure for 70 years. Here, the press captures a suffrage demonstration, circa 1905.

Bain News Service, Publisher. [Hedwig Reicher as Columbia in Suffrage Parade] Courtesy of Library of Congress

she was forced out of business within the year. Her efforts, however, have not been ignored by history. Although the times forced her to mask her gender, Cary is credited for being the first black woman to edit a newspaper. Years later, other women would make similar inroads into the mainstream media.

Journalist and activist Ida B. Wells-Barnett first became prominent in the 1890s due to African-American lynchings in the South. This pioneer black journalist was born in 1862 in Holy Springs, Mississippi. After completing her studies at Rust College near Holly Springs where her father sat on the board of trustees, Wells became a school teacher while also caring for her siblings.

Wells first began protesting the treatment of black southerners when, on a train ride between Memphis and her job at a rural school, the conductor told her that she must move to the train's smoking car. Wells refused, arguing that she had purchased a first-class ticket. The conductor and other passengers then tried to physically remove her from the train. Wells hired a lawyer and sued the Chesapeake and Ohio Railroad Company. The court decided in her favor, awarding her $500. The railroad company appealed, and in 1887, the Supreme Court of Tennessee reversed the previous decision and ordered Wells to pay court fees. Using the pseudonym "Iola," Wells began to write editorials in black newspapers that challenged Jim Crow laws in the South. She bought a share of a Memphis newspaper, the Free Speech and Headlight, and used it to further the cause of African-American civil rights.

Wells also worked to advance other political causes. She protested the exclusion of African-Americans from the 1893 World's Columbian Exposition in Chicago and three years later she helped launch the National Association of Colored Women (NACW). In 1909 Wells was a founding member of the National Association for the Advancement of Colored People (NAACP), and actively campaigned for women's suffrage.[13]

World War II Alters Women's Roles

With the onset of World War II, legions of women in the United States stepped into jobs and social roles once exclusively held by men—men who had left their jobs on the frontlines of business and industry to take positions on the frontlines of war. Posters appeared everywhere portraying strong, empowered women building war machines or fighting the Axis powers through industry. Rosie the Riveter, a fictional character based on Rose Will Monroe, a female riveter who helped to build B-29 and B-24 bombers for the U.S. Amy Air Corps, became a national icon for the new American woman. In one of the most famous depictions by artist J. Howard Miller, Rosie—a strong, attractive white woman—is shown with her hair in a bandana, her sleeves rolled up to reveal a slightly muscular forearm and the caption, "We Can Do It!" As a direct result of the war effort, America saw a major shift in the way that society, and women themselves, viewed women's role in the workplace, including the mass media.

The First Woman Television News Broadcaster

In a legendary example of single-minded dedication, while covering the breaking story of a looming military confrontation between India and Pakistan, Pauline Frederick (1908–1990) insisted on delaying emergency medical treatment after she fell and shattered her kneecap so that she could broadcast later that day her on-air report of the developing crisis. Recalling this and other highpoints of her early career, Frederick recollected, "Early in my career, when I was being blocked from going on the air, I was told a woman's voice does not carry authority; therefore, people wouldn't listen to [me]."[14] But people listened.

Although Frederick had degrees in political science and international law, she spent a large part of her career freelancing. In the 1940s and 1950s, the major broadcast networks were not interested in hiring full-time female correspondents. Nevertheless, Frederick was determined to get on the air, in spite of warnings such as "Stay away from radio, it doesn't like women." In 1945, while working as an assistant to a network radio commentator, Frederick talked her way into an overseas press junket and started filing her own stories. Shortly after that trip, when the regular ABC radio correspondent failed to show up for his assignment at the Nuremburg Trials, Frederick jumped in to cover the testimony of Hermann Goering, Hitler's second-in-command and the highest-ranking officer in the Luftwaffe.

15.9

WWII-era women had to step into the frontlines of the industries and jobs that their men left behind, inspiring future generations of women to join the workforce and take on roles traditionally dominated by men.

Hollem, Howard R, photographer. Pearl Harbor widows have gone into war work to carry on the fight with a personal vengeance, Corpus Christi, Texas. Courtesy of Library of Congress

Despite her international experience and proven record of accomplishment, Frederick's editors often assigned her to deal with "women-centered" issues. Eager to expand her repertoire, she convinced ABC to let her report on the stories that mostly male reporters were covering as long as she could secure exclusive access. When assigned to cover the final wartime voyage of the commissioned luxury liner *Queen Mary*, Frederick worked the angles in her typical fashion, securing herself an interview with then-five-star general and future president Dwight Eisenhower, who happened to be aboard the ship and traveling back to the United States.

In 1948, Frederick covered that year's national political conventions for ABC, which aired on television for the first time. As a result of her success with that assignment, ABC offered her a contract, making her the first full-time television network newswoman in history. In 1953, NBC hired Frederick to cover the United Nations. In 1954, she received the prestigious Peabody Award—a testament to her determination and commitment to journalistic excellence. Among her many accomplishments, Frederick was the first woman to moderate a presidential debate and the first woman elected president of the United Nations Correspondents Association. These achievements did little to secure her position with NBC, however. In 1975, the company forced Frederick out of her job because of her age and appearance. This discriminatory move demonstrated that television news still had a long way to go toward full equality for women. When asked about her departure from NBC, Frederick commented, "If a man is old, he's called interesting. When a woman is old and shows wrinkles, it's terrible, she's finished."[15]

Despite this setback, in 1977, Frederick returned to her roots in radio as the host of her own international affairs program, *Pauline Frederick and Colleagues*, on National Public Radio (NPR). She continued to anchor the program until she officially retired in 1981, at the age of 73. Pauline Frederick's story typifies most women's experience in broadcast media. The ongoing resistance from a male-dominated industry notwithstanding, Frederick persevered to become one of the most authoritative journalistic voices of the 20th century.

Women Struggle with Tradition in the 1950s

After the end of World War II and into the 1950s, the United States still demonstrated patriarchal tendencies. Defying these societal forces, women continued to push through gender barriers to obtain better, higher-paying and more prestigious positions. The media once again played an important role in changing public attitudes, particularly through its portrayal of women on television.

While an increasing number of women were asserting themselves as individuals and equals, just as many were seeking to restore their past roles as mothers and homemakers—the norm before World War II and the Korean War. For many women in the 1950s, the "American dream" meant a husband, children and a nice home in suburbia.

Women's roles on television in the 1950s reflected a growing tension between the traditional role of women and the more independent modern woman. While an increasing number of women were asserting themselves as individuals and equals, just as many were seeking to restore their past roles as mothers and homemakers—the norm before World War II and the Korean War. For many women in the 1950s, the "American dream" meant a husband, children and a nice home in suburbia. Popular television shows such as *The Adventures of Ozzie and Harriet* (1952) and *Leave It to Beaver* (1957) reinforced this supposed dream and idealized the "perfect American family." This ideal, however, competed against new voices who were speaking on behalf of women's independence and equal rights—one such champion was a feisty redhead named Lucille Ball.

In the fall of 1951, CBS television aired the first episode of the sitcom *I Love Lucy*, starring Lucille Ball and her real-life husband, Desi Arnaz. The show became an instant, nationwide hit. *I Love Lucy* followed the lives of Lucy Ricardo (Ball), a boisterous all-American redhead, and her Cuban husband, Ricky Ricardo (Arnaz). Ball's character in the show represented a clear break from the prewar stereotypical homemaker. She craved a career in show business, regularly questioned authority (particularly her husband's) and was not afraid to go to extremes to achieve her dreams. Lucy Ricardo's guileless exploration of a woman's place in the world became the subtext of the plot of each episode, while the charming cast and well-executed slapstick helped to safely and humorously challenge the beliefs of millions of Americans.[16]

In reality, Lucille Ball was already the woman that her TV character kept struggling to become. She was a clever and highly successful Hollywood businesswoman. When sponsors of *I Love Lucy* balked at investing more money to take the show national, Ball offered to finance the series through her own company, Desilu Productions, on the condition that Desilu would retain all of the syndication rights. At the time, TV networks rarely aired reruns, so CBS readily agreed to this deal. Ball's foresight paid off handsomely for Desilu Productions when her show went into seemingly endless reruns. In many ways, Ball's on- and off-screen personas made significant contributions to the advancement of women's rights—her Lucy Ricardo character opened American minds and hearts at that time to the idea of a new role for women within their own homes, while her career success set an example and helped open doors for aspiring media professionals.

Women Liberate in the 1960s

Few fans of the HBO series *Sex and the City* realize that the controversial best-selling book *Sex and the Single Girl*, written by Helen Gurley Brown, inspired the cable show. Brown began her professional career as a secretary and soon landed a position as the personal secretary to one of the managing partners at a large advertising agency. There, her writing skills so impressed her new boss that he gave her a shot at writing advertising copy. Brown won several awards and established herself as one of the top ad writers on the West Coast—not to mention one of the best paid.

Published in 1962, *Sex and the Single Girl* was a smash hit across the United States, in spite of its controversial and candid discussion of woman's independence and sexuality. In the book, Brown talks frankly both about women's sexual needs and about ways to use sex for career advancement in the male-dominated workplace. Brown's critics railed against the book's candid treatment of single women's sexuality, but women all over America embraced her book as a rallying point for the modern liberated woman.

After the enormous success of *Sex and the Single Girl*, Hearst Publishing, a leading magazine publishing company, asked Brown to revamp one of their failing publications, *Cosmopolitan*.[17] Brown dramatically reshaped *Cosmopolitan* from a conservative magazine targeting American families to a female-oriented equivalent to Hugh Hefner's *Playboy* magazine. The new *Cosmo* featured provocative pictures, controversial subject matter and practical advice on sex, fashion, careers and entertainment for the independent woman, packaged in a trendy, culturally relevant magazine. Under Brown's direction, advertising and subscription revenues soared. While feminists would later criticize Brown for perpetuating the stereotype that women use sex as a tool, Brown's vision encouraged women to reach out and claim ownership of career paths and social roles previously held only by men.

Shortly after Brown's rise to prominence, other voices for women's rights began to be heard in the media. Those advocates included Betty Friedan, another leader of the women's rights movement who had freelanced for *Cosmopolitan*. In 1963, Friedan wrote a book titled *The Feminine Mystique*, which provided a rigorous and well-argued diagnosis of women's issues in American society. In 1971, feminist Gloria Steinem co-founded *Ms.* magazine, which offered articles that reflected a harder-edged feminist ideology, but still targeted the average American female reader.

15.10

Critics argue that the portrayal of the leading ladies of *Sex and the City* still stereotype women, despite the fact that they openly talk about and act upon their sexual impulses. Do you agree or disagree with these critics?

London Entertainment/Alamy Stock Photo

Doors Widen for Women in the 1970s

In 1963, Lucille Ball became a mentor for innovative comic Carol Burnett. Four years later, in 1967, Burnett launched her own hit prime-time television show. *The Carol Burnett Show* became a weekly television staple throughout the United States, eventually winning 23 Emmy Awards. Like Ball, Burnett skillfully used comedy and her celebrity to open doors for women.

Women began appearing more frequently and in more prominent, leading roles—for example, Marlo Thomas in *That Girl* (1966–1971), Diahann Carroll in *Julia* (1968–1971) and Mary Tyler Moore in *The Mary Tyler Moore Show* (1970–1977). Each of these characters represented strong independent career women, whose lives proved compelling to viewers—and the shows soared in popularity as a result. In addition, *The Mary Tyler Moore Show* garnered great critical acclaim and won three consecutive Emmy Awards for outstanding comedy series (1975–1977). This program was groundbreaking because it was the first sitcom to feature a career woman who was not widowed, divorced or actively seeking a husband.

The 1970s also saw women making inroads into the television newsroom as well, with female reporters becoming on-air regulars. In 1976, Barbara Walters signed an unheard-of $1 million contract with ABC and became the first female anchor of prime-time evening news on a major television network.

Women Seek Equal Opportunity in the 1980s and Now

Though women accounted for nearly one-third of all journalists in the United States by the early 1980s, they still faced systematic discrimination and the stereotype of being "media eye-candy." As Patricia Melton, filmmaker, photographer, author and the founder of the international women's rights organization Peace X Peace, notes in her video segment for this chapter, women in the media were constantly being compared to

▶ **The Impact of Women in Media**
Filmmaker and author Patricia Melton explores the global impact of women on television.

15.11

Iranian-born Christiane Amanpour's reporting on Persian Gulf War brought her international recognition. Thereafter, she would report from other conflict zones, including Bosnia, Sarajevo and Jerusalem.

Mike Coppola/Staff

their male counterparts and expected to offer a "feminine," less fact-oriented perspective on the world. See how this perception is changing in the video segment titled "The Impact of Women in Media." ▶

Today, women in the United States and around the world continue to make great strides in breaking gender stereotypes—particularly in the mass media. Journalists such as award-winning international correspondent Christiane Amanpour (formerly of CNN and now with ABC) and CBS Lara Logan, to name two of many, are chipping away at the remaining gender bias by leading the way in serious news coverage, especially in subject areas such as war, crime and politics, where women reporters had previously been excluded. The proliferation of media technology in the Digital Age has opened the door for a whole new generation of global media producers, with women gaining a much greater opportunity to make significant contributions. (see Chapters 13 and 14). All over the world, from the United States to Qatar, from Beijing to Burundi, women are pushing the barriers toward true equality between the sexes, playing foundational roles in the establishment of media systems in developing nations, and continuing to make inroads into traditional media.

PIONEERS OF ASIAN-AMERICAN MEDIA

In 1972, the television series *Kung Fu* debuted on ABC. Set around the turn of the 20th century, the show followed the adventures of a Chinese Shaolin monk, who also happened to be a highly skilled martial arts expert, named Kwai Chang Caine. The role, however, was played by the late David Carradine—a white American actor. The series follows the storyline of how Caine flees from China to the United States in the late 1890s after avenging the dishonorable murder of his blind Shaolin master, Master Po, at the hands of the Chinese emperor's nephew. In his travels through the American West, Caine tries to track down his long-lost American half-brother, along the way becoming a champion of the oppressed—often poor Chinese immigrants mistreated by whites. Caine uses his Shaolin Buddhist spiritual grounding and martial arts skills instead of guns to fight the villain and save the day for these oppressed and powerless victims. In its day, the *Kung Fu* series enjoyed moderate critical and popular success, and it still enjoys a loyal following for its infrequent cable TV reruns. But the series' real lasting impact derived from its portrayal of Asians and Asian-Americans.

Mainstream Media Portrayals of Asians in America

Carradine's character Caine popularized certain notions of Asians and Asian culture to white Americans, who for the most part had little experience with either. Certainly, the characterizations of Caine as a smart, self-assured, well-trained and spiritually grounded hero, and the flashbacks to his Shaolin Buddhist training, encompassed many compelling and positive ideas, but they also fed popular stereotypes while conflicting with prejudiced beliefs that Asian immigrants were powerless victims. To try to understand how these conflicting views of Asians and Asian culture came about in American media, it is helpful to take a closer look at the popularization of the *Kung Fu* series and how certain social and political concerns influenced its production.[18]

While the most widespread account of the origin of *Kung Fu* is that the show was the brainchild of Hollywood screenwriter Ed Spielman, this account is not without controversy. In her memoir *Bruce Lee: The Man Only I Knew*, Linda Lee Caldwell claims that her late husband, the martial arts legend Bruce Lee, originally pitched the idea that would become *Kung Fu* to Warner Brothers Studio, but the studio rejected Lee's proposal. When the studio eventually retooled the concept and attributed it to Spielman, studio executives considered Lee for the lead role of Kwai Chang Caine, but decided that he looked "too Asian" for their audience. Instead, they chose David Carradine, a white American of strong European descent who had no martial arts training. Carradine would use yellowface—the common theatrical practice at the time of applying makeup and pulling back the skin around the eyes to give non-Asian actors and actresses the clichéd Asian look—to pass himself off as half-Chinese. Frustrated by Hollywood's resistance to Asian actors, Lee eventually returned to Hong Kong, where he would star in hugely successful films, such as *Fists of Fury* (1972). Whether Caldwell's claim is true, the circumstances that she describes are an accurate portrayal of the difficulties that have faced Asians in American culture and American media for the last two centuries.

Asian-American Media Begin With Chinese Immigration

Large-scale Chinese immigration to the United States began during the mid-1800s, driven by the lure of the California Gold Rush (1848–1855) and the pressures of the Opium War in China (1868). Like most immigrants, the thousands of Chinese laborers typically came to the United States with the hopes of establishing more prosperous lives than the ones they left behind—to them, America represented the "Gam San," or the "gold mountain." At the time, most of these immigrants were young males with very little education; many found jobs helping to construct the United States' first Transcontinental Railroad, which was completed in 1869.

After a time, many Americans began to react negatively to the growing Chinese population in the country and labeled Chinese immigration as the "Yellow Peril." This racist phrase, which was commonly printed in the papers of William Randolph Hearst, reflected the nation's fears of anything foreign—in this case, Chinese people. Authors and journalists eventually coined a new term for anti-Asian sentiment—the "Yellow Terror," as illustrated by the words of Mark Twain:

> The Yellow Terror is threatening this world to-day. It is looming vast and ominous on that distant horizon. I do not know what is going to be the result of that Yellow Terror, but our government has had no hand in evoking it, and let's be happy in that and proud of it.[19]

Such fears inspired the Chinese Exclusion Act of 1882, the first federal regulation directed toward curtailing foreign immigration in the United States. The act suspended Chinese immigration to the United States for what was supposed to be just a period of 10 years, but subsequent legislation later extended this period. It was not until 1943 before Congress finally appealed all exclusion acts and 1965 (with the passage of the Immigration Act) before certain restrictions were lifted. This law would once again change in 1990, when immigration caps were made more flexible.

The establishment of an Asian immigrant media resulted in part from the proliferation of distinctly Asian immigrant communities or separate neighborhoods with their own schools, banks, community centers and newspapers. To this day, "Chinatowns" exist in major cities throughout the United States, the oldest and most famous of which is in San Francisco. Other Asian immigrants followed this model: Today we can find "Japan towns" in many metropolitan areas, and "Korea towns" are present in sizable suburban centers.

15.12

A multitude of Asian groups call Chinatown, urban centers of Asian culture, home. Separation from mainstream culture contributed to the creation of an independent, Asian press.

Highsmith, Carol M, photographer. Chinatown, San Francisco, California. Courtesy of Library of Congress

15.13

After the Japanese attacked Pearl Harbor, anti-Asian sentiment filled American media.

Stricken from the air. Testifying to the extent of the Japanese sneak attacks are these three stricken U.S. battleships. Left to right: U.S.S. West Virginia, severely damaged; U.S.S. Tennessee, damaged; and U.S.S. Arizona, sunk. Courtesy of Library of Congress

These immigrant neighborhoods published newspapers and magazines in their respective languages, which in turn contributed to their segregation from the mainstream. In the late 20th century, Asian-Americans started to build a broadcasting presence, first on radio and then on television. Unfortunately, as with Native Americans, despite great strides made in recent years by Asian actors and media producers, the mainstream media continue to perpetuate popular Asian stereotypes.

Media Stereotypes Plague Asians in the Early 20th Century

Early American media depictions of Asian characters often identified them as villains—for example, Dr. Fu Manchu in *The Insidious Dr. Fu Manchu* (1913) and Flash Gordon's nemesis, *Emperor Ming* (1936). After the Japanese invaded China (1937–1945) and attacked Pearl Harbor (December 7, 1941), bringing the United States into World War II, negative imagery of Asians filled the media. Such Hollywood films as *Wake Island* (1942), *The Purple Heart* (1944) and many others produced during this period characterized Asians as the "enemies." As such, Asians became easy targets in both entertainment and news media.[20]

Negative stereotypes of Asians were reinvigorated in the 20th century following U.S. involvement in the Korean War (1950–1953), the Vietnam War (1963–1975) and Communist China's emergence as a major perceived threat to the United States during the Cold War (1947–1991). As shown by the casting in the *Kung Fu* television series and many other examples, Hollywood typecast ethnic Asian actors in villain roles using non-Asian actors in yellowface makeup in leading roles. This practice merely strengthened anti-Asian bigotry. Stereotyping of Asians in 20th-century American media crossed over into gender stereotyping, with Hollywood characterizing Asian men as less masculine and physically nonimposing. Asian women were portrayed as either sexually permissive, alluring and demure "Butterflies" or sinister, sexually deviant and conniving "Dragon Lady" characters. Anna May Wong, an accomplished American actress who played, among dozens of roles, the daughter of Dr. Fu Manchu in *Daughter of the Dragon* (1931), is a classic example of this media-driven stereotype. Unfortunately, these sexually charged portrayals of Asian women have had such a negative effect on

American social consciousness that approximately one-third of all pornography sold in the United States today involves female Asian models or actors.

Fortunately, in recent years, American audiences have witnessed a dismantling of this stereotype, albeit a slow one. The film remake of the television series *Charlie's Angels* (2000) is an example of a U.S.-produced film that attempts to reimagine the stereotypical Asian woman. Lucy Liu (who co-stars with Drew Barrymore and Cameron Diaz) plays Alex, a feisty, strong and intelligent member of a crime-fighting female trio known as Charlie's Angels. She is the contemporary Asian woman warrior, a term most commonly associated with the creative nonfiction work of the same name by writer Maxine Hong Kingston.

Maxine Hong Kingston is just one of several Asian-American writers whose work has earned her critical acclaim. Currently a professor emeritus at the University of California–Berkeley, Kingston's *The Woman Warrior* is taught across the disciplines, from Asian studies to Asian-American literature to gender and women's studies. It examines the lives of Chinese women in a historically patriarchal culture. While some critics have argued that this book overemphasizes the subjugation of the Chinese woman, thereby reinforcing Western stereotypes about Asian women in general, others have argued the opposite: Through Kingston's own autobiographical telling of the Chinese woman's experience from the perspective of an Asian-American woman, she has, in fact, elevated the status of women, empowered them and made them "warriors." Additionally, one critic notes that the stories very much echo the larger immigrant experience—as such, the book was fitting for a mainstream audience.[21]

Since Kingston's book was first published, many more Asian-American voices have emerged to tell their own stories of the Asian experience in the United States. The Asian American Writers' Workshop in New York City, for example, is a nonprofit arts organization (and the only one of its kind) that was established in 1991 for the purpose of showcasing Asian-American literature, educating people about the Asian-American experience and bringing to the forefront important voices that might not otherwise be showcased in the mainstream media.

Asian-Americans Break Through in 21st-Century Media

Today, Asians in American media have moved into more mainstream roles in popular media. They are often portrayed as either strong, beloved heroes, such as Jackie Chan or Masi Oka in the NBC television sci-fi series *Heroes*, or as model citizens—hard-working, responsible and highly educated. As examples of the latter, consider the images projected by broadcast journalists Ann Curry, Lisa Ling and Laura Ling and by actors Sandra Oh (*Grey's Anatomy*), George Huang (*Law and Order: Special Victims Unit*) and Kal Penn (*House*). Before Penn joined the cast of *House*, he was well known in his role as Kumar in the comedy films *Harold & Kumar Go to White Castle* (2004) and *Harold & Kumar Escape from Guantanamo Bay* (2008); the popularity of these films helped make him the first Indian-American actor to achieve success in the Hollywood mainstream. After two years of playing Dr. Lawrence Kutner on *House*, Penn left to join President Barack Obama's administration as associate director in the White House's Office of Public Liaison; he resigned this position in 2010 to return to acting.[22]

15.14

Kal Penn, the first Indian-American actor to achieve success in Hollywood's mainstream, temporarily left acting behind in 2009 to take a position in the White House Office of Public Engagement.

United Archives GmbH/Alamy Stock Photo

Comedian Margaret Cho represents a new independent voice in minority media: Not only is she Asian, but she is also bisexual. In the early 1990s, Cho, a popular Korean-American comic on the American club circuit, was asked to star in an Asian-American sitcom. In 1994, ABC launched the series *All-American Girl*, which featured Cho and the first all-Asian cast in U.S. television history, in network prime-time. Unfortunately, the show tanked in its first season, in large part to poor writing and constant format changes.

Cho documents her struggle to make the series successful in her hit one-woman specials on HBO and her book *I'm the One That I Want*. Cho reveals the pervasive biases that confront Asian-Americans as they try to take part in the mainstream American media. Cho tells how, after her first screen test, the producers were convinced that her face was too round and, therefore, that her look was "too Asian" to reach wider American audiences. Cho immediately began a crash diet to conform to the producers' expectations, losing 30 pounds in two weeks, and suffering acute kidney failure as a result. Midway through the season, the show's producers, who were convinced that her character was not acting "Asian enough," hired coaches to help Cho learn how to "act Asian." After this effort failed to produce the results the network wanted, the show's all-Asian supporting cast was replaced with an all-white cast, "to promote a greater contrast that would accentuate Cho's Asian-ness." Although *All-American Girl* made some strides toward offering a more balanced depiction of Asian-American life, a majority of viewers rejected the show, given its portrayal of Asian-American life from a primarily white American perspective.[23]

15.15

Margaret Cho, a Korean-American comedian and actress, is the antithesis of the stereotypical demure, Asian female.

Reuters/Alamy Stock Photo

PIONEERS OF GAY AND LESBIAN AMERICAN MEDIA

In 1971, a major California bank hired David B. Goodstein (1932–1985)—the son of a wealthy Jewish family from Denver, Colorado, and a Columbia University Law School graduate—as vice president for portfolio investment. Goodstein had served in the Army, practiced law in New York City, and helped raise funds for a number of social-service organizations within the civil rights movement. All in all, he was a perfect choice to head up the investment division of a major bank. But Goodstein was also gay, and as soon as his new employers learned this fact, they fired him. Goodstein reacted by channeling his anger into political action and was instrumental in gaining passage in 1974 of a bill that made legal in California consensual sex between adults of any sexual persuasion. In 1975, Goodstein purchased *The Advocate*, a Los Angeles-based gay magazine; over the next 10 years, he built into the largest circulating gay publication in the world. It remains at this pinnacle today.

Although Goodstein was a controversial figure, no one questions his contributions to the gay community. He staunchly believed that the best way to promote the gay rights cause was to use mass media to depict gays and lesbians, despite their sexual orientations, as mainstream Americans. This less confrontational approach brought Goodstein and *The Advocate* in frequent conflict with his more radical counterparts in the U.S. gay rights movement, including Harvey Milk. The gay rights movement, which officially began following the New York City Stonewall riots in 1969, not only sought to protect the civil rights of gays and lesbians, but also sought the end to the criminalization of homosexuality. Milk was one of its famously outspoken advocates. He did not hide his homosexuality, not

> Although Goodstein was a controversial figure, no one questions his contributions to the gay community. He staunchly believed that the best way to promote the gay rights cause was to use mass media to depict gays and lesbians, despite their sexual orientations, as mainstream Americans.

even while he served as San Francisco city supervisor. Milk was the first openly gay man elected to public office in California. On November 27, 1978, he was assassinated, along with Mayor George Moscone, at work in San Francisco City Hall. Before the assassinations, the conflict between Goodstein and Milk over how best to push the cause of gay rights in the media was legendary—and was featured in the award-winning 2008 biographical film *Milk*, starring Sean Penn.

The conflicts between these two renowned leaders of the gay rights movement exemplify the clash of ideas that challenges all mass media serving minority constituents: Is their primary role to celebrate and support the differences between their audience and the mainstream, or should they serve as a bridge to help the audience become accepted by the mainstream? Goodstein remained a clear proponent of the latter position, and *The Advocate* continues that bridging mission today.[24]

Gay Rights Are Human Rights

Gay and lesbian media began to emerge in the United States in 1924 when a Chicago postal worker named Henry Gerber (1892–1972) founded the Society for Human Rights. The Society for Human Rights published two issues of a magazine titled *Friendship and Freedom*, the first gay and lesbian publication in the United States, before Chicago police shut down the Society and destroyed all copies of the publication. Embittered by the experience, Gerber continued to try to rally Chicago's gay community to help model it after the vibrant gay community he had witnessed in Germany before immigrating to America as a young man.

One of the earliest gay and lesbian publications, which continues in operation today, is *Vice Versa*, founded by a Hollywood studio secretary named Edith Eyde. Eyde wrote under the pen name "Lisa Ben"—an anagram for "lesbian." Ben wrote that her intention in starting *Vice Versa* was to create "a medium through which [lesbians] may express our thoughts, our emotions, our opinions—as long as material was within the bounds of good taste."[25]

15.16

Sean Penn, who won an Oscar for playing Harvey Milk in the film *Milk* (2008), called for a statewide "Day of Remembrance" in honor of this first openly gay politician.

Moviestore Collection Ltd/Alamy Stock Photo

The Mattachine Society, founded in 1950, was the first national homosexual rights organization in the United States. Two years after its founding, and years before the ideological conflicts between gay rights movement leaders David Goodstein and Harvey Milk became public, two distinct factions emerged within this organization. The first took a confrontational approach to gay and lesbian rights. The second faction believed that the path to gay rights required integration with the mainstream, not confrontation. This split came at the height of Wisconsin Senator Joseph McCarthy's national anti-communist witch hunt, with more conservative members of the Society fearing that confrontational approaches would lead to the group being labeled communists. The two groups agreed to a friendly split, with the integrationists keeping the Mattachine Society banner and the radicals forming the organization One, Inc.

In 1953, One, Inc., began publishing the first nationally distributed gay and lesbian magazine, the self-titled *One*. Both the FBI and the U.S. Postal Service launched harassment campaigns against One, Inc., and the magazine. Eventually, the postmaster of Los Angeles ruled that *One* violated the federal Comstock Laws—laws established in 1873 that made it illegal for anyone to send material considered lewd or obscene through the mail. One, Inc., sued to have the postmaster's ruling overturned, and the Supreme Court finally overturned the ban in 1958.

Meanwhile, in 1955, the Mattachine Society began publishing its own magazine, *Mattachine Review*, for gay men. Around the same time, the Daughters of Bilitis, the first major lesbian rights organization in the United States, began publishing *The Ladder*, whose life ran from 1956 to 1972.[26]

The Sexual Revolution Gives Gay Rights Momentum

The sexual revolution of the 1960s gave momentum to the gay rights movement, and with that momentum came steady growth in the number of gay and lesbian publications produced in the United States. These new gay and lesbian publications reflected the radical, countercultural editorial voice of the times. One of the most well known of these publications was the *Los Angeles Advocate*, the forerunner to Goodstein's *Advocate* magazine. Dick Michaels and his partner, Bill Rand, started the *Los Angeles Advocate* after the Los Angeles police department wrongly arrested Rand for lewd conduct during a raid on a local bar in 1966. The raid was part of a larger campaign by law enforcement to harass homosexuals. Michaels, who had a Ph.D. in chemistry and had worked as an editor for a respected academic journal, immediately became involved in a local gay and lesbian group called PRIDE. Michaels took over the group's newsletter and the first issue of *The Los Angeles Advocate* came out in September 1967.[27]

A watershed moment for the gay and lesbian press, and the gay rights movement in general, came in the early morning hours of June 28, 1969, during an incident known today as the Stonewall riots. The Stonewall Inn was an underground bar in the Greenwich Village section of New York City. Even though the bar, like the many other gay bars in the neighborhood, was the target of occasional police raids, on this historic morning the police went beyond their usual harassing shakedowns and violently assaulted a number of the bar's patrons. When a woman whom police officers had pushed to the ground as she struggled to escape got to her feet, she yelled to the crowd outside the bar, "Why don't you guys do something?" As more police arrived, the crowd shifted from chanting and jeering into engaging in a violent battle with police, which quickly spilled into the street and escalated into a full-fledged riot.

Over the next few days, thousands of gays and lesbians rioted in the streets around the Stonewall Inn to protest years of abuse at the hands of the New York City police. All three major area newspapers—*The New York Times*, *New York Post* and *New York Daily News*—covered the riots as well as the resultant gay rights protests, and all did feature stories on the plight of gays and lesbians. These stories gained national attention in the mainstream media, leading to unprecedented national public exposure for gay rights activists all over the country.[28]

> In the aftermath of the Stonewall riots, the number of gay and lesbian publications in the United States exploded to more than 150 newspapers and magazines nationally by 1972.

In the aftermath of the Stonewall riots, the number of gay and lesbian publications in the United States exploded to more than 150 newspapers and magazines nationally by 1972. As earlier mentioned, David B. Goodstein purchased *The Advocate* in 1975 and redirected the magazine to reflect the developing upscale gay and lesbian lifestyle, including regional and national gay rights political agendas—a demonstration of how the gay and lesbian media began to adopt journalistic standards similar to those embraced by the mainstream media. With this change came a parallel move away from radical civil rights advocacy.

Today, advocacy organizations actively monitor all mass media outlets in an effort to prevent the misrepresentation and defamation of lesbian, gay, bisexual and transgender (LGBT) people. The largest and most successful of these monitoring organizations is the Gay and Lesbian Alliance Against Defamation (GLAAD). Founded in New York City in 1985, GLAAD initially focused on countering inaccuracies and factual misrepresentation about the AIDS epidemic in the mass media. Over the years, its mission has expanded to include campaigns that encourage more positive portrayals of LGBT individuals in both entertainment and news media and to work with local and regional media outlets to improve their coverage of their local gay communities. In 1990, the organization launched the GLAAD Media Awards to recognize media outlets for their fair and inclusive representations of LGBT people and communities. In 2010, for example, the GLAAD Award for Outstanding Documentary went to the producers of the PBS documentary film *Ask Not*, which explored the history of the infamous "Don't ask, don't tell" policy for gays serving in the U.S. military.

Gay, Lesbian and Transgender Media Enter the Mainstream

The outbreak of HIV/AIDS in the early 1980s posed an ethical dilemma for the gay and lesbian media. While some publications focused on supporting HIV/AIDS awareness, others chose to avoid reporting on the epidemic, for fear of losing advertisers. With the 1990s came a renewed focus on increasing the visibility of gays and lesbians in mainstream culture. In response to the debate on whether to ban gays from serving in the U.S. military, the Clinton administration established the controversial "Don't ask; don't tell" policy.

Mainstream businesses began tapping into the gay and lesbian community as a breakout market, and gays and lesbians began to appear in mainstream music, television and film. By 2006, the gay and lesbian market in the United States had grown to an estimated $660 billion. Lured by the potential of this previously taboo market, mainstream companies in the late 1990s began investing significant resources to target gays and lesbians with tailored advertising campaigns. By 2007, nearly 200 of the *Fortune* 500 companies were directly pursuing gay and lesbian consumers, with that number increasing ever since. Absolut Vodka, Levi's (jeans), American Airlines, Volvo and Expedia are but a small sample of the many mainstream companies whose advertising, marketing and public relations departments have developed campaigns to court the gay and lesbian market.[29]

15.17

The NYC Stonewall riots of June 28, 1969 represented a watershed moment for the gay rights movement—thrusting the gay cause into the mainstream media. Today LGBT causes are regularly covered.

Pacific Press/Contributor

The 1990s also saw the forward push of gay and lesbian artists into the mainstream media, including the introduction of homosexuality and homosexual themes in television and film. Trailblazing gay musicians, including Elton John, Boy George, Melissa Etheridge, George Michael and k. d. lang, have all have used their star power to campaign for gay and lesbian community issues. In 1997, comedian and sitcom star Ellen DeGeneres "came out" on *The Oprah Winfrey Show*, only to have her character on her sitcom *Ellen* (1994) do the same during an episode of the show two months later. Dr. Kerry Weaver, a regular character on *ER* from 1995 to 2007, played by actress Laura Innes, revealed that she was a lesbian in a controversial episode. *Will and Grace*, a sitcom that followed the lives of Will, a gay lawyer, and Grace, his straight female best friend, debuted on NBC in 1998 to become the most successful program portraying a gay lead character in the history of television. The series has had international impact on traditional attitudes toward homosexuality.

On the big screen, gay and lesbian storylines have also become more common in films geared toward broad mainstream audiences. Openly gay and lesbian actors and actresses such as Wanda Sykes, Ian McKellen, Rupert Everett, George Takei and Rosie O'Donnell enjoy successful careers in part because of their homosexuality, not just in spite of it. In 2005, *Brokeback Mountain* opened to tremendous media interest. The film, which portrayed two male cowboys who fall in love and struggle to come to terms with their relationship, was a financial and critical success, earning $178 million in global box-office sales, garnering eight Academy Award nominations, and winning three Oscars.

Until recently, American newscasters never revealed information about their sexual lives. Barbara Walters revealed in her 2008 memoir that she had had an affair with married African-American Senator Edward Brooke (R. MA) in the 1970s. Neither felt they could reveal their relationship at that time. And for decades, openly gay TV network news anchors were unheard of. Fast forward to 2011, when CNN revealed that its popular news hosts Don Lemon and Anderson Cooper are gay—with little or no loss of audience and very short-lived media attention, further demonstrating that a growing majority of Americans today easily accept gays and lesbians in the media.

CONCLUSION: ON THE PATH TOWARD GREATER FUTURE DIVERSITY

In the late 20th century, and now into the 21st century, the United States has become ever-more diverse. This trend has occurred in large part because of the way that media and communication have played a critical role in bridging the gap between minorities and the mainstream. While it is beyond the scope of this book to lay out the numerous struggles and successes of the countless minority groups that have representation in the United States, it is important to note that these groups played foundational roles in what we recognize as American history and the American experience. We have presented the stories of some of the larger minority groups here, exploring how each group has used mass media as both a platform through which to express its unique culture and as means to more fully integrate with and contribute to the broader social and cultural landscape.

While each minority group discussed in this chapter has experienced a unique journey toward equality, they have also shared similar challenges to some extent. We have chosen to focus our brief exploration of diversity and mass media on Native Americans, Latino-Americans, African-Americans, Asian-Americans, women and gays and lesbians; however, the same dynamics apply to the experience of the Irish-Americans, Polish-Americans, Italian-Americans, Jewish-Americans, Arab-Americans. . . . The ever-growing list of minority groups that are experiencing similar barriers to equality and integration is a very long one, yet each diverse community makes valuable contributions to the larger society, culture and media.

The media allow minority voices to be heard; expose mainstream society to positive images of those groups' communities, culture and heritage; and break stereotypes. Immigrant communities, in particular, have used the media to celebrate and perpetuate their rich heritages, thereby giving new generations the gift of their ethnic roots. The mass media are, therefore, perhaps the most important mechanisms driving diversity in America, as well as in much of the world, today.

CHAPTER SUMMARY	KEY TERMS
Pioneers of Latino Media in America The history and struggle of Latino-Americans in their quest to achieve ethnic equality in American mass media is explored. **Visual Media** **The Emergence of Latino TV** 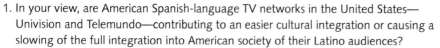 Univision's Mariá Elena Salinas explores the impact of Univision and Latino television on today's Latino-American communities. 1. In your view, are American Spanish-language TV networks in the United States—Univision and Telemundo—contributing to an easier cultural integration or causing a slowing of the full integration into American society of their Latino audiences? 2. In this video segment, Univision's popular prime-time news host Maria Elena Salinas describes the important role and mission Univision plays as a mass media educator. Is this a valid role and model for all network and cable news networks to undertake? If so, which English-language news network in the United States is closest to Univision's model? If not, why not? 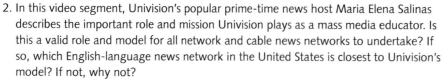	Spanish press in exile Spanish immigrant press crónica México de afuera Latino native press Operation Wetback telenovelas Kerner Commission

Pioneers of Black Media in America The story of the pioneers who fought for equal, fair and nonracist representation and full participation for blacks in American media is outlined. **Visual Media** **John Sengstacke and the *Chicago Defender*** Groundbreaking black newspaper publisher John Sengstacke tells the 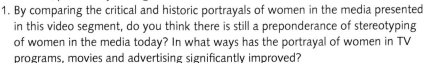 story of the role of the *Chicago Defender* in the Great Migration to the North. 1. Give two examples of black mass media organizations in television or publishing today that are working in the tradition of the *Chicago Defender*. 2. Compare the state of black mass media today with that during the time of the *Chicago Defender* described in this video segment.	objectification *Freedom's Journal* Reconstruction Jim Crow era *Chicago Defender* Great Migration Pullman porters Black Power movement
Pioneering Women in American Media The stories of some of the pioneering women who have fought to make American mass media gender neutral are studied. **Visual Media** **Women Stereotypes**  A critical look at historical and contemporary portrayals of women in the media, particularly through film. 1. By comparing the critical and historic portrayals of women in the media presented in this video segment, do you think there is still a preponderance of stereotyping of women in the media today? In what ways has the portrayal of women in TV programs, movies and advertising significantly improved? 2. Name two or three current prime-time TV dramas in which the female characters are presented in a way that negates previous stereotyping and explain why these specific female characters offer audiences such strong and even groundbreaking portrayals. **The Impact of Women in Media** Filmmaker and author Patricia Melton explores the global impact of women on television. 1. What is the global impact of the increasing number of leading women in the news media and in the media spotlight? Has Patricia Melton's vision been realized? 2. How is the changing role of women in the Islamic world impacting the evolution of culture in these countries? Are the now-frequent presentations by women news anchors and journalists in the Middle East effectively counterbalancing the traditional roles and views of women there?	women's suffrage movement
Pioneers of Asian-American Media The Asian-American struggle to enter into American mainstream media is analyzed.	yellowface "Yellow Peril" Chinese Exclusion Act of 1882
Pioneers of Gay and Lesbian American Media Looks at how gay and lesbian actors and comedians have brought LGBT characters and stories into popular American entertainment media.	*The Advocate* gay rights movement Mattachine Society Daughters of Bilitis Stonewall riots Gay and Lesbian Alliance Against Defamation (GLADD)

NOTES

1 Aleiss, A. (2008). *Making the white man's Indian: Native Americans and Hollywood movies*. Praeger.

2 Rollins, P. C. (2003). *Hollywood's Indian: The portrayal of the Native American in films*. University Press of Kentucky.

3 Kanellos, N., & Martell, H. (2000). *Hispanic periodicals in the United States, origins to 1960: A brief history and comprehensive bibliography*. Arte Publico Press.

4 Ibid.

5 Ibid.

6 Rodriguez, A. (2009). *Azcarraga, Emilio and Emilio Azcarraga Milmo*. Retrieved from www.museum. tv/archives/etv/A/htmlA/azcarragaem/azcarragaem.htm

7 Woolley, J. T., & Peters, G. (2009). Lyndon B. Johnson. *The American Presidency Project*. Retrieved from www.presidency.ucsb.edu/ws/?pid=28369

8 Burroughs, T. (2001). *Drums in the global village: Toward an ideological history of black media*. Doctoral dissertation, University of Maryland, College Park.

9 Douglass, F. (1857). *My bondage and my freedom*. Miller, Orton & Co.

10 Burroughs, T. (2001). *Drums in the global village: Toward an ideological history of black media*. Doctoral dissertation, University of Maryland, College Park.

11 Best, W. (n.d.). Chicago defender. In *Encyclopedia of Chicago*. Chicago Historical Society.

12 Schwarzbaum, L. (1992, May 1). "The Cosby Show's" last laugh. *Entertainment Weekly*.

13 Newseum Staff. (2016, May 9). Chips Quinn scholars program. *Newseum*. Retrieved from www. newseuminstitute.org/initiatives/chips-quinn-scholars-program-for-diversity-in-journalism/; Franklin, J. H., & Meier, A. (1998). *To keep the waters troubled: The life of Ida B. Wells*. Oxford University Press; Steptoe, T. (1982). *Black leaders of the twentieth century*. University of Illinois Press. Retrieved from www.blackpast.org/aah/barnett-ida-wells-1862–1931

14 The Paley Center for Media. (2009). *Pauline Frederick: Radio and television journalist*. Retrieved from www.shemadeit.org/meet/biography.aspx?m=29

15 Ibid.

16 Sanders, C. S., & Gilbert, T. (1993). *Desilu: The story of Lucille Ball and Desi Arnaz*. Harper Collins.

17 Garner, D. (2009, April 21). Helen Gurley Brown: The original Carrie Bradshaw. *The New York Times*.

18 Ono, K. A., & Pham, V. (2009). *Asian Americans and the media*. Polity Press.

19 (1906). Welcome home: Address at the dinner in his honor at the Lotos Club, November 10, 1900. In *The complete works of Mark Twain: Mark Twain's speeches*. HarperCollins.

20 Ono, K. A., & Pham, V. (2009). *Asian Americans and the media*. Polity Press.

21 Ling, A. (n.d.). *Maxine Hong Kingston*. Retrieved from http://college. cengage.com/english/heath/syllabuild/iguide/kingston.html

22 Ono, K. A., & Pham, V. (2009). *Asian Americans and the media*. Polity Press.

23 Ibid.

24 Retrieved from www.thepointfoundation.org/scholarships/goodstein.html; see also Thompson, M. (2008, November). Two men and a myth. *The Advocate*.

25 Marcus, E. (1992). *The Struggle for Gay and Lesbian Equal Rights, 1945–1990, An Oral History*. HarperCollins. Retrieved from queermusicheritage.com/viceversa.html

26 Streitmatter, R. (1998). Gay and lesbian press. In M. Blanchard (Ed.), *History of the mass media in the United States*. Fitzroy Dearborn.

27 Gay passion, gay pride. (2007). *The Advocate*.

28 Carter, D. (2004). *Stonewall: The riots that sparked the gay revolution*. St. Martin's Press.

29 Moses, L. (2007, June 25). Mission control: Advocate, OUT to undergo editorial tweaks. *Mediaweek*.

16

Working in Mass Media in the Digital Age

CHAPTER OUTLINE

Employment Trends in Mass Media

Newspaper Editor Loretta Harring, managing editor of the regional newspaper *The Capital*, discusses hiring practices.

TV Sports Anchor Joe Fonzi, sports reporter and anchor at San Francisco television station KTVU, gives insights on the job of a sports reporter.

NPR Radio News Host Michel Martin, talk-radio host of the NPR news program *Tell Me More*, discusses selecting news stories to cover.

Survey of Selected Media Industries
Achieving Success in the Media Industry
Conclusion: Make the Industry You Want

Documentary Film Producer, MTV Cheryl Horner Sirulnick describes the creative and technical processes of developing documentary projects.

Entertainment Public Relations Agent Marcus Bass of Spelling Communications describes working as an entertainment PR professional in Hollywood.

Radio DJ Sam Diggedy, radio DJ at KDON in Northern California, describes what it is like to be a popular Top 40 radio DJ.

Video Game Developer The founder of a leading video game company explains video game development and the importance of teamwork.

LEARNING OBJECTIVES

1. Describe the various career categories in mass media and the trends that are both altering the industry and affecting employment opportunities.
2. Explain how professional guilds and unions and similar organizations can help individuals secure jobs and build careers in various media industries.
3. Assess how professional portfolios or sample reels are put together in order to showcase talents and experience.
4. Describe the challenges and opportunities afforded new job candidates interested in building a career in one of the many mass media industries.

AS WE HAVE LEARNED

throughout this book, the mass media industry is changing. Yet, while its business models may have been transformed and the channels of media access may have become digitized and globalized, the industry's role in society remains ever pivotal. Through the mass media, citizens of the world develop a better understanding of their society, culture, government and political systems. They become more informed, and they are entertained. Additionally, we have learned how most mass media industries in the United States are, at their core, business enterprises. Most of you who are using this book and its companion media tools may well be majoring in mass communication. If so, you have taken the first step toward building a career in the many fields and subfields found within mass media.

This chapter *of Mass Media Revolution* surveys the principal career paths and employment opportunities currently available in today's mass media industry. It provides you with the information you will need to answer the following frequently asked questions:

• What are the career paths in mass media today?

- Where are these jobs found?
- What do I need to do to successfully land a job in mass media after I graduate?
- What are the employment trends for jobs in mass media in the near future?
- How much money can I expect to earn?

To answer these questions, you must first recognize that not only have the mass media as social, cultural and business institutions changed, but so have the prerequisite knowledge and skill sets possessed by the industry's professionals. The innovative technologies that have hurtled us into the Digital Age have simultaneously altered the production, distribution and economics of an entire industry. Four specific trends have hastened this transformation:

- **Media convergence.** As media platforms continue to converge, the skills required to work in media industries are also converging, requiring even entry-level job seekers to demonstrate multiple skills—skills that were considered separate specialties not so long ago.
- **Altered business models.** For media companies to remain competitive in a converged world, they—and the larger industries of which they are part—have had to change their business models. For example, because evolving digital technologies have made it possible for a single person to perform tasks that once required the work of many, companies can hire fewer people and invest more funds in technology.
- **Portfolio applications.** Submitting just a résumé detailing one's skills, past experiences and education is no longer enough. Mass media companies now look more closely at individual portfolios—generally digital or online collections of completed projects that demonstrate a specific skill set or knowledge base. Photographers, for example, might use a tool such as Zen Folio to showcase images shot under a variety of contexts and with multiple devices; Web designers might create their own dynamic Web-sites to illustrate Flash features, animation and so forth.
- **Going freelance.** Shifts in industry business models and changes in the economic landscape have made working as a salaried employee for a single company less attractive. More and more people working in the various mass media industries are finding that they have far more opportunities as freelancers or contracted workers. This trend is changing the concept and culture of the mass media professional.

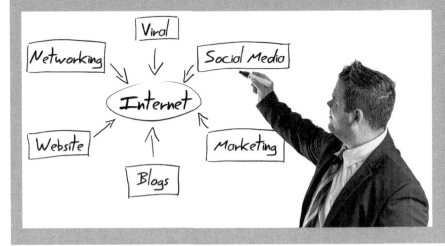

16.1
Mathias Rosenthal/Shutterstock.com

EMPLOYMENT TRENDS IN MASS MEDIA

Currently, anyone looking to build a career in the mass media can expect to find three types of earning tracks: as hourly and salaried wage earners, as contract professionals, and as freelance professionals. Mass media organizations are leading the transition from traditionally salaried to freelance and contracted positions. Freelancing has become a major employment trend among the mass media industries, opening the door to new employment opportunities.

Hourly and Salaried Wage Earners

Previously, hourly and salaried positions dominated the media professions. As a wage earner, whether on an hourly basis or an annual salary basis, the media professional becomes a direct employee of a company, organization or government agency and enjoys a variety of employer-provided benefits. These benefits often include paid sick leave and vacation, health insurance and some form of retirement program or pension. Employees must abide by the company policies and understand that they can be terminated with or without cause, depending on applicable state regulations. Promotion and salary increases typically reflect a combination of quality of performance and length of employment. Salaried employees are also usually covered under their employer's liability and errors and omissions (E&O) insurance policies, which offer protection against lawsuits that result from non-negligent performance of their duties as assigned by their employer. In this employment structure, the employer—not the employee—automatically owns any intellectual property created by the employee even when the employee is the author or creator of the material.

> In this employment structure, the employer—not the employee—automatically owns any intellectual property created by the employee even when the employee is the author or creator of the material.

Contract Professionals

Contract professionals are typically independent employees who have signed on to work for a company for a set period of time—for example, six or 12 months. While contracted professionals function in a way similar to wage earners, there are some differences:

- The contracted professional is not a direct employee of the company or agency.
- He or she must submit invoices to get paid, known as a fee-for-service payment.
- The contracted professional must pay quarterly taxes and pay for his or her own health insurance and retirement funds.
- The individual is not covered under the company's liability and E&O insurance policies.
- He or she may or may not retain ownership of intellectual properties created under contract.

Most contract professionals in mass media belong to professional associations or guilds—for example, writers belong to the Authors Guild of America; film, television and radio directors belong to the Directors Guild of America; television and film screenwriters belong to the Writers Guild of America; and photographers and video producers belong to the Professional Photographers of America. These professional associations and guilds offer many group benefits and insurance programs that are generally available to salaried professionals. Although some contract professionals work in offices or studios provided by the contracting companies, a growing number, upon the company's request, work off-site—either at home or in a separate office or studio. Offsite employees must also use their own equipment—whatever that may be. What motivates this trend toward offsite employment is cost. In short, companies save money on the rental or purchase of space and equipment.

Unlike with salaried employees, the terms regarding ownership of intellectual properties are stipulated by the specific contract signed. Copyrights to material of any kind created under the contract—articles, books, photographs, graphic designs, video productions, music compositions and so forth—may automatically belong to the contracting company, may belong to the contracted professional but with limited or exclusive license held by the company for a specific time, or may belong to both parties.

Freelance Professionals

Freelance professionals are independent contractors who work on specific projects and then move on to the next one when each project is completed. Like their contract professional counterparts, freelancers commonly join associations or guilds that provide many group benefits and insurance programs. In addition, these groups serve two other very important functions for both the freelancer and the hiring company or organization.

First, these associations and guilds establish skill-based certifications that ensure companies that they are retaining qualified professionals in the categories they require. Second, they set standardized compensation rates for the various skill levels, job assignments and type of media involved. For example, a commercial videographer signing on with an advertising agency to shoot a national commercial spot has a pre-established rate structure on which to base per-hour, per-day or per-week fees. Some associations and guilds also provide their members with invoicing and billing services; the guild bills and collects payments on behalf of its members and then deducts taxes and insurance contributions, much in the same way as a traditional company would do for its salaried earners.

16.2

Many media companies now hire freelancers and contract professionals because it is more cost-effective. Most freelancers and independent contractors work in their own fully equipped home offices.

Monkey Business Images/Shutterstock.com

These many services are invaluable to both freelance and contract professionals; thus, if you're seeking to start a career in the media industry as a freelancer or contracted employee, the first step would be to qualify for and join an appropriate guild. Some associations and guilds also negotiate master contracts with an entire media industry and, in doing so, perform the role of a national union. For instance, every five years the master contract between the Writers Guild of America and the movie studios and television networks comes up for renegotiation. A failure to agree to new contract terms can lead to a costly strike that stops the production of feature films and television programs. Usually such industry-wide strikes are short-lived because they are costly to both the guilds and the industries. They also create bad public relations and can even trigger government intervention.

> if you're seeking to start a career in the media industry as a freelancer or contracted employee, the first step would be to qualify for and join an appropriate guild.

SURVEY OF SELECTED MEDIA INDUSTRIES

In addition to general guidelines that will help you navigate the mass media industry, this chapter provides you with an overview of job categories. To further enhance your understanding of careers in the media, eight "Day in the Life" video segments have been produced for this chapter to give you glimpses of life in various aspects of the media field. The next few sections survey evolving roles in the following media industries: newspapers and magazines; television and radio broadcasting; film and video production; advertising and public relations; the music industry; photography; and video games.

Newspapers and Magazines

Traditionally, writers (reporters, columnists, feature writers) were solely responsible for the textual content of any article or story they wrote for the publications that employed them—and only for them. Other media

16.3

The newspaper and magazine industry is quickly becoming an industry of multimedia creators, where editors now take a greater role in deciding a publication's layout and ensuring that the design accommodates multiple media platforms.

Lou Linwei/Alamy Stock Photo

professionals working for the same publications would be responsible for producing the photographs, illustrations, charts and graphics that might accompany these articles. Task assignment and general management of content belonged to the editors, who were also responsible for mediating the content being published. In recent years, however, such role divisions have become less commonplace. For example, today it would not be unusual to encounter a writer who not only produces textual content, but also researches and does marketing and public relations. These days, many of the traditionally individual roles have morphed into something more akin to multiskilled media creators.

Working in Multiple Platforms
Writers in the Digital Age are now expected to develop content suitable for multiple—and multimedia—platforms, including the Internet. In such situations, writers must serve as their own first-line editors and occasionally be their own photo editors. In most cases, writers and editors must develop stories that can work in parallel media—from print publications to online Websites to broadcast cable and Web-based television. Traditionally, the task of formatting the layout of a publication fell in the hands of the designers. Now that the layout process, from small newsletters to major national newspapers and magazines, occurs in the digital realm, however, many writers and editors have taken on this responsibility. Editors whose job it was to assign stories and edit the work of the writers they managed are now also responsible for taking the lead in managing publication layout and graphic execution.

Broadening Their Specialties
In the past, publications often employed numerous editors and assistant editors with responsibilities for particular subject areas or "desks"—the international desk, the financial desk, the arts and entertainment desk. Today the trend is to collapse these specialized roles under the management of fewer editors, giving them greater responsibility over broader, more diverse subject areas. News analysts and correspondents are also finding that they are required to serve as their own researchers. In short, writers in the 21st century are expected to produce their stories with far less collaborative support than in years past. They are also expected to perform these multiple roles faster than ever before, while maintaining standards of quality and creativity.

Adapting to New Work Environments
Rapid advances in digital technologies are changing the work environments for writers, reporters, correspondents and editors. The biggest change they face is the decentralization and mobilization of their professions. Today, increasing percentages of the professionals in these industries perform their work in the field and at home, which means that the centralized support systems of large newsrooms, for example, are slowly becoming obsolete. Furthermore, while media industry jobs were once centrally located in major metropolitan areas, digital technologies and broadband communication have expanded their reach. Media industries may now be found in suburban and rural areas, and writers and editors can continue to work for their publishers even while residing hundreds or even thousands of miles away from the corporate headquarters.

As noted earlier, technological mobility is one of the major factors contributing to current employment trends—namely, the use of more freelance and contract professionals and fewer salaried staff. Since we live in a 24/7 news and information culture, however, this evolution has actually benefitted the industry. Digital technologies, greater mobility and the employment of self-sufficient, nonsalaried professionals enable publishers to produce their content faster and at less cost.

Digital technologies, greater mobility and the employment of self-sufficient, nonsalaried professionals enable publishers to produce their content faster and at less cost.

Career Outlook

According to projections by the U.S. Department of Labor, freelance and contracted employment opportunities are expected to grow by 8 percent between 2010 and 2018.[1] Competition for these positions is expected to increase, especially as the number of college graduates attracted to such positions increases. Fortunately, the explosion of Internet-based media outlets (blog sites, companion Websites, electronic and print-on-demand publications) and the parallel demand to fill these outlets with content have led to greater employment opportunities for individuals seeking viable writing careers. Despite the shifts affecting the media industry at large, local news remains popular. As such, many small newspapers have been able to survive even in the era of media convergence. The sustained viability of these smaller, community-focused newspapers and regional magazines has opened doors for experienced journalists and editors as well as recent graduates just entering the field.

According to the U.S. Department of Labor, in 2010, the median salary for writers and authors was $55,420, and editors' compensation ranged from $49,990 to $114,450. The median salary for technical writers in 2010 was $63,280.[2] Today, many writers earn income from multiple sources. Depending on their talent and self-marketing abilities, they may have the ability to exceed these median ranges. At the same time, they are also responsible for covering many of their own expenses, including health insurance. Memberships in professional associations (such as the Authors Guild of America and the American Society of Journalists and Authors) can help offset these expenses and provide other support services; as such, memberships in these organizations are currently are at an all-time high. ▶

▶ **Newspaper Editor**
Loretta Harring, the managing editor of one of the oldest continually published regional newspapers in America, discusses what she looks for when hiring recent journalism school graduates and the important roles still played by regional and local newspapers.

Television and Radio Broadcasting

Jobs in radio and television as well as at cable and satellite networks are very competitive. As with the print media industry, most broadcasting jobs historically existed in large metropolitan areas—namely, Los Angeles, New York, Chicago and Atlanta. Unlike the newspaper and magazine industries, where advances in digital technologies and the Internet have had a major impact, however, television and radio broadcasting have experienced only minor decentralization. In recent years, television production has followed its sister industry, movie production, to new industry centers—Wilmington, North Carolina, for example. With the steady migration of television and radio content onto the Web, employment opportunities in the broadcasting industry have grown.

Common Job Categories in Broadcasting

Anyone interested in pursuing a career in broadcasting will encounter a multitude of career tracks. This section provides a brief overview of some of the most common career fields within television and radio broadcasting:

- **Business operations.** Broadcasting companies rely heavily on their business teams. Business operations ensure that finances are properly managed and distributed and that all personnel remain informed

16.4

Migration of media content onto the Internet has led to increased opportunities in television and radio broadcasting. Here, a radio announcer delivers a newscast that will be streamed live onto the station's Website.

Tsian/Shutterstock.com

▶ TV Sports Anchor
Joe Fonzi, sports reporter and anchor at San Francisco television station KTVU, shares the challenges and excitement of working as a broadcast sports reporter.

The technical side of television and radio remains dominated by the trade unions and guilds, all of which provide career and certification paths for entry-level college graduates.

about market and media trends. Furthermore, they make sure that companies remain competitive and viable. Roles in business operations include positions in operations management, programming, marketing/advertising/sales and multiple management support occupations.

- **News.** Broadcasting is as much about the news as it is about entertainment. Individuals interested in this side of the industry may find opportunities as reporters (for news, weather, sports and lifestyle), photographers/videographers, story researchers and fact checkers, news writers, assignment editors and on-camera news analysts and commentators. ▶

- **Documentary and reality programming.** Production of documentary programs is no longer just a niche division of the film industry; with the growing audience interest in dramatic reality programming (for example, *Deadliest Catch* on the Discovery Channel), broadcasting careers focused on the development of documentary and reality programming have increased in number and scope. The advent of high-definition (HD) technology and the switch to digital broadcasting have made it feasible for networks such as Discovery and the BBC to bring shows like *Life* into people's living rooms—and have opened doors to new and exciting careers for mass media professionals working in this area.

- **Online radio.** The convergence of broadcast radio onto the Internet has broadened the market and thus the career opportunities in both music radio and news-talk radio. ▶

- **Technical operations.** Both the television and radio broadcasting industries require trained technical personnel, including but not limited to broadcast, video and audio engineers; FCC-licensed master control engineers; computer-based audiovisual (A/V) editors; technical directors and assistants; and set designers and builders. The technical side of television and radio remains dominated by the trade unions and guilds, all of which provide career and certification paths for entry-level college graduates.

Career Outlook

Annual compensation for occupations in the broadcasting industries varies greatly, depending on factors such as geographic area, size of operations and the union or nonunion nature of the contract. According to the U.S. Department of Labor, overall employment in broadcasting industries continues to increase by 10 percent annually, although the parallel trend of using technology to consolidate operations and limit the number of staff required is moderating this growth. In addition, the broadcasting industry leads all other mass media industries in the ongoing trend toward hiring more contract freelancers and employing fewer salaried personnel.

Film and Video Production

Closely aligned with the broadcasting industry is the film and video production industry, which has also experienced significant transformations in both its business models and the number and type of personnel employed in the industry. Despite these changes, employment opportunities in this field remain controlled by trade unions and guilds—even freelance production operations and projects unofficially rely on their standards. These organizations wield tremendous influence over hiring practices, determining required qualifications and standards and, of course, compensation levels and terms.

The U.S. motion picture and video production industry produces the largest number of feature films and the most television and video content in the world. The growth of television and cable/satellite outlets, along with continued advances in the technologies used to shoot, edit and distribute film and video content, have reduced the dominance of the major studios and enabled the growth of many small and medium-size independent production companies. This trend has also produced greater opportunities for employment.

While formal training from college and university programs is valued, of equal value in landing jobs in the film and video production industry is the ability to demonstrate skills and creativity through work samples, portfolios and production credits. These artifacts often carry more weight in employment decisions than the traditional résumé and educational transcripts.

▶ NPR Radio News Host

Michel Martin, talk-radio host of the NPR news program *Tell Me More*, explains how she decides the day's agenda, which includes carefully selecting the most important news stories of the day.

While formal training from college and university programs is valued, of equal value in landing jobs in the film and video production industry is the ability to demonstrate skills and creativity through work samples, portfolios and production credits. These artifacts often carry more weight in employment decisions than the traditional résumé and educational transcripts.

A Shift in Hiring Criteria

Film and video production is a complex, costly and high-risk endeavor; as such, candidates for employment in this field must demonstrate a balance of education and top-notch creative and technical skills. The graphic design and game development industries are following suit in demanding that entry-level employees demonstrate that they have real-world skills. In response, an ever-increasing number of college and university programs in film, video and related production programs are now focusing on helping their students build marketable portfolios and sample reels as part of their requirements for graduation.

A combination of rising production costs, rapidly growing competition and reduced production budgets has forced the film and video industry to streamline its operations; only the few high-budgeted feature films financed by major studios and their independent partners are immune to these challenges. Production companies today hire fewer personnel for each project—many of them freelancers—and retain only small management and support staffs between projects. This results in a mixed situation for professionals working in this industry. On the one hand, there are fewer permanent jobs in the industry, even though the industry is actually expanding. On the other hand, a wider number of employment opportunities are available for those people who are able to move easily from one project to the next, building stronger portfolios along the way.

16.5

Author J. Charles Sterin (center of group inside camera dolly track) directing a complicated scene with his all-freelance crew on location in Dallas, Texas for his PBS series *FutureProbe*, 1995.

J. Charles Sterin—1995

▶ **Documentary Film Producer, MTV**
Cheryl Horner Sirulnick, founder and executive producer of Gigantic! Productions for MTV, describes the creative and technical process of developing documentary projects.

Career Outlook

Digital technology is making it easy for just about anyone to become a filmmaker and distribute independent films on the Web, with YouTube leading the way in promoting this "do it yourself" trend. Yet out of the millions of independent videos that are produced and posted on such sites each month, only a fraction lead to careers in film and video. It remains a difficult industry to break into. Even so, the ongoing demand for talented people in this industry is unquestioned. ▶

As in the broadcasting industries, annual compensation for occupations in the broadcasting industries varies greatly. Careers in film and television production can be highly lucrative, but commonly require a significant investment in time and effort before they yield high-end compensation. The industry continues to grow, with small independent production companies offering the best entry-level employment opportunities. (See Table 16.1.)

Advertising and Public Relations

Much as in the film and video production industries, jobs in advertising and public relations (PR) are highly competitive. The scramble for jobs is partly due to the perceived glamour of the industry, and partly due to the potentially high compensation that such jobs can yield. Although small- and moderate-sized advertising and public relations firms can be found in any large metropolitan area, or as divisions within major corporations, the industry's major geographic centers reflect its historical roots: New York City, Los Angeles and Chicago. In fact, according to the U.S. Bureau of Labor Statistics, 19 percent of all advertising firms and 28 percent of advertising and PR jobs in the United States in 2010 were geographically centered in California and New York—the exception being the large branch of the industry that focuses its PR services on congressional and federal lobbying; this division, unsurprisingly, is centered around Washington, D.C.

A Shift in Services

Although jobs in advertising and PR are generally lucrative, employment prospects in these industries are marred by their uncertain job security and lack of stability. In the last two decades, mergers and acquisitions in the industry, as well as the convergence and integration of advertising and PR operations, have contributed to this industry's relative instability. Layoffs are commonplace, as accounts are lost or "stolen" by competitors and major clients that reduce their advertising budgets without warning.

Like all the other mass media industries discussed thus far, advertising and public relations have had to adapt their business models to accommodate advances in digital technologies and the growth of the Internet. Fortunately, in so doing, new and creative job opportunities have emerged. Both advertising and

Table 16.1 2015 National Indusstry-Specific Occupational Employment and Wage Estimates

Media and Communication Occupations		
Occupation	Required Entry-Level Education	2015 Median Pay
Announcers - Program Hosts	Bachelor's Degree	$30,080
Broadcast Engineering Technitians	Bachelor or Post-Secondary Technical School Degree	$41,780
Editors - Publications or Other Print or Online Media	Bachelor's Degree	$56,010
Film/Video Editors and Camera Operators	Bachelor's Degree	$55,740
Photographers	High School Diploma and Additional Training	$31,710
Public Relations Specialists	Bachelor's Degree	$56,770
Reporters, Correspondents, Broadcast News Analysts	Bachelor's Degree	$37,720
Technical Writers	Bachelor's Degree	$70,240
Writer and Authors	Bachelor's Degree	$60,250
Film/TV Producers and Directors	Bachelor's Degree + 5 years On-the-job Training	$68,440

*Source: Bureau of Labor Statistics, U.S. Department of Labor, 2015 Occupational Outlook Handbook

PR agencies, working as either integrated services or as stand-alone operations, are now diversifying their services to include market and business development and consultation as well as Internet advertising and site development. Alternatively, they may service clients from specific industries, such as film and television. ▶

Career Outlook

Entry-level employment in advertising and public relations follows a more traditional path than in some other mass media industries. New hires can expect to work long hours and should recognize that a high value is placed on teamwork and collaboration. They can expect to be asked to demonstrate multiple skill sets and an aptitude for innovative thinking. An entry-level job at a small firm can be an easier path to a career in this field, although such organizations do not offer the same potential for advancement as can be found at the larger firms.

Freelancing in advertising and PR is growing, but not nearly as rapidly as in other mass media industries. The reasons for this lag are twofold: Attracting and servicing potential freelancers represents a sizable expense, and firms tend to want to lock staff into noncompetition agreements that prevent them from working with other firms. Despite these obstacles and challenges, freelancers still manage to find opportunities in the field. Professionals with proven technical skills, including graphic artists and designers, photographers, market researchers, music composers and video producers, can find many opportunities in this industry. When they do, they typically work on a project-to-project basis.

According to the U.S. Department of Commerce, jobs in advertising and PR are expected to grow at a rate of 14 percent through 2020.

Client specialization is also on the rise, with smaller, more narrowly focused firms landing some larger accounts specifically because of their

16.6

A creative director and her team present magazine ad photos and designs to the marketing director of a major client.

Golden Pixels LLC/Alamy Stock Photo

▶ Entertainment Public Relations Agent
Marcus Bass of Spelling Communications describes his career and his experiences working as an entertainment public relations professional in Hollywood.

reputations in particular fields. The Miami, Florida-based advertising firm Crispin Porter & Bogusky (CP & B) perfectly exemplifies this trend. CP & B's innovative approach to advertising and PR won the company contracts with such international clients as Mini Cooper, IKEA and Virgin Atlantic—turning an otherwise very small firm into a major national and international industry player (see Chapter 8).

In advertising and public relations, as in all mass media industries, strong portfolios are essential for new entrants into the field. However, unlike the trend in many other mass media industries, advertising and PR employers still place a high value on educational records: Statistics show that graduates of industry-recognized advertising and PR programs have a bit of an advantage over nongraduates when it comes to competing for entry-level agency jobs.

Music Industry

The music industry includes a wide variety of professions and businesses: performance, publishing, distribution, management, composition. This section, however, focuses primarily on the technical and management paths of music broadcasters. Without individuals to fill these key roles, audiences would be unable to enjoy the music they receive through cable, satellite and online channels. Career tracks in the music broadcasting industry are found in the following areas:

- **Management and marketing:** station managers, music programmers, music agents and sales representatives
- **Technical production:** audio recording technicians, audio broadcasting engineers
- **Technical and creative development:** producers and directors of music videos
- **Hosting and presenting:** music show hosts, radio disc jockeys (DJs), video jockeys (VJs) ▶

▶ Radio DJ
Sam Diggedy, popular radio DJ at KDON Top-40 radio in Northern California, describes what it is like to be a popular radio DJ.

The U.S. Department of Labor and the U.S. Department of Commerce both categorize the music industry employment categories under a much broader designation, "arts and entertainment industry." As with the many career paths that fall under this broad category (composing, performance), participation in this industry requires an equal amount of talent and formal training—the latter from either colleges and universities or specialty schools dedicated to music and the performing arts.

Employment and Salary Trends

Employment trends in music closely follow both cultural and economic trends in society. In other words, when people have increased leisure time along with increased levels of disposable income, music sales increase. This equates to more people working full- or part-time in the music industry. Conversely, when the economy experiences a downturn, causing a greater percentage of the population to have less disposable income, sales of music decrease, with a parallel tightening of the jobs market in the industry overall. In addition, and as compared to other industries that are part of the mass media, the average earnings potential in the music industry is relatively low. The exception, of course, is those people working in the high end of the industry. This pattern is quite similar to the earnings potential for those working in journalism.

Employment trends in music closely follow both cultural and economic trends in society. In other words, when people have increased leisure time along with increased levels of disposable income, music sales increase.

As in most other industries making up mass media, job opportunities and earning potential in the music industry are greatly influenced by geography. For example, a radio DJ at a radio station that is operated by a large corporation such as Clear Channel will earn much higher wages than a DJ at a smaller, independently owned station—for doing exactly the same job. Similarly, a music-recording technician or audio engineer working as either a staff member or freelancer in one of the major media centers will earn significantly more money than a similarly qualified technician or engineer doing the exact same job in one of the many smaller markets across the country.

Career Outlook

Because of these geographic realities, there is a great deal of mobility in the music industry. Like other mass media industries, music attracts a large number of freelance and independent contractors, and a large percentage of performers and technical people move from job to job, and from city to city, in an effort to improve both their job opportunities and their annual incomes. This ebb and flow of professionals contributes to the view of the music industry as being less stable a job market than other industries in mass media.

Like their sister industries in mass media, the music industry is dominated by unions and guilds, both for performers and for technical workers. Unions in the music industry—most notably the American Society of Composers, Authors, and Publishers (ASCAP)—have had a long and very successful record of ensuring that members receive fair compensation. As mass media have entered the Digital Age, the music industry unions have also led the way in seeking and enforcing copyright protection.

16.7

You need not restrict your desire to build a music career to the music industry. You may find other opportunities in film, television and radio as a composer for a film soundtrack, a jingle writer for an advertising company, a sound engineer for a radio station or even a music critic for a magazine.

Brand X Pictures/Thinkstock

Other career tracks that tie directly to the music, but are not necessarily opportunities found within the music industry itself, include reporting on music and musical performers for magazines and newspapers; programming music for radio and television programs; specializing in music soundtracks for television and film productions; and recording music and serving as audio engineers for radio, television and film.

Photography

Photographers, photo researchers, and photo editors can be found working in all mass media industries, including publishing, advertising and public relations, television and film, videography, cinematography, video game development and Website development. In a Digital Age characterized by image manipulation and citizen journalism, photography plays a crucial role by contributing to the overall media message presented.

The evolution of digital technologies has had a tremendous impact on how photographers and photo editors do their jobs. Today most professional photographers use high-end digital cameras and software

16.8

Those seeking careers in the field of photography have a multitude of specialties to choose from, including marine and nature photography, which has increased in popularity with the recent spate of nature documentaries on cable television and film.

Rich Carey/Shutterstock.com

such as Adobe Photoshop to process their images. They also use a number of integrated software programs to archive, select and lay out images—for example, Adobe's fully integrated Creative Suite. Some art and fashion photographers continue to capture images using film cameras; however, with few exceptions, today's professional darkroom work is done digitally.

Career Categories and Skills

The professional photography field includes a number of specialized career tracks. These avenues include photojournalism and documentary photography, fashion photography, nature photography, sports photography, fine art photography, architectural photography, marine photography and advertising and product photography.

In most of these specialties, photo editors work in tandem with photographers to select and present photographs in the most effective way. These two professions have a long and tightly linked history, with some photographers becoming photo editors themselves. Today both photographers and photo editors must be exceptionally well versed in digital-image processing technologies—using both the camera and the computer—as well as adept in ancillary technologies such as lighting, rigging and high-resolution large-format photo printing.

Successful photographers come to the field with formal training in both art and technology. As in most of the careers in the industries that are part of mass media, training and degrees (or certificates) are important for entering the field, but portfolios are just as important. Those who hire or commission photographers need to see a portfolio to judge whether a candidate's skills and aesthetics are appropriate for the job. Historically, photographers have led the way in developing effective and innovative portfolio techniques. With the continued growth of the Internet, Web-based portfolios have become the norm for professional photographers working in all specialties. A compelling and effective Web-based portfolio would seem a basic requirement for gaining employment as a staff photographer—even at an entry level—or winning commissions as a freelancer. Not surprisingly, most of the better photography training programs at colleges and universities require students to build both effective physical and Web-based portfolios as a requirement for graduation.

> Successful photographers come to the field with formal training in both art and technology.

Career Outlook

The photography industry has historically been linked to other mass media industries that rely on visual images, specifically publishing, advertising, movies and television. As such, most of the industry has generally been centered around New York City, Los Angeles and Chicago. However, in recent years, photographers have succeeded in building strong careers throughout the country and the world, in both urban and rural regions. Specialized photographers, such as the ones identified previously, naturally gravitate to the hubs of their specialties. Thus, fashion photographers will base themselves in New York, Los Angeles, Paris and London, whereas maritime photographers might base themselves in areas such as Newport, Virginia;

Long Beach, California; or Miami, Florida. Many of the most successful photographers, regardless of specialty, have built their careers around the concept of mobility: They go to where the jobs are.

According to the U.S. Department of Labor Occupational Employment Statistics, the median annual earnings in the photographic industry has increased since 2010 to $29,130 with the most successful 10 percent of all photographers employed earning an average of $65,000. These annual earnings figures are for average direct salaries or freelance fees and do not take into account the additional annual earnings from archive licensing and publication royalties, which for many professional photographers can represent a significant additional income.

Numerous professional photography associations and guilds exist, such as the Professional Photographers of America (PPA), American Society of Media Photographers (ASMP), Advertising Photographers of America (APA) and Editorial Photographers (EP). These organizations offer professional photographers everything from group insurance, to continued education and certification programs, to copyright protection legal services, to job banks. Unlike in the television, film and music industries, however, photography associations do not fulfill a strong collective bargaining and fee-setting union role, but rather act as cooperatives that offer support to their members. Many states also have state-level associations for professional photographers.

Similar to the situation in the book publishing industry, where literary agents play a key role in helping launch and manage the careers of writers and novelists, professional photography careers can be launched by signing with a good photography agency. Signing with an agent with a strong industry reputation is often harder than getting your first big photography job. However, it is difficult, if not impossible, for photographers to market themselves as well as a photography agency can.

Landing a commission to work for a major magazine, especially one that is renowned for its photography, is another path to rapid career success. Photo editors are skilled at helping photographers build on their artistic strengths and work on their artistic and technical weaknesses. The close relationship between photographer and photo editor is the hub of success at publications such as *National Geographic* magazine and *Vogue*, and other leading photo-rich magazines around the world.

Video Game Industry

One of the fastest-growing mass media career clusters is in the video game development industry. Teams of professional writers, graphic designers and animators, computer programmers and special effects photographers, typically headed by a lead game designer, collaborate to create a basic creative gaming scheme. This means determining the overall theme, visual "look," main characters and principal playing rules.

Collaboration and Creativity

Designers, artists and programmers on the team work on sections of the game while writers create the game's background story narrative and character dialogues. Video effects artists

16.9

Video gaming is so popular among children, young adults and adults alike that gaming development has become one of the fastest-growing mass media careers.

Gabriel Bouys/Staff

and computer animators, working from drawn storyboards, build the tens of thousands of screen sequences aided by sophisticated computer-generated imagery (CGI) programs. Music composers and performers create the soundtracks while audio engineers marry the music, action/background sounds and character dialogues into seamless, multitrack interactive audio elements. Background artists and 3-D-model makers work to create the game "sets" that videographers then digitally capture, using camera and motion-control techniques pioneered by special effects artists in the film industry.

At the heart of the video game development team are the computer programmers and software engineers who build the programs that make all of the game components work in the virtual digital world. Depending on the complexity of the game and the sophistication of the game's virtual environments and action sequences, video game development can employ multiple teams of dozens of professionals working collaboratively—much like the creative teams and production crews working on feature movies and television programs.

The Career Demographic

Many of these creative team members come to video game development projects with solid academic training in their respective specialties, along with strong portfolios that effectively demonstrate their technical skills and creative talents developed from past projects. The game development industry primarily draws from a talented pool of people who are themselves avid video gamers. Not surprisingly, the demographics of the video game industry consists overwhelmingly of recent college graduates or individuals in their 20s and 30s, plus some older game developers who have worked their way up to lead their development teams. Those working at all levels in the industry experience a great deal of mobility, as either freelancers or salaried staff. As new projects go online, development teams also simultaneously form, dissolve and re-form.

Career Outlook

The U.S. Bureau of Labor Statistics does not yet report separate employment and earnings statistics for the video game industry. Annual surveys by video game industry associations, such as the Entertainment Software Association (ESA), Computer Game Developers Association (CGDA) and the Interactive Digital Software Association (IDSA), have reported that annual salaries for writers, designers and computer artists range from entry-level salaries of $35,000 to $40,000, to salaries of $85,000 or even more than $100,000 for well-established and highly accomplished professionals working in this field. Moreover, the game development trade associations report continued industry growth at a rate of 22 percent per year—and job opportunities continue to grow apace.[3]

Working in video game development means many weeks and months of long hours and intense team-based problem solving. To compensate for the required long hours and stressful working environments, and to help to attract the most talented people, most game development companies offer small royalty shares to their development team members.

> To compensate for the required long hours and stressful working environments, and to help to attract the most talented people, most game development companies offer small royalty shares to their development team members.

A new employment designation is emerging to serve in the converging industries of TV, film and video game development: multimedia artists and animators. According to the *2010 Occupational Outlook Handbook*, the median pay for multimedia artists is $58,510, with the job outlook increasing at a rate of 8 percent through 2020. It is interesting to note that nearly 59 percent of multimedia artists are self-employed freelancers.

As with all the other industries that make up mass media, geography plays a role in finding jobs in this industry. Video game companies tend to locate in and around San Francisco and Los Angeles, Seattle, Austin, Boston, and the Washington, D.C./Baltimore metropolitan area. These centers of development have sprung up adjacent to universities known for their strong undergraduate and graduate programs in the skill areas required. A growing number of major universities, such as the University of California–Irvine, the University of North Texas and Massachusetts Institute of Technology, as well as specialty colleges such as DigiPen Institute of Technology near Seattle, offer entire degree programs in video game development.

Many new graduates enter the industry as interns, which helps them break into the game developer community and further develop their portfolios.[4] ▶

ACHIEVING SUCCESS IN THE MEDIA INDUSTRY

To build a career in mass media, not only do you need the standard college training and degrees, certain personality attributes and a strong work ethic, but you also need to demonstrate your skills and talents through the creation of an effective portfolio, sample reels and Websites. Rogfer Cooper, director of the School of Media Arts and Studies at Ohio University, and Tang Tang, a professor in the Department of TV–Film at the University of Wisconsin, found that, beyond demonstrated talents and technical skills, personality attributes are a big factor in determining career success in mass media.[5] Their study confirmed that traits such as adaptability, reliability, articulateness, persistence, ambition and resourcefulness help ensure career success across all mass media industries—with ambition and resourcefulness being the most important factors.

▶ **Video Game Developer**
The founder of a leading video game company gives a tour of the process of video game development and a glimpse inside what it is really like to work on a video game development team.

Soft Skills, Hard Skills

Cooper and Tang's study demonstrated that although the vast majority of upper division undergraduate mass media majors report that they "intend" to build a career in one of the media professions, only 60 percent of graduates actually do so upon graduation.[6] The 40 percent who do not lack the required personality attributes—that is, the "soft skills" that will drive them to continue acquiring knowledge—and the "hard skills" that enable them to succeed professionally. This study confirms what those working in mass media already know: Successful careers are built on continued training, acquisition of new knowledge and skills and the ability to demonstrate the required talents, work ethic and drive.

Successful careers are built on continued training, acquisition of new knowledge and skills and the ability to demonstrate the required talents, work ethic and drive.

The drive to succeed is, in part, a logical outgrowth of the technological and collaborative convergence trends highlighted throughout this book. Continued convergence makes it especially important for individuals to work effectively across job roles and within multiple technologies.

Job seekers, especially in today's fast-paced mass media world, have the burden of proving that they are not only talented, but also adaptable; logical, yet creative; driven and capable; and independent, yet collaborative.

Making Money on Social Media

There are many ways to generate income through various social media platforms. Here are several tips to keep in mind when you're interested in making money with social media. Because social media is designed to build community by sharing comfort, support, information, expertise, and entertainment, you need to be authentic. Develop your social media "voice" so that it speaks to followers in unique ways. This can include showing your sense of humor, sharing your life challenges and mistakes, and even discussing what's going on in your life. Another tip is when those on social media are having fun, don't interrupt the fun by just talking about yourself, but join them in their fun or create your own fun.

Since the social media world is about paying-it-forward, give away something valuable such as the first chapter of your new book, and if they provide you with feedback, offer to send them a PDF copy of it. Use social media sites that attract your target audience. Twitter may be easier to use and more attractive to some, but if your Facebook is generating more traffic, especially those that will buy from you, then focus on it.

Build trust by delivering what you promise. Failure to meet obligations will affect your bottom line. Engage your target audience by getting them involved in what you are doing. Ask them questions on Facebook, ask for feedback on blog posts, or hold conversations on Facebook's Quora feature.

Build community by responding quickly when your followers post questions or concerns. Because social media is always on, be prepared to respond during evening hours and on weekends. Also, thank visitors that share your content or comment on your posts, and consider ways you can repay the compliment. Give value by focusing on your community, what their thoughts or pains are, how you can help them, while discovering why they are engaged with you.

Take time to plan your strategy, and update your plan as things change. You may want to meet with clients on a monthly basis to review results and plan for future projects. Also, have a contingency plan and respond quickly as things go wrong. Social media marketing tends to be less predictable, so be ready for the response.

And, lastly, use effective metrics to measure, analyze, and respond to your business that helps you focus your efforts in creating content that performs well. This includes listening to both positive and negative comments and answering questions quickly.

The Power of Portfolios

As mentioned throughout this chapter, outstanding portfolios can mean the difference between getting a job and not getting a job. Your portfolio can set you apart as a leading candidate among an eager and competitive pool of applicants.

To build a memorable and effective portfolio, follow these four steps:

1. Identify and collect examples of your best work.
2. Conduct industry research.
3. Organize your work.
4. Consider your portfolio presentation style.

Identify and Collect Examples of Your Best Work

First, get into the habit of identifying and collecting examples of your best work. Start with projects you completed during your undergraduate program. The best examples of your writing, photography, video projects, and computer art or animation projects should become the raw material for your portfolio. It is always important to seek feedback from others; ask them to help you determine which of your work samples most strongly express your talent and abilities. Current and former professors, fellow students and even parents can help you make more critical selections of your work.[7]

Conduct Industry Research

Next, conduct industry research. Which types of samples do potential employers in your desired field expect to see? Expectations evolve with corresponding changes in the industries, so familiarize yourself with market trends as you conduct your research. Use the Internet to find out how established and successful professionals in your field of interest are structuring their portfolios to address these trends. For example, a student wishing to start a career in photojournalism should study not only the Websites operated by potential publications or broadcast employers, but also the many portfolio Websites created by successful photojournalists. Similarly, a writer wishing to start a career in publishing should study the Websites of major and mid-sized publishers, regularly visit the Websites of the leading writers' associations and guilds and study the Websites of successful freelance writers to learn how they are presenting their work to the marketplace.

Organize Your Work

Determine an overall theme and structural style for your portfolio. Your theme will be largely influenced by what you have learned from your research. One of the challenges of portfolio building and maintenance today is that, like all mass media, your portfolio will have to "live" on multiple platforms; you will need to present your portfolio in hard copy during job interviews as well as via the Web. Stand-alone Websites are a good start, but are not enough. In addition, you'll want to create effective short-form "teaser" demonstrations of your work via industry job bank sites, using portfolio-based pages available on social networking sites such as Facebook and LinkedIn or using the portfolio-building pages that might be available on the Websites of professional associations related to your field of interest.[8]

The Internet allows you to construct a "modularized" portfolio from which you can easily select samples of your work and adapt them to fit the requirements of the specific medium in which you are presenting the portfolio: a bound hardcopy, Website, DVD—as well as the potential employer to whom you are delivering it. While developing your portfolio, always emphasize quality over quantity. Employers may spend only a few minutes initially reviewing hundreds of applicant portfolios before narrowing the field of candidates. To be successful, your portfolio has to quickly grab the potential employer's attention. It has to be visually memorable—even if you're pitching your writing abilities—because employers tend to quickly winnow the field of applicants to those few who make the best first impression, then go back and spend more time looking at or reading deeper into the few portfolios that initially interested them.[9]

> While developing your portfolio, always emphasize quality over quantity.

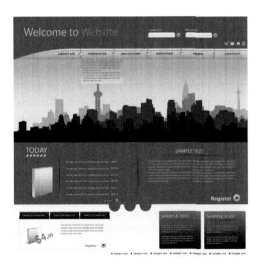

16.10

In this Digital Age, when applying for a position within the mass media industry, a strong portfolio that tells the story of who you are and why a company should want to hire you is key.

Jozsef Bagota/ Shutterstock.com

Consider Your Portfolio Presentation Style

Presentation style and structure are important. It is not just your work samples that will help market you, but also the effective and even innovative way in which you present your samples. Your Website or pages on large networking sites must also express your creativity.

A recent graduate looking for work as a writer, for example, may not have been published yet. Nevertheless, editors will look for the best new writers who present work samples that look as if they have been published. Just scanning in an article you wrote for an advanced journalism course will not make the grade: Instead, you must professionally typeset the article and lay it out in columns so that it looks as if it is an already-published feature in a major magazine or newspaper.

For a new photographer, merely presenting a collection of your best images will not be enough. Instead, you must create and present a visually compelling formal design layout as if your photographs had already been published. Similarly, if you aspire to work in film or television, your sample reel must be carefully edited, paced and accompanied by an archival musical score to look and sound like a trailer for a new movie or TV series.

Like the mass media, portfolios tell a story. Your portfolio is a tool you can use to tell the story of you, in a manner that will make your viewers, readers or potential employers want to know you better.

CONCLUSION: MAKE THE INDUSTRY WANT YOU

Building a career in one of the mass media industries requires a strong drive and a long-term commitment to work in fields that are constantly evolving and highly competitive. Entry-level jobs are commonly low paying and require long hours working in often-intense environments. Meanwhile, careers in mass media commonly involve accepting special challenges such as geographic relocation, frequent travel and lack of long-term job stability. To succeed, recent graduates entering this job market must be able to effectively demonstrate their talents and abilities via strong and creatively presented portfolios as well as through the key personality attributes that mass media industry employers are seeking. Mass media industries are dominated by talented and multiskilled people who, although innovative and independent thinkers, are also effective and collaborative team players.

It is the challenge of the work that makes media careers so fascinating. Success in mass media today requires an ability to adapt quickly to new challenges and differing job roles. This chapter has presented an overview of some of the key issues that undergraduate mass media majors should consider as they prepare for landing their first jobs and launching their careers after graduation. Those who win jobs in mass media will be those who are best at demonstrating their talents and abilities and at telling their stories in a way that makes potential employers want them on their teams.

CHAPTER SUMMARY	KEY TERMS
Employment Trends in Mass Media Employment trends and career paths in various mass media fields are presented with a discussion of what it takes to enter these fields. Visual Media **Newspaper Editor** Loretta Harring, managing editor of the regional newspaper *The Capital*, discusses hiring practices. 1. In the video segment, the managing editor of the newspaper *The Capital* describes her attempts to keep the newspaper relevant and financially viable in the 21st century. *The Capital* is a successful local/regional newspaper. Explain which aspects of the managing editor's approach could be applied to help keep larger print newspapers viable. Which aspects of Ms. Harring's approach would not translate to a larger newspaper, and why?	

TV Sports Anchor
Joe Fonzi, sports reporter and anchor at San Francisco television station
KTVU, gives insights on the job of a sports reporter.

1. In what ways is the job of a TV sports anchor different from a TV news
   anchor? How are they similar?

NPR Radio News Host
Michel Martin, talk-radio host of the NPR news program *Tell Me More*,
discusses selecting news stories to cover.

1. In what ways does the NPR news-talk radio program *Tell Me More*
   differ from such programs on commercial radio networks and/or in radio
   syndication? How do these differences impact the way the news is presented?

Documentary Film Producer, MTV
Cheryl Horner Sirulnick describes the creative and technical processes of
developing documentary projects.

1. The production of successful TV documentaries is a team effort. What
   skills, beyond technical abilities, are required to land and succeed in a production
   team member position? How does one go about acquiring these additional
   nontechnical skills?

Entertainment Public Relations Agent
Marcus Bass of Spelling Communications describes his experiences
working as an entertainment PR professional in Hollywood.

1. How does the daily work of a real-life Hollywood PR agent differ from
   agents as they are depicted in popular TV series and movies?

Radio DJ
Sam Diggedy, radio DJ at KDON in Northern California, describes what
it is like to be a popular Top 40 radio DJ.

1. What are a few of the critical differences between radio DJs of today—
   like Sam Diggedy in this video—with radio DJs from the Golden Age of radio?

Video Game Developer
The founder of a leading video game company explains the process of
video game development and the importance of teamwork.

1. Compare and contrast the video game production process at the small game
   company featured in this video segment with the game development process at
   Firaxis, a far larger game development and production company. (See Chapter 7.)

Survey of Selected Media Industries
Actual job statistics among the major career categories within mass media are provided
and discussed.

Achieving Success in the Media Industry
Explains the difference between "soft" and "hard" skills and discusses the importance of
building a work sample portfolio as a critical aspect of preparing oneself to apply for and
land a position in mass media.

NOTES

1 U.S. Department of Labor, Bureau of Labor Statistics. (n.d.). *Occupational outlook handbook, 2010–
   2011 edition*.
2 Extrapolated from U.S. Department of Labor, Bureau of Labor Statistics.

3 Liming, D., & Dilorio, D. (2011, Fall). Work for play: Careers in video game development. *Occupational Outlook Quarterly*.

4 Crosby, O. (2000, Summer). Working so others can play: Jobs in video game development. *Occupational Outlook Quarterly*.

5 Cooper, R., & Tang, T. (2010, Spring). The attributes for career success in the mass communication industries: A comparison of current and aspiring professionals. *Journalism & Mass Communication Educator, 65*(1), 40–51.

6 Ibid.

7 Gilliam, J. (2010). How to build a professional portfolio. *Helium Jobs & Careers*. Retrieved from www.helium.com/items/185287-how-to-build-a-professional-jobportfolio

8 Hunter, D. (2009). How to make a demo reel. *Media College*. Retrieved from www.mediacollege.com/employment/demo-reel.html

9 Ray, M. (2008). *What makes a good photography portfolio*. Retrieved from www.professionalphotography101.com/photography/portfolios.html

Glossary

33 1/3 rpm long-play disc   a device that made the syndication of full radio programs an affordable alternative for smaller radio stations in the 1930s.

360-degree campaign   a campaign that presents the client's message across a wide range of media platforms, including the Internet, television and radio, print and mobile devices.

acetate blank recording disc   a device onto which radio stations could record on the spot, earning it the name the "instantaneous" record.

acquisition   in film or television, the stage of the media creation process in which a producer acquires the rights to a story.

Action News   Magid's term for an audience-responsive news format; also called *Eyewitness News*.

active media platforms   platforms that allow for the exchange of information between users who share in creating the media content and messages.

actualities   a term coined by the Lumière brothers to describe their 10 short films displaying vaudeville theater acts.

AdSense   a Google advertising program that allows customer content sites to deliver text, images, videos and interactive advertising targeted to specific audiences with the goal of enticing consumers to click on their ad.

advertising   a type of communication that attempts to persuade individuals to take some form of action (buy, believe, consume) toward a product, idea or service.

AdWords   Google's main advertising platform that matches keywords in searches to Google client advertising; payment is based upon a pay-per-click model and accounts for a large share of Google's revenues.

affinity paths   messages and media that attract and focus the receiver's attention through clarity of image and information.

agenda setting   a theory that describes the ability of news media to influence the public agenda—research that demonstrates that the more frequent and prominent the coverage of a given news story, the more importance audiences will give the issue.

agent-based artificial life program   the use of computer modeling to study real-life systems; used in science fields, including physics and biochemistry, where the study of the actual systems is either impractical, very costly or both.

air checks   in radio, recordings of commercials sent back to advertisers to prove airtime purchased.

alternative music   a catch-all label given to the music that does not easily fit into the popular mainstream; also called *independent music*.

amplitude modulation (AM)   the primary broadcast technology used before FM; it offers limited sound range and muddled, static-riddled signals, especially during bad weather.

analog-based terrestrial broadcasts   a communication system in which broadcast signals are transmitted and received via antennas through radio waves.

animatronics   the use of computer-controlled electronics and robotics to give mechanized puppets lifelike movement, facial expressions and, in some cases, voices in real time.

anime   a Japanese film genre based on animation.

antiquity stage   the final stage of innovation during which technologies become obsolete.

antitrust laws   U.S. federal efforts to break up industry monopolies and allow for healthy competition in such as areas as steel, tobacco and oil.

appropriate technologies   the notion that just because innovation enables enhanced communication through mass media, it does not automatically mean that these systems are the best platforms for certain forms of communicating.

appropriation tort   a legal mechanism that protects individuals against identity theft and the use of the information for the benefit of anyone other than the individual who "owns" it.

arena rock bands   prominent fixtures of the 1970s music scene; these music groups rated high on production values and commercialization but low on creativity.

art house theaters   film theaters that specialize in showing foreign and lower-budget independent films; they are located mostly in urban centers.

Articles of Confederation   under the newly founded United States, the first attempt at a national government.

audience broadcasting   a type of media message that seeks the widest reach and the largest number of "eyes" or "ears" for an ad.

audience demographics   factors such as age, sex, race, educational levels, geographic location and psychographics, as well as attitudes, social and cultural values, interests and lifestyles, which content producers and advertisers use to identify exactly who their audience is and what they want.

audience share   the market share of the media audience.

author   any creator of an original work, regardless of the form of the work.

authoritarian system   a system in which the government totally controls all media content and uses the media to spread information to favor the government's authority.

author's rights system   a copyright system based on the French-Napoleonic legal system wherein the value of the created product can never be separated from the original author.

authorship   works that can be perceived, reproduced or otherwise communicated, either directly or with the aid of a machine or device.

avatar   a player's alter ego.

backpack journalism   a journalistic approach in which the individual field journalist performs all the roles of newsgathering, photojournalism and reporting that traditionally have been performed by a team of professionals. It is made possible by advances in digital cameras, portable photo and video editing systems, and Internet-based communications.

backward compatibility   the ability for a new format to work with older technologies.

bandwidths   smaller slices of the crowded range of broadcast frequencies.

Berne Convention   a treaty ratified in 1902 that attempted to reconcile copyright law conflicts and bring much of international copyright law into a cooperative treaty structure.

BGAN satellite terminal   a Hughes Company, satellite-based phone and Internet service that allows full phone and Internet access from anywhere in the world.

bias by selection   deliberately selecting which stories will appear during all points of a nightly news program.

Big Five   the five major film studios (Paramount, Loew's/MGM, Fox Film Corporation, Warner Bros. and RKO) that dominated Hollywood during its Golden Age.

Black Power movement   a subcurrent of the civil rights movement that encouraged Afrocentrism, black autonomy and violent activism.

blacklist   the purposeful denying of privileges to select parties.

block-booking system   a film distribution system that typically bundled five films together: a single high-quality A-film along with four lower-quality A- and B-films.

blockbusters spectacular, huge-budget film productions.

blog a Web log; a Website launched and maintained by individuals who have strong interests in and usually strong views about the topics on which they focus.

blogosphere the interconnected community of blogs.

Blu-ray optical disc an information storage format that offers improved image and audio quality with features unavailable on high-definition digital video discs (HD DVD).

Bollywood the Indian film industry based in Mumbai, which produces more than 1,000 films each year. The Indian equivalent of the Hollywood movie industry.

Book Rights Registry a database that documents the legal status of all works and arbitrates disputes between parties claiming rights to any work in the database.

breaking story a "new" major news story happening in the moment. It requires more airtime and commentary than stories that have been circulating for a while.

broadcasting spreading media content through telecommunications.

broadcasting region the geographic spread of television stations owned by a company.

broadsheets large-format newspapers, typically between 15 and 24 inches.

bylines the inclusion of the author's name with a newspaper article; it helps a newspaper reader to better understand the writer's complex work.

camera obscura an early photographic technique that used a pin-hole light box (camera) to study the behavior of light.

Carl Rowan (1925–2000) a journalist, author and government official. Rowan was one of the first black journalists to work at a major American newspaper, starting his career at the *Minneapolis Tribune* in 1948. In 1961, Rowan was appointed deputy assistant secretary of state by President John F. Kennedy and, in 1964, the director of the U.S. Information Agency (USIA) by President Lyndon Johnson. Rowan later became the first black American to serve on the National Security Council. After his stint in government, Rowan returned to journalism at the *Chicago Sun-Times*.

categorical imperatives Kant's principle that people are obligated to observe certain thoughts and actions, regardless of the outcome, because they are intrinsically right.

CD technology a recording technology that was able to reproduce digital audio with much higher fidelity than previous tape-based systems.

Celler-Kefauver Act (1950) U.S. federal legislation that sought to close loopholes that might result in conglomeration of businesses; also commonly referred to as the Antimerger Act.

censorship the effort to control or ban the flow of information.

Chicago Defender one of the largest and most influential national black-owned and -run newspapers in the history of the black media.

Chinese Exclusion Act of 1882 the first U.S. federal regulation that put curbs on foreign immigration.

citizen journalist a nonprofessional, untrained journalist who writes stories and shares information via the Internet or by submitting stories to mainstream news services such as CNN's "I-Reports" program.

Citizens United the Supreme Court ruling in *Citizens United v. Federal Elections Commission*, 558 U.S. 310 (2010) in which the court held that the First Amendment prohibited the government from limiting independent political expenditures by corporations and unions. This landmark and controversial ruling opened the door to very wealthy corporate partisans investing hundreds of millions of dollars in attempts to influence the outcome of elections at both the state and national levels.

click fraud a service that creates large runs of repetitive automated link clicks to a page, giving a false representation of the number of real-page views.

clickbot a program that runs a click fraud operation.

cliffhanger a suspenseful chapter ending in a serially published novel that encourages readers to purchase the next issue.

closed societies societies that discourage freedom of thought and expression.

cloud; cloud computing   the delivery and use of computing programs, applications and file and data storage capacity as a networked Internet-based service as opposed to programs, files and data being stored on individual users' computers.

code of ethics   a clear statement of guidelines developed to help individuals make ethical decisions.

Code of Federal Regulation   federal legislation that limits the disclosure of nonconviction information.

commercial press   a type of newspaper that reported on trade and business dealings and was paid for by the promotion of products and the sale of advertisements.

commercial radio   advertising-backed radio that helped to increase radio's financial base and spurred a rapid improvement in both the quality and quantity of programming.

commercial satellite radio   a radio technology developed in the early 2000s to capitalize on the desire of U.S. listeners for greater diversity in radio programming.

Committee on Public Information   a U.S. government committee headed by George Creel; it exercised a significant amount of control over Americans' perception of World War I and standardized war coverage across the vast array of publications in the United States.

Committee to Protect Journalists   an independent, nonprofit organization founded in 1981 to promote worldwide freedom of the press by defending and protecting the rights of journalists to report the news without fear of imprisonment or punishment.

Communications Act of 1934   federal legislation that empowered the FCC to regulate communication media, including radio and television (both cable and satellite).

compact disc (CD)   a recorded music medium that is the product of a cooperative partnership formed in about 1981 between Philips, which had acquired access to Laserdisc designs from MCA, and Sony.

Compatible Time-Sharing System (CTSS)   a system that allowed users of IBM mainframe computers remote access as well as the ability to leave messages for other users.

composite   a clever fusing of two separate photographs.

console   a computer system designed for interactive entertainment.

Constitutional Convention   also known as the Philadelphia Convention; a convention during which the delegates discussed core tenets of the proposed U.S. Constitution.

Consumerism   a system that creates and encourages the purchase of goods and/or services in increasing amounts.

contempt of court   an offense in which the offending reporter can be fined or jailed for ignoring a court order.

content coding   a technique used by researchers to analyze specific content delivered in the mass media so as to enable the scientific study of that content's effect on audiences.

content mobility   also known as three-screen convergence; an approach that supports relatively seamless transferring of video content between digital television, personal computers and mobile devices.

content sharing   the exchange of intellectual property among users over the Web.

contingency planning   a form of PR that develops action plans to address problems that are likely to confront organizations in the future; it includes crisis management.

convergence of content and businesses   a movement that is forcing the reinvention of business models and in some cases threatening the very existence of traditional forms of media.

copyright   a means of protecting the intellectual properties and the rights of individual creators and owners.

copyright infringement   unlawful use of another's intellectual property; also known as copyright piracy.

Copyright Law of the United States   federal legislation enacted by Congress in Title 17 of the U.S. Code in 1976 that defines authorship.

copyright legal tradition   in the United States and Britain, the view that intellectual creations are another form of "property" that can be bought and sold, licensed, transferred and inherited.

copyright piracy   see copyright infringement.

Corporation for Public Broadcasting (CPB)   the U.S. federal government's conduit for passing taxpayer funding into the public broadcasting system through station and programming grants.

covers   songs and tunes performed by artists other than the original.

crisis communications   a form of PR communication meant to stimulate interest in a product after a product line has been developed or to reform the image of a company in the wake of an emergency.

crónica   a popular genre and early staple of the Latino immigrant press that provided readers with satirical commentary on current events, issues and trends, often through fictional characters and stories.

crosscutting   an editing technique that establishes action taking place in multiple locations.

cross-genre films   films that are considered to fall within more than one category.

cross-platform   also known as multiplatform; a term used to describe video gaming devices that also support Blu-ray HD movies.

cultivation effect   a theory drawn from research on the long-term effects of television viewing that states that the more time people spend projecting themselves into the worlds they see on television, the more likely they are to believe that the social realities portrayed are "real," even if what they are viewing is in fact fictitious.

cultural aesthetics   what is considered "in good taste" within a specific cultural context.

cultural context   the social, religious and political rules that govern how people are expected to behave and respond toward one another.

cultural convergence   the breaking down of the demarcations between cultural contexts.

cultural hegemony   in a media context, typically the nation that controls or dominates the media throughout the world.

cultural imperialism   the spread of a culture into the society of another, generally without that society's consent.

culture   the integrated and dynamic social system of behaviors, characteristics, customs, language, artifacts and symbols that distinguish one social group from another.

customized ad viewing   a service that allows users to select which ads they will watch and when they will watch them while online.

daguerreotype process   a photographic process invented by Lois Daguerre; it involves the use of silver-coated copper plates, with images being developed by combining silver iodide and warmed mercury.

dangerous news   according to the Committee on Public Information, news that might contain information about military movements or possible threats against the president.

dark money   contributions to political campaigns from undisclosed hidden sources—to unduly influence American elections.

Daughters of Bilitis   the first major lesbian rights organization in the United States.

dead air   media downtime, during which no new news or information is being aired or released.

Declaration of Principles   Ivy Ledbetter Lee's foundational work that presented the first set of ethical standards for public relations.

defamation   any form of implied or explicit communication that damages a person's, organization's or product's reputation or standing in the community.

defamation with malice   deliberate wrongful action with the intention of harming another person.

demographic studies   studies that examine basic human characteristics, such as individuals' age, gender, race and income.

Designated Market Areas (DMAs)   210 U.S. TV markets used in establishing audience ratings.

development   in film or television, the stage of the media creation process in which the screenplay and characters are shaped, a story's background and potential shoot locations are researched, and production budget details are built.

Digital Divide   the gap that separates those who have financial and physical access to information technologies and those who do not.

Digital Divide 2.0   advances in technology and lower manufacturing costs that have yet to reach the poor and other disadvantaged subgroups of certain regions in the world.

digital immigrants generations transitioning into the Digital Age.

Digital Millennium Copyright Act (DMCA) in 1998, federal legislation that altered U.S. copyright law to criminalize the production and distribution of technology, devices and services whose intent was to bypass measures that controlled access to copyrighted works.

digital natives a term coined by Harvard professor John Palfrey that refers to the first generation to grow up in a world where digital technologies and the Internet were already in place.

digital subscription model a content-on-demand model that delivers digital content to users whenever and wherever they seek it.

dime novel mass-produced novel that cost 10 cents and was intended to accommodate customers of the rapidly expanding railroad system.

direct media revenue revenue from selling media products and content directly to the consumer.

direct-to-home distribution a film distribution system in which film catalogs are offered by services such as Netflix and streamed over the Internet.

distribution stage in film and TV, the stage of the media creation process in which the final project is released to theaters or premieres in the lead television network's programming schedule.

documentary photographer see *photojournalist*.

dramas television programs that generally hold the prime-time slots; they include everything from mysteries and action/adventures to political and crime thrillers.

dynamic adaptive learning self-directed selection of knowledge nodes and self-structured organization to increase one's ability to absorb and use new information.

e-books digital books whose features include the ability to store hundreds of titles on a single device, the ability to change font sizes, send e-mail and access the Internet.

economies of scale the ability to increase cost advantages by increasing production levels and sometimes expanding the business.

Editorial Advisory Board an oversight organization developed by DC Comics during World War II to ensure that all comic books met accepted standards for morality.

editorial process the phase of the publishing process during which draft stories are read and corrected (sometimes cut down or refocused) by editors.

editorial to publication cycle the amount of time it takes for a news story to be researched, written and published in a traditional newspaper.

editorializing expressing an opinion as if it were objective fact or an opinion about an otherwise objective account.

elaboration likelihood model a theoretical model of how attitudes and beliefs are formed, and how they might change, by the levels at which audiences use logical analysis against their preexisting attitudes and beliefs.

Electronic Frontier Foundation a nonprofit advocacy group made up of lawyers, policy analysts and activists working on behalf of media consumers.

electronic mail; e-mail originally a digital networked-based system for sending and receiving text-only messages, which has since evolved to accommodate images, video and audio.

electronic media integrated circuits, computers, the World Wide Web and the ubiquitous cyberspace.

embedded journalism a type of journalism in which reporters and photojournalists report from within the trenches or with the people about whom they are reporting.

ensemble cast a cast that includes many lead characters.

episodic television drama a dramatic television series consisting of 13 hours spread over 13 weeks.

equivalence Alfred Stieglitz's term that identifies photographs as visual metaphors built around their ability to elicit emotional reactions in the viewer.

Espionage Act federal legislation enacted under President Woodrow Wilson, which made it a federal crime to publish anything that "attempted to cause insubordination, disloyalty, mutiny, or refusal of duty in the U.S. Armed Forces."

exhibition license   a license that specifies when and where theaters will show a film.

Eyewitness News   see Action News.

Fair Use Doctrine   the category of copyright law covering certain cases of limited lawful use without license or release.

Fairness Doctrine   also known as the equal time law; a requirement that radio stations provide free airtime for all opposing views regardless of position or economic resources.

feature filmmaking   a type of film production in which films are made for theatrical distribution.

Federal Communication Commission (FCC)   a U.S. government agency that is empowered by the federal government to regulate the licensing and use of the broadcast spectrum of media by all nongovernmental organizations, companies or individuals.

Federal Radio Commission (FRC)   a federal agency that was the predecessor of today's Federal Communications Commission.

fiduciary responsibility   the legal requirement of all members of the board of directors for a company to make their best efforts to manage the firm and protect the interests of all shareholders.

File Transfer Protocol (FTP)   a standard set of procedures used for exchanging and manipulating files across a network of computers.

film distributors   members of the film industry who focus on getting as many movies shown on as many screens in as many theaters as possible.

film noir   "black film"; films that are typically cynical and menacing in tone and physically characterized by black-and-white visuals, low-key lighting and urban settings.

financial PR   PR that accurately and persuasively communicates events in the business world to other institutions as well as to consumers.

financing-distribution model   a film production business model that relies on outside financing to create a film.

Five W's (and one H) of journalism   the who, what, when, where, why and how of a news story.

folk music   a music genre characterized by untrained musicians whose compositions are passed down via oral tradition.

folk rock   folk music characterized by a harder, more electric sound.

format wars   a war between companies attempting to establish and promote integration of a leading technology.

Founding Fathers   the group who wrote the fundamental doctrines of freedom of speech and freedom of the press into the U.S. Constitution.

Four formats   commercial radio programming styles that use AAA (adult album alternative) music, news-talk, classical and urban music.

Fourdrinier machine   technology that made paper from raw materials much more quickly than previous machines.

Fourth Estate   a term credited to Scottish essayist Thomas Carlyle (1759–1881). It refers to the free press, which is deemed responsible for checking the balance of power of the other three estates: the executive, legislative and judicial branches.

Freedom of Information Act (FOIA)   federal legislation that opens government records that were previously closed to public scrutiny.

Freedom's Journal   the first black publication in the United States; it was founded in 1827 by two freemen living in New York.

French New Wave   a film genre created by young independent directors who drew their inspiration from art, literature and documentary films. The resulting films focused on complex character relationships, sexual passions and religious turmoil.

frequency modulation (FM)   the standard for quality radio broadcasting that replaced AM and would remain unchallenged until the advent of digital radio.

fundraising   PR that helps to facilitate capital drive campaigns, whether through organizational training or actual implementation.

future shock   a term coined by Alvin Toffler to describe an individual's personal perception of "too much change in too short a period of time"; Toffler extended the view that the majority of social problems are basically symptoms of future shock.

gag order   a restrictive judicial order that commands all the participants in a trial to have no contact with the news media.

gangsta rap   a musical form that offered a pessimistic, rage-saturated perspective on life.

Gay and Lesbian Alliance Against Defamation (GLAAD)   an advocacy group founded in New York City in 1985, initially to counter inaccuracies and fear-mongering about the AIDS epidemic in the mass media.

gay rights movement   a movement that sought to protect the civil rights of gays and lesbians as well as put an end to the criminalization of homosexuality.

genres   film types.

German expressionism   a film genre focusing on the dark side of the human experience, revolving around themes of madness, insanity and betrayal.

glasnost   Mikhail Gorbachev's policy of "openness" that loosened information control and made all government activities more transparent to the people of the Soviet Bloc.

global village   Marshall McLuhan's belief that as mass-media technologies evolve, enhanced cultural exchange will become more widely possible.

Godey's Lady's Book   one of the first American magazines that catered exclusively to female readers.

Golden Age   a period in which Hollywood filmmaking was dominated by the Big Five movie studios and that gave birth to talkies.

golden mean   according to Aristotle, in ethics, the balance between possible extremes.

golden rule   an ethical principle first practiced by Christians: "Do to others what you would want them to do to you."

Gore Bill   U.S. federal legislation (named for its author, Senator Al Gore) that continued funding for the establishment of regional hosting hubs and their related infrastructure and lifted the last barriers to full and open access for everyone to the Internet.

gossip column   a forum for entertainment-oriented news established by Walter Winchell; popular in tabloid journalism.

gramophone   the predecessor to the record player; the first technology to offer consumers interchangeable recording media in the form of a hard plastic disc as opposed to the cylinders of Edison's and Bell's inventions.

graphic novel   an expansion of the comic book genre that summarizes an entire story with a beginning, middle and end and often delves into subject matters and themes of a more mature nature.

Great Migration   the migration of approximately 1.3 million blacks to the North from the South between 1916 and 1930.

"greatest-happiness principle"   John Stuart Mill's ethical system that states the right course of action is the one that leads to the greatest happiness for the greatest number of people, within certain reason.

grunge   a musical subgenre characterized by distorted guitars, raw sound and lyrics reminiscent of punk rock.

hard rock   a style of music, made possible by improvements in stage production technologies, characterized by an amplified and distorted electric sound.

hate radio   the use of airwaves to broadcast ethnic propaganda, usually to incite violence.

Hays Code   the strict and censorious film ratings system established in the United States in 1922 by William H. Hays.

HD (digital) radio   satellite-based radio that offers consumers more program stations and choices than traditional radio.

heavy metal a style of music characterized by harsh instrumentals, outrageous costuming and often-violent lyrics.

hierarchy of human needs according to Maslow, a hierarchy beginning with basic physiological needs, which then moves through safety, love and esteem to self-actualization.

High Performance Computing and Communications Act of 1991 "The Gore Bill," which allocated $600 million for the creation of the National Research and Education Network (NREN) and served as the foundation for the "information superhighway."

high-context cultures societies wherein both the producers and the consumers (the audience) of media content (the actual words, images and stories) heavily depend on a shared understanding of the context within which that media content is presented.

high-definition digital video discs (HD DVD) a backward-compatible information storage format that offers higher-resolution video and audio quality as well as increased storage capacity over traditional DVDs.

high-fidelity premium record a record containing sound produced at advanced levels.

hip-hop a live break-beats form so named for its "hip" ("current") rhythmic tempo.

Hollywood studio system the handful of movie studios that virtually ruled the entire film industry in the first half of the 20th century, controlling everything from screenwriters' and actors' contracts to the ownership of movie theaters.

HTML Hypertext Markup Language; a relatively simple programming language that allows Web developers to specify how a document will appear when accessed by a wide variety of Internet browser programs.

HTTP Hypertext Transfer Protocol; a collection of communication and software standards that allows many different kinds of computers to communicate with each other over the Web.

hub-and-nodes distribution model a conceptual model used to illustrate how multiple related links can work together to achieve a common goal for mass benefit.

Hutchins Commission a U.S. government commission formed at the request of Henry Luce to investigate whether the press was functioning in society as the nation's Founding Fathers had intended.

hybrid films films that mix stylistic components often rooted in other media.

hyperlinks references or sources that can be accessed by clicking on a link.

hyperlocal journalism news and information publishing, usually via the Web, that is specifically oriented toward relatively small well-defined audiences either within a geographical location or special interest group, or both.

iconic images visual representations that are commonly encountered in the larger visual language of mass media.

image consulting grooming a client's image in ways that promote positive public perceptions of the client.

immersive virtual reality (IVR) the purist form of virtual reality, which combines sophisticated interactive appliances with realistic computer-generated environments, thereby engaging most of the human senses.

independent music also known as indie music; see *alternative music*.

indies independent movies.

indirect media revenue revenue primarily received from advertisers and advertising-related sales such as product placements.

Industrial Revolution a period of advancements in agriculture, manufacturing, mining and transportation that spanned the 18th and 19th centuries.

information filtering the weeding out of what one deems unwanted or irrelevant information; when practiced by a government, the goal is to keep people in the dark and to maintain the government's power over them.

information overload   the burgeoning quantity of information, along with the escalating number of mass-media channels and content that we face most days.

inoculation theory   a social psychology theory that attempts to explain how people's attitudes and beliefs change, or resist changing, in the face of persuasion, especially through the mass media.

integrated circuit (IC)   a miniaturized electronic circuit that forms the basic electronic building blocks of all electronic equipment, from computers to MP3 players to the digital control boards in cars.

intellectual properties   original works of creators and owners.

international intellectual property rights (IPR)   international laws that enforce copyright.

international media co-production treaties   agreements established by countries in an effort to respond to the economic challenges facing their respective native media production companies.

Internet   interconnecting networks that allowed university newsgroup communities (CSNET and BITNET) to communicate via a then-new file transfer protocol called e-mail.

Internet backbone   the network infrastructure of the Internet.

Internet browser   an application whose software allows information on the World Wide Web to be viewed, retrieved and moved.

"Internet haven"   a country that makes no effort at copyright enforcement.

Internet radio   the migration of traditional radio content to the Web.

inverted pyramid   reporting structure wherein the most important facts are presented in the lead sentences, followed by more elaborate details that support those facts.

I-Reports   a program developed by CNN in which news segments are generated by users and posted on the Internet; it includes blogs and video.

Italian neorealism   a film style characterized by nonprofessional actors in storylines about the poor and working class.

Jacob Riis   one of the first photojournalism practitioners. Riis was most well known for his images of tenement life among the immigrant populations of New York City's Lower East Side.

jazz   a musical genre that combined African-infused rhythms and instrumentation with a heavy dose of improvisation.

Jim Crow era   (1867–1965) the period that deemed blacks "separate but equal," in effect formalizing segregation in the United States for nearly a century.

journalistic ethics   the set of ethical responsibilities expected of the journalist when reporting on and writing about a story.

kaiju   Japanese monster films.

KDKA   the first licensed commercial broadcast station based in Pittsburgh, Pennsylvania, which made its debut on November 2, 1920.

Kerner Commission   a commission established by President Lyndon B. Johnson to investigate the increase in race-related violence in the United States.

kinetoscope   W. L. K. Dickson's viewing device for moving pictures.

knowledge industry   an industry rooted in the relationship between the media and business that enabled fairly unrestricted access to an ever-widening range of information and knowledge.

Latino native press   press that focused on securing the rights and voice of Latinos as guaranteed under the U.S. Constitution.

legal jurisdiction   a geographical area over which law can be applied.

libel   written defamation.

libertarian-based system   a mass-media model built on a commitment to present all views and cultural tastes of the audience.

life-blogging   the act of sharing the minutia of one's daily life with a circle of online "friends" in a very public forum.

lithography   a printing technology in which only the image to be printed requires ink; ink is not applied anywhere else on the plate.

lobbying   PR that focuses on communicating the interests, concerns and issues pertinent to particular individuals and organizations to local, state and national legislatures.

long-tail advertising   Internet-ad placement services.

long-tail journalism   a model drawn from economics to illustrate high-volume sales of small, specialty products via nonlimiting media and higher user activity (e.g., the Internet).

low-context cultures   societies in which the media that are produced and consumed are generally straightforward.

Madison-meets-Vine   the growth of product integration in television programs and movies.

magazinists   authors who specifically wrote content for magazines.

mainframe computers   large data processing systems with massive storage capacities.

manga   "whimsical pictures"; a form of Japanese art that has become an enormously popular subgenre of comics published in the United States.

manifest destiny   the belief that the nation was destined to expand.

manufacturing consent   a term coined by Noam Chomsky to describe how media can be used to set the public agenda.

market model   also known as the American-style media business model; a model in which the majority of media are funded through a combination of advertising revenue and subscription fees.

mass media   the communication platforms that enable the exchange of information and meanings (content) between individuals and groups.

mass media conglomerate   a single entity that owns the majority of the media industries.

mass media framing   when the media, particularly the news media, presents stories and issues to fit the "reality" that it wants the public—the receivers—to accept.

mass media networks   systems designed to communicate messages to a large number of people rapidly and simultaneously.

mass media systems   tightly overlapping networks of media resources.

massively multiplayer online role-playing game (MMORPG)   the genre of role-playing video games hosted on Websites that enable very large numbers of players to interact with each other in real time within the virtual reality environments of the game.

mass media platform   the entire gamut of technology-based communication media, from the telephone through sophisticated Internet technology.

Mattachine Society   the first national homosexual rights organization in the United States, founded in 1950.

matte shots   a filmmaking technique in which a large painting of an environment, including all elements from trees and roads to buildings, is installed as a background to a film.

maturity stage   the fourth stage of innovation, during which one particular mass media technology emerges as the clear winner, dominating the world market.

McCarthyism   a period during which scores of Americans in academia and especially the entertainment industry and government were unfairly accused of being communists and traitors.

media asset value   a value based on all the media properties produced and/or owned by a company in a given year, compared to the total costs of creation or acquisition.

media bias   the intentional or unintentional slanting of news reporting toward one side due to the political views or cultural beliefs of journalists, producers or owners of a media outlet.

media convergence   the phenomenon whereby mass media technologies—such as computers, radio, television, telephone and magazines—move closer and closer to becoming fewer and fewer interconnected platforms that, given the anticipated continuation of the trend, will eventually become a single system.

media dynamics   a perspective for studying mass media, referring to all the various processes and influences that go into shaping mass media content.

media effects   also known as media influence; ideas and theories about how mass media influence people as individuals, as families, as communities, as nations.

media ethics   principles that help individuals and cultures understand responsible behavior and actions in media.

media hegemony   dominance of the media by a particular group.

media law   law that regulates radio and television broadcasting to ensure that the content is in the interest of the public.

media literacy   a term commonly used to describe the identification, study and analysis of all the processes involved in creating and consuming media content across all media types and platforms.

media monopoly   a market model in which the production and distribution of a specific media industry is dominated by a single group.

media space   the multidimensional electronic environment whose center is everywhere at once, and whose boundaries are nonexistent.

mediated communication   the exchange of ideas and information quickly, effectively and across geographical and cultural barriers through technology.

mediated news content   news content that has been selected and reviewed by a professional news editor and to which editorial oversight has been applied in an effort to assure that the story is factual, focused and appropriately presented.

meme   a contagious idea. An element of culture, often an image or video clip that is passed from person to person, quickly becoming a shared experience of tens of thousands or even millions of people.

message   mass media content delivered to broad audiences via specific mass media networks.

México de afuera   ("Mexico outside") ideology that sought not only to protect Latino-Americans against the perceived loss of the Spanish language, but also to maintain the Mexican culture's close links to the Catholic Church.

microblogging   a much-abbreviated form of blogging, such as Twitter.

Miller test   a set of criteria used to determine obscenity-versus-freedom-of-speech cases.

mise-en-scène   a French term meaning "placing on stage"; everything set before a camera.

modem   a device that connects computers via telephone lines.

monomyth   according to Joseph Campbell, the story of the "hero's journey."

Moore's law   Gordon Moore's prediction that in our age of integrated circuits and computers, technology will follow a pattern of accelerating innovation.

morning zoo format   a lifestyle talk-show formula that employs sparse music playlists, zany staged stunts and running pop culture commentary.

Morse code   a character-encoding system that transmitted information via sound and visual signaling (dots and dashes) when sequenced in a particular way, representing specific letters and numbers created by Samuel Morse.

motion control   a filming process in which cameras move along specially constructed tracks and that allows for repeated shooting of scenes from various angles.

Motion Picture Patents Company (MPPC)   the brainchild of Thomas Edison, a cooperative group that allowed companies to pool resources and demand licensing fees from film producers, distributors and exhibitors outside their group.

motion picture technology   patented by Edison in 1888, perforated film that traveled from a sprocketed reel across a revolving shutter in front of a strong continuous light source.

Motion Pictures Ratings System of 1968   a film-rating system established in the United States that allowed studios to test the waters with more controversial content.

moving picture   the projection emitted through the photo-covered glass wheel of Muybridge's zoopraxiscope; as the hand crank is turned and each image is quickly projected from the glass wheel onto a screen, it appears as though the subject in the photo is moving.

muckrakers   reporters who attempted to educate America's middle class by writing serious pieces that exposed the relationships between the business world and the government, laying bare the rampant corruption and abuse of power by elected officials.

multimedia journalist   a reporting professional who has skills in many aspects of the media and is able to operate comfortably, creating stories that run on different media outlets at the same time—for example, in a newspaper's print and Internet editions as well as on an associated radio or TV news program.

multiple-source confirmation   the requirement that reporters confirm the facts in a story with at least three sources to help assure the reliability and credibility of those facts.

multitrack recording   magnetized tape-recorder technology that can simultaneously record multiple instruments and vocal tracks as one single, layered and cohesive whole.

music video   the synthesis of music and video that enabled television to take over quickly as the most popular way of promoting artists.

narrowcasting   a type of media message that encompasses narrowly directed messages to smaller, more clearly defined audience segments.

negligent libel   a situation in which defamation of or damage to the plaintiff occurs, but is unintended.

Net Roots Movement   the use of blogs as a form of political activism.

Netscape Navigator   the first Internet browser made widely available to the public.

network neutrality   the view that everyone should have equal access to all online content at equal speeds.

new journalism   the combination of convergent multiple news platforms, immediate audience feedback and criticism and required proficiency in multimedia technologies.

new media   the term encompassing all digital, interactive and converged media on the Internet.

new media model   the Internet media business model wherein media creators rely on the Web to reach and sell to their audiences directly.

news aggregator site   a Web-based site that does not produce its own stories or perform its own journalism, but instead compiles and presents news stories from other news sources.

news bulletin   a short news piece that avoids the longer, narrative style of traditional articles.

news magazines   a hybrid of the traditional newspaper and the quality magazine.

news spin   U.S. government influence over media content through regulation.

news syndicates   service cooperatives that allow member news organizations to share stories and resources.

Newspaper Preservation Act   federal legislation stating that for newspapers to participate in a joint-operating agreement (JOA), one of the papers had to demonstrate proof of financial trouble.

Newspaper Publicity Act of 1912   an act of federal legislation that made it mandatory for newspaper companies to disclose publication ownership and to label clearly advertisements that might be confused with news or editorial content.

newsreels   short film montages that featured brief, often sensationalized coverage of national and world events.

niche audiences   narrowly defined, highly targeted audiences.

Nickel-in-the-Slot   Louis Glass's predecessor to the jukebox; it started out playing only one short song yet sparked the coin-operated entertainment machine craze.

nickelodeons   theaters that charged 5 cents for admission.

Nielsen ratings   a measurement system that identifies television audience size and composition and provides programmers with daily and hourly snapshots of the viewing audience.

Noam Chomsky   a longtime MIT professor of linguistics and renowned futurist philosopher and cultural critic.

nodes   linked lists and tree data structures on the Web.

noise   the cacophony of messages that demand our attention and response.

nongovernmental organizations (NGOs)   groups created by nonparticipating and nonrepresentative individuals of a ruling administration or regime.

novel   long-form fiction. In their early incarnations, novels were often broken down into episodes for publication over several issues.

objectification   the reduction of peoples and cultures to mere objects.

obscenity   any behavior considered lewd, offensive or indecent.

obscenity laws   laws that prohibit behavior deemed by a culture to be socially unacceptable.

online social networking   digital environments that allow individuals to create public profiles for multiple forms of community interactions via the Internet.

op-ed page   in newspapers, the section comprising opinions and editorial views.

open society   a society, such as a democracy, that allows significant opportunities for the media to monitor and report on the operation of its government, in effect "opening" its actions to public scrutiny.

open-source model   an approach to content production and management that permits easy, widespread access to information.

Operation Wetback   the effort by the Dwight D. Eisenhower administration in 1954 to deport 3 million undocumented immigrants living in the Southwest back across the border to Mexico.

paid search optimization   the practice of increasing site traffic via Internet advertising.

pan-cultural systems   systems that extend beyond the physical borders of a cultural region.

participatory democracy   a system that permits and encourages a greater number of people to participate in the larger political process.

participatory virtual reality (PVR)   new media technologies accessed online or via digital storage devices that enable users to move through, explore and interact with computer-generated environments.

partisan bias   according to John Street, bias that occurs when a cause is deliberately promoted in the media.

partisan press   publishers that served as the media voice of American political parties and other groups with political or ideological agendas.

passive media platforms   platforms that allow for little or no direct input into the content from the user, such as when we watch a movie or television program.

payola   the practice of paying bribes to radio disc jockeys (DJs) and station owners to control which records would receive airplay over the radio.

pay-per-view   "pay as you view."

peer-to-peer (P2P)   user networks such as Napster and BitTorrent, where the content is not only shared between peers, but supplied and purchased by them as well.

penny press   newspapers that cost just one penny; they catered to a growing literate audience more interested in entertainment and knowledge than in politics or ideology.

phonograph   a sound recorder that recorded sound as notches on a tinfoil-wrapped cylinder the size of a cardboard roll of toilet tissue.

photojournalist   a reporter who uses images (primarily still images but also videography) to report on news and stories.

player progression   a characteristic of video games that focuses on the development of each player's game skills.

podcast   media content produced and released especially for the Web and Web-enabled portable devices.

political bloggers   commentators who frequently see themselves as a counterforce to mainstream media and are upfront about their biases.

political consulting   PR that advises politicians on how to best engage their constituencies.

POP   Post Office Protocol; an application used for receiving e-mail.

popular music   music that broadly encompasses all nonclassical music styles.

pornography   any form of media that depicts sexual behavior for the purposes of arousing an audience.

Postal Act of 1792   federal legislation that enabled newspapers to be sent within 100 miles of their publishing location at a cost of one cent per copy; everything outside this 100-mile range cost one and a half cents.

postproduction stage   in film and TV, the stage of the media creation process in which all of the material that has been shot is edited into a linear story.

"Potter's Box"   Ralph Potter's four-step system for ethical decision-making.

preproduction stage   the stage in the production process of media projects—TV programs, films, video games, etc.—that encompasses writing and development and all logistical planning that occurs prior to the onset of actual production.

printmaking   a printing technique refined by Gutenberg in which metal or wooden letters were placed in wooden frames, covered with oil-based ink and pressed onto paper with a large hand-cranked press.

print-on-demand   a printing process wherein a new copy of a book or other printed resource is not printed until an order for the text has been received.

printing press   Gutenberg's invention that revolutionized printing and gave birth to modern mass media.

prior restraint   a legal maneuver in which the government tries to stop someone from publishing or airing a story that it fears will damage it.

privacy   "the expectation that confidential personal information . . . will not be disclosed to third parties."

proactive PR   a type of PR that engages with the public and seeks to demonstrate good will.

product affinity   acceptance of a product's message or brand for the purposes of building a strong emotional relationship with it.

product placement   a highly effective way of creating audience affinity with a product or message without direct commercial advertising; also referred to as *product integration*.

product tie-ins   T-shirts, books, toys, and other items linked to a media project.

production financing stage   in film and TV, the point in the media creation process at which the producer lines up the lion's share of the funding for the project.

production stage   in film or TV, the stage of the media creation process in which all the story scenes are filmed (or shot in high-definition video) in a nonlinear sequence; also known as the principal photography stage.

propaganda   a type of communication that concentrates on persuading clients to support a very specific issue, such as a cause or a social movement, and most commonly a government's decision to go to war.

propaganda bias   according to John Street, bias that occurs when a story is reported with a deliberate intention of making the case for a particular party, policy or point of view.

proximity   McLuhan's theory of minimizing distance via digital media.

psychedelic sound   a musical style that experiments with multitrack technology and non-Western musical styles; produced with the aid of psychedelic drugs, which many musicians believed enhanced their creative abilities and artistic expression.

psychographic studies   studies that look at individuals' lifestyles, values, attitudes and personalities.

psychographics   the identification of audiences by geographic region, age group, gender, income levels, educational levels, race or ethnicity, social class and lifestyle.

public agenda   the list of policy issues that affect the people of a town, a city or a nation.

Public Broadcasting Service (PBS)   the United States' noncommercial educational broadcasting service, which is modeled after the BBC in the United Kingdom.

public figure   an individual who has chosen to place himself or herself in the public arena and benefits from the media exposure.

public opinion research   the study of statistically valid samplings of individual attitudes and beliefs, including their complex interconnections, commonly conducted by public opinion polling organizations, and the analysis of the results of such studies in an effort to predict future public behaviors, such as viewing a particular television show, voting for a specific candidate or purchasing a certain product.

public relations (PR)   an industry that focuses on building and managing clients' brands and perceptions.

public relations polling   an important means of acquiring data for companies and other branches of PR to help inform their approaches to cultivating public opinion.

public service announcements (PSAs)   noncommercial and presumably nonpolitical advertising.

public sphere model   a model in which media serve as the central environment or "space" in which ideas and views circulate in the form of information sharing and storytelling.

Pulitzer Prize   named after Joseph Pulitzer, an award given to the most highly recognized professionals in journalism and letters, drama and music.

Pullman porters   black men hired during the late 19th and early 20th centuries to service the Pullman trains, but who also smuggled black newspapers into Southern black communities.

pulp magazines   inexpensive fiction magazines printed on cheap wood pulp paper published between the early 1890s and the early 1950s.

punch cards   an early analog "memory" system.

questing   a characteristic of a video game that spans across a particular place or geographical area.

questionable news   according to the Committee on Public Information, rumors of U.S. activity at home or abroad and reports of technological advancements that could be appropriated by America's enemies during World War I.

Quora   Facebook's feature that allows users to update their status by putting up photos allowing friends to see what is going on in their daily lives.

race music   predecessor to rhythm and blues; music that catered to racial stereotypes.

Radio Act of 1927   federally enacted radio broadcast regulations that favored the networks and nearly drove small radio stations into extinction.

radio broadcasting   the unrestricted transmission of a radio signal to numerous receivers.

ragtime   a musical style that blended Tin Pan Alley standards with syncopation (a rhythmic arrangement in which the stress falls on a beat that would normally not receive it) and American plantation folk music.

rap   a musical genre built around improvisational spoken-word poetry.

Rashomon effect   the effect of the subjectivity of perception on our memories that accounts for why different observers of the same event often report strikingly different and equally plausible accounts.

ratchet reality TV   reality television programs that feature black and other minority women in unflattering, often stereotypical characterizations.

reactive PR   PR that attempts to rescue companies when crises occur.

read–write media culture   culture wherein media content producers supply the creative, entertainment and journalistic components to consumers via technologies that enable each person to be his or her own news editor or entertainment programmer.

reality television   low-budget television productions built around real people placed in unusual situations.

Reconstruction (1865–1877)   the period during which all freed slaves were granted federally protected civil rights, followed by the early Jim Crow era.

release   a written authorization that allows someone else to access and use your name, likeness and private information for commercial purposes.

remote news van   a self-contained television news field production unit (usually built into a small- to medium-size van) that includes cameras, lights, audio equipment video postproduction equipment and the ability to uplink live or recently recorded reports to its home station via satellite and microwave links.

return on investment (ROI)   financial term for when a company can economically produce high-valued media assets and higher revenues through the efficient use of its production resources.

rhetoric   the art of discourse, either written or oral, that attempts to inform, persuade or motivate the reader, listener or viewer. Rhetoric is also the term for the traditional academic study of social and civic discourse.

rhythm and blues (R&B)   the melting pot of the black American music scene of the 1940s and 1950s that included jazz, blues and gospel music.

rock 'n' roll   slang term for "sex," originating from blues music; may be traced back to a form of urban black music known as "rhythm and blues" (R&B).

routine news   according to the Committee on Public Information, general-interest news that could be printed without authorization during World War I.

Rule of Three   targeted audience capture = increased revenues from sales and/or advertising = content control.

Samurai cinema   Japanese warrior films.

satellite uplink boom   a retractable satellite or microwave-transmitting antenna built into a remote news van that the operator can elevate above natural obstructions such as buildings and trees.

satellite-based digital broadcasts   a communication system in which broadcast signals are transmitted and received via microwave radio relay technology.

scientific model of mass media communication   a model that uses hypothesis, observation and evaluation to help us to filter only the most meaningful of information.

scribes   ancient masters of the written word who had significant influence over the political, economic and cultural progress of their societies.

search engine   a device designed to search information on the Web.

Sedition Act   federal law that makes it a crime to attempt to stop and/or publicly protest recruitment by the U.S. Armed Forces.

sell-through products   units that are directly sold to the public.

serial fiction   a type of television program that cleverly unifies story elements, day after day, for thousands of episodes, into plots that continuously unfold and are never fully resolved.

Shannon–Weaver model   a communication model that includes the information source, the message, the receiver, the sender, the channel, the signal and any noise that may interrupt the communication process.

shield laws   laws (passed in most states) that give reporters some means of protection against forced disclosure of confidential information or sources in court or before Congressional committees.

shock jocks   radio jockeys known for their brand of racy, often controversial, comedy.

short-tail journalism   a model drawn from economics to illustrate large-volume sales of small quantities of multiple products as seen in traditional news organizations (e.g., newspapers or broadcast programs with limited pages and airtime).

shortwave stations   the many small, independent stations in North America and throughout the world broadcasting informational, political and religious programming of all stripes.

show runners   bankable talent.

situation comedies   sitcoms; comedies that feature regularly recurring characters in a familiar environment.

sketch comedies   short comedy scenes or vignettes.

skiffle   tough, beat-driven music developed by British musical artists and influenced by American rock 'n' roll, jazz and blues artists.

slander   spoken defamation.

Smith Act   a law that made it a federal crime to advocate the violent overthrow of the government, or any such actions related to such overthrow.

SMS   Short Message Service; another name for texting.

SMTP   Standard Mail Transfer Protocol; an application used for sending and receiving e-mail.

soap operas   serial fiction television programs, so named for the household detergent manufacturers that sponsored them; originally started on radio.

social cause promotion   PR that attempts to persuade the audience to accept an organization's views on a particular issue.

social contract   according to Thomas Hobbes, a contract between rulers and citizens wherein citizens abdicate all their natural rights to their leaders, who then use any means necessary to ensure the safety and continuation of society.

social group   two or more people who interact with one another.

social judgment theory   looks at how individuals weigh new ideas presented to us by others, especially through mass media, and compare them, or refuse to compare them, to one's current views and beliefs.

social learning theory   a theoretical model applied to the study and research of communication and mass media that looks at how people learn within a social context.

social psychology the scientific study of how an individual's ideas, thoughts, feelings, beliefs and behaviors are influenced by those of actual or imagined other people. The study of human behavior that results from social interactions.

social-responsibility system a mass media model wherein the government establishes and maintains mass media as part of its social responsibility.

soft-cost resources production crews and equipment and postproduction facilities.

Sound Broadcasting Act a British law that made it possible for privately funded companies to begin broadcasting regionally, with the goal of encouraging the development of an independent and commercially funded broadcast media.

sound recording the re-creation of sound waves including voice, music and sound effects.

sound-on-film technology developed by Lee De Forest, a technology that imprinted sound into light waves that could be recorded as visual images onto the same continuous film strip.

Soviet-Communist system a mass-media model developed in the former Soviet Union and rooted in the ideas of Karl Marx and Friedrich Engels, both of whom believed that "the ideas of the ruling classes are the ruling ideas." Under this system, mass media are to be publicly owned, unmotivated by profit and used solely to educate the masses and promote socialization and conformity.

Spaghetti Westerns low-budget films shot in southern Italy so as to visually mimic the American Southwest.

Spanish immigrant press press that served the needs of Spanish-speaking immigrants, offering them a sense of community and security in their adopted country as well as publishing stories of local community interest.

Spanish press in exile early immigrant press operated by South and Central Americans living in the colonies.

speakeasies illegal saloons and dancehalls where vaudeville and burlesque shows were performed during the Prohibition years.

spec script a treatment written on speculation or placed on the open market.

special effects simulations of events in film; also called FX or SFX.

spin misinformation that attempts to hide the truth of an event or an issue.

Star Chamber a secret tribunal of the British Parliament that prosecuted and punished individuals for printing seditious literature.

star system promotion of the image, rather than the acting, of notable film stars.

Stationers Guild an organization authorized by the British Parliament in 1156 to regulate and enforce licensing fees on printing.

Statute of Anne enacted in 1710, the first piece of European legislation to vest the rights to a work to the author instead of the printer.

stereotype system invented by Firmin Didot (1764–1836), a system that used a soft metal printing plate, with each plate representing an entire page of a publication including all text and graphics.

Stonewall riots protests against police-instigated violence directed toward patrons (mostly gays and lesbians) of New York City's Stonewall Inn on June 28, 1969. Thousands of gays and lesbians rioted in the streets around the Stonewall Inn to protest years of abuse at the hands of the New York City police.

streaming media content that is delivered in a constant, continuous manner over the Web.

studio engineers professionals who are able to cut out and replace errors in performances as well as create complex compositions that would be nonreproducible outside a studio.

subscribers individuals who commit to paying for a printed product (magazines) for a specified period of time at a specified cost.

subsidy publisher see also vanity press; a publisher that offers authors low-cost alternatives to publication of their manuscripts by the commercial publishing houses.

sweeps week in television, the annual seven-day ratings periods held during the first weeks of November, March, May and July.

syndicate a cooperative collective of small companies.

syndicated comic strips   comic strips that appear in multiple newspapers.

systems in development   the nascent media systems present in most developing countries.

tabloids   publications devoted to sensational news.

talent agent   an individual or firm that represents actors, television and film writers, directors and producers, photographers and models, authors, designers and professional athletes in all areas of the entertainment industry.

talk radio   a format based on discussions about topical issues of the day.

talkies   films with soundtracks that mixed location sounds (real or constructed) with dialogue and background music.

technological convergence   the situation in which media delivery tools and platforms move.

technological determinism   a theory that suggests that as technologies develop and advance, so must the structure and values of our society and culture, and so must we as human beings.

Telecom Reform Act   U.S. legislation that attempted to regulate some information and media content on the World Wide Web.

Telecommunications Act of 1996   U.S. federal legislation that deregulated the broadcast industry and removed the long-running restrictions on multistation ownership.

Telegraph   an instrument allowing for communication over distance through the use of electrical impulses via a cable developed by Samuel Morse.

telenovelas   program lineups directed toward a pan-Hispanic audience; comprised of Spanish-language variety shows and sports broadcasts.

telephone   developed in 1876, a device that could convert the human voice into electrical impulses of various frequencies and then back again into a human voice via radio waves.

teleprompters   scrolling screens from which news anchors read the news, a practice that allows them to engage more directly with their viewers.

teletype   telegraphic machines that printed messages typed on the transmitter's keyboard.

text messaging   also known as *SMS* (Short Messaging Service) and "texting"; the practice of transmitting messages via portable devices such as cell phones and PDAs.

textual analysis   also called content analysis, it is the research methodology used by social scientists for the study of content in communication and mass media.

The Advocate   a Los Angeles-based gay magazine and the largest circulating gay publication in the world.

the majors   refers to the three largest and dominant companies within the television, film and music industries.

theory of hostile media effect   observes that individuals holding strong biases toward an issue (also called "partisans") perceive media coverage as biased against their opinions, regardless of whether the perceived bias is real and whether the media coverage is actually balanced and nonbiased.

Tin Pan Alley   the music publishing district in New York City so-called for its tin-pan-clash-sounding piano music.

trade showing   the viewing of a film before it is purchased or rented.

treatment   book rights, a script or a story concept, usually developed and presented in abbreviated form.

tweet   a 140-character Twitter message.

Twitter   a free social micro-networking site where participants post short text-based updates.

"two-way street" principle of PR   articulated by Ivy Ledbetter Lee, the idea that the PR professional is a communications facilitator between clients and the public.

typewriter   a machine with an alphabetic keyboard that replaced handwritten work.

UNESCO   United Nations Educational, Scientific and Cultural Organization; an NGO that promotes peace and universal respect through collaboration, education and unfettered sharing of knowledge and ideas.

unwitting bias   according to John Street, the bias that occurs when hard choices have to be made about what (stories) to include and what to exclude.

URL   Universal Resource Locator; a system that gives every site in every document on the Internet a unique locatable "address" that anyone can easily access.

uses and gratifications model   a model developed by Denis McQuail, in which media consumers select and use media in an effort to gain specific gratifications of their individual needs.

utilitarianism   a tradition of ethics in keeping with John Stuart Mill's view that dishonesty is sometimes necessary in service of a greater good.

V-discs   musical recordings produced exclusively to entertain U.S. troops stationed around the world during World War II.

vanity press   see also subsidy publisher; a publisher that offers authors low-cost alternatives to publication of their manuscripts by the commercial publishing houses.

veil of ignorance   John Rawls's philosophy that suggests that to be ethical, a person must be ignorant of any individual characteristics that might influence his or her decisions.

vertical integration   a business structure in which one company operates and controls all the means of production, distribution and exhibition for a large segment of the news publishing or movie industry.

viral media   media messages shared through rapid replication via the Internet.

virtual reality   a computer-simulated environment.

visual culture   the aspects of our day-to-day lives that rely on some form of imagery to convey meaning.

visual literacy   the ability to evaluate, apply or create visual representations and to understand how they communicate meaning.

visual media   all forms of physical media, such as fine art, drawings, graphic illustrations, sculptures, visual icons and so forth.

visual windows   the technologies through which we view images and that influence our ability to extract meaning from multiple images.

Voice over Internet Protocol (VoIP)   voice communications that occur over the Internet.

Web 1.0   digital publishing and distribution as well as early forms of e-mail communication.

Web 2.0   also known as the "new" new media; includes greatly enhanced user participation via networked creativity, innovation, information sharing and content sharing.

Wikipedia   a nonprofit, open-content, Internet-based encyclopedia established by Internet entrepreneur Jim Wales and philosopher Larry Sanger.

wireless telegraphy   signals sent electronically through electromagnetic waves.

women's suffrage movement   a women's rights movement initially led by Elizabeth Cady Stanton and Lucretia Mott; the 70-year-long struggle for women to secure the right to vote.

World Wide Web (WWW)   a system of documents (Web pages) that live on the Internet containing text, images and multimedia, all interlinked and easily navigable.

writing for column length   writing to befit the physical space and layout of a newspaper or magazine.

writing to time   writing a story to befit the allocated airtime within a broadcast news cycle.

wuxia   Chinese martial arts films.

yellow journalism   an age of journalism during which independent media became potential vehicles for furthering the private agendas of those individuals who owned or had controlling interests in publishing companies.

yellowface   the theatrical practice of applying makeup and pulling back the skin around a performer's eyes to give him or her a clichéd Asian look.

"Yellow Peril"   a racist phrase commonly printed in papers published by William Randolph Hearst. It reflected the nation's xenophobic fears and stereotypical views of anything foreign, in this case, Chinese people. It was eventually replaced by the term "Yellow Terror."

Zone System   Ansel Adams's system of photographic composition, which separates ranges of light into 11 zones.

zoopraxiscope   debuted by Muybridge in 1879, an instrument that used bright light to project onto a white screen the photos on a glass wheel, which was turned with a hand crank.

Bibliography

CHAPTER 1

Blondheim, M., & Watson, R. P. M. (2007). *The Toronto school of communication theory: Interpretations, extensions, applications*. Toronto: University of Toronto Press.

Browne, R. B., & Fishwick, M. W. (1999). *The global village: Dead or alive?* Bowling Green, OH: Bowling Green State University Popular Press.

Brunner, C., & Tally, W. (1999). *The new media literacy handbook: An educator's guide to bringing new media into the classroom*. New York: Anchor Books.

Cavell, R. (2002). *McLuhan in space: A cultural geography*. Toronto: University of Toronto Press.

Chomsky, N., Belletti, A., et al. (2002). *On nature and language*. New York: Cambridge University Press.

Cohen, H., & Australian Key Centre for Cultural and Media Policy. (1999). *Revisiting McLuhan*. Nathan, Queensland: Australian Key Centre for Cultural and Media Policy.

Donaldson, C., McLaughlin, K., et al. (2002). *McLuhan's wake*. Montreal: Primitive Entertainment/National Film Board of Canada.

Fontana, M., Discovery Channel Education, et al. (2007). *Advanced media literacy: Discovery school: Language arts*. New York: Discovery School. Distributed by Insight Media.

Frechette, J. D., & ebrary, Inc. (2002). *Developing media literacy in cyberspace pedagogy and critical learning for the twenty-first-century classroom*. Westport, CT: Praeger.

Gordon, W. T., & Willmarth, S. (1997). *McLuhan for beginners*. New York: Writers and Readers Pub.

Grosswiler, P., & Institute of Policy Alternatives (Montreal, Quebec). (1998). *The method is the message: Rethinking McLuhan through critical theory*. New York: Black Rose Books.

Hesmondhalgh, D., & Toynbee, J. (2008). *The media and social theory*. New York: Routledge.

Hirji, F. (2011). Through the looking glass: Muslim women on television—an analysis of 24, lost, and little Mosque on the Prairie. *Global Media Journal: Canadian Edition*, 4(2).

Kress, G. R. (2003). *Literacy in the new media age*. London: Routledge.

Levinson, P. (1999). *Digital McLuhan: A guide to the information millennium*. New York: Routledge.

Lopez, A. (2008). *Mediacology: A multicultural approach to media literacy in the 21st century*. New York: Peter Lang.

Macedo, D. P. (2007). *Media literacy: A reader*. New York: Peter Lang.

Marchand, P. (1998). *Marshall McLuhan: The medium and the messenger: A biography*. Cambridge, MA: MIT Press.

Marchand, P., & McLuhan, M. (1996). *Understanding McLuhan in the electric world, change is the only stable factor*. New York: Southam Interactive.

Marchessault, J. (2005). *Marshall McLuhan: Cosmic media*. Thousand Oaks, CA: Sage.

McLuhan, M., McLuhan, E., et al. (1996). *The essential McLuhan*. New York: Basic Books.

McLuhan, M., McLuhan, S., et al. (2003). *Understanding me: Lectures and interviews*. Toronto: McClelland & Stewart.

Moss, J. G., & Morra, L. M. (2004). *At the speed of light there is only illumination: A reappraisal of Marshall McLuhan*. Ottawa: University of Ottawa Press.

Potter, W. J. (2001). *Media literacy*. Thousand Oaks, Calif.: Sage.

Potter, W. J. (2004). *Theory of media literacy: A cognitive approach*. Thousand Oaks, CA: Sage.

Potter, W. J. (2008). *Media literacy*. Thousand Oaks, CA: Sage.

Sanderson, G., & MacDonald, F. (1989). *Marshall McLuhan: The man and his message*. Golden, CO: Fulcrum.

Scannell, P., Schlesinger, P., et al. (1992). *Culture and power: A media, culture and society reader*. Thousand Oaks, CA: Sage.

Silverblatt, A. (2008). *Media literacy: Keys to interpreting media messages*. Westport, CT: Praeger.

Silverblatt, A., Ferry, J., et al. (2009). *Approaches to media literacy: A handbook*. Armonk, NY: M. E. Sharpe.

Stevenson, N. (1995). *Understanding media cultures: Social theory and mass communication*. London: Sage.

Strate, L., & Wachtel, E. (2005). *The legacy of McLuhan*. Cresskill, NJ: Hampton Press.

Taylor, P. A., Harris, J. L., et al. (2008). *Critical theories of mass media then and now*. New York: McGraw-Hill/Open University Press, pp. xi, 233.

Theall, D. F. (2001). *The virtual Marshall McLuhan*. Ithaca, NY: McGill-Queen's University Press.

Tyner, K. R. (2009). *Media literacy: New agendas in communication*. New York: Routledge.

Woodward, K. M. (1980). *The myths of information: Technology and postindustrial culture*. Madison, WI: Coda Press.

CHAPTER 2

Blanchard, M. A. (1998). *History of the mass media in the United States*. Chicago: Fitzroy Dearborn.

Briggs, A., & Burke, P. (2005). *A social history of the media: From Gutenberg to the Internet*. Cambridge: Polity.

Bunch, B., & Tesar, J. (2000). *Desk encyclopedia of science and mathematics*. New York: Penguin Books.

Edwards, B. (2004). *Edward R. Murrow and the birth of broadcast journalism*. Hoboken, NJ: John Wiley & Sons, Inc.

Emery, M., Emery, E., & Roberts, N. L. (2000). *The press and America: An interpretive history of the mass media*. Boston, MA: Allyn & Bacon.

Evans, H., Buckland, G., & Lefer, D. (2004). *They made America: From the steam engine to the search engine: Two centuries of innovators*. New York: Little, Brown and Company.

Fischer, D. H. (2005). *Liberty and freedom: A visual history of America's founding ideas*. New York: Oxford University Press.

Folkerts, J., & Teeter, D. L. (2002). *Voices of a nation: A history of mass media in the United States*. Boston, MA: Allyn & Bacon.

Frizot, M., Albert, P., & Harding, C. (1998). *The new history of photography*. New York: Konemann.

Gombrich, E. H. (1995). *The story of art*. London: Phaidon.

Grout, D. J., & Palisca, C. V. (2001). *A history of Western Music* (6th ed.). New York: W. W. Norton.

Ifrah, G. (1994). *The universal history of computing*. Hoboken, NJ: John Wiley & Sons, Inc. "Internet history." Retrieved from www.computerhistory.org/internet_history/

Josephy, A. M., Jr. (1994). *500 nations: An illustrated history of North American Indians*. New York: Alfred A. Knopf.

Kopplin, J. (2002). *An illustrated history of computers*. Retrieved from www.computersciencelab.com/ComputerHistory/History.htm

Marcus, A. I., & Segal, H. P. (1999). *Technology in America: A brief history*. Boston, MA: Harcourt Brace.

Neuman, J. (1995). *Lights, camera, war: Is media technology driving international politics?* New York: St. Martin's Press.

Newhall, B. (2006). *The history of photography*. New York: Museum of Art.

Rhodes, R. (1999). *Visions of technology: A century of vital debate about machines, systems and the human world*. New York: Simon & Schuster.

Star, P. (2004). *The creation of the media: Political origins of modern communication*. New York: Basic Books.

Taft, R. (1938/1964). *Photography and the American scene 1839–1889*. New York: Dover Publications.

Uth, M., & Cheney, R. (1999). *Tesla: Master of light*. New York: Barnes & Noble Publishing.

CHAPTER 3

Baylis, T. (1999). *Clock this: My life as an inventor*. London: Headline Book Publishing.

Brooks, R. (2004, November). The other exponentials. *MIT Technology Review*.

Brown, J. S., & Duguid, P. (2002). *The social life of information*. Cambridge, MA: Harvard Business School Press.

Clarke, A. C. (1986). *July 20, 2019*. New York: Omni Books/MacMillan.

Clay, R. A. (2003, February). Unraveling new media's effects on children. *Monitor on Psychology*.

Cole, J. Y. (2005). *Jefferson's legacy: A brief history of the library of congress*. Washington, DC: Library of Congress.

Epstein, J. (2005, January). The future of books. *MIT Technology Review*.

Fabun, D. (1970). *The dynamics of change*. Upper Saddle River, NJ: Prentice-Hall.

Feynman, R. P. (1999). *The pleasure of finding things out*. New York: Perseus Books.

Grafton, A. (2007, December 10). Future reading. *The New Yorker*.

Harrison, J., & Hirst, M. (2007). *Communication and new media: From broadcast to narrowcast*. New York: Oxford University Press.

Hudson, D. (1997). *Rewired*. New York: Macmillan Technical Publishing.

Kelley, T., Littman, J., & Peters, T. (2001). *The art of innovation*. New York: Crown Business.

Lessig, L. (2001). *The future of ideas*. New York: Random House.

Lessig, L. (2004). *Free culture: How big media uses technology and the law to lock down culture and control creativity*. New York: Penguin Press.

Levinson, P. (1997). *The soft edge: A natural history and future of the information revolution*. New York: Routledge.

Levinson, P. (1999). *Digital McLuhan: A guide to the Information Millennium*. New York: Routledge.

Levy, S. (2007, November 26). The future of reading. *Newsweek*.

McLuhan, M. (1964/1999). *Understanding media: The extensions of man*. Cambridge, MA: MIT Press.

Negroponte, N. (1996). *Being digital*. New York: Vintage Books.

Rhodes, R. (1999). *Visions of technology: A century of vital debate about machines, systems and the human world*. New York: Simon & Schuster.

Rohmann, C. (1999). *The world of ideas: A dictionary of important theories, concepts, beliefs, and thinkers*. New York: Ballantine Books.

Roush, W. (2005, May). The infinite library. *MIT Technology Review*.

Star, P. (2004). *The creation of the media: Political origins of modern communication*. New York: Basic Books.

Stephens, M. (2007, January/February). Beyond news: Journalists worry about how the Web threatens the way they distribute their product; they are slower to see how it threatens the product itself. *Columbia Journalism Review*.

Stepp, C. S. (2006, April/May). Center stage: The Internet has become an integral part of the way newspapers distribute their content, a phenomenon that's only going to increase. *American Journalism Review*.

Surowiecki, J. (2006, May). Philanthropy's new prototype. *MIT Technology Review*.

Toffler, A. (1970). *Future shock*. Mattituck, NY: Amereon.

Uth, M., & Cheney, R. (1999). *Tesla: Master of light*. New York: Barnes & Noble Publishing.

White, S. P. (2002). *New ideas about new ideas*. New York: Perseus Books.

CHAPTER 4

Barnhurst, K. G., & Nerone, J. C. (2001). *The form of news: A history*. New York: Guilford Press.

Baum, G. (2000). *The future of publishing and the electronic book*. Washingon, DC: Georgetown University.

Baum, M. (2003). *Soft news goes to war: Public opinion and American foreign policy in the new media age*. Princeton, NJ: Princeton University Press.

Beegan, G. (2008). *The mass image: A social history of photomechanical reproduction in Victorian London*. New York: Palgrave Macmillan.

Bernstein, R. (2008). *The New York Times: The complete front pages: 1851–2008*. New York: Black Dog & Leventhal. Distributed by Workman.

Bouquillard, J., & Marquet, C. (2007). *Hokusai, first manga master*. New York: Abrams.

Brake, L., & Demoor, M. (2009). *The lure of illustration in the nineteenth century: Picture and press*. New York: Palgrave Macmillan.

Bridges, J. A., Litman, B. R., et al. (2006). *Newspaper competition in the millennium*. New York: Nova Science.

Brigham, C. S., & Readex Microprint Corporation. (2004). Early American newspapers (1690–1876). Readex digital collections. *Archive of Americana*.

Brooker, P., & Thacker, A. (2009). *The Oxford critical and cultural history of modernist magazines. Volume 1: Britain and Ireland 1880–1955*. New York: Oxford University Press.

Burns, E. (2006). *Infamous scribblers: The Founding Fathers and the rowdy beginnings of American journalism*. New York: Public Affairs.

Chermak, S. M., Bailey, F. Y., et al. (2003). *Media representations of September 11*. Westport, CT: Praeger.

Clark, C. E. (1994). *The public prints: The newspaper in Anglo-American culture, 1665–1740*. New York: Oxford University Press.

Cloud, B. L., & Simpson, A. K. (2008). *The coming of the frontier press: How the West was really won*. Evanston, IL: Northwestern University Press.

Conboy, M. (2002). *The press and popular culture*. Thousand Oaks, CA: Sage.

Coopersmith, A. S. (2004). *Fighting words: An illustrated history of newspaper accounts of the Civil War*. New York: New Press. Distributed by W. W. Norton.

Copeland, D. A. (1997). *Colonial American newspapers: Character and content*. Newark: University of Delaware Press.

Corey, M. F. (1999). *The world through a monocle: The New Yorker at midcentury*. Cambridge, MA: Harvard University Press.

Cranberg, G., Bezanson, R. P., et al. (2001). *Taking stock: Journalism and the publicly traded newspaper company*. Ames, IA: Iowa State University Press.

Cumming, D. O., & Medill School of Journalism. (2009). *The Southern press: Literary legacies and the challenge of modernity*. Evanston, IL: Medill School of Journalism, Northwestern University Press.

Darnton, R. (2009). *The case for books: Past, present, and future*. New York: PublicAffairs.

Dary, D. (1998). *Red blood and black ink: Journalism in the Old West*. New York: Knopf. Distributed by Random House.

Davies, D. R. (2006). *The postwar decline of American newspapers, 1945–1965*. Westport, CT: Praeger.

Davis, E. A. (1995). *Science in the making: Scientific development as chronicled by historic papers in the Philosophical magazine, with commentaries and illustrations*. Bristol, PA: Taylor & Francis.

De Armond, A. J. (1969). *Andrew Bradford, colonial journalist*. New York: Greenwood Press.

Deegan, M., & Sutherland, K. (2009). *Transferred illusions: Digital technology and the forms of print*. Burlington, VT: Ashgate.

DeMatteis, J. M., Barney, J., et al. (1984). *The Marvel comics adaptation of 2010*. New York: Marvel Comics Group.

Douglas, G. H. (1999). *The Golden Age of the newspaper*. Westport, CT: Greenwood Press.

Emery, M. C., Emery, E., et al. (2000). *The press and America: An interpretive history of the mass media*. Boston, MA: Allyn & Bacon.

Entman, R. M. (2004). *Projections of power: Framing news, public opinion, and U.S. foreign policy*. Chicago: University of Chicago Press.

Felsenthal, C. (1998). *Citizen Newhouse: Portrait of a media merchant*. New York: Seven Stories Press.

Franklin, B. (2009). *The future of newspapers*. London: Routledge.

Freitas, J. (1997). *The American comic strip*. Santa Cruz, CA: Crown College.

Gerber, R. (2005). *Katharine Graham: The leadership journey of an American icon*. New York: Portfolio.

Goulart, R. (2000). *Comic book culture: An illustrated history*. Portland, OR: Collectors Press.

Harris, B. (1999). *Blue and gray in black and white: Newspapers in the Civil War*. Washington, DC/London: Brassey's.

Homer, W., & Tatham, D. (2003). *Winslow Homer and the pictorial press*. Syracuse, NY: Syracuse University Press.

Horton, S., & Yang, J. M. (2008). *Professional manga: Digital storytelling with Manga Studio EX*. Boston, MA: Focal Press/Elsevier.

Howard, N. (2005). *The book: The life story of a technology*. Westport, CT: Greenwood Press.

Huntzicker, W. (1999). *The popular press, 1833–1865*. Westport, CT: Greenwood Press.

Johanningsmeier, C. (1997). *Fiction and the American literary marketplace: The role of newspaper syndicates, 1860–1900*. New York: Cambridge University Press.

Johnson, S., & Prijatel, P. (1999). *The magazine from cover to cover: Inside a dynamic industry*. Lincolnwood, IL: NTC.

Kist, J., & Harvard University, Program on Information Resources Policy. (1993). *The role of print on paper in the publishing house of the future*. Cambridge, MA: Program on Information Resources Policy, Harvard University, Center for Information Policy Research.

Kuratomi, R. (2001, May 12). *The significance of comics. Santa Cruz Sentinel*.

Lamb, C. (2004). *Drawn to extremes: The use and abuse of editorial cartoons*. New York: Columbia University Press.

Leonard, T. C. (1995). *News for all: America's coming-of-age with the press*. New York: Oxford University Press.

Lindley, W. R. (1993). *20th-century American newspapers in content and production*. Manhattan, KS: Sunflower University Press.

Maier, T. (1994). *Newhouse: All the glitter, power, and glory of America's richest media empire and the secretive man behind it*. New York: St. Martin's Press.

Maihafer, H. J. (2001). *War of words: Abraham Lincoln and the Civil War press*. Washington, DC: Brassey's.

Manzella, J. C. (2002). *The struggle to revitalize American newspapers*. Lewiston, NY: E. Mellen Press.

Martin, S. E., & Hansen, K. A. (1998). *Newspapers of record in a Digital Age: From hot type to hot link*. Westport, CT: Praeger.

McQuaid, J. (2012, May 24). The digital future of The Times-Picayune. *Forbes*. Retrieved from www.forbes.com/sites/johnmcquaid/2012/05/24/the-digital-future-of-the-times-picayune

Merritt, D. (2005). *Knightfall: Knight Ridder and how the erosion of newspaper journalism is putting democracy at risk*. New York: American Management Association.

Messaris, P., & Humphreys, L. (2006). *Digital media: Transformations in human communication*. New York: Peter Lang.

Morris, R., Rushing, S. K., et al. (2008). *Words at war: The Civil War and American journalism*. West Lafayette, IN: Purdue University Press.

Munk, N. (2004). *Fools rush in: Steve Case, Jerry Levin, and the unmaking of AOL Time Warner*. New York: Harper Business.

Nasaw, D. (2001). *The chief: The life of William Randolph Hearst*. Boston, MA: Houghton Mifflin.

Nord, D. P. (2001). *Communities of journalism: A history of American newspapers and their readers*. Urbana, IL: University of Illinois Press.

Pace, A. K. (2003). *The ultimate digital library: Where the new information players meet*. Chicago: American Library Association.

Paddock, T. R. E. (2004). *A call to arms: Propaganda, public opinion, and newspapers in the Great War*. Westport, CT: Praeger.

Pitcher, E. W. R. (2003). *The American magazine and historical chronicle (Boston, 1743–1746): An annotated catalogue of the prose*. Lewiston, NY: Edwin Mellen Press.

Pitcher, E. W. R. (2006). *The New-York magazine, or, Literary repository (1790–1797): A record of the contents with notes on authors and sources*. Lewiston, NY: Edwin Mellen Press.

Pizzitola, L. (2002). *Hearst over Hollywood: Power, passion, and propaganda in the movies*. New York: Columbia University Press.

PricewaterhouseCoopers (2012). *Global entertainment and media outlook: 2012–2016. Newspaper digital circulation spending starts to offset print decline in EMEA*. Retrieved from www.pwc.com/gx/en/global-entertainmentmedia-outlook/segment-insights/newspaper-publishing.jhtml

Pustz, M. (1999). *Comic book culture: Fanboys and true believers*. Jackson, MI: University Press of Mississippi.

Ratner, L., & Teeter, D. L. (2003). *Fanatics and fire-eaters: Newspapers and the coming of the Civil War*. Urbana, IL: University of Illinois Press.

Raymond, J. (2005). *The invention of the newspaper: English newsbooks, 1641–1649*. Oxford/New York: Clarendon Press/Oxford University Press.

Reed, B. S. (1995). *Outsiders in 19th-century press history: Multicultural perspectives*. Bowling Green, OH: Bowling Green State University Popular Press.

Riley, S. G. (1992). *Corporate magazines of the United States*. New York: Greenwood Press.

Robinson, F. M., & Davidson, L. (1998). *Pulp culture: The art of fiction magazines*. New York: Collectors Press. Distributed by Universe.

Schelly, B. (1999). *The golden age of comic fandom*. Seattle: Hamster Press.

Silva, I., Vallejo, A., et al. (1990). *The history of the comics, volume 4*. West Long Branch, NJ: White Star.

Sloan, W. D., & Williams, J. H. (1994). *The early American press, 1690–1783*. Westport, CT: Greenwood Press.

Squires, J. D. (1994). *Read all about it! The corporate takeover of America's newspapers*. New York: Times Books.

Sylvie, G., & Witherspoon, P. D. (2002). *Time, change and the American newspaper*. Mahwah, NJ: Lawrence Erlbaum Associates.

Thomas, G., & Dillon, M. (2002). *Robert Maxwell, Israel's superspy: The life and murder of a media mogul*. New York: Carroll and Graf.

Time. (1995). *The face of history: Time magazine covers 1923–1994*. New York: Author.

Turner, H. B. (1999). *When giants ruled: The story of Park Row, New York's great newspaper street*. New York: Fordham University Press.

Wallace, A. (2005). *Newspapers and the making of modern America: A history*. Westport, CT: Greenwood Press.

Weldon, M. (2008). *Everyman news: The changing American front page*. Columbia, MI: University of Missouri Press.

Welky, D. (2008). *Everything was better in America: Print culture in the Great Depression*. Urbana, IL: University of Illinois Press.

Whyte, K. (2009). *The uncrowned king: The sensational rise of William Randolph Hearst*. Berkeley, CA: Counterpoint. Distributed by Publishers Group West.

Wilson, S. (2009). *The secret life of the American otaku or an obsessed Japanophile's ravings*. Santa Cruz, 'CA: University of California.

Wolf, G. (2003). *Wired: A romance*. New York: Random House.

Young, M. (2007). *Death, sex and money: Life inside a newspaper*. Carlton, Australia: Melbourne University Press.

CHAPTER 5

Alderman, J. (2001). *Sonic boom: Napster, MP3, and the new pioneers of music*. Cambridge, MA: Perseus.

Badal, J. J. (1996). *Recording the classics: Maestros, music, and technology*. Kent, OH: Kent State University Press.

Barrow, T., Newby, J., et al. (1995). *Inside the music business: Career builders guides*. London: Blueprint.

Bekker, P. (2007). *The story of music: An historical sketch of the changes in musical form*. Whitefish, MT: Kessinger.

Blue, H. (2002). *Words at war: World War II era radio drama and the postwar broadcasting industry black-list*. Lanham, MD: Scarecrow Press.

Burkart, P., & McCourt, T. (2006). *Digital music wars: Ownership and control of the celestial jukebox*. Lanham, MD: Rowman & Littlefield.

Buskin, R. (1999). *Insidetracks: A first-hand history of popular music from the world's greatest record producers and engineers*. New York: Spike.

Campbell, R., Martin, C. R., & Fabos, B. (2004). *Media & culture: An introduction to mass communication*. New York: Bedford/St. Martins.

Chang, J. (2005). *Can't stop won't stop*. New York: Picador.

Cogan, J., & Clark, W. (2003). *Temples of sound: Inside the great recording studios*. San Francisco, CA: Chronicle Books.

Coleman, M. (2003). *Playback: From the Victrola to MP3, 100 years of music, machines, and money*. New York: Da Capo Press.

Colombo, G. W., & Franklin, C. (2006). *Absolute beginner's guide to podcasting*. Indianapolis, IN: Que.

Creech, K. (2003). *Electronic media law and regulation*. Boston, MA: Focal Press.

Creech, K. (2007). *Electronic media law and regulation*. Boston, MA: Focal Press.

Dannen, F. (1991). *Hit men: Power brokers and fast money inside the music business*. New York: Vintage Books.

Day, T. (2000). *A century of recorded music: Listening to musical history*. New Haven, CT: Yale University Press.

Denisoff, R. S. (1988). *Inside MTV*. New Brunswick, NJ: Transaction.

Elborough, T. (2009). *The long-player goodbye: The album from vinyl to iPod and back again*. London: Sceptre.

Ertegun, A. M., Steinberg, S., et al. (2007). *Atlantic records: The house that Ahmet built*. Burbank, CA: Rhino Entertainment.

Farr, J. (1994). *Moguls and madmen: The pursuit of power in popular music*. New York: Simon & Schuster.

Fisher, J. P. (2001). *Profiting from your music and sound project studio*. New York: Allworth Press.

Floerkemeier, C. (2008). *The internet of things: First international conference, IOT 2008, Zurich, Switzerland, March 26–28, 2008: Proceedings*. New York: Springer.

Fuqua, C. S., & ebrary, Inc. (2005). *Music fell on Alabama: The Muscle Shoals sound that shook the world*. Montgomery, AL: NewSouth Books.

Gallagher, M., & Mandell, J. (2006). *The studio business book: A guide to professional recording studio business and management*. Boston, MA: Thomson Course Technology PTR.

Glover, J. (2005, September 1). Dear Constanze. *The Guardian*.

Gomery, D. (2008). *A history of broadcasting in the United States*. Malden, MA: Blackwell.

Gronow, P., & Saunio, I. (1998). *An international history of the recording industry*. New York: Cassell.

Heaton, T. L. (2004, November 14). TV News in a postmodern world: Part II. The case for MTV. *Donata Communications*. Retrieved from www.donatacom.com/papers/pomo2.htm

Himes, G. (2009, September). College radio grows up: WTMD reflects the profound changes happening to college and public radio stations. *Baltimore Magazine*.

Hoffmann, F. W., Carty, D., et al. (1997). *Billy Murray: The phonograph industry's first great recording artist*. Lanham, MD: Scarecrow Press.

Hull, G. P. (2004). *The recording industry*. New York: Routledge.

Hunter-Tilney, L. (2009, August 8–9). The vinyl countdown. *Financial Times of London*.

Inglis, A. F. (1990). *Behind the tube: A history of broadcasting technology and business*. Boston, MA: Focal Press.

Kahn, A. (2006). *The house that Trane built: The story of impulse records*. New York: W. W. Norton.

Katz, M., & ebrary, Inc. (2004). *Capturing sound: How technology has changed music*. Berkeley, CA: University of California Press.

Kelley, N. (2002). *R&B, rhythm and business: The political economy of black music*. New York: Akashic.

Kelly, M. B. (1993). *Liberty records: A history of the recording company and its stars, 1955–1971*. Jefferson, NC: McFarland.

Kennedy, R., & McNutt, R. (1999). *Little labels—big sound: Small record companies and the rise of American music*. Bloomington, IN: Indiana University Press.

Knopper, S. (2009). *Appetite for self-destruction: The spectacular crash of the record industry in the Digital Age*. New York: Free Press.

Kot, G. (2009). *Ripped: How the wired generation revolutionized music*. New York: Scribner.

Kusek, D., Leonhard, G., et al. (2005). *The future of music: Manifesto for the digital music revolution*. Boston, MA: Berklee Press.

Lake, S., & Griffiths, P. (2007). *Horizons touched: The music of ECM*. London: Granta.

Lewis, P. M., & Jones, S. (2006). *From the margins to the cutting edge: Community media and empowerment*. Cresskill, NJ: Hampton Press.

Marmorstein, G. (2007). *The label: The story of Columbia records*. New York: Thunder's Mouth Press.

Martland, P. (1997). *Since records began: EMI, the first 100 years*. Portland, OR: Amadeus Press.

McLaren, M. (2006, August 18). Punk celebrates 30 years of subversion. *BBC Online*.

Mickelson, S. (1983). *America's other voice: The story of radio free Europe and radio liberty*. New York: Praeger.

Milner, G. (2009). *The story of recorded music*. London: Granta.

Morley, P. (2001). *"This is the American Forces Network": The Anglo-American battle of the air waves in World War II*. Westport, CT: Praeger.

Morton, D. (2000). *Off the record: The technology and culture of sound recording in America*. New Brunswick, NJ: Rutgers University Press.

Morton, D. (2004). *Sound recording: The life story of a technology*. Westport, CT: Greenwood Press.

MTV. (2004, November 14). *Brainy encyclopedia*.

MTV. (2004, November 14). *Cable Network Information*.

Negus, K. (1992). *Producing pop: Culture and conflict in the popular music industry*. London/New York: E. Arnold.

Nussbaum, E. (2012, July 30). Tune in next week—the curious staying power of the cliffhanger. *The New Yorker Magazine*.

O'Connor, A. (2008). *Punk record labels and the struggle for autonomy: The emergence of DIY*. Lanham, MD: Lexington Books.

Posner, G. (2002). *Motown: Music, money, sex, and power*. New York: Random House.

Priestman, C. (2002). *Web radio: Radio production for Internet streaming*. Boston, MA: Focal Press.

Scaruffi, P. (2005). *History of popular music*. London: Omniware.

Scaruffi, P. (2007). *A history of popular music before rock music*. London: Omniware.

Schultz, B. (2000). *Music producers: Conversations with today's top hitmakers*. Emeryville, CA: Mix Bookshelf.

Smith, C. (2009). *101 albums that changed popular music*. New York: Oxford University Press.

Smith, J., & Fink, M. (1988). *Off the record: An oral history of popular music*. New York: Warner Books.

Steffen, D. J. (2005). *From Edison to Marconi: The first thirty years of recorded music*. Jefferson, NC: McFarland.

Sudano, S. (2004, November 14). *MTV and music videos: Past to present*. Retrieved from Retrieved from www.acsu.buffalo.edu/~sisudano/

Sutton, A., & Nauck, K. R. (2000). *American record labels and companies: An encyclopedia (1891–1943)*. Denver, CO: Mainspring Press.

Thompson, D. (2003). *Wall of pain: The biography of Phil Spector*. Berkeley, CA: Sanctuary; Publishers Group West.

Thompson, G. R. (2008). *Please please me: Sixties British pop, inside out*. Oxford: Oxford University Press.

Tiber, E. (1994). How Woodstock happened. *The Times Herald-Record* (Middletown, NY).

United States Congress, House of Representatives, Committee on the Judiciary, Subcommittee on Courts, the Internet and Intellectual Property. (2004). *Internet streaming of radio broadcasts: Balancing the interests of sound recording copyright owners with those of broadcasters: Hearing before the Subcommittee on Courts, the Internet, and Intellectual Property of the Committee on the Judiciary, House of Representatives, One Hundred Eighth Congress, second session, July 15, 2004*. Washington, DC: Government Printing Office.

United States Congress, Senate, Committee on the Judiciary. (2002). *Online entertainment and copyright law: Coming soon to a digital device near you: Hearing before the Committee on the Judiciary, United States Senate, One Hundred Seventh Congress, first session, April 3, 2001*. Washington, DC: Government Printing Office.

Verschuur, G. L. (2007). *The invisible universe: The story of radio astronomy*. New York: Springer.

Ward, B. (2004). *Radio and the struggle for civil rights in the South*. Gainesville, FL: University Press of Florida.

Weissman, D., Jermance, F., et al. (2003). *Navigating the music industry: Current issues and business models*. Milwaukee: Hal Leonard Corp.

CHAPTER 6

Aberdeen, J. (n.d.). The motion picture patents company vs. the independent outlaws. *Hollywood Renegades Archive*.

Aberdeen, J. (2000). *Hollywood renegades: The society of independent motion picture producers*. Palos Verdes Estates, CA: Cobblestone Enterprises.

Abramson, A. (2003). *The history of television, 1942 to 2000*. Jefferson, NC: McFarland.

Aitken, I. (2001). *European film theory and cinema: A critical introduction*. Bloomington, IN: Indiana University Press.

Altman, R., & Fields, A. (1989). *The American film musical*. Bloomington, IN: Indiana University Press.

Archer, M. (1933). Wisconsin man inventor of folding film roll Kodak features. *Wisconsin Magazine of History*.

Barnes, B. (2009, November 15). Burdened by billions in debt, MGM puts itself up for sale. *The New York Times*.

Basinger, J. (1994). *American cinema: One hundred years of filmmaking*. New York: Rizzoli.

Bignell, J., & Fickers, A. (2008). *A European television history*. Malden, MA/Oxford: Wiley-Blackwell.

Biskind, P. (2004). *Down and dirty pictures: Miramax, Sundance, and the rise of independent film*. New York: Simon & Schuster.

Blackstone, E., & Bowman, G. W. (1999). Vertical integration in motion pictures. *Journal of Communication, 49*.

Booker, M. K. (2004). *Science fiction television: A history*. Westport, CT: Praeger.

Borde, R., Chaumeton, T., et al. (2002). *A panorama of American film noir, 1941–1953*. San Francisco, CA: City Lights Books.

Bordwell, D., Staiger, J., et al. (1988). *The classical Hollywood cinema: Film style and mode of production to 1960*. London: Routledge.

Bridges, H., & Boodman, T. C. (1989). *Gone with the wind: The definitive illustrated history of the book, the movie, and the legend*. New York: Simon & Schuster.

Briggs, A., & Burke, P. (2007). *A social history of the media: From Gutenberg to the Internet*. Cambridge: Polity.

Browne, N. (1998). *Refiguring American film genres: History and theory*. Berkeley, CA: University of California Press.

Cagin, S., Dray, P., et al. (1984). *Hollywood films of the seventies: Sex, drugs, violence, rock 'n' roll and politics*. New York: Harper & Row.

Cameron, I. A. (1993). *The book of film noir*. New York: Continuum.

Cherchi Usai, P. (2001). *The death of cinema: History, cultural memory and the digital dark age*. London: British Film Institute.

Chun, J. M. (2007). *"A nation of a hundred million idiots"? A social history of Japanese television, 1953–1973*. New York: Routledge.

Compart, M. (2000). *Noir 2000: ein reader*. DuMont.

Cook, P., Bernink, M., et al. (1999). *The cinema book*. London: British Film Institute Publishing.

Couric, K., Foner, E., et al. (2004). *Freedom: A history of US*. Alexandria, VA: PBS Home Video.

Cumbow, R. C. (1987). *Once upon a time: The films of Sergio Leone*. Metuchen, NJ: Scarecrow Press.

Daniel, D. (1998). Motion picture competition. In M. Blanchard (Ed.), *History of mass media in the United States*. New York: Routledge.

Dixon, W. W. (2009). *Film noir and the cinema of paranoia*. New Brunswick, NJ: Rutgers University Press.

Edgerton, G. R. (2007). *The Columbia history of American television*. New York: Columbia University Press.

Elliott, K. (2003). *Rethinking the novel/film debate*. New York: Cambridge University Press.

Engberg, M. (1993). *The erotic melodrama in Danish silent film, 1910–1918*. Bloomington, IN: Indiana University Press.

Evenson, B. (1998). Hollywood studio system. In M. Blanchard (Ed.), *History of mass media in the United States*. New York: Routledge.

Finler, J. (1988). *The Hollywood story*. New York: Crown.

Folkerts, J., & Teeter, D. (2002). *Voices of a nation: A history of mass media in the United States*. Boston, MA: Allyn & Bacon.

Forrest, J. (2008). *The legend returns and dies harder another day: Essays on film series*. Jefferson, NC: McFarland.

Gabler, N. (1988). *An empire of their own: How the Jews invented Hollywood*. New York: Crown.

Gehring, W. D. (1988). *Handbook of American film genres*. New York: Greenwood Press.

Georgakas, D. (1992). Hollywood blacklist. In B. Buhle & D. Georgakas (Eds.), *Encyclopedia of the American left*. Chicago, IL: University of Illinois Press.

Geraghty, C. (2008). *Now a major motion picture: Film adaptations of literature and drama*. Lanham, MD: Rowman & Littlefield.

Giddings, R., & Selby, K. (2001). *The classic serial on television and radio*. New York: Palgrave.

Grant, B. K. (2003). *Film genre reader III*. Austin, TX: University of Texas Press.

Grieveson, L., & Wasson, H. (2008). *Inventing film studies*. Durham, NC: Duke University Press.

Guynn, W. (1990). *A cinema of nonfiction*. Rutherford, NJ/London/Cranbury, NJ: Fairleigh Dickinson University Press/Associated University Presses.

Haberski, R. J. (2007). *Freedom to offend: How New York remade movie culture*. Lexington: University Press of Kentucky.

Heller, D. A. (2006). *The great American makeover: Television, history, nation*. New York: Palgrave Macmillan.

Herbert, S. (2004). *A history of early television*. New York: Routledge.

Hill, J., Gibson, P. C., et al. (2000). *Film studies: Critical approaches*. New York: Oxford University Press.

Hilmes, M. (2003). *The television history book*. London: British Film Institute.

Hitt, J. (1990). *The American West from fiction (1823–1976) into film (1909–1986)*. Jefferson, NC: McFarland.

Irwin, J. T., & ebrary, Inc. (2006). *Unless the threat of death is behind them: Hard-boiled fiction and film noir*. Baltimore, MD: Johns Hopkins University Press.

Kaplan, E. A. (1998). *Women in film noir*. London: British Film Institute.

Kaufman, P. B., & Mohan, J. (2008). *The economics of independent film and video distribution in the Digital Age*. Tribeca Film Institute.

Landy, M. (1991). *British genres: Cinema and society, 1930–1960*. Princeton, NJ: Princeton University Press.

Magiera, M. (2009). DVD threatens film economics. *Video Business Volume*.

Marcus, M. J. (1986). *Italian film in the light of neorealism*. Princeton, NJ: Princeton University Press.

Marcus, M. J. (1993). *Filmmaking by the book: Italian cinema and literary adaptation*. Baltimore, MD: Johns Hopkins University Press.

Masnick, M. (2009). *NY Times* buys bogus movie. *Tech Dirt Volume*. Retrieved from www.techdirt.com/articles/20090205/0319043658.shtml

Meehan, P. (2008). *Tech-noir: The fusion of science fiction and film noir*. Jefferson, NC: McFarland.

Mills, M. (2009). HUAC & the censorship changes. Retrieved from www.moderntimes.com/huac/

Moore, B., Bensman, M. R., et al. (2006). *Prime-time television: A concise history*. Westport, CT: Praeger.

Moul, C. (2005). *A concise handbook of movie industry economics*. Cambridge: Cambridge University Press.

Mullen, M. G. (2008). *Television in the multichannel age: A brief history of cable television*. Malden, MA: Blackwell.

National Public Radio. (2009, April 18). Is the small screen replacing the silver screen? *Morning Edition*.

Neale, S., & British Film Institute. (2002). *Genre and contemporary Hollywood*. London: British Film Institute.

Niemi, R. (2006). *History in the media: Film and television*. Santa Barbara, CA: ABC-CLIO.

Nordin, J. (2009). *The first talkie. All talking! All talking! All talking! A celebration of the early talkies and their times*. Retrieved from http://talkieking.blogspot.com/2009/02/first-talkie.html

Nordisk Film. (2004). *Nordisk film history*. Retrieved from www.nordiskfilm.com/resources.ashx/Resources/NordiskFilm/Presse/Historie/historie_uk_PDF.pdf

O'Connor, J. E., & Rollins, P. C. (2005). *Hollywood's West: The American frontier in film, television, and history*. Lexington: University Press of Kentucky.

Palmer, R. B. (1994). *Hollywood's dark cinema: The American film noir*. New York: Twayne/Maxwell Mcmillan.

Palmer, R. B. (1996). *Perspectives on film noir*. New York: G. K. Hall/Prentice Hall International.

Patel, D., Benson, L., et al. (2007). *Cinema India: The art of Bollywood*. Melbourne, Australia: National Gallery of Victoria.

Pauwels, H. R. M. (2007). *Indian literature and popular cinema: Recasting classics*. New York: Routledge.

Pye, D., Gibbs, J., et al. (2007). *Movie and tone: Reading Rohmer: Voices in film*. New York: Wallflower.

Rango, T. (2009, November 9). Sony to offer film on Internet TV, then DVD. *The New York Times*.

Rolls, A., & Walker, D. (2009). *French and American noir: Dark crossings*. New York: Palgrave Macmillan.

Roman, J. W. (2005). *From daytime to primetime: The history of American television programs*. Westport, CT: Greenwood Press.

Rungfapaisarn, K. (2009, November 9). Big rise in piracy hits DVD-makers. *The Nation*.

Sanders, J. (2009). *The film genre book*. Leighton Buzzard: Auteur.

Sanders, S., & Skoble, A. J. (2008). *The philosophy of TV noir*. Lexington: University Press of Kentucky.

Scott, A. (2005). *Hollywood: The place, the industry*. Princeton, NJ: Princeton University Press.

Silver, A., & Ursini, J. (1996). *Film noir reader*. New York: Limelight Editions.

Silver, A., & Ursini, J. (2004). *Film noir reader 4*. New York: Limelight Editions. Distributed by Hal Leonard.

Silver, A., & Ursini, J. (2005). *Film noir reader*. New York: Limelight Editions.

Silver, A., Ward, E., et al. (1992). *Film noir: An encyclopedic reference to the American style*. Woodstock, NY: Overlook Press.

Smith, S. (2009). Blu-ray prices dropping to DVD levels. *The Tech Herald*.

Smith, S. (2009, September 23). DVD sales continue to drop, rentals on the rise. *The Wall Street Journal*.

Spicer, A. (2007). *European film noir*. Manchester: Manchester University Press. Distributed by Palgrave.

Stam, R. (2005). *Literature through film: Realism, magic, and the art of adaptation*. Malden, MA: Blackwell.

Stelter, B., & Stone, B. (2009, February 4). Digital pirates winning battle with studios. *The New York Times*.

Voytilla, S. (1999). *Myth and the movies: Discovering the mythic structure of 50 unforgettable films*. Studio City, CA: Michael Wiese Productions.

Walker, J. R., Bellamy, R. V., et al. (2008). *Center field shot: A history of baseball on television*. Lincoln: University of Nebraska Press.

CHAPTER 7

Achter, P. (2008). Comedy in unfunny times: News parody and carnival after 9/11. *Critical Studies in Media Communication, 25*(3), 274–303.

Anderson, J., & Rainie, L. (2012, February 29). *Future of the Internet—Millennials will benefit and suffer due to their hyperconnected lives*. Pew Internet & American Life Project. Retrieved from www.pewinternet.org/Reports/2012/Hyperconnected-lives.aspx

Banks, M. A. (2008). *Blogging heroes*. Indianapolis: Wiley.

Bolter, J. D., & Grusin, R. (2000). *Remediation*. Cambridge, MA: MIT Press.

Bonfadelli, H., Bucher, P., et al. (2007). Use of old and new media by ethnic minority youth in Europe with a special emphasis on Switzerland. *Communications: The European Journal of Communication Research, 32*(2), 141–170.

Boxer, S. (2008). *Ultimate blogs*. New York: Vintage Books.

Buckingham, D. (2007). Media education goes digital: An introduction. *Learning, Media, & Technology, 32*(2), 111–119.

Castronova, E. (2005). *Synthetic worlds*. Chicago: University of Chicago Press.

Chadwick, A. (2006). *Internet politics*. New York: Oxford University Press.

Chaplin, H., & Ruby, A. (2005). *Smartbomb*. Chapel Hill, NC: Algonquin Books of Chapel Hill.

Cheong, P. H. (2008). The young and techless? Investigating internet use and problem-solving behaviors of young adults in Singapore. *New Media & Society, 10*(5), 771–791.

Cochrane, P. (1999). *Tips for time travelers*. New York: McGraw-Hill.

Cotton, B., & Oliver, R. (1993). *Understanding hypermedia 2.000*. London: Phaidon Press.

Deibert, R., Palfrey, J., et al. (2008). *Access denied*. Cambridge, MA: MIT Press.

d'Haenens, L., Koeman, J., et al. (2007). Digital citizenship among ethnic minority youths in the Netherlands and Flanders. *New Media & Society, 9*(2), 278–299.

Esser, F. (2008). Dimensions of political news cultures: Sound bite and image bite news in France, Germany, Great Britain, and the United States. *International Journal of Press/Politics*, *13*(4), 401–442.

Franco, J. (2008). Extreme makeover: The politics of gender, class, and cultural identity. Television & *New Media*, *9*(6), 471–486.

Friedberg, A. (2006). *The virtual window*. Cambridge, MA: MIT Press.

Gezduci, H., & d'Haenens, L. (2007). Culture-specific features as determinants of news media use. *Communications: The European Journal of Communication Research*, *32*(2), 193–222.

Gómez-Barris, M., & Gray, H. (2006). Michael Jackson, television, and post-op disasters. *Television & New Media*, *7*(1), 40–51.

Greenfield, A. (2006). *Everware: The dawning age of ubiquitous computing*. Berkeley, CA: New Riders.

Hampp, A. (2008). Mags go from spreads to screens. *Advertising Age*, *79*(34), 8.

Hasinoff, A. A. (2008). Fashioning race for the free market on *America's next top model*. *Critical Studies in Media Communication*, *25*(3), 324–343.

Heim, M. (1998). *Virtual realism*. New York: Oxford University Press.

Hewitt, H. (2005). *Blog: Understanding the information reformation that's changing the world*. Nashville, TN: Thomas Nelson.

Hirst, M., & Harrison, J. (2007). *Communication and new media*. Melbourne, Australia: Oxford University Press.

Holtzman, S. (1997). *Digital mosaics: The aesthetics of cyberspace*. New York: Rockefeller Center.

Jenkins, H. (2006). *Convergence culture*. New York: New York University Press.

Jenkins, H. (2006). *Fans, bloggers and gamers*. New York: New York University Press.

Kaku, M. (1997). *Visions*. New York: Random House.

Klaassen, A. (2008). Can MySpace's grand experiment help save the music industry? *Advertising Age*, *79*(79), 80.

Krug, G. (2005). *Communication, technology and cultural change*. London: Sage.

Ksiazek, T. B., & Webster, J. G. (2008). Cultural proximity and audience behavior: The role of language in patterns of polarization and multicultural fluency. *Journal of Broadcasting & Electronic Media*, *52*(3), 485–503.

Kung, L., Picard, R. G., et al. (2008). *The Internet and the mass media*. London: Sage.

Lessig, L. (1999). *Code*. New York: Basic Books.

Lister, M., Dovey, J., et al. (2003). *New media: A critical introduction*. New York: Routledge.

mobiThinking.com. (2012). Global mobile statistics Part C: Mobile marketing, advertising, and messaging.

Moses, L. (2008). Shining example. *MediaWeek*, *18*(13), 7.

Orlick, P. B., Anderson, S. D., et al. (2007). *Exploring electric media: Chronicles and challenges*. Malden, MA: Blackwell.

Ornebring, H. (2008). The consumer as producer—of what? *Journalism Studies*, *9*(5).

Poole, S. (2000). *Trigger happy*. New York: Arcade.

Porter, D. (1997). *Internet culture*. New York: Routledge.

Rains, S. A. (2008). Health at high speed: Broadband Internet access, health communication, and the digital divide. *Communication Research*, *35*(3), 283–297.

Reports, N. (2003). Approaching the end of the "monomedia" era. *Nieman Reports*, *57*(4), 10–11.

Rochlin, G. I. (1997). *Trapped in the Net*. Princeton, NJ: Princeton University Press.

Rosenau, J. N., & Singh, J. P. (2002). *Information technologies and global politics*. Albany: State University of New York Press.

Shenk, D. (1997). *Data smog: Surviving the information glut*. New York: HarperCollins.

Slatalla, M., & Quittner, J. (1995). *The gang that ruled cyberspace*. New York: HarperCollins.

Sreekumar, T. T. (2007). Cyber kiosks and dilemmas of social inclusion in rural India. *Media, Culture & Society*, *29*(6), 869–889.

Tribe, M., Jana, R., et al. (2006). *New media art*. Hohenzollernring, Germany: Taschen.

Turkle, S. (1995). *Life on the screen: Identity in the age of the Internet*. New York: Rockefeller Center.

U.S. Department of Commerce, National Telecommunications and Information Administration. (2011, February). *Digital nation: Expanding Internet usage, NTIA Research Preview*.

Wardrip-Fruin, N., & Harrigan, P. (2004). *First person*. Cambridge, MA: MIT Press.

Wentz, L. (2008). Hispanic fact pack. *Advertising Age*, 3.

Wessler, H., & Adolphsen, M. (2008). Contra-flow from the Arab world? How Arab television coverage of the 2003 Iraq war was used and framed on Western international news channels. *Media, Culture & Society, 30*(4), 439–461.

Yun, H. J., Postelnicu, M., et al. (2007). Where is she? *Journalism Studies, 8*(6), 930–947.

Zittrain, J. (2008). *The future of the Internet and how to stop it*. Harrisonburg, VA: R. R. Donnelley.

CHAPTER 8

Berger, A. (2000). *Ads, fads, and consumer culture: Advertising's impact on American character and society*. Lanham, MD: Rowman & Littlefield.

Berger, W., Porter C. + Bogusky. (2006). *Hoopla*. New York: PowerHouse Books.

Bordo, S. (2003). The empire of images in our world of bodies. *Chronicle of Higher Education, 50*.

Brown, A., & Dittmar, H. (2005). Think "thin" and feel bad: The role of appearance schema activation, attention level, and thin-ideal internalization for young women's responses to ultra-thin media ideals. *Journal of Social & Clinical Psychology, 24*(8), 1088–1113.

Chang, S., Newell, J., & Salmon, C. (2006). The hidden history of product placement. *Journal of Broadcasting & Electronic Media, 50*(4).

Devlin, L. (2005). Analysis of presidential primary campaign commercials of 2004. *Communication Quarterly, 56*, 17–28.

Earle, R. (2000). *The art of cause marketing: How to use advertising to change personal behavior and public policy*. Lincolnwood, IL: NTC Business Books.

Franz, M. M. (2007). *Campaign advertising and American democracy*. Philadelphia, PA: Temple University Press.

Gitlin, T. (2003). *Media unlimited: How the torrent of images and sounds overwhelms our lives*. New York: Holt.

Grossberg, L., Wartella, E., Whitney, D., & Wise, J. (2006). *Media making: Mass media in a popular culture*. London: Sage.

Jewitt, C., & van Leeuwen, T. (2001). *Handbook of visual analysis*. London: Sage.

Johnson, F. L. (2008). *Imaging in advertising: Verbal and visual codes of commerce*. New York: Routledge.

Kaid, L. L., & Johnston, A. (2001). *Videostyle in presidential campaigns: Style and content of televised political advertising*. Westport, CT: Praeger.

Kawamoto, K. (2002). *Media and society in the Digital Age*. Boston, MA: Allyn & Bacon.

Legenbauer, T., Ruhl, I., & Vocks, S. (2008). The influence of appearance-related TV commercials on body image state. *Behavior Modification, 32*(3).

Levinson, P. (2001). *Digital McLuhan: A guide to the Information Millennium*. New York: Routledge.

Malefyt, T. D. D., Moeran, B., et al. (2003). *Advertising cultures*. New York: Berg.

Messaris, P. (1997). *Visual persuasion: The role of images in advertising*. London: Sage.

O'Shaughnessy, J., & O'Shaughnessy, N. J. (2004). *Persuasion in advertising*. New York: Routledge.

Page, J. (2006). Myth and photography in advertising: A semiotic analysis. *Visual Communication Quarterly, 13*.

Paletz, D. (2001). *The media in American politics: Contents and consequences*. New York: Longman.

Pavlik, J. (1996). *New media and the information superhighway*. Boston, MA: Allyn & Bacon.

Potter, W. (2008). *Media literacy*. London: Sage.

Reichert, T. (2003). *The erotic history of advertising*. Amherst, NY: Prometheus Books.

Reichert, T., & Lambiase, J. (2003). *Sex in advertising: Perspectives on the erotic appeal*. Mahwah, NJ: Lawrence Erlbaum Associates.

Ries, A., & Ries, L. (2002). *The fall of advertising and the rise of PR*. New York: Harper Business.

Roberts, K. (2005). *Lovemarks: The future beyond brands*. New York: PowerHouse Books.

Roberts, K. (2005). *Sisomo: The future on screen*. New York: PowerHouse Books.

Spurgeon, C. (2008). *Advertising and new media*. New York: Routledge.

Twitchell, J. B. (2000). *Twenty ads that shook the world: The century's most groundbreaking advertising and how it changed us all*. New York: Crown.

CHAPTER 9

Albarran, A. B., & Pitts, G. G. (2001). *The radio broadcasting industry*. Boston, MA: Allyn and Bacon.

Anduaga, A. (2009). *Wireless and empire: Geopolitics, radio industry, and ionosphere in the British Empire, 1918–1939*. New York: Oxford University Press.

Avery, R. K., Barbieri, R., et al. (2000). *A history of public broadcasting*. Washington, DC: Current.

Babe, R. E. (2009). *Cultural studies and political economy: Toward a new integration*. Lanham, MD: Lexington Books.

Balk, A. (2006). *The rise of radio, from Marconi through the Golden Age*. Jefferson, NC: McFarland & Company.

Ballmer, P., Barksdale, J., et al. (1999). *Microsoft vs. the Justice Department playing monopoly*. Princeton, NJ: Films for the Humanities and Sciences.

Barrow, T., Newby, J., et al. (1995). *Inside the music business: Career builders guides*. London: Blueprint.

Bartlett, R. A. (2007). *The world of ham radio, 1901–1950: A social history*. Jefferson, NC: McFarland & Company.

Berg, J. S. (2008). *Broadcasting on the short waves, 1945 to today*. Jefferson, NC: McFarland & Company.

Biermans, H., & Guerrieri, P. (2007). *The music industry: The practical guide to understanding the essentials*. DSS Publishing (Da Street Sound Ltd.).

Boddy, W. (2004). *New media and popular imagination: Launching radio, television, and digital media in the United States*. New York: Oxford University Press.

Brown, R. J. (1998). *Manipulating the ether: The power of broadcast radio in thirties America*. Jefferson, NC: McFarland & Company.

Bunzel, R. (2008). *Clear vision: The story of Clear Channel Communications*. Albany, TX: Bright Sky Press.

Burkart, P., & McCourt, T. (2006). *Digital music wars: Ownership and control of the celestial jukebox*. Lanham, MD: Rowman & Littlefield.

Burns, K., Lewis, T., et al. (2004). *Empire of the air: The men who made radio. Ken Burns' America collection*. Alexandria, VA: PBS Home Video. Distributed by Paramount Home Entertainment.

Cramer, R. B., Lennon, T., et al. (2000). *The battle over Citizen Kane*. Boston, MA: WGBH Boston Video.

Curtin, M., & ebrary, Inc. (2007). *Playing to the world's biggest audience: The globalization of Chinese film and TV*. Berkeley, CA: University of California Press, p. x.

Digital Music Report (2012). Retrieved from www.ifpi.org/content/library/DMR2012.pdf

Douglas, G. H. (1987). *The early days of radio broadcasting*. Jefferson, NC: McFarland & Company.

Dyck, A., Zingales, L., et al. (2002). *The corporate governance role of the media*. Cambridge, MA: National Bureau of Economic Research.

Ertegun, A. M., Midler, B., et al. (2007). *Atlantic records: The house that Ahmet built*. Burbank, CA: Rhino Entertainment.

Films for the Humanities. (2000). *Digital magic: The revolution in film and TV*. Princeton, NJ: Author.

Foege, A. (2008). *Right of the dial: The rise of Clear Channel and the fall of commercial radio*. New York: Faber and Faber.

Forna, P. (2007). *Consuming media: Communication, shopping and everyday life*. New York: Berg.

Foust, J. C. (2000). *Big voices of the air: The battle over Clear Channel Radio*. Ames, IA: Iowa State University Press.

Garnham, N., & Inglis, F. (1990). *Capitalism and communication: Global culture and the economics of information*. London: Sage.

Gibilisco, S. (1994). *Amateur radio encyclopedia*. Blue Ridge Summit, PA: TAB Books.

Great Britain, Department for Culture Media and Sport, British Screen Advisory Council, et al. (1998). *Proceedings of the European audiovisual conference*. Birmingham, April 6–8, 1998. Luxembourg: Office for Official Publications of the European Communities.

Hilmes, M. (1997). *Radio voices: American broadcasting, 1922–1952*. Minneapolis, MN: University of Minnesota Press.

Hilmes, M., & Loviglio, J. (2002). *Radio reader: Essays in the cultural history of radio*. New York: Routledge.

Hong, S. (2001). *Wireless: From Marconi's black-box to the audion*. Cambridge, MA: MIT Press.

Hoskins, C., McFadyen, S., et al. (1997). *Global television and film: An introduction to the economics of the business*. New York: Clarendon Press; Oxford University Press.

Hull, G. P. (2004). *The recording industry*. New York: Routledge.

Hutchison, T. W., Allen, P., et al. (2006). *Record label marketing*. Burlington, MA: Focal Press.

Jones, R. O., & U.S. Federal Trade Commission. (2007). *Marketing violent entertainment to children*. New York: Novinka Books.

Keith, M. C. (2000). *Talking radio: An oral history of American radio in the television age*. Armonk, NY: M. E. Sharpe.

Kennedy, R., & McNutt, R. (1999). *Little labels, big sound: Small record companies and the rise of American music*. Bloomington, IN: Indiana University Press.

Kenney, W. H., & ebrary, Inc. (1999). *Recorded music in American life: The phonograph and popular memory, 1890–1945*. New York: Oxford University Press.

Knopper, S. (2009). *Appetite for self-destruction: The spectacular crash of the record industry in the Digital Age*. New York: Free Press.

Lamb, R., Armstrong, W. G., et al. (1980). *Business, media, and the law: The troubled confluence*. New York: New York University Press.

Lasky, B. (1984). *RKO, the biggest little major of them all*. Englewood Cliffs, NJ: Prentice-Hall.

Lenthall, B. (2007). *Radio's America: The Great Depression and the rise of modern mass culture*. Chicago: University of Chicago Press.

Low, L. (2000). *Economics of information technology and the media*. Singapore/River Edge, NJ: World Scientific; Singapore University Press.

Madianou, M. (2005). *Mediating the nation: News, audiences and the politics of identity*. London/Portland, OR: UCL Press; Cavendish.

Mattelart, A. (1979). *Multinational corporations and the control of culture: The ideological apparatuses of imperialism*. Sussex/Atlantic Highlands, NJ: Harvester Press; Humanities Press.

McLaughlin, K. (2005). *Paperwork: Fiction and mass mediacy in the Paper Age*. Philadelphia, PA: University of Pennsylvania Press.

Miller, E. D. (2003). *Emergency broadcasting and 1930s American radio*. Philadelphia, PA: Temple University Press.

Miller, T. (2007). *Cultural citizenship: Cosmopolitanism, consumerism, and television in a neoliberal age*. Philadelphia, PA: Temple University Press.

Mitchell, J. W. (2005). *Listener supported: The culture and history of public radio*. Westport, CT: Praeger.

Motavalli, J. (2002). *Bamboozled at the revolution: How big media lost billions in the battle for the Internet*. New York: Viking.

Nair, B. (1980). *Mass media and the transnational corporation: A study of media-corporate relationship and its consequences for the Third World*. Singapore: Singapore University Press.

New York Center for Visual History, KCET (Los Angeles, Calif.), et al. (1994). *Film in the television age: American cinema, Part 8*. South Burlington, VT: Annenberg/CPB Collection.

Pecora, N. O. (1998). *The business of children's entertainment*. New York: Guilford Press.

Pendergast, T. (2000). *Creating the modern man: American magazines and consumer culture, 1900–1950*. Columbia, MO: University of Missouri Press.

Pocock, R. F. (1988). *The early British radio industry*. Manchester/New York: Manchester University Press; St. Martin's Press.

Pollard, A. (1998). *Gramophone: The first 75 years*. Harrow, Middlesex: Gramophone Publications.

President's Committee on the Arts and the Humanities. (2006). *Symposium on film, television, digital media, and popular culture, May 23–24, 2006, Los Angeles, CA: Summary report*. Washington, DC: Author.

Puddington, A. (2000). *Broadcasting freedom: The Cold War triumph of Radio Free Europe and Radio Liberty*. Lexington: University Press of Kentucky.

Rai, A. (2009). *Untimely Bollywood: Globalization and India's new media assemblage*. Durham, NC: Duke University Press.

Regal, B. (2005). *Radio: The life story of a technology*. Westport, CT: Greenwood Press.

Richter, W. A. (2006). *Radio: A complete guide to the industry*. New York: P. Lang.

Rudel, A. J. (2008). *Hello, everybody! The dawn of American radio*. Orlando, FL: Harcourt.

Sies, L. F. (2000). *Encyclopedia of American radio, 1920–1960*. Jefferson, NC: McFarland & Company.

Stone, D. P., Hartley, D., et al. (1998). *Film history: The story of film, TV and media*. Princeton, NJ: Films for the Humanities & Sciences.

Stone, D. P., Hartley, D., et al. (1998). *Radio history: Media waves, an introduction to mass communication*. Princeton, NJ: Films for the Humanities & Sciences.

Stone, D. P., McGraw-Hill Companies, College Division, et al. (1998). *Recording history: The story of film, TV and media*. Princeton, NJ: Films for the Humanities & Sciences.

Todreas, T. M. (1999). *Value creation and branding in television's digital age*. Westport, CT: Quorum Books.

Tune, C. A., & Practising Law Institute. (2007). *Technology and entertainment convergence: Business and legal issues for the next stage of "technotainment."* New York: Practising Law Institute.

U.S. Department of Commerce. (2001). *The migration of U.S. film and television production: The impact of "runaways" on workers and small business in the U.S. film industry*. Washington, DC: Author.

U.S. House of Representatives, Committee on Resources. (1999). *Providing for the collection of fees for the making of motion pictures, television productions, and sound tracks in National Park system and National wildlife refuge system units: Report (to accompany H.R. 154) (including cost estimate of the Congressional Budget Office)*. Washington, DC: U.S. Government Printing Office.

U.S. House of Representatives, Committee on Small Business. Subcommittee on General Oversight and Minority Enterprise. (1980). *Media concentration: Hearing before the Subcommittee on General Oversight and Minority Enterprise of the Committee on Small Business, House of Representatives, Ninety-Sixth Congress, second session*. Washington, DC: U.S. Government Printing Office.

Walker, J. (2001). *Rebels on the air: An alternative history of radio in America*. New York: New York University Press.

Wasko, J. (1995). *Hollywood in the information age: Beyond the silver screen*. Austin, TX: University of Texas Press.

Wildman, S. S., Siwek, S. E., et al. (1988). *International trade in films and television programs*. Cambridge, MA: Ballinger.

Wolf, M. J. (1999). *The entertainment economy: How mega-media forces are transforming our lives*. New York: Times Books.

Wolff, M. (2008). *The man who owns the news: Inside the secret world of Rupert Murdoch*. London: Bodley Head.

Yoder, A. R. (2002). *Pirate radio stations: Tuning in to underground broadcasts in the air and online*. New York: McGraw-Hill.

CHAPTER 10

Alterman, E. (2003). *What liberal bias? The truth about bias and the news*. New York: Basic Books.

Ang, I. (1996). *Living room wars: Rethinking media audience for a postmodern world*. Routledge.

Anton, F. (2006, August). Cultivating fear: The effects of television news on public's fear of terrorism. *Mass Communication and Society*.

Arpan, L. M., & Nabi, R. N. (2011). Exploring anger in the hostile media process: Effects on news preferences and source evaluation. *Journalism & Mass Communication Quarterly, 88*(1).

Auletta, K. (2003, May 26). Vox Fox: How Roger Ailes and Fox News are changing cable news. *The New Yorker Magazine*.

Banks, M. A. (2008). *Blogging heroes: Interviews with 30 of the world's top bloggers*. Hoboken, NJ: John Wiley & Sons.

Banning, S. A., & Sweetster, K. D. (2007). How much do they think it affects them and whom do they believe? Comparing the third-person effect and credibility of blogs and traditional media. *Communication Quarterly, 55*(4).

Benkler, Y. (2006). *The wealth of network: How social production transforms markets and freedom*. New Haven, CT: Yale University Press.

Bennett, W. L. (2007). *News: The politics of illusion*. Pearson Longman.

Bicket, M. W. A. D. (2006, August). The Bagdad Broadcasting Corporation: US Conservatives take aim at the BBC. *Mass Communication*.

Bowman, S., & Willis, C. (2003). *We media: How partisans are shaping the future of news and information*. The Media Center at the American Press Institute.

Boxer, S. (2008). *Ultimate blogs: Masterworks from the wild Web*. New York: Vintage Books.

Boysen, G. A., & Vogel, D. L. (2007). Biased assimilation and attitude polarization in response to learning about biological explanations of homosexuality. *Sex Roles, 57*(9/10).

Choi, J. H., Watt, J. H., & Lynch, M. (2006). Perceptions of news credibility about the war in Iraq: Why war opponents perceived the Internet as the most credible medium. *Journal of Computer-Mediated Communication, 12*(1).

Christen, C. T., Kannaovakun, P., & Gunther, A. C. (2002). Hostile media perceptions: Partisan assessments of press and public during the 1997 United Parcel Service strike. *Political Communication, 19*.

Clarke, T. (2007). *Lipstick on a pig: Winning in the nospin era by someone who knows the game*. New York: Free Press.

Crier, C. (2005). *Contempt: How the right is wronging America*. New York: Rugged Land Press.

Davis, A. C. (2012, March 1). Md. becomes eighth state to legalize gay marriage. *The Washington Post*.

Drehle, D. (2007). Weapons of mass media. *The Washington Post*.

Duncan, I. (2012, March 1). Maryland governor signs same-sex marriage law. *Los Angeles Times*.

Flanagin, A. J., & Metzger, M. J. (2000). Perceptions of Internet information credibility. *Journalism and Mass Communication Quarterly, 77*(3).

Gans, H. J. (1979). Multiperspectival news. In *Deciding what's news: A study of CBS Evening News, NBC Nightly News, Newsweek, and Time*. Pantheon Books.

Geer, J. D. (2003). Evaluating the credibility of online information: A test of source and advertising influence. *Mass Communication & Society, 6*(1).

Gillmor, D. (2006). *We the media: Grassroots journalism by the people for the people*. O'Reilly.

Giner-Sorolla, R., & Chaiken, S. (1994). The causes of hostile media judgments. *Journal of Experimental Social Psychology, 30*.

Grant, A. E. (2006, August). When news breaks, they fix it: The impact of *The Daily Show with Jon Stewart* on current events knowledge. *AEJMC, Mass Communication & Society Division*.

Grossberg, L., Wartella, E., Whitney, D. C., & Macgregor Wise, J. (2006). *Media making: Mass media in the popular culture*. London: Sage.

Gunther, A. C. (1992). Biased press or biased public? Attitudes toward media coverage. *Public Opinion Quarterly, 56*(2).

Gunther, A. C., & Chia, S. C. (2001). Predicting pluralistic ignorance: The hostile media perception and its consequences. *Journalism & Mass Communication Quarterly, 78*(4).

Gunther, A. C., Christen, C. T., Liebhart, J. L., & Chia, S. C. (2001). Congenial public, contrary press, and biased estimates of the climate of opinion. *Public Opinion Quarterly, 65*.

Gunther, A. C., Miller, N., & Liebhart, J. L. (2009). Assimilation and contrast in a test of the hostile media effect. *Communication Research, 36*(6).

Gunther, A. C., & Liebhart, J. L (2006). Broad reach or biased source? Decomposing the hostile media effect. *Journal of Communication, 56*.

Gunther, A. C., & Schmitt, K. (2004). Mapping boundaries of the hostile media effect, *Journal of Communication, 54*(1).

Halloran, L., (2011). Gay marriage activists: Minn. vote offers opportunity. *NPR*.

Hanson, R. E. (2008). *Mass communication: Living in a media world*. Washington, DC: CQ Press.

Hewitt, H. (2005). *Blog: Understanding the information reformation that's changing your world*. Nashville, TN: Nelson Books.

Ho, S. S., Binder, A. R., Becker, A. B., Moy, P., Scheufele, D. A., Brossard, D., & Gunther, A. C. (2011). The role of perceptions of media bias in general and issue-specific political participation. *Mass Communication and Society, 14*.

Kim, D., & Johnson, T. J. (2009). A shift in media credibility: Comparing Internet and traditional news sources in South Korea. *The International Communication Gazette, 71*(4).

Kiousis, S. (2001). Public trust or mistrust? Perceptions of media credibility in the information age. *Mass Communication and Society, 4*(4).

Kline, D., Burstein, D., De Keijzer, A. J., & Berger, P. (2005). *Blog! How the newest media revolution is changing politics, business, and culture*. New York: CDS Books.

Lee, T. (2005). The liberal media myth revisited: An examination of factors influencing perceptions of media bias. *Journal of Broadcasting & Electronic Media, 49*(1)

Leslie, L. Z. (2004). *Mass communication ethics: Decision making in postmodern culture*. Boston, MA: Houghton Mifflin.

Levin, M. R. (2005). *Men in black: How the Supreme Court is destroying America*. Washington, DC: Regnery.

Liebes, T., & Katz, E. (1990). *The export of meaning: Cross-cultural reading of Dallas*. Oxford: Oxford University Press.

Lord, C. G., Ross, L., & Lepper, M. R. (1997). Biased assimilation and attitude polarization: The effects of prior theories on subsequently considered evidence. *Journal of Personality and Social Psychology, 37*(11).

Love, R. (2007, March/April). Before Jon Stewart: The truth about fake news—believe it. *Columbia Journalism Review*.

Mackay, J., & Lowrey, W. (2007). *The credibility divide: Reader trust of online newspapers and blogs*. Presented at the ICA 2007 Annual Meeting.

Masci, D. (2009). *A contentious debate: Same-sex marriage in the U.S.* Pew Research Center's Forum on Religion & Public Life.

McHoskey, J. W. (1995). Case closed? On the John F. Kennedy assassination: Biased assimilation of evidence and attitude polarization. *Basic & Applied Social Psychology, 17*.

Media Research Center. (2008). *How the public views the media*. Retrieved from www.mediaresearch.org/biasbasics/biasbasics4.asp

Metzger, M. J., Flanagin, A. J., Eyal, K., Lemus, D. R., & McCann, R. M. (2003). Credibility for the 21st century: Integrating perspectives on source, message, and media credibility in the contemporary media environment. *Communication Yearbook, 27*.

Morley, D. (1980). *The nationwide audience: Structure and decoding*. British Film Institute.

Morley, D. (1989). Changing paradigms in audience studies. In E. Seiter, H. Borchers, G. Kreutzner, & E-M. Warth (Eds.), *Remote control: Television, audience, and cultural power*. Routledge.

Munro, G. D., & Ditto, P. H. (1997). Biased assimilation, attitude polarization, and affect in reactions to stereotype-relevant scientific information. *Personality and Social Psychology Bulletin, 23*(6).

Murrow, E. R. (2004). *Museum of broadcast communications*. Retrieved from www.museum.tv/archives/etv/M/htmlM/murrowedwar/murrowedwar.htm

Nyhan, B. (2012). Does the U.S. media have a liberal bias? *Perspectives on Politics, 10*.

Outfoxed: Rupert Murdoch's war on journalism [video documentary]. (2004). Disinformation Company.

Paletz, D. L. (2002). *The media in American politics*. New York: Longman.

Park, C.-Y. (2005). Decomposing Korean news media credibility in the Internet age. *International Journal of Public Opinion Research, 18*(2).

Patching, M. H. R. (2007). *Journalism ethics: Arguments and cases*. New York: Oxford University Press.

Pew Research Center for the People and the Press. (2005). *Bottom-line pressures now hurting coverage, say journalists*. Retrieved from http://people-press.org/reports/display. php3?PageID=825

Plous, S. (1991). Biases in the assimilation of technological breakdowns: Do accidents make us safer? *Journal of Applied Social Psychology, 21*(13).

Potter, D. (2007, December/2008, January). His way: How Roger Ailes' game plan created Fox's cable domination. *American Journalism Review*.

Purcell, K., Rainie, L., Mitchell, A., Rosenstiel, T., & Olmstead, K. (2010). *Understanding the participatory news consumer: How Internet and cell phone users have turned news into a social experience*. Pew Research Center.

Reynolds, G. (2003). *Ethics in information technology*. Boston, MA: Thompson Course Technology.

Richardson, J. D., Huddy, W. P., & Morgan, S. M. (2008). The hostile media effect, biased assimilation, and perceptions of a presidential debate. *Journal of Applied Social Psychology, 38*(5).

Rodman, G. (2001). *Making sense of media*. Boston, MA: Allyn & Bacon.

Schulman, D. (2006, May/June). Mind games. *Columbia Journalism Review*.

Smith, A. (2008). *New numbers for blogging and blog readership*. The Pew Internet & American Life Project.

Street, J. (2001). *Mass media, politics and democracy*. New York: Palgrave.

Vallone, R. P., Ross, L., & Lepper, M. R. (1985). The hostile media phenomenon: Biased perception and perceptions of media bias in the coverage of the Beirut Massacre. *Journal of Personality and Social Psychology, 49*(3).

Vedantam, S. (2006, July 24). Two views of the same news find opposite biases. *The Washington Post*.

CHAPTER 11

Alf, J., & Mapp, J. (2006). *The faiths of our fathers: What America's founders really believed*. Barnes & Noble.

Baer, W. S., & Rand Corporation. (1992). *Technology's challenges to the First Amendment*. Santa Monica, CA: Rand.

Barton Carter, T., Dee, J. L., & Zuckerman, H. L. (2000). *Mass communication law in a nutshell*. St. Paul, MN: West Group.

Barton Carter, T., Franklin, M. A., & Wright, J. B. (2007). *The first amendment and the fifth estate: Regulation of electronic mass media*. St. Paul, MN: Foundation Press.

Bobbitt, R. (2008). *Exploring communication law: A Socratic approach*. Pearson/Allyn & Bacon.

Bowman, J. S. (2005). *The Founding Fathers: The men behind the nation*. New York: World Publications Group.

Bruschke, J., & Loges, W. E. (2004). *Free press vs. fair trials: Examining publicity's role in trial outcomes*. Mahwah, NJ: Lawrence Erlbaum Associates.

Bunnin, B., & Beren, P. (1998). *The writer's legal companion: The complete handbook for the working writer*. New York: Perseus Books.

Burns, E. (2006). *Infamous scribblers: The Founding Fathers and the rowdy beginnings of American journalism*. New York: PublicAffairs.

Caddell, R., & Johnson, H. (2006). *Media law*. New York: Oxford University Press.

Carey, P. (2007). *Media law*. London: Sweet & Maxwell.

Carter, T. B., Dee, J. L., et al. (2007). *Mass communication law in a nutshell*. St. Paul, MN: Thomson/West.

Coombe, R. J. (1998). *The cultural life of intellectual properties: Authorship, appropriation, and the law*. Durham, NC: Duke University Press.

Copeland, D. A. (2006). *The idea of a free press: The Enlightenment and Its unruly legacy*. Chicago: Northwestern University Press.

Crawford, M. G. (2002). *The journalist's legal guide*. Scarborough, ON: Carswell.

Creech, K. C. (2007). *Electronic media law and regulation*. Boston, MA: Focal Press.

Dill, B. (1986). *The journalist's handbook on libel and privacy*. New York/London: Free Press; Collier Macmillan.

Douglass, E. P. (1989). *Rebels and democrats: The struggle for equal political rights and majority rule during the American Revolution*. Chicago: Elephant Paperback.

Elias, S. (1999). *Patent copyright and trademark*. Berkeley, CA: Nolo.

Feintuck, M., & Varney, M. (2006). *Media regulation, public interest and the law*. Edinburgh: Edinburgh University Press.

Fischer, D. H. (2005). *Liberty and freedom: A visual history of America's founding ideas*. New York: Oxford University Press.

Fletcher, G. P. (2002). *Our secret constitution: How Lincoln redefined American democracy*. New York: Oxford University Press.

Gillmor, D. M. (1996). *Fundamentals of mass communication law*. St. Paul, MN: West.

Ginsberg, B., & Lowi, T. J. (2000). *American government*. New York: W. W. Norton & Company.

Glasser, C. J. (2006). *International libel and privacy handbook: A global reference for journalists, publishers, webmasters, and lawyers*. New York: Bloomberg Press.

Goldstein, P. (1995). *Copyright's highway: The law and lore of copyright from Gutenberg to the Celestial Jukebox*. New York: Hill and Wang.

Goldstein, P. (2001). *International copyright: Principles, law, and practice*. New York: Oxford University Press.

Gunther, R., & Mughan, A. (2000). *Democracy and the media: A comparative perspective*. Cambridge: Press Syndicate of the University of Cambridge.

Hall, K. L. (2005). *The Oxford companion to the Supreme Court of the United States*. New York: Oxford University Press.

Harrison, M., & Gilbert, S. (2003). *Great decisions of the U.S. Supreme Court*. New York: Barnes & Noble.

Icenoggle, J. (2005). *Schenck v. United States and the freedom of speech debate: Debating Supreme Court decisions*. Berkeley Heights, NJ: Enslow.

Jassin, L. J., & Schecter, S. C. (1998). *The copyright permission and libel handbook: A step-by-step guide for writers, editors, and publishers*. Hoboken, NJ: John Wiley & Sons, Inc.

Judson, J. L., & Bertazzoni, D. M. (2002). *Law, media, and culture: The landscape of hate*. New York: Peter Lang.

Kanyongolo, F. E., & Article 19. (1996). *National security and legal protection of media freedom*. London: Article 19.

Lane, F. S. (2006). *The decency wars: The campaign to cleanse American culture*. Amherst, NY: Prometheus Books.

Lapham, L. H. (2004). *Gag rule: On the suppression of dissent and the stifling of democracy*. New York: Penguin Press.

Leaffer, M. (1999). *Understanding copyright law*. Albany, NY: Matthew Bender & Company.

Lessig, L. (2004). *Free culture: How Big Media uses technology and the law to lock down culture and control creativity*. New York: Penguin Press.

Lipschultz, J. H. (2000). *Free expression in the age of the Internet: Social and legal boundaries*. Boulder, CO: Westview Press.

Lipschultz, J. H. (2008). *Broadcast and Internet indecency: Defining free speech*. New York: Routledge.

Litman, J. (2001). *Digital copyright*. Amherst, NY: Prometheus Books.

Loewen, J. W. (1996). *Lies my teacher told me: Everything your American history textbook got wrong*. New York: Simon & Schuster.

Loveland, I. (1998). *Importing the first amendment: Freedom of expression in American, English and European law*. Oxford: Hart.

McDougall, W. A. (2004). *Freedom just around the corner*. New York: HarperCollins.

Middleton, K. R., & Lee, W. E. (2007). *The law of public communication*. Boston, MA: Pearson/Allyn & Bacon.

Moore, D. J. (2006). *Privacy: The press and the law*. St. Albans, VT: XPL.

Overbeck, W. (2005). *Major principles of media law*. Belmont, CA: Thomson Wadsworth.

Patterson, L. R. (1968). *Copyright in historical perspective*. Nashville, TN: Vanderbilt University Press.

Pember, D. R., & Calvert, C. (2007). *Mass media law*. New York: McGraw-Hill Higher Education.

Sadler, R. L. (2005). *Electronic media law*. London: Sage.

Samuels, E. (2000). *The illustrated story of copyright*. New York: Thomas Dunne Books.

Smartt, U. (2006). *Media law for journalists*. London: Sage.

Stone, G. R. (2004). *Perilous times: Free speech in wartime from the Sedition Act of 1798 to the War on Terrorism*. New York: W. W. Norton & Company.

Sweeney, M. S. (2006). *The military and the press: An uneasy truce*. Chicago: Northwestern University Press.

Tedford, L. T., & Herbeck, D. A. (2005). *Freedom of speech in the United States*. State College, PA: Strata.

Wilentz, S. (2005). *The rise of American democracy: Jefferson to Lincoln*. New York: W. W. Norton & Company.

Wood, G. S. (2004). *The Americanization of Benjamin Franklin*. New York: Penguin Press.

Woodruff, P. (2005). *First democracy: The challenge of an ancient idea*. New York: Oxford University Press.

Zelizer, J. E. (2004). *The American Congress: The building of democracy*. Boston, MA: Houghton Mifflin.

CHAPTER 12

Batchen, G. (2001). *Each wild idea: Writing, photography, history*. Cambridge, MA: MIT Press.

Bendavid-Val, L. (2001). *Stories on paper and glass: Pioneering photography at National Geographic*. Washington, DC: National Geographic.

Benjamin, W., Doherty, B., et al. (2008). *The work of art in the age of its technological reproducibility, and other writings on media*. Cambridge, MA: Belknap Press of Harvard University Press.

Brennen, B., & Hardt, H. (1999). *Picturing the past: Media, history, and photography*. Urbana, IL: University of Illinois Press.

Brothers, C. (1997). *War and photography: A cultural history*. New York: Routledge.

Burnett, R. (1995). *Cultures of vision: Images, media, and the imaginary*. Bloomington, IN: Indiana University Press.

Cadava, E. (1997). *Words of light: Theses on the photography of history*. Princeton, NJ: Princeton University Press.

Chiaramonte, G., Borgonzoni, P., et al. (1983). *The story of photography: An illustrated history*. Millerton, NY: Aperture. Distributed by Viking-Penguin.

Collins, K., & Henisch, H. K. (1990). *Shadow and substance: Essays on the history of photography in honor of Heinz K. Henisch*. Bloomfield Hills, MI: Amorphous Institute Press.

Coote, J. H. (1993). *The illustrated history of colour photography*. London: Surbiton.

Daval, J. L. (1982). *Photography: History of an art*. New York: Skira/Rizzoli.

Davenport, A. (1999). *The history of photography: An overview*. Albuquerque, NM: University of New Mexico Press.

Derrick, R., & Muir, R. (2002). *Unseen Vogue: The secret history of fashion photography*. London: Little, Brown.

Druckrey, T. (1996). *Electronic culture: Technology and visual representation*. New York: Aperture.

Durant, M. A., McDermott, D., et al. (1998). *McDermott & McGough: A history of photography*. Santa Fe, NM/New York: Arena Editions. Distributed by D.A.P./Distributed Art Publishers.

Edwards, E., & Hart, J. (2004). *Photographs objects histories: On the materiality of images*. New York: Routledge.

Eskildsen, U., Ebner, F., et al. (2008). *Street & studio: An urban history of photography*. London: Tate.

Evans, J., & Hall, S. (1999). *Visual culture: The reader*. London/Thousand Oaks, CA: Sage/Open University.

Films for the Humanities. (2002). *Decoding photographic images*. Princeton, NJ: Films for the Humanities & Sciences.

Frizot, M. (1998). *A new history of photography*. Köln: Könemann.

Gernsheim, H. (1982). *The origins of photography*. New York: Thames and Hudson.

Green, J. (1984). *American photography: A critical history 1945 to the present*. New York: H. N. Abrams.

Henisch, H. K., & Collins, K. (1990). *Shadow and substance: Essays on the history of photography in honor of Heinz K. Henisch*. Bloomfield Hills, MI: Amorphous Institute Press.

Hirsch, R. (2000). *Seizing the light: A history of photography*. Boston, MA: McGraw-Hill.

Howells, R., & Matson, R. W. (2009). *Using visual evidence*. Maidenhead: Open University Press.

Hoy, A. H. (2005). *The book of photography: The history, the technique, the art, the future*. Washington, DC: National Geographic.

Jeffrey, I. (1981). *Photography: A concise history*. New York: Oxford University Press.

Jeffrey, I., & National Museum of Photography Film and Television. (1999). *Revisions: An alternative history of photography*. Bradford: National Museum of Photography, Film & Television, National Museum of Science & Industry.

Lange, D. (1981). *Dorothea Lange*. Millerton, NY: Aperture.

Lemagny, J. C., & Rouillé, A. (1987). *A history of photography: Social and cultural perspectives*. New York: Cambridge University Press.

Lewinski, J. (1980). *The camera at war: A history of war photography from 1848 to the present day*. New York: Simon & Schuster.

Lister, M. (1995). *The photographic image in digital culture*. New York: Routledge.

Livingston, J., Fralin, F., et al. (1988). *Odyssey: The art of photography at* National Geographic. Charlottesville, VA: Thomasson-Grant.

Macdonald, G. (1980). *Camera: Victorian eyewitness: A history of photography, 1826–1913*. New York: Viking Press.

Marien, M. W. (1997). *Photography and its critics: A cultural history, 1839–1900*. New York: Cambridge University Press.

Marien, M. W. (2006). *Photography: A cultural history*. Upper Saddle River, NJ: Prentice Hall.

Mitchell, J. G. (2001). *National Geographic: The wildlife photographs*. Washington, DC: National Geographic Society.

Moyers, B. D., O'Neill, J. D., et al. (2006). *A conversation with Susan Sontag*. Princeton, NJ: Films for the Humanities & Sciences.

National Geographic Society. (1998). *Photographs, then and now*. Washington, DC: National Geographic Society.

National Geographic Society. (1999). *National Geographic photographs: The milestones*. Washington, DC: National Geographic.

National Geographic Society. (2003). *Through the lens: National Geographic greatest photographs*. Washington, DC: National Geographic.

Newhall, B. (1980). *Photography, essays and images: Illustrated readings in the history of photography*. New York/Boston, MA: Museum of Modern Art. Distributed by New York Graphic Society.

Newhall, B. (1982). *The history of photography: From 1839 to the present day*. New York: Museum of Modern Art. Distributed by the New York Graphic Society.

Nikpour, K., Cadigan, S., et al. (2004). *Photography and the brain: The language of photography*. Princeton, NJ: Films for the Humanities & Sciences.

Pollack, P. (1977). *The picture history of photography from the earliest beginnings to the present day*. New York: Abrams.

Raeburn, J. (2006). *A staggering revolution: A cultural history of thirties photography*. Chicago, IL: University of Illinois Press.

Raimondo Souto, H. M. (2007). *Motion picture photography: A history, 1891–1960*. Jefferson, NC: McFarland.

Roosens, L., & Salu, L. (1989). *History of photography: A bibliography of books*. New York: Mansell.

Rosenblum, N. (2007). *A world history of photography*. New York: Abbeville Press.

Sandler, M. W. (1979). *The story of American photography: An illustrated history for young people*. Boston, MA: Little, Brown.

Sandler, M. W. (2002). *Photography: An illustrated history*. New York: Oxford University Press.

Shires, L. M. (2009). *Perspectives: Modes of viewing and knowing in nineteenth-century England*. Columbus, OH: Ohio State University Press.

Shore, S. (2007). *The nature of photographs*. London: Phaidon.

Shore, S., & Center for American Places. (1998). *The nature of photographs*. Baltimore, MD: Johns Hopkins University Press.

Steichen, E., Royal Photographic Society of Great Britain, et al. (1997). *Edward Steichen: The Royal Photographic Society collection*. Milan, Italy: Charta.

Stroebel, L. D., Todd, H. N., et al. (1980). *Visual concepts for photographers*. New York: Focal Press.

Williams, V. (1994). *Warworks: Women, photography and the iconography of war*. London: Virago.

Wolf, H. (1988). *Visual thinking: Methods for making images memorable*. New York: American Showcase. Distributed by Rizzoli International Publications.

Zakia, R. D. (1974). *Perception and photography*. Englewood Cliffs, NJ: Prentice Hall.

Zakia, R. D. (2002). *Perception and imaging*. Boston, MA: Focal Press.

Zakia, R. D. (2007). *Perception and imaging: Photography—a way of seeing*. Boston, MA: Focal Press.

CHAPTER 13

Allan, S., & Thorson, E. (2009). *Citizen journalism: Global perspectives*. New York: Peter Lang.

Alysen, B. (2006). *The electronic reporter: Broadcast journalism in Australia*. Sydney: University of New South Wales Press.

Artwick, C. G. (2004). *Reporting and producing for digital media*. Ames, IA: Blackwell.

Atkins, J. B. (2002). *The mission: Journalism, ethics and the world*. Ames, IA: Iowa State University Press.

Barlow, A. (2007). *The rise of the blogosphere*. Westport, CT: Praeger.

Briggs, M., Schaffer, J., et al. (2007). *Journalism 2.0: How to survive and thrive: A digital literacy guide for the information age*. College Park, MD: J-Lab: The Institute for Interactive Journalism, Philip Merrill College of Journalism, University of Maryland.

Bruns, A. (2005). *Gatewatching: Collaborative online news production*. New York: P. Lang.

Bury, C., Donvan, J., et al. (2006). *The bloggers new rules, or no rules?* Princeton, NJ: Films for the Humanities & Sciences.

Carroll, P., De Palma, B., et al. (2008). *Redacted*. Los Angeles, CA: Distributed by Magnolia Home Entertainment.

Close Up Foundation. (2000). *Reporting from the hot spots: Close up conversations*. Alexandria, VA: Close Up Publishing.

Cohen, E. D., & Elliott, D. (1997). *Journalism ethics: A reference handbook*. Santa Barbara, CA: ABC-CLIO.

Cooper, S. D. (2006). *Watching the watchdog: Bloggers as the fifth estate*. Spokane, WA: Marquette Books.

Foust, J. C. (2005). *Online journalism: Principles and practices of news for the Web*. Scottsdale, AZ: Holcomb Hathaway.

Friend, C., & Singer, J. B. (2007). *Online journalism ethics: Traditions and transitions*. Armonk, NY: M. E. Sharpe.

George, C. (2006). *Contentious journalism and the Internet: Toward democratic discourse in Malaysia and Singapore*. Seattle, WA: University of Washington Press.

Gillmor, D. (2004). *We the media: Grassroots journalism by the people, for the people*. Beijing/Sebastopol, CA: O'Reilly.

Harsch, J. C. (1993). *At the hinge of history: A reporter's story*. Athens, GA: University of Georgia Press.

Hewitt, H. (2005). *Blog: Understanding the information reformation that's changing your world*. Nashville, TN: T. Nelson Publishers.

Hoyt, M., & Palatella, J. (2007). *Reporting Iraq: An oral history of the war by the journalists who covered it*. Hoboken, NJ: Melville House Publishing.

Kline, D., Berger, P., et al. (2005). *Blog! How the newest media revolution is changing politics, business, and culture*. New York: CDS Books.

Kolodzy, J. (2006). *Convergence journalism: Writing and reporting across the news media*. Lanham, MD: Rowman & Littlefield.

Lambros, V. (2008). *The impact of new media on the practice of journalism*. Fairfax, VA: George Mason University.

Lee, P. S. N., Fung, A. F. H., & Leung, L. (2009). *Embedding into our lives: New opportunities and challenges of the Internet*. Hong Kong: Chinese University Press.

Li, X. (2006). *Internet newspapers: The making of a mainstream medium*. Mahwah, NJ: Lawrence Erlbaum Associates.

McCain, T. A., & Shyles, L. (1994). *The 1,000 hour war: Communication in the Gulf*. Westport, CT: Greenwood Press.

Morrison, D. E., & Tumber, H. (1988). *Journalists at war: The dynamics of news reporting during the Falklands conflict*. London: Sage.

Paterson, C. A., & Domingo, D. (2008). *Making online news: The ethnography of new media production*. New York: Peter Lang.

Quandt, T., & Schweiger, W. (2008). *Journalismus online: Partizipation oder profession?* Wiesbaden, Germany: Verlag für Sozialwissenschaften.

Quinn, S. (2006). *Conversations on convergence: Insiders' views on news production in the 21st century*. New York: Peter Lang.

Quinn, S., & Filak, V. F. (2005). *Convergent journalism: An introduction*. Burlington, MA: Elsevier/Focal Press.

Raphael, M., Rowland, M., et al. (2004). *Frontline reporting*. New York: History Channel; Distributed by New Video.

Seierstad, Å., & Christophersen, I. (2005). *A hundred and one days: A Baghdad journal*. New York: Basic Books.

Sites, K. (2007). *In the hot zone: One man, one year, twenty wars*. New York: Harper Perennial.

Ward, S. J. A. (2004). *The invention of journalism ethics: The path to objectivity and beyond*. Montreal/Ithaca, NY: McGill-Queen's University Press.

Weingarten, M. (2006). *The gang that wouldn't write straight: Wolfe, Thompson, Didion, and the New Journalism revolution*. New York: Crown Publishers.

Wilkinson, J. S., Grant, A. E., & Fisher, D. J. (2009). *Principles of convergent journalism*. Oxford: Oxford University Press.

Wulfemeyer, K. T. (2006). *Online newswriting*. Ames, IA: Blackwell Publishing Professional.

CHAPTER 14

Acland, C. R. (2003). *Screen traffic: Movies, multiplexes, and global culture*. Durham, NC: Duke University Press.

Ahlmalm, A. (1997). *The culture of global advertising and the advertising of global culture*. McMinnville, OR: Linfield College.

Appiah, A., Gates, H. L., et al. (1996). *The dictionary of global culture*. New York: Knopf/Random House.

Bailey, D. (2004). *The open society paradox: Why the 21st century calls for more openness—not less*. Brassey's.

Crane, D., Kawasaki, K. I., et al. (2002). *Global culture: Media, arts, policy, and globalization*. New York: Routledge.

Demers, D. P. (2002). *Global media: Menace or Messiah?* Cresskill, NJ: Hampton Press.

Everette, E., & Dennis, R. W. S. (1998). *Media and democracy*. Piscataway, NJ: Transaction Publishers.

Flew, T. (2007). *Understanding global media*. New York: Palgrave Macmillan.

Fox, E., & Waisbord, S. R. (2002). *Latin politics, global media*. Austin, TX: University of Texas Press.

Franklin, S., Lury, C., et al. (2000). *Global nature, global culture*. London: Sage.

Gunther, R., & Mughan, A. (2000). *Democracy and the media: A comparative perspective*. Cambridge: Cambridge University Press.

Hachten, W. A., & Scotton, J. F. (2002). *The world news prism: Global media in an era of terrorism*. Ames, IA: Iowa State Press.

Hackett, R. A., & Zhao, Y. (2005). *Democratizing global media: One world, many struggles*. Lanham, MD: Rowman & Littlefield.

Hakanen, E. A., & Nikolaev, A. G. (2006). *Leading to the 2003 Iraq war: The global media debate*. New York: Palgrave Macmillan.

Harindranath, R. (2006). *Perspectives on global culture*. New York: Open University Press.

Herman, E. S., & McChesney, R. W. (1997). *The global media: The new missionaries of corporate capitalism*. Washington, DC: Cassell.

Hoskins, C. (1997). *Global television and film: An introduction to the economics of the business*. New York: Oxford University Press.

Jong, W. D., Shaw, M., et al. (2005). *Global activism, global media*. Ann Arbor, MI: Pluto Press.

Lewis, J. (2005). *Language wars: The role of culture in global terror and political violence*. Ann Arbor, MI: Pluto Press.

Lynch, D. C. (2006). *Rising China and Asian democratization: Socialization to "global culture" in the political transformations of Thailand, China, and Taiwan*. Stanford, CA: Stanford University Press.

Machin, D., & Van Leeuwen, T. (2007). *Global media discourse: A critical introduction*. New York: Routledge.

Mead, R. (2013, February 4). Brave new world—live from Gaza. *The New Yorker Magazine*.

Merrill, J. C. (1995). *Global journalism: Survey of international communication*. New York: Pearson Education.

Munshi, S. (2001). *Images of the "modern woman" in Asia: Global media, local meanings*. Richmond, VA: Curzon.

Neuman, J. (1996). *Lights camera war: Is media technology driving international politics?* New York: St. Martin's Press.

Newsom, D. (2007). *Bridging the gaps in global communication*. Malden, MA: Blackwell.

Orum, A. M., Johnstone, J. W. C., & Ringer, S. (1999). *Changing societies: Essential sociology for our times*. Lanham, MD: Rowman & Littlefield.

Price, M. E. (2002). Media and sovereignty: The global revolution and its challenge to state power. Cambridge, MA: MIT Press.

Seib, P. M. (2008). *The Al Jazeera effect: How the new global media are reshaping world politics*. Washington, DC: Potomac Books.

Siochru, S. O., Girard, B., & Mahan, A. (2002). *Global media governance: A beginner's guide*. Lanham, MD: Rowman & Littlefield.

Steven, P. (2003). *The no-nonsense guide to global media*. Oxford: New Internationalist/Verso.

Stone, D. P., Jones International Ltd., et al. (1998). *Global media: Media power*. Princeton, NJ: Films for the Humanities & Sciences.

Street, J. (2001). *Mass media, politics and democracy*. New York: Palgrave.

Thompson, J. B. (1995). *The media and modernity: A social theory of the media*. Stanford, CA: Stanford University Press.

Thussu, D. K. (1998). *Electronic empires: Global media and local resistance*. New York: Arnold.

Timmerman, K. R. (2003). *Preachers of hate: Islam and the war on America*. New York: Crown Forum.

Wark, M. (1994). *Virtual geography: Living with global media events*. Bloomington, IN: Indiana University Press.

Weaver, D., Löffelholz, M., & Schwarz, A. (2008). *Global journalism research: Theories, methods, finding, future*. Malden, MA: Blackwell.

Westfield, M. (2000). *The gatekeepers: The global media battle to control Australia's pay TV*. Sydney/London: Pluto Press Australia; Comerford and Miller.

White, J. D. (2005). *Global media: The television revolution in Asia*. New York: Routledge.

World Bank Institute. (2002). *The right to tell: The role of mass media in economic development*. Washington, DC: World Bank.

CHAPTER 15

Allen, D., Rush, R. R., et al. (1996). *Women transforming communications: Global intersections*. Thousand Oaks, CA: Sage.

Bentz, V. M., & Mayer, P. E. F. (1993). *Visual images of women in the arts and mass media*. Lewiston, NY: E. Mellen Press.

Bukowski, C. (1978). *Women*. Santa Barbara, CA: Black Sparrow Press.

Byerly, C. M., & Ross, K. (2006). *Women and media: A critical introduction*. Malden, MA: Blackwell.

Carilli, T., & Campbell, J. (2005). *Women and the media: Diverse perspectives*. Lanham, MD: University Press of America.

Carter, C., & Steiner, L. (2003). *Critical readings: Media and gender reader*. Maidenhead: Open University Press.

Carter, C., Branston, G., et al. (1998). *News, gender, and power*. New York: Routledge.

Cashmore, E., & ebrary, Inc. (1997). *The black culture industry*. New York: Routledge.

Chambers, J. (2008). *Madison avenue and the color line: African Americans in the advertising industry*. Philadelphia, PA: University of Pennsylvania Press.

Cole, E., & Daniel, J. H. (2005). *Featuring females: Feminist analyses of media. Psychology of women book series*. Washington, DC: American Psychological Association.

Columbia University. *Archives: University protest and activism collection, 1958–1999* (Bulk dates 1968–1972), p. 29.

Conor, L. (2004). *The spectacular modern woman: Feminine visibility in the 1920s*. Bloomington, IN: Indiana University Press.

Cooney, S., & Kelly, R. (1971). *A checklist of the first one hundred publications of the Black Sparrow Press: With 30 passing remarks by Robert Kelly*. Los Angeles, CA: Black Sparrow Press.

Daley, P., & James, B. A. (2004). *Cultural politics and the mass media: Alaska Native voices*. Urbana, IL: University of Illinois Press.

Dates, J. L., & Barlow, W. (1983). *Split image: African Americans in the media*. Washington, DC: Howard University Press.

Davies, K., Dickey, J., et al. (1987). *Out of focus: Writings on women and the media*. London: Women's Press.

Entman, R. M., & Rojecki, A. (2001). *The black image in the white mind: Media and race in America*. Chicago: University of Chicago Press.

Faas, E. (1978). *Towards a new American poetics: Essays and interviews: Charles Olson, Robert Duncan, Gary Snyder, Robert Creeley, Robert Bly, Allen Ginsberg*. Santa Barbara, CA: Black Sparrow Press.

Farrar, H. (1998). *The Baltimore Afro-American, 1892–1950*. Westport, CT: Greenwood Press.

Frith, K. T., & Karan, K. (2008). *Commercializing women: Images of Asian women in the media*. Cresskill, NJ: Hampton Press.

Fujioka, Y. (2005, December). Black media images as a perceived threat to African American ethnic identity: Coping responses, perceived public perception, and attitudes. *Journal of Broadcasting and Electronic Media*.

Gill, R. (2007). *Gender and the media*. Malden, MA: Polity Press.

Gross, L. P., & Woods, J. D. (1999). *The Columbia reader on lesbians and gay men in media, society, and politics*. New York: Columbia University Press.

Hall, A. C. (1998). *Delights, desires, and dilemmas: Essays on women and the media*. Westport, CT: Praeger.

Hamlet, J. D. (1998). *Afrocentric visions: Studies in culture and communication*. Thousand Oaks, CA: Sage.

Harne, L., & Miller, E. (1996). *All the rage: Reasserting radical lesbian feminism*. London: Women's Press.

Harris, P. (1999). *The queer press guide 2000*. New York: Painted Leaf Press.

Hellwig, T., & Thobani, S. (2006). *Asian women: Interconnections*. Toronto: Women's Press.

Hine, D. C., Hine, W. C., & Harold, S. (2004). *African American odyssey: Media research update* (2nd ed.). Upper Saddle River, NJ: Prentice Hall.

Howell, S. (1990). *Reflections of ourselves: The mass media and the women's movement, 1963 to the present*. New York: P. Lang.

Hunt, D. M. (2004). *Channeling blackness: Studies on television and race in America*. New York: Oxford University Press.

Inness, S. A. (2004). *Action chicks: New images of tough women in popular culture*. New York: Palgrave Macmillan.

Jacobs, R. N. (2000). *Race, media, and the crisis of civil society: From Watts to Rodney King*. New York: Cambridge University Press.

Jeter, J. P. (1996). *International Afro mass media: A reference guide*. Westport, CT: Greenwood Press.

Kanellos, N. (1998). *Thirty million strong: Reclaiming the Hispanic image in American culture*. Golden, CO: Fulcrum.

Kelly, R. (1979). *Kill the messenger who brings bad news*. Santa Barbara, CA: Black Sparrow Press.

Kepner, J. (1998). *Rough news, daring views: 1950s' pioneer gay press journalism*. New York: Haworth Press.

Kitch, C. L. (2001). *The girl on the magazine cover: The origins of visual stereotypes in American mass media*. Chapel Hill, NC: University of North Carolina Press.

Lazarus, M., Wunderlich, R., et al. (2000). *Beyond killing us softly: The impact of media images on women and girls*. Cambridge, MA: Cambridge Documentary Films.

Lueck, T. L., & Association for Education in Journalism and Mass Communication. (2004). *"Her say" in the media mainstream: A cultural feminist manifesto*. Columbia, SC: Association for Education in Journalism and Mass Communication.

Lumby, C. (1997). *Bad girls: The media, sex and feminism in the'90s*. St. Leonards, Australia: Allen & Unwin.

Ma, S. M. (2000). *The deathly embrace: Orientalism and Asian American identity*. Minneapolis, MN: University of Minnesota Press.

Macdonald, M. (1995). *Representing women: Myths of femininity in the popular media*. New York: E. Arnold. Distributed by St. Martin's Press.

Mansfield-Richardson, V. (2000). *Asian Americans and the mass media: A content analysis of twenty United States' newspapers and a survey of Asian American journalists*. New York: Garland.

Marriott, D. (2007). *Haunted life: Visual culture and Black modernity*. New Brunswick, NJ: Rutgers University Press.

Munshi, S. (2001). *Images of the "modern woman" in Asia: Global media, local meanings*. Richmond: Curzon.

Murphy, J. E., & Murphy, S. (1981). *Let my people know: American Indian journalism, 1828–1978*. Norman: University of Oklahoma Press.

Mwendamseke, A. N. S. (2003). *Mass media and female images: Reality and possible reforms*. Iringa, Tanzania: Iringa University College.

Myrick, R. (1996). *AIDS, communication, and empowerment: Gay male identity and the politics of public health messages*. New York: Harrington Park Press.

Nelson, S., Half Nelson Productions Inc., et al. (1998). *The black press soldiers without swords*. San Francisco, CA: Half Nelson Productions. Distributed by California Newsreel.

Noriega, C. A. (2000). *The future of Latino independent media: A NALIP sourcebook*. Los Angeles, CA: UCLA Chicano Studies Research Center.

Nuñez, L. V. (2006). *Spanish language media after the Univision: Hispanic broadcasting*. New York: Novinka Books.

Ono, K. A., & Pham, V. N. (2009). *Asian Americans and the media*. Cambridge: Polity.

Onwurah, N., Onwurah, K. S., et al. (1993). *And still I rise*. New York: Women Make Movies.

Oppliger, P. A. (2008). *Girls gone skank: The sexualization of girls in American culture*. Jefferson, NC: McFarland & Company.

Portales, M. (2000). *Crowding out Latinos: Mexican Americans in the public consciousness*. Philadelphia, PA: Temple University Press.

Prasad, N., & Stiftung, F. E. (1992). *A pressing matter: Women in press*. New Delhi, India: Friedrich Ebert Stiftung.

Pullen, C. (2007). *Documenting gay men: Identity and performance in reality television and documentary film*. Jefferson, NC: McFarland.

Rhodes, J. (2007). *Framing the Black Panthers: The spectacular rise of a Black Power icon*. New York: New Press. Distributed by W. W. Norton.

Ríos, D. I. A., & Mohamed, A. N. (2003). *Brown and black communication: Latino and African American conflict and convergence in mass media*. Westport, CT: Praeger.

Rodriguez, A. (1999). *Making Latino news: Race, language, class*. Thousand Oaks, CA: Sage.

Rodriguez, C. E. (1997). *Latin looks: Images of Latinas and Latinos in the U.S. media*. Boulder, CO: Westview Press.

Rofes, E. E. (1998). *Dry bones breathe: Gay men creating post-AIDS identities and cultures*. New York: Haworth Press.

Ross, K. (1996). *Black and white media: Black images in film and television*. Cambridge: Polity.

Ross, K. (2002). *Women, politics, media: Uneasy relations in comparative perspective*. Cresskill, NJ: Hampton Press.

Ross, K., & Byerly, C. M. (2004). *Women and media: International perspectives*. Malden, MA: Blackwell.

Rush, R. R., Oukrop, C. E., et al. (2004). *Seeking equity for women in journalism and mass communication education: A 30-year update*. Mahwah, NJ: Lawrence Erlbaum Associates.

Santa Ana, O., & ebrary, Inc. (2002). *Brown tide rising: Metaphors of Latinos in contemporary American public discourse*. Austin, TX: University of Texas Press.

Sarikakis, K., & Shade, L. R. (2008). *Feminist interventions in international communication: Minding the gap*. Lanham, MD: Rowman & Littlefield.

Soruco, G. R. (1996). *Cubans and the mass media in South Florida*. Gainesville, FL: University Press of Florida.

Standard Rate & Data Service. (1993). *Hispanic media and markets*. Wilmette, IL: Author.

Streitmatter, R. (1995). *Unspeakable: The rise of the gay and lesbian press in America*. Boston, MA: Faber and Faber.

Streitmatter, R. (2009). *From perverts to fab five: The media's changing depiction of gay people and lesbians*. New York: Routledge.

Subervi-Vélez, F. A. (2008). *The mass media and Latino politics: Studies of U.S. media content, campaign strategies and survey research: 1984–2004*. New York: Routledge.

Tasker, Y., Negra, D., et al. (2007). Durham, NC: Duke University Press.

Tebbel, C. (2000). *The body snatchers: How the media shapes women*. Sydney: Finch.

Thornham, S. (2007). *Women, feminism and media*. Edinburgh, Scotland: Edinburgh University Press.

Uganda Media Women's Association. (1998). *Report on a workshop for women leaders and the media: Moving into the 21st century*. Held at the Hotel Equatoria, November 21–22, 1997. Kampala, Uganda: Media Women Association.

Valdivia, A. N. (1995). *Feminism, multiculturalism, and the media: Global diversities*. Thousand Oaks, CA: Sage.

Valdivia, A. N. (2000). *A Latina in the land of Hollywood and other essays on media culture*. Tucson, AZ: University of Arizona Press.

Veciana-Suarez, A. (1987). *Hispanic media, USA: A narrative guide to print and electronic Hispanic news media in the United States*. Washington, DC: Media Institute.

Ward, B. E. (2001). *Media, culture and the modern African American freedom struggle*. Gainesville, FL: University of Florida Press.

Williams, L. (2001). *Playing the race card: Melodramas of black and white from Uncle Tom to O. J. Simpson*. Princeton, NJ: Princeton University Press.

Women's Institute for Freedom of the Press. (n.d.). *Media report to women*. Silver Spring, MD: Communication Research Associates.

Zilber, J., & Niven, D. (2000). *Racialized coverage of Congress: The news in black and white*. Westport, CT: Praeger.

Zoonen, L. V. (1994). *Feminist media studies*. London/Thousand Oaks, CA: Sage.

CHAPTER 16

Basalla, S. E., & Debelius, M. (2007). *"So what are you going to do with that?": Finding careers outside academia*. Chicago: University of Chicago Press.

Bendinger, B. (2004). *Advertising and the business of brands: An introduction to careers and concepts in advertising and marketing*. Chicago: Copy Workshop.

Bollinger, L., & O'Neill, C. (2008). *Women in media careers: Success despite the odds*. Lanham, MD: University Press of America.

Bone, J., Fernández, A., et al. (2004). *Opportunities in film careers*. New York: VGM Career Books.

Burns, J. B. (2007). *Career opportunities in journalism*. New York: Ferguson.

Camenson, B., DeGalan, J., et al. (1995). *Great jobs for communications majors*. Lincolnwood, IL: VGM Career Horizons.

Cappo, J. (2003). *The future of advertising: New media, new clients, new consumers in the post-television age*. Chicago: McGraw-Hill.

Cohen, D. S., Bustamante, S. A., et al. (2009). *Producing games: From business and budgets to creativity and design*. Boston, MA: Focal Press.

Collins, A., & Halverson, R. (2009). *Rethinking education in the age of technology: The digital revolution and schooling in America*. New York: Teachers College Press.

Crouch, T. L. (2008). *100 careers in film and television*. Barron's Educational Series, 2nd edition.

DeSena, C. (1996). *The comedy market: A writer's guide to making money being funny*. New York: Berkley.

Dzyak, B. (2008). *What I really want to do on set in Hollywood: A guide to real jobs in the film industry*. New York: Back Stage Books.

ebrary, Inc. (2003). *Resumes for advertising careers with sample cover letters*. Chicago: VGM Career Books.

Ellis, E. (2004). *Opportunities in broadcasting careers*. New York: McGraw-Hill.

Farr, J. M. (2007). *Top 100 computer and technical careers: Your complete guidebook to major jobs in many fields at all training levels*. Indianapolis, IN: JIST Works.

Farris, L. G. (1995). *Television careers: A guide to breaking and entering*. Fairfax, CA: Buy the Book Enterprises.

Feiertag, J., & Cupito, M. C. (2004). *Writer's market companion*. Cincinnati, OH: Writer's Digest Books.

Ferguson, D., & Patten, J. (2001). *Opportunities in journalism careers*. New York: McGraw-Hill.

Goldberg, J. (1997). *Real people working in communications*. Lincolnwood, IL: VGM Career Horizons.

Greenspon, J., & ebrary, Inc. (2003). *Careers for film buffs and other Hollywood types*. Chicago: VGM Career Books.

Gregory, G., Healy, R., et al. (2007). *Careers in media and film: The essential guide*. Los Angeles, CA: Sage.

Gregory, M. (2008). *The career chronicles: An insider's guide to what jobs are really like: The good, the bad, and the ugly from over 750 professionals*. Novato, CA: New World Library.

Heller, S. (2007). *Becoming a digital designer: A guide to careers in Web, video, broadcast, game and animation design*. Hoboken, NJ: Wiley.

Heron, M. (2006). *Creative careers in photography: Making a living with a camera*. New York: Allworth Press.

James, A. (1932). *Careers in advertising, and the jobs behind them*. New York: Macmillan.

Katz, H. E. (2003). *The media handbook: A complete guide to advertising media selection, planning, research, and buying*. Mahwah, NJ: Lawrence Erlbaum Associates.

Katz, J. A. (1984). *The ad game: A complete guide to careers in advertising, marketing, and related areas*. New York: Barnes & Noble Books.

Liming, D., & Dilorio, D. (2011, Fall). Work for play: Careers in video game development. *Occupational Outlook Quarterly*.

McKinney, A. (2002). *Real resumes for media, newspaper, broadcasting and public affairs jobs: Including real resumes used to change careers and transfer skills to other industries*. Fayetteville, NC: PREP.

Milar, M., & Brohaugh, W. (1978). *Photographers' market 1979*. Cincinnati, OH: Writer's Digest Books.

Mogel, L. (1998). *Creating your career in communications and entertainment*. Sewickley, PA: GATF Press.

Mosko, L., & Schweer, M. (2005). *Novel and short story writer's market 2006*. Cincinnati, OH: Writer's Digest Books.

Noronha, S. F. R., & ebrary, Inc. (2003). *Opportunities in television and video careers*. Chicago: VGM Career Books.

Noronha, S. F. R., & ebrary, Inc. (2005). *Careers in communications*. New York: VGM Career Books.

Orlik, P. B. (2004). *Career perspectives in electronic media*. Ames, IA: Blackwell.

Pattis, S. W., & ebrary, Inc. (2004). *Careers in advertising*. Chicago: VGM Career Books.

Rush, A., Hodgson, D., & Stratton, B. (2006). *Paid to play: An insider's guide to video game careers*. New York: Prima Games.

Scholastic. (2010). *Hot jobs in video games*. New York: Scholastic Reference.

Seguin, J. A. (2002). *Media career guide: Preparing for jobs in the 21st century*. Boston, MA: Bedford/St. Martin's.

Stratford, S. J. (2009). *Film and television: Field guide to finding a new career*. New York: Checkmark Books.

VGM Career Books & NetLibrary Inc. (2003). *Resumes for advertising careers with sample cover letters*. Chicago: VGM Career Books.

Warley, S., & Vault. (2005). *Vault career guide to journalism and information media*. New York: Vault.

Willins, M. (1997). *The photographer's market guide to photo submission and portfolio formats*. Cincinnati, OH: Writer's Digest Books.

Writer's Digest Books. (2010). *Photographer's market guide*. Cincinnati, OH: Author.

Writer's Digest Books. (2010). *Writer's market guide to getting published*. Cincinnati, OH: Writer's Digest Books.

Yager, F. (2003). *Career opportunities in the film industry*. Facts on File.

Index

Page numbers in italic indicate a figure. Page numbers in bold indicate a table.